GOVERNING
EDUCATION

Try asking serious questions about the
contemporary world and see if you can
do without historical answers.

Philip Abrams (1982, 1)

To Margaret and Norman McPherson
and to the memory of
Sadie and Abraham Raab

GOVERNING EDUCATION

A SOCIOLOGY OF POLICY SINCE 1945

Andrew McPherson

Charles D. Raab

EDINBURGH UNIVERSITY PRESS
1988

© Andrew McPherson and Charles D. Raab 1988
Edinburgh University Press
22 George Square, Edinburgh

Set in Linotronic Times Roman
by Edinburgh University Press
and printed in Great Britain
by Redwood Burn Limited, Trowbridge

British Library Cataloguing
  in Publication Data
McPherson, Andrew
  Governing education.
  1. School management and organization—
  Scotland
  I. Title.   II. Raab, Charles
  371.2'009411   LB2903
ISBN 0 85224 515 7
ISBN 0 85224 572 6 Pbk

Contents

Acknowledgements

We have incurred many debts of gratitude in bringing this book to completion. In particular we must thank all those who shared their knowledge and experience with us on an attributable basis, often over many hours. They are the late John Brunton, Gilbert Bryden, James Clark, the late William Dewar, the late David Dickson, Sir Norman Graham, George Gray, John McEwan, Bruce Millan, Sir William Murrie, Allan Rodger, David Walker and Sir Henry Wood. Although we could not offer this public acknowledgement to three of these persons during their lifetimes, we would wish their families and colleagues to know how highly we valued their participation. In the same spirit we also thank Lady Robertson for making available some of the papers of her late husband, Sir James Robertson. We are also grateful to the following for valuable, but non-attributable, interviews: Joseph Dunning, Alex Eadie, Sir Alex Fletcher, Farquhar Macintosh, Douglas McIntosh, Robert Middleton, Ian Morris, Sir James Munn, John Nisbet, the late George Reith, David Robertson and Andrew Walls. Others who gave us the benefit of their personal knowledge include Christopher Fyfe, the late Eric Gillett, John Gibson, Angus Mitchell, the late Alexander Mowat and the late James Scotland.

Many colleagues and friends provided help and valuable criticism. They are Michael Adler, Malcolm Anderson, Robert Anderson, Robert Bell, Patricia Broadfoot, Tom Burns, Penelope Cazaly, James Cornford, Bruce Curtis, Henry Drucker, Noel Entwistle, David Feingold, Judith Fewell, Lesley Gow, David Hamilton, Walter Humes, Grant Jordan, James Kellas, Maurice Kogan, Alastair Macbeth, Neil MacCormick, Colin MacLean, James Mitchell, George Moyser, Jennifer Ozga, Richard Parry, Susan Pringle, David Raffe, Stewart Ranson, David Regan, Anthony Seldon, Alexander Stewart, Rosemary Wake, Douglas Willms and John Young.

For permission to quote copyright material, we are grateful to David Allen, Robert Bell, Sir Charles Cunningham, Marie-Elisabeth Deroche-Drieux, Judith Fewell, Michael Keating, Alistair Laing, John Lloyd, Ian McDonald, James Mitchell, Tom O'Hagan, Hamish Paterson, Susan Pringle, Ian Seeley, Rosemary Wake, J. E. Weighand, Alf Young, John Young, the British Broadcasting Corporation, the British Library of Political and Economic Science, The Controller of Her Majesty's Stationery Office, the Open University and the Times Educational Supplement (Scotland).

Acknowledgements

The Scottish Education Department gave us access to certain restricted files, and allowed us to refer to them in our writing. The M.Ed. dissertation by the late Donald McKenzie was a valuable source.

We are also grateful for assistance with obtaining information to Judith Cripps, Ian Flett, Isobel McKendrick, Sir George Sharp, the Educational Institute of Scotland, the Scottish Education Department, the Scottish Examination Board and the Scottish Office. Other help was provided by Aberdeen City Libraries, Edinburgh City Libraries, Edinburgh University Library, Moray House College of Education Library, the National Library, the Scottish Office Library and the Scottish Record Office. Geoff Dodds and Stuart Smith gave technical assistance with tape recordings.

The photographs are reproduced with the permission of Aberdeen Journals Ltd (James R. Clark), Glasgow Herald and Evening Times (John S. Brunton, Dr David Dickson, Professor William McClelland, John S. McEwan, The Rt Hon. Bruce Millan MP, Sir William S. Murrie, Sir James J. Robertson), Allan G. Rodger (himself), Scotsman Publications Ltd (Dr William McL. Dewar), Scottish Education Department (Sir William F. Arbuckle, Sir John Mackay Thomson), Ian Southern (Sir Norman W. Graham) and J. Thomson (Gilbert S. Bryden).

This book could not have been physically produced without the meticulous care and attention of Moira Burke, Margaret Chisholm, John Harker, Carole Holliday, Linda McDonald, Margaret MacDougall, Cathie McIntosh, May O'Donnell and Lillias Wylie. We owe a particular debt to Caroline Clark, who bore the main burden of processing countless drafts of the text for electronic transfer, and to Joan Hughes, who proofed and administered our work. Any errors or deficiencies that remain are solely our own responsibility.

The research originated in work funded by the former Social Science Research Council (now the Economic and Social Research Council) in the Centre for Educational Sociology at Edinburgh University (grant HR 3262). The Moray Fund of the University provided two invaluable grants. Support from the Carnegie Trust for the Universities of Scotland helped to defray the initial costs of publication.

Finally, our special thanks are reserved for our families, whose support and forbearance made the whole enterprise possible.

Preface

I sometimes wished that I could just make up my mind about
something and say that that would be the end of it, instead of
saying, 'Well, this is what I think ought to happen, now please
consult people about this'; and then they come back about a year
later and say that they are sorry, but everybody is all over the
place, which is what normally happens, you see. It is very difficult
to describe all this . . . but that doesn't mean to say that things
don't happen. I am not suggesting that your views, at the end of
the day, have no influence at all, that people just carry on as if
they didn't have them. I think, at the end of the day, the system
does change, and change significantly, but it can't just be done by
administrative or Ministerial fiat, you know. It just doesn't work
like that.   Bruce Millan, Junior Minister 1966-70, and Secretary
of State for Scotland 1976-79

Well, if it doesn't work like that, how does it work? How are things made to
happen if everybody is normally all over the place? If administrative or
Ministerial fiat are not enough to change the educational system, what is?
And what is the significance of change?

In his first term of office Millan was responsible for the implementation of
comprehensive reorganisation, introduced by what arguably was the most
important Ministerial fiat in education since 1945. In his second term he saw
the period of expansion that had started in the late 1950s come finally to an
end in government retrenchment and concern for standards and efficiency.
Thus, if Ministers made things happen, they also found things happening to
them. If they made things change significantly, they were also concerned for
the significance of change. And what was true of Ministers was also true in
some measure of teachers, parents, pupils, and much of the public at large.

This book is about these questions and the answers to them. We deal both
with the substance of education, its schools and teachers, its curriculum and
examinations, and also with its governance, with the institutions and procedures through which policies for education were formed, effected or
thwarted. Most of our story is about Scotland, but many of the questions we
address have a wider reference, some of them British, some universal. All
of our story is about education, but much of it engages broader issues of
policy as well.

Educational purposes are not self-implementing. Likewise, the machinery of government grinds more than thin air. Decisions about curriculum, examinations, and comprehensive education are educational, but they also have implications for control and power. Conversely, governmental changes such as the founding and abolition of administrative bodies, and changes in administrative philosophy and style, ultimately affect what happens in schools themselves. Our book is an account of these reciprocal influences in one society, a study of its culture and practice at the points where education and government met. It is also an attempt to deal with these abstract generalities through the concrete experience of individuals. Thus much of the book consists of people talking, principally officials, teachers and a Minister. In reflecting as we do on our discussions with them, we try to understand the ways in which the 'system' has shaped their beliefs and actions, and to understand also the ways in which they, for their part, have shaped the system.

This task has drawn us outwards towards history (history is 'out there' as well as 'back there'), and outwards also to the wider governmental context. For most of this century Scotland's historically distinctive educational system has been administered from Edinburgh, but as a devolved and territorial element in a framework of United Kingdom government which subsumes England as well. Thus many aspects of continuity and change after 1945 have been common to both countries, arising either directly from the coordination of legislation, administration and finance, or indirectly from the commerce of people and ideas. At the same time, however, Scottish educational policy has been made by its own cast of characters, in its own setting and, for the most part, with its own script as well. We find in it, therefore, both the particulars of Scottish experience, and also the themes of British experience realised in Scotland in particular form.

Two such themes are expansion and partnership. Expansion describes the growing private and public commitment to education which saw the proportion of the British national income spent on education between 1948 and 1976 rise roughly from three to eight per cent. It saw two raisings of the school-leaving age (ROSLA), in 1947 and 1973, and also a rising demand for post-compulsory education. This started in the 1950s, steepened in the 1960s, and then levelled off in the 1970s, but continued to climb slowly. Expansion was also apparent in school curriculum, examinations, and organisation. Schools offered more subjects and courses. The proportion of young people in Scotland gaining certification (awards in public examinations) increased over the period from around five per cent to around seventy per cent. And, with comprehensive reorganisation in the 1960s, it was officially recognised, though more decisively in Scotland than in England, that all secondary schools should offer a broadly comparable service. The new and explicit expectation was that secondary schooling in Britain could do more things for more pupils. Neither the debate over standards and accountability in the 1970s nor youth unemployment in the 1980s have since shrunk public requirements of the service back to their earlier levels. Though confidence in these aspects of the service may have weakened, Britain in the late 1980s nevertheless stood on the threshold of a commitment to a system of education and training that would in effect constitute a raising of the period of compulsory learning by two further years.

The causes and consequences of post-war educational expansion are much debated. The demand for equality of opportunity was an important factor, and so too was a concern for economic performance. But expansion required governments to find more resources and to use them more efficiently. In Britain the problem became especially acute in the late 1950s as the children of the post-war baby boom approached secondary education. A renewed effort to solve it in the 1960s contributed in Scotland to a major reorganisation of educational governance. This established much of the framework through which the remaining problems of the century would be addressed, though it still retained deep roots in Scotland's political and administrative past.

Partnership, a second theme, is a description that has been given to the government of education in England and in Scotland, both before and after the changes of the 1960s. Partnership describes relations between central and local government across a number of policy areas, not only education. It refers to the division of responsibility for policy and provision between central and local government, and it implies some measure of agreed purpose and of shared power. Where education is concerned teachers are sometimes included in the official description of the partnership, and sometimes not.

Partnership can be contrasted with centralisation. In this context centralisation implies that power resides decisively in central government, and that local government and its employees, including teachers, are not much more than the agents of central government, having little or no autonomy of their own. Most commentators on the Scottish educational system in the twentieth century have regarded it as centralised, often because they make a comparison with England, implicit or otherwise. Many interpreters of English education have regarded it as a partnership. However, a number have argued a recent trend towards centralisation in England, some dating it from the mid-1970s, but others from the late 1950s, or earlier still.

Here the Scottish experience of central-local relations is apposite. A number of the changes in England that may signify a trend towards centralisation have their counterparts in Scotland some years or decades earlier. The centralisation thesis, however, concerns more than the field of education alone, and more than an institutional relocation of functions between central and local government. Some writers argue that there has been a wider shift in the locus of control over education from 'society', including parents, schools and teachers, to government; and a second shift within government, from educational professionals and officials who owe their primary allegiance to the field of education, to officials acting on behalf of a government machine in which managerial and economic considerations have gained ground against those of social welfare. In effect, it is argued that the education system itself has lost power.

There are affinities between these arguments and what are known as 'corporatist' theories of power. Corporatist theory comes in several variants. But all broadly hold that power is exercised by means of close collaboration between government and dominant producer groups. In this context, the post-1945 expansion of education and welfare is seen as the attempt of this alliance to maintain its position, broadly by 'schooling pupils to order'. Some writers have disputed the extent to which corporatism contradicts another model of the relationship between social groups and government, the model known as 'pluralism'. Pluralism too comes in several variants. But they all share the view that social power and political power are separable, and that the one does not decisively determine the other. They also maintain that no one group is permanently excluded from power. Pluralism asserts that the exercise of power is not unilaterally determined by any one social or political grouping, but is characterised by conflict, bargaining and compromise among a shifting plurality of political and social groups. In this respect, the partnership model of British educational governance, asserting as it does the dispersion of power between several agents, can be claimed as a special case of the pluralist position; and so also can the role of the state in promoting educational expansion. Here the argument is that disadvantaged groups have been able to use the state to ameliorate inequalities of access to educational opportunity; though only ameliorate, and not eliminate, because all policy outcomes, so pluralism argues, are characterised by compromise, and by consequences that were not originally intended.

In the opening and closing parts of this book we relate our study to the wider debate between pluralism and corporatism, and to questions of educational and social inequality. But we have not attempted an exhaustive resolution of the issues of grand theory that are at issue here. One reason for this is that the debate concerns all areas of government and society, not just education. Another is that our study is primarily empirical, and epistemological difficulties in the theories themselves leave empirical evidence with an uncertain role in arbitrating between them. Also, the sweep of evidence required for their adjudication is far broader than we could attempt given the present state of writing on British, and especially Scottish, education. Nor have we undertaken a wider review of the distribution of power in Scottish society. Nevertheless, we think it important to offer our evidence as an empirical contribution to the wider debate from one area of policy. There may also be some interest in our attempt to relate individual identity and the micro-politics of personal relationships to a wider analysis of power. But even here our primary focus is on what our informants told us about their actions and beliefs, and on the related institutions and policies.

This brings us to a central feature of the study. There are few British accounts of relations between individual policy-makers in education, and none, so far as we know, which presents the mutual attitudes and relationships of policy-makers on an attributable, non-confidential basis, using interview material which they have approved for public release. Maurice Kogan's corpus of work on educational policy in England comes closest to this and, indeed, has greatly influenced our approach. But other major accounts, both of England and Scotland, have either left the individual policy-makers out, or else have portrayed them as caricature creatures of a 'role', or an 'interest', or of some other abstraction. Our own study attempts to bring individuals back in, and we have been fortunate in being able to draw on the accounts of some twenty persons who were significantly involved in the making of policy for Scottish secondary education between 1945 and the early 1970s. They include politicians, civil servants and local-authority administrators, members of Her Majesty's Inspectorate of Schools (HMIs), and teachers who became nationally involved (see appendix 1).

Several of these persons had died by the time we began our investigation in the mid-1970s, though they had left behind them various sorts of record. However, the main evidence we present comes from interviews that thirteen of them gave us, on an attributable basis, in all but two cases after they had retired. We also conducted non-attributable interviews with twelve other persons who were active in different periods before and after the mid-1970s. Much of the attributable evidence is unique, and indispensable to an understanding of our period, and especially of those events that are still covered by the thirty-year rule that restricts public access to government records. Most of our interviewees had known and interacted with each other over many years, and in a variety of roles. Their testimonies constitute a unique set of perspectives on the reciprocal influences flowing between government and education, and on the way in which a wider 'policy community' was formed and maintained. This community included central-government officials, but also outsiders who helped them in the transaction of their business with the world of education, and some who hindered them too. The membership of this community was regulated in various ways, and its members acted within a common understanding of the possibilities and purposes of education and its governance.

One reason for the length of our book is that we reproduce *verbatim* extracts from the attributable interviews, sometimes as a narrative device, but also because the testimonies are historically important in their own right. Memory is mortal, of course, and the interviews do not pretend either to individual or collective omniscience. Where possible, we set them against other documentary evidence, and also against each other, for the conflicts of the period are sometimes compounded by conflicting memories of events. Where we juxtapose the testimonies our text can also be read as a reconstructed dialogue that is partly a portrayal of the events themselves, and partly a symposium on them.

To turn to the structure and argument of the book, part I is introductory. Chapter 1 is theoretical. It discusses the idea of partnership, and it reviews pluralist and corporatist accounts of policy-making, paying particular attention to Kogan's work. It also shows how substantive disagreements between various explanations of policy are related to disagreements over the logical status of explanations as such. Two questions are fundamental. First, power has as much to do with things that do not happen, as with things that do. How then is one to allow the evidence of human experience to arbitrate explanations of policy, whilst at the same time avoiding the trivialisation of the concept of policy that occurs when it is detached from considerations of power? Second, how can human experience 'arbitrate' explanations of anything, when the whole point about conflict is that people often disagree about what is 'really' happening? Our own position is outlined at the end of the first chapter and is developed thereafter. In summary it is that individuals, institutions and issues each have explanatory significance; that politics matter, even though there have been long periods when the influence of party politics on policy has been small; and that the explanation of policy and power requires an account not only of what happened, but also of what might have happened. This in turn requires that one find a way to discipline one's imagination of alternatives that were always unimaginably numerous. In sum, the explanation of policy is not to be found solely in the beliefs, intentions and actions of the policy-makers of the time. A wider reference is required in history, social institutions and the practice of the schools. What one does about the problem of 'reality' we leave, with a relief that others no doubt will share, to the very end of the book. Nevertheless, readers who find that they are not helped by the discussion of theoretical and methodological issues as such may prefer to start their reading with the summary of chapter 1, looking backwards, perhaps, only after they have worked some way forwards.

Chapter 2 attempts a sociological account of Scottish education and government up to 1945. A major theme is that of conflict and compromise between two opposing principles for the organisation of education, one emphasising local community and common provision, the other elite recruitment and bipartite or selective provision. This conflict influenced the emergence and form of the central authority in the later nineteenth century, with lasting effects on the policies it pursued, and on its relations with the rest of the system. The chapter deals with historical configurations of individuals, institutions and issues, and it implicitly argues the deficiency of analyses that disregard any of these three elements. The elements neither harmonised logically with each other, nor changed concurrently. Institutions were answers to yesterday's issues, future leaders the students of past ideas. For individual and society alike, the continuous present consisted of different pasts overlaid upon each other and upon different visions of the future. This is what gave depth to the present, and lent it impetus in some places and inertia in others. In trying to identify the facilities and constraints that inhered in these configurations, our purpose is to attempt to distinguish in subsequent chapters between the power that individuals had by virtue of their position, and the power they won for themselves; between the options that confronted them, and the options and choices they themselves made. That is, we try to give the distinction between what happened and what might have happened a logical and empirical grounding, and with it the discussion of policy and power.

Chapter 3 describes our methods of research.

Part II is a case study of the negotiation and exercise of power, set in the context of reconstruction and change in secondary schooling in the twenty years after the Second World War. Much of chapter 4 consists of the story of this period as told to us by John Brunton. It serves to introduce many of the principal events, and it illustrates how educational change required prior changes in educational governance, and in turn precipitated further changes therein. Also, Brunton himself was centrally involved in these events as Senior Chief Inspector of Schools. He has been credited by others with the leading role, and he has assumed, at least in some eyes, a quasi-heroic stature.

Chapter 5 then sets Brunton and his account against the views of him that were held by his colleagues in the Scottish Education Department (SED) and by others outside. From this there emerges a more complex picture of shifting conflicts, opportunities and alliances. These explain how Brunton won the power to implement change, and also how that power was conditional and constrained, leading sometimes to outcomes he had not originally sought. Brunton's reputation was in part a function of these conflicts. Different representations of the situation were constructed and exploited at the time as part of the struggle for power. After Brunton's retiral his period of office came to symbolise for some a vanished age in which educational policy had been made by professional educationists. But this was only one side of the man, one facet of the phenomenology of conflict, and one part of the wider story of change.

Part III then broadens the analysis in two ways. First, it describes how the conflicts and changes of Brunton's era reflected wider tensions and changes in the internal organisation of central government. Second, it brings in the crucial issue of resources, and examines the role of the SED in mediating relations over resources between central government as a whole and the Scottish local authorities. Chapter 6 outlines changes in the position of the SED within Scottish government. It traces the development of the Scottish Office from the pre-1939 era of virtually independent Departments to the present more federal organisation under the Secretary of State. At the same time as power was passing from Brunton the man, control within the SED was passing from inspectors, and from administrators with a professional background in education, to career civil servants whose backgrounds lay in administrative generalism and management. Meanwhile the Department itself was losing some of its former autonomy, and was becoming less isolated within the Scottish Office as a whole. This too affected the balance of influence within the Department between inspectors and administrators.

Chapter 7 focuses on the relationship between the Inspectorate and the administrative side of the SED. Scottish government in general has been characterised in terms of its 'administrative primacy'. The allegiance of inspectors to education, and their influence with administrators, are two factors that must be assessed in judging the extent to which this description applies to educational policy. Did inspectors fulfil their claim to be the 'spearhead' of the teaching profession, inserted at the very centre of the government machine? Or was their job to govern education on behalf of the administration? We consider the new emphasis on management that administrators brought to the Department, and the way in which inspectors sought to regain their influence over policy as the old order gave way to new persons, assumptions, and structures after Brunton had gone.

The Inspectorate-administrator relationship, and the influence of educationists more generally, are also functions of Ministerial style. Chapter 8 discusses national politics and considers the contribution of Ministers and MPs to the shaping of relations and policies. Social and economic issues have always had a high priority in Scottish politics. This priority has influenced both the character of the Scottish Office machine, which claims to 'fight Scotland's corner', and also the attention that Ministers have given to education; or, to be more precise though paradoxical, the lack of attention. After 1945 Scotland shared in the general British consensus over education's role in post-war reconstruction, but also in the widespread view that education was not a major party-political issue. Thus the initiative passed to the educational policy community with its own, traditional, priorities. Even though party-political inputs in Scotland became more important from the 1960s onwards, political accountability in education remained weak, partly because of the character of parliamentary mechanisms in general, and partly because of the survival of earlier habits and values.

Chapter 9 is the first of two chapters in which we discuss how the problems of resource provision were tackled at, and between, central and local levels. It describes changes in the way in which Scotland and its local education authorities acquired recurrent central funding. It also discusses the allocation of capital expenditure for the building of schools, and the Department's influence over education authorities' building programmes. The chapter shows how the processes for gaining and managing educational resources could bring the Department into conflict with the education authorities, as well as with competitors in other quarters of central and local government. In its turn, the competition in these quarters drew Department and education authority closer together for some purposes. Good relations with the Department could help protect education locally from raids by housing, and a good Department could help maintain education's share, both within the Scottish Office, and in wider governmental circles. For its own part, a good Department needed effective education authorities both to make a timeous forward case for resources, and also then to use them timeously.

With one main qualification, central-local relations over building and resources could be described as a partnership. The qualification is that our evidence on the extent of central-local disagreement over building goals is unsatisfactory. However, in the area of the salaries, supply and geographical distribution of teachers, conflicts between teachers, the local authorities and the Department were clearly in evidence. Chapter 10 explores this theme. There were chronic teacher shortages until the mid-1970s. Teachers wanted more money. They were reluctant to move to the areas where the Department thought they were needed, and favourably staffed local authorities did little to help, and something to hinder. Issues of salaries, supply and distribution, however, were less politically explosive in the 1940s and early 1950s than they were thereafter. This was partly because the effects of deficiencies of staffing and remuneration were absorbed by three sectors of the system whose disadvantage was at that time widely regarded as morally tolerable. Women teachers had not yet acquired equal pay; and the brunt of the shortage was borne by junior-secondary schools (short-course schools for pupils who failed the transfer examination at twelve), and by the West of Scotland.

In the 1960s, however, the moral climate changed and the political temperature was raised by educational expansion, by the drive towards educational equality, by new national policies of public-pay restraint, and by increasing teacher militancy, especially in the West. Chapter 10 describes the mixed success of the Department's attempts to tackle salary and supply issues in the 1940s and 1950s, and the major change of approach that it was obliged to make in the 1960s. Crucial to the new approach was the Department's annexation of the right and capability to define local need.

The resource issues discussed in chapters 9 and 10 have direct implications for several of our main themes. First, Departmental policies affected area inequalities. Efficient authorities got more. Better housed authorities got more. Better schools attracted better teachers, and in turn produced more teachers. Second, curriculum itself was treated increasingly as a resource problem, and the locus of curricular initiative tended to follow the changing locus of resource decisions. Third, overt conflict was precipitated by the Department's differences with the teachers over pay and mobility. Also, the Department thought that the local authorities were reluctant to put a collective national interest above their individual local needs. Conflict in its turn led to a fundamental reappraisal of the Department's internal capabilities and external relations. This reappraisal fed into the new structure of governance that emerged in the 1960s. It gave the Department's partners a greater presence at the centre. But it also fragmented the centre into discrete units between which the major links were Departmental officials and inspectors, and the minor links were other members of the policy community.

In part IV we explore the new structure of governance, concentrating increasingly on substantive educational issues and on interactions between governmental structures and educational provision and practice. Chapter 11 sets the scene by analysing the logical structure and historical continuity of the SED's bipartite or selective approach to secondary schooling up to the 1960s. It shows the links between the policies for certification, curriculum and selection. It also shows the links between these policies as a whole and the Department's use of the Advisory Council on Education, 1918-61. For many years this use had been severely constrained by external opposition to the Department's bipartism. This in turn meant that the Department had resisted policies with expansionist implications, because expansion would entail its working with outsiders who could not be trusted. Expansion would also require the Department to broaden its competence, in two senses. Internally, it would have to increase its range of expertise in order to provide for its new pupil clientele. Externally, it would have to ensure that the statutory educational rights and obligations of an enlarged clientele were met. This function was 'regulatory', but it also had 'promotional' implications for the Department's relations with both the local authorities and the national fringe bodies.

By the early 1960s it was clear to the Department that it could no longer resist the implications of expansion, and that it must reconstruct its relations with the wider education system. The Advisory Council was replaced by three bodies, the General Teaching Council (GTC), the Scottish Certificate of Education Examination Board (SCEEB), and the Consultative Committee on the Curriculum (CCC). Chapter 12 discusses the origins of the GTC in government's disputes with teachers over the latter's pay, professional status and influence on policy. The Department's difficulty in finding the teachers and other resources to sustain expansion brought the two sides into open conflict, and eventually obliged the Department to concede to teachers statutory rights of advice and of professional self-regulation. Nevertheless, the implications of the new Council for the balance of influence in any educational partnership require careful evaluation. The Council was itself an uneasy compromise between different principles of representation; there were often conflicts of interest between the several parties represented on it; the formal powers of the Council were limited; and the Department was still able to exercise several means of informal control. However, the Council survived, partly because of strong Ministerial support from a former teacher, and partly because it relieved the Department of work.

Like the GTC, the new Examination Board was also a statutory body, and also relieved the Department of work. It was first appointed by a Conservative Government, but the Labour Government of 1964-70 was to find it unacceptably wilful. Moreover, expansion gave the Board scope. In chapters 13 and 14 we show how the growth of certification in the 1960s and early 1970s extended the Board's influence over schooling at the expense of the CCC, the Secretary of State's main advisory body on curriculum. This mattered to the Department because the CCC was intended to be both a channel and a cover for Inspectorate influence over the curriculum. Moreover, the Labour Government was pressing for an end to bipartism. Ironically, in developing a new policy, the Department found itself opposed by trusted supporters of the old dispensation whom it had originally helped to place on the Board. With a further change of government, and with ROSLA in 1973, conflict came to a head. It led to a protracted attempt to rebuild a consensus on the purposes of secondary education. This attempt started with the appointment in 1975 of the Munn committee on the curriculum and the Dunning committee on assessment and certification. By the mid-1980s it was still not complete.

In the two decades after comprehensive reorganisation in 1965 much of the traditional character of Scottish secondary education was confirmed. The curriculum remained subject-based and non-vocational, and assessment for national certification remained largely external. Yet south of the Border there were strong trends in this period towards internal assessment and the integration of subjects. And, in the early 1980s, the Manpower Services Commission began its attempt in both countries to shift the secondary curriculum towards technical and vocational education.

What, then, gave Scottish secondary education its character after 1965? Why did Munn and Dunning's national reviews begin only a decade after comprehensive reorganisation? And why did they conclude as they did? Chapters 13 and 14 develop answers to these questions in terms of interactions between education and government. Particularly important was the way in which the 'representation' of interest groups was negotiated by central government as it restructured the system of advice. The solution that the Department reached in the mid-1960s weakened the CCC as an agency of curriculum development. It also left its imprint on the CCC's own educational thinking, thinking that Munn was eventually to legitimate. Furthermore, in reaching its compromise with outside interest groups, the Department was constrained to use particular criteria for the recognition of educational expertise and personal trustworthiness among outsiders. These criteria influenced the types of educational professionals who became involved with the SCEEB and the CCC; the areas of Scotland and the sectors of education from which they came; the areal and educational needs of which they consequently were aware, or which they recognised as valid; and the types of policies they then pursued. To question these criteria was to question the authority of the Inspectorate. But this was already severely eroded by changes within central government and the Department, and by educational expansion outside. Departmental administrators, however, still depended on Inspectorate performance. The new national advisory structure had been segmented in order to preserve central government's influence. Eventually, however, this segmentation would give the Inspectorate scope to reassert its position, both outside and inside the Department, for the task of linking the disaggregated elements of national advice fell mainly to the Inspectorate.

Meanwhile the Inspectorate had yet another difficulty to negotiate. Their authority derived in part from their educational expertise, and their expertise was rooted in a secondary-education system whose selective character was at least as old as the century. Chapter 15 describes the Scottish system of selective and comprehensive (*omnibus*) schools as it was until 1965 when the Labour Government initiated the abolition of selection in Scotland and the rest of Britain. The chapter shows how central government was content for some years after 1945 to leave the management of selection to the local authorities. It analyses the substantial political and professional support that there was for selection, and it discusses the contribution to this consensus of the scientific and progressive movement in educational thought that was associated with the development of intelligence tests. The selective system attracted little Scottish criticism until the early 1960s when the new O-grade examination at sixteen years began to encourage certificate presentations from junior-secondary schools. Even then, the main spur to reform within Scotland at both local and national levels was the mounting critique of selection south of the Border.

Chapter 16 analyses the way in which the policy for comprehensive reorganisation was developed and applied in Scotland. It attempts to identify the contributions of politicians, officials and educationists, both locally and nationally. It also assesses the significance of these events for some of our main themes: for the degree of Scottish autonomy in the educational policy process; for interpretations of Scottish education in terms of pluralism, corporatism and centralisation; and for the mutual influence of educational and governmental forms. The Labour Government intended comprehensive reorganisation to mark a decisive break with the bipartite and selective policy that the Department had pursued over the decades. But there was a sense in which the new policy was implemented before it was formulated. Labour wanted a policy that gave equal priority to all pupils, and not just to an academically able minority. In the mid-1960s it was far from clear what this meant, or how it could be achieved. Nevertheless, the shift in the mid-1960s ruptured the value-consensus in the educational policy community. This happened at precisely the time that central government was enlarging the membership of the community in order to share the increased burden and range of work consequent upon expansion. An untried governmental structure was thus despatched in pursuit of an unexplicated policy, certain only of the fact that it could not immediately return to the one body of experience and practice in which its authority was founded.

In part v we draw together the implications of our analysis for the issues raised at the beginning of the book. First, in chapter 17, we analyse the functions of the educational policy community up to the mid-1970s. In doing this we begin to make explicit connections between a micro-sociology of interpersonal relations, and a macro-sociology of power. The policy community was an important mediator of relations between government and society. Its anthropology helped to shape government's perception of education, the policies that were formulated, and the practices that flowed from them. We discuss two features of the community in particular. The first is the ontological basis of its values and beliefs in a distinctive 'egalitarian' interpretation of Scottish identity, the Scotland of the 'democratic intellect'. The second is the stratificatory process of appointment and preferment which established the individual membership of the policy community, and its internal relations of trust and deference. We show how ontology and stratification were mutually reinforcing. We also show how a policy community characterised by trust and deference was logically necessary to a system of representative democracy that aimed to base policy on expertise. The policy community resolved in practice what was, in logic, a fundamental inconsistency between the theory and practice of representative democracy. We identify the ways in which the concepts of 'representation' and 'expertise' were sociologically constructed so as to make collective policy action possible in spite of this logical difficulty. But the sociological construction of these concepts in turn structured the representation of Scotland that was achieved through the policy process. By this we mean two things. First, a particular, selective, and demonstrably incomplete picture of Scotland and its education system was represented as the empirical reality. Second, this view was sustained by individuals who were not representative, either by opinion or individual characteristic, of the group affiliation that was the public justification for their admission to the policy community.

Chapter 18 then examines individual and collective relations between members of the Department and the main pressure groups: the two largest teachers' associations, the local authorities, and the directors of education. The policy community was the community of individuals who mattered, and it was also the forum in which the interests of groups were represented, reconciled, or rebuffed. Relations between individuals could be critically important to relations between groups and government. A skilful negotiator could hope to win concessions from the Department by exercising a judicious combination of group demand and concession. But knowing when to settle depended on interpersonal trust: trust that a concession now might yield a benefit later; and trust that a willing Department, constrained as it was by its wider governmental setting, had nothing more to give. For most policy outcomes, consultation and negotiation were far more important than formal politics. The parliamentary mechanism was used by interest groups, but mainly to press the Department into consultation back up the line in Edinburgh. Political inputs at the local-authority level were comparatively unimportant, and were in the main mediated by a small number of directors of education. Within the policy community the standing and representation of groups' interests were often indistinguishable from the reputations and actions of individuals. Moreover, the same individual might be selected to play multiple corporate roles. Thus, crucial to an understanding of the wider issues of pluralism, corporatism and centralisation is a knowledge of how the Department regarded particular individuals, of how they played their representational roles, and of where they placed their loyalties, to their wider constituencies outside, and to the policy community within. The chapter presents evidence on these issues. It also shows how the career paths of individual members of the Department, and their earlier informal relations with outside members of the policy community, helped them to play their formal Departmental roles. Individual career and institutional role were not, in the final analysis, separable; nor, finally, were institutional role and individual friendship or respect. If formal institutional structures were answers to yesterday's problems, they also depended on yesterday's relations to keep them working on the morrow. The passing of generations made institutional reform more possible, but also more necessary.

A purely synchronic (i.e. static or 'snapshot') analysis of institutional structures could not capture these interdependencies, nor the problems and possibilities they presented to government. In chapter 19 we catalogue the overt and covert techniques used by the Department in its attempts to shape policy outcomes by shaping the policy community. We also review the significance of the policy community itself for the claims of pluralism and corporatism. Much of the membership, thinking and activity of the policy community was influenced by the Department. But the Department's repertoire of controls was finite; it sometimes made mistakes; and its policies might be resisted or transformed in the course of implementation. Also essential to an assessment of the distribution of power is a judgement of the intended and unintended outcomes of the policy process, as they were realised both in the practice of teachers, and in the experience of those they taught.

The final chapter draws our arguments together in the light of developments in British educational policy up to the time of writing. It also summarises our view of the relationship between policy, history and theory.

Several disclaimers about coverage are necessary. We have given most attention to secondary education, and have not attempted to cover systematically the sectors of primary, further, higher and adult education. Much of our detailed discussion ends in the mid-1970s at the point where the attributable evidence of our informants tapers off. We drew the final line firmly across the page just before the 1987 General Election. Also, we are conscious that primary source material remains that we have not consulted. For reasons described in chapter 3, our manuscript was shown to the Scottish Office before publication. We were not required to make any changes in what we had written, nor have any changes been made in response to the reactions we received, other than the correction of one factual error in chapter 14.

Finally, our main regret is that we have taken so long to produce what we have written. With the passing of time, several of our informants have died. Those who remain will no doubt have despaired of us and our endeavour. Our delay has been a discourtesy for which we apologise. What is worse, it has made it impossible for some of our informants to respond, and may well have discouraged those who happily still live from setting down their further thoughts. We hope they will do so, and will see some value in what we ourselves have made out of what they told us.

Was this how it was? Was this how it really was?

Edinburgh, May 1987

Part I

Introductory

One

Policy, History and Theory

> Without the historical test, theory may be beautiful but may be beyond validation and understanding. Without the theoretical test, history may be busy but blind.   Harold Silver (1983, 245)

Introduction: Beyond Partnership

The government of education in Britain is commonly described as a partnership. The term has various meanings, however, some of which are disputed. The arguments here are related to fundamental disagreements over how education is controlled and should be controlled. Thus partnership is an important theme.

Partnership refers, first of all, to the division of formal responsibility for education, as indeed for other services, between central and local government. This division takes two forms. First, statute vests some powers in the central authority, and others in the local authority. But partnership signifies something more than this division alone, because it would be misleading to apply the concept to situations of continuing conflict between the central and local authorities. An element of common purpose is implied by the idea of partnership, and not merely a formal division of responsibility. Second, many of the powers that statute vests centrally are in practice exercised by the local authority acting as the agent of central government. This may constitute a partnership but, again, only insofar as the agent shares a common purpose with the principal, that is, central government. If partnership is to apply to the making of policy, as distinct from the implementation of policy made by others, the relationship between the central and local authority that it describes must allow some scope for choice of goals on the latter's part. It is not enough that the local authority mechanistically agree and implement whatever the central authority decides. The local authority must also be able to influence purposes, and to implement policy with some discretion. In practice, no doubt, any discretion that the local authority enjoys as the agent of central government in some matters is reinforced by the local authority's statutory powers in other matters. The local authority's right to act independently of central government in certain instances makes it more important for central government to win the consent of the local authority in other instances where the local authority is formally no more than an agent of the central authority.

3

Partnership thus embraces a division of formal authority between central and local government, and also an interdependence between the central authority and its local administrative agent. The division of authority indicates some division of power and influence as well, as does the interdependence of central authority and local agent. Partnership therefore implies a system in which authority, power and influence are, to some extent, distributed or decentralised, and, until recently, this has been regarded by many commentators as an essential characteristic of English education.[1] North of the Border the matter is more uncertain. For the moment, however, suffice it to say that in Scotland also there is a division of authority and function between central and local government, and that these arrangements have been described as a partnership since the inception of the modern local authority (see chapter 2).

Some writers include a third party in the partnership, namely school teachers.[2] This makes things more interesting because relations between three parties admit of more possibilities than relations between two. For one thing, coalitions of two against one are possible in triangular relationships. For another, the inclusion of teachers, or indeed of any other non-governmental group, adds further dimensions to partnership's reference. Teachers are employees of local authorities. They have a very limited statutory authority over educational provision in England and Wales, and not much more in Scotland. To count them as partners with government is therefore to raise questions of power and influence, and questions of professional knowledge and practice. Teachers organise themselves in order to exert a collective influence on policy, both locally and nationally. They claim something like a monopoly of professional knowledge and skills. And, as individuals in the classroom, they practise education with considerable autonomy. This practice may itself 'aggregate' in ways that influence policy. The influence may not always be what teachers intend, and it may not always be a direct influence. Nevertheless, it can be powerful, usually as a conservative force, but not always so. There have been times when teachers themselves have claimed in as many words to be partners with central and local government. Sometimes these claims have been conceded in as many words, sometimes they have not. Such claims and concessions are themselves part of the rhetoric of educational politics, but they should not be dismissed as mere rhetoric. Partnership talk is also part of the action.

Power and practice are difficult things to study empirically, far more difficult than formal authority and its related administrative systems. Statutory authority is inscribed using agreed procedures and terminology, and it is interpreted by recognised public persons called judges. To be sure, it is also interpreted by somewhat more obscure persons called officials who often enjoy considerable discretion. But at least an exploration of formal authority knows to which persons and institutions it should turn at the start. There is in consequence no shortage of accounts of the formal governmental structures for educational policy-making in Britain.[3] But, with the more intangible issues of power and practice, the point of departure is more uncertain. So too are the methods of proceeding and the limits to the enquiry. If a study of power is to include teachers, whom should it exclude: pupils? parents? business and industry? the 'middle class'? the 'working class'? 'bureaucracy'? 'capitalism'?, 'society' itself? Each of these configurations may influence policy, and political activists may well say that they are acting on behalf of one or more them, as the current politics of education in England well illustrates.

Our own study is empirical and is mainly about educationists, officials and politicians. How they decided for or against certain policy options is an important part of the story. It is also the part that is easiest to substantiate, in principle if not always in practice. But the story of their decisions is not the whole story. Policy was shaped in other ways as well. In particular, there were the options and issues that did not get onto the agenda for decision. Some of these were consciously recognised as options, and consciously excluded or disregarded at an early stage. In principle these also can be evidenced, especially when their exclusion approximated a decision. Other options, however, were excluded because they were never consciously entertained. Nevertheless, they may have been systematically excluded, sometimes as a result of a shared background and set of assumptions among the decision-makers, sometimes as a result of the character of the policy-making institutions through which they worked. It could be argued that such exclusions should be disregarded on the grounds that they are potentially infinite, and that, logically, one cannot adduce evidence to explain why individuals reject options of which they are not aware. To do so, however, would be to trivialise the concept of policy-making. The awareness of policy-makers has itself changed over time. Policy-making is an aspect of power, and the control of awareness is a means of power, whether consciously or unconsciously used. We try, therefore, to look beyond the decisions of particular individuals to the historical evolution of the social institutions through which they worked; and we also try to identify regularities in the antecedents and consequences of their decisions, whether or not these were fully understood or intended.

This chapter discusses the ideas and secondary sources on which we have drawn for these purposes. Two main problems arise. First, the historical and social-scientific literature is small and rather disparate where educational policy is concerned.[4] Second, the explanatory statuses of history and social science are themselves in dispute.[5] We cannot settle the methodological issues. But neither can we wholly ignore them, because the views that writers hold on the nature of history and social theory correlate with their accounts of partnership, and also with the ways they define and explain the substance of educational policy.

In the next section we outline the intellectual pedigree of pluralism and

5

corporatism, two theories of government that have a bearing on partner-ship. We then examine the explanatory claims of history and of social theory. After that we focus on two bodies of empirical work on education in post-war Britain. Maurice Kogan is the foremost contemporary British writer on the government and politics of education, and he is a leading proponent of pluralism. We discuss his contribution, paying particular at-tention to the way in which his position on social theory and history relates to his pluralism. Thereafter we examine what sociology has had to say about relations between education and power. For some twenty years after 1945 British sociology adopted a social-democratic perspective on education that was itself an influence on educational thinking and politics. Later this perspective, and pluralism generally, came under attack, both as an expla-nation of British educational politics and as a political ideal. We discuss two examples of the critique. But we postpone until chapter 2 our introduction to Scotland and its schools.

Pluralism, Corporatism and Interests

Explanations of policy-making can broadly be divided into those that assert the interpenetration of political and civil society, and those that assert either that they are separate, or else that they are only trivially related as far as power is concerned. Prominent in the former category are explanations framed in terms of elites or social classes. The most common form of explanation in the latter category is pluralism.[6] Pluralism has many variants. Some variants assert that politics are independent of the social order, and that the political power that individuals can achieve by allying with others has no necessary relation to their positions in civil society. Politics are then viewed as a process of bargaining between groups, and between groups and government. From time to time the groups reconstitute themselves accord-ing to the issue of the moment and the need to enlarge or remake alliances in order to achieve desired outcomes. In some variants of pluralism, issues in the political arena largely determine the constitution and reconstitution of the interest groups. In other variants, the composition of political interest groups is influenced by more enduring groupings of civil society, for example of kinship, ethnicity, social status, occupation and social class. But even here the assumption is that there is no social group that cannot achieve significant political power, if not by itself then in coalition with other groups.

In the shorter term, such processes imply that inequalities of power and resources between groups and between individuals are not cumulative. In the longer term, however, pluralism has to worry about the stability and rationality of plural systems. This is partly because 'external' social change may upset the balance of power between groups, but mainly for the logical reason that the outcome of inter-group and group-government bargaining is, by definition, always a compromise. It is therefore something which no-one originally had wanted and for which no-one could have planned, except in the shorter term. On this view, the outcomes of policy accumulate, at best, in an incremental but disjointed way, revealing only in retrospect, and only if one is lucky, some fortuitous coherence or rationality that might perhaps be sharpened by subsequent reform. At worst, nothing increments. Thus, below the surface of pluralist compromise, there lurks the possibility of a growing Hobbesian anarchy in which alliances become briefer as the outcomes of collective action are increasingly recognised as unwanted and non-rational, offering too little of a pay-off to make further attempts at alliance-building worthwhile. Pluralism asserts equilibrium and compromise, but is haunted by the spectre of irrationality, ungovernability and social dissolution. Indeed, in extreme versions of pluralism, government itself is regarded merely as another group contending for power.

Nineteenth-century social science offers two explanations of why political and social orders survive. One explanation is benign and one pathological, but both emphasise the political significance of the institutions of civil society, and both still have currency. The benign explanation is that civil society, and especially family, kinship and community, give an enduring coherence to the political alliances individuals form. In particular, civil society is characterised by a moral order of normative beliefs about individuals' rights and obligations, and this moral order in turn sustains consent to the distributive inequalities that are an apparently universal feature both of social groups and of political alliances. The pathological explanation, by contrast, attributes the survival of an unequal political and social order not to consent but to the coercion that it sees in civil relationships. In Marxist accounts this coercion is derived from individuals' relations to the means of production, and it is realised through a state apparatus for physical and ideological control. Some critics claim that this apparatus includes the education system itself.

These are enduring concerns. One form that they have taken in the last decade or so is that of a debate between pluralism and what has come to be known as corporatism.[7] Essentially the corporatist interpretation of politics is a restatement of class and elite theory that plays on the logical insecurity of pluralism, and offers a third explanation for the survival of the political and social order. Like pluralism, corporatism comes in several variants. One version of it concedes an historically finite validity to pluralism. It allows that, at some stage in the development of the modern state, politics may once have resembled the pluralist model, and may still do so in its outer form or in particular sectors of policy-making. But corporatism also asserts that, especially in the period following the Second World War, the governments of the liberal democracies have tried to persuade the leaders of the many 'producer' groups in the pluralist cosmos to recognise their common interest, with each other and with government, in achieving a stable and long-lasting relationship in which demands can be bargained and conflict contained. This tendency is claimed to be most pronounced in the field of

7

economic and industrial policy, where the representatives of labour and capital are said to have become closely involved with government in making and administering agreed policies. But there have also been tentative efforts to apply corporatist concepts to social-policy fields, and to broach the relationships between corporatism, the professions, and non-governmental bodies. Some theorists of corporatism hold that the close involvement of groups with the polity may serve the interest mainly of their leaders, and less so that of the followers, whose demands are more controlled than promoted and whose disciplining is necessary if bargained policies are to be carried out. Others regard it nevertheless as a growing and necessary feature of government: only through corporatism, it is argued, can governability survive. Yet others take the view that the common good, or at any rate the interests of those groups which are excluded from privileged bargaining, are not served by corporatism. 'Consumers' of goods or services are typically counted among the disadvantaged. A further view is that the corporatist bargains that are struck between government and the leaders of social groups, in time result in the emergence of new political elites based on new life-styles and social identities.

In general, however, corporatism is one solution to Hobbesian anarchy. 'Liberal' or 'societal' versions of corporatism describe processes which lock interest groups and the state into a closed set of voluntaristic relationships based on consent. Such versions often argue that power is to some extent dispersed, because the state rules indirectly through groups that play a crucial part in implementing policy. The groups' indispensability is recognised in the process of bargaining and enables them to achieve many of their aims. In 'authoritarian' or 'state' versions, however, groups' interests are repressed as they are co-opted into relationships based on the coercive exercise of state power. Later, in part v we offer an analysis of relations between political and civil society in the area of education and we try to draw out the implications of these relations for pluralist and corporatist interpretations.

History and Theory

If these were the only issues in the field, then our review of theory would be a relatively clear-cut matter, taxonomically speaking. Unfortunately, there is a methodological complication. Philosophers of social science disagree over the possibility of describing human reality objectively, and disagree too over what would constitute an explanation of any particular reality. Most writers on educational policy neglect these issues. Among those who do not, methodological positions do not neatly coincide with substantive differences of theory and interpretation, and this further complicates the picture.

One reaction might be to dismiss social theory altogether and to set oneself to write history instead, sticking to the facts. But in history, too, there are comparable disputes, and even approaches that think themselves innocent of theory are ultimately marked by it. For many historians the hallmark of good work is a scrupulous attention to detail. This leads them, they say, to find in their subject matter a complexity that renders persons and events unique.[8] The methodological individualism of this position is both a practical discipline in the use of evidence, and a moral stance on human aspiration and agency. However, a history that is driven solely by the methodological assertion of serendipity and human idiosyncrasy is clearly unsatisfactory. No explanation of human events can avoid assumptions and generalisations that function as social theory, if only implicitly. As the historian of education, Harold Silver, has put it:

> Educational policy, social democracy, capitalism, are questions of theory, and 'theory' has no more of a hold on reality than has 'history'. They are all, equally, questions of history, which has no more of a hold on reality than has theory. Without the historical test, theory may be beautiful but may be beyond validation and understanding. Without the theoretical test, history may be busy but blind. The history of education has to examine its own organizing concepts (including, for example, that of 'education'), and at some point engage both with the broad reaches of policy, and with the close and detailed description and analysis of the processes of education, and of people's experience and perceptions of them. The most dangerous moments are when theory *claims* to be history and when policy *claims* to be experience. (Silver 1983, 245, his emphasis)

Silver would probably acknowledge, however, that the nature of reality is itself contested, not only between historians and social theorists, but also between theorists of different persuasions. At the heart of these debates lie fundamental disagreements over which persons and events should figure in an explanation, and how they should be described. Thus data may arbitrate theory, but they may also be created by theory, insofar as theory finds a particular significance in events and redescribes them accordingly.

A central issue here is the phenomenon of complexity. Some writers regard complexity as an irreducible aspect of human experience, whereas others prefer to regard it merely as a feature of the way in which observers have chosen to describe the world. Of course, all descriptions reduce complexity and therefore have the paradoxical quality of being at odds with that which they describe. For those who believe that complexity is integral to human events this paradox gives something of an advantage to methodological individualism's distrust of social theory. However, the view that 'reality' is constituted by an ideographic complexity is itself a conjecture. One may equally conjecture that its complexity is illusory or ideological, a consequence of the observer's busy concern with detail, or of his failure to generate the right concepts for grasping the underlying lawfulness of the world. Thus theory cannot be avoided, especially in an empirical study like this.

9

Complexity and Indeterminacy in Kogan's Pluralism

Maurice Kogan is a former civil servant from the Department of Education and Science (DES) who subsequently moved into academic life. His work on the politics and administration of education constitutes the most informative statement we have on policies for education in England and Wales between 1945 and the early 1980s.

Kogan himself would probably deny that he offers a model or theory, at least in a strongly determinist sense. He has distanced himself from attempts to 'turn familiar events into theoretical fodder' (Kogan 1982), and has inclined instead towards the view that policy events have an intrinsic complexity which does not easily yield to the simplifications of analysis:

> The sources of policy generation are so difficult to locate, let alone place in any logical pattern, that detecting the changes in values, or the pressures by which change is effected, is more a matter of art than of analysis. (Kogan 1975, 23)

Nevertheless, the model he offers draws explicitly on pluralism. His starting point is close to the partnership model, though with one important reservation (discussed below). There are, he says, three main sets of agents in the policy-making system, the DES, the local education authorities, and the teacher organisations (Kogan 1975, 23). This alone, he claims, is evidence that power is dispersed and that the system is pluralistic to some degree. Moreover, he argues, the three main agents themselves invoke pluralism to order their relations with each other. Thus, he has two reasons for claiming pluralism as the best approximation of how the system has worked in reality. Pluralism is a theory *of* the world because the observer can identify several main actors, and pluralism is a theory *in* the world, used by the actors themselves.

Kogan takes pluralism to be rooted in English historical experience: the English system of education evolved over a long period during which central government was only one of several major sponsors of educational provision. Hence power was dispersed. This dispersal in turn permitted a diversity of local provision, which it was difficult for central government to comprehend or to modify subsequently through strong central directives. Moreover, Kogan argues, education is intrinsically unlike other areas of social provision in that, being universal, it serves a variety of different groups and reflects a variety of values (Kogan 1983a, 70-2). Also, he asserts, central government itself acknowledges the truth of these generalisations and accepts that they must limit both its knowledge and its power. It has long conceded that its peculiar contributions to policy-making were to procure resources, to lay down minimum and maximum standards, and to sanction developments as they emerged from the system (Kogan 1978, 122, 129, 146-9). Hence 'the relationship between the centre and the periphery is firmly based on a belief in the power of the periphery. . . . to the credit of the British [*sic*] system, that is the established doctrine which now prevails' (*ibid.*, 160). Thus pluralism is presented as an emergent descriptive (proto-scientific) and prescriptive (constitutional) theory, which has served to explain the world well, and served to guide action in it.

Kogan is reluctant, however, to call these arrangements a 'partnership', arguing that 'partnership' implies a parity of power (*ibid.*, 136). Rather he acknowledges that, among the three main agents of the formal policy-making system, the DES 'wields determinant authority and great power' (Kogan 1975, 238). Thus, although his model asserts that power is dispersed, it does not assert that it is evenly dispersed. He grants that power is also unevenly distributed in that 'the pluralism of the system does not extend to many of the main actors in the processes of education' (*ibid.*, 231). Parental influence is mainly local, for example (*ibid.*), and the main interest groups vary in their ability to bring opinion to bear. Indeed, Kogan talks of 'legitimised and non-legitimised interest groups' (*ibid.*, 73 and 75-7), of 'contrived pluralism' (*ibid.*, 229) and of 'inside groups who run the whole thing' (Kogan 1978, 162). Such language suggests some misgivings over the assumption of dispersal. He argues that 'the formal educational policy-making system . . . forms a strong system of consensus which provides collective strength' (*ibid.*, 119). When he notes outsiders' perception of educational government's 'cohesion to the point of being a closed system' (*ibid.*), he comes even nearer to identifying a corporatist tendency. 'All the same', he concluded in 1975, 'the system is pluralistic inasmuch as authority and power are distributed among well-defined institutions at different levels. . . . They benefit from the assumption that power should be distributed and they are watchful of encroachments on their access to decision-making' (Kogan 1975, 231-3). Since 1975 he has not significantly modified this position.[9]

Kogan is well aware of the problems of delimiting 'educational policy' as a subject matter that is distinct from the world of educational practice and from the wider political system. He has thus attempted to extend his explanations and, in Silver's words (see above), 'to engage both with the broad reaches of policy, and with the close and detailed description and analysis of the processes of education, and of people's experience and perceptions of them'.

By extending the idea of policy-making to include educational practice, Kogan acknowledges that 'education is essentially an inter-personal activity between teacher and pupil conducted in individual institutions such as schools and colleges maintained by local authorities' (Kogan 1978, 121). Thus he finds that many educational policies, for example for comprehensive education and for the primary school,

> demonstrate where, at present, so much of the power lies. For an essential point about the development of educational policy is that whilst many of the main issues have been clarified and determined at

the centre . . . many policies and practices have been developed in the
schools and the local education authorities. (*ibid.*, 122)

Teachers and local authorities thereby contribute to the pluralism of the
system not only in their collective capacities as partners in national policy-
making, but also in their individual capacities as actors in a widely dispersed
system. Thus, when the concept of policy is broadened to include 'practice'
and 'policy-development', power over policy-making is found to be dispersed, not only between these three agents at the national level, but also
between this level and other levels of activity, including the individual local
authority, the school, and the individual teacher. 'The most important
changes in British education', he writes, 'have been bottom-up . . . on the
larger social objectives endorsed and pushed by central government . . .
there has been virtually complete failure' (Kogan 1983b, 73).

When Kogan says that the dispersal of power makes the politics of
education 'difficult to comprehend' (*ibid.*, 123), he is describing a dilemma
both for the external commentator and for actors in the system itself. The
dispersed practice of education is a logical feature of the system's pluralism,
and builds indeterminacy into it. This is because actors at one level never
quite know what is going to be coming up or down the line from another.
Thus knowledge, or the lack of it, and communication, or the lack of it, have
a central role in his analysis.

Here it is useful to clarify two senses of pluralism that figure in Kogan's
work. The first sense describes a national system in which groups' interests,
including those of the local education authorities, are negotiated at the
national level. It assumes the mutual orientation of the participants in the
context of a belief in the existence of a national system, and of their
voluntaristic contributions to decisions. It should be noted, however, that,
under certain conditions, this first sense of pluralism is virtually indistinguishable from liberal corporatism (see above). In the second sense, the
pluralist model is of dispersed centres of decision-making in which the
decision-makers dispose of sufficient resources, and have the statutory or
professional authority, to control their respective domains. This model thus
begs the question of the senses in which it describes a 'system' in respect
either of the actors' orientations, or of any systematic element in the net
outcomes of dispersed decision-making. Empirically this model is a candidate to describe situations where the notion of 'system' itself is disputed
between central government and local education authorities or other actors.
The central authority may wish, in the name of certain values, to 'systematise' across the other units, whereas the latter may not because they see
systematisation as a bid for overall control. Thus 'system' itself may become
a contested concept. What to Millan looked like people 'all over the place'
(see preface) may well from the other end have looked like genuine differences over values and policies. Tawney said that anarchy was one of the last
bastions of English liberty. This approximates the second sense of pluralism

distinguished here with its uncertain location somewhere between Hobbesian disorder and a society that is sufficient of a 'system' to be able to flourish on dissent.

Kogan's extension of the idea of policy-making to include educational practice helps to underpin his pluralist case. So also does his second extension, which is to include a broader idea of social stasis and change. Precisely because it is difficult to comprehend, the dispersed and indeterminate system is argued to be a conservative one, governed more by habit than by design. 'Analysts', Kogan writes, 'tend to look for change whereas continuity and conservatism most usually predominate' (Kogan 1978, 137). To focus on the changes which formal policies seek is to disregard the fundamental inertia to which all formal policy changes are marginal. The system of institutions and practices, values and rules, is an historical accumulation or sedimentation of compromise solutions to past conflicts (*ibid.*, 117-18). Again this is offered, not only as Kogan's view, but also as a description of the understanding of actors within the system, especially the DES. Central government, Kogan says, does not seek radical change, though it may on some occasions behave more 'promotionally' than on others.

Hence, it is argued that the plural system is in equilibrium and that an important part of that equilibrium is the logical inability of any one actor within it to comprehend the totality of its structure and workings: plural systems are sustained by the inertia of institutionalised ignorance. This does not mean that predictions cannot be made about them, but they will not, cannot, be predictions about particular events. Indeed, Kogan concludes his book *The Politics of Educational Change* (1978) by saying that 'almost all of the changes in this book could not have been predicted fifteen years ago. Speculation about educational futures even in the relatively short term is hazardous' (*ibid.*, 158). This indeterminacy does not mean that explanations of particular events cannot be given. They can. But they will tend to be *ad hoc* or *ad hominem*, and they will not specify all the causes (Kogan 1975, 21-2). Small wonder Kogan is concerned for the governability of such systems and for the 'disjointed incrementalism' by which change occurs (*ibid.*, ch.11).

In his theoretical statements, Kogan gives little space to the third source of indeterminacy in educational policy-making; namely changes in the economic, political and social life of the nation that are 'external' to education and its governance. Nevertheless, he clearly regards these as major. Much of *The Politics of Educational Change* is concerned with issues that are '"institutional" and political rather than educational', all of them echoing some of the main themes of British politics at large (Kogan 1978, 118).

Finally we note that Kogan's pluralism does not set out to explain or predict exogenous influences such as these, even though they may make for major educational changes. Nevertheless, his broadening of the concept of 'policy' to include practice, stasis and change does drag the meaning of the

13

word dangerously close to the idea simply of 'what happened'. It therefore looks at times as though his pluralism should be judged by its ability to explain educational change in general. This is an absurdly severe test and one which it is bound to fail. Nevertheless, it is a test that has been imposed in a recent attempt to displace Kogan's pluralism with a more pessimistic account of the idea of partnership. Before coming to this, however, we must first retrace our steps to examine how various strands of social theory have converged in the present debate over the status of pluralism and of alternatives to it.

The Sociology and Politics of Education

Until recently British sociology of education paid little attention to policy-making. Nevertheless sociology is important because it treats the relationship between civil and political society as problematic.

The sociology of education in post-war Britain is commonly understood in terms of three phases of development. The first derived from a Fabian tradition of academic enquiry and political involvement. Sociologists working within this tradition after 1945 were perhaps less concerned to study educational policy than they were to influence it, mainly through critical evaluations of the implementation of the Education Act of 1944 (e.g. Glass 1954; Halsey, Floud and Anderson 1961). They did not produce a sociological literature on policy-making and the state. But they did make the pluralist assumption that the state could, in principle, act independently of dominant social-class interests, and that social-democratic welfare policies had the potential to mitigate social-class differences in life-chances by making education at different stages equally available to all social classes. The state was not the executive committee of the bourgeoisie.

Education figured in this account as a consumption right of citizenship. But it was also given a part to play in a market economy which maintained incentives through (limited) differences of occupational reward. It was argued that an educational system that was equally accessible to all children, whatever their parents' position in the occupational hierarchy, would satisfy parental ambitions for their offspring. It would also ensure that youthful merit eventually reached the occupational level at which it could be most effectively employed. Technology required increasing skills of the work force. Educational systems sorted and developed this 'human capital', directing individuals to occupational levels appropriate to their skill and effort. Part of the surplus from the resultant economic growth could be reinvested in further reductions of cultural disadvantage, leading both to further growth and to greater political stability. For some twenty years after 1945 the two major political parties broadly agreed on this account.

In the 1950s and 1960s, however, the account was increasingly embarrassed by studies that showed the persistence of social-class differences in educational attainment, in Scotland as well as in England (e.g. Macpherson

1958; Douglas 1964). Various strategies of reform were mooted. These included comprehensive reorganisation, recurrent education, and the extension of state provision to include both a broader, more 'social', definition of education, and a wider range of clients, including pre-school children, parents and other adults. The expectation was that the state might compensate 'culturally disadvantaged' young people by enriching their early lives, and also those of their parents and of other adults in the community (Halsey 1972; Grace 1978, 78-86). These strategies pointed towards expanded provision, and still assumed that inroads on the social and economic order of capitalism could be achieved through electoral democracy and a government bureaucracy that was indifferent between political parties, social classes and any interest of its own (Halsey, Heath and Ridge 1980). They also, however, implied an enlarged and more intrusive role for the state itself.

The second phase in the post-war development of the sociology of education in Britain is more easily characterised by its somewhat self-conscious and overstated dissociation from what had gone before than by any single theory or method. It was diversely influenced by structuralism, phenomenology and symbolic interactionism. There was, nevertheless, a common concern to shift the terms of the debate from questions of educational opportunity, to questions of knowledge and social relationships. The explanation of the persistence of social-class differences in attainment was henceforward to be sought in the definition of knowledge and excellence that was incorporated in state and private schooling; a definition that was held to be philosophically arbitrary but systematically biased against working-class pupils (Young 1971).

In some ways this position was a diversion. It implied that there were no further questions that could usefully be asked about educational attainment within prevailing definitions of knowledge; and it directed study towards the 'politics' of interpersonal relationships in the classroom and away from the politics of the state, even though the latter had, by then, received little systematic attention. The principles of the distribution of power were to be sought, not in the tangible machinery of government and the formal processes of politics and administration, but in informal social relations and in impalpable structures of knowledge. Like the first phase, this second phase had little interest in the formal government, politics and administration of education, nor in the 'assumptive worlds' of those involved therein. Nevertheless, its rejection of a realist, 'objective' theory of knowledge in favour of an epistemological relativism weakened the social-democratic paradigm. If science were arbitrary, so too was technology, and the economic order could not, therefore, present the educational system with an objective requirement for individual merit. At the same time, external events began to confound social democracy's expectations of economic growth and redistribution: growth slowed, recession deepened, and it was realised that sizeable sections of the community were falling through the safety net of citizenship. Jencks' and his associates' *Inequality* (1973) showed that the educational system's promotion of talent had had little influence on life-chances in the USA; and Braverman's (1974) account of de-skilling in the labour market questioned technology's requirement for the human capital of education and skill.

If not by reference to social-democratic theory, how was one to explain the prevalence of state educational systems in advanced industrial societies, or explain the fact of the major expansion of these systems after 1945? In the third phase of sociological writing on education two sorts of account filled the vacuum. They can be described as neo-Marxist and neo-Weberian, but these are somewhat doctrinaire labels that understate the internal variety and overlap of these accounts. The neo-Marxist explanation of educational growth entailed a redescription of reality. It recast the liberal 'delusions' of democracy in more sinister light, as the ideology of a dominant group; and it represented the permeation by the state of ordinary social relations as the hegemony of this group. The post-war expansion of education, indeed much of the history of state education, could thus be read as the extension or retention of the dominant group's social control. It was argued that there was a 'correspondence' between, on the one hand, the habits of deference, order and acceptance inculcated by hierarchically organised educational systems, and, on the other, the worker predispositions that maintained public order in the face of economic exploitation (Bowles and Gintis 1976). Radical historians and others in the USA extended this critique to the significance for social control of welfare agencies and professionals in general, and the critique took root in Britain too (Karabel and Halsey 1977; Silver 1980, ch.5).

Perhaps part of the attraction of 'correspondence theory' was that it supplied a powerful explanatory metaphor where explanations were now wanting, for it was only one of several attempts in the 1970s to account by means of a single explanation both for the pursuit and for the apparent failure of social-democratic policies. But the attractions of correspondence theory were mixed. It replaced the possibility of action and reform in education with inevitability and passive despair. A theory was needed that restored the possibility of human agency. For some critics, many of them Marxist in orientation, a criterion of the truth of that theory was that it should sustain educational action tending towards the liberation of the working class (Reynolds and Sullivan 1980; Sharp 1980).

The current Marxist debate is part of a wider evaluation of structuralist explanations of social inequality, as distinct from explanations that are rooted in individual agency (Anderson 1980). One concern is whether ameliorative political action through social-democratic institutions modifies inequality or sustains it. At issue is the degree of autonomy enjoyed by politics and schooling, and the extent to which this autonomy may be constrained by dominating ideologies that permeate civil society in general and state officials in particular (Ahier 1983). Social-democratic theory had not asked such questions because it assumed that state officials did not have a vested interest in the maintenance of social inequality. Also at issue is the extent to which the respective interests of capital and the state are internally homogeneous and mutually supporting. Again this is a question that directs attention to the ways in which state officials, including teachers, interpret their role in relation to capitalism. Grace (1978), Ozga and Lawn (1981), and Lawn and Ozga (1986) are among the few studies to engage these questions with empirical research. The main self-avowedly Marxist analyses have been theoretical (e.g. Harris 1982). Nevertheless, much Marxist writing on education is willing to relax holistic, monocausal assumptions about the nature of social relations in the short and medium term, and to allow considerable explanatory autonomy to individual agency. At an empirical level it is difficult to see how the resultant explanations differ from those that pluralism might offer.[10]

The most important neo-Weberian alternative to the social-democratic account of education is to be found in the theory of 'credentialism' associated especially with the work of Randall Collins (1975, 1979). Here too the economic order figures prominently, but only as a dynamic that sets an agenda of problems for the political order, and not as an imperative that determines the solution of these problems. Collins assigns as much importance to conflicts over the distribution of rewards as he does to conflicts over their production. Following Bourdieu and Passeron (1970), he regards economic rewards as part of a larger currency of 'cultural capital' which may be appropriated in various ways. In conflicts over its distribution, groups formed by such criteria as language, ethnicity or other cultural attributes, are no less important than social-class groups. He then interprets the political order as the product of 'second-order' alliances between different groups as they pursue their own interests.

This is where the growth of organisations is important, Collins argues, and the growth of public examinations too. Access to organisations increasingly influences access to resources; and organisations themselves are increasingly the site of conflicts over reward distribution. A winning strategy is to 'fix' the public criteria of success in ways that favour one's own group within the organisation, and the organisation itself within wider society. Thus educational systems and certification expand partly because low-status groups have an interest in acquiring the social recognition (and hence the control of reward distribution) that attaches to publicly recognised certificates; whilst high-status interest groups wish to maintain a relative advantage over lower groups by raising and manipulating certification requirements for entry to valued positions. The possession of credentials correlates with individual success in life, not so much because credentials measure a talent for productive and therefore well-rewarded activity (broadly speaking, the social-democratic view), but more because they confer the positional capacity to influence the distribution of rewards in one's own favour.

National systems of certification therefore turn out to be central to the political process. They adjudicate and resolve competing claims on rewards, and they dampen what otherwise might be violent swings in temporary advantage from one interest group to another. But they also become the locus of conflicts over the appropriate criteria for public success. Neo-Weberian theories therefore direct our attention towards the control of public examinations, and they give certification a significance for interest-group politics in general. They suggest that corporatist 'incorporation' might be looked for, not only in politically explicit agreements between government and interest-group leaders to play the power game collusively, but also in the consent that is given implicitly by teachers and pupils to public examinations, and to the particular criteria of success incorporated in these examinations. In Bourdieu's analysis the social institution of certification is central to his analysis of power: 'academic qualifications', he writes, 'are to cultural capital what money is to economic capital' (Bourdieu 1977, 187). The micro- and macro-politics of certification is therefore an important theme of later chapters.

Recent Critiques of Pluralism in Education

The most important sociological attempt in recent years to formalise a pluralist account of educational politics is undoubtedly Margaret Archer's formidable comparative study of the development of the educational systems in England, Denmark, France and Russia (Archer 1979). Her thesis, however, has much in common with those of Kogan and Collins, and we reserve further mention of her work to chapter 2 on Scotland where her discussion of centralised and decentralised systems is apposite. Here, meanwhile, we comment briefly on two recent critiques of the pluralist interpretation of educational politics.

In *Education, Politics and the State: The Theory and Practice of Educational Change*, Salter and Tapper (1981) criticise the 'inability of interest group theory to incorporate the forces which lie behind the apparent balancing of rival group interests'. The result, they say, is that 'the issues of process and change over time remain enigmatic' (*ibid.,* 90). They argue that, in making an explanatory link between the conflicting demands of interest groups and actual policy outcomes, interest-group theory must resort to 'conceptual sops' like the 'climate of opinion'. Such sops mop up the problem of explaining the 'gap between cause and effect in the group-policy relationship' (*ibid.,* 91). This criticism is explicitly directed at Kogan's pluralism and at its inability to explain educational change.

What in effect Salter and Tapper try to do is to replace the conceptual sop of public opinion with a more rigorous account of the way in which ideology links cause to effect. 'The main thesis is simple', they write, 'the dominant bureaucratic apparatus in the shape of the Department of Education and

18

Science increasingly controls the process of educational change' (*ibid.*, vi). The external dynamic of these changes, they argue, is the protracted economic crisis which has left central government, here equated with the DES, as the agency best placed to interpret the changing needs of capitalism and to organise schooling to meet these needs in the light of other external demands, for example, of demography and finance. But the interests of central government do not perfectly coincide with the 'objective demand of the dominant economic order' (*ibid.*, 221), for 'though it is naturally in the interest of major government bureaucracies to respond to the economic order on which their survival ultimately depends, they may also view their interest in terms of the maintenance and extension of their own power' (*ibid.*, 221-2). Central government is better placed to pursue its own interests than any other group because, 'as the manager of the arena in which these demands are negotiated, the state apparatus (the DES) . . . can nonetheless interpret these pressures in ways which suit its own bureaucratic ambitions' (*ibid.*, 92). These developments have 'an internal logic', and can 'in no way be seen as part of a rational balancing of opposing group interests' (*ibid.*, 92). Rather, 'policy formation in education is becoming an activity encapsulated within a limited set of structures, permeated by bureaucratic values which emphasize the importance of scientific rationality, efficiency and professional expertise. These are the parameters which control the rate and direction of educational change' (*ibid.*, 93).[11]

There are a number of difficulties in this position, but we will comment only on two. First, the thesis is essentially historical: there is a trend towards the orchestration of educational policy-making by the DES because bureaucrats pursue their own interests. Yet most of the evidence the authors discuss relates only to the 1970s, and their account of DES officials is based almost entirely on official documents and secondary sources. They seem in effect to concede that the system was pluralist until the 1970s, but their clearest statement on this is unfortunately rather vague (*ibid.*, 41-2). Second, the thrust of the critique of Kogan's pluralism is that he is unable to explain how the DES 'aggregate[s] the knowledge, feelings, resistances and resource feasibility of the 30,000 institutions, the complex political system' (*ibid.*, 90; see also Kogan 1975, 238). But, as we suggested earlier, it is too severe to require of a theory of policy-making that it show how all educational practices and all educational change are incorporated in policy. They are not, and insofar as they are not, the problem of how the DES 'aggregates' is not that much of a problem. Nevertheless, the Salter and Tapper study is important. It attempts to explain a trend in government behaviour which many of their readers may feel they recognise, and certainly neither Kogan, nor other major pluralist writers, have anything very convincing to say about the fate of partnership under Mrs Thatcher.[12]

Our reading of the book *Unpopular Education* by the Centre for Contemporary Cultural Studies (CCCS 1981) is that it regards pluralism of all

varieties as limited, both analytically and morally. The cccs group redescribes English educational policy since 1945 as an unstable succession of
makeshift 'settlements' that temporarily contained and depoliticised popular responses to the continuing crisis of late capitalism. The events of the
1960s and 1970s made people more aware of the fragility of these settlements. But, the cccs group says, it is not schooling itself which has changed
in recent years. Its history since the Second World War has been an un-
changing one of 'discontinuities – a series of breaks and reversals, stagna-
tions and advances, crises and settlements' (*ibid.*, 247). What has changed
has been public awareness which now sees that 'the state [cannot] be
regarded as a neutral organ to be "won" by any side in an electoral battle'
(*ibid.*, 246). People, they claim, would be more likely today to embrace 'the
presumption that the administrative apparatuses of the state are self-in-
terested, duplicit, and secretive. The key problems now posed concern ways
in which political demands are refused or defused, or how, once conceded,
they are turned against their own purposes' (*ibid.*, 247). And they write:
'the shadowy figure of the DES has always been crucial to an understanding
of the formation and implementation of educational policy' (*ibid.*, 179).

These two studies have much in common. Both accept Braverman's
account of de-skilling, and a neo-Weberian position on the politically
stabilising function of certification. Both opt for a 'loose' correspondence of
schooling with the capitalist social order, but are vague on the class structure
of this order. Both regard the 'guerrilla warfare of the classroom' as a
conflict over the reproduction of social-class relationships, and both agree
on a trend towards the 'enclosure' or 'encapsulation' of policy-making by
professionals (inspectors, teachers, officials) as they sever education's links
with popular democratic culture and forms. However, whereas Salter and
Tapper regard formal politics as a trivial rhetorical accompaniment to the
'inevitable logic of the policy-process' (above), the cccs study pays much
more attention to the party and popular politics of the period, and to the
'hegemony' of capitalist social organisation. Hegemony is achieved through
the considerable 'ideological work' of the construction of alliances between,
on the one hand, class-dominated state agencies such as law and schooling,
and, on the other, forms of social domination in civil society, such as
patriarchy. By supporting liberal, social-democratic educational policies,
both major political parties after 1945, but especially the Labour Party,
sustained this hegemony. Labour conflated 'education' with 'state schooling' and stressed 'the politics of access at the expense of struggles over
content, context or control' (cccs 1981, 65). This 'statist' politics reduced
education to 'a consumer good, a mark of status and a means to personal
social mobility. . . . All sense of education as a lived process (occurring in
and out of schools) was completely lost' (*ibid.*, 72). Social-democratic
amelioration is presented as the ideology of professional politicians of all
parties. They feared the social resentment that might be caused by a

meritocratic educational system, and believed in their hearts that the 'cultural deprivation' that caused educational failure was a euphemism for cultural inferiority. This ideology, the CCCS group argues, sustained attempts to turn whole areas of the working class into the pliable clients of state agencies and state professionals; and in this endeavour Maurice Kogan, when an official, himself played a small part (*ibid.*, 126).

This 'statism' could be represented as a form of corporatism, though the CCCS study does not use this terminology. Nor does it discuss the pluralist model as such. We infer that the CCCS group regards Kogan's work as a descriptively more-or-less accurate account of one part of the policy system; the differences of interest between the groups in the policy-making arena merely reflect aspects of the division of labour among professionals (*ibid.*, 164), or struggles between different sections of capital. Such differences are as nothing when compared to the interests that separate professionals and capital from the mass of the working class. Thus to call the system 'pluralist' would be descriptively incomplete, and analytically and morally trivial. The CCCS group argues that post-war education took only one of the possible forms that were imaginable and attainable. When set against these alternatives, the historical 'reality' of post-war education must be redescribed (as 'statist schooling'). The major determinants of educational stasis are thus to be found outside the formal polity, and the major problem for the student of policy-making is to explain and reverse the removal of the working-class interest from the agendas of policy and practice. Thus the CCCS explanation involves a redescription of educational 'reality', and the test of the value of this redescription is its capacity to reinstate the working-class interest.

Summary and Discussion

We can broadly distinguish three approaches to the explanation of education, policy and the state. The first is characterised by an emphasis on the essential indeterminacy of human events. If policy does not just fall off the back of lorries, it does require to be explained with due regard to the complexity of events in the real world. This world is intrinsically ideographic, but it can be validly known through individual experience. Its complexity is real, and is not a result of ideology's obscuring individuals' perceptions of some simpler, underlying truth. Thus all that is required to explain policy outcomes is reference to individuals' beliefs and intentions. These cannot be consistently predicted from any group affiliation they may have. Much, therefore, will always be left unexplained. Stable patterns and trends may occasionally be discernible, ordered perhaps by an aggregating mechanism such as government consultation or public opinion, perhaps by a great man with a firm grasp or wide vision, perhaps by an underlying theme such as progress. However so, any pattern will be more apparent to the historian who attempts to view events with hindsight and detachment. The study of contemporary events is premature history, therefore, and

21

social theory a flirtation with ideology.

The second and third approaches, by contrast, assume the lawfulness of human events and explicitly embrace social theory. They assume that there is an order in human events that lies beyond the comprehension of any single individual involved in them. Reference to the beliefs and intentions of these individuals is therefore insufficient to explain regularities in the antecedents and consequences of their actions.

The second approach focuses on a political arena that is assumed to be separable from civil society. Power is dispersed among groups within this arena. This dispersion may result from the decentralised historical origins of the system, or perhaps from a general acceptance of a constitutional model of partnership which the main groups concerned try to observe. Dispersion means that, whilst particular events will appear unpredictable, a prediction can be made about the net consequences of events over the long-term: no one group will benefit more than another. This is a pluralist position. But one version of corporatism also belongs within the second approach. Because of the inherent instability of a system that is always unpredictable in the short term, governments that seek predictability may incorporate the leaders of interest groups in decision-making procedures, and thereby drift towards corporatism. Alternatively, the effectiveness of the application of rationality to the solution of problems may tip the balance in favour of official dominance. There is a presumption, however, that neither equilibrium, nor disequilibrium, nor incorporation, in the longer term favours any one group more than another. Corporatist relations are not necessarily dominated by a particular class-, bureaucrat-, or status-group. Maurice Kogan's work spans these first two approaches, though it is, of course, mainly empirical in character.

The third approach places more emphasis on the interdependence of political and civil society. Thus social-democratic sociological theory argues that rudimentary equalities in civil society (for example, equality before the law) were incorporated in an emergent welfare state. This in turn further stabilised civil society by limiting the effects of social-class inequality through the enrichment of citizenship. Educational policy is then understood as the outcome of the interplay between citizenship and inequality, between a public interest on the one hand, and individual or group interests on the other. The neo-Weberian accounts we have discussed are similar. Policy is regarded as the outcome of inter-group conflicts and alliances. But political conflicts and alliances are constrained by 'alliances' in civil society, such as the alliance achieved through the social institution of certification. The outcomes of alliances made in the formal political arena may veer towards the interests of dominant civil groups but do not necessarily do so. Neo-Marxist accounts may also refer to struggles between interest groups. In the CCCS account, however, these groups represent only the different sections of capital; the working-class interest is largely excluded from influence in the arena of formal politics. The interpenetration of civil and political society explains much of this exclusion. Ideology distorts working-class representations of their true situation and their perceptions of their 'real interests'. The pattern of civil domination and subordination limits the problems that are to be resolved in the formal political arena, and biases their solution towards capital. Pluralism may explain the resolution of minor differences of interest between professionals or sections of capital, but it does not challenge the dominant group. In Salter and Tapper's account the differences of interest within and between capital and professionals are not minor. But it is not fully clear what these differences are, or whether they upset the pluralism to which, in the main, Salter and Tapper appear to subscribe.

Complicating these substantive and theoretical differences are two methodological issues, one concerning the validity of the social world, and the other the validity of human experience. Writers' positions on these issues entail different definitions of policy and different views of evidence. Their positions correlate with their substantive theories, but not perfectly so. Broadly three methodological stances can be distinguished. First there is methodological individualism. As we have indicated, this asserts that human events are intrinsically ideographic and must be understood solely through the evidence of the beliefs and intentions of the individuals involved. The second and third positions posit a social world. This world inheres in regularities in human events that are supra-individual in the sense that no actor comprehends them all. The second position accepts the validity of human experience of this world, even though it is incompletely comprehended. The third position does not. Rather, it believes that human experience, or human reality, may have to be redefined; that reference may have to be made to what individuals would experience (perceive, believe, prefer and do) were their experience not constrained by this social world. Pluralist interpretations typically take one or both of the first two positions; corporatist interpretations one or both of the second two. In the first two positions, policy is defined in terms of events occurring within the formal polity, and the boundary of this polity with civil society is treated unproblematically. In the third approach, the conventional understanding of the polity is itself regarded as problematic and as an aspect of the exercise of power. With the boundary between political and civil society either dissolved or relocated, educational practice and experience may also require redefinition; hence the 'politics' of the classroom, and notions of 'statist' schooling and classroom 'resistance'.

Steven Lukes (1974) has well described the implications of these methodological positions for the definition and explanation of power. It is easiest to adduce behavioural evidence if one focuses on the actual choices people made between actual options. But such a focus confines the empirical study of policy outcomes to issues where options existed and were known.

Such options are typically articulated as a result of competition or conflict. But such a focus is unduly restrictive because an important aspect of power is the capacity to shape or suppress competition, and with it the development of options. Herein, however, lies a dilemma. How can one adduce evidence from actual human behaviour in respect of options that did not develop, and in respect of behaviour that did not occur? At first sight the choice seems to lie between a study that respects evidence but trivialises the concept of policy by detaching it from wider questions of power; and a study that reaches towards the intangibles of power, but that thereby floats free from any grounding in the evidence of what the individuals in question believed, wanted or did.

In practice, however, the dilemma is not as stark as it might appear. First of all, there are lessons that can be learned from the way choices were made between articulated options. Much of the evidence of this book assesses such choices. Also, it is possible to show how some options failed to materialise as such, and to do this without detaching oneself entirely from the discipline of behavioural evidence. Partly this involves attention to sequences of events wherein an early decision, such as ruling an option out, shaped subsequent events. Partly it requires attention to assumptions that may have been unconsciously or unquestioningly held, and to beliefs that were held mistakenly. Relevant also is evidence from periods when existing assumptions and practices were challenged or destabilised, as happens to have been the case in Scottish education at roughly twenty-year intervals from the 1890s onwards. What is required most of all, however, is an analysis of the social world; that is, an analysis of the facilities and constraints that inhered in individuals' situations, not all of which they apprehended or chose. The task of the following chapter is to analyse the social world of Scottish education and government as it had come to be by 1945 when our study starts. Later in the book we show how this world had also shaped the identities of many of the individuals who made Scottish educational policy in the years after 1945, and had carried them into the policy community. Through this structuring of personal identity and group affiliation, civil and political society were linked to each other and thence to the schooling of later generations.

NOTES
1. Short, Boyle and Crosland are among the former Ministers who used the term 'partnership' with approval to refer to this system (Boyle and Crosland 1971, 126 and 187; Fowler 1974, 9). Selby-Bigge, the Permanent Secretary of the Board of Education from 1911 to 1925, praised the 'active and constant partnership' between the Board and local authorities that had been provided by the 1918 Education Act. But the financial relationship was problematic (Selby-Bigge 1927, 114-18 and 186-8). A more recent Permanent Secretary, Pile (1970-76), has likewise emphasised that the education service is a partnership both in statutory terms and in the working out of relationships in

practice (Pile 1979). Whilst other officials do not necessarily use the term 'partnership', the concept of distributed and shared power is at the heart of their descriptions of the educational system (e.g. Briault 1976; Weaver 1976). Briault, a local-government officer, sees this distribution as a source of strength, but notes the checks and balances that exist within a consensus that includes the schools. Academic observers, also, use the partnership model in describing central-local relations (e.g. Kogan 1978; Regan 1979; Fenwick and McBride 1981). Many acknowledge that partnership, or the 'balance of power', has been under great strain over the past ten years or so as a result of the extension of central control (e.g. Bogdanor 1979; Broadfoot 1980; Kogan 1983b). Some go further to conjecture its severe erosion or demise (Ranson 1980; Fenwick 1985; McNay and Ozga 1985, 1-7). Others, however, in government and elsewhere, seek to revive partnership through the clarification of powers and the extension of membership (DES/WO 1977; Aldrich and Leighton 1985). Kenneth Baker, who was appointed Secretary of State for Education in 1986, has said that he wishes to extend the range of partners. But he has also equated partnership with the principal-agent model (*TES* 25 July 1986). Meanwhile, writers on central-local relations in areas other than education alone have cast doubt on the utility of partnership as an analytical model. Thrasher (1981) points to its ambiguity and to its rhetorical use by central and local participants. He asks that it be clarified, or else abandoned. R. Rhodes (1981) abandons it in favour of a more sophisticated model of 'power-dependence' based on exchange theory.

2. For example, Briault (1976), and Fenwick and McBride (1981). Pile (1979) describes a central-local government partnership 'with the teachers through their national organisations increasingly involved as a third element' (*ibid.*, 24). Regan (1979), however, does not include teachers in the partnership. Bell and Grant (1977, 166) doubt whether the kind of triangular relationship described by Briault is really a partnership so much as a situation of occasional warfare in which teachers form shifting alliances. Lawn and Ozga (1986) see the recognition of teachers as partners in terms of central government's strategy of indirect rule, through which it has promoted only a restricted idea of teachers' professionalism. They argue that, with the contraction of the educational system in recent years, teachers' unequal status is more clearly seen as central government exerts greater control over the teaching force.

3. Among the main descriptive accounts for England, and with Wales usually included by implication, are Kogan (1975, 1978), Pile (1979), Regan (1979), and Fenwick and McBride (1981). Bell, Fowler and Little (1973) and Bell and Grant (1977) focus more widely and include not only Wales but also Scotland, Northern Ireland, Eire, and other systems in the British Isles. Scotland is described in Milne (1957), Hunter (1972) and Humes (1986).

4. For reviews see Davies (1982), Marsden (1982) and Parkinson (1982). Parkinson comments that 'the most striking feature of the British literature in this field is how relatively little of it there is. . . . We know little about the role of political parties or of pressure groups in policy-making and indeed relatively little about how the formal government apparatus of decision-making works. For example, despite its growing significance the precise role of the Department of Education and Science in policy-making remains unexplored. Equally significant, there has been hardly any analysis of the inter-governmental dimension of policy-making. The relationships between central and local government and the shifting balance of power between the two is crucial to any understanding of virtually any policy initiative during the past two decades, and yet little is known about them. This is most visibly true in one of the most

controversial policies in the post-war period: the comprehensive reorganisation of secondary education. There have been some studies of national, and rather more of local authority policy-making, but hardly anything which deals at a theoretical level with the interactions of the two levels of government in this policy area. Yet, in the final analysis, this dimension has critically affected the implementation of national policy. The same is true about many other important policies introduced during the post-war period' (Parkinson 1982, 114-15). The situation has changed little since 1982, but for subsequent empirical analyses that engage theoretical questions, see Hargreaves (1983), Shipman (1984), Ranson (1985b), Broadfoot (1986), McCormick (1986), Ranson and Tomlinson (1986), and Rhodes (1986, ch.8).

5. An accessible general introduction to the issues is Abrams (1982). Following Mills (1970), he argues persuasively that sociology and history share a common enterprise in the explanation of events, structures and individual behaviour. Historical sociology 'is the attempt to understand the relationship of personal activity and experience on the one hand and social organisation on the other as something that is continuously constructed in time' (*ibid.*, 16).

6. A recent definition of pluralism refers to 'the existence of a plurality of relatively autonomous (independent) organizations (subsystems) within the domain of a state' (Dahl 1982, 5). In one form or another, pluralism has provided one of the principal paradigms of political science for several generations. It has strong roots in interest-group theory, reviewed by Margolis (1979, ch.5) and by Richardson and Jordan (1979, ch.1). Pluralism was refurbished in America from the late 1950s on as a renewed challenge to social-class and ruling-elite analyses of power structures that were put forward by, for example, Hunter (1953) and Mills (1956). Dahl (1958) was the main critic. Through empirical studies of decision-making in local communities, he and his colleagues showed that power was dispersed, and was not wielded by a single elite that held sway across a range of issues (Dahl 1961; Polsby 1963). The relationship between pluralism and democracy has frequently been discussed, and the democratic claims of pluralism criticised (Dahl 1956, 1982; Schattschneider 1960; Connolly 1969; Lowi 1979). Some saw pluralism as, nevertheless, an elitist theory of democracy (Walker 1966; Bachrach 1967). Others developed this argument by reconsidering the theory of political power. They showed how issues were kept off the agenda of public discussion by tactical, structural, or ideological means, thus systematically reinforcing the power of some relative to that of others (Bachrach and Baratz 1962, 1970; Lukes 1974).

7. The corporatist literature to which we refer differs from pre-1945 theories of the corporate state. Sometimes called 'neo-corporatism', it considers the role of groups in the political processes of advanced capitalist society, and focuses primarily upon economic and industrial policy-making at the national level (e.g. Winkler 1976; Middlemas 1979; Crouch 1982). One leading writer, Schmitter, describes it as 'a system of interest and/or attitude representation, a particular modal or ideal-typical institutional arrangement for linking associationally organized interests of civil society with the decisional structures of the state' (Schmitter 1979a, 8-9). But Schmitter prefers to talk about 'intermediation' rather than 'representation', because interest groups in corporatist relations with the state acquire functions of resource allocation and social control (Schmitter 1979b). There are, however, many alternative definitions and conceptions of corporatism. Among the main sources for these, and for empirical applications, are Schmitter and Lehmbruch (1979), and Lehmbruch

and Schmitter (1982). Both contain a large number of references to a wide literature. The first of these sources mainly explores theoretical issues, whilst the second mainly compares different countries. It is arguable that the complexity of the subject has contributed to its conceptual unclarity and to terminological confusion. There are many schools of corporatism (Lehmbruch 1982). It may be partly for this reason, and partly because there is, likewise, no single model of pluralism, that writers disagree on the extent to which the two concepts overlap. While Schmitter recognises that corporatism shares common properties with pluralism, he nevertheless distinguishes between pluralism and corporatism in terms of the number and nature of the interest groups, their relation to the state, and their role in representing interests (Schmitter 1979a, 13-16). Others see little new in corporatism that pluralism does not deal with (Jordan 1981, 1983; Martin 1983a, 1983b), a view that is rejected by those who find corporatist theory fruitful (Crouch 1983). Cawson (1978), Richardson and Jordan (1979, ch.8), Harrison (1980), Grant (1985b) and Self (1985) discuss both theories. Crouch (1985) proposes an analytical model of relationships between capital and labour which clarifies some distinctions between pluralist and corporatist forms of bargaining. Other recent developments widen the canvas to include non-economic and non-industrial sectors (e.g. Newman 1981, ch.10; Cawson 1982), and move from the 'macro' level to the 'meso' in assessing the extent to which corporatism exists in particular industries and policy areas, and in localities (Cawson 1985a, 1985b; Grant 1985a; Rhodes 1985b; Saunders 1985; Simmie 1985).

8. For example, in her study of nineteenth-century elementary education, Gillian Sutherland comments that 'what passed for ideas in many men's minds were often fragments rather than systems, tangled up with half-stated assumptions and prejudices sometimes inconsistent with each other, but none the less powerful for all that'; and she advises that, 'the respective weights to be attached to vested interest, deeply-felt commitment, or ideology can only be worked out *for each individual, one at a time* . . .' (Sutherland 1973, 1 and 346, our emphasis). See also the discussion in Abrams (1982, ch.10).

9. In writings published in the late 1970s and early 1980s, Kogan has commented on the threats posed to pluralism by tendencies towards a more closed system of decision-making and towards greater central control of finance and curriculum. However, he still saw the fundamental robustness of its pluralism as one of the abiding qualities of the educational system of England and Wales (Kogan 1978, 1979, 1983a, 1983b).

10. The point is also made by Hargreaves and Hammersley (1982) in their criticism of *Unpopular Education* (cccs 1981) which we discuss below. Hargreaves (1982) contains a fuller analysis of the ways in which the neo-Marxist thesis of the relative autonomy of political and cultural factors, including schooling, 'are designed to admit complexity while excluding pluralism' (*ibid.*, 117). The programme for research that Hargreaves sets out in his conclusion, and to which he has subsequently contributed (Hargreaves 1983), corresponds to our understanding of our own enterprise: 'one useful way of putting relative autonomy to work empirically would be through careful analysis of educational policy-making and its effects upon school practice in particular historical periods. This would make it possible to elicit the ways in which policy is formulated and implemented on the basis of limit-confirming assumptions policy-makers hold about the relationship between schooling and the social structure, and in the context of various constraints that derive from that social structure. The ways in which particular policies and accumulations of policies

27

provide a context for school practice, affecting in no small part the shape of the latter, could then be traced through' (Hargreaves 1982, 123). For discussions of Hargreaves (1982) see Dale (1983), Nash (1984) and Fritzell (1987). Other contributors to the debate on neo-Marxist theory and method include Dale (1982), Davies' (1983) review of Apple (1982a, 1982b), and Archer's (1983) discussion of the work of Bernstein and Bourdieu. The exchange between Silver (1981, 1983, ch.5) and the authors of *Unpopular Education* (Baron *et al.*, 1982) is also relevant to the general problem of how conflicting theories are to engage with each other and with evidence.

11. These arguments resemble those of recent writers on the autonomy of governmental structures, and specifically of state bureaucracies. Nordlinger (1981) proposes a 'state-centred' perspective on policy-making, in which government officials are not constrained by societal preferences and pressures. In Nordlinger's view the state can also change society's preferences to enhance its own autonomy. The relationship between the autonomy and development of the state, the internal workings of bureaucracy, and corporatism is a relatively recent subject of study (Birnbaum 1982; Cawson 1982, chs 4 and 5; Cawson 1985c). The conception of bureaucrats as rational actors seeking to expand the influence of their organisations is central to the writings of a number of American theorists of administration (Downs 1967; Niskanen 1971; Peters 1978). Bureaucrats compete with politicians for control of policy, and are in a strong position to win. However, 'the' bureaucracy is not united. Competition and conflict occur between agencies or bureaux as each seeks to aggrandise or protect its programme and budget. Kogan finds cultural and structural reasons for criticising the borrowing of such theories. He argues that British civil servants are not proprietorial about 'their' programmes, and that the DES is not homogeneous in its viewpoints and motivations (Kogan 1981, 165-6). For the latter reason he rejects Salter and Tapper's view of the DES as monolithic (Kogan 1982). Ranson (1985) shows that there was a DES 'departmental view' of education for the sixteen-to-nineteen age-group, which entailed greater central control in the pursuit of policy objectives. However, the agreed view did not prevent conflict between branches of the DES over how the policy should be implemented.

12. We regret that, in drafting this chapter, we overlooked Salter and Tapper's (1985) revision of their 1981 argument. This revision, which does draw upon interviews, attaches more importance than the earlier study to the Manpower Services Commission (MSC) and to party politics. But it does not deal with the difficulties we raise, nor does it signal a change in their theory.

Two

Scotland

Public sector education in Scotland is a partnership between
central and local government.   Scottish Office (sто 1984, 2)
Control from the centre is a reality.   Leslie Hunter (1972, 38)

Introduction: Beyond Centralisation

The government of education in Scotland, like that in England, is officially
described as a partnership.[1] Partnership implies a dispersion of power and
responsibility. Yet most commentators agree that the Scottish system is
more centralised than the English.[2] Part of the explanation for this apparent
contradiction is that such descriptions have a rhetorical function in the
politics of the systems themselves, asserting the claims and counter-claims
of conflicting groups. Also, the terms themselves are imprecise. We have
explored these themes in relation to English experience and the idea of
partnership. In this chapter we extend the discussion to Scotland and to the
historical origins of its educational and governmental institutions. These
emerged in response to challenges and conflicts that have had lasting consequences for the story to come.

What commentators agree by Scottish centralisation is roughly as follows:
Scotland is a small country with a long history of public educational provision characterised, in the nineteenth century, by greater public access and
greater uniformity of practice than in England. The creation of the Scotch
Education Department in 1872 and of the Scottish Office in 1885 allowed
subsequent developments to continue along separate and characteristically
Scottish lines, steered by the early Secretaries of the sED who enjoyed
something of an administrative despotism between 1885, when the first was
appointed, and 1921, when the second retired. They bequeathed to their
successors powerful tools of control, a widespread habit of obedience among
educationists outside, and a secondary-school system that enjoyed a level of
development that was both uniform and high by British standards of the
time. During these years central influence was also increasing by default
owing to the slower development in Scotland of the local authority. In
England, local school boards were replaced in 1902 by larger and more
powerful county authorities. But school boards in Scotland lasted until
1918. There were over nine-hundred of them, and nearly all were too small
to play a major part in the developments that were taking place. Thus, in

Scotland, it was not the local authority but the central authority that assumed control of teacher training (graduate and non-graduate) in 1906, that developed the non-university institutions of higher education called 'central institutions' after 1901, and that took a leading role in promoting secondary-school provision. Even when the local control of Scottish education was finally passed to thirty-five *ad omnia* authorities in 1929 (from 1919 to 1929 there were nearly forty specially elected *ad hoc* authorities administering education alone), many were still too small to make much impact. This continued until their demise in 1975, when they were replaced by nine regional and three island authorities.

Other features, too, are said to have enhanced the power of central-government officials in Scotland. Scotland has a proportionately larger central Schools Inspectorate than England and, unlike England, has no local-authority inspectors, although the Scottish local authorities began to appoint educational advisers in the late 1960s. Public examinations are a powerful means of control in education. Until 1965 the Scottish Inspectorate conducted all national school examinations in Scotland. Since then, there has continued to be only one examining body for schools, statutorily independent, but with central-government representation on it. National curriculum advice since 1965 has been given by a non-statutory body, appointed by the Secretary of State for Scotland and linked to the Inspectorate. There are no school governors for maintained schools in Scotland.

These are mainly arguments about the institutional inheritance. But there is also an important and closely allied argument about the anthropology and normative standards of what we have called the Scottish educational policy community. It is that Scotland is a small country in which everybody values education, knows everybody else, and can easily be got together to thrash things out. Thus, it is claimed, the education system is one in which people naturally 'look to the centre' for a lead, and, as a result, educational policy in Scotland is more often led from the centre than it is in England. This, it is argued, is partly because people want it that way, and partly because there are fewer alternatives to this state of affairs. There are said to be fewer hindrances too, insofar as Scottish provision, being more uniform, is more easily comprehended and steered from the centre. The crucial point, however, is the assertion that central initiative commands consent, and is therefore expected, natural, legitimate. It is one of the most cherished of official arguments, and one that permeates both the discourse of policy and various histories and textbooks.[3]

There is some truth in the centralisation model. But, like the idea of partnership, the idea of centralisation takes one only so far, and it begs as many questions as it answers. In particular we can ask, to what centre does Scotland look and work? There are a number of candidates.

First there are the universities. For much of the past century the distinction between the SED and the universities has not been important to educational policy. The Department harnessed the universities' prestige to its own purposes in 1889, when it persuaded them to accept the Departmentally controlled Leaving Certificate for admissions purposes. Thereafter, a pupil's wish to enter university on leaving school required that pupil and teacher alike conform to Departmental requirements. Since 1889 the interests of the universities and the Department have diverged only occasionally. But this is mainly because the focus of policy has hitherto been on age-groups that were too young to be of direct interest to the universities. It is more likely that universities and Department will be at odds with each other in the future as the issues of student selection and course provision are decided for the post-compulsory sectors. This has obvious implications for any explanatory model that holds that one condition of the Department's power is its influence over national certification.

Within the Department itself there are arguably two centres: the administration and the Inspectorate. At times one can see more daylight between them than at others. There was a lot in the mid-1950s and early 1960s, and judgements of any change since then must be an empirical matter. Then there is the Scottish Office itself, controlling the purse to which its five spending departments want access. There is also a political centre of fluctuating importance. It contributed something during the Second World War (see part II), but little in the two decades that followed. Thereafter, a Labour centre was crucially important to the implementation of comprehensive reorganisation in Scotland because of its political alignment with most of the local authorities. More recently a Conservative centre has been important, partly because the resistance of many local authorities to its policies has led to a politics of central imposition. But, even when the central and local authorities have been politically aligned, other groups have limited the political centre's influence. For example, for some years the official policy of the Labour Party in Scotland has been to end denominational schooling. But it has done nothing to implement that policy for fear of alienating its substantial Catholic support. Finally, within the framework of the United Kingdom, there is the centre (or even centres) constituted by the various departments of government, by the Manpower Services Commission, and by the political parties.

If the idea of one Scottish centre is problematic, so also is the view that the only partners to the centre are weak relative to those in England. In the past this may have been true of the smaller and more remote authorities. But it was not self-evidently true before 1975 of Lanarkshire, Aberdeen, Edinburgh or Glasgow nor, since regionalisation, of Strathclyde. The argument is often made that the English system is more pluralist than the Scottish because of the strength of the English local authorities. But the DES is not faced, even in the Inner London Education Authority, with an authority like Strathclyde that speaks for almost half the country. Moreover, size alone debars neither the councillors nor the officials of any local authority from action through their national organisations.

One can make the same sort of argument about other Scottish groups. Against the foregoing catalogue of centralist tendencies we may set an equally persuasive list of Scottish features which could plausibly be appropriated by arguments stressing partnership, pluralism and decentralisation. These features have included: independent universities administered, not by the S E D, but by the University Grants Committee (U G C) within a United Kingdom framework; a large teaching force, and a better qualified force, relative to England; a major national teachers' union, the Educational Institute of Scotland (E I S); national advisory councils and committees; a national research council, founded in 1928, and for much of its life supported independently of central government by the E I S, the local authorities, directors of education and others; the local authorities themselves, albeit many small, but with national organisations and a collective potential; a national Association of Directors of Education (A D E S); a national press; and, finally, special provision for Scottish business in the Westminster Parliament where, after 1945, an increasing proportion of Scottish M Ps were themselves school teachers, and were retained as spokesmen for educational interests.

In other words, if we describe the Scottish policy world purely in institutional terms, then its potential for partnership and pluralism is not self-evidently less than the English. It may be, of course, that the case for English pluralism has been exaggerated, as Bell and Grant (1977, 87) suggested some time ago, and as many have claimed of events since then. Or it may be that terms like partnership and centralisation are insensitive to what may be really quite minor variations in British political culture. Kogan, for example, describes the English system as pluralist, but also as one in which the D E S wields great power and determinant authority (Kogan 1975, 238). At first sight, such a description is no less applicable to Scotland. What is certain, however, is that any tendency for Scottish policy-making to be Departmentally led, and for Scots to look to the S E D for a lead, did not just happen. Nor was it dictated by an impersonal logic of Scottish institutions, civil or political. Rather, it represents a triumph for the Department over considerable institutional odds. Where that triumph has been achieved, it has resulted partly from the way in which the Department has shaped the institutions of governance, and partly from the work it has had to do to make these institutions run in particular ways.

That work, and its related triumphs, has always had a cost for the Department, a cost in the form both of opportunities foregone, and of responsibilities reluctantly assumed. In a system in which people look to the centre, changes of policy and provision are liable to impose greater burdens on the central authority than they do in systems where there are multiple local agencies. Thus the S E D has continually been required to measure the desirability or inevitability of changes in the schools against the implications for its own resources and control. One result has been that the political work that Departmental officials have had to do, in order to try to control a potentially pluralist set of institutions, has itself conditioned substantive educational policy, and has conditioned, in particular, central government's attitude to the largest change of all, namely expansion.

The prospect of an expanding school system has always threatened a heightened level of activity and expenditure, both potentially disruptive for a Department working within a relatively fixed establishment and grant. Where these could not be significantly enlarged, and where expansion could not be resisted, the Department had no alternative but to search for new allies and human resources outside government itself. If expansion were to proceed along the lines it desired, the central authority had to influence outsiders' demands, the currency of issues in the public domain, and the standing of the people who argued for and against particular policies. And, even if the Department could not grow larger, it still had to grow wiser, or more expert, if it were to provide for the greater range of pupils and circumstances that came with expanding enrolments. Otherwise it might surrender authority to providers outside who claimed a newer or more appropriate expertise.

All these considerations could be satisfied in some degree by the admission of outsiders to the councils of the Department. Once this began to happen, as it did in the 1950s, 'looking to the centre for a lead' might continue to signify a deference to the central authority and its acolytes. Alternatively, it might indicate a centrally negotiated and coordinated pluralism, in the first sense of the term distinguished in chapter 1, or even a shift towards corporatism. Clearly, what is crucial here is the relationship between officials and outsiders within central government and at its fringes. This relationship, and the wider consent it commanded, is one theme in the story that follows.

But this is to anticipate. The main argument of the present chapter is that mid-Victorian Scotland was confronted by a choice between two conflicting ways of relating educational systems to the social order, the one stressing open access, community and local control, the other stressing restricted access, individualism and central control. The former position emphasised the virtues of a traditional view of Scottish democracy: the good society was one in which educational provision at all stages was generous and open, and one in which each community had a school of equivalent status. The latter position held that democracy was more efficiently served by making separate provision for different types of education and different types of community, and by sponsoring only some individuals to the highest levels. A partial settlement of this conflict had emerged by the 1890s, but the settlement was contested, both nationally and locally, in the following decades. The resultant conflicts, and the political work that the Department had to do to maintain its influence, limited its room for manoeuvre with the teachers and local authorities. This had a lasting effect on the way in which the machinery of governance was used after 1918, and on the Department's attitude to particular individuals, ideas and practices. It also led to an ideological redefinition of the nature of the Scottish educational tradition that favoured the Department's position. But it was not until the late 1950s that the SED began to grope towards a solution to the governmental impasse, impelled by expansionary forces which it could no longer contain. The expediential solution at which it arrived in the turbulent circumstances of the mid-1960s established the system of educational governance broadly as we have it today. But a legacy of earlier conflicts also survived.

The next two sections are preliminaries to the central argument. First we outline the administrative and political position of Scotland and its educational system within the United Kingdom. Then we turn briefly to social theory to consider how we may distinguish empirically between the potential for partnership that inhered in the institutional legacy, and the relationships that actually transpired.

Scotland in the United Kingdom

Since 1870 there has generally been separate but coordinated legislation for education in Scotland and England (Knox 1953, 241-2), and this coordination has extended to non-statutory initiatives as well. Recent years have seen the simultaneous introduction in the two countries of comprehensive reorganisation (1965), the raising of the school-leaving age (ROSLA) (1972-73), and the government programmes for the young unemployed that culminated in the Youth Training Scheme (YTS) (1983). The expansion of provision for further and higher education in England and Scotland in the 1960s followed similar timetables, and even relatively minor innovations made their appearance at about the same time in the two countries.

Devolved provision for government and administration in Scotland originated in the compromises that a London-based government made with Scotland's distance and distinctiveness after the union of the Scottish Parliament with the English Parliament in 1707. It was reinforced by a nineteenth-century concern to keep united a kingdom that was threatened by the centrifugal forces of Celtic nationalism. Since then the major British parties have periodically competed for the middle ground of Scottish politics by offering measures of political and administrative devolution, though mostly confined to the politically non-prestigious areas of health and welfare, education, agriculture, housing, and relatively minor economic matters (Kellas 1968, ch.7; Donaldson 1969; Harvie 1977; Dickson 1980). In the late nineteenth century, and indeed, for much of the first four decades of the twentieth, Scotland had its own Minister, and was administered by a number of boards, and later departments. During this period the formal powers of the Minister grew, and by the outbreak of the Second World War, the reorganisation of the modern Scottish Office was completed (Hanham

1969; Gibson 1985, ch.III). It was located mainly in Edinburgh and was directly responsible to the Secretary of State for Scotland. This post normally has full Cabinet status. Since 1951 it has been supported by a Minister of State and usually by three junior Ministers. Since 1941 a junior Minister has usually had immediate Ministerial responsibility for education and at least one other department of the Scottish Office. The Scotch Education Department (renamed Scottish in 1918) was located mainly in London until the early 1920s. By 1939 it had moved to Edinburgh, retaining a London base at Dover House. The Scottish Schools Inspectorate was founded in 1840 and has always been based in Scotland (Bone 1968). The legal powers of the SED have broadly resembled those of the DES (though it is said that officials in both the SED and the DES like to describe the other institution as a backward form of their own).[4] There are regular contacts between officials of the two Departments. A recent observer has suggested that DES thinking may pre-condition SED thinking on major problems and policies, but that 'it is difficult to pin down the extent of DES influence on Scottish education and it doubtless varies with personalities and issues' (Macbeth 1983, 171-2).

There were always persuasive arguments for the separate administration of Scottish education. Compared with England, the nineteenth-century school and university systems in Scotland were well developed, and public representatives were more closely involved in their management and finance (Anderson 1983a, 1983b, 1985b, 1985c). Responsibility for the school system has remained in Scotland, but the Scottish universities have been controlled this century within a United Kingdom framework administered at one remove originally by the Treasury, and later by the central authority for education in England. Nevertheless, some distinctive university elements survived. Two of the principal institutions served by Scotland's universities in the nineteenth century, the Law and the Church, retained their independence, and a third, medicine, had its own professional collegiate structure in Scotland. With the growth of compulsory state education, the universities supplied in increasing numbers the manpower needs, and later the womanpower needs, of a fourth relatively independent sector of Scottish life, the school system itself (Mackay 1969, ch.4; Anderson 1983a, chs 7 and 8; Bell 1983, 1986; Corr 1983).

An important channel for the supply of graduate teachers was the three-year Scottish Ordinary or General degree. After 1892 the degree became a 'collection' of discretely examined subjects, very different from the philosophy-centred general education that many nineteenth-century Scots had wanted to preserve (Davie 1961, 1986; McPherson 1972; Anderson 1983a, 270-1 and 280-2; Anderson 1987). Nevertheless, it was to remain one of the distinguishing features of the Scottish university system in the twentieth century, and one that was held to justify the broad subject requirements of the Higher Grade of the Scottish School Leaving Certificate (SLC) examination. The Honours degree, also remodelled in 1892, was awarded

35

usually after a four-year course, the 'extra' year being justified partly by reference to the shorter period of secondary schooling in Scotland (i.e. five or six years, compared with seven or eight in England), and partly by the desirability of maintaining a broad university course, at least in the first two years. Almost a century later, when making recommendations in 1985 for the future form of the government of higher education in Scotland, the Scottish Tertiary Education Advisory Council (STEAC) reaffirmed the importance of these 'distinctive features . . . of Scotland's educational tradition' (SED 1985, 5). They were not considered important enough, however, to persuade the Government to accept STEAC's recommendation that, subject to certain conditions, ultimate responsibility for the Scottish universities should be passed to the Secretary of State for Scotland.

Another feature that distinguished the Scottish system from the English was religion. Although the Church Disruption (schism) of 1843 was eventually to weaken the public influence of religion, the varieties of Scottish Calvinism were quite distinct from the Anglicanism of the South. Religious participation was higher in Scotland, and the government of the established Church more 'democratic' in that there were no bishops, non-ordained persons had a place in Church government, and the Church itself was held to be largely separate from the state (Donaldson 1960a, 70-103; Smout 1972, 213-22; Smout 1986, ch.VIII). With Irish immigration, especially into west-central Scotland, the proportion of Catholics in the population began to grow. Today about one-fifth of the population in compulsory schooling is educated in Catholic schools, but this proportion touches forty per cent in the west-central half of the country. Though by no means dead, the religious issue has been less contentious in twentieth-century Scotland than in England. R. A. Butler had to give more attention to church schools than to any other problem in his preparations for the 1944 Education Act (Butler 1971, 96 *et seq.*). But Scotland had broadly solved these matters by 1918. Unlike England, the school boards that were established throughout Scotland under the Act of 1872 were allowed to take over the management of voluntary schools. Most Presbyterian schools were transferred. Then, in 1906, the Protestant denominations relinquished direct control of teacher training to a system of 'Provincial Committees' under the SED (Cruickshank 1970, ch.5; Bell 1986, ch.4); and in 1918 full provision for denominational (in practice, Catholic) education within the state system was made (Dealy 1945, ch.V; Treble 1979; Fitzpatrick 1986, ch.4).

A further distinguishing feature of Scottish education has been its emphasis on a national, public, system (Saunders 1950). Although the model of the English private school penetrated Scotland, and although some Scots were educated at such schools in England, there was less money for private endowments in Scotland. There was also less inclination to support private institutions, rather than the public system that had been established in the aftermath of the Presbyterian revolutions of the sixteenth and seventeenth centuries. The first *Book of Discipline* had called in 1560 for a system that gave universal access to elementary education, and that gave the able child the opportunity to acquire higher learning both at school and at university. The universities themselves were always publicly controlled, and this was reinforced by the Universities (Scotland) Act of 1858 (though later, the University College at Dundee was initially a private foundation). In their conception of the form and purposes of higher education, moreover, the universities were well adapted to the needs of a poor, but educationally ambitious society (McPherson 1973). Throughout the nineteenth century the aspirations of the national school and university system, and what was, by then, its somewhat tattered reality, were fiercely defended by Scots who argued the case for state support with a sceptical and sometimes uncomprehending London government. Scottish liberalism had little patience with the English view that the involvement of the state in educational provision at levels above the elementary should be minimal, and that the provision of secondary education in particular should be left to market forces. The enhancement of access to education through a reformed, public and national system was an important but continuously frustrated item on the agenda of mid-Victorian Scottish politics (Davie 1961; Anderson 1983a, 1983b).

This protracted dispute over the incorporation of Scottish civil forms within the framework of a United Kingdom polity strengthened the view that the fate of Scottish identity was linked to the fortunes of the educational system. It also imparted a powerful impetus both to administrative devolution and to the thinking and practice of the inter-war system in which the Scottish policy-makers of the third quarter of the twentieth century were to have their own school and university education. Scottish education was thereby to remain 'one of the best-defined "arenas" of Scottish life, and one which most strongly maintains the boundary of the Scottish political system' (Kellas 1984, 230; see also Raab 1982b).

The Social Origins of Educational Systems

Archer's (1979) study under this title is an application of systems theory to the history of education in four countries from the early nineteenth century onwards. Since it was published she has developed her thinking in several other works (Archer 1981, 1982, 1983), and has also issued a shorter version of the original book (Archer 1984). Her theory provides one basis for distinguishing between the potential of inherited institutions to support or inhibit centralised or decentralised action, and the actual events of their history.

Archer attempts to explain patterns of relationships between the various agents of educational policy and practice over lengthy historical periods. These periods are characterised, first, as an 'emergent' phase before the state became the principal provider of education; followed by a 'developing' phase, lasting roughly to the mid-twentieth century and during which pri-

mary and secondary education systems were constructed; and then by a
'contemporary phase'. Writing of the first phase she says:

> The domination of the Church was lengthy in medieval Europe without
> it producing significant growth. The pre-condition of take-off is there-
> fore competitive conflict between at least two corporate groups for
> educational control, a stage first signalled by the post-Reformation
> battle between Protestants and Catholics whose shared aim of produc-
> ing religious orthodoxy multiplied the number of schools in existence.
> (Archer 1982, 9)

Not everyone accepts a 'group-conflict' explanation of educational expansion (e.g. Boli, Ramirez and Meyer 1985; Anderson 1986). However,
group conflict has a further significance in Archer's argument, which is that
the nature of this conflict conditions whether the state educational system
that subsequently emerges is centralised or decentralised. Moreover,
Archer claims, the character of the centralised or decentralised state system
in its emergent and developing phases, persists to the contemporary phase
and, in principle, allows one to characterise its present and future workings.
What Archer's theory promises, therefore, is a way of using history to
describe the potential for action of Scottish education in 1945, but in a way
that would not confine our analysis solely to what actually happened thereafter.

What sorts of group conflict, then, led to the emergence of a centralised
or a decentralised system? There were two strategies by which groups could
assert themselves:

> . . . *substitution*, which consists in devaluing the existing monopoly by
> competition in the educational market, by building and maintaining
> new schools and recruiting, training and paying new teachers to staff
> them; or *restriction* which involves the use of legal machinery to deprive
> the ownership group of its educational facilities. . . . In substitution
> educational control is challenged by market competition: in restriction
> the aim is a legal transfer of control. (Archer 1982, 10, our emphases)

In educational systems with 'substitutive' origins, Archer argues, the state
typically played a minimalist role, ceding control to existing local providers,
and making provision itself only when gaps were left unfilled. Because
groups provided for themselves in such systems, provision was finely tailored to their discrete, local demands. Institutions and courses tended therefore, to be well differentiated, or specialised, but also poorly articulated one
with another, and often overlapping and inefficient. Overall, such systems
were pluralist, but only in the second sense of the term distinguished in
chapter 1 because, at that stage of their development, they were also
'unsystematic'.[5]

In the second 'phase', private (individual) demand for education began
to take off, and the state, which was starting to spend public money on
education, began to 'systematise' the specialised substantive elements that

had grown up piecemeal. Nevertheless, Archer asserts, the systems that emerged from substitutive origins were still decentralised in the second phase of development. The variety of substantive provision could not be fully 'comprehended' (understood and managed) from the centre alone. Central governments had therefore to recognise that local providers were legitimately involved (as agents of the central authority and/or authorities in their own right) in the policy-making of what had become unified, though not yet 'fully' systematised, national systems. Thus educational practice, and its legacy of institutions and ideas, shaped and limited the scope of subsequent educational politics. Typical examples are Denmark and England.

Systems having 'restrictive' origins faced the opposite problem. By Archer's definition they were centralised, systematised and unified (see note 5). But, as private demand for education began to take off, the state found that its educational provision was not sufficiently diversified or specialised to meet the demands of groups other than the founding elite. Change did not tend to occur, however, through new departures in practice among educational professionals or other local agents; their fund of alternative ideas and practices was too small. Instead, change came mainly through the negotiation of political demands at the centre. This was often a lengthy process, characterised by long periods of stasis broken by dramatic change that was centrally led. Even then, the central directives were often too broadly framed to meet the circumstances of particular categories of pupils, schools and curricula, though the aspiration of central government was always to achieve the finer categorisations that would give it more intimate control. Typical examples are Russia and France.

Archer's theory has been criticised,[6] but it remains a valuable heuristic, especially in respect of the implications of substitution and restriction for the ensuing character of educational politics and practice.

Scottish Origins and Conflict

An immediate problem in applying the theory to Scotland, however, is that one cannot satisfactorily describe the origins of the Scottish system of public education solely in the terms of the restrictive strategies of an elite, nor of the substitutive strategies of the market. The original Reformation settlement was theocratically inspired, and popularly sustained thereafter. Its constitutional status was initially dubious, and its political viability was always contingent upon the English sovereign authority, both before and after the Act of Union had redefined the boundaries of the Scottish political system (Donaldson 1960b, ch.ix; Mackie 1960, ch.ix; Smout 1972, chs ii, iii and ix). Moreover, the eighteenth-century consolidation of public education also fits uneasily with Archer's typology. She observes that unopposed domination by a group led typically to 'a low level of provision such that education did not touch the lives of the vast majority of the population'

(Archer 1982, 9-10). But it was during a period of Presbyterian hegemony in the eighteenth century that the national system in Scotland was considerably extended. Provision was made through the public system, and the play of the market was restricted. This strategy confirmed the Scottish system in an important feature that Archer ascribes to centralised systems with restrictive origins: relative to England, Scotland in the early nineteenth century had fewer substitutive educational networks associated with diverse social or religious groups.[7] Such networks were later to develop from the Disruption and from responses to industrialisation, Irish-Catholic immigration and the demands of an urban middle class. But they were late arrivals and, as we have seen, they did not become so deeply embedded that central government could not largely absorb them in little more than a generation.

We can say, therefore, that mid-nineteenth-century schooling in Scotland was more uniform than schooling in England, even though central government as yet played little part in educational provision, and even though local government, at the level of the parish, was in many places overextended. However, schooling was not centralised, in the sense of being organised around central government, though it had a higher potential for such an arrangement as the influence of organised religion declined. This potential was strengthened by the widespread belief that there should indeed be a single public system, that it should embody systematic relations between its several parts, and that it should be based on the standard administrative unit of the parish. The potential originated, however, not in the restrictive control of a single elite, theocratic or otherwise, but in a high degree of consensus over the part that a public and national education system should play in a civil society that lived by religious precept (Saunders 1950, part IV; Smout 1972, ch.XVIII).[8] As religion declined, so the way was opened to the Department to assert its claim to custody of the national system in times of change.

Population grew in the nineteenth century, and its distribution shifted on two axes: from the country parish to the town and city; and from the North and East to the central belt, and especially to the west-central industrial conurbation centred on Glasgow. These changes confronted Scottish civil society, and education in particular, with a major crisis of identity and purpose. A first resolution of this crisis was achieved by the 1890s, but it was to be contested in the following generation, with lasting repercussions.

The crisis had two dimensions. One concerned the continuing implications of the political Union. Should solutions to problems be sought within a Scottish or a United Kingdom framework? If the latter, would civil society in Scotland long resist assimilation to the South (Phillipson 1969)? The other question was how the civil and spiritual order of the traditional parish might be reproduced in the city. In the early nineteenth century, Thomas Chalmers attempted to introduce the parish school and the parish welfare system into Glasgow in order to regulate the urban poor (Saunders 1950, ch.4). It was a thankless task. But Scottish literature from the early nineteenth century, through MacLaren, Barrie and Buchan, and up to Bridie in the 1950s, was nostalgic for a simpler form of social solidarity. The Glasgow conurbation, in particular, was not assimilable to traditional ideas of identity and social responsibility, and many regarded it as a material and moral blackspot, before and after 1945 (see chapter 17).

As for schooling itself, the state made a commitment to universal elementary education in the 1870s. But what was not settled in Scotland, nor between Scotland and England, was the form that elementary and secondary education should take. This issue was complicated by the continuing dispute over the future of the national university system and its links to the parish and burgh schools. Various considerations were involved, religious, governmental and educational. Following Anderson (1983a) they can be resolved into two conflicting prescriptions for the national system, each resting on a distinctive conception of the relation of education to the social order.

The traditional view, as we may call it, was that a reformed school system should continue to make access to higher learning available school by school, along the lines of the parish school (Anderson 1983a, chs 5 and 6). This entailed a view of secondary education as an open-ended continuation of elementary schooling, tailored to the socio-economic circumstances of pupil and parish, locally available, and free of rigid rules requiring the allocation of pupils of different ages to different educational stages or levels. A similar view of the university was also implied: there should be no entrance examination or requirement of graduation; students should be able to enter or leave at different academic levels, working their way piecemeal through university if necessary, and living in the cheapest possible way, cheek by jowl with the community (McPherson 1973). Thus prescriptions for the organisation of elementary, secondary and higher education were related one to another, and the whole was based on the view that education should be made available in ways that reduced social distinction and that increased access. Hence, local schools should be allowed to grow 'from the bottom up', as local demand for longer courses increased, and in order to increase that demand. As many pupils as possible should be given an opportunity for as long as possible. Educational selection should be postponed and should not be irrevocable. Curriculum should remain general, and authority in teaching and learning should be of knowledge, and not of social distinction (McPherson 1972). Writing in the late 1950s when 'some of the old issues ha[d] come to life again', this and more was what George Davie evoked by the title of his celebrated study *The Democratic Intellect* (Davie 1961, 7).

The alternative, bipartite view was associated with what Anderson calls the 'secondary education party' (Anderson 1983a, chs 5 and 6). It was that the state should separate elementary from secondary education, and 'raise the standard' of the latter by linking it to a new academic requirement for university matriculation. This would have the incidental effect of attenuating the connection between the university and the local parish school, which often could offer only rudimentary secondary courses. Henceforward, the ladder to university would rise exclusively through the secondary school, though the position of the able but poor 'lad o' pairts' (Anderson 1985a) would be preserved by reforming educational endowments into competitive bursary schemes. Selection of pupils for entry to secondary schools would be required, but the overall scheme would still be public and national. In it were many of the elements of a 'social efficiency' platform (Finn 1983). Specialist secondary schools would concentrate resources, and give economies of scale. With economy, new subjects such as the sciences and languages could be developed in the secondary curriculum, thereby preparing pupils better for university. Secondary-school teaching would be restricted to such pupils. Pupils not bound for university would be offered a non-secondary, post-elementary curriculum of vocationally relevant courses. The selection of pupils to different types of course would enhance social efficiency, not merely by ensuring economies of expenditure, but also by promoting individual talent to its appropriate level, and by preparing it accordingly for its next career step. Integrated with these elements was the conception of a stratified teaching force that was internally differentiated in terms of the qualifications of its members to teach the various specialisms and stages generated by this model.

One may describe an educational system that adopts this second strategy as a system of 'sponsored mobility': that is, a minority of individuals is selected at an early age (on grounds that may or may not be wholly 'meritocratic'), and their subsequent progress through education to elite positions is 'sponsored' by the disproportionate allocation of resources to them (Turner 1960). Sponsored-mobility systems may be contrasted with 'contest-mobility' systems in which larger proportions of individuals are prepared in order to contest with each other for valued educational or occupational positions when selection finally occurs. In sponsored systems, a large proportion of pupils is debarred from competition at an early age, and the basis of future social differentiation is laid down early in the pupil's personality, reinforced often by concomitant educational and residential segregation. In contest systems, social differentiation is postponed and access to educational facilities is shared. In this sense, then, the different positions that Victorian Scotland took on elementary and secondary schooling rested on opposing, but distinctively Scottish, views of how society should organise social differentiation and social mobility. 'System' was not a value-neutral term. Both views were still apparent in Scottish secondary schooling after 1945, with the sponsorship principle in the ascendant as a result of its promotion by the SED.

Settlement of the Conflict: Educational Issues

Under its first two Secretaries, Sir Henry Craik (1885-1904) and Sir John Struthers (1904-21), the s E D pursued a bipartite policy for the development of secondary education, based on ideas of social efficiency, social differentiation and sponsorship. In some ways, this was the easier course. A reformed group of some sixty secondary schools had emerged from the work of three government commissions on educational endowments in the 1870s and 1880s, largely in response to demands from the urban middle classes (Anderson 1983a, ch.5). For the most part, the provision of higher education in parish schools survived only in the Highlands and the North East; and secondary teaching was starved of public resources, Parliament having withheld adequate state support from Scottish secondary education for decades. In England, moreover, an emergent model of open secondary schooling for lower social groups was to be displaced by a revitalised grammar-school sector, following the demise of the school boards in 1902 (Banks 1955).

Craik, however, made his own contribution to the Scottish settlement. In 1888 he introduced the Scottish Leaving Certificate (s L c), a national examination for secondary-school pupils, conducted by the Department. Then, in the following year, he linked secondary school to university by persuading the universities to accept the examination at the Higher Grade for the university matriculation requirement introduced by the Universities (Scotland) Act of 1889 (Dobie 1967). Until 1924 the s L c Higher Grade was set at a higher standard than the universities' own Preliminary Examination (Osborne 1966, 126) and, in the early 1960s, Highers courses were 'still largely framed for pupils aiming at a university entrance qualification' (s E D 1965a, 32). Nevertheless, the Leaving Certificate and its successors were one of the main ways in which the Department tried to influence the organisation and curriculum of the secondary school, and this remained true even after the examination passed out of its direct control in 1965 (see chapters 4 and 13).

One reason for the Department's reliance on certification as a means of control was that other parts of the settlement proved less tractable than the link it had made between secondary school and university. Three aspects of the Department's policy were particularly controversial: its impact on local communities, its impact on social class, and its impact on access.

The Department disliked schools in which resources were used inefficiently. It therefore disliked small schools, and wanted to locate secondary provision in centres of population. In some socio-spatial circumstances this might indicate one *omnibus* school to serve a single community. But, where a community was small and there was a larger centre of population nearby, the policy implied the Department's opposition to a secondary school for the smaller community. The secondary pupils from the smaller community would have instead to travel to the secondary school in the larger centre. Thus the policy on resources had a local and regional dimension, and for decades it exposed the Department to the criticism that it had some responsibility for continuing rural depopulation.

The policy also entailed, as we have said, an insistence on pupil differentiation and selection. On transfer from primary school, secondary and non-secondary pupils (after 1945, certificate and non-certificate pupils) should be separated, whether or not they entered an *omnibus* school. This policy had similar implications for local community. Common provision would only encourage the proliferation of small secondary schools 'grown' from non-secondary ones. Scarce resources, for example of buildings and trained teachers, would again be spread inefficiently around. The procurement and efficient deployment of resources continued to preoccupy the Department after 1945 (see chapters 9 and 10), and it continued to regard the reduction of the number of secondary schools as a sure path towards efficiency.

The definition of a completed secondary education that the Department wished to impose after 1900 required secondary pupils to remain at school for three or four years beyond the minimum leaving age. This definition was socially regressive. By lengthening the period during which pupil and family were required to invest in education and to forego earnings, the new definition favoured wealthier families. It also favoured wealthier communities, and this was of crucial importance during a formative period in the construction of state provision for secondary education in the early decades of this century. Local schools were more likely to be designated as secondary if they showed some prospect of producing, in sufficient numbers, pupils who could fulfil the requirement of an extended investment. Thus the policy of social efficiency was overtly universalistic, but covertly particularistic, favouring particular social groups and particular local communities; and deliberately so, Paterson (1983) argues. A stratified system of schooling was thereby mapped onto communities that were believed by the state to have different potentials for secondary education. Mining communities, for example, were unlikely to acquire a secondary school. The evidence is that school and community interacted thereafter to reproduce, and probably to reinforce, local variations in community and social-class orientations towards the value of schooling (McPherson and Willms 1986).

The policy of centralising secondary-school provision, and restricting it to an elite, also had implications for access and expansion. Archer (1982) has pointed out that a pre-condition for expanding enrolments is the provision of universal, sequential, or end-on, relations between educational stages. The Department's insistence on two separate ladders from primary school, the narrow one leading to higher education, and the broader one terminating on entry to the labour market at fourteen years (and later at fifteen years), meant that the Department's opposition to local schools that were uneconomically small was also an opposition to expanding (lengthening) pupil enrolments. The Department was quite explicit about this, for example in its efforts to kill off the expanding demand for supra-primary levels of education after the First World War. It wanted to restrict secondary provision to the intellectual elite, estimated in 1926 by Craik (by then an MP) to be around five per cent, and certainly not more than ten (Craik 1926, 154). It also wanted to close courses that were 'intermediate' between the primary and secondary levels, courses which kept open, on contest-mobility lines, the possibilities of entry to secondary education. Such courses, a chief inspector complained, only encouraged the 'masses' to follow the 'classes', thereby inflating pupil demand for courses the Department thought inappropriate to them (Fraser 1920, 37). What the Department thought the masses needed after the social and moral disruption of the First World War was 'a spell of self-repression' and severe instruction in the duties of citizenship (*ibid.*, 31). It was to take a similar line after the Second World War as well, when the Sixth Scottish Advisory Council on Education confronted it with proposals to unify the two post-primary sectors around a single, progressive and comprehensive, model of universal secondary education that would substantially expand enrolments (see chapter 4).

Thus one of the Department's aims was to try to suppress expansion that threatened to breach the two main categories of post-primary schooling (secondary/non-secondary and, after 1945, certificate/non-certificate). A second aim, however, was to seek expansion that could be contained within these two categories and that was necessary if the Department were to see statutory requirements fulfilled. In fact, it was never to achieve either of these aims before its bipartite policy was overtaken by comprehensive reorganisation in 1965. Throughout the twentieth century one of the main motors of policy change has been the stubborn refusal of pupils to embark on courses thought proper to their intellectual level, and to complete the courses on which they did embark.

A third aim of the Department throughout this period was to shift the 'vertical dimension' of the organisation of schooling from 'stage' to age. This was legislated for in the 1870s, but it had not been achieved a century later. In the traditional system, a young person progressed up the vertical dimension, that is, from one institution or one teaching group to the next, not according to age, but according to stage, or level of performance. The practice of promotion by stage survived to influence transfer from primary to secondary school. The age of transfer in Scotland was finally set to about twelve years, whereas England moved back to eleven years. But, as late as the 1960s, and despite decades of pressure on local authorities from the SED, only about sixty per cent of Scottish pupils on three-year ('junior') secondary courses had entered them at a sufficiently early age to complete them before they reached the minimum school-leaving age. They had been held back in primary school in order to give them a later, and therefore better, chance of qualifying for the senior-secondary (five-year) certificate course (Osborne 1966, 94-100).

In this respect, many local authorities operated a system of stage promotion based on the contest-mobility principle of giving as many pupils as possible a chance for as long as possible. The survival of contest-mobility norms can also be seen in the large proportions of the age-group, relative to England, that were admitted to public secondary certificate courses between 1918 and 1965 (Osborne 1966, 98; McPherson 1973). In the 1920s the Department complained that admission to certificate courses was too generous (SED 1921). It was still complaining about this in the 1960s (SED 1961b, paras 85 and 86).

The conflict over stage promotion had implications for curriculum and methods of teaching. Stage promotion implies a greater homogeneity of pupil ability and motivation in a teaching group; age promotion implies a greater heterogeneity. Thus one finds the SED, both before and after 1945, urging that school classes be constructed on the principle of age promotion, and that the content and difficulty of courses be more finely tuned to the wider variation of pupil abilities that resulted from promotion by age. It also argued that selection and fine-tuning should take place earlier in the primary- and secondary-school courses. Many schools, however, resisted, and based their practice on the contest-mobility principle that selection and differentiation be postponed for as many pupils as possible, and for as long as possible. Many teachers pitched the course in the final year of primary school at the 'pre-qualifying' stage, and were criticised for it (SED 1956a, 10 and 11). Similarly, senior-secondary (grammar school) teachers were criticised for teaching all their pupils as though they were potential university entrants until the year of their leaving examination (in Scotland the fifth year, i.e. when pupils were seventeen: SED 1959b, paras 16 and 33; 1965a, 32). Comprehensive reorganisation for a time halted the SED's insistence on earlier differentiation. But the general problem of harmonising the difficulty of courses with the selection of pupils to them had still to be addressed in the Munn and Dunning reforms of the 1970s and 1980s (Gray *et al.*, 1983, parts I and II).

Archer (1979, ch.8) suggests that a characteristic of centralised education systems is that their legislative and other directives are often grossly tailored to categories of pupils and outcomes. Superficially this might seem to fit the Scottish case after 1945, the case of a system in which a major policy instrument, the national certificate, was designed to carry able pupils to university, but to do little else for them, and nothing at all for the large majority of pupils. Curriculum for less able pupils therefore tended to be a pale imitation of academic courses, even though the Department wished otherwise. The Department, hoist on its own petard, complained bitterly of teachers' conservatism. Archer contends that such complaints are also a feature of the politics of centralised systems (*ibid.*). But we must remember too that one reason for the apparent grossness of the secondary system, organised as it was in 1945 around the dominant idea of getting pupils into higher education, was the continuing dispute between the Department and its critics over the proportions of pupils that should be allowed to prepare themselves for higher education.

Our contention is not that the whole of twentieth-century educational policy in Scotland can be construed simply as a mid-Victorian battle continuously refought, although this is an aspect of the matter. Nor is the continuity of many of the issues the central point, though this again is important. For example, the non-secondary, post-primary schools of the inter-war period became the junior-secondary schools of the period after 1945 and, even fifteen years after comprehensive reorganisation, their legacy was still apparent in their pupils' attainments (McPherson and Willms 1986). Our main point follows from the fact that the 1890s settlement was contested and fragile, and left the Department much political work to do if it were to be maintained, let alone advanced. If we are to understand the extent and nature of centralisation in the Scottish system, the significance of the system's many pluralist features, and the extent of its autonomy, then we must treat these aspects of its governance as features that were forged, not in an historical vacuum, but in a continuing and keenly contested dispute over the form and purposes of the public education system.

Settlement of the Conflict: Issues of Governance

Anderson describes how Craik's plans for the centralisation of secondary-school provision were overturned in 1892 by M Ps who felt that 'the separate development of secondary education was alien to the Scottish democratic tradition . . . [and who] favoured local control over bureaucratic centralisation' (Anderson 1983a, 212). 'If there ever had been a chance of concentrating secondary work in a small number of schools', Anderson concludes, 'it disappeared with the events of 1892' (*ibid.*, 219). Craik 'had been defeated by the power of localism, and he did not forget or forgive this' (*ibid.*, 214).

One legacy of this defeat was a Departmental distrust of local control often bordering on contempt. Another was that the schools inherited by the county authorities that were formed in 1918, had had even longer to engender local and professional loyalties. In the early 1920s the new local authorities opposed the Department's policy for providing post-primary schooling in secondary and non-secondary sectors that divided irrevocably at twelve years, or thereabouts. The local authorities wanted a third, 'intermediate', sector, that would take the promising fifteen-year-old on to the completion of a full secondary course (AEAS 1925b, 13-15). They also wanted to open up an alternative route to university for the early school leaver *via* evening continuation classes (AEAS 1925a, 15-19). Both proposals would have maintained the contest-mobility principle of postponing selection. In terms of market position, teachers had much to gain from the expansion this implied. They too opposed the Department, arguing for 'a full secondary education for all pupils' (*SEJ* 11 January 1924). But the 'withering fire of criticism' directed at the Department came from many quarters, and echoed older arguments for the social solidarity of the traditional system (Wade 1939, 122; Young 1986, ch.2).

The conflict over educational and social purpose helped to set the structure of educational governance until 1965, and the uses to which the Department put it. By 1918 the elements of what could have been made to work as a partnership model had emerged. The 1918 Act provided for an Advisory Council of which two-thirds of the members should be qualified to represent educational interests. One argument in the campaign for a Council was that the Department was out of touch and at odds with significant Scottish opinion, nationally and locally (Douglas and Jones 1903, ch.v; Young 1986, ch.1). Not surprisingly, the Department itself doubted the need for such a body. The SED already consulted on major issues with the local authorities and the teachers. It saw little reason to duplicate consultation with outsiders, and it feared that a Council might provide them with a platform. It was right to be concerned. Opponents of the Department's bipartite policy captured the first Council (1920-24). From it they launched their blueprint for a unified and expanding secondary system. Again the Department neither forgave nor forgot, and it determined to run subsequent Councils on a tighter rein (Young 1986, chs 2 and 3; see chapter 11 below).

On the whole the SED succeeded, and the Scottish Advisory Council was given much less scope than its counterpart bodies in England and Wales, the Consultative Committee (1900-44), and the Central Advisory Council (1944-68) (Kogan and Packwood 1974). Indeed, the case for restriction was emphasised by the consequences of the SED's one subsequent failure to control its own advisory body. The Sixth Scottish Advisory Council of 1942-47 seized substantial control of its own affairs, and it produced a blueprint for universal secondary education that blended progressive educational thought from England, America and elsewhere, with the rhetoric and practice of Scottish democracy. But what especially embarrassed the SED were the Sixth Council's proposals to unify the secondary-school system, to increase and lengthen secondary-school enrolments, and to multiply the number of local secondary schools. Another nineteenth-century issue had again come to life. In the short term the proposals were dismissed by the Department, and were promoted by teachers and local authorities in word more than in deed. Thirty years later, however, the emergent shape of Scottish secondary education in the final decades of the twentieth century bore some comparison with the model proposed in 1947. Evaluating and explaining this resemblance is a necessary component of any general judgement on the pluralism of the Scottish system.

For much of this century, external opposition to the Department's substantive policies for education limited the use it could make of outside bodies, and this limitation, in its turn, helped to sustain the substantive divide. Conflicts between the SED, teachers and the local authorities over secondary-school expansion made the Department reluctant to take outside advice, and reluctant to allow its advisory bodies significant influence. This, in turn, restricted the opportunities for schools to develop a fund of alternative ideas and practices, an alternative body of convincing experience. It also made policies with expansionist implications even more unacceptable to the SED. With the new logistic burdens imposed on it by the 1918 Act, the SED was obliged to transfer the conduct of the qualifying examination for secondary education from its Inspectorate to the local authorities. If the Department were to remain of a size considered reasonable in British government, further expansion would require a further devolution of powers, devolution to agents in a potential partnership who had yet to prove that they could be trusted. As the primary and secondary systems grew larger after 1945, the burden on the Department increased. Nevertheless, Departmental suspicion of expansion and administrative devolution continued. Part of the story we tell is how the Department was eventually forced to accommodate these pressures and to search for a solution to the questions of control that they posed. Whom could the Department trust, and through what sort of executive and advisory machinery should the trusted few, and later the trusted many, make their contributions? How were the options for educational change to be assessed when the fund of alternative ideas and practices was too small to convince? By the early 1960s answers to these questions were urgently necessary. People were expecting too much to come from the centre, the Department complained, and it set about encouraging other agents for change to think of themselves as partners (see part IV).

Finally, one clarification is necessary. It would be wrong to take away from this chapter only the impression of a beleaguered Department promoting a sponsorship model in the face of the concerted opposition of teachers, local authorities and public opinion in general. Over certain issues an interest group and the Department might see each other as potential allies. At the end of the First World War, for example, teachers looked to the Department for protection from their school-board employers (SRO 1917), whilst the Department, for its part, thought it might influence opinion in the Labour Party by cultivating good relations with the EIS (Stocks 1970). Rather, we have pointed to the logical interrelations of the issues – local control, access and opportunity, expansion, selection and differentiation, age-promotion and curriculum – and we have suggested that there is an underlying dimension to the positions people took on them. But we are not suggesting that educational politics inevitably reduced to a clash between polar opposites, between an open, contest-mobility model on the one hand, and a bipartite, sponsored-mobility model on the other. Nor are we suggesting that a person's views on any one issue activated predictable views on the others. Rather, we are pointing to the logical basis out of which coalitions might form between different groups for whom these different, but related, issues were important. Such coalitions were feared by the Department and sought, sometimes, by its critics.

To talk of an underlying dimension is partly our own abstraction. But it is not mere abstraction, because it also describes a conflict that contemporaries themselves recognised. Educational issues were explicitly discussed in terms of their implications for social solidarity and social mobility, for a traditional and open community on the one hand, and for a nationally efficient society on the other. However, groups did not necessarily align themselves as the logic of the issues might indicate, nor feel equally strongly on issues where logical entailment was recognised, nor act from a single motive. Indeed, the interrelatedness of the issues often makes the inference of motives difficult, and all the more so because an effective educational politics would try to persuade people of the relatedness of the issues in an attempt to form coalitions. Conversely, an effective Departmental counter-politics would try to attenuate relations between issues, partly by argument, and partly by denying to potential opponents an institutional forum, such as an unsupervised Advisory Council, where coalescence between groups might occur.

Thus, for much of the Department's life, it has been engaged with its critics in a protracted ideological battle over the legitimacy of its custody of the national system, arguing that its policies did not break with the tradition of Scottish democracy so much as fulfil that tradition in a changing world. It is no accident that what was probably the Department's most fulsome claim for its stewardship of national values was made in the most contentious of its directives for the separate development of secondary schooling, Circular 44 of 1921 (see chapters 11 and 17). The Circular set back the cause of common secondary schooling but did not, however, defeat it. Contest-mobility norms survived in the practice of the schools, and the argument over common schooling extended into the years after 1945, impelled initially by aspirations for social reconstruction, and in the longer term by the expansionary implications of secondary education for all.

NOTES
1. See the epigraph, and also the S E D memorandum to the Royal Commission on Local Government in Scotland (R C L G S 1968a, 39). Neither statement included teachers in the 'partnership', though this was sometimes conceded, especially when it was necessary to placate them – see, for example, the Secretary of State for Scotland, John Maclay (P D 1961). Other applications of 'partnership' to Scotland include Morgan (1927, 197), A D E S (1947, 16), Bone (1968, 233) and Macbeth (1983). A contemporary and sceptical view is Humes (1986, *passim*).
2. See Knox (1953, 236-7); Osborne (1968, 79); Scotland (1969, 185 and 273); Bell and Grant (1977, 91); Gethins, Morgan, Ozga and Woolfe (1979, 19 and 22); and Humes (1986).
3. Hence Norman Graham's complaint, cited in the epigraph to chapter 9, that 'it is really remarkable that people should expect so little to come from the periphery and so much from the centre'. See also the Rendle report's comment

in 1981 on 'the willingness of the periphery in Scotland to look to the centre for a lead' (s o 1981, 59). The report asserted that 'although the broad statutory powers are similar in the two countries, the influence of central bodies including government, on the educational system in Scotland has tended to be more powerfully exerted, and more readily accepted than it has in England : indeed a central lead – in curriculum matters among others – is positively looked for' (*ibid.*, 7). The argument also surfaces in the Crawley report (s ED 1986, paras 2.1 and 5.6). As to non-official sources, Osborne (1966, 34) writes that 'there is a willingness to allow a far greater measure of authority to be centralized in the hands of the Department than would be tolerated in England' ; and he concludes that 'the Department has governed the schools with a heavier hand because it has been expected to do so' (*ibid.*, 40). Again, Hunter (1972, 38-9) writes of teachers that 'it tends to be assumed that the Department knows best, and thus its views are generally accepted. . . . Thus control from the centre is a reality; but it would be wrong to regard this control as in any way a stranglehold'. A similar position pervades Bone's (1968, ch.10) account of the Inspectorate, and James Scotland's (1969, ch.17) analysis of the Scottish educational tradition.

4. The most recent comparisons of powers are Bell and Grant (1977), Gethins *et al.* (1979), Fenwick and McBride (1981), and Macbeth (1983).

5. Archer (1979, ch.4) distinguishes centralisation from two other features which, she says, are common to all state educational systems, 'unification' and 'systematisation'. Broadly, unification means that educational institutions are subsumed within a single governmental structure under the state. By this definition, one might say that Scottish education today is not fully unified, though education in the United Kingdom is ; but much depends here on the extent of the autonomy of the s ED within the governmental framework of the United Kingdom. Systematisation means that government seeks to impose a logic upon relations among the various institutions such that the whole 'system' is greater than the sum of its parts, and relates to government. Thus we arrive at this definition of centralisation : 'Unification is not synonymous with the centralization of education, although the former is clearly a pre-condition of the latter. The concept of centralization denotes specific relations between the unified parts. "A centralized system is one in which one element or sub-system plays a major or dominant role in the operation of the system. We may call this the *leading-part*, or say that the system is *centred* around this part. A small change in the leading-part will then be reflected throughout the system, causing considerable change." A centralized system is thus a special type of unified system, but not all unified systems are centralized' (Archer 1979, 175, her emphases).

6. See King (1979), the exchange between Archer (1980) and King (1980), and Anderson (1986).

7. Not all historians would agree. Two questions are at issue here : the impact of eighteenth-century Scottish schooling, as indicated by levels of adult literacy ; and the role of private-sector schooling in the eighteenth and nineteenth centuries. Smout (1972, 427) writes : 'Between them, the parochial schools and the adventure schools of the Lowlands were able to maintain a rural society in which almost everyone seems to have been able to read and write from at least as early as the mid-eighteenth century, despite all the subsequent social demographic and economic changes before 1830. That was a remarkable achievement, certainly not parallelled in England, and probably parallelled in very few societies anywhere in the world, except for Prussia, parts of

Switzerland and a few Puritan areas in the United States'. He also suggests that the demand for adventure-school (i.e. private) education was 'a measure of the success of the Kirk and the parochial schoolmasters in persuading the peasantry that education was desirable' (*ibid.*). Houston (1982, 101), however, maintains that 'the advance of Scotland to its clearly pre-eminent literacy in the mid-nineteenth century' probably started later and was 'concentrated in the late eighteenth and early nineteenth centuries'. He also suggests that the contribution of private schooling cannot be ignored, either in Scotland, or in other systems that lacked a statutory public system but that nevertheless achieved levels of literacy comparable to that in Scotland (*ibid.*, 95-102; see also Houston 1985). A similar point is argued by West in relation to Scottish provision before the Education Act of 1872 (West 1975, ch.6). This is contested by Anderson, who emphasises the importance of church schools in the mid-nineteenth century. Anderson concludes that 'private schools never established themselves as the leading sector, or impressed the public by their efficiency. . . . Thus *laissez-faire* ideology did not seem particularly convincing or attractive to Scottish opinion, which sought the way forward rather in adapting and modernizing the tradition of public provision' (Anderson 1983b, 534).

8. There is a further, and crucial, respect in which the traditional Scottish system was not centralised in Archer's sense (see note 5). The Scottish Schools Inspectorate was founded in 1840, and the S E D in 1872. But, at that stage, they were far from constituting a 'leading part' which could easily effect a rapid change throughout the entire system. Indeed, the idea of a system has only a limited application to the disaggregated parochial units of the time, oriented though many were to the Knoxian idea.

Three

Methods

The cure for ignorance about how something gets done is to talk with those who do it. . . .   Heclo and Wildavsky (1974, xiii)

The Department never explain.   Sir George Macdonald, Secretary of the S E D 1922-28[1]

In the chapters that follow, we make extensive use of attributable interview material collected from a number of leading figures in Scottish educational policy-making. Clearly we would not have bothered to talk to them had we not thought that they would explain, and that their explanations were essential to the cure for ignorance. The main purpose of this chapter is to discuss our methods and procedures, and the logical status of the evidence we take from the interviews and other sources. The chapter concludes with a description of how the material is presented, including the typographical and other conventions used in the text of parts II to v. We start, however, with a brief look at our other sources.

Secondary and Primary Sources

Although education is one of the largest items of Scottish public expenditure, and has long been regarded as an essential element in Scottish identity and nationhood, policy-making for education in Scotland did not begin to receive systematic attention until the 1980s. Before then most writers on policy either ignored Scotland, or else assimilated it unthinkingly to a British model usually, nevertheless, described as English. Osborne (1966, 1968) and Bell and Grant (1977) are the principal exceptions. The fault, however, lay mainly north of the Border and with the 'acts and facts' approach of standard secondary sources such as Knox (1953), Mackintosh (1962), Bone (1968), Scotland (1969), Hunter (1972) and Findlay (1973). This body of work did not convey a sense of the processes of policy-making, and it did little to question the received wisdom about the basic structure of the system and the soundness of the service it delivered. Its main characteristic, however, is that there is not much of it.

The state of the Scottish literature is in part a consequence of the policy process itself. Scottish education and government are little esteemed by the British political elite, and accounts of decision-making for Scottish education rarely figure in published diaries, memoirs and biography. Moreover,

Scottish education until the 1960s operated in relative independence, not only of education in England, but also of government in Scotland. Its secondary literature was written, in the main, by educationists for students of education. Questions of government and power belonged to another world that was distant and obscure. There are no Scottish equivalents of the 'official' accounts of the central authority for education in England and Wales written by former Permanent Secretaries (Selby-Bigge 1927; Pile 1979). Scottish officials, moreover, are less frequently called to account by Parliament than are English officials. The public domain is thereby deprived of a source of insight whose importance is apparent from the few examples extant. The valued published evidence of the Parliamentary Select Committee's investigation of the Scottish Schools Inspectorate in 1968 is a case in point (SCES 1968).

For these reasons, the Scottish policy process does not readily generate evidence that might sustain a systematic public discussion of that process. Further reasons for this will become apparent in part v. Whether this situation explains the quality of academic writing on Scottish policy-making, we do not know. It is patchy in its coverage, more often descriptive than analytical, and stimulated more by the currency of political issues, like devolution, than by a concern to cumulate a tradition of systematic research. In the 1980s, however, there has been a welcome mood of reassessment from which has emerged a body of scholarly writing on the history of Scottish education and policy. Its fruits include studies of the system in late Victorian and Edwardian times (Anderson 1983a), of the relationship between the Scottish universities and the SED (Bell 1986), of the Advisory Council 1918-61 (Young 1986), and of the SED during the Second World War (Lloyd 1979). There is also much work of quality and interest in unpublished theses (e.g. Wake 1984). Humes and Paterson edited and contributed to an important collection of 'revisionist' essays in 1983, and Humes himself has recently published a yet more revisionist critique of the 'leadership class' in Scottish education (Humes 1986). Our main objection to Humes' method is that it is based on the two axioms that the Department never explains, and that talking to its decision-takers compounds ignorance with sin (Raab 1987a).

Among the published primary sources we have used are a wide variety of official reports produced by governmental and fringe bodies, and by various groups. The annual reports to Parliament of the SED up to the late 1970s are particularly important. They are referenced with the suffix 'a' in each year. Parliamentary debates have conveyed a sense of the political currency of issues and events, but we have not examined them exhaustively. The press, in particular the *Times Educational Supplement (Scotland) (TESS)* and the *Scottish Educational Journal (SEJ)*, is informative on events. Interviews given to journalists by public figures have supplemented the interview material we collected ourselves, and feature articles written by prominent persons have been useful.

As to unpublished materials, the official Departmental files are held in the Scottish Record Office (SRO), and are normally available only after thirty years have elapsed. Although we have not consulted these exhaustively, they have yielded material of great interest. Chapters 4 and 11 use such material, but the records for the period after 1945 have yet to be fully exploited. Chapter 11 also includes material from official files that, whilst still subject to the thirty-year rule, has been made available to us at the discretion of the SED, and on the understanding that the names of officials not be revealed. In addition, we have used information on memberships specially supplied by the Inspectorate and the Examination Board, and other information supplied by individuals. This included policy documents and ephemeral material in the possession of the interviewees. We also saw some minutes of the CCC.

Our evidence on what was happening in the schools after 1945 comes mainly from official statistics, and from two bodies of research, one conducted by the Scottish Council for Research in Education (SCRE) (Macpherson 1958; Maxwell 1969), and the other by the Centre for Educational Sociology (CES) at Edinburgh University. *Tell Them From Me* (Gow and McPherson 1980) is a record of how the pupils of the 1970s experienced their schooling. *Reconstructions of Secondary Education* (Gray *et al.*, 1983) describes curriculum, examinations, school organisation and labour-market entry for Scottish pupils at various points in the 1950s, 1960s and 1970s. *Fourteen to Eighteen* (Raffe 1984a) updates much of that story. Further afield, Keith Hope's (1984) study, *As Others See Us*, is a valuable reminder that Scottish meritocracy after 1945 had some basis in fact. The present book addresses the policy side of the story that is told in *Reconstructions*. Both books originated in a programme of collaborative research that the CES conducted from 1975 to 1982 as part of an enquiry into relationships between policy, practice and social explanation.

Choice of the Interview Method

We had several reasons for choosing the interview as our principal method of research.[2] If individual agency were to be taken at all seriously in explaining policy, we needed to know about the 'assumptive worlds' of policy-makers; Young and Mills have used this term to denote the intermingled beliefs, perceptions, evaluations and intentions that comprise policy-makers' understanding of the policy milieu (Young 1977; Young and Mills 1978). Secondary sources told us nothing about this, and few primary sources were able to show how these understandings operated in the inner workings of the policy machine.

A second reason for using interviews was that the other sources could tell us quite a lot about what was done, but less about what was not done, and less still about the how and why of the matter. Also, they told us quite a lot about central government, but less about local authorities, fringe bodies and interest groups. Primary and secondary sources informed our thinking, and often provided a first basis for many of the interview questions. In turn, what we learned from the interviews led us towards written sources to verify an account, or to extend our understanding. But the existing written accounts did not take us very far into the dialectic of belief and action. They did not cover many crucial events or perceptions, nor did they reveal motives. Moreover, we needed to interpret the documents themselves in the light of the political processes in which they were generated, and this is not easy without access to the persons involved.

When we began our interviews in 1976, virtually all of the official papers from 1945 onwards were closed to public access under the thirty-year rule. Although we were aware at the outset that government departments had the discretion to vary these conditions, we doubted that we would be allowed to see more recent files. In 1976 our relationship with the SED was strained as a result of earlier research to which the Department had taken exception (McPherson 1984a). Rightly or wrongly, we believed that we had to create sources for research, not merely locate them.

We were encouraged in this by the fruitful precedent of Maurice Kogan's interviews with leading figures in English educational policy-making. In one book, two former Ministers of Education, Edward Boyle and Anthony Crosland, discussed their activities as Ministers in the 1950s and 1960s (Boyle and Crosland 1971). In another, the chief education officers of several local education authorities talked about their policy-making activities (Kogan and van der Eyken 1973). These studies and later ones (e.g. Bush and Kogan 1982) were unique in putting on record the first-hand accounts of principal participants elicited, and arguably enhanced, through skilled and knowledgeable interviewing.

Our decision to use interviews was also influenced by the well-known study of decision-making in the Treasury and Whitehall by Heclo and Wildavsky (1974). Their interviews were non-attributable. We felt, however, that statements made in the knowledge that they were to be publicly attributed and assessed had a firmer status as evidence than those which were clandestine or anonymous. We have used non-attributable interview material. However, the text of an on-the-record interview is more robust. It can be used by others as a primary source that has an independent existence in the public domain. This imposes a discipline on any user, ourselves included.

Possibly at the expense of frankness, it also imposes rigour upon the interviewee, for whom the interview is a form of public account. But this poses a problem, for not all policy-makers are free to give their accounts in public. It is worth recalling the climate in which our interviews were conducted. Civil servants especially are bound by Section 2 of the Official Secrets Act 1911 not to disclose, without authorisation, information entrusted in confidence to them, or obtained in the course of their work. The Act also makes it an offence knowingly to receive such unauthorised information. On entering and leaving the civil service, officials sign a declaration that the terms of the Act have been drawn to their attention, although the Franks report notes that the declaration has no legal force and is misleading (DCOSA 1972, paras 34-6 and appendix VI). Section 2 has been criticised as a 'catch-all' which, by being both broad and unclear, inhibits far more disclosure of official information than is necessary for the security of the state or the requirements of good government (*ibid.*, chs 2 and 3). The late 1970s saw a major and successful prosecution under the Act (Michael 1982, ch.3), and several abortive attempts to replace Section 2 with a more precise statute.

However, there were also countervailing developments. In 1977 the 'Croham Directive' was promulgated, under which the Head of the Home Civil Service urged Departmental heads to publish background documents to policy decisions (*ibid.*, ch.11). Around the same time, issues concerning official secrecy and confidentiality became more widely discussed as a result of the publication of Ministerial memoirs. Ministers do not normally reveal what goes on in Cabinet, nor the details of their relations with officials over policies. But an unsuccessful prosecution to stop the publication of Richard Crossman's *Diaries of a Cabinet Minister* (Crossman 1975) left several matters of law and practice unclear (Young 1976). A committee of Privy Counsellors, chaired by Lord Radcliffe, was subsequently appointed to consider the principles which should govern such publications (CPCMM 1976; Michael 1982, 100-2). That committee underscored the importance to good government of confidential relationships, but frowned upon litigation as a way of preserving them. Instead, it reinforced the moral obligations that flowed from them by tightening up the system of vetting, and by introducing a non-statutory period of fifteen years following the governmental events in question during which Ministers and officials would refrain from publishing information that might breach confidence (CPCMM 1976, para.92). Information that had to do with the opinions of colleagues about items of public business, with advice tendered or received, and with judgements about those who served under them, was to be regarded as particularly sensitive (*ibid.*, para.56).

The climate of events led us to expect that the SED would take an interest in our investigation, and perhaps be concerned about it. We cannot be certain whether the emergence of controversy over official secrecy and 'open government' influenced the attitude of the SED or of the interviewees towards our research. However, it meant that we and they were well aware that interviews with central-government figures inevitably involved the Department as a third party which had discretion to authorise disclosures of information to outsiders. The currency of these wider issues influenced our own approach by reinforcing our decision to adopt a fairly elaborate procedure for negotiating the contents of the interview transcripts.

All this, however, should be kept in perspective. This is not the inside story of HMI5.

Conducting the Interviews

When we started in 1976 we had neither a target number of interviews nor firm quotas of categories of persons to be approached. It was more important that each person would agree to talk to us, and that their experience would allow them to talk in some breadth and depth. Our main criterion was that, in their main employment or other appointments, they had held positions that had *prima facie* been important in the making of educational policy. This meant that we should try to see persons who had had careers in the Inspectorate or on the administrative side of the SED, in local government, colleges of education, secondary education, and educational research, or who had been employed by professional or non-governmental organisations. We were also interested in their experiences as appointees to committees, boards and councils. Another important criterion was that they had retired from service in the education system or had otherwise moved on. We hoped that they would thereby have more time to see us, to review whatever documentary evidence they themselves held, and to discuss and edit their transcripts. By and large we were not disappointed in this. We also thought that, being retired, they might be more inclined to talk freely, letting their thoughts range over their experience in an assessment that was freed from the immediate preoccupations of office.

Holders of certain positions were obvious candidates for interview. Thus, we wished to see Sir William Murrie and Sir Norman Graham as former Secretaries to the Department for the period up to the early 1970s, and John Brunton and David Dickson as former Senior Chief Inspectors. We wanted to talk to William Ross as a former Secretary of State for Scotland who had been closely interested in education. In effect he refused, but we did interview Bruce Millan, who had been responsible for education in the Scottish Office as a junior Minister under Ross, and who later became Secretary of State. We also knew about, or had some acquaintance with, several other persons of interest. William Dewar had been a head teacher in three areas of Scotland and had been active nationally. David Walker had spent many years in the local administration of education before becoming the first full-time Director of the SCRE. Douglas McIntosh was a prominent figure for almost three decades, first as Director of Education for Fife, and later as a college principal. He was also active nationally on the Advisory Council, in the Examination Board, and in educational research.

We chose the names of others from among persons who were recommended to us in the course of the interview programme. These included George Gray (Secretary of the Scottish Council for the Training of Teachers (SCTT) and Registrar of the General Teaching Council (GTC)), Gilbert

Bryden (General Secretary of the EIS), and Alex Eadie MP (one-time Chairman of the Fife Education Committee). Sir Henry Wood was included as a former principal of the largest college of education in Scotland, and as a key member of several bodies concerned with the training of teachers. A similar reason suggested Allan Rodger's inclusion: his career, first as lecturer in Moray House College of Education, and thereafter as a senior SED administrator dealing mainly with school-building, finance and teacher-training, gave him a central position in the policy process and a wide knowledge of people and events. We wanted to look at the administrative side of local authorities and James Clark (Aberdeen), John McEwan (Lanarkshire), and George Reith (Edinburgh) were suggested to us as Directors of some of the larger education authorities with different characteristics and problems. Clark, in particular, had also been active nationally.

There was not, however, a one-to-one relationship between the persons we interviewed, and the positions they had held (see appendix 1). Several, obviously, had held the same post, and many had moved about the education system in the course of their careers, occupying roles in different sectors, and sitting on various public bodies. Most of them could therefore tell us about several areas of decision-making. As we shall see, there had been a remarkable criss-crossing of careers, producing a body of common experiences and acquaintances that extended back, in several cases, to well before the Second World War. Many of the interviewees figure in each other's accounts of events, and most were part of a network that linked their different organisations in some degree.

We conducted sixteen interviews with the intention that the transcript made from the tape-recording should become an attributable source. A further nine interviews were conducted with no intention of attribution, and these interviews were not recorded, or transcribed.

The attributable transcript of each interview is the product of a negotiation that went through several stages. In each case we first wrote to the prospective interviewee to explain the aims and method of the research. Two former Ministers refused. One pleaded the pressure of other business; the other failed to make an effective reply to several letters. Otherwise, every person to whom we wrote readily agreed to a brief preliminary discussion. In this we enlarged upon our earlier letter, and also learned more about the person's career, thereby supplementing what we already knew from published sources, and from other persons' comments. During this 'dry run' the scope and terms of the main interview were discussed. In particular, it was agreed in all but one case that the transcript of the tape-recorded interview would remain the property of the interviewee until a final version had been agreed and approved, whereupon the approved transcript would be at our disposal for direct quotation in subsequent publication.

Each person whom we intended to interview attributably agreed to a second, main, interview. Before this took place, we sent him a memorandum of proposed topics. In return, some persons sent us additional biographical information and copies of publications or other relevant documents. The interviews varied in duration from about two to fifteen hours. Most were conducted in one day in an informal atmosphere in university rooms. The longer ones required several sessions, and two were spread over several weeks. In the early interviews, with Dewar, Brunton, Murrie and Wood, we were less active than we were later in cross-questioning, in trying out interpretations and hypotheses, and in pressing questions and evidence. At first we had to enter the system and find our bearings. As we developed our own knowledge and interpretations we were, perhaps, better able to focus the interview, and to elaborate, confirm or challenge viewpoints in our own questioning. We were also able to bring into play material from earlier interviews in order to obtain comparisons on specific points and to elicit reactions to our provisional interpretations. An example is our discussion with Rodger in chapter 5 about the ways Brunton gained power and influence.

After each interview a transcript was made from the tapes and was edited for accuracy. The transcripts ranged in length from about forty pages to about three-hundred-and-twenty pages. Slight cosmetic changes were made and a typed copy was sent to the interviewee who was invited to make any changes he wished. Some interviewees were asked to clarify certain points or to supply additional information, and in a number of cases new material resulted from these requests. In particular, several persons also volunteered to write more. We incorporated such changes in a revised version of the transcript and, where valuable material had been altered or deleted, we asked that passages be reinstated or rewritten. This was almost always possible; very little has been totally lost, though sometimes one must read between the lines of a carefully phrased statement. Finally, in all but three instances, a retyped copy of the version agreed for public quotation was produced.

To explain these three exceptions: one person felt unable to edit more than about one-half of his initial transcript. He had spoken freely and frankly about other named persons, and he found it impossible to modify certain passages without losing the point of the information he had given. We return to this episode later on. A second lacked the time to do this work, but said we might use his unedited material, subject to his final approval of the particular passages for quotation. This was an arrangement that we were anxious to avoid in general. We wished to retain our freedom to interpret evidence which had been released to the public domain on its own merits, and to do this without fear that the evidence might be withdrawn in the light of how it appeared in the context of our book, or of other public information. For different reasons the third interview would not have lent itself easily to rendering in written form without a considerable input from ourselves. We decided to clear with these persons any passages from the original, unedited, transcripts that we had selected for attributable quotation. In the event, hardly any direct quotations have been drawn from the three uncompleted interviews. The remaining thirteen interviewees all finally agreed with us a version of their interview that we could quote without further reference to them. Only two interviewees asked to read draft chapters of the book, and this led to one area of change in our final manuscript (see chapter 10, note 3).

Although the transcribed interviews form the largest part of our primary evidence, they are not the only attributable accounts upon which we have drawn. We also use material collected by others. This includes minutes of evidence given before parliamentary select committees or Royal Commissions by some of our interviewees, and by others. It also includes material given in a BBC television broadcast by Sir James Robertson (Robertson and Wright 1962) and in a radio broadcast for the Open University recorded by Bruce Millan (Millan 1973). An interview given by Sir Charles Cunningham, a former Scottish Office official, is also used (Cunningham 1980). It was taken from the transcript of the interview he gave to Anthony Seldon as part of the British Oral Archive of Political and Administrative History (BOAPAH), located in London. We also listened to the recorded memoir of Gordon Campbell, a former Secretary of State for Scotland, which forms part of *Scotland's Record* in the National Library of Scotland (Campbell of Croy 1978). Nine other persons who were, or are still, active in educational policy-making, were able to provide us with information, especially about the 1970s and 1980s (see appendix 1). As pre-arranged, the substance of those conversations is not used directly or attributably.

An Evaluation of the Interview Method

How good were our interviews? As we have already suggested, the ethical and methodological aspects of this question are closely related. We had first to persuade people to talk to us. Dewar was the first to do so; one of us had earlier had some dealings with him over a common interest in examinations. In the course of our interview with him, Dewar offered to approach Brunton on our behalf. Independently of this, a fortuitous social encounter with Murrie had allowed us to make an approach; and Murrie, we believe, consulted with Brunton whom we had also interviewed by that time. In his own interview, Murrie offered to speak to Graham. Thereafter such intercessions were less necessary. In our initial letter we simply listed the persons who were already helping us, among them two former Secretaries to the SED and a former Senior Chief Inspector, and this seems in general to have been persuasive enough. However, Murrie had suggested we speak to Rodger, and Dickson helped with our approach to him. 'They are quite harmless', was the way Dickson told us he would describe us to Rodger. We were not sure whether to be pleased or disconcerted.

Our approach has a number of implications. First and foremost, people have helped and trusted us, and this has influenced all of our decisions about the presentation of evidence. We were not inviting the persons we interviewed to be indiscreet, nor for the most part would they have wished to be so. In a sense our research was tapping the trust which binds members of the policy community together across dispersed structural locations and even across lines of conflict on particular issues. We, in our turn, were trusted and vouched for. Moral considerations apart, that trust had to be maintained if we were to use material attributably, and to preserve the possibilities for future research by ourselves and others. Nevertheless, our approach could clearly lead to circularity, bias and incompleteness in our substantive conclusions. If help and trust took us into the policy community, were we also 'taken in' in other ways? Was it gullibility that rendered us harmless? Did we really reach the persons that mattered? And has the criterion of 'multiple role occupancy' by which we selected some of the interviewees, led us to overestimate the interconnectedness of the system and the variety of the careers that it allowed?

We certainly would not claim that these men alone formed a decision-making group that ran Scottish education, nor that any such group could be precisely identified. Nevertheless, while we reserve judgement until part v on the question of interconnectedness, it is evident that the interviewees were well informed, and that most had figured prominently in many of the events with which we were concerned. With the possible exception of Ross, we think it unlikely that an alternative set of persons would have given us a substantially different idea of Scottish educational policy.

All the same, we are aware of some important gaps among the informants who supplied attributable testimony. For example, none worked from a primary-school, further-education, or university base; none was a woman; and none was involved in Catholic education, this being especially important in the West. Nor did we interview a Conservative Scottish Office Minister attributably. The relative indifference to educational policy that was characteristic of Conservative Ministers of the 1950s and 1960s had led us to doubt the value of interviews with them. The previously mentioned Campbell memoir, dealing with the early 1970s, reinforced this assumption (see chapter 8). Nevertheless, this was a mistake. Possibly, also, we were wrong to neglect Members of Parliament, other than Eadie. Many MPs had earlier careers in teaching, on education committees in local government, or in teacher politics. David Lambie, for example, has been MP for Ayrshire Central since 1970, and was a teacher in the west of Scotland. He was active in the EIS and the GTC, and was Chairman of the Scottish Labour Party in the mid-1960s. We also came to feel, as we analysed the material in part v, that we should have made more of an effort to broach the educational politics of the west of Scotland in the material we had collected.

A further self-evident deficiency arises from the fact that several important figures of the period had died by 1976. One was Sir William Arbuckle, who succeeded Murrie as Secretary of the SED (1957-63), and who was part of a crucial central-government triumvirate (with Murrie and Brunton) in the 1950s (part II). Another was Sir James Robertson, Rector of Aberdeen Grammar School and principal author of the 1947 Advisory Council report on *Secondary Education* (SED 1947b). We were fortunate, however, that his widow was able to make letters and papers available to us, and also that the transcript of the television interview with Sir James has survived. Another major figure was William McClelland, Professor of Education at St Andrews University, Executive Officer of the National Committee for the Training of Teachers (NCTT) from 1941 to 1958, and one of the most influential persons in educational research between the wars. These three emerged from our interviews as persons whose influence must be recognised in any account of the period. No doubt there are others: W. B. Inglis, Principal of Moray House College (1951-66) for example. Among those whom we did not interview, although it might have been possible to do so, were: Sir David Anderson, first Chairman of the Examination Board; Alec Young and Andrew Cameron, formerly Directors of Education for Aberdeenshire and Dunbartonshire, respectively; Ronald Dingwall-Smith, for many years an Assistant Secretary in the SED and, later, Principal Finance Officer in the Scottish Office; and other prominent members of the Inspectorate.

The potential for bias in our method has both a substantive and a methodological aspect. If, indeed, we have entered a policy community, how are we to confirm what its members say? 'Triangulation' is a common answer to this question; the view, that is, that if one sets out different perspectives on an event according to the different vantage points of the participants, then the truth of the matter will emerge in the round, at the intersection of these perspectives. It is an attractive solution, and one we use in this book. But by itself the method guarantees nothing. Within a community that is caught in the grip of an idea, no amount of triangulation will guarantee an independent perspective on events. Think, for example, of a village seized by cup-tie fever. Few enquirers from outside would back village opinions of its team with money. They would first want some independent reality test, or at least to hear a dissenting voice or two. Within the village itself they may not find one. No-one there wants to upset confidence in a team that yet has battles to win.

Our own work has faced us with similar dilemmas, dilemmas that are simultaneously substantive (to do with our description and interpretation of policy-making and its community), methodological (to do with how we procure evidence and assess its import), and ethical (to do with personal relationships of trust and obligation in which we have participated). These dilemmas also involve the difficult issues of conflict, competence and confidentiality. An independent reality test, of a sort, is provided by the official

documents that are already publicly available, and by those that are subsequently released into the public domain. However, official records are
selectively written and selectively archived. They have no superior claim to
objective 'truth' and cannot, therefore, even if they were available now,
fully solve the problem of how we validate the evidence from the interviews
(Seldon and Pappworth 1983, ch.3). In one way, therefore, we are fortunate
that there was evidence, not only of disagreement among the interviewees,
but also of conflict. The status of the evidence on agreements and disagreements is fourfold. First, there are personally attributable views that were
related to us on the explicit understanding that they would enter the public
domain. Such material is used at length in the following chapters. Second,
in places we convey non-attributable information that was intended for
public use (though, as we have said, such information is somewhat dubious
as a main source of evidence). A third category is information that was
given to us in confidence, but that was intended to inform our general
judgements. We feel fairly sceptical about this sort of evidence too, and
have not relied greatly upon it. The little that is used is treated non-attributably. Fourth, there is indirect evidence that arises, not from what we were
told, but from procedural aspects of the interviews themselves, and from
events that occurred during the negotiation of the research.

To explain: it quickly became apparent that a variety of considerations
lay behind prospective interviewees' offers of assistance. The motive could
indeed be a relatively detached intellectual interest in the way things had
worked: at least one person seemed to us to regard his participation as an
extension of his public service, as a way of educating the public about the
workings of representative democracy. There were several other persons,
however, who, we thought, saw themselves as the architects of an education
system that had subsequently been destroyed or altered, in a way that, they
thought, incriminated the administrative side of the SED. Their evidence
was offered partly as a testament to the past. But, in at least one case, we are
sure that it was also offered as a continuation of the fight, as an indication
that defeat had not been acknowledged. In that instance the interviewee
knowingly refrained from obtaining official clearance for his final transcript
from the SED before approving it for public use. In the light of the difficulties
caused by this and by subsequent events, the Department used another of
our interviewees, also a former official of the SED, to bring ourselves and the
Department together to discuss the issue. The outcome was satisfactory to
both sides.[3]

Thus it was clear that the events of the 1950s and 1960s were far from dead
in the late 1970s. History was 'out there' as well as 'back there', not least the
tension between Inspectorate and administration in the SED. Relations
between the two groups were affected by changes in the structure of Scottish
and British government that began in the 1950s (see part III). But personalities and changes of personnel also contributed (see part II), and the issue

was played out in relation to major changes in the substance of educational policy, especially comprehensive reorganisation and ROSLA (see part IV). Opinions, and differences of opinion, on personalities, structures, and substantive educational policies were thus intermingled.

This raises further questions. In the contacts that were arranged for us, or suggested to us, were we being guided to particular protagonists in an argument that was not yet done? How heated had the argument been, and how should we assess the judgements of persons' motives and competence that it generated? Also, how should we assess the meta-judgements, the more general theories of personalities, power and policy-making that were offered? 'I don't like policies being labelled with the names of individuals', Graham, the career administrator, objected at one point in our interview when we characterised a policy as 'Bruntonian'. He thought we would be misled in our judgements if we 'personalised' too far, a view, interestingly, that is shared, though from a somewhat different vantage point, by the CCCS group in *Unpopular Education* (CCCS 1981, 14). Other interviewees, however, considered that the way specific persons performed their roles had been crucial to the working of the system. Clark, for example, concluded an assessment of Brunton, saying: 'Again we have the importance of the personality of an individual as a major factor'. Moreover, Clark also thought highly of the personal contribution Graham himself had made to central-local relations (see chapter 7). Bryden, too, saw the changes of the mid-1960s largely in terms of personalities and personal relationships. He attributed the shift in the balance of power to the passing of sympathetic former educationists like Arbuckle and Rodger on the administrative side, and to the replacement of Brunton as HMSCI by the less forceful Dickson. Brunton himself concurred in this latter judgement (see chapter 7).

The general point we are making here is this: as a method of validation, triangulation requires the observation of an event from several 'points of view' (roles, positions, perspectives, interviewees) that are dispersed, so to speak, in space. Ideally this space must encompass all relevant dimensions. But we did not move from one point to the next at random. At times we were guided by surviving participants who still cared about the issues. We cannot be sure that the interviews have sampled points in all dimensions of the argument. Moreover, the locations or positions of these points are problematic. The vantage points had themselves become dispersed in 'policy space' as a result of policy arguments. The points of view have thus to be located and defined by reference to the dimensions of an argument that is itself an object of enquiry. In part II, for example, a lot hangs on whether certain persons, among them Brunton and Rodger, are speaking as educationists or as administrators. Both men had an early background and career in education, but Brunton finished as Senior Chief Inspector (educationist) whereas Rodger ultimately became an Under-Secretary (administrator). For reasons explained in part III, this distinction was possibly less pronounced in Brunton's time than it is today. But the distinction today is partly the product of an earlier argument about the division of labour and the distribution of power, an argument in which Brunton and Rodger themselves figured. Only if we know about the historic dimensions of that argument, and Brunton and Rodger's position in it, can we assess whether our juxtaposition of their accounts constitutes a triangulation, that is, an intersection of perspectives from standpoints that are independent both of each other and of what is observed.

This being so, we face something of a problem, for it seems that our judgement of the potential of our interviews to produce valid and verifiable statements about the policy-making world is itself dependent on our prior substantive judgements about the nature of that world, about what it contains and where we are in it. In the dominant view of science, however, a valid substantive judgement is required to be independent of, and to follow from, the use of a valid method. What, then, is the cure for ignorance? When the Department speaks, in what sense does it explain?

Our dilemma, of course, is characteristic of sociological and historical enquiry. But the interview does have one advantage over the inert documentary record, because it allows the enquirer to question and observe in the light of hypotheses which take this dilemma into account. One may thereby make available evidence that is, in a limited sense, independent of the historical events and of their reconstruction by those who were involved.

Several 'procedural' aspects of the interviews were also illuminating. The interviewee's decision not to seek official approval of his transcript is one example. Occurring at an early stage in our research, this incident enhanced our understanding of alignments in disputes that had taken place years before. 'The Departmental chaps', said Gilbert Bryden, 'were far too clever to let you guess what was going on and, of course, they were trained not to'. In some respects we also found this. The Official Secrets Act, as we have explained, admits of considerable flexibility of interpretation. Some Departmental officials were more flexible than others, and this flexibility was associated, we think, partly with the personal 'affect' of the issues under discussion, and partly with the degree to which the interviewees continued to identify, after retirement, with the norms and obligations of their main career roles. This influenced what was said, how it was said, and how we were, implicitly, invited to interpret it. The career administrators tended to speak in measured, lapidary phrases, often punctuated by long silences. The phrasing was considered and often spare, and the implicit meaning, we think, high. Their transcripts required little editing, by them or us, for content or for style, and were among those that were most efficiently and expeditiously delivered to us in a form that could be readily agreed for public use. We had a strong sense, from all this, of persons who were *still in office*, of persons whose socialisation to the norms and customs of the administrative civil service was enduring, and who still performed in that role. 'If the times had fallen differently', said Murrie, 'you might well have had Brunton as head of the Scottish Education Department'. In addition to being H M S C I, Brunton had also had an administrative career, and he handled his interview (an early one for us), in much the same way as Murrie and Graham. At the same time, however, he broached the sensitive question of inspector-administrator relationships more directly than did the two former Secretaries, though choosing his words with equal care; and he took considerable pains over the precise wording of accounts of sensitive events and issues in subsequently preparing the version of his transcript for publication.

All of this is relevant to the meaning that the reader is invited to take from the transcript evidence. But it may also help with the problem of disengaging the validity of our method from the validity of our conclusions, so that the former may contribute to, and not just derive from, the latter. We are suggesting that, in a very limited way, procedural aspects of the interviews give us a further, and partially independent, perspective on the historic events; independent insofar as we, as interviewers, could form our own judgements of character and personality, of competencies, and of where allegiances lay, basing these judgements not only on the interviewees' careers and statements, but also on our own observations of their behaviour. Thus it seemed to us, for example, that one test of whether there had been difficulties between educationists and administrators, and of how people lined up on either side of this issue, was not what they said about it, but whether they were prepared to discuss it (on or off the record). Also relevant, if they were prepared to discuss the issue, was the extent of the investment they made in the considered editing and phrasing of their statements on the matter.

Another procedural aspect of interest was the breakdown of communication between an interviewee and ourselves. Following his interview, one person edited his transcript reluctantly and intermittently. He finally abandoned it, saying that the entire interview had been given on the assumption that it would not be publicly quoted, and that the authentic account of events that the interview had been acknowledged to capture, could never be publicly rendered. We were certain, however, that the understanding that we had reached with this person before the interview had not differed in any way from all the other instances in which arrangements for publication proceeded without dispute. Rather, we think it was the troublesome authenticity of the content of the interview that caused the breakdown in relations.

We mention this case as an extreme example of something that, in a less pronounced way, featured in all the interviews, quite simply because it is a feature of all communication: that is, the interpretation, negotiation and renegotiation of the purposes and terms of the relationship. More usually this is done by conversational and other gambits that avert breakdown and allow discussion to continue. Thus a pause, a gesture, a silence may all be informative even though such 'information' is not easily publicly rendered.

Similarly the response, 'I don't know', may speak volumes, and sometimes did, we think, when it was given to our questions.

What, in this context, are we to make of lapses of memory? Two aspects of this question may be distinguished. First, there is the general problem of events receding in time, with an attendant forgetfulness, acknowledged or unacknowledged, on the part of those who were involved. Obviously this will feature in any study which asks retired persons to reflect on events over some thirty years. With two qualifications, however, we do not regard the methodological problem of how one verifies such recollections as being qualitatively different from that of verifying any interview data. The qualifications are, first, that other participants in the historic events may be scattered, deceased or otherwise prevented from commenting. Second, the informant himself may, through illness or death, be removed from a continuing discussion of what happened.

The second aspect of the problem of memory relates to lapses, or possible lapses, of which the recollector is aware. 'Memory', Crossman observed, 'is a terrible improver – even with a diary to check the tendency' (Crossman 1975, 12). Memory has to do with the selective operation of present attention and interpretation on a past which was itself at the time selectively perceived, interpreted and stored. What remains, and what is forgotten, tell us something about both past and present, though it may not be easy to disentangle these. Moreover, as we have suggested, the interviewees varied in their views of how far past the past was, and this in turn seems to have been related to the affect and importance of issues for them. Thus some persons refreshed their memories before the main interview by looking over papers they had kept (and had kept, one presumes, selectively). An example is George Gray, who, among his other positions had been Secretary of the SCTT from 1959 to 1967, the body that authorised the building of the new colleges of education in the 1960s. When we interviewed him in 1977, these were under threat of closure. Had they been intended as temporary or permanent institutions? This was a question of the hour, and a question on which Gray had apparently briefed himself well before speaking to us. He had kept the papers that allowed him to do so. On the other hand, others had not kept papers, and in this and other ways had clearly distanced themselves from earlier roles. Again, such procedural information assists understanding, though, it must be added, retired civil servants are not allowed to retain official papers.

Also informative were the conjectures or hypotheses with which interviewees tried to supply gaps in their knowledge or memory. For example, in developing our own thinking about Brunton's power, we conjectured that it resided partly in the fact that the fortuitous pattern of his career for a time had given him the identity both of an inspector and of an administrator (see chapter 5). In the eyes of his colleagues his position was essentially ambivalent. In a subsequent interview we were brought up with a start when one of them broke off an account of how Brunton had tried to get innovation moving, to remark that he could not remember whether Brunton at the time had been HMSCI or Assistant Secretary. A trivial and 'mechanical' lapse of memory? Confirmation of Brunton's ambivalence? An indication of the marginality of the issue? Or something of all of these?

Several sorts of hypothesising went on in the interviews. In one sense all efforts of memory involve an hypothesising of the past. It was not unusual for officials to answer, when their memories were stretched, that 'we would not have done this', or 'this would have been our practice'. Doubtless such responses often tell one something about the events themselves. But they are also sometimes indicative of a normative perspective on those events; an indication of what would have been done 'as a rule' and, only possibly, of what was actually done. Alternatively, the response may indicate that it was not so much memory that was stretched, as a willingness to reveal the facts of the matter. A second sort of hypothesising aimed less at supplying deficiencies of memory, and more at supplying historic deficiencies of knowledge; that is, at supplying things that could not easily have been known by the participant even at the time. Attributions of motives and perceptions to other persons are examples. Third, our informants also hypothesised about more general processes. These conjectures, again, were informative for their manifest content, and also sometimes for what they indicated about the interviewee's own thinking. Also revealing were interviewees' confirmations or rejections of hypotheses that we ourselves felt increasingly confident to offer. Occasionally, too, their reactions gave some indication of the world they had taken for granted. It had never occurred to one director of education, for example, that the Scottish policy community might have had a strong axis in the East (see part v).

Thus the interviews generated hypotheses about the way policy had been made, and information about the interviewees' 'assumptive worlds'. They also gave us indications of the extent to which people had reflected at the time on what they had been doing. One example of this is Allan Rodger's account of how he once calculated the proportion of his time as an SED civil servant that was spent in 'defensive activity'. Another is his recollection of having once, as an intellectual diversion, drawn up a reckoning of all the directors of education, assigning them points for various qualities (see chapter 17). But this is to venture towards the area of personal competence, an area that is as important to an understanding of policy, as it is difficult to discuss publicly. We reproduce interviewees' judgements of the competence of their contemporaries sparingly, and only when they assist a wider interpretation.

To summarise our discussion of method, we have suggested that there are interdependencies between methodological problems, ethical problems and problems of substantive interpretation. The interview method extends the tests to which one may subject one's interpretations of the past, but its use is clearly circumscribed by personal obligations of trust and confidentiality. The interdependencies dictate, however, that the extent of these obligations cannot be determined solely by abstract ethical argument. It also depends on one's explanations of the social world, and these explanations cannot be wholly determined by independent evidence. They derive also from one's axioms. Hence the importance of subjecting one's conclusions to the test of iterative dialogue: 'Was this how it really was?'.

We acknowledge, in other words, that there must be an element of arbitrariness both in our handling of sensitive information, and in the conclusions we reach. In a sense, what we are offering is premature history and can be criticised as such. On the other hand, one may regard history itself as an attempt to construct and reconstruct a discussion of events that life itself has terminated prematurely, before all the hypotheses have been canvassed, and before all the participants have been called to account, to each other and to the future. That eventuality is perhaps where reality lies. Were there time we should reach it. As it is, we must act. Time obliges us to make our own arbitrary decisions about what can be said with confidence and what can be said with propriety. But the interviews themselves have postponed the closure of the discussion, and the moment at which the events they describe fall inert into history. When others dust away the sand, they will find that the fragments have a story to tell.

Method of Presentation

Our use of the attributable interviews differs from Kogan's. Each of his interview-based works deals with the performance of a particular role by different individuals, and moves outward from the role to its interconnections throughout the education system. The oral accounts of interviewees, presented consecutively and organised around topics, reveal a wider structure of processes and events, and also some of the personal connections that linked Ministers or chief education officers to others. For example, in presenting sequentially the interviews with chief education officers, Kogan and van der Eyken (1973) underscored the separate and parallel work of these persons in their education authorities. Each dealt with the same central department. But the extent to which local officers knew or observed each other, interacted professionally, or participated in the same events, does not emerge well from the sequential treatment.

Our own interviewees interacted regularly with each other, and it therefore made sense to interweave their accounts, rather than present them sequentially. Most of the following chapters are, in effect, collages organised around events or topics. Each draws heavily upon the testimonies of several persons, and many include substantial extracts from other oral evidence, such as select-committee minutes. These are treated in the same way as our own interviews, except that we indicate their source and do not change their typography. Where a source is not indicated for a statement by an interviewee, the source is the interview he gave to us. The chapters also contain a substantial amount of our own commentary and discussion by way of introduction, conclusion, and linkage. The passages we have written are identified by a justified right-hand margin, whereas the transcript texts have a ragged right-hand margin. Passages taken from transcripts often, but not always, include the question we put to the interviewee, prefaced by 'Q.'. They always include the interviewee's name in capital letters at the beginning of his answer (for example, 'BRUNTON'). The end of a transcript passage is signified by the indented new paragraph that follows. There are no paragraphs within text from the transcripts.

Composing a narrative from an assemblage of texts has required us to omit phrases and sentences from the original where they were not strictly necessary. We have also sometimes rearranged the order in which passages appear in the original, for example when we bring together remarks on a particular theme that was discussed in more than one place in an interview. The use of a series of dots indicates an omission. Three dots ('. . .') indicate an omission within a sentence, and four dots indicate an omission across one sentence or more, sometimes even across a number of pages. Dots do not signify pauses in the flow of an interviewee's speech. These we have not attempted to represent. We have not indicated the omission of material at the beginning and end of quotations from transcripts or from other sources. Nor have we indicated any reordering of statements, though such reorderings are always accompanied by dots indicating accompanying omissions. We have also, on occasion, made small technical adjustments, such as altering the first letters of words from upper to lower case and *vice versa*, for stylistic reasons, and adding or substituting our own words in square brackets in order to clarify an item or improve continuity. In addition, in a few places we have felt at liberty to make slight changes in the wording of our own questions, thus departing from the approved transcript. This has been done mainly in order to improve the fit between the question and the context in which it appears in the chapter, or where the original question contained a minor factual error which should now be corrected. Obviously such changes have a potential for abuse, and we have been careful to try to retain the sense of the original question where such changes have been made. We think that the few changes were all trivial and do not misrepresent the dialogue between ourselves and the interviewee, nor invalidate his answer. As the approved transcripts are sources in the public domain, the propriety of our entire work of editing and selection is open to scrutiny.

NOTES
1. ADES (n.d., 12).
2. 'Oral history' methods and specialised interviewing are considered in Dexter (1970), in Seldon and Pappworth (1983), in Moyser and Wagstaffe (1987), and in Raab (1987b).

3. When we met members of the Department at their request to discuss this matter in 1978, they ensured that we were made aware of the rules constraining publication of confidential information. Before the meeting took place, an official had told us that the SED sought a 'gentleman's agreement', precisely the term used by Radcliffe in describing how the rules about memoirs should be effected (CPCMM 1976, para.59). Insofar as our role as interviewers and ultimate users of the information linked us to the interviewee in question, it was not inappropriate for the Department to have sought such an agreement with us. We regarded the uncleared transcript as a final and unamendable one agreed between ourselves and the interviewee. The Department did not press this issue, but they indicated the passages they found objectionable. We reached an understanding with the Department that they might see our manuscript before publication, and that we would have regard, at that stage, to their views. We were grateful to the Department for its attitude, which was constructive and helpful in an awkward circumstance. In the event, the Department suggested only one small factual correction.

Part II

Education, Reconstruction and Change:
A Case Study

On September 1st 1939, regulations made under the Education (Scotland) Act of 1936 designated all post-primary education in Scotland as secondary, and raised the school-leaving age from fourteen to fifteen years. On the same day, Germany invaded Poland. War was declared two days later and, on October 12th, the leaving age was returned to fourteen years. Thereafter, the 1939 Code that had prescribed 'secondary education for all' remained in operation, 'though it was recognised that its provisions and purposes could not be fully implemented' (SED 1941a, 5).

The immediate concern of the SED, or of what was left of the SED now that a number of its officials were seconded to war work, was to get the school population away from urban areas and the threat of bombing. But, by 1942, the tide of war had turned, and plans were being laid for social and educational reconstruction (Addison 1975; Gosden 1976). Archer writes that the Labour Party used its position in Churchill's wartime Coalition Government to 'transmit the external pressures for large scale reforms and "no tinkering" to the political centre' (Archer 1979, 581). This was also the case in Scotland, where Tom Johnston was the Labour Secretary of State. He had accepted office under Churchill on the understanding that he would be given a free hand to develop plans for the economic and social regeneration of Scotland (Harvie 1981b, 1981c). One of his initiatives in 1942 was to appoint a Sixth Council of the Scottish Advisory Council on Education (Lloyd 1979; Young 1986). It sat until 1946, dealing with fourteen remits and producing four major reports, on the training of teachers, technical education, primary education, and secondary education (SED 1946b, 1946c, 1946d, 1947b).

These reports came too late to influence the Education (Scotland) Acts of 1945 and 1946 which, in the main, applied the principles of the 1944 Education Act for England and Wales to Scottish circumstances (Knox 1953, 227; Lloyd 1979, chs 9 and 10). But these principles were mainly administrative. Other than sanctioning secondary education for all and a minimum leaving age of fifteen years, measures that were already effected in Scotland, though suspended because of the Second World War, the English Act of 1944 was mainly notable for the further powers it gave to the Minister and the Board of Education. In particular, it placed on the Minister the duty to 'secure the effective execution by local authorities, under his

73

control and direction, of the national policy for providing a varied and comprehensive educational service in every area'. Johnston decided not to adopt this clause in the Scottish Bill leading to the 1945 Act. Instead the powers of the Minister were defined through specific clauses whose number alone gave the impression of substantially increased central control (Lloyd 1979, ch.9). The Scottish legislation indeed increased the Minister's powers, but it is an open question whether they exceeded the potential for central control inherent in the English Act.

The legislation of 1944-46 said little about the form and content of secondary schooling. Thus the Scottish Advisory Council had some scope to influence policy in the early days of peace. But what this would mean in practice was not clear. Between the wars, its counterpart body in England, the Consultative Committee, had fed a succession of broadly progressive reports into the public debate on education (Kogan and Packwood 1974). By contrast, the Scottish Advisory Council, after a stormy start in the 1920s (see chapter 2), had worked on narrow remits and had published little (Young 1986). But the major reports of the Sixth Council each addressed a broad sector of educational provision, and for the first time delivered progressive educational thinking to the Scottish public between official covers. What would official and public reaction be?

Chapter 4 opens with a teacher's account of the impetus that the Second World War gave to hopes in one locality for social and educational reconstruction. These hopes were to find national expression in the work of the Sixth Council, and especially in its report on secondary education. The principal author of that report, James Robertson (later Sir James), then describes its genesis, philosophy and recommendations. The report is important for several reasons: it argued for progressive policies as a fitting development of a national and democratic education system; it captured the public imagination in Scotland and overseas; and it anticipated many features of education in the 1960s and 1970s, among them comprehensive schools, a core curriculum, and internal assessment for public examinations. But little positive was done about the report for at least five years following its publication. Extracts from the evidence of John Brunton and Allan Rodger then give, respectively, the views of a school inspector and an SED administrator on the SED's responsibility for this inactivity. A 'classical lobby' was important, and so also was the influence of external examinations. Evidence from public records throws further light on the Department's thinking and on reactions from educationists.

The second half of the chapter presents Brunton's account of the failure to implement the Council's proposals, and of how he later initiated change. Brunton was the longest serving Senior Chief Inspector of Schools (1955-66). He was centrally involved in reforms that had their origins in the early 1950s, and their first impact in the following decade. His narrative therefore serves to introduce many of the policies, structures and personalities of the first twenty years of our period. He describes how a reorganisation and revitalisation of the Schools Inspectorate was a precursor to changes in curriculum and examinations, and how these changes in turn necessitated changes in structure. These structural changes included s E D working parties that brought non-s E D educationists into the policy-making process, and the founding of two bodies, the Examination Board in 1963, and the Consultative Committee on the Curriculum (c c c) in 1965. Brunton's evidence reveals how his initially piecemeal and opportunist attempt at improvement developed into a more general strategy for change. This strategy tended to displace the career administrator, and to reserve a prominent place for the professional educationist, especially the inspector, and especially Brunton himself. To move in this direction he had to overturn or circumvent old relationships, and to form new ones. He stole the administrators' clothes, although, as we shall see, they eventually stole them back.

Brunton claimed that he was working towards decentralisation and the implementation of the Sixth Council's recommendations for secondary education. But his methods and achievements were mixed, and questions have been raised about his motives as well. These issues are taken up in chapter 5 where a number of Brunton's contemporaries have their say. There we suggest that the way Brunton presented himself to them was decisively influenced by the internal politics of the Department. We also suggest that educationists outside the Department assimilated Brunton's public *persona* to a Whiggish historiographical tradition of Scottish educational improvement led by great men. This tradition was itself a creation of the educational politics of Craik and Struthers at the turn of the century. But it was also a tradition that the Inspectorate had an interest in maintaining, and worked to maintain. A further purpose of part II is thus to show how an ideology of benign leadership from the centre has influenced both the primary and the secondary accounts of the period, and therefore requires reassessment.

Four

Policies and People 1945–65

We should not encourage the view that even the lessons of the war
are likely to necessitate any very drastic changes in . . . the
[Schools] Code. . . .   Sir John Mackay Thomson, Secretary of
the SED 1940-52[1]

Reconstruction

William Dewar was appointed Headmaster of George Heriot's School in
Edinburgh in 1947 and he later worked closely with Brunton. During the
Second World War he had been responsible for Greenock Academy, an
old-established secondary school serving a port near the mouth of the
Clyde. He told us how he had become involved there in the movement for
reconstruction:

DEWAR. When I joined the Headmasters' Association I started to meet
people with desires similar to my own, to get things clarified, to throw off
many of the restraints that there were, for example, a near reverence for the
Inspectorate. But in the period getting towards the end of the War, and
immediately after the War, there was a tremendous upsurge. . . . Now the
Emergency Relief Organisation and the Air Raid Patrol organisations in
Greenock had forty-three senior personnel, of whom I was one. In 1943 we
established the Forty-three Club which met once a fortnight. . . . From this,
a group of us started to say, 'Now what can we do for this area, once this War
is over?' The town divided into two halves – east end and west end.
Everything to the east was poor property with a very big Irish population as
also in its neighbouring town of Port Glasgow; whereas the west end had the
well-to-do people; and those of us who were involved in this felt there was
something better than this unhappy division. Moreover the town was going
to have to be rebuilt after the bombing and this was an opportunity to
rebuild the life. . . .

Q. One detects the same sort of hope for a new beginning in the 1947
Advisory Council report on *Secondary Education.*

DEWAR. Indeed. Several of those who were involved in that were . . .
headmasters that had worked on during the War, and most of them had
been heads before the War. J. J. Robertson was, in a way, the dynamic
behind [the report].

Robertson was Rector (i.e. Head Teacher) of Aberdeen Grammar

School at the time of his appointment to the Sixth Scottish Advisory Council in 1942. In later articles he described how the Council came to produce its reports on teacher training (SED 1946b), primary education (SED 1946d) and secondary education (SED 1947b). We reproduce extracts from Robertson's writings here in interview-text form:

ROBERTSON. The Education (Scotland) Act of 1918 provided for the setting up of an advisory council 'consisting as to not less than two-thirds of the members of persons qualified to represent the views of various bodies interested in education', and the Department [SED] 'was to take into consideration any advice or representation submitted to them by the advisory council'. . . . When, in November 1942, that great Scottish Secretary, Tom Johnston, reconstituted the Advisory Council on Education, it was after the 1918 pattern, with all the interested parties duly represented among its twenty-three members.[2] . . . The Secretary of State gave us a commission almost as wide as the field of education, by comparison with which remits to later councils seem enviably tidy and manageable. . . . We were superbly led by our chairman, the late Sir William Hamilton Fyfe, classical scholar, fellow of Merton, well-loved head for eleven years of Christ's Hospital, and then vice-chancellor successively at Kingston, Ontario and Aberdeen. . . . He it was who, being determined that the major reports should reveal something distinctive and unitary in form and content, decreed that three of us should chair overlapping committees and do all the drafting. . . . The three big reports[3] took shape in the later years of the war when hope and growing confidence had given place to certainty of victory. And with that certainty came awareness that all the brave words about the preciousness of our way of life, the new-found national unity, and the greatness of our debt to the common folk, must presently translate themselves into social and educational action or stand discredited. The recognition found expression in notable departmental pronouncements and a great Education Act which provided for the raising of the leaving age and committed Scotland irrevocably to the revolutionary concept of all education as one, and of secondary schooling as but a stage within it and not as an extra for a privileged minority. If anything more was needed to make us live and work 'with a vision of greatness', it came with the Secretary of State's insistence, despite our groans, that the 'teaching of citizenship' must have priority over our deliberations on the primary and secondary school. So it was that a body of men and women, mostly middle-aged or elderly, did try, without forgetting their Scots respect for the things of the mind, to think sustainedly of education as nothing less than the totality of what a liberal democracy will seek to do in the nurture of all its young. That was the hour [Robertson 1969a]. The broad lines [of the report on secondary education were] the acceptance of Christian Democracy as the ideal and the best safeguard of an individualism neither anti-social nor escapist; education's concern with the whole person and all the diversity of persons over the whole life-span; the remedying of premature and excessive use of the specialist teacher; the need to correct an over-intellectualised schooling by giving a larger place to the physical, the practical, the affective, and the aesthetic; and the obligation to concentrate for the time being at least on the needs of the many, since the schooling of the gifted few had been education's care for centuries [Robertson 1957]. The secondary education the advisory council envisaged was simple in conception: for all, four years of quite general schooling, with more justice done to the aesthetic and practical sides; then, for those who wished it and would profit by it, two years of reasonably specialized work in course of which the pupil might insensibly grow into the student. Believing, like our English opposite numbers, that the seventeen-to-eighteen year was soon enough for the external[4] examination to invade the schools, we proposed to assess the twelve-to-sixteen stage by internal tests, externally moderated and then at eighteen a searching external examination. . . . While the curriculum between twelve and sixteen would not ignore wide differences in intelligence, within these years all would have a broadly similar schooling. Science would be general science only: integrated social studies were preferred to separate history, geography and civics: there was no thought of splitting up any practical subject: and timetables allowing of no lifting and laying of subjects at the end of [second year] and almost none at the end of [third year] showed how strongly we favoured a smooth, straight run up to sixteen [Robertson 1966]. Now, it is broadly true that those who were most sensitive to the sociological challenge of education were the most cordial in their welcome of the report, while those for whom education was primarily the professional practice of the schools were noticeably cooler towards it [Robertson 1957].

Robertson's report also recommended the *omnibus* school as 'the natural way for a democracy to order the post-primary schooling of a given area' (SED 1947b, para.164);[5] it proposed 'a more permanent and fully representative advisory machinery' for examinations, with teachers contributing at least one third of the membership (*ibid.*, para.249); and it suggested that the Inspectorate be renamed, because teachers 's[aw] in the perpetuation of this name some derogation from their own status' (*ibid.*, para.659).

When the report was published, John Brunton was an HMI in Perth. But he was also a member of an SED committee in Edinburgh that was set up in 1947 to consider the report. He described the Department's reaction:

BRUNTON. In 1947, the Secretary [Mackay Thomson] and the Senior Chief Inspector [Watson] were very conservative in their outlook. They were both very confirmed classics [i.e. classicists] and so was J. J. Robertson. He was a classical scholar of some eminence, and the Secretary and the Senior Chief Inspector thought that from certain points of view Robertson had let down the side, so to speak. . . . He had not treated secondary education and particularly the teaching of classics and mathematics sufficiently seriously in their view, and he had made proposals for the development of these subjects particularly, but also of other subjects and of secondary education generally, which were not in harmony with the classical tradition. To some extent the failure to implement the report was attributable to this excessive conservatism on the part of the Secretary and the Senior Chief Inspector and also of the man who was more or less designated to succeed as Senior Chief Inspector in 1948 who was another classic [George Pringle, HMSCI 1948-55]. They objected very strongly to most of the suggestions that were made about the Inspectorate.

Q. Did the Secondary report reflect J. J. Robertson's own thinking or a consensus of the Advisory Council?

BRUNTON. It was a consensus of the views of the Advisory Council, but it was undoubtedly in line with Robertson's own thinking. Robertson was a very disappointed man when nothing much was done about his recommendations. But, of course, it must be borne in mind that the timing of the report was to some extent unfortunate because in 1947 a great deal of attention was being devoted to matters arising out of the 1945 Education Act. There were all sorts of things to tidy up in the schools; for example, to get masses of over-age pupils out of the primary schools; to do something about the dreadful two-year post-primary departments which were tacked on to primary schools; and to get improvements in buildings and in staffing. Then in 1947 of course came the great upheaval caused by the raising of the school-leaving age, and that gave rise to frightful problems, not only of courses and methods of teaching in the schools, but of the mere provision of accommodation for the extra pupils. The problems at that time were very great, and these didn't leave much time for dealing with really fundamental matters concerning attitudes and teaching in secondary schools. All that, coupled with the ultra-conservative attitude of the Department and the lack of any lead to the Inspectorate, meant that the report was regarded as a valuable document but that nothing much was done about its recommendations. At the end of 1950 the Department did [prepare] a circular [SED 1951b] commending the report to the attention of the educational world and generally endorsing many of its recommendations, but very few active steps were taken to encourage people to go ahead and do something, and furthermore, there was no real pressure from the teaching profession to do anything about it. . . .

Q. The impetus for innovation would have to come from the centre and from the Secretary . . .

BRUNTON [interjecting]. Yes, undoubtedly so in the circumstances of the time.

Q. . . . rather than from the opinion represented in the Advisory Council, or from the teaching profession?

BRUNTON. The report was presented to the Secretary of State and it was dealt with as all reports are within the Department concerned. The influence, the authority, of the Department at that time were very strong and teachers looked to the Department for leadership, and I'm afraid strong leadership was not forthcoming. Moreover, the Advisory Council was disbanded after the report was presented, and most of its individual members were neither vocal nor very active.

Q. What impact did the report have on you as a local H M I?

BRUNTON. Oh, profound! I was unhappy about the findings of the Senior Chief Inspector and the Secretary. I thought much more could have been done about it even at the time.

Q. There was no move from the centre?

BRUNTON. I was one of seventy people; there were others in the Inspectorate who thought as I did but we weren't in influential positions at that time. We tried to do something in our fairly limited spheres, particularly at subject level, but could not affect broad areas of policy. And there was at that time no machinery for securing a consensus of views of the Inspectorate. . . . The report was certainly discussed by directors of education and teachers, but not much was done beyond discussion. Some individual teachers in schools tried to do something at subject level, but individuals within a school haven't terribly much effect unless they get some backing.

By 1945 Allan Rodger was an Assistant Secretary in the S E D. We asked him about reactions to the report:

Q. One of the things that obviously preoccupied the directors of education was the proposed Leaving Certificate. They were concerned that no indication was given of its standard in relation to the old Leaving Certificate.

RODGER. I should think that that would probably be, in various groups, the most important consideration; it would be, from the university point of view, one of the most important points also.

Q. Of course, Robertson thought that linking a Leaving Certificate to university entrance qualifications was educationally unsound.

RODGER. Educationally unsound. Yes. Perhaps that might be said. But the universities nevertheless had to consider what they would do with whatever Leaving Certificate the Department might produce; and if they couldn't approve of whatever certificate the Department might produce, they had to do something on their own – they had to modify their own Preliminary Examinations, which existed in those days. Nobody wanted Scottish pupils to face two examinations: a Leaving Certificate and a separate university entrance exam.[6]

Q. At the same time, the Department itself was holding discussions with the local authorities on the reform of the Leaving Certificate, on the assumption that Robertson's report could not be implemented.

RODGER. Yes, but I repeat that members of the Department did not wish the pupils . . . to face two examinations. Therefore the Department had to proceed along a line acceptable to the universities.

Q. So the Department was, in a sense, continuing on its own lines with examination reform, not so much in opposition to the Secondary report but independently of it.

RODGER. I would not say 'in opposition to' but 'independently', with our eyes on the universities.

Q. Did that perhaps reflect Mackay Thomson's influence, amongst others? You said that he was particularly interested in the Leaving Certificate?

RODGER. Possibly you have hit on something here. . . . At the time of the Education Act, Sir John Mackay Thomson was the Secretary of the Department. He was a very able man with an excellent Oxford record in classics. He was a pleasant man, very conservative both with a big 'C' and a small 'c'. He was interested in the classical work of the schools, in the work of independent schools, and in the Leaving Certificate. He had been Sixth Form Master in Fettes and then Rector of Aberdeen Grammar School. But for a Secretary of an Education Department, he did not have wide interests in education. . . . Mackay Thomson would not willingly give up the Leaving Certificate, and I think probably . . . Watson, despite his brilliance and his constant endeavour to favour high attainment, was . . . extremely traditional. Anything new was suspect and, almost certainly, wrong.

Rodger agreed with Brunton that change would have required a strong lead from the SED itself, and so too did our other informants who commented on this, among them James Clark, who in 1947 was Depute Director of Education in Aberdeen:

CLARK. The report . . . had a very good initial press. . . . SED leadership should have encouraged every local authority in the country to see to what extent implementation of aspects, or as much of the report as possible, was a feasible proposition in their area; and what the factors were that prevented this, whether it was staff resources, building resources or whatever. But there was no leadership from the SED; I think that's the only place that it could have come from, at this stage. There was the equivalent of virtual silence for a period.

However, despite public enthusiasm for the language and sentiment of the report, the Department was not under great external pressure to act. One reason for this was that teacher opinion was divided. There were seven teachers on the Sixth Council, and four of them had held the presidency of Scotland's largest teachers' association, the EIS. For almost thirty years the EIS had been the sole teachers' union but, with the advent of secondary education for all, a separate Scottish Secondary Teachers' Association (SSTA) was formed in 1946. Broadly speaking, the SSTA was intended to represent the interests of those who taught courses for national certification, the elite teachers, in other words, of the pre-war system. William Dewar, and James Robertson himself, were among the founding members of the SSTA, and a high proportion of its leading figures were 'classics'. The two associations differed in their reactions to the report. An editorial in the EIS journal welcomed the report. It observed that 'the policy of the Institute has been endorsed in many particulars', and concluded that 'we confidently hope and expect that much of the report will presently be accepted as the official policy for secondary education in Scotland' (*SEJ* 21 March 1947). The SSTA, however, condemned the report's attempt to squeeze the 'lads and lassies o' pairts[7] into a Procrustean bed made to measure of the many' (SSTA 1947). It disliked in particular the reduced status that an integrated curriculum would offer to the honours graduate and subject specialist. Following this attack Robertson left the SSTA and rejoined the EIS. But SSTA teachers had individual influence in the Department (see chapter 18), and a 'classical axis' was important. David Dickson told us that 'the generation of classics people before my time, would be very unwilling, I imagine, to accept the reduced importance he [Robertson] gave to the classics. I don't mean inspectors only; a lot of the secondary headmasters and the classics teachers seem to have felt the same too.' George Gray, another founding member of the SSTA, confirmed this:

GRAY. The classic saw, if he thought ahead, a contraction of his field of operations, because of the extension of other fields of operation. And so the report got [a] rather unfavourable doing from the SSTA. . . . Subject-orientated teachers and headmasters and so on, with vested interests, as I had, let's be candid, saw in it a revolution in the secondary schools.

Evidence has survived on the reactions of the directors of education (ADES 1947). It indicates that these were too varied, and too concerned with the practicalities of implementation, to lead to concerted pressure for action. But at least their national association gave them the potential to form a collective view and transmit it to the Department. Wood told us that no such machinery had existed for the teacher-training colleges,[8] nor for the Inspectorate in which, as we have seen, the view at the top was paramount.

Not only was the profession itself divided and poorly placed to put pressure on the Department, but influential politicians had themselves been diverted. Tom Johnston had given an initial impetus to the Council's work and priorities (Harvie 1981b; Lloyd 1984; Young 1986, ch.5), but the Council's main conclusions were not framed in time to influence the legislation of 1945 and 1946. Moreover, Johnston almost lost the 1945 legislation altogether because of his preoccupation with the mooted restoration of *ad hoc* local authorities (Lloyd 1979, 458). His *Memories* (Johnston 1952) indicate a somewhat superficial interest in educational questions and, in any case, he left national politics in 1945. His Labour successor as Secretary of State was Joseph Westwood. He instructed Mackay Thomson that any reform should ensure that all school leavers would have something to show for their efforts (SRO 1950, 26 July 1947). But the Departmental papers do not suggest that Ministers in office did anything more to influence the Department's response to the Advisory Council's proposals.[9]

Thus the field was left to the senior officials of the SED. Mackay Thomson had been reluctant to see a Sixth Council appointed, partly because the

Department had already laid its plans for post-war advance, and partly because he was reluctant to risk a reopening of the religious issue that had been settled in Scotland in 1918 (Lloyd 1984). However, he had eventually come to accept a new Council as the lesser of two evils, as a way of being seen to respond to popular demands for reform which he believed Scotland had already achieved, or else did not require. Even then, he was not reconciled to the wide and reforming role that Tom Johnston had encouraged the Council to take (*ibid.*). 'We should not', he wrote forebodingly in 1945, 'encourage the view that even the lessons of the War are likely to necessitate any very drastic changes in either the Code or the Memorandum' (see note 1). It was the outbreak of the Second World War, after all, that had led to the suspension of universal secondary education in Scotland. In Mackay Thomson's view what educational and social advance required was a return to pre-war standards, and this could best be achieved by implementing the 1939 Code. Until Mackay Thomson's retirement in 1952, the annual reports of the Department to Parliament show a preoccupation with the restoration of standards at once academic and moral.

Thus recollection and record alike confirm Mackay Thomson's 'conservatism'. When the *Secondary Education* report was published he set up a committee of inspectors and administrators to formulate the Department's response. Its members included Rodger, Gilbert Watson (HMSCI 1945-48), and William Arbuckle, who was later to become Secretary of the Department (1957-63). Another member was Brunton himself. Although the committee minutes contain nothing to suggest that Brunton's contributions were influential, his standing in the Department was clearly somewhat higher than the 'one of seventy' that he mentioned to us. The committee first met in June 1947, and by the following April had prepared a draft response for Ministerial approval. But it was clear from the outset that the Council's report was doomed. At its first meeting the committee welcomed the report's recognition 'that there are limits to what can be demanded from the school in the way of regenerating society', and it insisted that change should neither impair provision for the able minority nor undermine the bipartite distinction between three-year and five-year post-primary courses (SRO 1950, 9 June 1947). Watson in particular argued strongly against the recommendation for an internally assessed certificate at sixteen years. Both he and Mackay Thomson, who regularly communicated his views to the committee, vigorously opposed the Council's proposal to establish an advisory examinations board.

The root of Watson's and Mackay Thomson's opposition to change was their dislike of the consequences for Departmental control of the expansion they anticipated. The committee thought it 'probable that a fair proportion of pupils would now stay on at school until sixteen' and that national certification at sixteen years was a possibility (SRO 1950, 18 July 1947). But Mackay Thomson, recalling the pre-war Intermediate Certificate (see chapter 2), feared that the large number of candidates would swamp the Inspectorate, and that the Treasury would not authorise the necessary increase in establishment (SRO 1950, 13 February 1948). An examination board, on the other hand, would only offer undue influence over schools to industry, the professions and commerce (SRO 1950, 6 October 1947). Watson, too, was opposed to giving a Board responsibility for a national examination at sixteen:

> The risk attending this last course was that the Department, as a result of no longer controlling the examination which the great majority of pupils would take, would largely lose effective control of the curriculum of most pupils under sixteen, which might come in practice to be dictated by the examination board. (SRO 1950, 18 July 1947)

The Department eventually gave its formal response to *Secondary Education* in Circular 206 of March 1951. The delay of four years was itself an indication of the Department's attitude. The circular damned the report with faint praise for its philosophy, and made it plain that schools were not required to innovate (SED 1951b, para.16). The decision on *omnibus* schooling was left to the local authorities. Whilst changes in curriculum and teaching methods were suggested, these were not for the 'intellectually able minority'. Such pupils, the circular said, were 'not ill-served by those traditional forms of secondary education which were designed for them' (*ibid.*, para.2). Perhaps most important of all, the circular made no reference to the proposed 'four-plus-two years' structure of national certification. Instead it argued that 'at the time when the Council submitted their report the raising of the school leaving age to sixteen still appeared likely to take place within the not too distant future'. The circular continued, 'But now that it is clear that the leaving age must remain at fifteen for some considerable time, the Secretary of State considers that . . . secondary education should continue to be organized . . . in courses extending normally over three years and five years' (*ibid.*, para.22). Later, Robertson denied that the Council's proposal for national certification for all sixteen-year-old pupils had presupposed the raising of the period of compulsory education to sixteen years. On the contrary, he said, the Council intended such an examination to encourage pupils to stay on to sixteen for as long as the minimum leaving age was fifteen years (Robertson 1957; SRO 1961a, Third Meeting, 1959). Nor, as we have seen, had Watson or Mackay Thomson thought that the first national certificate examination must coincide with the end of compulsory schooling, although they did think that would be a tidier arrangement.

Circular 206 did little more than tell influential educationists what they had already learned three years earlier in their consultations with the Department. Arguably the important Departmental response to the Advisory Council came, not in the circular, but in the history of the Leaving Certificate which the Department published in 1951 as a chapter of its annual report (SED 1952a). Occasioned ostensibly by the change in that year from a 'group' to an individual-subject certificate, this history can be read as a refutation of the values and theory underlying the Council's recommendations. The Council had wished to sever the link that Craik had made between school certification and university matriculation, arguing that it had since distorted the school curriculum (SED 1947b, para.253). But the Department asserted the importance of the connection (SED 1952a, 21), and retorted that the Certificate had been 'one of the strongest influences in the broadening of secondary courses' and the raising of standards (*ibid.*, 20). It also warned that, when standards had been entrusted to teachers themselves in the decentralised administration of the Leaving Certificate during the War, the teachers had allowed the pass rate to rise by five per cent (*ibid.*, 19).

The change from a group to an individual-subject examination in 1951 had been recommended by the Advisory Council in 1947, as the Department did not neglect to point out. But it had its origins in the (Norwood) report of the Schools Examination Council in England in 1943 (BE 1943) and in the subsequent deliberations of the Roseveare Committee on the report. Co-ordination of Scottish with English arrangements was uppermost in Mackay Thomson's mind. He had fed Roseveare's thinking to the SED committee that was considering the *Secondary Education* report (SRO 1950, 3 and 7 October 1947), and this seems by May 1948 to have swung the committee in favour of an examination in individual subjects. The committee was not, however, persuaded by the English plans to introduce an O-level examination for sixteen-year-olds. This meant that, after 1951, the first national certificate available to Scottish pupils was normally taken only after two years of post-compulsory schooling, at about seventeen years of age, whereas in England, the new O-level examination was available one year earlier. One consequence was that 'early' leaving from Scottish certificate courses in the 1950s was high by comparison with early leaving from the English grammar school (Douglas 1964, 126). But the SED papers do not suggest that the implications for early leaving were anticipated when the decision against an examination at sixteen years was made. The overriding concern was the strain on resources that was threatened by the post-war 'bulge' and by lengthening pupil enrolments, and the loss of Departmental control that such expansion threatened.

Brunton and the Origins of Change

Nevertheless, Rodger told us, the Departmental view was not unanimous:

RODGER. There were certain folks, however, who were still not at the top, and therefore not able to exert top influence, but exerting all the influence that they could towards the implementation in large measure of J. J. Robertson's report. They included Arbuckle, Brunton, and myself. Watson was succeeded by Pringle, who had a somewhat broader view of education than Watson. He was also a very distinguished classicist and also something of a traditionalist. He was succeeded by Brunton, when things changed very rapidly.

In 1944 Henry Wood (later Sir Henry) came from Manchester to Jordanhill Teacher Training College in Glasgow. His impressions of the Scottish system at that time give some idea of the task Brunton faced:

WOOD. In the primary field the schools were pretty formal compared to English primary schools, and in Glasgow at least there were male graduate headmasters appointed usually at the age of about fifty-five. The whole thing seemed very static. In secondary schools the main difference was the absence of the sixth form, and the fact that there was a group certificate with a strong classical and mathematical background, which more or less ignored science. You could do maths and physics as a combined subject. There wasn't the scientific outlet in the secondary schools. There was a distinct absence of local further-education colleges as compared with the South, and, on the whole, the whole system was very much centralised with the Inspectorate running the Leaving Certificate examination. Teacher training was conducted under regulations that had been first devised in 1905 and really changed very little. There were things on the other side as well; for instance, the Scottish Inspectorate were nearer the teachers and nearer the schools than the corresponding people in the South.

Q. How did that work?

WOOD. Well, I think it was because they had been recruited as subject teachers for examination purposes so they had been in the schools. In the South until the War the English Inspectorate was mainly Oxbridge and very often with little, practically no, experience of schools. So although there was tight control in Scotland it was never sort of god-like as it was apt to be in the South.

John Brunton was appointed Senior Chief Inspector in 1955:

BRUNTON. When I became SCI I immediately set about reorganising and revitalising the Inspectorate and trying to provide leadership in redirecting their attitudes and activities. It wasn't so much a structural reorganisation as just a reorientation of their duties, and an attempt to change the attitudes and the activities of the Inspectorate. I had started this before I became Senior Chief Inspector. For example, [as Assistant Secretary 1951-55] I proposed and had accepted some fairly big changes in reporting procedures. And I went very closely into the problem of what we called 'wastage' in the senior-secondary school. Great numbers of very able youngsters were leaving at the age of fifteen, whenever they could, and I came to the conclusion that they were doing it in the first place because of the Leaving Certificate examination and its form, and secondly, because their courses weren't very appropriate; they weren't catching their interest or inspiring them to continue their education. And I managed to get the chief inspectors at that time to agree with my view that a change in the examination structure would probably be necessary, and that certainly some close consideration had to be given to courses of study in the senior-secondary school. I also appointed a very carefully selected committee of inspectors to examine the problems of the junior-secondary school. This was the only way in which anything could be done at that time (through appointing a committee of inspectors to look at it) because it hadn't crossed anybody's mind within the Department that teachers might have something of value to contribute.

Q. Could you tell us about curriculum development in the senior-secondary school?

BRUNTON. That came about gradually; it wasn't a thing that happened immediately. Soon after I became Senior Chief Inspector I got the Department to agree that we should introduce an examination in the fourth year of the secondary school. Traditionally, both the Lower grade and the Higher grade of the Certificate were taken in the fifth year, and they were quite rigid examinations with a very rigid structure. We came to the conclusion that it would be of great assistance if the first examination could be moved a year forward, so as to hold out a carrot to those who were leaving at the age of fifteen and get them to stay on. That decision was taken after I had done a quite careful investigation into the feasibility of doing something of this kind, because a lot of people thought that it would not be possible to provide a national examination in the fourth year in Scotland. But I conducted a quite careful investigation with ready co-operation from the schools and from examination boards in England in respect of the Ordinary-level of the General Certificate of Education, and proved quite conclusively that it could be done. The findings were fully discussed with teachers and directors of education, and the decision was taken to introduce the fourth-year examination. That was a crucial decision, because I immediately said that the new examination structure would have an obvious effect on the curriculum of the senior-secondary school and we ought to examine what that effect would be. And so it was decided to appoint what I called a 'working party' to examine the curriculum of the senior-secondary school. I called it a working party because I was determined it wasn't going to be a committee whose report would be pigeon-holed; and the big breakthrough came when, after a real struggle within the Department, I got it agreed that we should have teachers and directors of education on this working party.

Q. Who was the struggle with?

BRUNTON. Oh, within the administration of the Department, because this had never been done before. It was a very big breakthrough and the consequence was that there has not been a single committee appointed within the Department, even now, to consider problems of curriculum and so on, which has consisted exclusively of inspectors. From that time forth teachers have always been involved.

Q. What was your purpose behind involving teachers? Was it to gain wider acceptance for an initiative coming from the Department?

BRUNTON. Yes, that partly, but also because obviously teachers who were engaged with these problems in the classroom, the front line so to speak, had far more direct knowledge of what was needed and of the probable impact of anything that might be proposed. There was also, vaguely at first, but becoming clearer with time, a desire to secure the co-operation of teachers and to enhance their professional consciousness by involving them in work of this kind. After I became s c I I encouraged the [teacher-training] colleges to raise their academic standards, and about 1958 I abolished their subjection to inspection. In doing so, however, I insisted that inspectors should have the right to go into the colleges freely and consult the staffs about matters of common interest. Thus, the inspectors could go and say, 'Here are my problems; what can you do to help me?' or 'What are your problems and what can I do to help you?' The result was a much more fruitful relationship with the college staffs, and before long members of these staffs were actively engaged in curricular work along with school teachers, headmasters, directors of education and inspectors.

Q. We get the impression that you picked particular bright young inspectors and threw your influence behind them in the development of new curricula in, for example, physics and chemistry.

B R U N T O N. May I explain just how all this came about? It arose out of the decision to introduce the new fourth-year examination and the subsequent report of the working party on the curriculum of the senior-secondary school [s E D 1959b]. The working party's recommendations removed the rigidities from the curriculum, gave it a new fluidity and flexibility, and gave to headmasters and teachers a new freedom to plan courses suited to the needs of their pupils at different levels of ability. They also introduced teachers to new ideas about the approach to their pupils and to the teaching of their subjects. These recommendations, which were largely in line with the Advisory Council's thinking, were greeted with much interest and in some instances with much enthusiasm, and were quite widely and rapidly adopted largely, I am sure, because they came from a body on which teachers had been quite substantially represented. The result was an almost immediate, and very noticeable, improvement in the whole atmosphere of the senior-secondary schools, and a rapid increase in the number of pupils remaining on at school after the age of fifteen [see s E D 1965a, 32]. The new fourth-year examination required new syllabuses, and I set my various subject committees to work to produce them. The traditional drill was for examination syllabuses to be drafted by the Inspectorate and then discussed with the teachers before they were finally approved, and the time was not yet quite right for changing this procedure. I hoped that the new syllabuses would be progressive and encourage new approaches to teaching, and was very disappointed when this did not happen in most of the subjects; the new draft syllabuses were, with a very few exceptions, little more than somewhat simplified versions of the old ones. I was even more disappointed when the teachers accepted them with relatively few criticisms. But I had regarded this examination as an opportunity to modernise the curriculum, and not to go ahead with all the classical physics and mathematics and so on that had for so long been traditional in the old examination for the Lower grade. So the first breakthrough again came when a new inspector of physics was appointed, [Donald] McGill [HMI 1959-62]. When McGill came to see me first of all after he was appointed, he said to me how disappointed he was with the new syllabus in physics, and I said to him, 'Well, you're a man after my own heart. This is precisely what I think myself. There is only one member of the science Inspectorate who agrees with me' – he was a chemist, A. J. Mee [HMI 1946-69]. And I said to McGill, 'Have you any thoughts about what we might do?' He said, 'Oh yes, I have thoughts.' So I said, 'Go and put them down and let me see them'. And McGill brought his thoughts in broad outline, and I considered them very carefully and discussed them with one or two other people. And then I said to him, 'Look, develop these and go and take them round the schools, the universities and colleges, and discuss them with various people and see what the reaction is'. He reported that the reaction was on the whole very favourable. So I arranged a conference of influential teachers of physics from universities, colleges and schools at which the new ideas were discussed in great detail and were recommended for adoption. Subsequent development was placed in the hands of a carefully selected group of inspectors and teachers, who produced and published a new Ordinary-grade syllabus, and then set to work to organise training courses for teachers to introduce them to the new ideas, and issued explanatory memoranda and leaflets which were subsequently translated into textbooks with the co-operation of the educational publishers. The new proposals represented a very major departure from the traditional syllabus, and in order to avoid giving too big a shock to the mass of the teachers in the schools, it was decided to introduce the new syllabus as an alternative one which the schools could take or not take as they wished. Within a very short time work was started on a new syllabus in chemistry. The procedures adopted were more or less the same as in the case of physics, and the end result was similar. . . . The next big development came in mathematics. This time the inspector most directly concerned had the sympathetic interest and support of a widely representative committee on mathematics which had recently been set up to consider means of increasing the supply of teachers of mathematics [see chapter 10]. The procedures adopted were similar to those in the sciences, and the carefully selected group of teachers was even more influential in carrying forward the new ideas [see Mee 1964]. By this time other members of the Inspectorate were considering their own subject specialisms, and revision of syllabuses was very much in the air. During the next year or two major changes were proposed, were fully discussed and developed along with appropriate teachers, and were adopted in a variety of subjects such as biology, history, geography, modern languages and technical subjects. And then our minds turned towards considering how all this should, and could, be developed down into the junior-secondary school. . . . Before all this happened, teachers who were influential in the councils of the EIS had been calling on the SED to 'give them a lead' particularly in the modernisation of the teaching of mathematics and science. They had now been given the lead they wanted. Only a minority of teachers adopted the new syllabuses when they were first introduced, but the number of 'converts' increased substantially within a year or two. . . . With the new Ordinary-grade syllabuses launched, the next logical step was to consider the development of these syllabuses for the Higher-grade examination. The teachers for the most part saw the sense of this and raised no real opposition. The difficulties which did arise came from the attitudes of the universities, where various professors did not think that the proposed new Higher-grade syllabuses provided a suitable preparation for continued study in university courses. I had to point out that the schools had to do more than prepare pupils for universities. They had also to cater for those who would go forward to other forms of further and higher education, as well as for those who would not necessarily continue their formal education in any institution at all. . . . However . . . we reached a consensus of view about the Higher-grade syllabuses, and they were eventually introduced.

Towards a New Structure for Advice

We asked Brunton whether he had a grand design, when he became HMSCI, for a reorganised structure of advice:

BRUNTON. I had no such grand design to begin with. My first preoccupation was to improve communication and consultation within the Inspectorate, and between the Inspectorate and teachers in the schools. Other improvements in consultation were made simply by seizing opportunities for improvement as developments in the system took place, and as each one took place trying to foresee its likely repercussions and prepare for them. As I have said, I saw the Inspectorate as the spearhead of the teaching profession, providing ideas and encouraging teachers to co-operate in developing them. But I was certainly anxious to arrive at a point where teachers would themselves suggest possible improvements and would not always look to the Inspectorate for a lead. To begin with, I had no thought of an examination board as such. But I was thoroughly convinced that the conducting of a national examination was no proper function of the Inspectorate.

Q. So you wanted to devolve that function but you didn't know to what sort of body?

BRUNTON. When the new examination was [being] established, it very rapidly became apparent that the Inspectorate just couldn't cope because of the increase in the number of candidates. So when the [committee of the] Advisory Council was appointed [in 1959] to consider the post-fourth-year examination structure, I suggested to the members that they should consider who should run the examinations. When I first suggested this they looked blankly at me as if they didn't know what I was talking about; and so I gave them a couple of papers, the first telling them how the examinations were conducted, and the second making certain suggestions for the future. I suggested, with the agreement of the Secretary, the constitution of an examination board of some kind [s ro 1961a, 3 February 1960], and my suggestions were more or less written into the report, and this is how the Examination Board was born. When this was recommended by the Advisory Council (s ed 1960b, paras 50-7), I may say, it met with considerable opposition within the administration of the Department, but the recommendation was fairly quickly adopted. . . . I wanted to get people appointed to the Inspectorate who were concerned with, or had experience in, the primary school and in other parts of the system. But we couldn't do it because of the Leaving Certificate examination. We had to cover every subject in the examination, and with a limited staff you could only do it by appointing people with proper qualifications to cover the subjects. . . . The whole thing was rigid from that point of view. I wanted to do things in special schools. Ultimately I managed to do them and, in the end, I started to appoint people with primary-school experience as vacancies arose. But this took an awful lot of doing. And, even when I got it accepted by the Inspectorate that this should happen, you have no idea of the opposition I met from the Civil Service Commission who were ultimately responsible for all Civil Service appointments. I was proposing to interview people for the Inspectorate some of whom didn't have any degree at all, let alone an Honours degree. [The Examination Board] . . . arose firstly out of my conviction that conducting a national examination wasn't a proper thing for the Inspectorate to be doing; secondly, that it was taking up an unreasonable amount of Inspectorate time which could be used better elsewhere; thirdly, out of the impossibility of the Inspectorate continuing to carry on the examination; and fourthly, out of my conviction that, if there is to be a national examination, it ought to be conducted by the national educational system, and this was a heaven-sent opportunity of bringing the universities, the colleges, the teachers, industry and commerce in to consider things within the schools, far more than they had ever done before.

The Examination Board assumed responsibility for the conduct of examinations for the Scottish Certificate of Education in 1965 (see chapter 13). In the same year the Consultative Committee on the Curriculum (ccc) was established as a non-statutory Departmental committee to give advice on the curriculum (see chapter 14). In England this function fell to the Schools Council that had been set up in 1964, with strong local-authority and teacher representation. We asked Brunton about his approach to the ccc:

B runton. This was one of my last acts. I think it was the last major proposal I made within the Department. I had been quite a close observer of the fairly recently established Schools Council in England. This was a very large organisation with a very large infrastructure, and it did not seem to me that anything of that kind was necessary in Scotland, because we were smaller and much more intimate, and the various parts of the educational system were much more closely in touch with each other. All the directors of education, all the main representatives of the teachers and the headmasters and so on, we were seeing constantly, and it didn't seem to me that a great infrastructure of this kind was necessary. But I felt that something was required. We had got relations between the Department and the Research Council [the Scottish Council for Research in Education] onto a proper footing, we were encouraging the Research Council to go ahead and do more practical things; we had encouraged the colleges of education to develop their research; and through such contacts as we had we were encouraging the universities to do this also. We had set up the Examination Board which had responsibility over a large area of senior-secondary education. It seemed to me that some body was required on which all these different interests would be represented, which would have a general oversight of the curriculum, and which would be at least a relatively independent body of real authority giving powerful advice to the Secretary of State. When this proposal was first made within the Department, it met with intense opposition from certain members of the administration, but after many arguments it was agreed that this body should be established. I suggested that we ought to appoint as chairman of this curriculum body some eminent person from the educational world. But the administrators who had opposed me had the last word and argued that it would give prestige to this new body if the Secretary of the Department were to take the chair. I knew that this was a big mistake but could not prevent it happening.

NOTES
1. Mackay Thomson to Parker (SRO 1945, 24 August 1945).
2. Young (1986, ch.5) points out that the constitution of the Sixth Council differed in several respects from that of the First Council appointed under the 1918 Act. Young's thesis is an invaluable account of the work of the Advisory Council and of its relations with the SED over the period 1918-61. Another important source for the early events discussed in this chapter is Lloyd's (1979) account of the SED during the Second World War.
3. Robertson did not apparently regard the report on technical education (SED 1946d) as one of the Sixth Council's 'major' reports.
4. The original reads 'internal', but 'external' is clearly intended.
5. However, para.157 of the report stated: 'we are fortified by the evidence of two witnesses who out of a particularly wide experience hold that any unqualified condemnation of the junior secondary school at this stage would be premature and insufficiently based. Stress must be laid on the fact that the new short-course schools have had a relatively brief trial and under conditions both confused and adverse.' The report also had reservations about the cost of upper-school provision in small comprehensives. The strength of the report's case for comprehensives is best appreciated by reading it at length. But there is little doubt that it was weakened by the position it took on junior-secondary schools.

6. There is, however, evidence that the universities may have liked the Council's proposals. The *Scotsman* of 14 March 1947 reported that an official of Edinburgh University 'thought it very likely that the universities would welcome the withdrawal of the Senior Leaving Certificate and its replacement by a School Certificate at the end of the fourth year and a Higher School Certificate at the end of the Sixth Form Courses. In all probability the proposed Higher Certificate, provided the examination had the appropriate contents, would be accepted by the universities as corresponding to the University Preliminary Examination.' Rodger's comment may be applicable, therefore, only to university entry requirements relating to the Lower Grade. We owe this reference to John Young.
7. On the 'lad o' pairts' see chapter 17, and Anderson (1985).
8. There was the National Committee for the Training of Teachers but this was dominated by William McClelland. McClelland was appointed chairman of the Seventh Advisory Council 1947-51, but his views on the future role of the teacher-training colleges were anathema to the Department (see chapter 11).
9. See also Young (1986, 371-4).

Five

People and Power

> In my opinion, Brunton was probably the last of the chief inspec-
> tors who was able to stand up fully to the administrators in the
> Department. . . . Opposing this imposed policy, or effort at
> policy-making, stands the rather lonely figure of Brunton, de-
> manding that the educational sphere in Scotland must not be
> deprived of developments and improvements on the purely edu-
> cational front. George Gray, General Secretary of the SSTA
> 1945-59, Secretary of the SCTT 1959-67, and Registrar of the GTC
> 1966-72

Introduction

Many of Brunton's contemporaries outside the Department shared his view
that it was a mistake for the Secretary of the Department to chair the new
CCC. They saw this move as part of a growing trend towards the control of
the advisory function by SED administrators. Wood, for example, told us
that Graham's decision surprised him, and that chairing the CCC was 'an
obvious function of the Senior Chief Inspector'. Like Gray, Wood thought
that a watershed was reached in 1965. He told us, 'since Brunton has gone I
would say that the professional civil service has come to dominate the
Department'. This was also the view taken by Gilbert Bryden, General
Secretary of the EIS 1961-74. How influence within the Department shifted
after Brunton's retiral we discuss more fully in part III in the context of a
broader review of governmental change. In this chapter we make an initial
assessment of Brunton's account of how he initiated change and promoted
the influence of the Inspectorate, the 'spearhead of the teaching profession',
as he called them. Looking back on Brunton's chief inspectorship, some of
his contemporaries were later to assign it a quasi-heroic status, not unlike
the view that Morgan in an earlier generation had taken of Craik and
Struthers (Morgan 1929). However, James Scotland's history (Scotland
1969) refers to Brunton only once, as the chairman of the 'Brunton' report
From School to Further Education (SED 1963b). Scotland himself traces the
origin of the Examination Board, not to Brunton, but to evidence presented
to the Eighth Advisory Council by the Association of Directors of Education
(Scotland 1969, 187); and he says little about the origins of the CCC. On the
other hand, James Scotland's history in general has little to say about
politics and personality. To what extent, then, was Brunton the central

figure that he himself described, or even the legendary figure that others maintained? How did he acquire such power as he exercised, and how was it constrained? What were his purposes, methods and achievements? And what relationship was there between legend and reality?

Views of Brunton from outside the SED

We look first at the views of several people outside the SED, starting with Dewar:

DEWAR. I would say that the change in the machinery was something that found its dynamic from Brunton. . . . The Inspectorate were being asked to do more and more to guide [the] local authority, because the local authority did not have the know-how. . . . There was only one place I could get my guidance, namely from the HMI; and Brunton was with me there. . . . This was what he was after: to get the inspectors into the schools. . . . [A] few of them had vision but a very large number of them had been too long in their districts. . . . [I was] asked by Brunton to let Heriot's take a special examination that he was asking several schools in Scotland to take, to compare our Lower Grade Leaving Certificate with . . . the GCE O-level; and Heriot's became one of those in the experiment.

Q. So it first came from Brunton to you, did it?

DEWAR. This was so. He said, 'Look, we are going to see whether an examination of this standard would be something that fourth-year pupils could take'. . . .

Q. Was Brunton responsible for deciding on the remit, structure and function of the Examination Board?

DEWAR. I would say so. He was really the power behind the throne at that time.

We asked Bryden:

Q. Would you agree that, right from the time Brunton became Senior Chief Inspector, he was anxious to get more teacher involvement?

BRYDEN. Oh yes, yes, that's true. There is no doubt about that. . . . Brunton was a much more teacherly Senior Chief Inspector than any of the others.

Q. Was teacher participation a scandalously new idea in the mid-fifties?

BRYDEN. It was probably regarded as an idea that everyone should support, but that no one did. . . . But Brunton managed to achieve a far greater measure of teacher participation.

Q. Did the EIS see a lot of him on a personal basis?

BRYDEN. No, not particularly. I think we had him once at a congress. He and I got on very well. I knew a lot of him and we met frequently.

Thus what Bryden particularly remembered was not formal contacts between the Institute and the HMSCI, but his own personal contact with Brunton. James Clark, Director of Education for Aberdeen, made a similar comment:

CLARK. I felt that the Inspectorate in Brunton's time [was] much more knowledgeable about the local situation and the feeling in the local authority, and the inspectors came to see the directors more often. Brunton himself came more often.

Q. By comparison with the way that the Inspectorate had been under Pringle, who preceded Brunton, did you feel the effects of a shake-up . . . that inspectors had been too long in their districts, that it was moribund?

CLARK. Yes, I think so, and when Brunton took over there was fresh thinking and there was much more drive and a broader outlook. Brunton himself was getting around very much more, in my view, than any Senior Chief Inspector before or since . . . (I had better qualify that a little, because I saw a lot of David Dickson subsequently.) But I think that Brunton really brought a breath of fresh air into the Inspectorate. . . . The one-to-one contact between somebody like myself and Brunton, I found extremely valuable.

In his evidence to the Parliamentary Select Committee on the Inspectorate in 1968, Wood had said: 'The great change in the last fifteen years has been to try and get something moving. There is no doubt that the initiative in this respect came from the Inspectorate. . . . I would say that a great deal of the change in Scottish education since 1958 stemmed from the Senior Chief Inspector' (SCES 1968, Q.218). In conversation with us, Wood confirmed Brunton's account of the role he had encouraged the colleges of education to adopt:

WOOD. One of his [Brunton's] first acts was to come and talk to [William] Inglis [Principal of Moray House College, Edinburgh, 1951-66] and myself about whether there should be inspection of colleges or not, and we all agreed that it was the formal inspection that ought really to stop, and that this would lead to greater co-operation between the academic staff of the colleges and the Inspectorate. This in fact happened, and in all the curriculum committees that Brunton established the college subject specialists played quite a significant part; and I would have said this came in the main through the Inspectorate and Brunton rather than from the local authorities or the Scottish Council for the Training of Teachers [SCTT].

The SCTT was founded in 1958 when it replaced the National Committee for the Training of Teachers (NCTT) as part of a general reform of teacher training (see chapter 12). From his perspective as the first Secretary of the SCTT, George Gray put the emphasis differently from Wood, but he broadly agreed with Wood's judgement of Brunton's standing:

Q. Where do you think that this policy for the de-control over the colleges came from? Was it a question of Brunton's looking for support from the colleges for the sorts of curricular changes that he was trying to force through? Was it a *quid pro quo*?

GRAY. In my opinion, Brunton was probably the last of the chief inspectors who was able to stand up fully to the administrators in the

Department. The administrators are dominated by the Secretary of State and he is under the control of the Treasury. . . . Opposing this imposed policy, or effort at policy-making, stands the rather lonely figure of Brunton, demanding that the educational sphere in Scotland must not be deprived of developments and improvements on the purely educational front.

Q. Was it Brunton who was responsible for the loosening of control in the colleges?

GRAY. I don't think so. A. G. Rodger, Under-Secretary, was largely responsible. I think . . . [it] was just simply the logical outcome of Robbins [CHE 1963] and the current notions about autonomy. Incidentally you [then] get a national Scottish Council [SCTT] to undertake a certain number of the coordinating functions which the Secretary of State undertook previously, and therefore release the Inspectorate for other roles.

Q. So the change from the NCTT to the SCTT was part of the general strategy of releasing the Inspectorate?

GRAY. I think that came into it, but it wasn't surely the basic motive.

With some differences of emphasis, four of these five views saw Brunton's contribution very much as Brunton himself had volunteered. The exception was Gray, who thought that Brunton had used the opportunity presented by a more general reorganisation of relationships that was already afoot. But even Gray acknowledged that Brunton championed education. Among our non-Departmental interviewees the one other dissentient opinion was that of Douglas McIntosh, voiced some ten years earlier in 1968, just two years after he had completed a twenty-two year spell as Director of Education in Fife. Having then succeeded Inglis as Principal of Moray House College of Education, he accompanied Wood in 1968 to give oral evidence to the Select Committee on the Inspectorate. There he took issue with Wood's view, quoted above, that change had stemmed from Brunton. McIntosh said, 'I would not agree with that at all. . . . I do not think this flow was coming from any particular body; I think everybody moved in and helped' (SCES 1968, Q.218). McIntosh, however, was an unabashed critic of the Inspectorate, and his view must be assessed in the context of his general purpose in that session, which was to argue for a shift in the balance of influence from the Inspectorate on the grounds of its incompetence: 'They require training; they get no training. . . . They get no opportunity for refreshing their scholarship. From the moment they join the Inspectorate their capital begins to run down. . . . I know that the people at this table have far more qualifications because of our training than any of them' (*ibid.*, Qs 232 and 238). This critique can be traced back to an older conflict, described in chapter 11, between the Department and the scientific and progressive movement of the inter-war period. McIntosh worked with the leading figures of that movement, and he always held that the training that it gave in research was the best authority for decision-making in education.

Departmental Conflict and External Alliances

We asked Brunton:

Q. How do you explain the fact that, as Senior Chief Inspector, you were able to take such an initiative over a period of ten years when, it seems, ultimate power lay with the Secretary and the Under-Secretaries of the SED?

BRUNTON. The ultimate authority lay with the Secretary, not the two Under-Secretaries. I myself had the status, though for a time not the emoluments, of an Under-Secretary. But that apart, I think that the answer to your question is to be found in the simple word 'communication'. . . . I instituted a regular monthly conference of chief inspectors when we met regularly in solemn conference to discuss matters of policy. We met of course very frequently apart from this. The communication within the Inspectorate was very much improved. I instituted conferences, residential conferences of my staff; sections of the staff to begin with, and, after a year or two of getting them used to this sort of thing, a regular annual three-day conference in which we all met together; and we knew each other, which had never happened before. We knew each other, we knew our thinking, we put forward the ideas that we wanted to be followed, and I got them really a coherent body working as one force. . . . The administrators were aware that . . . the Inspectorate had become a united body following a coherent policy which had been thrashed out in hours of discussion. But I worked in harmony with them [the administrators] and took pains to discuss with them what was happening or was proposed, and to iron out differences of opinion wherever possible, for example, by inviting them to meetings at which policy developments were being discussed, including my residential conferences of the staff. [The administrators were aware also that] such influence as I exerted derived very largely from the support and the sympathetic agreement of many friends throughout the educational system, in the teachers' organisations, in schools and colleges, even in universities and latterly in industry and commerce. . . . I think for the first time in history I could say that a Senior Chief Inspector had visited every district in Scotland. I went out and saw my staff at work and met the directors of education. The directors of education, when they came into St Andrew's House, would just naturally drop into my room and discuss any problems they had to discuss, and I had my finger on the pulse of the whole of Scottish education. Through all these conferences and meetings one was able to initiate ideas, to suggest things and to get things going.

We put this explanation to Bryden:

Q. Do you think Brunton's arm was strengthened in the Department by the relationship that he enjoyed with educationists generally, and in particular with teachers?

BRYDEN. He made a great thing of bringing the teachers as far as possible into all sorts of educational decisions, and I shouldn't be at all surprised if he managed to be extremely influential in the Department by giving the administrators the impression that he had the teachers on his side, and that what he said would be supported by the teachers.

Q. You said, 'the impression'. Are you suggesting that there was a bit of impression-management?

BRYDEN. Oh I think probably there was a good deal of management. . . . He gave his administrative colleagues the impression that he had far more shots in his locker than he actually had. He had good shots in his locker, but I think probably not as many as they thought. If they had called his bluff, I think they might have called it with some success. . . . But these are quite difficult issues, sometimes, unless you were actually in the Department and knew what was going on. And then you had the Departmental chaps who were far too clever to let you guess what was going on and, of course, they were trained not to.

In addition to his constituencies 'in the country', Brunton mentioned a second important source of support:

BRUNTON. Above all, I took care to keep the Secretary in touch with what was in the wind, and to secure his informal agreement to particular developments before they were formally announced or put into effect. I cannot recall one single instance during the eleven years of my service as SCI when the Secretary interfered with the major work of the Inspectorate or refused to approve any major development proposed. There were one or two occasions when important advances were disputed by certain members of the administration; but on each occasion the advance was approved because it had the Secretary's backing. . . . I had four and a half years of experience as an Assistant Secretary within the Department before I became SCI. I therefore knew both sides, the administrative and the professional. My responsibility as Assistant Secretary was for schools and examinations. Decisions on all matters of policy, both administrative and professional, were at that time taken by the administration, though the SCI was consulted before decisions on professional matters were taken. But [as Assistant Secretary] I gradually developed a procedure for sitting in on the discussions of the SCI and the chief inspectors and putting proposals to them for changes in the work of the Inspectorate and in aspects of the educational system; in other words, giving them a voice in the formulation of educational policy. After I became SCI in 1955, it quite quickly became accepted that all matters concerning the Inspectorate and all professional educational policy were my responsibility, subject to the ultimate control of the Secretary of the Department who, as a matter of fact, rarely interfered, mainly because he was always consulted beforehand about matters that legitimately required his decision or approval. I had very good relations with the administrators, but they understood and respected my sphere of responsibility as I did theirs.

100

These carefully chosen words on the shifting locus of decisions before and after Brunton became Senior Chief Inspector in 1955 should be juxtaposed with Brunton's earlier comment in this chapter that, once he had become Senior Chief Inspector, he 'took pains to discuss with them [the administrators] what was happening or was proposed . . . for example, by inviting them to meetings at which policy developments were being discussed'. We asked Brunton to tell us more about his relationship with the Secretary, the relationship that made it possible for him to preserve this newly acquired influence for the position of Senior Chief Inspector:

BRUNTON. I served as SCI under three Secretaries. I was appointed [in 1955] by Sir William Murrie [Secretary of the SED 1952-57], under whom I had served for a time as an Assistant Secretary, and who was familiar with my thinking on education. Murrie was a very able administrator. If one had ideas to put forward, he would consider them carefully and, if he agreed, would say, 'Yes, carry on', and that was that. And that's how a lot of things happened. The day after I was appointed he invited me to 'do something about the Inspectorate' and was in complete sympathy with what I tried to do. He was also in complete agreement with the various developments that took place subsequently. He was succeeded by Sir William Arbuckle [1957-63], who had been appointed to the Inspectorate only six months before me and with whom I had worked very closely over the years. As an Under-Secretary in the Department [1952-57] his thinking had been closely aligned to mine and there was therefore no difficulty at all when he became Secretary. Arbuckle was succeeded by Sir Norman Graham [in 1964].

What was the basis of Brunton's relationship with Murrie and Arbuckle? The spirit of reconstruction had not been the only legacy of the Second World War. The War had physically shifted the school population and the careers of those who administered the schools:

MURRIE. I had started in the Scottish Office in London, and I had served from 1935 until 1944 in the Department of Health in Edinburgh; and I had rubbed shoulders with inspectors from the SED who, in 1939, were seconded to the Health Department, to help in carrying out the evacuation scheme. Indeed, from 1938, we knew that we were going to have an evacuation scheme for school children and my division of the Health Department worked pretty closely with the Education Department people. . . .

Q. Who were your eyes and ears in the first few months you were Secretary?

MURRIE. Very largely Arbuckle, who was an old friend of mine. . . .

Q. Could we talk about Brunton? He was Assistant Secretary in 1951. He was already *in situ* when you came in in 1952.

MURRIE. He was one of the little group I mentioned who, at the beginning of the War, came and worked as administrative officers in the Department of Health. I think he dealt with hospitals. He then went back to be an inspector after the War. He then came into the Department as an

Assistant Secretary. And it was a very deliberate choice to make him Senior Chief Inspector. He seemed, at least to me, much the best person because he had the knowledge of both sides.

Q. And you told him to reorganise the Inspectorate. Is that right?

MURRIE. No. I wouldn't take credit for this. I think Arbuckle was the main person, but Arbuckle and I felt that he was the person to do this.

Q. Would it have been at Arbuckle's suggestion, then, that Brunton sat in on the Senior Chief Inspectors' conferences while he was still Assistant Secretary in the Department? This apparently was a new departure, and an attempt to bring the Inspectorate into the discussion of policy-making at an earlier stage.

MURRIE. I think, probably, yes, but I couldn't swear to this. I think that Arbuckle and Brunton and I saw very much eye-to-eye . . . in this field.

Q. What seems to happen, when Brunton goes over to be Senior Chief Inspector, is that he takes with him some decision-making which he himself described as having previously reposed with the administration. Was there a transfer of decision-making to the Inspectorate as a result of his move?

MURRIE. Not a conscious transfer of particular topics, but certainly a feeling [that] Brunton knows both sides of the coin and we can trust him to take more decisions than his predecessor.

Q. Brunton and Arbuckle between them introduced the principle of having teachers on working parties. Opinions differ as to where this idea came from. Would you credit them both?

MURRIE. Yes.

David Dickson was an area inspector in Fife when Brunton appointed him to chair the Inspectorate working party that published *Junior Secondary Education* in 1955 (SED 1955b). He was eventually to succeed Brunton as Senior Chief Inspector in 1966. We asked him how it was that Brunton's career had moved several times between Inspectorate and administration:

DICKSON. Well, to some extent of course these matters are accidental. Brunton came back in because Pringle, his predecessor as HMSCI, died in office. If Pringle had . . . served a normal period as Senior Chief, it is, I think, doubtful whether Brunton would have moved back again into the Inspectorate. He might have been too old to do that you see. . . . Mind you, when one talks about Brunton and Arbuckle having all this influence, one has to remember that they were in touch at the same time with a lot of other people not only in the Inspectorate but also in the colleges of education and among the directors of education. All sorts of things were discussed with them unofficially as well as formally. . . .

Q. It's one thing to go out and consult, it's another thing actually to bring some of these people into the machinery at the centre, as began to happen in the fifties. Was this Arbuckle's initiative or Brunton's?

DICKSON. Both, I should say.

Q. How important was Murrie's giving Brunton unquestioned backing for what he wanted to do?

DICKSON. Oh, very important indeed, and Arbuckle at least as much.

Q. When Arbuckle became Secretary?

DICKSON. Yes . . . and even before, when Arbuckle was in the Department under Murrie. Arbuckle had a great deal of influence on Murrie, I think.

Q. Yes. Indeed, this is what Murrie said.

DICKSON. I would have thought so too. Arbuckle would have had a great deal of influence on me too. Indeed he did have. . . . I always think of Arbuckle along with Brunton as the two men who, at that difficult period, moved the Department and other people as well in the direction in which we ultimately went. . . .

Q. Who would you say was the prime mover?

DICKSON. Ah, that's very difficult, I would think that Brunton would put forward the ideas rather than Arbuckle, but Arbuckle would be the one who sorted them out and said, 'Well, I think what we should do is so-and-so, and so-and-so'. They were a very good pair indeed.

Thus Brunton was commonly regarded, along with Arbuckle, as a central figure. Murrie and Dickson saw the thinking of the two men as of a piece, though they were inclined to give Arbuckle the edge as the prime mover within the Department. But perhaps this is not surprising. For much of his career, Arbuckle held higher office than Brunton, ending it as Secretary of the Department. It is equally natural that Brunton should have been the more salient figure of the two in the eyes of educationists outside the Department. Brunton made it his business to cultivate his contacts with this wider world to a degree that a Departmentally based senior administrator would perhaps have found difficult; though it is possibly significant that Sir Norman Graham, Arbuckle's successor to the Secretaryship, also made a reputation for frequent and extensive contacts with the educational world at a time when he was actively questioning the influence of the Inspectorate within the Department (see chapters 6 and 7).

A full assessment of Brunton's aims, methods and legacy must take account of further aspects of educational policy at this time, and also of the new machinery of advice. We come to these in later chapters. But from our early interviews several hypotheses had emerged about the sources of Brunton's power. We discussed these with Allan Rodger. Rodger was Assistant Secretary in the SED from 1945 to 1959, and then Under-Secretary from 1959 to 1963. The discussion deals first with the locus of power in the Department, and then with the changing structure of advice. It ends with two views of Brunton's educational thinking. These throw some light on his role in the formation of policy. They also help explain why that policy was to depart in several fundamental respects from the spirit of the *Secondary Education* report of the Advisory Council, despite Brunton's claim that his aim was to implement it:

Q. Had Brunton been unhappy as Assistant Secretary?

RODGER. No, I don't think so. I think perhaps he enjoyed his importance as an Assistant Secretary, and he enjoyed as Assistant Secretary his power to achieve what he wanted. I don't for a moment think he was unhappy. But from the time he became the head of the Inspectorate, he was out to make the Inspectorate important, and I think that was why he welcomed, for example, the change from Mackay Thomson to Murrie. Mackay Thomson was an educationist in the sense that he had worked in education as a teacher and headmaster. Murrie was not; he was an administrator. And Brunton probably took a different view from either Arbuckle or myself about this. We thought that a Secretary was possibly best who had a background in education. Brunton took the view that a Murrie appointment was good because, not being an expert himself, he had to call in the Inspectorate as his experts. So Brunton saw this kind of change as a means of aggrandising the importance of the Inspectorate and his importance as its Chief.

Q. Brunton said that before he became the SCI in 1955 almost all of the decisions in the Department had been taken by administrators. How could Brunton as Senior Chief Inspector exert the influence that he did? It occurred to us that part of the explanation lies in the fact that Brunton's changes had actually started when Brunton was still an Assistant Secretary, when, if you like, he enjoyed authority within a traditional context.

RODGER. Yes, that I think is true. I am sure that some at least of the changes which Brunton brought about as Chief Inspector germinated in his mind as Assistant Secretary.

Q. That is to say, Dickson's work that resulted in the *Junior Secondary* report had been initiated by Brunton when he was Assistant Secretary. The reform of the Inspectorate had been started by Murrie and Arbuckle, but also suggested by Brunton, and in some respects begun by him whilst he was still Assistant Secretary.[1] He then, very unexpectedly, moved across from Assistant Secretary to Senior Chief Inspector. Was there not a period of weeks, or months, or possibly even years, in which some of the aura of authority that had gathered around him as Assistant Secretary, carried across to his position as Senior Chief Inspector?

RODGER. Yes, that may be true. You see, during that period . . . Brunton was the Assistant Secretary in charge of schools. Murrie would therefore be dependent on Brunton and might perhaps stop there rather than proceed right on to the Inspectorate. Brunton therefore, as you say, gathered an authority which he carried over with him; and therefore, when he became Senior Chief Inspector, he was acting perhaps both as Assistant Secretary and Senior Chief Inspector.

Q. What we are also suggesting is that, perhaps in 1955 or 1956, it wasn't yet finally clear where Brunton's eventual career would lie. The way Murrie put it was that, if times had fallen out differently, you might have had Brunton as head of the Department.

RODGER. That is possible, but at the time I imagine that, when Brunton accepted the post of Senior Chief of the Inspectorate, he was deliberately preferring that avenue to any possibilities of administrative promotion. . . .

Q. So here we have a man, Brunton, Senior Chief Inspector, whose ultimate position in the Department had come to be independent of the post he happened to hold.

RODGER. Yes, that is quite possible.

Q. And this is part of the explanation of how, for a period of about ten years, the Inspectorate enjoyed a greater freedom than before or since.

RODGER. Yes, that may be right, but I should have thought (though this was after my day) that the prestige and power of the Inspectorate remained high in Dickson's time [HMSCI, 1966-69].

Q. Can we ask you about the part that was played in Brunton's strategy by teachers' representation on his working parties? It seems to me that you can have teachers on working parties for a number of reasons: one of them is that you believed genuinely in teachers' professionalism, that they should, in some sense, be self-determining, and have a say . . .

RODGER. Yes.

Q. . . . in matters concerning them. But there are also all sorts of other reasons why you would want teachers on your working parties: one might be . . .

RODGER. One might be sheer show.

Q. Exactly; to legitimate in advance your curriculum reforms with the profession. Another is that it is a more effective way of dissemination; the more people are involved, the more likely it is that a thing will get done.

RODGER. Yes.

Q. Another reason is that this is one of the ways in which you get good ideas from people who are working at the chalk face, if you like.

RODGER. Yes.

Q. Another reason, perhaps, is that Brunton needed as large as possible a constituency of people outside the Department who were involved with him and who were receptive to his ideas. In other words, being so widely and deeply involved was not simply a way of legitimating his ideas and getting things done. It was also a way of protecting his position *vis-à-vis* the administrators in the Department; building a constituency which he could use.

RODGER. I think that the points you have made tell the story correctly, but I wouldn't say that all of the points are of equal importance. I think that Brunton was more influenced by casual conversations with people, which matured in his mind later, and particularly with the Inspectoral viewpoints, than with the other things which you have mentioned.

Q. And yet he spent an awful lot of his time going around.

RODGER. Yes. . . . Certainly, much more than Pringle; probably more than any of his predecessors. Part of that was to gather ideas; part of that was to disseminate his own thoughts amongst others; but part of it was simply, I think, to enable him to say to Ministers and to say to the Secretary that he had discussed this with so-and-so. . . .

Q. Would you say, then, that Brunton was a genuine believer, at the end of the day, in teacher professionalism? That this was something he wanted to work towards, genuine teacher representation?

RODGER. I would doubt that. I would think that, at the end of the day, he was always working towards Bruntonianism.

Q. Would you see that as another form of centralised activity, based upon a strong central task-force of inspectors?

RODGER. Well, Brunton wanted to be the centre himself. There wasn't much thinking of the Department as a central task-force.

Q. Did you attend the annual meetings of the Inspectorate to which he invited members of the administration? Were these very orchestrated affairs which would be working towards something which Brunton wanted at the end of the day?

RODGER. Oh yes, very much so. I would think so. Brunton got things done; got things done apparently democratically. But I think that there was a good deal of appearance of democracy, rather than of any very strong faith in democracy in Brunton's own mind.

Q. Couldn't one say, perhaps, that it was more than appearance; that he was forced to work with the tools that were there at the time? At that time there were very few tools. What he had to do first was to put the Inspectorate's house in order; make the Inspectorate into an organisation that was capable of stimulating curriculum reform, of providing a lead; and, in order to do this, he had to behave autocratically in some ways?

RODGER. In some ways. He certainly did much to organise the Inspectorate, to acquaint them with the problems which he felt were important, and to inspire them to think these out and give him the results of their thoughts. He taught the Inspectorate that they were an important body, and he really made them feel important.

Q. How much opposition was there from the administrative side of the Department to the idea of teacher-representation on working parties?

RODGER. None that I know of. But this really is a question that came to a head after I retired. (I retired in 1963 you know . . .).

Q. Brunton told us that there was opposition to this, but he didn't mention exactly where it was coming from. One thing that he did say was that the Secretary of the Department insisted that he chair the working parties that were set up. And perhaps one of the reasons why the working parties were hand-picked and chaired by Brunton or by hand-picked men, was that this was such a new idea that Murrie and, later on, Arbuckle, insisted that the man whom they could trust, Brunton, be in control. To some extent the autocracy was forced on him.

RODGER. To some extent autocracy was forced upon him. But I think it would be in keeping with Brunton's general viewpoint that he should be chairman of bodies which the Secretary did not chair. And I think that this would also be in keeping with his view of the importance of the Inspectorate. . . . He had in the Inspectorate several extremely good people who gave him ideas. Dickson was one. Indeed this very last week when I saw Dickson, Dickson was telling me about his own appointment as Senior Chief Inspector. He said, 'I never expected to be Senior Chief'. I asked, 'Why that?' 'Because', he said, 'I thought Brunton would be all against me; and I knew that he would have quite a part to play'. Dickson and Brunton often disagreed. Often enough Brunton wouldn't admit that he had done so, but in the end he often acted on the advice he had got from Dickson. [James] Shanks [HMI 1946-62, HMCI 1962-72] was another, and [James] Forsyth [HMI 1945-72]. Now, these are two chaps who are very, very capable of producing very good educational ideas. Brunton encouraged them to do so at these meetings; and Brunton would gladly absorb their good ideas and bring them into operation. . . . I would say that he and Dickson were probably the two most successful Senior Chief Inspectors that we ever had, although they were very, very different people. I wouldn't say that Brunton was himself primarily an originator but, when other people provided him with ideas, he was excellent at knowing whether they were good ideas. If somebody else suggested them, and they were good, they would reappear as Brunton's own in two years' time. . . . He would recognise good original thinking and, most important of all, he got things done. After he recognised that something was good, and after it could be regarded as Bruntonian – even although it was probably not Bruntonian originally – then he got it done. He achieved much, and for this I admired and respected him. . . . The personal relationships between Arbuckle and Brunton were pretty good, although I happen to know that Arbuckle shared the view that I have just expressed, that he was very good at producing other people's ideas as his own. . . . Arbuckle and Brunton proved to be a good and creative team, wherever the creative elements originated. . . .

Q. Sir Henry Wood said of Brunton that most of the curricular changes that happened in Scotland since the mid-1950s had stemmed from the Senior Chief Inspector. Is that a judgment that appeals to you?

R ODGER. Well, I would say that they had stemmed from the committee of which Brunton was the chairman. I wouldn't say that they necessarily stemmed from Brunton himself. . . . If Wood emphasised Brunton's contribution he was telling a considerable part of the story, but not all. Dickson's work on the junior-secondary curriculum was of great importance. In my opinion, Dickson was an excellent, down-to-earth educational thinker who thought carefully and well about what was appropriate with pupils of high, or of moderate, or of low level of ability.

This assessment of the derivative quality of Brunton's educational thought is also suggested, if in slightly different language, by a comment of

Clark's:

CLARK. I think that you will find that quite a number of my ex-colleagues would agree with me that Brunton was probably the most outstanding Senior Chief Inspector in the post-war era. . . . He commanded a great deal of trust and was respected for his integrity.

Q. Did you see in him the figure of a theorist as well?

CLARK. I saw him as a thinker. I saw him as one who was somewhat of a theorist, who knew the necessity of trying to develop theory as a background to what he saw as the solution of problems, if I can subdivide it in that way. He thought a very great deal about his job and about education in Scotland. He was not an outstanding educational theorist but, outstandingly, he saw the necessity for theory.

Discussion

The quality of mind that had struck both Clark and Rodger, surely, was preeminently that of the successful administrator: the ability to select and harmonise ideas and purposes over broad areas of provision, if necessary subordinating intrinsically good ideas to the requirements of the overall scheme into which they must fit. It was just such an ability that Rodger discerned in Murrie. He told us: 'Murrie's particular way of tackling a problem was to invite everybody in the Department who might be expected to have a specialist knowledge of the field to give him a memorandum. . . . He then picked up all the good ideas and built them up into a unity, and that would be the policy. But, in that final production, he had contributed little except brilliant analysis. He had put into it little or no creative thought himself'.

We do not suggest that this description will also serve as the perfect account of Brunton's thinking. But it begins to place him closer to a Murrie than to a Dickson, say, or to others whose entire career was to be in the Inspectorate. Brunton's general reputation outside the Department put the emphasis differently, on Brunton the educationist, the 'lone figure' fighting to sustain the educational interest. There was an element of myth-making in this, inevitably perhaps because the generality of educationists outside the Department saw only part of the picture. Moreover, Brunton himself stood to gain from such a reputation in his struggles with colleagues in the Inspectorate and administration. His closer allies outside saw this, and were well aware of his management of impressions. But they also thought that more than mere impressions were involved, and they respected his determination. Clark told us 'Brunton was not a man who gave in easily, and if he thought he was right, he would keep hammering away at something; the dog with the bone is something that jumps to mind'.

Inside the Department, again perhaps inevitably, what was more evident was not Brunton's educational commitment, but his determined defence of the area of competence he had annexed from the administration. In this

defence, however, impression-management may again have been important, if we are right in our contention that Brunton exploited the ambiguity
of his current and prospective authority in order to advance his policies. He
had moved from Inspectorate to administration before becoming HMSCI;
he might have done so again thereafter, or so it seemed at the time. To the
generalist administrator Murrie, Brunton was the educationist who knew
both sides of the coin. To an Inspectorate that resisted, or failed to develop,
the curriculum reforms he desired, he was an HMSCI who had come to the
post unexpectedly from a high level of administrative authority. He had
already started the uncomfortable process of change whilst at that level, and
for a while there was some prospect that he would return to the administrative side with an even higher rank.

We should not expect, therefore, to be able to strip away the layers until
the inner truth of the man is exposed in the form of an unambiguous
allegiance to one side or the other of an educationist-administrator duality.
Brunton himself turned different faces to his audiences, according to
circumstance, and he used impression-management to help unlock
the inertial relations between government and education. Contemporary
judgements of Brunton vary, not just because he was seen from different
angles by different parties, and therefore incompletely by each. They
also vary because he caused them to vary. We cannot simply add up
these separate, partial judgements in the hope that a rounded judgement
will thereby emerge. Nor can we easily infer his priorities from his actions,
given the constrained circumstances in which he found the SED in the early
1950s.

One final, and tantalising, piece of evidence may be mentioned, a letter
Brunton wrote to Sir James Robertson in July 1963, days after the publication of the Brunton report (SED 1963b).[2] In it Brunton said that he thought
that 'everything that is happening in secondary education in Scotland at the
present time is directly attributable to the work done by the Advisory
Council between 1942 and 1947'. Was this a private moment between two
friends, a moment when the public face no longer mattered, and the best
clue therefore that we have to what Brunton was trying to achieve? Was it,
alternatively, a generous courtesy to a man whose public honour would
probably not erase his disappointment over the fading of the ideal of
reconstruction? Or did Brunton intend his words as a final settling of
accounts between the educationist whose prose had animated a vision of the
future, and the official who had done something to realise it in a piecemeal,
compromised but hopefully incremental manner?

A final answer cannot be given, not only because the letter is only a letter,
but also because the idea of 'implementing' the Council's report is itself not
simple. The report is open in places to a variety of interpretations, and some
of its recommendations were mutually inconsistent. Clark told us, 'I probably had as much to do with J.J.Robertson as anybody, and there is no

that he had a feeling of great disappointment at the treatment of the secondary report'. Robertson, for his part, thought Brunton 'the most quietly resolute progressive the Department has yet given us' (Robertson 1969d, 226). But he was nevertheless disappointed in the progress that had been made up to the late 1960s for all but the 'top fifteen percent' of pupils, saying that it lacked 'vision and the willing mind' (*ibid.*). Towards the end of his life Robertson read the reality of reform differently from Brunton.

Nevertheless, Robertson's report had been important to the Department, for two reasons. The Department was statutorily obliged to 'have regard' to the recommendations of the Advisory Council in framing its own policies. Officials were never slow, therefore, to point to the authorisation that their policies might find in an earlier Council recommendation. More important, however, was the fact that the report's vision of reconstruction had animated a set of traditional Scottish values on which much of the Department's own claim to authority was based. The merits of competing policies were judged in part against these traditional values, as they had been judged earlier in the century as well (see chapter 2). Both the primary and secondary reports of the Sixth Council claimed to offer a realisation of Scottish egalitarianism. However fundamental the SED's objections might be to particular Council recommendations, the Department would always risk less by presenting its objections as matters of detail and timing, and as matters of means, not of ends.

Thus earlier conflicts continued to influence the Department's strategy and rhetoric after 1945, and the pursuit of that strategy in turn generated its own contemporary history. Written in the mid-1960s, Tom Bone's *School Inspection in Scotland 1840-1966* observes of the post-1955 period that 'what was done in the senior secondaries may be viewed as an attempt to give effect, in a modern context, to the recommendations of the Advisory Council in 1947' (Bone 1968, 234). One can almost hear Brunton speaking here. Perhaps one can. In his acknowledgements, Bone especially mentions the help of Arbuckle and Brunton, and also of Robert Macdonald. Macdonald was the son of Sir George Macdonald, Struthers' successor as Secretary of the Department (1922-28), and he had himself been a chief inspector under Brunton (1949-62). Bone tells us that, during Brunton's Senior Chief Inspectorship, 'a sense of partnership between inspectors and teachers' was achieved for the first time (*ibid.*, 233); and also that the progress of the period 'resulted largely from the impetus that the inspectors, in their new partnership with teachers and college lecturers, have been able to give to development' (*ibid.*, 240). In Bone's account, the makers of Scottish education no longer moved autocratically towards progress, but democratically, as leading partners with a 'natural' authority:

> The inspectors have normally been the leaders, as is only natural because of the width of their experience and their coordinating position. . . . Inspectors may not be feared any more, but, as a body, they

are accorded a more healthy respect than ever was the case in the past. (*ibid.*, 233 and 236)

Thus, as Brunton's inspectorship passed into history, its rhetoric attained the respectability of history, a history to which the Inspectorate could turn in its new claims to authority, and which soon penetrated textbooks produced in the colleges of education for the next generation of teachers (Hunter 1972, 31-9; Findlay 1973, 37).

What happened to the Inspectorate's claims within and outwith the Department, we discuss in parts III and IV. But the present case study reminds us that the history of these claims must be treated as part of the 'primary' policy action, and not only as the detached account of that action, written after the event. What is true of 'looking to the centre for a lead', is also true of the themes of 'partnership' and 'progress'. All have a dual or symbiotic character where rhetoric and reality merge, the primary event and the secondary interpretation. All are in some respect ideological. Brunton advanced his power by appealing to these ideas and to values that had been reinvigorated by the Sixth Advisory Council and the Second World War. Some of his allies outside the Department, in their turn, interpreted the self he presented to them in terms of an older historiographical tradition. This was the tradition of Morgan's *Makers of Scottish Education* (1929), a tradition in which great men like Craik and Struthers had led the advance towards the Knoxian ideal (Morgan 1927, 1929; Stewart 1927). As we shall see, the circumstances and repercussions of Brunton's departure helped to harden this story into legend. Many of his allies lost the direct line of communication and influence they had formerly enjoyed with the Department. To celebrate Brunton was to deprecate the changed arrangements.

For all that, Brunton, so one of his colleagues stressed to us, was a humble man, personally shy, somewhat isolated, and far from the outstanding public speaker that Robertson was. How he construed Robertson's report, and how far he was moved by its ideals, we cannot finally say, although it is interesting that he did not accept our description of it as 'visionary', and did say that he thought that much more could have been done immediately. Whatever the reasons for his frustration over the Department's inactivity, it is perhaps in this frustration that we find a clue to the importance that he attached to the pragmatic principle, to the subordination of the ideal to the practicality of the next step towards that ideal. If his thinking and responses were essentially those of an administrator, of a man preoccupied rather more by means and process than by content and ends, much of the explanation lies in the inadequacy of the resources and structures of the time to the task of providing mass secondary education for the first time in the history of the state. The general problem of finding and using resources was immense, as we shall see in part III, and Brunton's own experience as the inspector responsible for Glasgow had left him with a particularly jaundiced view of the ability of local authorities to make proper provision (see chapter

9). But we shall find in part IV that the means that Brunton used to work towards new machinery for innovation and advice made their own contribution to the form which that machinery was eventually to take. The directive style of his working parties, for example, was to leave its mark on the constitution and activities of the CCC. Similarly, his use of the certificate examination as a major means of educational reform was to work against the realisation of principles that Robertson's report had regarded as fundamental, eventually displacing any comprehensive and progressive ideal with a form of education that many pupils experienced as bipartite in form, and statist in its content and outcomes.

NOTES
1. The same was true of the decision in 1955 to introduce a fourth-year examination in the near future.
2. Brunton's letter was occasioned by an exchange of letters in the *Scotsman* between Sir Garnet Wilson (5 July 1963 and 13 July 1963) and Sir James Robertson (10 July 1963), following a *Scotsman* leader of 2 July 1963 on the publication of the Brunton report *From School to Further Education* (SED 1963b). Wilson had been a member of the Sixth Advisory Council, and he wrote to complain that the Sixth Council had dismissed the case for pre-vocational education that the Brunton report had now apparently revived.

Part III

Government and Resources

We have highlighted the activities of one influential person in central government, and described how he sought to exploit relationships inside and outside the Department in order to promote his ideas. But policy processes cannot be understood solely in terms of alliances and manoeuvres seen at close range. The focus must be broadened to include the structures within which these interactions occurred, and which provided many of their possibilities and constraints. The way in which resources were obtained and distributed must also be examined.

The organisational divisions of central government within Scotland, and between Scotland and Britain, marked off separate institutional bases for action. One element in these arrangements was the Inspectorate. The SED and the Scottish Office as a whole were others. The parliamentary and administrative apparatus of British government were two further arenas of decision-making which impinged on Scottish education, albeit ones which did not have as their main purpose the administration of Scotland or of its educational system. Nor did the characteristics and interrelationships of this sprawling 'centre' remain fixed. They altered under the pressure of changed political, economic and administrative circumstances, and under the influence of officials, politicians and others who shaped them to serve different purposes at different times. For those whose principal concern was the educational system, these alterations affected the work they had to do to gain the support of others.

A further factor was the involvement of central government with local authorities and teachers in negotiations over policy and over the allocation of resources. Here, too, the separate parts had scope for autonomous action, but they were also interdependent. Their ability to work together affected the chances for Scottish education to get what it wanted in the wider arenas of British government and politics. Moreover, the resolution of some of the largest problems depended crucially upon the course of relationships among the several actors. There were problems of equity and of substantive change in curriculum and school organisation. To solve them the Department had to work both through and against the teachers and the local authorities.

Our discussion in chapter 6 relates the account of Brunton in part II to the changing patterns of influence within central government. The SED had remained a relatively isolated, professionally led department down to Brunton's time. However, new assumptions about the role of the Scottish Office and about administrative careers were to have powerful repercussions on the SED, and also on the Department's relationships with the educational policy community outside. In particular, as chapter 7 shows, the influence of the Inspectorate was curtailed by these wider changes, and its independence placed in some doubt after Brunton had gone. Later, however, it was able to assert itself on new bodies and in national educational developments, relying for influence less on dynamic personal leadership than on institutional linkages across the policy community.

Chapter 8 considers the part played by Ministers, Parliament and national politics. Until recently, Ministerial inputs to policy were infrequent. For many years, education was not controversial in party-political terms, and Ministers found more pressing issues to engage their political interests. However, Ministers were crucial in connecting the Department to Westminster and Whitehall. They represented Scottish interests in those circles, and transmitted government policy pressures to Scotland.

Parliamentary activity played little part in the formation of educational policy, but educational issues frequently provided topics for debate and criticism. For much of the period after 1945, Parliament's interest was mainly in resource questions, predominantly those concerning the provision of buildings and the supply and payment of teachers. These were also uppermost on the administrative agenda. Chapter 9 explains how financial resources for current and capital expenditure were obtained, and controlled through an extended vertical chain whose end-points were the Treasury and the classroom. This chain, however, was vulnerable to lateral pressure from other spending priorities at national and local levels. Moreover, its ability to lift the burden of educational expansion depended on how securely its links of trust and helpfulness were connected along its length. Keeping the chain serviceable depended partly on national economic and political circumstances; but it also required Scotland to win its case in Whitehall, the Department to support education's claims in Edinburgh, and the cities and counties to use resources efficiently. There was much political work to do all round, not least for the Department. We show how it attempted to do this, both by collaborating with the education authorities and by controlling them.

In chapter 10 we continue our discussion of resources by showing how teachers' salaries were negotiated, and how the Department tried to cope with chronic deficiencies in the supply and distribution of teachers. The SED, the education authorities, and teachers' representatives were all involved in questions of pay and provision. But relations were often severely strained by the national economic situation and by the limited influence of the Department at the Treasury. Yet much depended on a solution to these resource problems: not only the success of substantive policies to reduce inequities and to cope with expansion, but also the goodwill of teachers and education authorities in promoting further developments.

Six

The Changing SED

There was a danger, under the system which obtained until the forties and fifties, that the S E D would become increasingly in-grown and parochial, separate in its attitudes and in its officers from the rest of the Government service. The changed pattern of recruitment has obviated this danger.   Scottish Education De-partment (S E D 1968b)

Introduction

Part II discussed changes in action, advice and control that accompanied the school reforms that started in the 1950s. In this chapter and the next, we consider the wider context of governmental reform in which these changes took place. Brunton's institution-building enhanced the Inspectorate's in-fluence over policy innovations in the later 1950s and early 1960s. At the same time, however, questions were being raised about the Department's separate position within the Scottish Office. This position owed much to the hold its education specialists had earlier had on posts in its senior adminis-trative ranks. However, their grip was beginning to loosen by the time Brunton became Senior Chief Inspector. This change was not an isolated one but was part of a broader movement of Scottish Office reform which gathered pace as the 1960s wore on. It is in terms of these wider trends that the full significance of new relationships within the Department must be assessed.

Writing in 1978, Kogan said that the D E S and its predecessors were considered to be remote from the Whitehall mainstream, prestigious, but not usually a springboard for Ministers or civil servants aspiring to higher office (Kogan 1978, 149-51). A similar case of moribund aloofness has been diagnosed in Scotland: 'sleepy hollow' was how the S E D was reputedly known after 1945 to others in the Scottish Office (Morris 1976). One reason why Murrie was brought back was to remedy this, and Graham's Secretary-ship saw the process of integration advance not only within the S E D, but between it and the Scottish Office generally. These changes accompanied the Department's attempt to clear its decks, as educational provision ex-panded, by hiving off various executive tasks to new fringe bodies (see chapters 12 to 14), and by encouraging the local education authorities to be more self-reliant (see chapter 9).

Influence over central educational policy owed something to the happenstance of careers and to contingencies of personality and personal relationships, though even these individual considerations were to some extent sociologically ordered (see part v). In addition, of course, systemic bureaucratic factors of structure, recruitment and promotion were of great importance. The internal and external aspects of the Department were highly interdependent: to question the position of the Department within St Andrew's House was also to question the internal arrangements by which the Department constituted itself and conducted its business. Much of the Inspectorate's influence over policies derived from the prominence which those arrangements had given it within the Department. Organisational changes across the Scottish Office therefore challenged, and for a time limited, the scope of Inspectorate influence. But so, too, did the interplay of careers and personalities within the Department.

The SED's historic isolation was linked to its custom of growing its own administrators. But, once Brunton had left in 1966, the continuing bifurcation of inspectors' and administrators' careers that had started in the 1950s exposed the Inspectorate's position in central policy-making to critical scrutiny. So, too, did the inter-Departmental changes we discuss here and in chapter 7. In this chapter, we explore the broader Scottish Office context by looking, first, at the way in which the Department broke with tradition in the recruitment of its leading administrative officers. Change in promotion practices in the lower administrative ranks of the Department had begun in the early 1940s. It became more marked in subsequent decades when the selection of Secretaries like Murrie and Graham, whose experience lay outside education, reinforced the feeling that the SED's atypicality could no longer be justified. The intention was to move educational administration towards the work of other Departments and into the sphere of modern public-administration thinking. We show how the consolidation of the Scottish Office as a powerful agency of devolved administration reinforced this, reducing the autonomy of the Department but falling short of an overriding centralisation of policy-making within St Andrew's House.

An 'Independent' Department

For many years, the SED was the 'secret garden' of the bureaucracy. It was a more independent-minded department than any other and, until the 1950s or 1960s, was left largely to its own devices by a Scottish Office which itself possessed few of the attributes of an overarching body. Allan Rodger and Sir William Murrie each recalled aspects of the history of the Department, going back to the days before 1939 when it was a committee of the Privy Council:

RODGER. Modern compulsory education came to Scotland with the 1872 Act. Soon a Scottish Education Department was set up of 'My Lords', . . . a body which seldom if ever met, and so the control of education rested with the officials. . . . It is only within the last fifty years that the Secretary of State has become a powerful Minister corresponding to other important Cabinet Ministers. Thus there was a period of fifty years or so when the Department had no masters except the virtually mythical 'My Lords', and certainly had no Ministerial control in the modern sense. . . . The letter that the Department sent out in the old days was: 'My Lords say . . .'. Now, 'My Lords' were a group of people who never met but, technically, they were the Department. While undoubtedly there was a time when the Department thought of itself as a powerful independent body, this notion was fading before 1952.

MURRIE. The Scottish Education Department was rather proud of having been a department before the other Scottish departments were created. It had been not under the Secretary for Scotland, but under a subcommittee of the Privy Council of which the Secretary for Scotland was Vice-President. And in its bones it had the feeling that it was an independent department, and not a group of civil servants who were carrying out the wishes of Ministers. But I don't want to exaggerate this; it was something that one sensed rather than an unwillingness on their part to co-operate. I think they went on feeling that there was a thing called the Scottish Education Department, which had a policy in a way that the Department of Health, the Home Department or the Department of Agriculture did not. Each of these regarded itself more as the servant of the Secretary of State, though even in the Health Department and the Agriculture Department there was a lingering feeling of independence. They had been semi-independent boards until the twenties – and because they had operated in Edinburgh, while the Secretary for Scotland was mainly in London, they didn't feel quite the same integration with him that people like myself, who were originally officers of the Scottish Office in Dover House in London, felt. We were living with the Secretary of State, and we couldn't conceive of ourselves as independent of him. The other departments had to some extent the feeling of an independent entity, and I should say that Education felt it a bit more than the others, but I don't attach a tremendous amount of importance to this.

Q. Was this a feeling that continued after your arrival?

MURRIE. It was lingering, when I came. I think it was dying, but you still occasionally found people who would say, 'the Department would not approve of this'.

Q. Can you give examples in which this sense of independence would be apparent in the workings of the Department?

MURRIE. It's difficult to say, and it may be that it is partly due to the mystery, in the sense of *métier*, of education. The large body of inspectors, who have been teachers and who are dealing with matters in which they are experts, and Ministers probably don't know so much about, tend to have rather a different attitude from the all-purpose civil servant who is serving a Minister and carrying out the Minister's will, and probably doesn't know very much more than the Minister does about some of the things that he's doing. It's only a matter of degree.

What was the view of Rodger, who had had no Whitehall experience?

RODGER. I had never thought of it in these terms. I did not realise that it was constantly in Murrie's mind that the Department existed to do the Minister's will, in contrast to the view that the Department was something that existed to be a power in its own right. I can perfectly see that Murrie would think in these terms. Undoubtedly there was a time when officers of the Department thought of the Department as being a power in its own right. . . . This was possibly still to some extent true, though I think that our notion of the Department as an independent body had been, for some years, giving place to the idea that we were a body serving the Secretary of State.

The Recruitment of Department Secretaries

Chapter 5 showed that the style and relationships of individual officials had implications for change in the larger patterns of the institutional landscape. The possibility of curricular revision had, in part, depended upon the close relationship between Brunton, the Senior Chief Inspector from 1955, and Arbuckle, who was promoted to Under-Secretary when Murrie became Secretary of the Department in 1952. The unusual circumstances of administration during the Second World War had already given these three experience of working together, and each reciprocated the trust of the others. Despite opposition to his various initiatives, in particular from administrators within the Department, Brunton could normally rely on the support of Murrie and Arbuckle in winning his point.

The relationships among these three men, brought together by different career-paths in Scottish administration, continued through a crucial turning point in Scottish education in the late 1950s and early 1960s. Brunton's period as Senior Chief Inspector saw a transformation of the Inspectorate, and a redistribution of functions within central government and among fringe bodies. Also, Murrie's arrival as Secretary marked the first break with a tradition of recruitment which had brought education specialists to the Secretaryship as far back as 1885. Arbuckle, who followed Murrie as Secretary in 1957 after many years on the administrative side, was the last former inspector to rise to the top post in the Department.

Until well into the period after 1945, the Scottish Office was unusual in that the Whitehall ideal of administrative generalism had little purchase among its top ranks. But it was the SED that clung longest to the characteristics of a department run by professionals who had a background in the substantive specialism of its field. Elsewhere in central government, by contrast, what used to be called the administrative class of the British civil service was the preserve of the generalist who could turn a hand successfully to anything, 'from pig prices to fire brigades', as Rodger scornfully remarked. Experience of the government machine, sensitivity to political circumstance, clarity on paper, and ease of communication with others in the 'village' of Whitehall, all equipped the generalist to play policy-making roles at the top. Such civil servants were not specially trained in the subject-matter of a department, although they could acquire deep knowledge of it through long service. But their stock-in-trade was breadth, not depth (Profitt 1968; Fry 1969, ch.5; Self 1972, chs 5 and 6). Some senior Scottish Office officials matched their Whitehall counterparts in these respects, and some had served in United Kingdom departments. Others, like the SED's ex-inspectors, acquired some of the characteristics of the generalist administrator after entry to a relevant department from subject-specialist walks of life. But a full test of the usefulness of generalism in Scottish administration was not possible as long as inter-departmental transfers were infrequent. Recruitment and promotion had long reinforced a departmentalism which came naturally to Scottish Office administrators. Their orientations were less to other Scottish Office departments than they were to their cognate departments in Whitehall, to their Scottish specialist clientèle, and to the Scottish local authorities.

Most of the SED Secretaries before Murrie, but only Arbuckle thereafter, had served with the Inspectorate before moving into administrative careers (*Civil Service Yearbook*, various dates; *Who's Who*, various dates). Whilst Sir Henry Craik (Secretary 1885-1904) had never been an inspector, he had spent most of his working life in close involvement with the essential functions of education. Craik's attempt to realise his national-efficiency conception of the educational system figured in chapter 2. His policy was consistent with resource rationales that generalist administrators themselves might have proffered. Nevertheless, Craik was regarded in Scottish educational circles as an educationist-in-administration, a 'maker of Scottish education' in Morgan's hagiographic estimation (Morgan 1929). Another such was the former inspector Sir John Struthers (Secretary 1904-21) who followed Craik. These two were heads of the SED who built up the national educational system:

> They have not regarded it as their function merely to distribute Government grants in accordance with conditions laid down by Parliament, and to co-ordinate the action of the local authorities -- they have initiated developments of far-reaching importance, and have done much to form the educational policy of the country. (Morgan 1929, 221; see also Munro (n.d.), 144-7; Macdonald (1937); Headlam (1937))

How they balanced educational with resource considerations is open to debate. However, modern and more critical estimations of Craik and Struthers similarly testify to their absorption in the pursuit of educational and social aims through their dominant positions in central administration (Dobie 1967; Findlay 1973; Anderson 1983a; Finn 1983).

Sir George Macdonald (1922-28), a numismatist and classical archaeologist of international repute, followed Struthers in the Secretaryship. Like Craik, he had never been an inspector, although early in his career he had been short-listed for an Inspectorate post. A schoolmaster in Kelvinside Academy, Glasgow, and then lecturer in Glasgow University, he was out-posted to Edinburgh as Assistant Secretary in the SED from 1904 whilst Struthers remained at Dover House in Whitehall. Controlling secondary-school inspectors and the Leaving Certificate, he 'had been a driving force within the Department long before he became its head' (Bone 1968, 131; see also Curle 1949). Sir William McKechnie (1929-36) had begun an academic career at the turn of the century in Edinburgh and Glasgow Universities, and had then joined the Inspectorate where he served for over twenty years. His successor, Sir James Peck (1936-40), was the first non-classicist in the Secretaryship, but he had lectured at Glasgow University in mathematical physics, and had been an inspector before serving with the London County Council Education Department and the Edinburgh School Board. Peck's middle career was as a civil servant in various fields before his return to education as an official in the SED six years before he became its Secretary.

We cannot say whether Peck's appointment as Secretary marked a first attempt to bring a person of somewhat wider administrative experience to the top of the Department. However, perhaps it is wartime exigency which explains why his successor exemplified the older pattern. Sir John Mackay Thomson (1940-52), another classicist, had taught in Edinburgh at Fettes College before becoming Rector of Aberdeen Grammar School. He then went to the Inspectorate, subsequently moving sideways and working his way up the Department's administrative hierarchy to the Secretaryship over some fifteen years. However it may be, a pattern had long been established in which the SED drew its Secretaries from among those who had been heavily involved with the substantive aspects of education as practitioners and as officials. Indeed, it was not only the Secretaries who had inspectorial or educational experience: the small SED complement of administrative civil servants throughout the 1930s and into the early years of the Second World War included a substantial proportion (two or three of the six or seven) who had come up via the Inspectorate.

Changes of real consequence in staffing and promotion began during the Second World War. Rodger saw a connection between these developments and the appointment of the Department's Secretary:

RODGER. Until 1942 or 1943 (it was certainly during the War), the Scottish Education Department had a small Secretariat (of administrative rank) but no junior members of the administrative class. There were no assistant principals or principals. Under the Secretariat were executives. . . . In those days the Secretariat was chosen from the Inspectorate (or other outside sources), or posts were filled by the promotion of outstanding executives. I remember when, during the War, the best of our branch chiefs (called chief executive officers) were made principals, and so for the first time the Department had an administrative hierarchy. It was after the War that we got our first assistant principal. Since then the Department have had their quota. As soon as a group of first-class young administrators grew up, they naturally wished for the same chances of promotion as they would have in another department, and so 'importations' from the Inspectorate would have been resented. Thus a day was bound to come when an administrative civil servant would be appointed Secretary. Murrie's appointment in 1952 was the first. Thus I see Murrie's appointment as an inevitable consequence of the modern structure of the service in SED.

However, the appointment of 'an administrative civil servant' from within SED, after a career in various branches of educational administration, might have been far less of a break with the past than the more obvious 'importation' of a man like Murrie as Secretary. Murrie had had no experience in the education field, and presumably had fewer contacts with the community of educational practitioners outside the Office who had been accustomed to seeing 'weel kent faces' emerge into the Secretaryship. The Permanent Secretary of the Scottish Office in 1953 was Sir David Milne, whom Murrie knew, having succeeded him as Principal Private Secretary to the Secretary of State in 1934. How did Murrie view his own arrival back in Scotland at the head of the SED in 1952?

Q. Yours was in a sense an unusual appointment in that you were coming from outside.

MURRIE. Not as unusual as you suggest, because I had started in the Scottish Office in London, and I had served from 1935 until 1944 in the Department of Health in Edinburgh, and I had rubbed shoulders with inspectors from the Scottish Education Department, who, in 1939, were seconded to the Health Department to help in carrying out the evacuation scheme.

Q. On your appointment, Grainger-Stewart remained as Deputy Secretary [1949-59] in the SED, whereas you had had no direct previous experience of education.

MURRIE. This is perfectly true. . . . I don't know why I was sent to the Scottish Education Department, except that it was apparently thought that I had better go back to Scotland after eight years in London, and this was the right sort of level at which I should go back.

Q. You see the circumstances in terms of your own personal career rather than the circumstances that obtained in the SED?

MURRIE. Yes.

Rodger broadly confirmed Murrie's account:

Q. Did you, at the time, see Murrie's appointment as the first serious attempt, if you like, to pull the Scottish Education Department into line with practice in the UK?

RODGER. I didn't see that at the time: indeed there were superficial

changes earlier than 1952. I saw it later, but not at the time. The Deputy
Secretary, when Mackay Thomson retired, was Grainger-Stewart . . . an
advocate by profession . . . and it was my feeling at the time that the
Treasury – after all the Treasury [was] largely responsible for the appointments to the top jobs all over the civil service -- that the Treasury had come
to the conclusion that Grainger-Stewart was not the most suitable Secretary.
If, therefore, the Department was not providing, from its own ranks, the
next Secretary, a Secretary had to be provided from elsewhere. . . . Now I
think that the Treasury probably felt also that in those days, in Scotland,
there was probably a sufficiently Scottish nationalistic feeling to make them
select a Scotsman – if not the best man in Whitehall, then the best Scotsman
in Whitehall. Murrie was a Scotsman, so. . . .

Q. And, of course, he was known to Sir David Milne.

RODGER. Yes. And David Milne was a very powerful person. So Murrie
came. But, at the time, I didn't see this as a move that was to be continued,
but I rather took it to be a personal thing: it was a deliberate choice on the
part of the Treasury (and Milne) of somebody other than Grainger-Stewart.

Q. Perhaps it also reflected the fact that the Department, during the War
years and the immediate post-war years, hadn't had the staffing, and had
been so stretched in its commitments, that it had not been able to sponsor
its future Secretaries.

RODGER. That's possibly true, although some of the younger people –
take Arbuckle, for example – were holding very responsible posts outside
the Department. You see, Arbuckle was an Assistant Secretary in the
Department of Health. He was seconded, as a principal, to the Department
of Health to deal with evacuation matters [1939]. But he was appointed
there as an Assistant Secretary [1941], and gave that up to come back into
the Inspectorate [1943]. . . . He then became an Assistant Secretary with us,
but he was an Assistant Secretary in the Department of Health before he
was an Assistant Secretary with us.

Q. I see Arbuckle's appointment as Secretary in 1957 in succession to
Murrie as, in a way, a return to the former position.

RODGER. That is what we thought. I am now inclined to think that it
wasn't. Arbuckle's appointment possibly did not reflect a reversal of policy
but an appointment in his own right.

Q. But it could also be seen as a continuation of the newer situation,
because Arbuckle had had experience outside the Department?

RODGER. Outside the Department. Yes. . . . I should imagine that . . .
Murrie would have an important say in who was to be his successor, and
here his personal liking for, and high professional regard for Arbuckle
would come in. That might be how it came that Arbuckle came back, and
some of us thought that perhaps this was a return to the old procedure,
which it wasn't. . . . What has happened since Murrie came in 1952 is that
the process has spread downwards. You see, even after Murrie came,

promotions within the Department were made from within . . . a post (say)
of principal was filled from the Department's staff, but after Murrie had
gone and after Arbuckle had gone, the process of widening the scope of
staffing has spread throughout the Scottish Office . . . any post now, from
the very intermediate levels upwards, is open, not to Departmental people
only, but to the whole Scottish Office.

Murrie's explanation for the changed staffing practices was essentially the
same as Rodger's:

Q. Arbuckle, who was Secretary until 1963, was the last Secretary to have
had some prior service in the Inspectorate. Was there a conscious change of
policy after him, possibly related to the closer integration of the SED with
the Scottish Office as a whole?

MURRIE. No. I would explain it rather on the ground that during the
fifties and sixties there was a greater tendency to move administrative
people around, in and out of the four Scottish departments, and that you
didn't in any particular department look only within that department for a
head. It was the job of the Permanent Under-Secretary of State to judge
who was the best person anywhere within the Scottish Office, or even
outside the Scottish Office, to take one of these jobs.

Q. Does this indicate that the Inspectorate does not produce persons
fitted to be Secretary?

MURRIE. There was no conscious feeling of this and it seems to me that
you might well have had Brunton as head of the Scottish Education
Department if the times had fallen differently. He seems to me to be an
example of someone who was both an inspector and an administrator.

Dickson had a more direct explanation of the change:

DICKSON. There was . . . a feeling on the administrative side that there
was no particular reason why they should go on bringing people into the
Office from the Inspectorate. There were enough people in the administration to provide good Assistant Secretaries without any help from us.

Q. Was this a bit of administrative trade unionism?

DICKSON. I would say so. Yes. A perfectly understandable one. The
time came when transfer from the Inspectorate to the Secretariat stopped.
Brunton was to have been, anyway, the last man moved over from the
Inspectorate to the administration. . . . There was a clear understanding that
no more HMIs would be moved.

Q. You don't think it was unfortunate that after Brunton there was a
clearer division of careers?

DICKSON. No, no. It would have been unfortunate if steps hadn't been
taken to correct the situation, so to speak.

Dickson's feeling mirrored that of Norman Graham, who succeeded
Arbuckle as Secretary in 1964, and alongside whom Dickson worked as
Senior Chief Inspector from 1966 to 1969. Under Graham, co-operation,
and even integration, were strongly encouraged (see chapter 7). Although

Rodger was unable to describe the extent of Murrie's influence as Permanent Under-Secretary of State (1959-64) in the choice of Graham, there is no doubt that a Permanent Under-Secretary plays an essential part in such matters. Moreover, Rodger's account of Murrie's philosophy points towards Murrie's support of a break with the past:

RODGER. Now, I have discussed this with Murrie: Did he think that it was a good thing for a person to move departments, as he had done, or did he think it was a good thing for persons to rise in their own Department? And I knew that he took a differing view from me.... His attitude ... was, 'I don't see that it's necessary that the person who is head of a department should have been brought up in that department's techniques and mystiques'. He said, 'It's not surely necessary that the head of the Department of Health should be a doctor; it's surely not necessary for the head of the Department of Agriculture to have been a farmer'. Therefore he did not think that it was necessary for the head of the Education Department to have been a teacher or someone in the educational world.... He also said, 'I have now served in a few departments – the Department of Health, and then the Cabinet Office, and so on'. He said, 'Really, the processes of thinking to solve a problem of administration are the same whether that problem is in agriculture, education, health, police, or whatever'. He held that there were certain qualities required to think out administrative problems, whatever these administrative problems might be.

Q. How new a view was this in the Department?

RODGER. That was possibly not so much a new view as one that we had not thought about. I think – accustomed as the Department had been right from its start to deal with its own problems – that there was a widespread feeling in the Department that you jolly well had to have this background, this knowledge before you were really fit to be the supreme person.

Graham found this 'quite exceptional' in the civil service. He said that the growth of administrative and financial problems made it more difficult for inspectors to transfer to the administrative side of the SED, and that cross-posting was 'quite deliberately' done in the Scottish Office to enlarge the experience of civil servants (SCES 1968, Q.97). Although it had not been lacking in Arbuckle, the former teacher and inspector, breadth of administrative experience now became a very important qualification for the top post. As we have seen, Rodger's considered view of the appointment of Arbuckle as SED Secretary was that it did not signify a return to a narrow basis of recruitment, but that it marked a transition to the practice of searching further afield for a suitable person.

Like Murrie, Graham had served in the Scottish Health Department before the War, and had wartime experience in Whitehall. He then returned to Health in 1945, where he spent the next eighteen years before transferring to the SED to become its Secretary:

Q. How much of it was new, as compared with your experience in Health?

GRAHAM. Obviously, a considerable part of it is new. The people you deal with are new, but many of the problems are essentially the same problems dressed up in different clothes. . . . Everybody, virtually, concerned with social policy . . . was responsible to the Secretary of State and there were a lot of people who had seen the problems from different angles. They had worked on housing, they had worked on the health service, they had worked on social work, they had worked on education – not necessarily on all four, but as it happened, I myself had been concerned with all four; and there are a good many other people who had been concerned with at least three of these areas. . . . I think it comes naturally for people to work together and to be conscious that a particular problem has other facets than the one that they are immediately concerned with.

The Secretaries who came after Graham had also moved round the service. Martin Fearn's (1973-76) first post was with the Indian Civil Service in wartime. He later returned to spend about twenty years in the Scottish Home Department (later Home and Health (SHHD)) before transferring to the SED in 1968. Angus Mitchell (1976-84) had broad experience of Scottish Office work, gained not only in social-policy fields but also in Agriculture and Fisheries (DAFS) and, more briefly, in the Scottish Development Department (SDD). But Mitchell differed from generalists like Murrie, Graham and Fearn, in that he had accumulated, in all, some twenty years' experience in the SED before becoming its Secretary. However, very little of his time was spent in direct relation to schooling, and from 1969 he was in charge of the Social Work Services Group (SWSG) which was attached to the Department, going to Home and Health for a short period before returning to the Secretaryship. When Mitchell retired, his place was taken by James Scott. Scott had come to the SDD after many years' service in India and in New York with the Commonwealth Relations Office, and had spent the 1970s and early 1980s in the SDD and then the Scottish Economic Planning Department (SEPD). Like Murrie and Graham, he had no previous SED service before taking over as Secretary.

Structural Change and the Scottish Office 'Federation'

Métier or no, from the 1950s on, the SED acquired its 'all-purpose civil servants', persons who, like Graham, found it natural to make comparisons between administration in different parts of the public sector. Graham himself explained the changes as reflecting 'a change in the circumstances . . . education is probably a much more political issue, poses bigger problems in the use of resources, is more closely involved with the other aspects of social policy'. This explanation points towards a second and related reform. The similarity of administration across departments could provide the rationale for cross-posting civil servants. Moreover, it was also being argued in British administrative circles that the interdependence of problems and of policies required that policy-making, management and public expenditure be planned and coordinated across a wider field (Stacey 1975, ch.6; Brown and Steel 1979, chs 10 and 11; Greenwood and Wilson 1984, ch.3). This, it was held, would improve effectiveness and efficiency. In principle, such 'corporateness' should not have been too difficult to achieve in Scotland, especially as administrators were beginning to move round the departments. We asked Graham:

Q. Does this mean that forward planning in Scotland is done without having to rely upon an elaborate machinery of planning the way it has developed in Whitehall?

GRAHAM. Well, a good deal of it can be done within the ambit of the Scottish Office because somewhere in the Scottish Office most of the responsibilities rest; and it's relatively easy to achieve the coordination which involves in Whitehall different departments and different Ministers.

On the other hand, the historical distinctiveness of the Scottish departments impeded a collective approach. Until the outbreak of the Second World War, Scotland had been administered by a loose collection of departments and, formerly, boards (Gibson 1985, chs 2 and 3). Before the 1930s, there had been few pressures to bring departments into line and to subordinate them to an overarching structure. But in 1932, John Buchan (MP for the Scottish Universities; later Lord Tweedsmuir) urged the relocation of Scottish administration in Edinburgh, and its consolidation in one building. This, he argued, would symbolise Scottish nationhood and be a more efficient and convenient way of promoting 'a Scottish policy' (quoted in *ibid.*, 75). The appointment of a Scottish Commissioner under the depressed-areas legislation of 1934, coupled with the arousal of Scottish 'middle opinion' during the 1930s slump, lent strength to the idea of a more unified administration with a more promotional role (Harvie 1981a, chs 2 and 4; Harvie 1981b; Gibson 1985, ch.3). The Commissioner was based in Edinburgh and maintained close contact with the Agriculture and Health Departments, and also with the Secretary of State. The latter opened an Edinburgh branch office in 1935. Councils and committees bridged the worlds of government, industry, labour and the professions in promoting the revival of Scotland's economic and cultural life.

The expansion of government's role led to a reconsideration of administrative structures. The Secretary of State, Sir Godfrey Collins, (1932-36), appointed a committee under Sir John Gilmour, a former Secretary of State (1924-29) to survey the machinery of Scottish administration (CSA 1937). In 1937 it made recommendations for the remodelling of the Scottish Office that ensued in 1939. Gilmour's report wanted to tighten the accountability of the individual Scottish departments to the Secretary of State. But it firmly opposed the idea that they be merged into one unit, and rejected the idea of an 'imposing pyramid with a supreme administrative head' (*ibid.*, para.49). The relatively weak 'Permanent Secretary' it envisaged would hold a higher rank than the Secretaries of the departments, but would not command a central secretariat. In the delicate arrangement which was formulated in the late 1930s to overcome departmental isolation, the integrity of the departments as separate bodies was reaffirmed within a more coordinated administration in a new building, St Andrew's House. Whilst they were no longer to be statutory creations, each department had access to the Secretary of State, performed separate personnel work under the control of its Secretary, and kept its separate financial Supply Vote.

Let us recall that Rodger's main explanation of administrative changes was in terms of factors internal to the civil service. Yet he also conjectured that in 1952 it was politically appropriate to appoint 'the best Scotsman in Whitehall'. And he thought that nationalism may have had a further consequence:

RODGER. One wonders if – and here is a new thought . . . has the rise of Scottish nationalism meant that the top brass in London has thought that instead of having four Scottish departments with only a titular head, we should have a pronounced and strong Scottish Office with bits? I think that 1952 was perhaps the beginning of regarding the four Scottish departments, not as four departments at all, but as a Scottish Office. So it could be pointed out to the people of Scotland: 'You've jolly well got your own Scottish Office'.

It is plausible to see Scottish Office integration as owing something to the upsurge of Scottish nationalism, but perhaps premature to date its inception from the 1950s. The signing of the Scottish Covenant in 1949 by some two million people had dramatically highlighted the demand for a Scottish Parliament (Kellas 1984, 131). But Westminster's response in 1952 was to set up a Royal Commission under Lord Balfour (RCSA 1954). In declaring itself satisfied with existing arrangements whereby the four Scottish departments maintained clearly separate identities under the Secretary of State, the Balfour report repeated, almost word for word, the convictions expressed by Gilmour.[1] It may, however, have been indicative of changes to come that, shortly afterwards, Sir David Milne, the head of the Scottish Office at the time, emphasised the role of the Secretary of State and the notion of teamwork in the Scottish Office, over and above the functions of individual departments (Milne 1957).[2] As the Scottish Office began to take a leading role in economic affairs and to promote regional policy, the distinct practices of the departments came to be seen as grit in the machinery of government. The functional scope of the Scottish central authority expanded in the 1960s and 1970s with the creation of the SDD, the SEPD (now the Industry Department for Scotland (IDS)), the Scottish Development Agency (SDA), and other fringe bodies (Gibson 1985, chs 6 and 7; McCrone 1985; McCrone and Randall 1985). Nationalism became electorally more significant (Kellas 1984, 132-9) and reinforced demands for solutions to Scotland's economic and social problems. A weightier and ostensibly more integrated Scottish Office, operating under more promotional Secretaries of State, themselves advised by less shadowy Permanent Under-Secretaries, was seen as an instrument for change. It contrasted sharply with the pre-1945 (and, indeed, pre-1960s) governmental milieu in which the SED could remain an independent fiefdom.

The increasing prominence of the Permanent Under-Secretary of State arose from changes which were intended to provide an enlarged functional scope, and an enhanced authority, for corporate Scottish Office activity that overarched the individual departments. Here is Rodger:

RODGER. Now, when I first was in the Department, the man who was head of the Scottish Office was Sir Horace Hamilton [1937-46]. He was succeeded by Milne [1946-59]; he was succeeded by Murrie [1959-64]; Murrie by Sir Douglas Haddow [1965-73]. In the days of Horace Hamilton and when David Milne first began, we in the Department didn't think – perhaps at my level I was just ignorant – that these people mattered at all. They were outsiders, and it was only in David Milne's later days, and in Murrie's days, that that post became important to the Department. . . . We knew that the person in that post was just as likely as the Secretary of State himself to call the Department's policy in question. . . . You see, Sir Horace Hamilton did not regard himself as being above the four Secretaries of the four Scottish departments – he insisted that he was *primus inter pares*. But later the man in that post was *primus*.

Q. Would this change have accompanied a change in the way in which Secretaries of State thought about their own role?

RODGER. It may have. . . . A Secretary of State may have taken a new view of what this top civil servant should do. Indeed, I used to think that the top official was a very underemployed man, but not later. Possibly as time went on and the Minister's responsibilities grew, he had to turn more and more to his top permanent official.

Departmental reorganisation and the creation of new machinery for economic regeneration had already begun during Murrie's period as Permanent Under-Secretary. However, the main change occurred during Sir Douglas Haddow's period in office (Macdonald and Redpath 1979, 132; Parry 1987, 120-5; Gibson 1985, 142). Haddow's long service in the Department of Health had begun in 1935, and was interrupted for three wartime years (1941-44) which he spent in the Private Office of the Secretary of State. He later became Secretary in Health (1959), and then went to the SDD (1962) as Secretary, before arriving at the top post in the Scottish Office. In Haddow's time there, and after, there were important reforms in inter-departmental coordination, and in personnel and financial procedures. These are well documented by Macdonald and Redpath:

The Gilmour report . . . recognised that the Secretary of State had a general function of promoting Scotland's interests. They described this function as 'penumbral' and thought that . . . the Permanent Under-Secretary of State, (who was otherwise mainly a co-ordinator) should advise him on it rather than any of the departments. . . . This penumbra became the area in which Secretaries of State took perhaps the greatest interest, and wielded the most influence . . . until eventually it developed into a department with executive functions [the SEPD]. Meanwhile the Permanent Under-Secretary of State was emerging from the penumbra. The setting up of the Regional Development Division in 1964, reporting direct to him . . . met the wishes of the Under-Secretary of the time for some more definite task. And the co-ordinating task itself was becoming more onerous, starting with the Plowden Report of 1961 which recommended a system of financial forward estimates by programme. By the late 1960s the public expenditure survey system was in full operation. . . . The Secretary of State was being presented by his departments with several programmes, whose English equivalents – each presented by a different Minister – could well be in competition with each other; so clearly some co-ordination was required, and this fell to the Permanent Under-Secretary. Then in 1968 came the Fulton Report with its emphasis on personnel management and organisation – and the Secretary of State had four departments, each with different management policies and office procedures. It was a timely coincidence, perhaps, that the next Permanent Under-Secretary [Sir Nicholas Morrison, 1973-78] had a special interest in management; but the build up of Central Services to meet these needs had already begun to take place. (Macdonald and Redpath 1979, 102 and 132)

In the 1970s there were further moves towards the unification of the Scottish Office. A Scottish Office financial Vote was created, and a more formal 'management group' of department Secretaries, supported by a permanent staff, superseded the informal weekly meetings of previous years. The new public expenditure procedures brought a far greater emphasis upon coordination across the Scottish Office through a centralised Finance Division. In the mid-1970s, the consolidation of a new Central Services organisation housing the Finance Division and statistical, management and other services, was intended to give Scottish Office operations a greater degree of corporateness as well as an enhanced managerial emphasis. Inter-departmental transfers of administrators had become more frequent and, by the beginning of the 1970s, personnel work was integrated across all departments, so that 'the 1970s generation of entrants felt little of the old departmental loyalties' (Parry 1987, 123). Macdonald and Redpath summarise the changes:

Thus from the simple concept of 1939 – four departments with a one-man co-ordinator and a few common services – there had emerged a federal organisation unique among government departments. . . . The federal structure – even if it just grew – was in many ways well suited to the unique diversity of the Scottish Office functions. All staff were assigned to the Scottish Office and had extended chances of experience and promotion, which was helpful not only to the staff themselves but in the process of co-ordination and exchange of views between departments; while at the same time the customers were still dealing with individual departments, to which their functions gave a distinct character. (Macdonald and Redpath 1979, 133-4)

Discussion

It has often been said that the Scottish Office, with its single political head, has an inherent advantage over United Kingdom departments, whose coordination must take place across the Cabinet table and through complex, often cumbersome inter-departmental committees and negotiations. By increasing its coordination, the Scottish Office may have indeed been perfecting this advantage. In so doing, it enjoined upon the SED a horizontal context of policies and administrative routines. Along with the changes in staffing, this helped to bring the Department into the fold and to increase its resemblance to the other departments.

External and internal pressures alike moulded a more centralised and coordinated Scottish Office than had formerly existed in the 'confederation' of departments loosely gathered under the Secretary of State. Gilmour's Scottish Office was somewhat more cohesive, an administrative counterpart to the crystallisation of 'middle opinion' around the promotion of planned public intervention for economic and social regeneration in the 1930s. But Gilmour did little to overcome departmentalism. A generation later, the urgency of the economic and industrial problems of the 1960s and 1970s found a political and administrative response in a more highly geared refashioning of the Scottish Office. This response was, once again, fuelled partly by nationalism. It wore away some of the SED's distinctiveness, and changed its position in the Scottish Office. But pressures from within the SED also contributed to the change. The expansion of educational provision increased the scale of educational expenditure, and the proportion that was borne centrally. This sharpened the competition for resources and, in the less favourable economic and public-expenditure climate of the late 1960s onwards, widened the frame of reference within which the Department's claims were scrutinised.

'Federalism', however, is a form of organisation that falls some distance short of unification, and there is nothing which suggests that the Scottish Office 'federation' of departments is merely a temporary resting-place on the road to a tightly centralised structure. Moreover, federal arrangements may be ambiguous even when there is a written constitution that stipulates the distribution of powers and functions. Where we are dealing, not with constitutions, but with a mixture of political power and bureaucratic folkways, the degree of central control and the autonomy of the constituent parts are renegotiable, and vary as political and other circumstances change. The rationalisation of policy-making through new techniques of analysis, financial control, and personnel and office management, has developed at a slower pace than some in Whitehall and St Andrew's House may have wished. Whilst there may be more coordination amongst Scottish Office departments, the primacy of functional divisions has persisted. There is no regular machinery for the centralisation of substantive policy-making above the SED and the other departments, and the well developed departmental networks have not been displaced as the main system through which policies are negotiated and decided. It is still not unrealistic to talk of 'departmental' policies, views and initiatives. Perhaps the most telling point is the observation that 'the customers were still dealing with individual departments'.

On the other hand, the 1945 Education Act and the raising of the school-leaving age in 1947 brought many new 'customers' to the SED. A Department geared in the inter-war period to the traditional functions of primary education for all and secondary education for some, acquired an enlarged responsibility after the Second World War in the form of universal secondary education. Schooling was now expected to do more things for more pupils. But secondary education was still selective and, until comprehensive reorganisation, little was expected of the junior-secondary sector beyond the 'training of character'. The 1960s once again brought new kinds of customer, and greater demands from traditional ones. The Department was drawn, somewhat reluctantly, into new central initiatives on the curriculum and examinations (see chapters 13 and 14). Further education expanded rapidly, as did advanced and higher education in the central institutions. At the same time, a reshuffling of functions in the Scottish Office gave the SED more museums and galleries to look after; and the development of policy for juvenile justice and personal social services provided administrative reasons for grafting the SWSG onto the Department's structure in 1968 (Gibson 1985, 148-9; Macdonald and Redpath 1979, 110-11).

The SED had a larger administrative complement in the 1970s. Whereas, in the 1930s, six or seven administrative-class civil servants had led the SED, by 1965 there were twenty-five in the grades of principal and above. In 1975, there were forty-eight in those posts, falling to forty-two in 1985 as the SED declined in numbers, like the Scottish Office and the civil service generally. Administrative careers could progress within this enlarged Department, but cross-postings also made the Department a way-station, or a destination, for some whose experience of different policy fields covered the Scottish Office.

Some of this experience was gained in the administration of industrial and economic redevelopment. The origins of regional economic policy can be found in the 1930s, but it gathered pace under Scottish Office auspices in the 1960s. Changing ideas about central administration, and increasing central provision of resources, together resulted in a more corporate and promotional view of government which was bound to impinge sooner or later upon an expanding education service. Education itself embraced a 'human capital' philosophy from 1945 on. But it also pursued the goal of an ever-more-perfect academicism for the top quarter or so of pupils, rather than the development of technical or vocational forms of provision for the able. Expansion aggravated the problems here, bringing more pupils into academic courses with which they could not cope. Industry, in particular, failed to penetrate the secret garden of the school curriculum. The Toothill report (sc(di) 1961) was an early, but failed, attempt to relate education to industry. Only in the late 1970s did the distance between the two again become a serious cause for concern. Economic recession deepened in the 1980s, the problems of youth unemployment increased, and the decay of regional policy was symbolised by the collapse of flagship projects in steel, engineering and automobiles. The generation of administrators that had hoped to lead Scotland's revival after 1945 were by now in senior positions in the Scottish Office, and seem to have placed some of the blame for this decay on a still-separate sed. A fresh attempt was made to draw the Department towards the Scottish Office. Starting in 1979, education and industry were brigaded together under one junior Minister (only, however, to be separated again in the Ministerial reshuffle of September, 1986), and in 1984 a new Departmental Secretary came across from the economic-planning and development areas of the Scottish Office.

Some of the most important changes occurred, as we have seen, with the implementation of a new philosophy of the Secretaryship. Although the Scottish Office fell far short of unity, the efforts made in that direction were enough to put paid to Inspectorate claims upon the top post. But, if the sed was no longer to be formally led by specialists, what role in central policy-making would fall to an Inspectorate which Brunton had moulded into a corporate body with aspirations to leadership of the educational policy community? We consider this question in chapter 7.

NOTES

1. 'We consider that . . . the existence of the four Departments is now more firmly than before an accepted feature of Scottish administration. . . . The case for a merger could be established only if there was an obvious lack of co-ordination in the Scottish Departments. There is no evidence of this. . . . If the Head of the Department is to be responsible for the efficiency and working of the staff under his control he must have his own Establishment Division. Any other arrangement would inevitably impair his authority. . . . We can see no advantage in an . . . arrangement whereby the Votes of all the Scottish Departments would be administered centrally' (rcsa 1954, paras 188, 191 and 192).

2. 'The four Scottish departments have no legal existence independent of the Secretary of State. . . . The functions of the Department of Agriculture, for example, . . . are simply the functions of the Secretary of State wearing his agricultural hat. . . . The identity of the Secretary of State with his departments is perhaps not yet fully understood, although it has been a constitutional fact since 1939. There is still prevalent in Scotland a vague belief that departments can act on their own authority and make decisions against which there is an

appeal to the Secretary of State. . . . Unity in diversity is in fact one of the characteristics of the Scottish Office. The diversity is mainly one of function. . . . If there are any deeper differences they are rapidly dying out. What is more important to remember is the unity – the ways in which the four departments act together as the Scottish Office, and what they have in common' (Milne 1957, 5 and 22).

Seven

The Inspectorate in the SED

We, the inspectors, tended to think of the Scottish Education
Department as being the Inspectorate with some administrators.
The administrators didn't think that way, and . . . from about 1950
were strongly thinking quite the opposite, but now I think we've
probably got a much more sensible system. David Dickson,
HMSCI 1966-69

Introduction

Brunton served as Senior Chief Inspector under three Secretaries from 1955
to 1966. This period marked a transition from the older concept of the
Department as a body led by persons whose careers had originated within
the educational world, to one that incorporated more orthodox civil service
assumptions. Developments in the Scottish Office overtook Brunton's vision of the Inspectorate's position at the centre of things. Now that its virtual
freehold on the Secretaryship had lapsed, further limits were placed upon
the Inspectorate's influence by Graham's scepticism of Departmental practices, and by the administrative theory to which he subscribed.

In this chapter we present a more detailed picture of Graham's impact
upon relations within the Department. We examine how a new conception
of integration brought more of the Inspectorate into closer contact with a
Departmental administration that was itself becoming more managerial in
emphasis. Some inspectors were inducted into administrative ways, although permanent positions on that side of the Department were now
virtually closed to them. For a time, these changes left the Inspectorate in a
more subordinate position than it had enjoyed under Brunton. Whilst it was
involved with central administration on a broader front, a new administrative climate, together with the political direction of policy for comprehensive reorganisation, for a time reduced the scope for Inspectorate initiatives.
From the mid-1960s on, authority was seeping away from the Inspectorate,
both outside the Department and within it. However, by the later 1970s
there were signs that the administrators had not been able to maintain their
penetration of the Inspectorate, nor control its activities to an extent consistent with Graham's notion of a well integrated Department. The Inspectorate was heavily involved in the new advisory machinery, and had recap-
tured a leading role in the development of national policy for examinations

and the curriculum. By the end of the 1970s the Inspectorate was leading the policy community again. In part IV we discuss the extra-Departmental aspects of this story. In this chapter we focus on the Inspectorate's loss of authority within the Department after the retirement of Brunton.

The Senior Chief Inspector and the Secretary

Rodger said that Brunton welcomed Murrie's arrival as Secretary because, as an administrator rather than an educationist, Murrie would have to rely heavily upon his inspectors, and particularly upon Brunton as Senior Chief Inspector. Rodger thought that Brunton saw an opportunity here to enhance the importance of the Inspectorate in central decision-making. Brunton himself had remarked to us in 1976: 'I had very good relations with the administrators, but they understood and respected my sphere of responsibility as I did theirs'. He brooked no interference with his control of substantive educational policy, although he took pains to keep administrators in touch with proposals generated within the Inspectorate. Harmony, however, was contingent upon the relationships he had built with Murrie and Arbuckle, whose ultimate consent and support were essential. The accounts in chapter 4 testify to a certain truculence and astute entrepreneurship as Brunton sought to further his aims, sometimes, evidently, in the face of opposition from other administrators. For Brunton, collaborative teamwork meant principally his taking the lead, followed by Inspectorate colleagues, in relations with outside practitioners whom he had enlisted in his projects. At the centre of government, collaboration did not imply the self-effacing role of helpmeet to generalist civil servants who might expect to call upon a technical branch to make an expert contribution, no less but no more, from the back room of the Department.

Brunton described the place he had achieved for the Inspectorate in an anonymous article published by the EIS in the year of his retirement. He asserted the preeminence of the Inspectorate at the zenith of its leadership, and claimed for it a substantial degree of initiative in the formation of educational policy within the Department and outside:

> From being a close-knit body which tended to live and work separately from its fellow workers in the educational world – the administrators on the one hand and the teachers on the other – the Inspectorate has of its own volition entered into new relationships with both these partners. . . . Both as an extension of the administration and as part of the national pattern of education it has shared in all the movements which political and professional thinking have in recent years accelerated. . . . Does change in policy bring change in the Inspectorate, or is it the other way round? Both hinge on the issue by the Department of memoranda embodying current professional thinking, which can – potentially at least – alter the character of our whole traditional system. Inspectors promote the policy contained in them as a central aim of their day-to-

day business. But they are also instrumental in the compilation of these documents, for their unique knowledge of the schools, and their relationships with people in all parts of the educational system which enable them to sound opinions freely, contribute most of the evidence upon which the recommendations are based. (EIS 1966a, 2-3)

Through the enormous range of its responsibilities and its participation in virtually every activity, the Inspectorate had 'drawn a net tightly over the whole of Scottish education'. Brunton went on: 'No limit has yet been set to the Inspectorate's activities . . . it may, indeed, have no need of one, for some time to come at any rate' (*ibid.*, 5).

Brunton here was thinking of the Inspectorate as a separate partner in the system of educational governance. Yet, even before he had written these words, changes had begun which affected its position at the centre and challenged the authority which Brunton had built up over the years. The Senior Chief Inspector had to defend his *modus operandi* when faced with the questions raised by the new Secretary, Norman Graham, during the years 1964 to 1966, when the two men overlapped in the Department. Brunton does not seem to have enjoyed with Graham the same degree of mutual confidence that had existed with the previous Secretaries, although at one point in our interview he played down the extent of disagreement or of institutional rivalry:

BRUNTON. Sir Norman Graham . . . came over from the Health Service with no previous experience of education. To begin with, he found rather puzzling and somewhat uncongenial a situation in which a professional Inspectorate wielded very considerable influence alongside the administration without being in any way subservient to it. He took exception to some of our Inspectorate procedures until he learned that there were good historical reasons for them and that they were often designed to fit in with the ideas and procedures of bodies with whom the Inspectorate had to co-operate. But he generally supported the policies that were being pursued, though I sensed that he had reservations about the situation within SED, which departed in some significant respects from orthodox civil service practice.

James Clark came into contact with several Secretaries and Senior Chief Inspectors in the course of his career as Aberdeen's Director of Education. He explained how the leadership of the Inspectorate was challenged by Graham's scepticism. Graham opened up his own lines of communication to the local educational world:

CLARK. I think that it would be true to say that when Norman Graham came in . . . he was asking a lot of questions, and he wanted answers to these questions. He was perfectly right to ask them and to expect answers. . . . He had had a lifetime, up till then, of experience in the civil service, but not in education. The Education Department was different. Education operated rather differently from the other services, and I would think, from my contacts with him, that there was a genuine desire, on Graham's part, to try to understand what it was all about. . . . It would have been very easy for him to have come in and just accept things as they were.

Q. Whom, in the Department, could he rely on to be his eyes and ears?

CLARK. Graham did not rely entirely on people within the Department for answers to his questions. I would contrast him here with Martin Fearn [SED Secretary 1973-76], whose appointment, of course, was bound to be shorter-term; some people say 'stop-gap'. I would have thought that Graham was broader minded than Fearn, and saw that, if he was going to get as complete a picture as he could of the educational set-up, he had to get outside the Department, as well as take advice and get information from within it. I think, probably, that Graham would have been rather more sceptical of advice from the Inspectorate, than any of the other Secretaries. I don't mean by that that he didn't take advice from the Inspectorate; he did. But I think, on the occasions that I knew a little about, he still asked questions, and he didn't accept comment from the Inspectorate on a particular situation, development or idea, just like that because they were members of the Inspectorate and were professional educationists associated with the Department.

Clark's comments on the Secretaries and Senior Chief Inspectors he knew provide an insight into the effect of generalist civil servants, and of personal qualities, upon the central control of the educational system. His remarks on Graham's style, and on Dickson as successor to Brunton, point to a shift of power between the two sides of the Department in the 1960s:

Q. Over a period of thirty years you've seen Mackay Thomson, Murrie, Arbuckle, Graham, and Fearn as Secretary of SED. How much difference did it make to a local authority who was the Secretary of the Department? I have the impression that Murrie was much more anxious to get to know the local authorities than his predecessor.

CLARK. Yes. I don't think that there is any doubt about that. It so happened that Mackay Thomson did, in fact, have some knowledge of the Aberdeen situation, because he had been on the staff here. But I think that Murrie, coming in as an administrator, did make a very big effort to get to know the problems of individual authorities. He was an administrator rather than an educationist, but I think that he encouraged what he thought to be sound educational development, and got to know his authorities. My impression of Arbuckle is that he knew a fair bit about the authorities before he became Permanent Secretary, and perhaps this made it, in a sense, inevitable that he didn't appear to be getting around the authorities as much as Murrie. This is obviously a subjective judgement. Then, when it came to Graham, my own experience of Graham was that he undoubtedly tried to get to know the root of the problems that were facing him. . . . I think that Norman Graham's main contribution to the centre-local-authority situation was the raising of issues . . . making us think in a rather different way about the relationships between central and local government, and, perhaps, examining some of our powers and operations against the background of his queries. . . . Graham, when one met him . . . in a one-to-one situation, was very likely to ask pertinent questions on some educational issue of the day, and how Aberdeen was facing up to it and what was the local reaction to it and so on. This was, I think, sound policy on his part, of getting to know what was happening. . . . I probably saw more of him on issues that affected Aberdeen, than any of the others.

Q. The people at the centre had to listen to what Brunton was saying, because Brunton had mobilised a great deal of opinion. Did Graham's development of contacts with local authorities, and his seeking of advice outside the Department, represent an awareness that this is what you have to do if you want to control the balance of influence between the Inspectorate on the one hand and the administrators on the other?

CLARK. I think, yes. You see, people at the top are in an extraordinarily difficult position, because in many cases, unless they go out and seek information and opinion, they will receive what those below them think they ought to know.

Q. Was it your impression that under Brunton and Arbuckle, the lines of communication to the administration had been through Brunton much more than, say, they would have been through Dickson?

CLARK. I think that in Brunton's time it was predominantly through Brunton.

Q. Did you feel that, with David Dickson, the centre of influence had moved back towards the administration, as compared with Brunton's day?

CLARK. I would think so. Dickson's influence was of a different kind. He came out and he talked more to teachers and heads, particularly at the time of the junior-secondary blue book [SED 1955b] and so on, with which he was intimately concerned. He did a lot on that and the issues that were raised by that. . . . He came . . . as Senior Chief Inspector . . . more than anybody else with the exception of Brunton, but his approach was entirely different from Brunton's. . . . I hope I'm not doing David an injustice here. Brunton, I think, went deeper than Dickson and tended to see the long-term implications of certain aspects of educational development rather more clearly than Dickson. . . .

Q. How far do you think that might be a reflection of the fact that Brunton became the Senior Chief Inspector at a younger age than Dickson, and could anticipate a longer period?

CLARK. He had a long period. I think this is a fact, but I think it is also in the nature of the man. In a sense, David Dickson, in those days, could be the able, flamboyant, extrovert, hail-fellow-well-met; everybody fell for his charm, and, you know, he projected a good public image in this way.

Q. The wind was blowing pretty hard with Circular 600 and ROSLA in the offing. Whereas (this is hypothesis) Brunton would have stood against it,

Dickson was prepared to bend with it.

CLARK. I would agree with that. . . .

Q. And another difference, of course, would be that Dickson had Graham as his Secretary, and he did not have Murrie-Arbuckle backing.

CLARK. This is true.

Graham was Secretary for a relatively long period (1964-73) during which there were three senior chief inspectors: Brunton, who was approaching retirement, David Dickson (1966-69), and John Bennett (1969-73). Was there any significance in the fact that the succession of Senior Chief Inspectors became more rapid following Brunton? We compare the views of Brunton, Bryden and Graham:

Q. You were Senior Chief Inspector for eleven years. Now that's a very long run, longer than anybody else has had there, and in a sense one needs a long period of time to effect changes.

BRUNTON. Yes. I got it accepted that nobody should be appointed, ever, as Senior Chief Inspector who couldn't give to the job a minimum of five years but, unfortunately, each of the next two men lasted only three years. . . . I fear that there was a loss of initiative even in consolidating what had been gained. . . . There has been in recent years a loss of a sense of direction. . . . After I retired in 1966 there happened what I feared might happen – the administration within the SED became much more dominant, the direction of policy became much less clear-cut in the professional field, and the Inspectorate's effort lost some at least of its momentum.

Gilbert Bryden echoed Brunton's assessment:

Q. Would you agree with the view that, since Brunton went, the balance of power and influence in the Department has shifted back towards the administration and away from the Inspectorate?

BRYDEN. I would agree with that, yes.

Q. What would you attribute that to, looking at it from the outside?

BRYDEN. Well, I would be inclined to attribute it to the retirement of Arbuckle and Rodger, partly. You see, there were no longer chaps like Arbuckle and Rodger in the administration. There were teachers of course in the top ranks of the Inspectorate . . . but the Senior Chief wasn't as important a man as either the Under-Secretary or the Secretary. And I'm inclined to think it might have been a personality matter too. David Dickson, who was a very, very popular Senior Chief, probably didn't press things to the same extent as some of his predecessors did. And I think the chaps who succeeded David Dickson were not all that heavyweight.

On the other hand, Graham gave a different picture when he was asked about Brunton's successors:

Q. Is there any significance in the fact that, after Brunton's period as Senior Chief for some eleven years, the next two Senior Chief appointments were for three years at a time? Brunton's view was that, if you were going to do anything as Senior Chief Inspector, three years wasn't long enough to see policies through.

GRAHAM. This again seems to be personalising too far. I should have thought the doctrine was [that] the right appointment was 'the best man at the time'. If he had only a relatively short period to go, that was perhaps a pity. One couldn't be sure about that. John Bennett, for example, chose to retire. When he retired, I think, if he had wanted to, there would have been no reason why he shouldn't have stayed longer than he did. But the other thesis seems to presuppose that everybody has got to have a new policy and do his thing over a period. Conceivably it would be different in the old days when perhaps the Senior Chief Inspector was the only inspector in the Department; whereas, nowadays, a great many inspectors have experience of working in the Department at different levels; and it can't be nearly as difficult as it once was to adapt to a somewhat different role for the inspector who had been, for virtually all of his time, in the field. . . . There is a tendency outside to assume that the professionals and the administrators are necessarily at daggers drawn, which is quite wrong. It was a very happy relationship. . . . I would say a very enjoyable relationship. I think most of my administrative colleagues would subscribe to that. Ask Dr Dickson how it looked from the other side.

Fulton's Proposals and the Department

Dickson shared Graham's conception of teamwork that involved both sides of the SED in a single enterprise. He told us that 'the important thing is that the inspectors and the administrators should co-operate, and shouldn't stand shouting at one another from a distance'. By contrast, Brunton had won control over areas of policy. Brunton's view was that inspectors not only promoted Departmental policies amongst practitioners but played a powerful part in their formation. Dickson, however, talked more in terms of the Inspectorate's advising administrators, who, in the refashioned relationship which came about in Graham's time, were more firmly in control.

In chapter 6 we saw how the recruitment of administrators, and their cross-posting between departments, had supplanted the leadership of education specialists in the SED. It is worth noting that, from the mid-1960s on, a much wider debate was taking place in the civil service over the qualities that were desirable in administrators and professionals, and over the proper form of relations between the two. Ironically, generalism came to fruition in the Scottish Office at a time when it was being vigorously criticised as obsolete in the administration of the contemporary state. The Fulton report argued that administrators should have something more than experience-based knowledge of how to work the government machine and advise Ministers. Depending on the area of government in which they worked, they should be formally trained either in economic and financial administration, or in social administration, and should be skilled in management (CCCS 1968).

Fulton referred to these qualities as 'professionalism', but the report's concept of this was not coherently explained. It included more of the deep knowledge of a subject than Murrie or Graham thought important for an administrator to have. But it also involved a broader understanding of social policy, and greater skills in management, than inspectors traditionally possessed. Rigid career distinctions between administrators and specialists would be broken down through the promotion of a new managerialism throughout a reformed civil service. Although Fulton was highly controversial and met with considerable resistance, policy analysis and resource management became by-words, and many of the report's recommendations on structure and training were implemented, at least in part (Fry 1985, chs 1 and 3).

Graham's belief in the essential similarity of administration across different Departments, and in the importance of coordination between them, could in one sense be construed as support for the traditional concept of the civil servant as the versatile all-rounder. His wish to ensure that financial and administrative aspects were not overshadowed by the professional, educational aspects of policy is consistent with the traditional view. Graham brought a generalist's wider experience to a Department which was steeped in substantive specialisation, although, as we have seen, he invested much effort in learning about it from the ground up. But he also brought an interest in modern managerial and analytic techniques which foreshadowed Fulton and the reforms of the 1970s. In a lecture to the Royal Institute of Public Administration (RIPA) published in 1965, Graham called for a new intellectual grounding for educational administration, imported from worlds in which techniques of policy analysis and organisation had been developed:

> If, now, in more practical field-work of the kind known as operational research, we could make the same effort as an earlier generation did in fundamental research [on learning and intelligence], it would be of immense benefit. We ought also to subject the day-to-day business of the schools, . . . and, perhaps, even methods of teaching and class organization to detailed rigorous analysis, properly applied by people who understand the background and the objectives – analysis of the same kind as, applied in other fields, has done so much to improve efficiency as well as to ease the burden on all those engaged. . . . We may well be to an increasing extent concerned with management. Training in the principles of management and in the application of new management techniques has clearly come to stay. (Graham 1965, 304 and 309)

The Staffing Survey of the early 1970s, which we discuss in chapter 10, embodied this philosophy and brought sophisticated analytic techniques to bear upon the perennial problem of allocating teachers to schools and classrooms.

In their interviews, Murrie and Graham invoked Fulton in support of the temporary service of inspectors on the administrative side of SED. This may have been a bit disingenuous, because Fulton had argued for more permanent policy-making responsibilities for specialists. We have already seen that permanent administrators were no longer to be drawn from the Inspectorate. However, short secondments of high-flying inspectors as principals in the Department were still seen as useful. They would not be starting on a new career-path, but their isolation would be eroded, and they would come to appreciate administrative considerations alongside educational ones before resuming their careers as HMIS.[1] Earlier, in their evidence to the House of Commons Select Committee on Education and Science (SCES), Graham and Dickson had cast doubt on the willingness of inspectors to come over to the administrative side, and had emphasised salary obstacles to lateral movement into the top grades. Graham said:

GRAHAM. We have . . . deliberately brought in one member of the Inspectorate . . . to give him some idea of how the office worked, how the office viewed the problems, and what mattered in the educational system at the end he did not normally see. The first of those people has now gone back to the district inspectorate. It was a great advantage to the office, I think, to have his experience; it was a signal success. He has himself said that he feels a great deal the better equipped from having had this experience. . . . They were selected . . . as inspectors whom we thought might go a considerable way in the Inspectorate and would be all the better for having this experience [SCES 1968, Qs 97 and 103].

In fact, the preservation of the professional/administrative boundary in the Scottish Office as a whole is confirmed in Macdonald and Redpath's account; although, as we shall see later, the term 'independence' that they use lends itself to different interpretations:

The Fulton report . . . recommended that professional staff should have a greater role in management and should in some cases be employed in administrative divisions within the line management. This happened to a limited extent in the Scottish Office. . . . The professionals did not appear on the whole to regret the fact that Fulton had not been applied more widely. They appeared to value highly the independence of their professional advice, which did not derogate from their close involvement in policy formation; and they were concerned to organise themselves in ways which facilitated their links with administrative staff. (Macdonald and Redpath 1979, 129)

Within the SED, this was done by having more inspectors available as advisers in the Department. Graham saw the physical relocation of chief inspectors in the centre not only as a way of preventing their isolation, but also as an improvement upon the situation that had obtained under Brunton. It would bring professional educational considerations more systematically to bear upon administration without merging the career hierarchies.

142

As he told the 1968 Select Committee, Graham wanted to broaden and institutionalise the points of contact between the two sides: no longer would a Senior Chief Inspector be virtually the only person to whom a Secretary could initially turn for professional advice within the Department. By the same token, no longer would a Senior Chief Inspector 'gate-keep' communications between the two sides to the extent that Brunton had done, 'insupportably' in Graham's view:

GRAHAM. We have felt increasingly the need for professional advice readily available within the office . . . we have now a much stronger professional element within the office than we had when I first came to the Department. Then the only inspector was the senior chief inspector, and in the nature of his duties he was often not there. That seemed to me a great weakness in that we wanted professional advice sometimes quickly and the fact that it all fell on one man was really insupportable [SCES 1968, Qs 20 and 98].

The Department's memorandum to the Select Committee also linked the new procedures to the ending of permanent transfers of inspectors to the administrative side:

perhaps as a result of this, more thorough arrangements are now made to ensure consultation between the administrators and the inspectors.

. . . In particular the Chief Inspectors are increasingly being consulted beforehand about policy circulars, memoranda and similar publications and about any pending legislation. (*ibid.*, 5)

The memorandum went on to explain that the close liaison of inspectors with the various Divisions of the SED was 'of the greatest importance in helping to ensure the smooth working of the administrative machine, both locally and nationally' (*ibid.*).

Dickson confirmed the picture of a broad interface. But, whereas Brunton had written about the Inspectorate's entering into relationships with administrators 'of its own volition', Dickson saw this as the attempt of a somewhat worried Inspectorate to regain some influence once recruitment practices had changed:

DICKSON. We had to consider how our influence and advice could best reach the administration, and it was out of this that the practice arose whereby the chief inspectors in charge of primary, secondary, and further education were stationed in St Andrew's House or York Buildings. . . . It's silly to have a good HMI and take him into the [administration] and lose him. You're far better making him a chief inspector and keeping him as a chief inspector, but basing him in the office where he will work with the administrators.

Q. I gather that, when Brunton was Senior Chief Inspector, he was virtually the only representative of the Inspectorate permanently based with an office in St Andrew's House.

DICKSON. That is true.

Q. Does that mean that there was an unworkable burden on him?

DICKSON. Yes, but by and large he made it work. Most people would have found it unworkable. But I think that the Senior Chief Inspector's job, even in my time, was a very, very heavy load. But then, of course, HMIs in Scotland always have had a heavy load. I told you that at one time I had three big jobs on. In England they would have had at least four inspectors doing what I was doing, because they had enough numbers to provide specialists.

Q. So, when you became Senior Chief Inspector, some of the links between the Inspectorate and the administration would have been direct between the two persons concerned, rather than filtered through the Senior Chief Inspector as they would have been to a greater extent under Brunton?

DICKSON. That's a difficult one. Day-to-day relations would certainly have been like that, but if any large issue was involved it would have come through the Chief Inspectorate. It would have come to the Senior Chief and been discussed by the chief inspectors who at least in those days met monthly.

Influence and Independence

How was the influence of the Inspectorate changed by attempts to integrate it into the policy machinery of the Department? How long did any integration last? Graham used the ambiguous term 'insupportable' when referring to the funnelling of advice through the Senior Chief Inspector. For Graham, apparently, a single source of internal advice was an unreliable part in a smooth-working machine, and it interfered with the ability of administrators, as the Secretary of State's advisers, to take firmer control over policy-formation within the Department. Dickson said, however, that Brunton had been able to shoulder the burden of work. Perhaps, therefore, it was not so much a mechanical problem as one that involved differences of personality and of substantive views of education. But had the man who had 'drawn a net tightly over the whole of Scottish education' not woven its filaments into a myth of Inspectorate influence and independence, a myth which educationists outside the SED had amplified because it sustained their aims and self-image?

As we saw in chapter 5, George Gray emphasised Brunton's role in counterposing educational to financial considerations, even in relatively expansionist years. In Gray's view, Brunton was 'the last of the chief inspectors who was able to stand up fully to the administrators' who were transmitting Treasury pressures that came via the Secretary of State. Treasury pressures aside, the emergence of strong political and Ministerial initiatives on secondary schooling in the mid-1960s coincided with the other changes we have discussed to circumscribe further the Inspectorate's control of its own activities. In 1966, Bruce Millan became junior Minister with responsibility for education. He thought that inspectors should maintain an independence of judgement, 'but they should certainly at the end of the day, be following . . . the policy of the Government'. We give his views on relations between Ministers and inspectors at greater length in chapter 8.

In their evidence to the 1968 Select Committee, officials of the teachers' organisations measured the Inspectorate's position against an ideal of complete independence from government, which some of them, rather naively, saw as supported by the Victorian curiosity of the Sovereign's appointment of inspectors. But this aside, most of these teacher officials agreed that inspectors now worked more closely within the bounds of government policy; this both constrained criticism and impeded the communication of professional advice on policy. The Scottish Schoolmasters' Association (SSA) complained most vehemently in its memorandum, arguing that teachers were losing confidence in an Inspectorate that was simply a tool of the SED's officials (SCES 1968, 93 and 96). On the other hand, Gilbert Bryden of the EIS seemed resigned to the situation as he saw it:

BRYDEN. We doubt if there is all that much independence in practice. It is clearly impossible, I think, for the Inspectorate to express views on education that are radically different to the views held by the Government. So that we do not know how far the independence of the Inspectorate goes.
. . . I do not really see how you can entirely divorce the Inspectorate from the policies of the Government. If the Government is to have anything to do with education, it seems to me that the Inspectorate cannot run counter to the findings of the Government [*ibid.*, Qs 320 and 323].

Dickson's evidence to the Select Committee affirmed his preference for an influential and functionally integrated Inspectorate, rather than an ineffective independence. In the following exchange, he and Graham were responding to questions put by Gilbert Longden, an English MP who was a member of the Select Committee:

DICKSON. I am no great believer in the wisdom of having educationists sitting separately producing their ideas about what should be done in education, and paying no attention whatever to all the difficulties of administration, finance, etc. on which all their ideas must in the end depend.
. . . I would not like my people to be sitting on the sidelines making airy fairy pronouncements about education. I would much rather have them in the middle of the battle helping and prodding the administrators. . . . I do not see us essentially as an arm of the Secretary of State. . . . There is no intervention at all as far as expressing [our] views to the Department is concerned; [we] frequently do. We feel entirely independent in this matter. What may happen to those views in the formulation of national policy is another story.

LONGDEN. Their independence has been impugned by certain of our witnesses who cast doubt upon whether they are in fact free to exercise independence of judgment and action?

DICKSON. If you mean by this when an inspectors' panel, say a panel of modern language inspectors, sits down and agrees upon a particular matter of policy and after that that any individual inspector on that panel can go round schóols advising them to the contrary, that obviously would be an impossible situation. But the panels of inspectors themselves would agree upon the professional matters of the teaching of modern languages entirely on their own. They would not be influenced politically or administratively [*ibid.*, Qs 49, 50, 57 and 58].

In giving his own views on the matter, Graham invoked his experience in Health:

GRAHAM. I think it was taken for granted that the professional advisers in the Department, i.e. the medical staff, expressed their views as medical men, but I cannot remember anybody ever making an issue of the fact that they were somehow independent. It was as closely an integrated machine as we could make it [*ibid.*, Q.65].

From the mid-1960s on, the Inspectorate's influence seemed to depend less upon the dynamism of a Senior Chief Inspector to whom administrators might defer as he moulded professional thinking at the centre, and more upon the institutionalisation of inspectors' advisory roles, both within the Department and on the newly created bodies outside. But the resocialisation and retooling of the Inspectorate evidently had not gone far enough by the early 1970s. On whichever side of the Department they served, Graham wanted HMIS, whose careers had developed through mainly educationist routes, to share the administrators' concern with resources and management. He returned to the theme of his RIPA lecture in a 1971 article written with John Bennett, the Senior Chief Inspector, following a visit they had made to North America. They referred to local authorities, but their remarks were intended for internal Inspectorate consumption, and the significance of their determination to convert ex-teachers to managerialism would not have been lost on inspectors:

Whatever the resources deployed, both in Ontario and in Maryland, there was much more concern than one would find in the average education authority here to reckon and compare the cost and to maintain at the centre a strong organisation for the purpose. There was no feeling, as there is here, that administration is at best a necessary evil and most of the time something of a luxury – and this attitude is perhaps the more striking when nearly all the 'administrators' are themselves professionals, i.e. teachers by origin. (Graham and Bennett 1971, 3)

Graham turned to the Scottish Office Management Services Unit to analyse the organisation of the Inspectorate in relation to its roles in central decision-making, resource management, and educational innovation. The Unit noted the Inspectorate's 'close working partnership with the administrative divisions of the SED in such important broad areas as curriculum development, school building and teacher supply' (SOMS 1973, para.5.2). But it also found that the Inspectorate lacked aims, direction and cohesion.

A debilitating fragmentation seemed to affect it:

> Individuals have often been left to make their own interpretations of the purpose of their jobs and to strike their own working priorities, virtually without senior direction or support . . . many Inspectors show limited awareness of being part of a single service . . . they frequently pursue their own specialisms, with resulting gaps in understanding of what colleagues, sometimes based in the same office, are doing and how it might impinge on their own work. (*ibid.*, para.5.3)

The report argued, however, for a further strengthening of the Inspectorate's corporate profile and central policy contributions. On the report's recommendation, an echelon of deputy senior chief inspectors was created in order to reduce the span of the Senior Chief Inspector's responsibilities. The number of chief inspectors working at central headquarters was also enlarged.

But even this reorganisation failed to satisfy the 'Rayner' scrutiny of the Inspectorate, which was carried out in 1981 by Peter Rendle, a retired SED official (SO 1981; Pickard 1983; *TESS* 1 April 1983). Rendle's report showed that the reforms of the mid-1970s had not resulted in a smoother integration of the central educational machinery. Was this because the internal problems of the Inspectorate itself, which had been noted in the 1973 report, had been successfully overcome? Had it regained its corporate self-confidence? Brunton, let us recall, had insisted on participating in the Inspectorate's own deliberations when he was an Assistant Secretary before 1955. As Senior Chief Inspector, however, he kept administrators at bay whilst bringing the Inspectorate 'out of the dinosaur age', in the phrase used by one of the new deputy senior chief inspectors of the mid-1970s, Andrew Chirnside, when he recalled his early days under Brunton (quoted in Reid 1975). If the Inspectorate lost the initiative to the administrators in the later 1960s, ten or more years later the administrators did not regard it as the biddable collaborator that the Department had envisaged. Rendle's report echoed Graham's complaint of the 1960s that the Inspectorate was too narrowly interfaced with the rest of the Department, and had pre-empted policy initiatives:

> The burden of strategic liaison with the Department seems to rest almost wholly on HMSCI who also has a substantial managerial burden.
> . . . Administrators need to have their eyes lifted to more distant horizons. This must be a task of the Inspectorate as a whole and not left too much to HMSCI. (SO 1981, paras 5.22 and 8.10)

Between the two sides of the Department, the report argued, 'collaboration is patchy and . . . sometimes non-existent in the policy and programme planning fields' (*ibid.*, para.8.10). Departmental administrators were frozen out of participation in the Inspectorate's own key planning groups, whilst the Departmental Planning Committee, which was set up in the early 1970s and which the SED Secretary chaired, was an inadequate body and was too much concerned with short-term issues:

> There is an apparent lack of well developed lines of communication between the Inspectorate and the administration at all levels – except for *ad hoc* enquiries. Initiatives are launched by the Inspectorate and staff are committed to lines of action without the administration being adequately aware of where the action might eventually lead. (*ibid.*, para.8.2)

Although its influence had waned after 1965 with the implementation of Circular 600 and with the establishment of the Examination Board, the Inspectorate's release from many of its traditional tasks left it available for advisory and developmental roles which in later years expanded dramatically. Inspectors were able to reassert their influence in the policy process through the numerous positions they held on a wide variety of outside bodies. In all, the 113 inspectors held 337 assessorships in 1967 (SCES 1968, 10); and the figure reached some 450 by 1981 (SO 1981, appendix J). There are strong indications that, by working through these bodies, and by orchestrating the Munn and Dunning Development Programme from the Department (*ibid.*, appendix E), the Inspectorate was able to recast Brunton's net over the system and to regain a dominant position in the educational changes of the late 1970s and 1980s. We examine its role in national policy for certification and the curriculum in chapters 13 and 14.

Summary and Discussion

For a period after 1945, the position of the Inspectorate remained strong. Proportionately more numerous than its English counterpart, it did not share its role with local inspectors. These did not exist north of the Border where the main development of education-authority advisorates began only in the 1970s. The Department drew upon the Inspectorate for its leaders. Under Brunton inspectors achieved a more corporate presence, building a reputation as policy innovators at the centre and as *animateurs* amongst practitioners, some of whom they involved in centrally led developments. Brunton's Inspectorate took many of the initiatives, but it enjoyed the support and protection of a Departmental administration which had no competing projects to pursue.

By the mid-1960s these conditions were changing. Administrators tried to curtail the power of the Inspectorate, and their efforts were assisted by changes occurring across the Scottish Office. These changes, in turn, stemmed both from administrative reform in British government and from Scottish Office initiatives in economic development. But the actions of particular individuals were instrumental as well. The Inspectorate's wings were clipped. No longer were SED Secretaries to be ex-inspectors. Whilst a few inspectors were to continue to serve as administrators, this service was now to be only temporary and was designed to socialise them to the ways of administration. A resource-conscious administration attempted to draw the

Inspectorate into the hierarchy of Departmental decision-making, and preached it a lesson in managerialism. Evaluators were brought in from outside to take the measure of the Inspectorate, to propose its reform, and to redefine its role.

A comparison with England is relevant here. Commentators have seen English H M Is up to the 1970s as relatively non-interventionist, although one ex-Minister, Gerry Fowler, has argued that, even at that time, the Inspectorate was more active than was commonly conceded (Fowler 1975). At any rate, its involvement in central policy-making within the D E S was not very evident until the emergence of political controversies over policies and standards in the 1970s. Since then, the English Inspectorate has maintained a higher profile. Under Sheila Browne, its Senior Chief Inspector for nine years until 1983, it played a greater part in national development and monitoring. In the late 1970s, one-quarter of the Inspectorate was gathered into the centre to work on national enquiries (Salter and Tapper 1981, 197). It gained a reputation for independence and openness by publishing politically controversial reports on schools and on the effects of public-expenditure restraint upon local authorities' educational provision.[2] But is this reputation justified? Rhodes' study of the English Inspectorate depicts 'puzzles about its position which never seem quite to be resolved'; the Inspectorate 'retains independence of judgment on matters within its professional competence, but is accountable to the Secretary of State. It must, therefore, work within the framework of departmental policy, and also contribute to that policy' (G. Rhodes 1981, 113). The Inspectorate has been formally involved in the D E S machinery for planning. But Rhodes cannot be precise about the extent to which inspectors' views have been effectively brought to bear. He argues that this is because,

> unlike enforcement inspectors, there is no core function which schools inspectors have to perform. Enforcement inspectors have certain statutory regulations to administer and have powers and sanctions correspondingly. They have at least this specific duty to carry out. Schools inspectors do not. It is to that extent a more open question how political and administrative considerations operate to determine the scope of the inspectorate's work. Within the inspectorate and in the relations between it and Ministers and the rest of the department there is no set pattern but rather a continuously evolving approach to questions of functions and priorities. (*ibid.*, 113-14)

Salter and Tapper, on the other hand, are in no doubt as to the course of this evolution. They argue that the English Inspectorate's functions and priorities were, in the 1970s and 1980s, firmly set for it by the D E S, which used H M Is to legitimate a new central *dirigisme*. Using Gramsci's term, they see the Inspectorate as 'organic intellectuals' who provided the D E S with an ideology of education to help the Department increase its control. The bureaucratic values espoused by the D E S 'emphasize the importance of scientific rationality, efficiency and professional expertise' (Salter and Tapper 1981, 93). In embracing these, they claim, the D E S developed a managerial and planning approach to educational governance which required the elaboration of mechanisms for monitoring the system and for gathering and disseminating information (*ibid.*, ch.5). They go on to argue that the Department made a bid for power over its 'partners', the teachers and the local education authorities. But, if the D E S were to speak with a louder voice, it required keener eyes and ears. Thus the Inspectorate became the linch-pin, but its 'myth of autonomy' had to be preserved, 'since it enhances the supposed objectivity of the information on which the Department rests its policy proposals' (*ibid.*, 111; see also 233-4). Embarrassed by critical reports from the Organisation for Economic Co-operation and Development (O E C D) in 1975 and from the Select Committee on Expenditure in 1976, the D E S went public with a 'Great Debate' (*ibid.*, 199). Salter and Tapper argue that this was done in order to help effect a political and ideological transformation.

Scotland, however, managed without such fanfares. There were no authoritative and public outside reports begging a response, and there was no crisis, real or imagined, over 'standards'. Although, in the aftermath of R O S L A, there was concern for truancy and indiscipline (S E D 1977d), there was no Great Debate. This is not to say that a job of ideological reconstruction was not being done in Scotland in the 1970s; it was. But its origins were more diverse than those suggested for the ideological crisis in England, and its form was quite different. We deal with this in chapter 20.

If there were a crisis of capitalism, we may suppose that it affected Scotland no less than England and Wales. But, although developments north of the Border bear some resemblance to Salter and Tapper's picture, there are important differences as well, especially differences of timing. Salter and Tapper attribute the changes in the central government of education in England partly to the effects of the adverse economic and demographic factors of the 1970s, and partly to the 'needs' of an ambitious D E S bureaucracy seeking more power. In Scotland, however, the new managerial emphasis of the S E D and the Scottish Office dated from the 1960s, and had begun to affect the position of the Inspectorate well before the onset of economic crisis. The Department's preoccupation with perennial resource questions concerning the building and staffing of schools had long involved the Inspectorate in supervising, encouraging and controlling the local authorities (see chapters 9 and 10). By the turn of the 1960s, the Department had moved decisively towards a closer central specification of school-staffing complements. It justified this in terms of resource-efficiency and managerial rationality in the face of the impending rise in the school-leaving age. At around the same time, it invented a new structure of promoted posts to cope with some of the problems of teachers' careers and school management (see chapter 10). These problems had arisen from the shift to fewer and larger secondary schools after comprehensive reorganisation, and they were exacerbated by ROSLA. In the 1980s, however, the Inspectorate was sharply critical of the managerial performance of promoted teachers (SED 1984).

Central management remained an important theme in Scotland in the 1980s, and the Inspectorate was expected to play a major part in it. Humes points out that the Secretary of State's 1983 policy statement on Rendle's scrutiny of the Inspectorate tacitly invoked an investment-return model of education; it described HMIS' tasks in terms of providing an audit, promoting cost-effectiveness, and indicating norms of quality for practitioners to achieve (Humes 1986, 74). However, the Inspectorate was not merely a pliant instrument with no impulses of its own towards leadership. Judgements of the extent of its independence must take account of the powerful role it was allowed to play in shaping and controlling the networks of consultation and advice, of its management of the new system for curriculum and examinations, and of its work on the Action Plan (see part IV). All these served to reinsert it in the central policy-making process.

How far the Inspectorate remained independent in carrying out its advisory and promotional functions, however, is still an open question. The Secretary of State's statement on Rendle considered that it was 'essential to preserve the Inspectorate's independence of professional judgement', for this contributed to the Inspectorate's effectiveness and to its esteem (SSS 1983, para.2.1). We cannot assert that the Minister was merely trotting out the simple 'myth of autonomy' in order to mask an opposite, but equally simple, truth that the Inspectorate was merely an instrument of ideological control. For the Inspectorate's role gave it resources which were not negligible, and in recent years it has shown signs of deploying them to bolster its position. Nevertheless, it kept from public view any misgivings it had about the effects of expenditure restraint. In any case, 'independence' and 'autonomy' do not have clear meanings in the subtle and sometimes ambiguous relations between a special *corps* of civil servants, such as inspectors, and the administrative 'regulars', Ministers, practitioners and others with whom they work.

We cannot say whether the SED's move to new methods and rationales was 'necessary' according to any logic of bureaucratic aggrandisement, although we have shown the circumstances that brought it about and the consequences for the Inspectorate after Brunton had gone. Perhaps the administration in the SED was indeed refashioning its approach to governance, and using the Inspectorate as its agent in reconstructing its ideology. But perhaps not; we have no direct evidence to support such an unequivocal interpretation of its purpose. Central intervention and economic efficiency were not coins that needed new minting, and the signposts for change in the 1970s were less conspicuous than they were in England.

Scottish evidence therefore casts doubt upon Salter and Tapper's interpretation. To their credit, however, they realise that attempts to explain

151

the Great Debate come up hard against a stubborn indeterminacy of fact:

> Glancing through the jumble of facts, no particular pattern readily emerges: the pressures span the economic, political, demographic and educational spheres; no one factor is obviously more important than another in precipitating the Debate and any suggested connection is bound to be descriptive and speculative. If there is a dynamic present then it is well hidden. But perhaps we and the Marxists are being over-optimistic and over-theoretical in searching for a dynamic in educational change. Perhaps change occurs when a largely accidental aggregation of external pressures reaches a level which forces the education system to adapt itself accordingly. (Salter and Tapper 1981, 193)

This sounds remarkably like the pluralism they condemn in Kogan (see chapter 1 above).

In chapter 6 and in this chapter we have examined the Inspectorate's changing role within central government. Earlier, our account of Brunton's activities and of the hiving-off of functions from the centre drew attention to the Inspectorate's relations with those outside. These relationships, with teachers and with local authorities, further complicate the question of the Inspectorate's independence. For advice was proffered (or rejected) and influence exerted (or countered) in this external dimension as well; and, there too, the independence of the Inspectorate was asserted (or denied). Inspectors acted, or were expected to act, variously and sometimes conflictingly, as patrons, brokers, partners, information-gatherers, disseminators, and even as inspectors, as they dealt with the different parts of the policy community.[3] The nature of that community, which we examine in parts IV and V, casts further light upon the changing role and influence of the Inspectorate, as does the Ministerial context, which we discuss next.

NOTES

1. Two inspectors appear to have moved permanently to the administrative side as Assistant Secretaries. One of them was A. K. Forbes, the man to whose earlier secondment in the 1960s Graham referred. He became an Assistant Secretary at the end of 1974 (although he was still listed as a Chief Inspector in the *Civil Service Yearbook* until 1978) with responsibilities for teacher supply and training, and briefly for schools. He left the Department to direct the Prison Service in 1980 and died in 1982. The other, R. D. Jackson, moved in 1978 to an SED Assistant Secretaryship in charge of social work services for the elderly and the handicapped, and then to do personnel and services work in the Prison Service in 1982. A small number of inspectors spent time in administration before resuming careers in the Inspectorate. Some went on to become chief inspectors and one, John Ferguson, became Senior Chief Inspector in 1981.
2. See the interviews with Sheila Browne in O'Connor (1983) and in Hodges (1983). See also Browne (1983). England preceded Scotland in publishing the results of inspections; Rendle did not recommend it and the initiative came from Ministers. We were told that a Ministerial instruction was given to the

Department and its inspectors not to write reports criticising the effects of local education expenditure cuts.

3. MacLean's collection of terms by which inspectors described themselves in 1976 included 'consultant, coordinator, cooperator, catalyst, digestor, enabler . . . encourager, helper, honest broker, guide, link (or liaison) man, meter-reader, operator, observer, reporter, refresher, stimulator, trouble-shooter, visionary, watchdog' (MacLean 1976a; see also MacLean 1976b and 1976c).

Eight

Ministers, Officials and Parliament

There are political issues, and strictly educational issues, and as a
Minister you shouldn't pretend that you are an educationist.
  Bruce Millan, Secretary of State for Scotland 1976-79

A Minister is trying, nearly all the time, to please.
  Allan Rodger, SED Under-Secretary 1959-63

Introduction

In the years following Brunton's retirement in 1966, relationships between
the Inspectorate and administrators remained somewhere between the
poles of daggers drawn and smooth integration. More inspectors were
brought into the Office, and in 1968, 1973 and 1981 there were reappraisals
of the Inspectorate's functions and organisation. But the distribution of
power between the two sides also owed much to their involvement in issues
and movements outside the Department. The balance of influence depended, too, on the way the Minister used the resources of his office in
making and administering policy. His contribution, in turn, depended partly
upon his own interest in educational matters, and partly upon the place of
education in the political agenda.

In the British system of party government, the Minister connects the
official machinery with the world of party politics, and is responsible for
what the bureaucracy does. Whilst he has the final say, he is highly dependent upon the support, protection and advice he receives from officials.
They may know far more about the subject for which he is publicly responsible, and have more regular contacts with the policy community outside
government. In turn, officials act in the Minister's name and cannot ignore
his authority. They need his political *imprimatur* for the departmental
policies they seek to implement, and they depend upon him to further their
department's interests, and in our case Scotland's interests also, in Downing
Street, Westminster and Whitehall (Mackintosh 1968, 533-54; Self 1972,
ch.5; Brown and Steel 1979, 126-34). This mutual dependence allows officials to work on the Minister as well as to him. Ministers cannot take it for
granted that they will hold sway. Recently there has been much discussion
of the role officials play, and should play, in a system of parliamentary
democracy. Whilst critics across the political spectrum have claimed that the
civil service is too powerful, others have argued that party-political and

Ministerial deficiencies create a vacuum which the permanent bureaucracy fills by default (Crowther-Hunt 1980; Young and Sloman 1982, 19-31 and 86-98; Fry 1984; Greenwood and Wilson 1984, 77-84; Fry 1985, ch.2).

Transactions between Ministers and officials are influenced by several factors which we consider in this chapter: those that pertain to the climate of political decision-making, to persons and roles, and to the working patterns of the Scottish Office. After a brief overview of the place of education in Scottish party politics, we examine the Ministerial dimension by looking at the part played in educational policy by Secretaries of State and junior Ministers since the Second World War. We consider the special factors that predisposed Scotland to 'administrative primacy' over some issues.[1] We also glimpse some of the interactions between officials and Ministers before going on to examine the treatment of Scottish education in Parliament. Parliamentary involvement in questions of educational resources figures in chapters 9 and 10, where we consider the dealings of the Scottish Office with London-based government.

Education and Party Politics

Immediately after the Second World War, it was a Labour Government that was charged with implementing the new system of universal secondary education. However, faced as it was with severe economic and housing problems, it could not give education first priority. In Scotland new political initiatives in education did not emerge to challenge the conservatism of the Department (see chapter 4). In any case, political energies were absorbed more in the housing programme than in education (see chapter 10). In Harvie's estimation, the political parties were stagnant through the 1950s, leaving public affairs 'tranquil' and 'politically quiescent', except for the occasional clamour of nationalism. Despite its electoral success in 1945, the Labour Party in Scotland was bereft of personalities, and its organisation had collapsed. The Liberals were weak, whilst the Conservatives, though back in power from 1951, had a minority of Scottish seats, drew their representatives from amongst the gentry and the professions, and were remote from many of the country's social and economic problems (Harvie 1981a, ch.4). Thus parties did little to aggregate Scottish political opinion and transform it into policies. There was, it is true, a strategy for post-war redevelopment. Many of its roots were Scottish and owed a great deal to the consensus politics established in the 1930s through the agency of 'middle opinion' (Marwick 1964; Addison 1975, ch.1). The Labour Secretary of State, Tom Johnston (1941-45) had gathered former Secretaries of State into a 'Council of State' to consider policies for economic regeneration. The consensus embraced organisations, interest groups and leaders of opinion outside government circles, as well as the Scottish Office itself. But the strategy was primarily directed at economic and social policy, rather than at the specifics of education;[2] and it was the Scottish Office which provided the main element of continuity from pre- to post-war years (Johnston 1952, ch.18; Campbell 1979; Harvie 1981a, chs 2 and 4; Gibson 1985, chs 3-5; Saville 1985).

Some light is shed on the generally non-partisan atmosphere of post-war policy-making by Sir Charles Cunningham in an interview with Anthony Seldon in 1980. Between 1942 and 1957, Cunningham was Deputy Secretary and then Secretary of the Scottish Home Department (SHD):

CUNNINGHAM. There was remarkably little political controversy about the trend of development that was thought likely to be in Scotland's interests after the war . . . it was, I think, remarkable how close agreement there was . . . there was a sort of upsurge of hope. . . . It was beginning to seem a little bit as the kind of country it might once have been. . . . I think that the mood of optimism was continuing up almost . . . indeed I think actually – to the time at which I left Scotland in 1957.

SELDON. To what extent did you feel in the twelve years after the war . . . that the conduct of policy at the Scottish Office was political, Party political?

CUNNINGHAM. Hardly at all. I think that all the Ministers in that period were concerned to do what they conceived to be in the best interests of Scotland . . . and I do not remember any particular acute political controversy over Scottish affairs. There were differences of emphasis, naturally . . . but a broad agreement between the Parties as to where we wanted to go and how we might set about getting there . . . we were fortunate in the Scottish Office in that both Ministers and civil servants, apart from their official relationship, had a genuine desire to contribute to the prosperity and wellbeing of their country [Cunningham 1980, 8 and 10-12].

Our research does not enable us to judge whether Cunningham has exaggerated the apolitical character of government after the Second World War. Nevertheless, there is little doubt that education was of minor party-political importance in comparison to housing, health, and the infrastructure of the economy. Expansion of provision following the 1945 Education Act, ROSLA in 1947, and post-war demographic changes set the agenda for educational administration. But education was in some ways an appendage to the main thrust of Scottish policy, and its claim upon resources was insecure (see chapter 9). Within education, reconstruction came to mean 'roofs over heads'. With the Department's lack of response to the Advisory Council's 1947 report on secondary education, there was no vehicle to carry new ideas further. Education remained on the agenda in a general way as an integral part of Scottish national identity (see chapter 17) and, later, MPs sprang to the defence of Scottish education in the face of perceived threats from the 1958 revision of local-government financial allocations (see chapter 9). But these interventions registered a concern more with resources than with change. Labour was divided on the question of selection for secondary education, though arguments for its abolition gradually gained ground. In the mid-1950s, the Scottish Labour Party attacked selection and fee-paying, and urged the adoption of comprehensive schooling (LPSC, n.d.). Some of its Members of Parliament found opportunities to press the point in parliamentary debates. However, the Party had not resolved its position on these questions, and it was still some ten years away from holding the power in Westminster to put change into effect (see chapters 15 and 16).

Comprehensive reorganisation in 1965 brought education to the centre of the political stage and overturned existing consensual relationships. Yet the running on this policy was made in the South, and many in Scotland, even on the Labour side, thought it not entirely applicable north of the Border. Working-class ambitions were thought to be attainable through greater access to the traditional ladder, and many education authorities in Scotland could boast that the proportion of their pupils gaining entry to senior-secondary courses was higher than the proportion of English pupils entering grammar schools (see chapter 15). Teachers' grievances over pay and conditions intensified in the 1960s and were debated in Parliament. But they were contained and settled through consultation between their representatives and the government machine. Teachers' renewed militancy over salaries and conditions of service aroused public controversy in the early 1970s, but their cause was not taken up strongly in party arenas. The Labour Party held power at the time of the 1970 strike and did not support the teachers. Some of its prominent MPs strongly opposed the strike, whilst the Conservatives could only give lukewarm support to such action (Deroche-Drieux 1976, 146-7).

However politically-charged were the educational issues of the 1960s, they were still a sideshow to the concern of the Scottish Office and of politicians to promote regional and industrial development (see chapter 6). In the 1970s, political devolution took pride of place, owing its inspiration to the revival of nationalist electoral fortunes (Kellas 1984, chs 7 and 8). As in the rest of Britain, however, the oil crisis of 1973 and the squeeze on public expenditure constrained new policy departures. But the ways in which the educational system might adjust to falling pupil numbers presented politically sensitive choices. So, too, did the abolition of fee-paying schools and, in the 1980s, the local implementation of parental choice, and teachers' pay and conditions of service. On the other hand, there was no 'Great Debate' in Scotland on standards or on educational accountability. The Munn and Dunning reforms of secondary-school curriculum and examinations proceeded as a managerially run national development programme, and not as a political issue. The debate over Munn and Dunning 'was a matter for the professionals' (Forsyth and Dockrell 1979, 18). However, the burdens that this programme placed upon teachers gave them, and their political supporters, valuable ammunition in their campaign for an independent pay review in the mid-1980s.

We do not assert that party differences have not mattered, for Labour and Conservative Governments have pursued varying legislative paths and have sometimes given priority to different educational goals and sectors. In part to counteract political influence, educational professionals and administrators have often preferred *ad hoc* local education authorities and the representation of teachers' interests on local education committees (Douglas and Jones 1903; SERC 1917; RCLGS 1967, Qs 11-29; 1968b, Qs 3961-4000 and Qs 4058-65). The deeper partisanship that resulted from local-government reorganisation in 1975 has made it more difficult for professionals to mediate the local political input into education. Nevertheless, public education has not usually been a strong Conservative subject, and the Labour Party has not always formulated a clear or unified line in educational policy. Nor has it always given a prominent place within its deliberations to major matters of substantive reform. Drucker notes that the debate on education at the 1978 Scottish Conference of the Labour Party lasted all of thirty minutes, and made no mention of the Pack, Munn and Dunning reports of the previous year which had set the agenda of educational development (Drucker 1979, 105). The Scottish National Party gained much ground in Scottish politics in the 1970s, recruiting to its ranks many who were involved in the education service. It was odd, therefore, that a Nationalist collection of policy papers published in that period of devolutionist ferment should omit to say anything on education.[3]

With this as background, we now consider the part played by Ministers.

Scottish Office Ministers

The status within government of the Education Minister for England and Wales has not always been high. It was perhaps at its lowest in the later 1940s and well into the 1950s: Florence Horsburgh was denied a seat in Churchill's Cabinet from 1951 to 1953 (Seldon 1981, 270-82). However, many English Education Ministers since then have left their mark on policy.[4] Some moved education closer to the centre of the political stage, whilst others found it there and took the initiative in policy-making. Up to the time of James Callaghan in 1976, Prime Ministers showed little interest in education and rarely pronounced upon it in public. Since then, education has held a prominent place on the political agenda, and its Ministers have remained in the limelight.

Judgements about the importance of the education portfolio are more difficult to make for Scotland because there is no 'single-function' Education Minister. However, since the 1960s, issues such as teachers' pay and conditions, closures of colleges of education, and the position of fee-paying schools, have unavoidably involved interventions by Ministers and confrontations with interest groups and local authorities. Ministers have also intervened in questions of selection, school organisation, pedagogy, the curriculum, the examination system, and new forms of post-compulsory education and training. Their initiatives in some of these areas have been dramatic because they have upset established expectations that substantive innovation would be controlled by professionals without political 'interference'. Kellas does not include Ministers, or indeed other politicians or laymen, amongst the 'principal policy-makers in Scottish education'. These he enumerates as SED administrators and inspectors, local directors of education, and teachers' organisations (Kellas 1984, 230). From the late 1970s on, however, such a view seems much less tenable than once it was.

In order to assess the importance of Ministers in Scottish educational policy-making, we may look back over forty-five years to consider the extent to which Secretaries of State for Scotland and junior Ministers devoted particular attention to their education remits.[5] Tom Johnston's early reputation as a radical Labour propagandist and MP was superseded by the one he gained as an innovative and energetic administrator during the Second World War. His Secretaryship involved him in a wide set of undertakings concerned with the economic regeneration of Scotland, leaving him little time to pursue his interest in education, or to follow through on his reconstitution of the Advisory Council (Young 1986, ch.5). He wanted curricular change, but he ran up against a conservative Department, a conservative classical lobby, and an educational system in which support for progressive reforms was disaggregated. Johnston himself favoured the idea of teaching citizenship in schools but got nowhere with it (Johnston 1952, 153). He was responsible for a major piece of legislation, the Education Act of 1945, which was the Scottish version of Butler's 1944 Act in England and Wales. He himself seems to have wanted to take education out of local politics, and his preoccupation with the possible restoration of the *ad hoc* local authorities almost lost the legislation. On his resignation, it was Lord Rosebery, Secretary of State in Churchill's brief post-coalition Government of 1945, who saw the 1945 Bill through to the Royal Assent (Lloyd 1979, chs 9 and 10; Gibson 1985, 112)

None of Johnston's successors in the post-war Labour Government was of comparable stature. Then, too, in comparison with Johnston's period, it was not so easy for Scotland's voice to be heard in government. Attlee's programme of social reform was run centrally from Whitehall. Joseph Westwood (1945-47) had been Joint Parliamentary Under-Secretary during Johnston's tenure. He is credited with 'a keen interest in education' (Pottinger 1979, 103), but he put most of his energies into housing, an emphasis which helps to explain the squeeze on educational resources in the late 1940s which we discuss in chapter 9. It was to Westwood that the Advisory Council reported on secondary education, but the SED was in no hurry to give its response. Westwood was succeeded by Arthur Woodburn (1947-50), Johnston's former Parliamentary Private Secretary. Woodburn does not seem to have had any substantial educational involvement (Pottinger 1979, ch.11); nor does his successor, Hector McNeil (1950-51) (*ibid.*, ch.12).

Margaret Herbison, however, was actively engaged in education as McNeil's junior Minister (1950-51). Her concern over the shortage of teachers led to a direct involvement in the origins of the Special Recruitment Scheme (see chapter 10). A former Glasgow teacher who represented Lanarkshire North in Parliament, she was active on the back benches and in the higher councils of the Party in opposing the Labour Government's support for selective secondary schooling. Even while in office under McNeil, she campaigned for school reorganisation along comprehensive lines (Parkinson 1970, ch.5). With Labour in opposition in the mid-1950s, she was one of the champions of an end to selection (see chapter 16).

Unlike Labour Ministers in the Scottish Office, few Conservative Ministers attended local-authority schools, and most were educated in England, so their first-hand knowledge of the details of the Scottish educational system had been limited (Kellas 1984, 43-4). James Stuart (later Viscount Stuart of Findhorn) had a relatively long run in office (1951-57) during the consensual years of which Cunningham spoke (Stuart 1967; Pottinger 1979, ch.13; Seldon 1981, 130-40). He was a weighty figure in Churchill's Cabinet and had an enlarged Ministerial team to whom he delegated functions; James Henderson Stewart had responsibility for education as Joint Parliamentary Under-Secretary (1952-57). Stuart is said to have got on extremely well with Milne, Cunningham and other officials, but education, according to Seldon, 'was not a subject that particularly interested Stuart, and neither did Henderson Stewart make it one of his priorities' (Seldon 1981, 136-9). Stuart's memoirs have nothing to say about the running of education (Stuart 1967). In our interview, however, Graham told us that his impression was that Henderson Stewart and Niall Macpherson (later Lord Drumalbyn) (1955-60) as junior Ministers both took a considerable interest in their education remit. Henderson Stewart, in fact, had served on the Sixth Advisory Council, and later involved himself in the appointment of the Eighth and last Council (see chapter 11; also Young 1986, ch.10). The fact that Henderson Stewart was a National Liberal is said to have distanced him personally and politically from the Conservative Secretary of State (*ibid.*, 134); but Macpherson, too, was a National Liberal. Lady Tweedsmuir (1962-64) was another Conservative junior Minister who had a keen concern for education, perhaps arising from her Aberdeen constituency interests (see chapter 9). Murrie sheds further light on Stuart's period in a way which recalls the view of Cunningham, who was Murrie's colleague:

MURRIE. Reflecting on the years 1952 to 1957, I would regard them as not a period of great innovation, but a period in which we were trying to put into practice, or to get the education authorities to put into practice, new ideas that had been spawned in the late forties. . . . We were trying to digest, assimilate, and disseminate.

Following Stuart, John Maclay (later Viscount Muirshiel) (1957-62) and

Michael Noble (later Lord Glenkinglas) (1962-64) served during the years which saw Brunton consolidating the Inspectorate's position as leaders of educational change. Under Maclay and Noble, planning and regional development became the principal foci of Scottish Office activity (Pottinger 1979, chs 14 and 15; Gibson 1985, chs 5 and 6). But we have no evidence which points to an active Ministerial role in the formation of policy when Brunton was working towards the introduction of the O-grade, refashioning the secondary curriculum, and propounding the idea of the 'vocational impulse'. Although regional planning attempted to develop a strategy for education, all this meant in practice was that the SED's policies were implanted in the wider economic plan.[6]

We asked Murrie:

Q. To what extent did Noble have a policy in education, and was it different from Maclay's?

MURRIE. I don't remember that he had any particular policy that he wanted to push as distinct from Maclay, nor when Maclay succeeded James Stuart do I remember any change of emphasis. . . . [Ministerial initiatives] were comparatively rare in the field of education. . . . One Ministerial initiative I do remember: that was Henderson Stewart's idea that it would be good thing if the EIS and the SSTA could agree to form one union. . . . It was a very political thing and something that a Minister might well think of. . . . It didn't come to anything, but I instance this as a Minister initiating a policy.

Yet it would be surprising if the Secretary of State and the junior Minister were not involved at first hand in the reorganisation of the machinery of policy advice towards the end of the Conservatives' tenure in 1964. This included the suspension of the Advisory Council, the creation of the Examination Board and the emergence of a new curriculum committee (see part IV). However, Ministerial activity did not figure in our interviewees' accounts of these changes, and we have little information about the extent of politicians' contributions to them.

The political pace of education quickened after 1964 when William Ross (later Lord Ross of Marnock) was Labour Secretary of State (1964-70) (Pottinger 1979, ch.16). Ministers became more heavily engaged with educational change. This period included not only the early years of the new advisory machinery but also the run-up to ROSLA in 1972-73. Most important of all, it saw the implementation of comprehensive reorganisation (see chapter 16). These were also the years of 'downward incrementalism', the extension of certification to proportions of pupils far larger than originally envisaged (Gray *et al.*, 1983, ch.4). This extension was not decreed by Ministers, but Millan told us that it had their support (see chapter 13). Ross' close connections with the educational world, and his personal interest as a former teacher, were important factors in the establishment of the General Teaching Council (see chapter 12). Millan told us about Labour Ministerial involvement in policy-formation and implementation, but we are not able to present first-hand accounts of the part played by Ross or by Judith Hart, the junior Minister who dealt with education before Millan (1964-66).

The Conservatives returned to office in 1970. Gordon Campbell (1970-74) (later Lord Campbell of Croy), at one time a civil servant, appears to have seen himself as the Conservative Government's ambassador in Scotland, not as a Secretary of State prone to intervene actively in policy-making (Pottinger 1979, ch.17). The tape-recorded memoir of Campbell's time in office is virtually silent on the subject of education (Campbell of Croy 1978). In 1973 he could do nothing to prevent the decision of Glasgow's Labour administration to abolish selection and fee-paying (see chapter 16). When the Government changed hands in 1974, Ross was back as Secretary of State until 1976, and was followed in that office by Millan. In the later 1970s, the economic downturn and the squeeze on public expenditure made themselves felt in all areas and not least in education. Retrenchments occurred in the education authorities and in the colleges of education, and teachers pressed their interests more vehemently, all against a climate which thrust devolution to the top of the agenda of Scottish politics. The Secretary of State and his Education Minister were in the firing line and could hardly avoid involvement in decisions on substantive, procedural and resource issues.

Only with the return of the Conservatives to power in 1979 was there prominent Conservative leadership in educational affairs, with George Younger (1979-86) and Malcolm Rifkind (from 1986) as Secretary of State and, in succession, Alex Fletcher (1979-83), Allan Stewart (1983-86) and John MacKay (from 1986) as Minister for Education. This period included curriculum and examination changes following the Munn and Dunning reports, the Action Plan for pupils aged sixteen-plus (SED 1983), and the Education (Scotland) Act of 1981 which gave legislative effect in Scotland to the Government's policies for parental choice and for assisted places in fee-paying schools. These were major Ministerial initiatives. But perhaps the most prominent engagement of Ministers themselves in the day-to-day affairs of Scottish education in the mid-1980s was in the prolonged teachers' strike over pay and conditions.

Ministers and Officials

Ministerial influence depends crucially on relationships with officials in the Department. Here is Millan's view:

MILLAN. Any Minister wants to make sure that he is in charge of his Department, and that he isn't being run by civil servants or by anybody else. That I think is a very important role of the Minister. Not necessarily to get involved in all the detail . . . but certainly to see that the main lines of policy that are being followed are his, and his party's, and his Government's, and that the permanent establishment, as it were, isn't running the show the whole time.

Millan's words hint that it might be difficult for a Scottish Office Minister to retain political control of the 'show'. If so, the problem stems not only from the general circumstances of Ministerial office, but also from the conditions under which Ministers hold Scottish posts. As elsewhere in British government, Scottish Office Ministers come and go, whilst the civil service is permanent. A century's worth of Scottish Secretaries came and went in relatively rapid order: up to 1985 thirty-two persons had held the office (of whom three held it more than once), as against fourteen Permanent Secretaries and only eleven SED Secretaries. Whilst the disproportion was slightly less from 1940 onward, Scottish Ministers were still relatively transient. Kellas observes that 'Scottish Office duties are of course considerable, and an extended stay in the office may be almost essential if a Scottish Secretary is to become more than the tool of his civil servants' (Kellas 1984, 42). Ross had long experience, spread over two periods of office, and more recently, Younger's tenure made him the longest serving Scottish Secretary since Lord Balfour of Burleigh (1895-1903).

What is probably a more significant difficulty than transience is the division of the Secretary of State's attention amongst the several functions for which he is responsible. The Secretary of State at the DES has overall charge of only one function, and has several junior Ministers to look after its different sectors. By contrast, the Secretary of State for Scotland has a very wide brief of which education is only one part. He must generally defend and promote Scottish interests in Cabinet. In addition, he is responsible within Scotland for agriculture and fishing, transport and housing, law and order, and health. Economic and industrial development have become increasingly important parts of his role since the 1960s. The Ministerial team he leads expanded from the 1950s on, and now consists of at least one Minister of State and several junior Ministers. They are more specialised, but even they double up on functional responsibilities and may not be particularly interested in education. For many years, health and education were paired, but from 1979 to 1986 industry and education were in one Minister's charge, reflecting changed conceptions of policy relationships (Keating 1976; Ross 1978; Ross 1981; Keating and Midwinter 1983, ch.2; Kellas 1984, ch.3).

A third circumstance is geographical, and has affected the formality of contacts between officials and Ministers, as Murrie explained:

MURRIE. Because Ministers in the Scottish Office have to be in London most of the time, and most of the staff is in Edinburgh, we tended, in all Departments, to work through submissions. . . . You wrote a two-page memorandum saying, 'This is the point, you can do this and that, we would advise you to do this. And may we have your decision?'. '. . . The Minister might bring it back on Friday and say, 'I want to discuss this with someone in the Office'.

Q. Was this not a slightly inconvenient arrangement? Martin Fearn [SED Secretary 1973-76] suggested that it meant that the civil servants had to commit things formally to paper rather prematurely, because they couldn't just go down the corridor and speak informally with the Minister at an early stage in their thinking [*SEJ* 28 October 1976].

MURRIE. I always thought that it was a good arrangement, because it made you think about things and clear your mind before you went to the Minister.

Graham felt that communications between London and Edinburgh were very good, but Millan and Dickson took a different view:

MILLAN. It is much easier for English Ministers who can ring a bell and say, 'I want someone to come along and see me in five minutes'. You can't do that when they are four hundred miles away. . . . Inevitably, because of the set-up in the Office, unfortunately an awful lot of things are done on paper. I think that we probably had less discussion than we ought to.

DICKSON. The real difficulty about discussions with Ministers was that of getting hold of the Minister; he was up here only once a week and he had other departments besides SED to deal with. It was sometimes therefore very difficult to get hold of him for as much as five minutes. But he was always very approachable.

Q. Do you feel that he could have dealt with more?

DICKSON. Oh indeed yes, given the time. One used to feel the advantage which the DES people had, in that their Minister was in their building practically every day, and they could see him much more easily and more informally.

The details of what civil servants say to Ministers are virtually a closed book, and it is not possible to convey more than an impression of Departmental discussions with Ministers. But the interviews do provide useful indications of the nature and tone of these exchanges and of the opportunities for administrators and inspectors to contribute to decision-making. Brunton described his dealings with Ministers when he was an Assistant Secretary:

BRUNTON. We had at one time a Parliamentary Under-Secretary who could be troublesome from a civil servant's point of view. Whenever he saw a newspaper article relating to any aspect of education he immediately sent down and asked for an explanation. The normal civil service practice was to write a memorandum in reply, but this resulted as often as not in a lengthy exchange of papers with the Minister. But I found that if one gave the Minister a face-to-face explanation – a five-minute conversation – the Minister was in most cases perfectly satisfied. One could go and discuss educational questions with Ministers and satisfy them without over-much bother. I found it quite possible to convince them of the validity of proposals for change and development by parading the facts and advancing cogent arguments. In the great majority of cases decisions were taken on the educational merits of the case in question. Nowadays I have the impression that policies are all too often laid down by Ministers, and the schools are left to fit their practices and procedures to the policies without sufficient regard to the educational considerations.

Rodger discussed his role under three Secretaries and commented upon the way they dealt with Ministers:

Q. What scope did you have as an Assistant Secretary to influence the Minister?

R ODGER. I had quite a lot of scope to try, because Mackay Thomson was the Secretary till 1952 and he gave me a very free hand. . . . In [his] day, I would not have hesitated to put a minute direct to the Minister . . . I could rely on [Mackay Thomson's] support, but, really he had very little real interest in building. And when he was in office, I did all the speaking and all the writing. . . . Mackay Thomson, whatever his faults, was quite strong in a matter that interested him, but in most cases he was prepared to let the Assistant Secretary do the talking and then let the Minister decide as he pleased, and leave the Assistant Secretary to carry out the Minister's wishes. Arbuckle was definitely strong; he was prepared to argue his point of view against a Minister's obvious inclination. . . . If he was to see a Minister, he had a short preliminary discussion with the Under-Secretary and the Assistant Secretary concerned, and he made up his mind the line to take. He stuck firmly, very firmly, to that line when he saw the Minister but, if in the end he was overruled, then, as a good civil servant, he did as the Minister wished. . . . It was only after Murrie came that I was relegated, so to speak, to the position of Assistant Secretary. . . . I would not have thought of [putting a minute] except through Murrie. When the Minister had found time to consider a submission, he would probably phone down for somebody who knew all the facts. . . . The subordinate officer was not under any need to refrain from speaking, just because Murrie happened to be there. . . . If I had a point of view to express to the Minister when Murrie, the Minister and I were all together, I was perfectly free to do it. Knowing the man, I found it surprising that Murrie was not strong with Ministers.

Were inspectors similarly able to put their views to the Minister? We have seen that Brunton was able to shape important areas of policy as Senior Chief Inspector. He claimed to have been able to satisfy the Minister in a five-minute conversation, but also complained about political direction of policy in more recent times. We asked Dickson, his successor as Senior Chief Inspector, about his own relations with the junior Minister in charge of education:

Q. How often would you have seen Millan face-to-face?

D ICKSON. A great deal depends on what's going on at the time. I would have thought five or six times a year at least.

Q. What sorts of issues would you have taken him?

D ICKSON. Well, the development of comprehensive education . . . how

it was moving, how it wasn't moving, relations with particular authorities.
. . . You would discuss with him, of course, any operation in which you
would be willing to set up a working party. You would even discuss with him
the formation of the working party. . . . Towards the end of my time with Mr
Millan, there were no difficulties at all about approaching him informally
and unofficially. . . . It was seldom, I think, that he took the initiative [to see
me]; normally the movement would come from me. He had an awful lot to
do and he was never looking for something to fill in his time with!

Millan said that his views did not coincide with Dickson's about everything. In chapter 16 we look in greater depth at the comprehensive reorganisation of secondary education following Circular 600 in 1965. But Colin
MacLean's comment on the role of the Inspectorate in comprehensive
reorganisation hints at an estrangement between Millan and his inspectors:

> Here the inspectors, somewhat puzzled gauleiters, were enforcing not
> an Act but a mere circular, not the letter of the circular so much as its
> spirit. Neither they nor the profession in Scotland had contributed in a
> formal or definable way to the thinking behind the policy. On the other
> side of Mr Graham and his civil servants were politicians at St Andrew's
> House who had themselves given virtually no thought to this national
> policy. It was in no way an identifiably Scottish policy. (MacLean
> 1976b)

Millan, on the other hand, asserted that there was a broad agreement on
this particular issue in Scotland from which the Inspectorate did not dissent,
and he went on to comment upon the ambivalent position that inspectors
held as both professional experts and dutiful civil servants:

MILLAN. I didn't have any great disputes with the inspectors about, for
example, comprehensive reorganisation. . . . Their view on this was
basically the same as the directors', and the education committees', and the
general public. . . . But they also knew my view which was that, while I
wanted that to be done, and as rapidly as possible, I was not asking people
to do things which were educationally impossible . . . [or] which they found
professionally objectionable. . . . Now, on the other hand, I think that one
of the problems can be that, since inspectors, like administrative civil
servants, are civil servants who are meant to carry out what the government's policy is, you can sometimes get government policy carried out too
enthusiastically rather than not enthusiastically enough. . . . It is up to the
politicians to say that this is what we think ought to happen in these
particular fields where professional expertise is obviously absolutely
essential, and it is up to the professionals to say that it is good or bad, or 'it
can be done' or 'it cannot be done', or 'this is what our view is'. I think that
there should be a frank exchange of views, but I don't think that it is then
for the politicians to encourage the Inspectorate to go so enthusiastically for
something that they lose their own professional balance on the matter. I
think that may not always be the politicians' fault. I mean there is a tendency

to say, 'Well, this is what the policy is and we must see that it is implemented'.

Millan argued that it was important for the Minister to involve inspectors
in policy discussions and not rely solely on administrators as the channel for
Departmental advice, a channel which the formality of 'submissions' reinforced.[7] He offered a general view of the role of professionals in the policy
process, and of the boundary between their sphere of competence and that
of the 'lay' Minister:

MILLAN. The administrators are involved all the time. The bits of paper
come basically from the administrators, rather than from the Inspectorate.
In other words, there are not many papers that come straight to the Minister
that are signed by the Senior Chief Inspector . . . so you have to make an
effort to bring the Inspectorate in . . . to argue the thing out with a lot of
people, and not just to accept what is on the bit of paper . . . I think that it
is up to [the Minister] to see that the advice that he is getting does genuinely
represent a consensus of view within his own Office. . . . You see, there is a
tendency for arguments within the Office to be sorted out before anything is
presented to the Minister, and then he gets a piece of advice which looks as
if it's unanimous, but there have usually been all sorts of arguments going
on beforehand. You can't avoid that completely. . . . But I think certainly it
is sensible to involve the Inspectorate as the professional side of the
Department as well as the administrators. Quite often there is a tendency
for the administrators to take over completely. I like to think that I involved
the Inspectorate more, in the discussions with Ministers. . . . On things that
were genuinely educational, as distinct from strictly administrative, I tried
to make sure that the Inspectorate was present, and that I was getting their
view. . . . The Inspectorate obviously have a professional view, and that is
what they are there for . . . and I think that if you as politicians or administrators are doing things which they professionally think are bad or disastrous, they ought to tell you that, and they shouldn't just go along with what
you want them to do because that happens to be your political standpoint.
. . . I am talking strictly professionally now; I am not talking about matters
like whether it's good to have, say, an assisted-places scheme which the
present Government is doing. Supposing the Inspectorate took the view
that it was highly undesirable. All right, that's very much a political kind of
decision but it has an impact on what happens in the schools, and I think in
that case that, if the Inspectorate are against it, then they should say to the
Ministers that they think that this is undesirable, and, if the Ministers still
say this is what we want to do, then they should implement the policy. . . . I
don't accept the view that you should just listen to the professionals and
that's it finished. I mean you are as well not being there then. They have got
a role, and you have got a role. There are political issues, and strictly
educational issues, and as a Minister you shouldn't pretend that you are an
educationist in the professional sense, because you are not. If you are any

167

good as a Minister, you will know something about education at the end of the day, but you are not a professional teacher. You have to listen to advice, and if you are constantly getting into rows or disagreements . . . with your professional people, I think that that is very unhealthy.

Millan's comments suggest that, with the inclusion of professional educationists in deliberations, the Minister-civil servant relation was a somewhat complicated *ménage à trois*. The mutual accommodation of administrators and professionals was a matter in which the Minister and his political priorities played an important part. Millan felt he had to support inspectors as a counterweight to the tendency towards administrative predominance, yet not go so far as to leave the initiative in the professionals' hands. The pattern of mutual influence depended as much, or more, on the variable ways in which administrators, inspectors and Ministers performed their roles as it did on the institutional structures which set the stage on which they performed.

Parliament and Education

However skilled they were in handling relationships within the Department, Ministers' political reputations depended more upon their performance in Parliament. There, too, they received the support of their officials as they faced challenges from the Opposition, and sometimes from their own backbenchers. Relatively little Scottish parliamentary business is dealt with on the floor of the House of Commons. The bulk of it is handled in committees, of which the Scottish Grand Committee is the most prominent. It has gained a reputation as 'the place where the elected representatives of the Scots meet and speak together . . . a forum for the debating of government policy' (Edwards 1972, 322 and 325). The Committee is the main setting for debates of several kinds: on bills, on various topics called 'matters', on the estimates, and on committee reports. Was it an effective forum, and did MPs get close to the mark? Here is Rodger's description:

RODGER. Now, there was one big annual parliamentary occasion, as far as Scotland was concerned, and this was the . . . Scottish Estimates Debate. . . . The Department normally sent down a team a day or two before the debate. . . . We were really briefing Ministers and making and modifying their speeches, if the Ministers sought changes. Then we were present at the debate. . . . During my period of office, I was always there, because . . . right up to the time of my retiral . . . the two most important subjects discussed were building and shortage of teachers, both of which were within my province. Both were resource questions, and both had chronic shortages. The papers were always full of stories about groups of children in such and such a place with no school for them to go to, or with no teachers to teach them. These were the sorts of things, you see, that the newspapers were good at getting hold of.

But Rodger thought the Estimates debates were, 'on the whole, desperately poor; the dreariest things that you could imagine'. He said that fewer than half the Scottish M Ps turned up, and that some only went through the motions of participating in order to please their constituents, who expected their Member to air local difficulties. The illustration Rodger gave touches on the problem of building, which we discuss in its own right in chapter 9:

RODGER. [The EIS] were briefing [their] parliamentary spokesman, and so to that extent, there was one person anyway, who was going to be able to speak with some knowledge – speaking, of course, from a particular point of view. . . . Most of the other speakers who spoke at all, had probably come with a brief from their locality; although they may have spoken in more general terms, their real purpose was to air some difficulty in their own locality. Often enough, they had been briefed by their director of education. This local briefing arose more commonly in Glasgow than anywhere else: we knew that Stewart Mackintosh of Glasgow [Director of Education 1944-68] briefed Glasgow M Ps who were in opposition, to raise questions. It might be that Glasgow wasn't getting enough steel to build their buildings; the M P would then raise the difficulties about materials and then talk about these in general.

Rodger went on to describe how debates were sometimes stage-managed:

RODGER. All of us who were in the official box made notes on the points within our field that were made by the M Ps, and, as they made them, we all wrote little chits which gave the Minister . . . a reply to the point made. . . . In his winding-up speech, he tried to cover as many as possible of the points that had been raised, giving the answers that we had provided. In some few cases he would say – as we had openly put it to him to say – 'This is a subject we shall look into; and I shall write to you later'. . . . Now this may amuse you: I have been approached in the official box, by a member of the Opposition saying, 'Now you know all about this; we know damn all about this. Would you give me headings for a speech to make, criticising things where you think the Government could properly be criticised? Of course, I know you'll give me things where you feel you've got the answer.' And I would scribble out a few things, and this chap would stand up for about twelve minutes and make a speech on these, and even before he had made his speech, I had given the answers to the Minister. . . . If it is a county like Fife, which is interested in education and where the public have been taught to be interested in education, well, a Fife M P will probably feel that to maintain his own prestige in his own area, he has got to show an interest in education. He knows damn all about it, so he comes to me, asks me what he can say, knowing quite well that I will only tell him things about which I can give a jolly good answer. . . . Now that happened not once or twice, but a number of times. This shows how artificial the debates were.

Rodger was just as disparaging about Members' performance at Question Time as he was about the quality of debates. Question Time is a ritual which is not suited to probing policy in depth. Scottish members could confront the

Secretary of State only infrequently, and their chances of getting oral answers on educational topics were relatively poor because of the breadth of his responsibilities. Parliamentary Questions were fed into the bureaucratic machine where officials spent a great deal of time providing answers. Rodger said that 'PQS' numbered anywhere from five to fifty in a week, but that many were misconceived:

RODGER. One of our problems was that when asked a silly question, did you give a silly answer relevant to the question? Or did you answer the question which you thought that he meant to ask? Now, strictly we were always told to answer the question that we were asked, but I have tried, at times, to work in – provided that I wasn't becoming too loquacious – something which gave some of the real answer, as well as the strict (unhelpful) answer to the stupid question. . . . We knew the kinds of things that the teachers and the authorities were talking about. The question had a bearing on the current topic, but the chap who was asking the question obviously didn't understand really what it was all about, and so he asked the kind of daft thing that had only the appearance of being connected with the real issue. He wasn't really asking the guts and substance of the thing at all.

Whereas local councillors, with the help of their directors of education, have sometimes been able to consider fundamental issues of educational policy (see chapter 15), the occasions on which MPs could do so have been few, and even these have not always been adequately exploited.[8] Scottish MPs have suffered from especially heavy workloads, much of the work being done on bills (Burns 1960; Edwards 1972; Keating 1975). Millan agreed that there was not enough time available for debating educational issues, but he did not think that education was especially disadvantaged in that respect. He doubted that debates were useful:

MILLAN. Members of Parliament like to discuss and debate issues which are currently controversial rather than debating the long-term future of the education system. I am not sure that you get very good debates, unless the debates are about fairly concrete issues like trying to close colleges of education, for example. So there aren't enough general debates, and they tend . . . to be . . . on fairly strict party lines, although in fact there is a whole element of educational policy which doesn't actually divide on party lines. . . . But you are not going to get debates about, say, the development of the comprehensive system that are going to be directly terribly helpful to the Minister. That sounds rather disparaging, but I think parliamentary debate in education has not played – whether we like it or not – a tremendous influence, I think, either south or north of the Border.

Our evidence so far suggests that MPs made little positive contribution to educational policy. Yet, from 1945 to 1983, an increasing number of them had been directly involved in education. In that period, the proportion of the seventy-one Scottish MPs who had been in teaching or in related educational occupations grew from roughly one in fourteen to one in seven. The proportion of Scottish parliamentary candidates with these backgrounds rose even more steeply, from roughly one in eighteen to more than one in five, with heavy concentrations amongst the Labour and Scottish National parties (*The Times* 1945 to 1983).

Rodger concluded that only about one-third of Scottish M Ps were 'actively interested' in education, or were capable of making an informed contribution in Parliament on educational issues of wider significance. Rodger is not alone in arguing the impotence of parliamentary deliberation. Another view, however, is that M Ps play an effective part by concerning themselves with the local implementation of national policies, and by taking up local and pressure-group demands in Parliament. On this view, the contribution of M Ps should not be judged solely by the quality of debates. Rather, Parliament supplies the Member with the authority to amplify demands. But the arbitration of issues thus placed on the agenda takes place elsewhere, in the case of Scottish education mostly through consultations some four-hundred miles to the north (see chapter 19). On this second view, pressure groups play a major part in bringing matters to the attention of M Ps. The E I S, for example, has long maintained close links with Parliament. From 1959 to 1975, the Institute retained several M Ps across the party spectrum as paid parliamentary advisers. Since then, its liaison has been carried on informally (Belford 1946, 204-5 and 409 ; E I S 1975).

On neither of these views does Parliament make policies. But it can, sometimes deflect them. Rodger described the potential danger to Ministers :

R O D G E R. They know jolly well that if they displease any important group, whether teachers or local authorities in general, or a large and influential local authority like Glasgow, the aggrieved group will get hold of some Opposition M P who will make things hot for the Minister in the House ; therefore, rather than encourage his opponents to get talking points, a Minister is trying, nearly all the time, to please.

The raised political temperature of education since the mid-1960s may have made it harder for Ministers to placate interest groups and constituents. Members of Parliament could be useful allies in the skirmishes that outsiders had with government. One illustration of this is Millan's attempt to close colleges of education. Millan's proposal in 1977 triggered a dramatic campaign by the colleges, who used the media, public demonstrations and M Ps to good effect. The influence of pressure-groups, the Catholic Church, and parliamentary constituencies overcame the party loyalty of some Labour M Ps. They joined with the Opposition to win a reprieve for the colleges by forcing the Government's defeat in an adjournment debate on the floor of the House (Cope 1978). This was a notable achievement which embarrassed the Government and affected its plans for teacher education. But that was all. The setback was only temporary. The victory in Parliament was not carried through to a successful conclusion outside, for colleges were eventually closed. Although the campaign illustrates the success of extra-parliamentary pressure at a time when the Government did not have a secure majority, it does not testify to a sustained parliamentary capacity to make policies.

Kogan's view of the effectiveness of English M PS runs parallel to this. He argues that their impact on educational policy in the 1960s and 1970s was not clearly discernible, and was probably weak. Questions and debates kept officials and Ministers on their toes, and thus exerted a general pressure on the DES. Whilst this contribution was important, M PS gravitated towards matters concerning resources and constituency problems, and eschewed systematic enquiry into the larger, national issues (Kogan 1975, ch.9; Kogan 1978, 140-6):

> Parliament at most reviews, criticises and helps to aggregate and articu-late feelings about policy. Essentially it reacts to, rather than initiates, policy. So far, indeed, are M PS from decision-making, that it is uncertain whether they have even enough authority to review and criticise effec-tively. (Kogan 1975, 25)

Some have looked to the Select Committee system to reinforce Parlia-ment's ability to review and criticise the actions of the Executive. Select Committee investigations enable M PS to look more deeply into policy and administration by questioning civil servants and, more recently, Ministers. But committees only cover small patches of ground, have limited powers and staff support, and have often found their recommendations brushed aside or lost to public view. However, committee investigations do assist parliamentary scrutiny and have thrown light on several areas of English education and its governance. Scottish education, on the other hand, has been less well served in this way. For example, there was no Scottish counterpart to the critical and widely publicised report of the Expenditure Committee in 1976 on policy-making in the DES (SC on Expenditure 1976).

A new departure was made in Parliament in 1979 with the creation of a large number of departmentally related Select Committees. It is debatable whether these have helped backbenchers to influence policy. What is evi-dent, however, is the discrepancy between the way English and Scottish M PS have dealt with the respective Education Departments. From 1979 to 1983, the new Committee on Education, Science and the Arts produced nineteen reports on education in England and Wales. These included a major investi-gation of curriculum and examinations for the fourteen- to nineteen-year-olds, which was terminated only by the dissolution of Parliament. The remit of the new Scottish Affairs Committee, however, covered all the work of the Scottish Office, and therefore precluded concentrated scrutiny of any one function. It published eight reports, of which only one, on youth unemploy-ment and training, bore upon education (Lightfoot 1983; Englefield 1984; Drucker and Kellas 1985; Rush 1985).[9]

Discussion

We have no basis for arguing that national politicians have been less effective in education than in other areas of policy. Nevertheless, sustained deliberation over the content of education in Scotland has not been a feature of its party politics. For a time, the post-war consensus kept education out of politics. Although this changed, political differences in education were, for the most part, much less important than those in other fields. The role of MPs as vehicles for local and group interests cannot be wholly discounted. However, our evidence for education does not contradict the view of other commentators, that Parliament is generally in a weak position to control and scrutinise the Executive and to contribute substantially to the formulation of policy. The unsuitability of Parliament as an arena for discussing educational topics in any depth was sometimes used as an argument for an Advisory Council (see chapter 11). But, by the 1960s, the Council route was closed, leaving Scotland virtually bereft of public national fora for educational debate.

One view of this might be that national politicians played no part because there was no central part to play; that the reality of the system was that of dispersed pluralism. However, our conclusion is that such a part was indeed played by central government, both British and Scottish, in that it made crucial decisions that shaped the educational system as a whole. But, in the main, the central roles were not played by national politicians in the thirty years after 1945. The structures and processes of government made it difficult for them to be effective on substantive educational policy, even when their personal or political interests propelled them towards education.

For a long period, the initiative in policy-making lay mainly within the policy community of officials and educationists that linked government with society, and from which Ministers and politicians were for the most part excluded. The assumptions shared by those who were administratively or professionally concerned with education enabled them to resist or mould political inputs. However, government and Parliament exercised formal authority, and this was not a negligible resource. Ministers could, on occasion, override the established Departmental policy, whilst political currents affected both the national agenda of educational and social issues, and the status of policy alternatives that have pressed for entry into the decision-making arenas. These currents flowed swiftly in the 1960s, and became turbulent in the 1980s. But, whilst Ministers were prominent as policy-makers at times of heightened political controversy over education, neither they, nor the system of parliamentary politics, successfully countered 'administrative primacy' in the central governance of Scottish education. The Department guarded the gateways to the formal process of decision-making, and exercised a powerful influence over the informal channels through which initiatives were taken. It also influenced the structures and the composition of the policy community. Through these controls, and through the deference which the Department thereby commanded, it resisted political challenges, though it did not always defeat them (see chapters 16-19).

The former Conservative Secretary of State, Gordon Campbell, did not believe that Scottish Office officials misused their power or behaved more bureaucratically than those in Whitehall. But he, too, thought that 'an aggrieved farmer in Scotland or a parent or teacher with a problem could be excused if he felt that he could only deal with a faceless bureaucrat in the Department . . . in Edinburgh and that it was a long way round to require an MP at Westminster to pursue the matter' (Campbell of Croy 1978). 'Faceless bureaucracy' and physical remoteness were, of course, two of the main antagonists to the political control of affairs within its own borders which the devolutionists of the 1970s and the 1980s wished to restore to Scotland. It was argued that an elected Assembly in Edinburgh could make a difference. Perched on the doorstep of the officials in St Andrew's House, it would be armed with powers and resources, surrounded by attentive media, and supported by an interested yet critical public. It was thought that, in this way, the actions of the Executive would have been more effectively scrutinised, and the political control of policy facilitated, though not guaranteed.

The attention that Parliament has always paid to resource questions is not misplaced. In registering their concern about many of the abiding problems of educational provision, Members have responded to the expectations that constituents and interest groups, not least the teachers and local authorities, have had of them. But this has had only a general influence upon policy and practice, given a distribution of power in education which has placed a great deal outside the direct control of central government, and in the hands of the local education authorities. The engine rooms for educational policy at central and local levels were staffed by officials, and fuelled by resources provided through the United Kingdom political system. What light does the process of providing resources shed upon the governance of education and the formation of policy? These are the main questions to which we turn in chapters 9 and 10.

NOTES
1. Allen identifies six main features of the governance of Scotland: centralisation, administrative primacy, exclusiveness, secrecy, corporatism, and authoritarianism. He writes: 'the highly centralised nature of the administration itself and the overwhelming importance in Scottish government of administrative action produce what we may call a "bureaucratic illusion": that politics in Scotland is, and hence its study should be, all about administration' (Allen 1979, 27).
2. A plan for the post-war years had been produced by the Labour Party in Scotland in 1941. It dealt mainly with industrial location and development, but

also pronounced on education. It called for a 'new educational outlook' to sweep away the hierarchical 'class idea of education' in which able or affluent children could rise through elementary, secondary and university levels. It wanted secondary education to be made general between the ages of twelve and fifteen, and a number of vocational 'universities' to be founded (LPSC 1941).

3. Kennedy (1976) promised an education paper for a subsequent volume. However, it never appeared.

4. These include Sir David (later Lord) Eccles (1954-57; 1959-62), Sir Edward (later Lord) Boyle (1962-64), Anthony Crosland (1965-67), Margaret Thatcher (1970-74), Shirley Williams (1976-79), Sir Keith Joseph (1981-86) and Kenneth Baker (from 1986). See Boyle and Crosland (1971), Kogan (1975, 1978).

5. We use the undifferentiated term 'Minister' generically to refer to the Secretary of State, to the Minister of State, to the Joint Parliamentary Under-Secretaries of State who had Departmental responsibilities, and to the functional Ministers whose titles replaced that of Joint Parliamentary Under-Secretary in 1979. Alternatively, we use the term 'junior Minister' to refer to all but the first.

6. The most influential thinking in the early 1960s on regional development was done in the Toothill report, produced by the Scottish Council (Development and Industry) in 1961 with the support of the Scottish Office (SC(DI) 1961; McCrone 1969, 1985). Toothill devoted a chapter to education, endorsing educational developments that were underway, including the O-grade and new syllabuses in science and mathematics (SC(DI) 1961, ch.16). It argued for a 'stronger vocational bias' in junior-secondaries (*ibid.*, para.16.08), for more technical education; and for closer contact between education and industry.

7. In his study of policy-making in housing, planning and transport, Eric Gillett, Secretary of the SDD from 1976 to 1980, observes that Bruce Millan as Secretary of State 'was not a Minister likely to be driven where he did not want to go or to be overwhelmed by the amount of detailed evidence put to him by his officials' (Gillett 1983, 56).

8. Keating shows how MPs wasted the chance of a wide-ranging debate in 1973 during the passage of the bill that reorganised local government. This legislation established Regional Councils with education as a main function. The committee stage 'provided an opportunity for a thorough debate on the organisation of Scottish education under the new local government system, an opportunity lost. Returning from their Easter recess, the Opposition allowed themselves to be tripped up by a piece of procedure involving the grouping of amendments and so lost the chance of debating a substantial series of amendments, including a new schedule, which the government had tabled. The rest of the sitting was then spent discussing the question of religious representation on the new education authorities, a debate which, for all the two and a half hours spent on it, satisfied no one' (Keating 1975, 161).

9. In 1980-81, the Committee also published evidence taken on the closure of colleges of education, but did not produce a report. The Committee's predecessor, the Select Committee on Scottish Affairs (SCSA) of 1969-72, had been established by a Labour Government as a sop to reemergent nationalism. During its brief life, it looked only into economic planning and land resources, although it considered the question of industrial training in relation to the former, and took evidence from the SED for its report (SCSA 1970a, 1970b; Kellas 1984, 88).

Nine

Finance, Buildings
and Central-Local Relations

There is still a disquieting tendency in the Scottish educational
world to look to the Department to take the initiative in far too
many things. . . . It is really remarkable that people should expect
so little to come from the periphery and so much from the centre.
Sir Norman Graham, Secretary of the SED 1964-73[1]

Introduction

Our discussion so far has omitted any consideration of how resources for
education are acquired and distributed. However, Sir Norman Graham told
us that these were the questions that had occupied most of his time as
Secretary:

GRAHAM. Teachers, buildings, money, auxiliaries. . . . In the late sixties
we produced a whole new memorandum of guidance on accounting and
financial procedures for all the great number of bodies that we financed;
central institutions, colleges of education, approved schools, the lot. But a
great deal of time was spent on the size of the building programme, how it
should be allocated, where the emphasis should be; and, of course, I think
the major problem would always be the demand and supply problems of
teachers.

Likewise, Sir William Pile, Permanent Secretary of the DES from 1970 to
1976, noted the 'growing recognition' in his Department of the essential
function of resource planning: formulating objectives, framing national
policies to meet them, providing long-term costings to aid Ministerial
choice, and presenting the resource needs within central government (Pile
1979, 59).

This chapter and the next focus attention upon procedures for financing
current and capital expenditure and upon the supply, payment and distribution of teachers. Our main purpose in doing this is to illustrate the relationships among central levels of the system in St Andrew's House and
Whitehall, and between central government and the local authorities who
ultimately spent the money, erected the buildings, and employed the
teachers. We also highlight some of the changes in these relationships
insofar as they reflected impulses towards, or away from, centralised governance. The revision of existing procedures raised questions about differentials between Scotland and England, about the share-out of public expendi-

ture between education and other claimants, and about deeply rooted inequalities of educational provision across Scotland. In addition, educational expansion and economic difficulty exposed the way local authorities used resources, and gave the Department a greater incentive to take the lead in promoting efficiency and effectiveness.

In this chapter we discuss, first, the provision of finance for Scottish education from central sources. To do this we consider the Goschen formula that lasted until 1958 as the principal determinant of the Scottish education grant for current expenditure. (Teachers' salaries were always the largest single item of current expenditure, and these are treated separately, in chapter 10.) Our discussion of the circumstances of Goschen's demise brings in the local level as well. We explain changes in the method of distributing central finance, and look at the question of resource differentials between education authorities. Aberdeen and Lanarkshire stood at opposite ends of the continuum, and we draw upon our interviews with their former directors of education here and elsewhere in the chapter. We then touch on the Whitehall and Scottish Office environments within which the Department has acted in the years since Goschen to secure education's share of public expenditure.

Next we consider capital expenditure. Particularly in periods of educational expansion, a main focus of the SED's dealings with the Treasury and within the Scottish Office was the programme for new and improved schools. This set the overall limit for Departmental authorisations of local authorities' proposals. Because capital investment played a central role in national economic regulation, Treasury policy exerted a powerful influence over the total size of the school-building programme. Especially in periods of severe expenditure restraint, capital programmes were more vulnerable than current spending. Macro-economic factors and financial decisions taken in arenas far removed from Scottish education therefore constrained the implementation of educational policies. So, too, did scarcities of labour and materials, and political decisions about their allocation amongst competing demands. The changing size and location of the school-age population generated new patterns of demand for education which posed expensive problems in adapting an antiquated stock of schools. Authorities in the urbanised western and central parts of Scotland often found themselves in particular difficulties in this respect, and there were persistent inequalities between local education authorities. We concentrate particularly upon the interdependence of central and local government in the building of new schools. The SED aimed to improve local performance in the provision of accommodation, and across a broader front as well. But any renegotiation of relationships with the local authorities posed the question of how far the centre could relinquish control whilst still retaining the capacity for influence over the system as a whole. Our concluding discussion considers the implications of this issue for the themes of centralisation and partnership.

The Goschen Formula

For many years, Ministers did not have to argue their case with the Treasury in order to obtain most of Scotland's share of central-government grants for education. After 1918, the Goschen formula had annually and automatically given Scotland eleven-eightieths of the amount by which the annual grant for England and Wales exceeded the grant that had been given in 1913-14. The Goschen settlement was based on a proportion which had sometimes been used after 1888 to reckon the amounts of various Treasury grants for Ireland, for Scotland, and for England and Wales. The most important application of Goschen over the forty-year period to 1958 was to fix the aggregate main education grant for Scotland. It was sometimes argued that Scotland's educational development was held back by the financial tie to a South that was less ambitious to improve its public education system, and whose educational provision was cheaper. Pottinger notes that the Secretary of State in 1932, Sir Archibald Sinclair (later Viscount Thurso), had alarmed the SED when he asked whether Scotland might not do better with a needs-based grant (Pottinger 1979, 50). For Goschen was a quiet way of doing well without begging too many questions. The proportion approximated the countries' population proportions as they had been when it was originally determined.[2] But the population ratio had steadily declined below the Goschen ratio from early this century onward (Halsey 1972, table 2.1), and Scotland would have got less had the formula been adjusted accordingly. Murrie described the Department's view:

MURRIE. The system [Goschen] went on, illogical though it seemed to many of us, because in fact it paid. If you had instituted a system under which the needs of Scotland were each individually assessed and money provided for them, we should probably have had less money (at least that is what people thought) than by getting the Goschen proportion of the Ministry [of Education]'s expenditure.

The advantage was to some extent offset by a Scottish school population that was proportionately larger than that in the South. However, this difference was diminishing. The maintained-school population of Scotland in the early 1960s was only about three per cent higher than it had been in 1920, whereas that of England and Wales had grown by twenty per cent (Vaizey and Sheehan 1968, 100), a reflection of how far behind Scotland England had been in the inter-war period. The great expansion of secondary education in the South after the Second World War was disproportionately beneficial to Scottish educational finances, certainly until 1958 and possibly thereafter as well. However, some people regarded this benefit as no more than a partial compensation for an earlier Scottish expansion that had not been adequately funded at the time.

The aggregate Goschen share came to the SED. Rodger described the mechanics of its disbursement amongst the education authorities:

RODGER. Now, having got the eleven-eightieths as a grand-total sum, it was then left to us to distribute it as we cared. The allocation as between one branch of Scottish education – let us say salaries, which was the biggest piece of spending, maintenance of schools, purchase of . . . books, all of that kind of thing – the allocations as between one subject and another were really left to the Department. When I say 'to us', I should really say that we were usually acting in conformity with the authorities' desires, for they were putting in detailed estimates, and we were summing these up for Scotland; and, if the sum total for the teachers' salaries was a, and the sum total for some other thing was b, then it seemed to us that a to b was a ratio which would come out of our total sum. . . . The grant for equipment for the school-meals service was fixed at 100 per cent, whereas most other branches of educational work attracted grants at the rate of about sixty per cent. . . . Each [local authority] got a proportion of the global sum . . . [depending] upon a somewhat complex formula. Obviously one of the main factors in the formula was population. But that was not the only factor, because to have, as in Glasgow, your average school of 1000 or more, involved one kind of expenditure; and in Sutherland, where the average school has ten to twenty pupils, there was a different kind of expenditure, as, quite obviously, your proportion of teachers to pupils might be quite different. Therefore there had to be a different formula for extremely rural areas, from what there was in the towns and cities.

Q. Would you then tell the authority: 'This is your overall share of the global amount; and within it, so much will be salaries'?

RODGER. No. They were very largely left free to determine, in accordance with their estimates, how they would divide this money between this, that and the other thing. . . . They could then shift between categories within education, but they couldn't raid education in favour of health.

Q. But after 1958 they could.

RODGER. After that, yes.

The General Grant to Local Authorities

Rodger supposed that it was a Ministry of Education official, David Nenk (Under-Secretary 1955-60), who influenced the Treasury against Goschen. However, the formula was a casualty of a reform that had much wider objectives than that of ending the special financial arrangements for Scottish education. Rhodes argues against the view that the main protagonist of these changes was the Treasury, and explains them as the outcome of a tripartite agreement between the Treasury, the Ministry of Education and the Ministry of Housing and Local Government (MHLG) (Rhodes 1976, para.96). How the inter-departmental arguments were put, what the Scottish inputs were, and how the internal Scottish Office debate developed, cannot yet be documented. But central government sought a firmer grip upon the level of public expenditure in an expanding welfare state, and wanted to plan it more systematically over periods longer than one year. The Public Expenditure Survey (PESC) system, to which we return later, was to be one outcome of this wish. But it was preceded by a major reform of the financial relationship between central and local government which changed the system of central government grants to local authorities, and affected the financing of current expenditure on the education service (*ibid.*, paras 87-102; Regan 1979, 197-201). Simultaneous White Papers on both sides of the Border proposed a new general grant[3] which would amalgamate the service-specific, mainly percentage grants, with the intention of emancipating the local authorities from the grip of detailed central controls (MHLG 1957; SHD 1957). Some 85-90 per cent of the grants in question had been for education; this earmarking would now end as local authorities exercised choice within the general grant they would receive. Percentage grants, it was argued, had become too large in proportion to local rates, and were seen as 'an indiscriminating incentive to further expenditure' (MHLG 1957, para.3). They left too little responsibility with the local authorities for finding the money and for deciding their own priorities between services.

This was now to be remedied, and Treasury planning would benefit from having the level of general grant determined for two-year periods. The partial re-rating of industry was meant to give local authorities larger rate incomes and to take some of the pressure off the Exchequer. The Government rejected the accusation that it aimed to reduce the level and proportion of central grants, and to throw a greater burden on ratepayers. However, the wording of its proposals encouraged such fears, as did some of its arguments in the parliamentary debates on the Bills. Despite the Government's reassurance that education would not be let down, the education lobbies in both countries opposed the change as an attack on standards and on the further development of the service. Funds for education, they said, would be vulnerable to competition from other local services seeking expansion. For Scotland, a further matter of concern was the determination of the aggregate sum coming from the Exchequer. Although it was denied at first by John Maclay, the Secretary of State, (PD 1957a), he later told Parliament that the Goschen formula was to be abolished because there would no longer be an identifiable English education grant upon which to reckon Scotland's traditional proportion (PD 1957b).

Thus, for those in the education service, the new legislation aroused anxiety on three levels. First, would Scotland as a whole be treated worse than before? Second, how would funds be distributed amongst local authorities? And, third, would the education budget in each local authority be safe from competition with other categories of spending, or from local pressures to reduce the rates?

On the question of Scotland's treatment, whilst at times between the wars it might have conferred little benefit, the Goschen formula had become a totem. Yet it was not merely rhetoric when MPs and others sprang to defend it from abolition in the late 1950s. In comparison with the rest of the country, Goschen had also allowed a considerably higher proportion of local educational expenditure in Scotland to be met from the Exchequer rather than from the rates (Boyle 1966, 70-1). Thus Arthur Woodburn, Secretary of State from 1947 to 1950, lamented the formula's demise as a 'crime against Scotland' during the committee stage of the Local Government and Miscellaneous Financial Provisions (Scotland) Bill in 1958. Before 1945, Woodburn said, Scotland may have been held back by the lack of development in England. But, if Goschen went, Scotland could no longer expect to profit automatically from English improvements which incurred higher expenditure, such as the take-over of denominational schools long since achieved in Scotland. He added:

> it has been one of the tenets of the Secretary of State for Scotland that he held on like grim death to the Goschen formula. . . . Scotland needs more money on education than England and Wales. They have advantages, economic and otherwise, that we do not have. The only thing that we have to keep up our country's prosperity is education. (PD 1958a)

In the event, the 1958 changes did little to disturb national financial allocations. Whilst Goschen itself was dead, the aggregate general grant from the Treasury for Scottish local-authority expenditure was based on historic levels of central funding, and thus tended to carry forward the relativities of earlier years. Spending on education in Scotland and in the South continued to grow, taking an increasing share of public expenditure in the 1960s and 1970s (Regan 1979, ch.xi). Although the Secretary of State had to lobby more strenuously within government, Scotland remained a financially favoured part of the country into the 1980s if the relativities of central-government expenditure are judged solely on a population basis (Jackson 1979, table 3; Heald 1980a, tables 1 and 3; Parry 1982). Whether it was favoured in relation to need is not so easily decided (Heald 1980a, 1980c).

On the second point, the new method by which the aggregate Scottish amount was allocated to the local authorities also constituted a threat to educational interests, especially in authorities which had expanded their education service in the past. Again, however, no abrupt changes were afoot. The formula for distributing the grant amongst local authorities was designed to fit authorities' existing education expenditure, so as to minimise financial disturbance at the outset of the new system, and only gradually to effect any redistribution amongst authorities. This, it seems, had always been the practice of those who devised such formulae (Boyle 1966, 76). The general grant was an equalisation grant, but not strongly so, and the amount of differential aid it gave to local authorities with different demographic characteristics was rather small. John McEwan, former Director of Education for Lanarkshire, recounted his dismay that the formula perpetuated

Aberdeen's advantage and failed to shift resources to his own hard-pressed authority. He told us how he had briefed his County Clerk to propose to St Andrew's House a formula which would have reflected the higher proportion of school children in Lanarkshire's population. But he believed this was rejected because the Scottish Office wished to protect Aberdeen. Rodger, on the other hand, said he doubted whether St Andrew's House had thought this way.

Aberdeen figured prominently in the parliamentary discussion of the 1958 Bill as a symbol of Scottish educational advance which MPs across party lines thought threatened by the financial proposals. It was said that Aberdeen would now be penalised, having to find the money to sustain the high level of development it had achieved in earlier years, whilst 'niggardly' authorities like Renfrewshire would gain through the workings of the distribution formula. The Conservative member for Aberdeen South, Lady Tweedsmuir, praised the city with its low pupil-teacher ratio as 'a delectable place for teachers'; it would now suffer a loss, despite the work it had done 'with the approval of Government' (PD 1957c). From the other side of the House, Tom Fraser (Labour, Hamilton) regretted the implications of the change for Aberdeen, which had 'more fully implemented the 1945 Act than any other education authority in Scotland' and, in doing this, had been 'supported by the occupants of St Andrew's House ever since 1945'. It had 'built the schools, recruited the staff and created the expansion, but this expansion has to be paid for . . . in the future' (PD 1958c). He warned of the continuing cost of this expanded level of service which, under the new arrangements, would fall increasingly on Aberdeen itself. In this context Aberdeen also meant Scotland.

In more general terms, MPs expressed their fear lest the general grant would limit the centre's contribution to local coffers, presenting local authorities with the difficult choice either of increasing the rates or of foregoing improvements in education. This points to the third area of concern, the erosion of education's protected budget at both levels, but particularly at the local level. This was seen as endangering the educational partnership between the Department and the local education authorities. George Thomson (Labour, Dundee East) suspected that the Bill's proposals would subordinate the SED to the SHD as a result of the new procedure for transferring Treasury funds through the Department which had responsibilities for local government (PD 1958b). Rodger's description of the new arrangements underlines this:

RODGER. The authorities got a grand-total grant from the Government, and they could divide that between education, health and so on as they pleased.

Q. And that money didn't come through the SED?

RODGER. No. It went from the Treasury to the Scottish Office; and from the Scottish Office to the local authority. . . . But insofar as a particular authority was concerned, it was not allocated as between education, health, street cleaning, and so on. The object was to free local authorities from government control. . . . They got the grant total and could divide it between A, B, and C as they pleased. . . . [The s ED] could not even say that *x* per cent of an authority's total grant should go on education.

Q. Although you were saying earlier on that the s ED didn't exercise much control before that.

RODGER. They never really did exercise any close financial control, except perhaps in building.[4]

The ending of protection meant that the fortunes of the local education service came to depend more heavily upon financial decisions made within the local authorities. Some education departments were better placed than others to defend their corner. James Clark, Aberdeen's Direction of Education, explained how things worked out under the new system:

CLARK. Of the urban authorities, Aberdeen is pretty well top of the list throughout. And in part this was due to the policies deliberately adopted by the [Education] Committee. . . . I opposed the block grant because obviously I saw that it was going to mean less government money coming into the Aberdeen coffers, particularly as we had an Education Committee in Aberdeen that was keen to spend money on certain aspects of education. . . . The pupil-teacher ratio in Aberdeen was very favourable in these years. . . . I knew as Director that [the Education Committee] did not want the pupil-teacher ratio to be down-graded. . . . Under the block-grant system . . . there was a grant made to the local authority as a whole, with no allocation to education, even although educational factors had contributed to the calculation of the grant. Now, whereas at one time in the Aberdeen finance committee, it was possible for the director to say that the cost to the [local authority] of this particular development would be such and such, and the grant accruing would be sixty per cent or whatever, after the block-grant system came in, it was not possible to do this in this way. Therefore it could have been a major difficulty for the development of education in Aberdeen, if we had had a Finance Committee that became more difficult in the allocation of funds to education.

However, this never happened. Clark attributed his good fortune to Aberdeen's high regard for education, to the procedures of its finance committee, which enabled him to pilot his expenditure proposals to a successful conclusion, and to their trust in his experienced judgement. Much, however, was owing to his ability to gain the agreement of other top local officials and elected members in the early stages of the preparation of the education estimates. Another factor was Aberdeen's willingness and ability to sustain higher rates in order to develop its services.

Lanarkshire was in some respects similar. Its elected members believed in education as a means of working-class advancement. McEwan declared that his relations with county treasurers were excellent, and he described how they collaborated closely with him in the production of estimates. He reported that, for many years, treasurers took the view that 'their job was to find the money that the education committee said they wanted to spend'. On the other hand, elected members' enthusiasm for educational spending waned in the early 1960s. McEwan associated this with the coming of the general grant.

Scotland at the Treasury

At the central level too there was a different climate in the 1960s, as closer Treasury control of spending was sought through a new procedure for planning capital and current expenditure. The PESC system is known by the initials of the Treasury-based public expenditure survey committee which ran it. It was intended to make explicit the resource implications of policy decisions, and to provide a comprehensive view of spending over a rolling five-year period. This became the basis for Cabinet deliberations which set the annual totals of public expenditure, after which crucial bilateral negotiations took place on each programme between the Treasury and the spending departments. Education was one such programme; Scottish Office expenditure as a whole came to be separately treated as a programme in 1978.[5] The agreed results of these negotiations, and any disagreements, then went back to the Cabinet (Heclo and Wildavsky 1974, ch.5; Barnett 1982; Pliatzky 1982, ch.2). We asked Millan how much scope this system left to a Minister to increase resources:

MILLAN. Well, he doesn't have very much scope for increasing resources on his own. . . . It is very difficult for an individual Minister to swim against the tide. But, of course, the Government can decide that a particular service will be more . . . or less favourably treated than others, and in that sense, of course, the Minister responsible for education must fight for his own service, and whether he will do it successfully or not will depend partly on the objective circumstances, and partly on his effectiveness as a Minister.

Q. Whom does he fight with? His colleagues? Or is it a question of going to the Treasury?

MILLAN. Oh, I think in the first instance the Treasury. . . . Any Minister for any spending service is in competition with his Cabinet colleagues, as well as with the Treasury. . . . But the Secretary of State for Scotland is in a different position from other departmental Ministers, because he is responsible for the whole lot, and it is really up to him then to decide at any particular time where the priorities ought to be; and there is, within the public expenditure system, a certain amount of scope for the Secretary of State's making that kind of decision for himself, and not being bound by general Cabinet decisions on priorities at that particular time.

By the time Millan had become Secretary of State in 1976, PESC's efficacy had been overtaken by inflation and by large increases in expenditure programmes (Wright 1980, ch.6; Barnett 1982; Pliatzky 1982). We cannot determine how far PESC had ever been effective in bringing new ways of determining priorities to bear upon the education budget. But Denis Healey, Chancellor of the Exchequer from 1974 to 1979, said that the means he devised to enable the Cabinet to decide priorities, between health, education and housing, for example, never worked; to succeed, one would have had to 'stop the machine' (Young and Sloman 1984, 64).

The 'machine' is constructed more on the principle of piecemeal, sequential negotiation than that of comprehensive comparisons and rational choice. PESC did not so much transcend as incorporate these bargaining procedures. Graham, Rodger and Millan all participated in them. We asked Graham, first, how Scottish innovations were viewed in Whitehall:

GRAHAM. If I were a Treasury official and I were confronted by a proposal from Scotland for expenditure, I would not feel I was doing my job unless I took into account the possibility that . . . this innovation . . . would have consequences south of the Border; that you ought not, from the Treasury point of view, to look at the Scottish situation in isolation, unless you were quite sure that it is in isolation.

Q. Was there a continuing need to explain characteristic aspects of the Scottish system to the Treasury, for example, with respect to the provision for teacher training or teacher remuneration?

GRAHAM. It would have to be done from time to time on particular occasions, but there is some continuity in the Treasury and there is a good understanding of the Scottish position.

Dickson instanced satisfying the Treasury that there were valid curricular reasons for the superior Scottish provision of science classrooms. Rodger recalled the ease with which he got the Treasury to approve an increase in the size of the Inspectorate by more than ten per cent during Brunton's time as Senior Chief Inspector. Also, he confirmed that the relationship between the SED, the Treasury, and the Ministry of Education was delicate, and he described how it was handled:

RODGER. In general, they weren't aware of Scottish educational conditions until we pointed them out. If, for example, we were asking for something, and we were arguing about it and we made the point: 'This is being done in England, and people in Scotland will be annoyed if England seems to be getting a better deal', then they appreciated this argument. But possibly the difference was not one that they themselves were even aware of. . . . They were more conscious that England shouldn't be left behind Scotland, simply because whatever Scotland did had to be multiplied by something like eleven for it to be done in England. . . . The Treasury . . . never wanted to raise either expectations or annoyance on either side of the Border. . . . There is a dislike on the part of politicians of stirring up hornets' nests, and they didn't want to stir up hornets' nests in Scotland. Indeed, in many of the main rooms of the Ministry of Education, there was above the door, in big writing, 'REMEMBER SCOTLAND', a thing that they tended to forget. We were always annoyed if the Ministry did something, and we were not informed beforehand. . . . There was an unwritten rule between England and Scotland that we kept telling one another, beforehand, what we were contemplating. I think that we stuck to this better than they did, because it was easy for the major partner in size to forget the minor.

Q. There was never a question of approval being involved?

RODGER. Oh no. We were independent of England, and the Ministry was independent of us. . . . If something that we had proposed was heartily disliked by England, they would say so but there was no effort at compulsion. If the Ministry felt compelled to act, I think that they would tell the Treasury, and it would be via the Treasury that an effort would have been made to stop us.

Millan did not recall that the Treasury was difficult to deal with:

Q. In discussions with the Treasury, was there a need to explain and justify the separateness of Scottish provision?

MILLAN. There were certain things that we did . . . which are much more favourable for Scotland than England, and I don't remember them ever being seriously questioned. . . . School bursaries, for example, which is . . . on a more expensive basis in Scotland. . . . I don't remember the Treasury, or anybody else, ever trying to stop us doing what we were doing. . . . If you are talking about periods when there is tremendous restraint on public expenditure, and when you are being asked to make savings . . . then it is difficult to introduce innovations unless you have a bit of spare money. The Treasury are normally reasonably relaxed about innovations that are not too expensive, if you can find savings elsewhere.

Building Schools: Resources and Planning

Between 1946 and 1955, some 200000 new school places were created. About 20 per cent of the new ones were constructed in the Hutting Operation for the Raising of the School Leaving Age (HORSA) scheme, under the auspices of the Ministry of Works (SED 1966a, table 17). The SED and local authorities struggled to provide 'roofs over heads' to accommodate post-war population growth. Problems of accommodation continued to occupy them, as the population 'bulge' moved from the primary to the secondary schools. More space was also needed for the increasing numbers of pupils who were staying on after the school-leaving age, and for the raising of the leaving age itself. By the end of 1965, a further 478000 places had been added (*ibid.*), and 642000 more were completed in the next decade (GSS 1976, table 88; SED 1980e, table 2).

As Rodger remarked, central government exercised closer control over capital expenditure than it did over current spending. The total amount available for school building each year was determined by negotiation between the SED, the Scottish Office, and the Treasury. Each education authority required the Department's permission, called 'loan sanction', to borrow money for school-building projects (Griffith 1966, 90-3). The interest charges on these loans then became part of the local authority's current expenditure in subsequent years. Although the approval procedures were not identical to those in England, S E D administrators and inspectors, like those of the D E S, negotiated with the local authorities over their building programmes and individual projects (*ibid.*, ch.2; Regan 1979, ch.VIII). We illustrate these procedures below. But we look first at the situation facing central and local government immediately after the War. Rodger was in charge of school building for the Department:

R O D G E R. The Socialists came into power. . . . Now, the big thing that they were hearing about from all of their constituencies, was that . . . there was an enormous shortage of housing. Therefore the Scottish Ministers were all out to build houses . . . [not] schools. . . . There were shortages of steel, shortages of concrete, shortages of brick, shortages of wood; and, in a way, shortage of money too. . . . Committees were set up in London to allocate [these] to departments. . . . Now, the Scottish Office, unfortunately, was dealt with as an entity by the Treasury. I used to say to my colleagues in the Ministry of Education, 'I wish I were in your shoes, because you at least know what you want for education, and, although you won't necessarily get it, you will certainly get an allocation which is then yours. Whereas, I come down to fight for Scottish education and, at the end of the day, it is given as part of a Scottish Office grant, and the Scottish Office itself starts to quarrel about how much of this is to go to housing, how much to schools, and so on'. . . . Time after time, I put up to Ministers a statement of how many bricks I would require for the building of schools, and the Ministers would say, 'No, we'll halve that and put the half that we are saving into housing'.

Rodger said that Scottish Office officials tried to come to amicable agreements about the division of the total allocation of capital investment amongst the Scottish departments, but that, under the Labour Government at any rate, raids on education's share of money and materials had Ministerial blessing and benefited the housing programme. Alongside such 'pinching', however, there was also 'friendly reallocation' by which Rodger agreed to transfer unused resources to the Health Department for house building:

Q. Presumably this would allow you to ask for quite a lot, in the knowledge that you could always get it spent through housing, if you couldn't actually use it for putting up schools.

R O D G E R. Well, you might think that, but it doesn't work out that way. Suppose I asked for much more than I really needed . . . this was going to be spotted by the Treasury, because my figure was going to be considered alongside the Ministry of Education's figure, not alongside the Scottish Department of Health's figure. . . . They certainly were not going to give us a surplus that we could hand over to some other Scottish department. The Treasury had a further check on us. We had to make a return each year of the amount of each of the rationed materials we had used; thus demands in excess of accomplishment were readily spotted. These days of scarcity made the administration of building much more difficult than it was later.

The planning and building of schools took place at the local level, where the priority given to housing posed problems for the school-building programme. These were particularly acute in Glasgow, whose Labour administration, Rodger said, were diverting the available materials to housing:

RODGER. Vast new housing areas had been built without schools. They were completed without a shop or a school or a church or a community centre! Glasgow housing pinched all of the decent sites, and left all of the rotten sites for education. . . . This is one of the reasons why Glasgow's school-building programme was so long in getting off the ground . . . [Stewart] Mackintosh [Director of Education, 1944-68] could hardly get on with his job . . . for fighting the housing people to see that he was left sufficient spaces in the new areas. . . . In Householwood, there was one big uneven outcrop of rock on which you couldn't easily build houses. . . . That was the school site. The rock had to be hewn away and blasted away before you could build the school at all. And I think that in that case, something like £150 000 was spent before a start could be made to the building of the school. . . . Some of the first big schools that they built in Glasgow after the War (between 1950 and 1955) were built at phenomenally high cost as a result of the difficulties of the sites.

Rodger recalled that there was only limited scope to plead a special case to the Treasury for hard-pressed cases like Glasgow. Within the Scottish total, specific cost controls and other regulations comprised the context for the SED's relations with the local authorities. Rodger described how the authorities were allocated their shares:

RODGER. The Scottish Education Department was allowed, out of national resources, to spend £x million in the year. Then we had to allocate that £x million to the various local authorities . . . mainly, but not entirely, in terms of what they proposed to do. In fact they nearly always proposed to do far more than they could do. . . . The inspector would go to the architects' department and say, 'How far on are the plans for such-and-such school?' And the architect might say, 'Well, you know I've been so busy on that, that, and that, that I haven't got round to that yet'. . . . It was from information of that kind, as a supplement (and corrective) to what the authorities said that they wanted, that we eventually determined what this authority would get.

The varied capabilities of education authorities and the great difficulties some of them experienced were persistent problems for the central Department. The SED could not be indifferent to what was happening locally, for it had overall responsibility for the development of the national education service. Gaps between allocations to education authorities and what they then accomplished could not be hidden from the Treasury, and would reduce the credibility of the Department's bids for more. The SED would be acutely embarrassed just when there was an urgent need for new construction. As we will show, the Department sought strategic and structural solutions to these problems. Dickson, however, described an *ad hoc* measure:

DICKSON. When some authorities failed to take up all their allocation of money, we would sometimes try to divert the money to authorities who needed more buildings and could provide them timeously.

This happened with materials as well, as Rodger explained:

RODGER. I would say that in 1947 and 1948, Glasgow was so far behind in the planning and the preparation of things that, even if you had had 100000 tons of steel to give them, they couldn't use it, so it did go to the authorities ready to use it. It was no use to give it to Glasgow.

Aberdeen provided the best illustration of an authority which *could* use it. Rodger told us, 'I used to thank God for Aberdeen'. Clark, who became Assistant Director there in 1945, confirmed that Aberdeen was asked on occasion if they could build more 'because there was money available and other authorities weren't quite so streamlined'. We asked him:

Q. So it's not simply a question of motivation and local readiness to support a higher rate, but partly a question of speed and efficiency as well?

CLARK. Yes. . . . The building inheritance . . . was . . . comparatively good. . . . The immediate post-war problems were undoubtedly [firstly] the erection of school buildings quickly in connection with the very rapidly expanding new housing areas. . . . Immediately at the end of 1945 the Education Committee had tentative plans for some dozen or thirteen new school buildings; they were right in on the ground floor about the importance of a building programme and its implementation. . . . There was a very close liaison between the Housing Committee and the Education Committee at that stage. When a new estate was planned . . . there would be areas allocated, as far as possible in the best places in the estate, for educational buildings.

This was in striking contrast to Glasgow. Rodger explained it:

RODGER. Aberdeen had a very good combination of a convener of their Education Committee, a director of education, and an outside architect, who were all keen on buildings and who worked well together. Thus Aberdeen got their buildings done at a time when other counties weren't ready to start, and I would have had mighty poor Scottish figures if I had not had Aberdeen boosting them. . . . During that period, very little was done in Scotland in the way of building permanent complete schools. What was done, was done largely in Aberdeen.

Rodger had nothing but praise for Aberdeen's use of private architects. Several SED annual reports in the mid-1950s show that the Department's complaints about local authorities' planning centred on technical staffing inadequacies, poor coordination and their reluctance to employ private architects (SED 1954a, 1955a, 1956a, 1957a). The success of Aberdeen seems to have influenced the SED to urge more streamlined procedures upon the local authorities who lagged behind in planning and building. Several were large authorities located in the West.

Lanarkshire was one of them. Its difficulties, McEwan thought, could be traced not only to the block grant for current expenditure but also to a deficient capital allocation for Scotland as a whole and for his county in particular. He argued that the SED's calculations did not take into account Lanarkshire's population growth, nor its circumstances: large towns, and a need to provide many new schools. Lanarkshire had, in fact, invested heavily in the 1950s in primary schools, but McEwan acknowledged that there were obstacles, and said that secondary-school provision was 'shockingly inadequate':

MCEWAN. Once, when we tried to use our Members of Parliament to press the Scottish Education Department to allocate more 'investment' to us, they came back with what was, presumably, the answer that they had got from the Department, namely that we couldn't build any faster anyway . . . that capital allocations in past years had not been fully spent – we were slow in getting the plans drawn – and there is some truth in that.

Rodger laid some of the blame for problems at the local level upon factional political conflict amongst the Left. This was particularly acute in Dunbartonshire and Lanarkshire, 'the two counties whose politics bedevilled things more than in any other county in the country'. Disputes occurred in Lanarkshire, as elsewhere, about the location of schools, and about the use of outside builders and private architects:

Q. Did you use private architects?

MCEWAN. We had, at one stage, before the stopping of the building programme in 1960, nineteen different architects working for us, including the county architect. The council then made a *volte-face* and only the county architect, from then on for a period, was working for us, and that was a bit of a bottleneck, because it's impossible to develop a big staff overnight to take on the variety and quantity of school building that we were needing to deal with. And then, later, private architects were brought in again; and it was at the time when the county architect's department was working on its own . . . that the Scottish Education Department gave this kind of snide answer [about our inability to build faster].

The Department brought pressure to bear upon local authorities like Glasgow to use the private sector for designing and constructing schools. Particularly in the West, education authorities were given special planning help from central government. A crucial task fell to the Inspectorate and, once again, Brunton's role was all-important:

RODGER. You see, quite a lot of the work had been falling on the directors, in the building field. They had to determine how many HORSA huts they wanted – that was their first post-war job – and then they had to keep an eye on new building developments. Glasgow was building big new suburbs. What was the population of these suburbs going to be? How many schools were they going to require? Glasgow had the further problem of trying to guess the Protestant/Roman Catholic ratio in new areas. . . . Now, I found, sitting at the centre, that some directors had a gift for this sort of thing, and did it well, and that other directors did it badly. And when I found that a director was not good at it, I got the inspector to think about it quite independently, and then perhaps approach the director and see whether they, together, could reach agreement. In point of fact, much of the useful building thinking in Glasgow after the War, was done by the district inspector and not by the director of education; the district inspector being [John] Boyle, then Brunton. . . . We took care to send there a succession of people who could do this kind of work well. . . . I would give a great deal of credit for getting Glasgow out of the mess, to Brunton.

Q. What about Lanarkshire?

RODGER. Lanarkshire didn't do particularly well. [William] Hepburn [Director of Education, 1945-50] was a very able man, but this was not Hepburn's strong side, and I wouldn't say that it was the strong side of McEwan, who followed Hepburn. We had rather able chaps as inspectors in Lanarkshire, the first of whom was [John] Gunn, who had quite a flair for this. [A. Speirs] Kelly was pretty good, but Kelly wasn't forceful. . . . Brunton was forceful. If a thing had to be done and Stewart Mackintosh wasn't doing it, in effect, Brunton did it. . . . Brunton might say, 'You jolly well must get this done', and point out strongly the consequences of failure. . . . My total experience in the Department forced me to think that, with exceptions of course, authorities were not very able to plan and execute things for themselves. It may be a criticism of the Department that our people did too much for them. But there were certainly some areas that would have been in a sad mess if they had depended solely upon the local officials. . . . The longer time went on, the more sure the local authorities and we both became that what was important was to be thinking ahead.

There is some evidence that the education authorities themselves had wanted central government to do more about the difficult building problem. As far back as 1936, the Association of Directors of Education urged that information on building designs be pooled and that the SED set up an exhibition room for the purpose. They also wanted central advice. The Department was willing to offer it, but also thought that the local authorities should take the lead in developing new types of buildings (ADES n.d., 61). During the Second World War, a special committee appointed by Tom Johnston to advise on post-war school buildings brought together persons from both levels of government, and also teachers and architects. Its report recommended better procedures at and between central and local levels, repeated the call for a stronger, Departmentally based, system of information and advice, and even proposed an advisory committee to work in parallel to a Departmental school-planning section (mw 1945, 9).

There was a similar urgency south of the Border. In 1979, Sir William Pile described the English situation of the late 1940s and the arrangements that were generally to continue for at least the next twenty-five years:

> The circumstances of the immediate post-war period called for greater central control, to ensure that national educational policies were carried out within the severely limited financial and material resources available, but also for greater co-operation between the centre and the local providers of schools. A simple administrative framework was needed which would concentrate the leas' resources on the most urgent jobs and then leave them free to get schools built with the minimum of control from London. (Pile 1979, 75)

Like its English counterpart, the sed sought a national strategy for building, although less vigorously so. It found a solution which went beyond the *ad hoc* shunting of money and materials, and the crisis-management of the 1940s and early 1950s. The solution involved shaping relations within and between the Department and the education authorities in order to improve local capabilities and performance. This function was performed by administrators and technical specialists who undertook to raise the national effort through new systems of planning and construction. But, all the while, the role of district inspectors was crucial in the day-to-day planning and implementation of building programmes at the local level. Whilst local authorities welcomed help from the centre, they resented detailed controls and cumbersome procedures.[6] Rodger's description of the beginnings of change show how the Department was able to exert its influence more effectively, and with less conflict, through consultations at an early stage of the planning process:

RODGER. There was increasing feeling from the end of the War, that the Department should exercise less authority, delegate more, let its constituent bodies be more responsible. . . . It became clear to me, by 1950, that sometimes discussions that were verging on the acrimonious could arise between me representing the Department on the one hand, and an authority on the other, about the plans for a school; and I wondered how we could get rid of this. . . . The authorities had got in the habit, in pre-war days, of thinking out their educational requirements; carrying these out in the form of a building, or at least they put forward their proposals. . . . After the War, we were paying more attention to detail, and I found that, if an architect had gone to the length of planning a building in detail, and if at that stage we started to find fault with it, he didn't like it. . . . I found, on the other hand, that if we spoke to the same architect before his next school was built, he could probably mould his thoughts quite agreeably. Therefore it occurred to me that we ought really to try and change our code of practice. A committee was set up. . . . And we built up a code of practices, and it was simply this. If a school was required, the first job lay between the director of education and the inspector to determine how many children there would be. When this was resolved the second question was: what kind of school should it be? . . . Was it going to be comprehensive or what? Therefore, how many rooms would be needed? We felt that, by these initial discussions, the educational requirements would be determined amicably by discussion, before any work was done at all by the architect.

Despite the new code, local complaints about building procedures and about the Department's performance were expressed to the House of Commons Estimates Committee in 1952-53 when the Committee investigated school building. Although Murrie and Rodger defended the Department, local-authority spokesmen gave evidence about delays in the approval process and about difficulties in obtaining clear and stable cost guidelines from the SED. James Frizell, Edinburgh's Director of Education from 1933 to 1961, showed remarkable persistence over many years. He had been associated with both the 1936 and 1945 recommendations for a Departmental information and advisory centre, and he repeated this plea to the Estimates Committee. Murrie said that a step had been taken towards this, but the Committee's report strongly criticised the SED for not having developed a branch in which architects, administrators and inspectors could collaborate to coordinate and advise local authorities (SC on Estimates 1953).

Further steps were taken in the 1950s. The SED appointed a technical officer to help authorities during the construction stage, and a building-development team was established. It designed and supervised the building of exemplary schools in Hamilton (Lanarkshire) and Kirkcudbrightshire, and a trades college in Dundee. It gained generalisable experience for itself, and arranged for a large number of other authorities to observe and learn from what was being done. However, David Dickson, the first inspector to join the team when he was district inspector in Fife, cast some doubt on its efficacy in comparison with the Ministry of Education's Architects and Buildings Branch (Maclure 1984). The Scottish local authorities preferred the Ministry's bulletins.

Nevertheless, handbooks, circulars, exhortation and advice came in considerable quantities from the SED, and six working parties were set up jointly with authorities, mainly in the West and the central belt, to overcome delays in planning. But, when the Estimates Committee returned to the question of school building in 1960-61, the old complaints about red tape and frustrating controls were renewed (SC on Estimates 1961). The SED's witnesses admitted that overcrowding in St Andrew's House had caused the architects to be inefficiently boarded-out elsewhere, hinted that they were hard pressed, and acknowledged difficulties in getting planning clearance from other Scottish Office departments. Basically, however, they rejected the criticisms. Arbuckle talked of the early stages of the approval process as a point at which Departmental experience was placed at the disposal of the local authorities. The SED told the Estimates Committee that local-authority representatives on a working party a few years before had welcomed or acquiesced in central planning-control and did not see it lying heavily upon them (*ibid.*, Q.1814). Local authorities themselves were blamed for plans that outstripped their own capabilities and for poor coordination across their own fragmented committee structures.

On the whole, the report sided with the Department's critics, and found the SED's procedures inferior to those of the Ministry of Education. A powerful stimulus had already been given to the building programme, and a further rationale for central guidance, in the 1958 White Paper, *Education in Scotland: The Next Step* (SED 1958b). However, the recommendations of the Estimates Committee's report seem to have been an important specific cause of further changes in Departmental procedures. Whilst firm central control of costs was retained, procedures became simpler and more flexible as the building system geared itself to accommodate higher pupil numbers in the later years of the 1960s and beyond.

Size and Type of School

Was the development of central mechanisms of influence and control intended to shape educational practice by shaping physical provision? How much did the Department and the education authorities agree on the size and type of school? Maclure's study of post-war English school-building shows the mutual influences between educational practice and spatial design (Maclure 1984). Arbuckle told the Estimates Committee that the SED's inspectors passed to the buildings side of the Department any architectural or building implications of new curriculum ideas, such as changes in the balance of subjects (SC on Estimates 1961, Q.1815).

At a broader level, decisions regarding school organisation, the leaving age, the size and staffing of schools, and the pattern of local-authority provision affect physical accommodation, and are constrained by it. In England and Wales, negotiations between central and local officials over building programmes were conducted within a framework set by government policy (Griffith 1966, ch.2). Both sides normally agreed on the priority of meeting 'basic needs', or the provision of roofs over heads, to accommodate local changes in population and in housing. But local authorities' school-building priorities were sometimes overriden by the central department. Whilst there was considerable continuity in national building policies over the decades, there were also changes in emphasis as the attention paid to different sectors and stages of education fluctuated (Regan 1979, ch.VIII). Although the process of negotiation allowed central government to assert its policies, and thereby to shape education authorities' priorities, Regan argues that major conflicts between central government and the local authorities were rare, 'save for the massive exception of comprehensive education. A policy lead from the department usually provokes a willing response from LEAS' (*ibid.*, 125). Griffith notes that education authorities usually conform to central policy, but says that 'this is not necessarily evidence that they would do so were the actual selection [of projects] in their hands' (Griffith 1966, 160). But, he argues, even if they were free to choose, they would probably not diverge very far from DES policies.

Our own evidence in this area is too patchy for firm conclusions to be drawn about Scotland. The fragments we have contain indications both of agreement and disagreement between the Department and the education authorities. Here is Rodger:

RODGER. During the War there had been a building committee in the Department, and it published – towards the end of the War, or immediately after the War – a booklet on primary-school building. This body began to study secondary schools, but the committee petered out – quite deliberately – because HORSA huts for the raising of the school-leaving age in 1947, and the work which had been done in Hertfordshire and England, became the patterns. The Scottish body was just not thinking in the modern terms. But one important thing that this body did on primary schools, was to say that the ideal size, in their view, was a two-stream school – that is to say, two classes per year, fourteen classes under the headmaster. While that advice was made known to the authorities, it wasn't passed out in the form of an edict, and there was nothing to prevent Glasgow, or Edinburgh, or any other place, from developing three-stream schools, or four-stream schools if they wanted. But, undoubtedly, this general idea had its effect, and a very, very large number – after 1952, when we were really getting into building – of the schools were fourteen-classroom schools.

The committee to which Rodger referred, and on which he sat, was the one mentioned earlier that Tom Johnston had appointed. In secondary schools it assumed a 'mixed *omnibus* school of 750 to 1000 pupils' (MW 1945, 8), somewhat larger than the 600 or so that the Advisory Council was to recommend (SED 1947b, 31). In his evidence to the Estimates Committee, Rodger stated that the SED had not announced a definite maximum size, but that the Advisory Council's suggestion was uneconomically small because it produced small classes at the top of the school, each of which had to occupy a room (SC on Estimates 1953, Q.330). He also argued that, whilst the 1945 report on buildings 'formed the basis of the Department's policy' after the War, the buildings it proposed were very costly (*ibid.*, Q.1598).

According to Rodger, Conservative Ministers in the early 1950s said, 'let an authority do what it thinks best in local circumstances', and Murrie confirmed this:

MURRIE. I doubt whether we would have [said], 'Instead of building two small ones, build one big one'. . . . We would have asked the inspector to comment on the priorities by looking at the programme they had sent in. . . . They would almost certainly have consulted him at an earlier stage. . . . School building was designed to provide for the needs as they were then known, not to impose an educational policy on the local authorities. . . . My recollection is that, when I came to the Department in 1952, it was accepted and established that local authorities would want to build both junior-secondary . . . and senior-secondary schools, and that if they suggested two junior-secondary schools rather than one comprehensive school, and if the inspector concerned thought this was what they would need, we would not say to them, 'We are not going to approve this'. . . . I think we would have said, 'This is what the local authority want. If it is not unreasonable, we will let them have it'.

We asked Dickson:

Q. Was school building an instrument of central policy control?

DICKSON. It wasn't . . . it was an area in which there was a good deal of central control stemming from the financial limitations on it.

On the other hand, teacher shortages and Departmental encouragement led to some local centralisation of secondary-school provision, and the application of building regulations could be used as an instrument for this. Spokesmen for the Association of County Councils told the Estimates Committee in 1961 that the SED's space requirements were often too high and too rigidly enforced to make the remodelling of small rural schools feasible, thus forcing centralisation upon a county. It was said that modifying orders, relaxing the regulations, were only reluctantly given by the SED. The Department denied this, but it did argue that there was no justification for modifications in the construction of new schools (SC on Estimates 1961, Qs 1529-36, 1744-6).

A degree of permissiveness in the type of provision to be made was a safe course for a Government which was not seeking to change direction. Local authorities could be relied upon to reproduce a selective, bipartite system. Even Labour-controlled councils did not wish to change tack before the 1960s, if then (see chapters 15 and 16). Aberdeen did not build any secondary schools for twenty years after the War, although Clark speculated that, had they done so, 'serious consideration' might have been given to the *omnibus* school.

When Labour came to power in the mid-1960s, Circular 600 and the run-up to ROSLA provided new opportunities, as well as imperatives, for firm guidance on building policies. We consider secondary reorganisation at length in chapter 16, where we note Millan's complaint about the number of small junior- and senior-secondary schools inherited by the Labour Government. He argued that it was easier for the Department to get its way when starting afresh with new schools for ROSLA, although he did not seek to force six-year schools on areas where geography disallowed. Whilst there was no specific building programme for secondary reorganisation, building approvals and capital allocations were used to promote the national policy. Circular 609 in 1966 couched this policy in terms of a projected forty per cent annual increase of the building programme until 1970. This rise was intended to meet the needs generated by the increase and geographical shift of population, by ROSLA, and by the replacement of older stock: 'Any substantial new development for essential needs should be planned not only to provide immediately for larger rolls and the raising of the age, but also to serve, ultimately if not straightaway, as a unit in a system reorganised on comprehensive lines' (SED 1966d, para.15(c)).

'From Negative and Particular Control to Positive and General Guidance'

Irksome though its specific controls were, the Department attempted to help the local authorities to improve their building programmes. For its own part, by doing good for others, the Department may also have been doing well for itself, attempting to acquire a reputation as a forward-looking, managerial department presiding over an education service to which an efficient and effective national building operation was crucial. For the centre to concentrate upon major issues of policy and resource management, it was necessary to enhance the capabilities of the periphery so that some of the specific controls could be safely relaxed.

Griffith has suggested a rough classification of the attitudes of government departments towards local authorities (Griffith 1966, 515-28; see also Regan 1979, 33-5). A *laissez-faire* department interferes little with local affairs in the field. A regulatory department controls and inspects the local administration of the service, enforcing standards but not getting too closely involved with the work of the local authority. A promotional department, of which Griffith considers the DES to be the best example, is constantly and actively concerned with encouraging, advising, and helping the local authority to carry out its functions. Working relationships between centre and locality are close.

The formal distribution of powers in the education system, as well as the structure of the political game, ruled out a *laissez-faire* approach by the SED to the local authorities. The two levels depended on each other for the fulfilment of the educational objectives they both shared, and for some of those that they did not share. This 'power-dependence' (R. Rhodes 1981, ch.5; 1985a) brought central and local members of the policy community together in negotiations involving resources that included finance, information, political and legal power, and less formal means of bureaucratic influence. These were not equally divided between central and local government. Moreover, the centre was in a better position to deploy strategies for their use, and ultimately to change the rules and structures within which it conducted its relationship with the education authorities. The SED combined regulation with promotion. It moved towards the latter, but retained much of the former. Nevertheless, there was room for the SED and the local authorities to disagree about the significance of particular procedural changes: were they carrots or sticks?

We should recall that the Government had claimed that the general grant would enable more initiative to be taken locally over spending priorities and policies, and that it would increase the ability of the financially weaker authorities to develop their services. Members of the Labour Opposition had feared that central government would abdicate its responsibilities to authorities, some of which were unwilling or unable to take the initiative to develop the education service. On both sides of the House a central lead had been seen as desirable : there was an urgent national interest in the development of education, and what happened in one authority had consequences for others. To the extent that this lead was not only desirable but inevitable, some had argued that any talk of decentralisation was chimerical.

But decentralisation was in the air in the mid-1960s, for the Department could fulfil its aspiration to reach the higher peaks of policy development and management only by off-loading more of the burden of routine tasks to others outside. The SED was beginning to do this with new fringe bodies which helped to relieve the Inspectorate (see part IV). However, inspectors remained crucial to the building programme as the main channel between the Department and the local authorities. Relations between central and local government became more coordinated in the 1960s. In Graham's time there were more joint development projects for secondary schools, and later also for primary schools to which attention shifted under the Conservative Government in the early 1970s. In addition to appointing its own research officer, the Department developed links with United Kingdom agencies. The Consortium of Local Authorities Special Programme (CLASP) system of industrialised building involved eleven British local authorities in consortium work, under National Building Agency control, for building extensions to secondary schools. In the early 1960s, Glasgow and Lanarkshire were its only full members from Scotland.

On a wider front as well, Graham tried to grasp the nettle of the SED's often difficult relationship with local authorities. He argued that they were too tightly controlled from the centre, but he saw the problem partly in terms of their unwillingness to cut the umbilical cord. In his RIPA lecture he said :

> there is still a disquieting tendency in the Scottish educational world to look to the Department to take the initiative in far too many things. . . . it is really remarkable that people should expect so little to come from the periphery and so much from the centre. More of the detail of control, more of the business of day-to-day trouble-shooting and decision-taking, and more of the settling of what are essentially local issues . . . will have to go away from the centre if, within a Department of reasonable size, we are to give the time that needs to be given to the questions which are of real significance both on a national scale and in the longer term. . . . We would hope to move steadily from negative and particular control to positive and general guidance. (Graham 1965, 303 and 302)

Dickson gave an illustration and a partial explanation of the problem:

DICKSON. I would personally like to have seen local authorities coming to us and saying, 'Look, we would like experimentally to organise our schools on a four-term basis'. But I couldn't get any authorities to do that even when I asked them to. . . . Too often we had to produce the ideas. . . . I think this is really what Norman Graham was thinking about. . . . One of the difficulties, of course, with the local authorities as they were, when there were thirty-five of them, was that the director of education tended to be very much immersed in the detail of administration, and consequently had little time or opportunity to sit back and consider wider issues and larger questions. . . . Whereas we could much more easily devote a day or two occasionally to what we called 'meditation'. . . . the capability [of local authorities] would depend to a large extent on the ability of their officials. They varied, naturally.

Q. And it also depended on their education committees?

DICKSON. Oh indeed, yes. They varied a great deal in the extent to which they were interested in trying anything new. . . . It wasn't a case of rural areas being backward and urban areas forward-looking. . . . A great deal depended on individuals, especially on the interests of the director of education and of the chairman of the education committee.

The proposed reform of local government gave the Department a further chance to express its views. In its evidence to the (Wheatley) Royal Commission on Local Government in Scotland (RCLGS 1968a), the SED argued that the existing system of thirty-five education authorities was now outmoded. Graham reinforced this point in his oral evidence. He argued that the problem was not the unwillingness so much as the inability of many education authorities to cope with expansion and new developments. Many were too small and financially too weak to sustain adequate administrative and specialist staff, and had to rely for guidance upon the Department's administrators and inspectors. Moreover, local directors were often too closely involved in detail to be able to think about broader principles. Graham claimed that a more efficient education service and a stronger system of local government would result if larger administrative units were created. Some detailed central controls could then be abolished, although the centre would still need to sustain overall supervision and control, 'partly because of the money involved and partly because of the importance of education as a service in the national interest' (RCLGS 1968b, Q.3925). But Graham thought that local authorities' statutory and direct financial responsibilities in education should entail more local decision-making in matters concerning, for example, buildings, school closures, timetabling, schemes of educational provision, or minor capital works (*ibid.*, Qs 3923-4). Dickson told Wheatley that greater self-reliance at the local level would relieve the Inspectorate and allow it to concentrate on the problems that lay ahead (*ibid.*, Q.3735).

In our interview, Graham voiced a slight doubt about education authorities' eagerness to assume greater responsibilities:

Q. Did the local authorities take kindly to the measures that increased their ability to take decisions?.

GRAHAM. There are a lot of . . . unpopular decisions, and it is convenient sometimes for an authority to be able to blame central government rather than to have to take responsibility themselves. . . . Occasionally it suits them to be able to say, 'We would have liked to build a new school but the Scottish Education Department won't let us . . . at this juncture'. On the other hand, I think as the authorities realised the possibilities, the more forward-looking, certainly, welcomed change, as it came about.

How significant were the changes to a more promotional mode? Graham had offered a *quid pro pro* in his RIPA lecture: 'the more we can lay down general standards and requirements for, say, the building of primary schools, the less need there is to scrutinise and amend an education authority's plans' (Graham 1965, 302). In our interview, Dickson said it was 'not far from being the truth' when we suggested that what was being decentralised was relatively trivial in comparison to what was being retained at the centre:

Q. What was your view, and what was Brunton's view, as Senior Chief Inspector at the time?

DICKSON. That we should get rid of the trivial things, but that we would not want to give up our influence. We wouldn't use the word 'control' for obvious reasons. We don't in fact control so much as advise.

To some extent, the Department's desks were cleared of what Graham called 'obsolete administrative weapons' (*ibid.*, 306). Graham told us that this enabled the SED to devote more attention to the curriculum, to teacher demand and supply, and to studying 'the throughput of the system . . . what proportion of pupils were getting what sort of qualifications'. But there was little scope for an immediate increase in local autonomy, given the stronger thrust of national educational policy which started in the mid-1960s. Expansion was largely financed by the Exchequer. Whereas, in Britain as a whole in 1966, grants stood in relation to rates in a ratio of about one to one, by 1976 it was about two to one, and in Scotland about three to one (CLGF 1976, table 26; 347). The (Layfield) Committee on Local Government Finance (CLGF) commented that centralisation of control had accompanied this increased financial stake, despite government's expressed intentions to relax controls and offer some selective relief from minor irritations (*ibid.*, ch.5 and 87). Layfield learned from Scottish Office spokesmen that an easement of the very detailed control on the capital side was not likely to happen 'in major fields like education where we would still have an interest in detail, schools to be built and so forth' (*ibid.*, appendix 10, 46).

Graham argued strongly for the reorganisation of local government, but he retired before it took place.[7] The Scottish Office, including Graham's successor Fearn, saw the new local-government system as part of a wider enhancement of decision-making at the local level (*ibid.*, appendix 10, 55 and 59). But economic problems soon put severe limits upon the extent to which this promise could be fulfilled; and national crises of confidence in education, though much less severe in Scotland than in England, also affected the extent to which local authorities could be unleashed. However, the SED did relax its approvals procedures in 1977 in the light of the increased capabilities of the new and larger education authorities. Individual building projects now had to be sent for approval only at one stage, prior to the acceptance of tender, instead of at three or four stages. Provided that a project could be certified by the local authority to be up to standard and within cost limits, approval was given without examination of plans (SED 1976c). On the other hand, the SED's relations with education authorities were circumscribed by national economic and financial pressures which were channelled through the Scottish Office's Finance Division. The relaxation of scrutiny of local authorities' projects occurred within a new Scottish Office financial planning system which strengthened central government's strategic control over the totals of capital expenditure. The sharp reduction of those totals, in the years of retrenchment that followed, circumscribed local discretion, and central government used its new tool as a weapon in the fight to curtail local spending as a whole (Heald 1982, 150-1; Midwinter 1984, 11-12). Layfield was told about a new and firm Scottish Office rule that 'nobody in any part of the Office may issue a circular to a local authority which in any way involves them in spending more money without obtaining sanction from the Finance Division' (CLGF 1976, appendix 10, 25). The Scottish Office evidence to Layfield hinted at a conflict between the professional advisers in education and social work, who encouraged local spending, and the administrators and financial managers in the Department and the Scottish Office, who applied tighter constraints.

Summary and Discussion

We do not argue that, but for scarcity, political and administrative energies would have bent to the promotion of progressive policies after 1945. Nevertheless, resource shortages that were often severe provided much of the context for educational policy in that period. Shortages were a brake upon expansion, a major impediment to meeting needs however defined, and a major focus of energy and thought. To ameliorate shortages, central and local government drew together in a common effort. More research is needed to judge the extent to which centre and locality disagreed over the location, size, or type of accommodation to be built, and whether any such disputes involved fundamental differences of educational purpose. However, although relations between the SED and the local education authorities were often marked by friction, we have come across little evidence to indicate that the two pursued divergent goals. There were disputes over the centralisation of provision in rural areas, but there seem to have been few differences of opinion over the size and type of schools. The major differences in priorities were between education and housing, and this drew the SED towards whatever allies it could find among the local education authorities.

Accordingly, our assessment of partnership in this area must allow for the possibility that ends were not generally at issue between the SED and the local education authorities. However, the SED's thinking on central-local relations in policy areas where there were sharper disagreements over goals was arguably influenced by its experience on resources. For its frustration with some of the education authorities over buildings led it to devise ways of getting its influence in more effectively. In this, the role of the inspector loomed large as the principal channel of communication between the Department and the director of education. It was a channel that could also carry authoritative messages from the centre about more substantive educational matters.

The Department played a pivotal role between the education authorities, where most of the resources were ultimately spent, and the wider central arenas of the Treasury and the Cabinet, where the main decisions on aggregate resources were taken. In governmental circles, the Department, and the Scottish Office as well, competed for a share of public expenditure. Although, for a time, much of the SED's share came automatically, funding depended in part upon what was happening in English education, and in part upon the place of education in the national list of political priorities. In local arenas, the efficient and effective use of money and materials depended to an extent upon competing priorities, but also, on the buildings side, upon technical and administrative capabilities. In addition, although they tried, neither the education authorities nor the SED could do much, if anything at all, about certain adverse factors: demographic change, new developments in housing and planning that required new schools or alterations to old ones, and the inherited stock of often obsolete educational facilities. Nor was it easy to erode resource inequities between localities. They were both the cause and consequence of other educational and social differentials, and it is ironic that the provision of new schools appears to have been least effective in the communities that were most in need of rehousing.

The Department's dependence upon local performance for its own success in wider governmental arenas meant that few of the local authorities could be left on their own to get on with the provision of accommodation. In promoting building activities, however, the SED had also to apply standards, regulations, and cost controls. In these were embedded constraints as well as facilities. These overlapped with educational policies arising from professional and political arenas in determining what form accommodation should take, how the money should be spent, and who should have it.

National economic stringency together with rising educational demand meant that the Department oscillated between two modes, often emphasising regulation more than promotion. In the periods of greatest difficulty with buildings it found itself heavily involved on the ground, and its solution to local authorities' problems was one born of frustration and necessity: supervise closely, help the worst, prepare them to do better in future, and thank God for Aberdeen. But this was perplexing at both levels, for a small Department found itself overburdened, and the local authorities were themselves often frustrated by the way helpful promotion merged with bureaucratic regulation.

Rodger's 1950 code was a more diplomatic, though no less effective, way than hitherto for the Department to assert its influence. But the Department, at that stage, seemed reluctant to develop the more general promotional activities which might, in the long run, enable it to extricate itself from the morass of detailed supervision and nursing of local building programmes. Some local education authorities wished for more, not less, central guidance, and for protection against competing local services. Long accustomed to suckling for their sustenance, they raised a false alarm that the general grant of 1958 was threatening to wean them before time. They prophesied the ruination of the partnership which, as in the days of the *ad hoc* authorities, was felt to embody a special relationship between the Department and themselves.

The education authorities looked to the centre as the spokesman for Scottish education in the wider political process and as the leader in educational policy, though they did not wish to concede to it all rights to determine policy and standards. The SED was also the source of advice on the use of resources, a possible ally of local education departments in their battles with rigid planning by-laws, and the spokesman for Scottish interests at the Treasury. But the SED was sometimes holding back its assistance and rolling out its own red tape instead. Central government was the main financial benefactor, but some suspected that the Department was playing favourites, and they resented it.

As expansion gathered pace in the 1960s, the building programme accelerated, posing afresh a problem for the SED. For, by that time, a new Secretary found the Department bogged down by its dependents' expectations of leadership. He hoped instead to define a more creative policy-management role for the Department. The SED aimed to stimulate the local authorities to meet increased needs, but responsibilities could not safely be left in their hands without widening geographical disparities. Central controls and criteria were not relaxed very much. Moreover, with new policy departures in the mid-1960s, the time for decentralising the initiative seemed inappropriate. In the 1970s, larger and more powerful units of local government were created. They were able to do more for themselves, but no sooner had they dressed themselves up than they found they had nowhere to go: pupil numbers began to fall, inflation rose sharply, and government exerted far tighter control of expenditure than hitherto. The number of new places created in schools fell by half from 1974 to 1978, and the number of places in projects that were started in 1978 was just over a quarter of the number started in 1974 (s ED 1980e, table 2). It was estimated that schools were occupied to only about eighty per cent of capacity in 1978 (*ibid.*, paras 4.1 and 4.2). By the 1980s, the problem was no longer to build schools, but to close them.

Partnership in decision-processes for finance and buildings did not extend in any significant way to teachers, an exclusion about which they complained to the Estimates Committee at the beginning of the 1960s. We will revisit this point in chapter 12, where we consider the relationship between the teaching profession, advice and decision-making. But teachers' salaries were a major charge on current expenditure, and their representatives were directly involved in negotiating them. In the next chapter, therefore, we continue our discussion of resources by looking at salary negotiations and at the problems of teacher supply and distribution.

NOTES

1. Graham (1965, 303).
2. The history of the Goschen formula is obscure, but Mitchell's (1985) account helps to clarify its origin. The formula was first used in 1888 to distribute probate duty between England and Wales (eighty per cent), Scotland (eleven per cent), and Ireland (nine per cent). Although it was based on the countries' general Exchequer contributions, the formula was also close to their proportions of population. The inadequacy of statistics of territorial taxation revenues (Heald 1980b, 18) meant that comparisons of Goschen with population proportions were easier to grasp and to deploy in public argument. However, it is not clear how or why the original formula, expressed as a ratio (Scotland's eleven to England and Wales' eighty) was transmuted to the more generous 'eleven-eightieths'. The latter expression was often used after 1888, and was written into Education Acts in 1918 and in 1946. Heald notes that 'the practical influence of the Goschen formula is astonishingly badly documented' (Heald 1980c, 11). Further afield than education, calculations of Scottish income for public expenditure purposes have sometimes depended on formulae and rules of thumb predicated upon an English base. Although it has always been open to argument and to more precise determination, on a population basis Scotland seems at times, through the use of these rough-and-ready conventions, to have ridden a profitable piggy-back on English expenditure, or on transfer payments between levels of government within England (Boyle 1966; Rhodes 1976).
3. This became the rate-support grant in 1967.
4. Byrne has this to say of the change to the general grant: 'The supposed greater freedom from central control proved largely illusory because central control of capital investment remained and indeed increased, and because control through regulations of central government departments was directly linked to policy decisions and not to financial considerations' (Byrne 1974, 356; see also ch.v).
5. The innovation of the 'Scottish block' occurred in anticipation of devolution. It replaced the separate negotiation and allocation of funds for each Scottish functional programme. Instead, expenditure within the responsibility of the

Scottish Office was given as a total, within which the Secretary of State had some discretion to switch amongst programmes (Heald 1980c; Parry 1982; Keating and Midwinter 1983, ch.10). The Scottish total was determined by a quietly introduced formula, which Heald (1980c, 12) calls the 'Barnett formula' after the Chief Secretary to the Treasury, Joel Barnett. It gave England eighty-five per cent, Scotland ten per cent, and Wales five per cent of any annual changes in 'comparable' expenditure programmes. What Scotland received therefore depended upon the outcome of negotiations between 'English' Ministers and the Treasury, but Heald shows how Scotland is better protected than are England and Wales by the application of the formula during a period of public-expenditure cuts.

6. This discontent was reflected in the thinking of special committees on local government manpower that met in the late 1940s in both countries (West Midland Group 1956, 244-50).

7. In May 1975, a top tier of nine regional and three island authorities, all with responsibilities for education, replaced the earlier system. The regions were divided into districts, which had no education functions. An anomaly of the new system was the vast size of Strathclyde Region, which incorporated the Glasgow conurbation as well as a large rural hinterland. It contained some 2500000 people, almost half the population of Scotland. The population of the Borders Region, by contrast, was only about 100000. Local-government reorganisation also involved the abolition of the three local-authority associations. Their role in preserving a local-authority view and in negotiating with the Scottish Office was taken up by a new organisation, the Convention of Scottish Local Authorities (COSLA). The new local government system is discussed in Keating and Midwinter (1983, part 3).

Ten

Teachers: Salaries, Supply and Distribution

I think that the Department were gravely concerned about teacher supply probably from the War onwards. . . . I remember one civil servant who was in the SED for a long, long time. I met him a couple of years back when he had been out of the Department for some years, and he said to me, 'Is it really true that there is a teacher surplus? Is it really true? All the years I was in the Scottish Education Department the one thing that we all thought about was the shortage of teachers.' Gilbert Bryden, General Secretary of the EIS 1961-74

Introduction

Most of the funds spent by local authorities come from central government; more money is spent on education than on any other local service; and teachers' salaries have always been the largest fraction of local educational expenditure. In 1920, salaries took seventy-four per cent of educational expenditure, and the proportion did not fall below half until 1964-65 as other costs rose (Vaizey and Sheehan 1968, 100; Cumming 1971, 5-6). With the expansion of education after 1945, it is not surprising that the provision and remuneration of teachers loomed large in parliamentary debates on education and on the agendas of administrators in the SED. Here the circularity of education showed itself: producing more teachers tomorrow meant staffing the schools adequately today. It also required an expansion of teacher-training facilities, and improvments in the financial and other conditions of teachers' service.

Like buildings, teachers were a resource whose provision activated governmental participants both inside and outside the educational world. But unlike capital investment, for which the main decision-making procedures tended to exclude teachers, the supply, training and payment of teachers brought their representatives into regular contact, and sometimes conflict, with the education authorities and the SED. In an administrative view of education, teachers may be a 'resource' to be deployed in a classroom. In an educational view, they may, in addition to their teaching role, be an instrument for development and innovation, as they were in the days of Brunton and, more recently, of Munn and Dunning. But these functional perspectives must also be seen in relation to the aspirations and actions of teachers themselves as contenders for political influence over the shaping of their careers and over the substance of education itself. Thus the 'resource' acts and reacts, organises itself, makes some claims successfully but has many others denied, and bargains its support for other participants against the demands it makes upon them.

We discuss teachers at various places in parts III, IV and V. This chapter concentrates on their salary negotiations, and on the problems of supply and distribution. In chapter 12, our attention is focused upon the formation and role of the General Teaching Council (GTC) from the mid-1960s on, and, in particular, on its position as the Secretary of State's adviser on teacher supply and training. In our discussion of the policy community in part V, we consider the Educational Institute of Scotland (EIS) and the Scottish Secondary Teachers' Association (SSTA) as interest groups. There we focus upon the interpersonal trust that underpinned the negotiations of their spokesmen with the Department's officials. We also assess the influence of the associations in national policy-making.

In this chapter, we first look at the negotiation of teachers' salaries. Two sets of considerations influenced the negotiations. First, the profession often found it difficult to aggregate a collective interest beyond the lines of fragmentation that were evident between school sectors, between levels of qualification, and between teachers' organisations. Second, there was a changing relationship between the employing local authorities and the levels of Scottish and British government at which the overall financial and policy decisions were taken. Following our discussion of salaries, we show how the Department attempted to overcome the persistent shortage and uneven distribution of teachers. Inadequate staffing threatened to undermine attempts to equalise opportunity and to innovate. Although the problems were to prove largely intractable, the Department's efforts to solve them led it, in the early 1970s, to supplement piecemeal expedients with a more systematic approach that applied national standards of staffing. All the while, however, the Department searched for better ways of analysing and forecasting demand and supply, as an essential prerequisite for policy-making. We show how the SED came to rely less on what outsiders told it about staffing requirements, and more on its own standards and calculations. This linkage between information and central control, and the more formal style of management it entailed, contributed to a change in the relationship between the SED and the teachers. Teachers were becoming less deferential, but also increasingly apprehensive about their place in the system. Relations with the local education authorities also changed in the 1970s, with implications for local curricular and staffing initiatives; for the staffing needs of a school were now to be defined by a national formula which severely limited the extent to which they could be determined by consultation between the head teacher, the director of education and the local education committee.

Negotiating Teachers' Salaries

Some figures help to put the salaries question into perspective. At prices then current, Scottish local-authority recurrent expenditure on education stood at £17.5 million in 1944-45, of which teachers' salaries were about £10.5 million (SED 1951a, 60). Ten years later, the amounts were about £52 million and £26 million (SED 1956a, appendix 2); in 1964-65, £120 million and £55 million (SED 1966a, appendix 2). By 1985, they had reached about £1,044 million and £510 million (CI 1986, appendices 5 and 7). Inflation apart, these changes reflected the growth of the teaching force and of better salaries in an education system which was itself expanding greatly, especially at the more expensive secondary- and further-education ends. Thus teachers' salary negotiations had major financial implications for the economy as a whole.

Teachers were paid according to the level of their certification. From 1906 to 1965, teachers trained in categories named after chapters of the training regulations, which were amended from time to time. Generally speaking, a Chapter Four teacher taught in a primary school after a three-year course or, if a graduate (and, after 1924, men had to be graduates), a one-year course. Article 39 enabled a Chapter Four teacher who had done two years of a subject at university to qualify to teach it in the lower years of secondary school. First- or second-class honours graduates took a year of training (two terms after 1958) and became Chapter Five subject specialists. Ordinary and third-class honours graduates could follow the Chapter Four/Article 39 route. Chapter Six teachers did not need a degree but were professionally qualified in a technical speciality and trained for up to a year.

National minimum salary scales had been established as far back as 1919 and had lasted until 1945. Just before the outbreak of the Second World War, pressure exerted by the EIS and the ADES led to the establishment of the National Joint Council (NJC) to negotiate teachers' salaries. Through it, the EIS sought to achieve a common maximum salary for graduates and non-graduates, but issues concerning war-service pay soon took precedence on the NJC's agenda. In 1943 the Advisory Council recommended that the minimum scales be replaced by standard scales which would apply uniformly across the education authorities. Tom Johnston, the Secretary of State, assented in principle, and also restructured the NJC to enhance its representativeness and prestige. The NJC was given an independent chairman, Lord Teviot, under whom triennial salary awards were negotiated and proposed to the Secretary of State (Belford 1946, 397-402). Conditions of service were also within the NJC's scope, and remained within the ambit of its successor organisations until 1968, when the Scottish Teachers' Service Conditions Committee (STSCC) was established as a non-statutory body (SED 1969a, 91).[1]

For a period of some twenty years after 1945, the EIS was the only teachers' body with seats at the salary-negotiation table. It formally represented all categories of school teachers as well as those who taught in further-education institutions. The EIS's membership stood at over 25 000 in the 1940s. This increased slowly but fairly steadily to about 35 000 in the early 1970s. It rose to more than 45 000 by 1984, or more than eighty per cent of the Scottish teaching force (Deroche-Drieux 1976, 45; Humes 1986, 137). Founded in 1847, the EIS saw itself as a professional association, or institute, whose concerns for the advancement of education went far beyond questions of salaries and working conditions. In its early decades, its membership embraced the gamut of educational institutions, and included professors, inspectors, Ministers and SED Secretaries. But, for much of this century, the strongest sectoral base of the EIS has been among non-graduate women teachers in primary schools, and geographically, in the west of Scotland. From the 1950s on, the Institute became more militant over issues concerning salaries, conditions, and the 'dilution' of the profession in a period of severe teacher-shortage (see chapter 12). Whilst strikes became part of its repertoire of techniques, serious internal clashes over the desirability of industrial action often pitted the leaders against the more militant, and politically more left-wing, teachers in parts of the urbanised West (McKenzie 1974).

In comparison with teachers in England and Wales, where the largest organisation, the National Union of Teachers (NUT), claims fewer than half the teaching force as members, Scottish teachers have a much more unified presence (Ozga 1985). The vast numerical superiority of the EIS, and the monopoly of the channels of official consultation with the Department which the Institute enjoyed until the 1960s, reinforced this unity to the satisfaction both of the EIS and the SED. Yet, within and outwith the EIS, professional unity was always precarious, and only sometimes achieved in practice. It was not until 1917 that the EIS reabsorbed some smaller associations that had split off from it before the turn of the century. Between the Wars, pressure groups crystallised within the Institute to advance the interests of different sections of the profession which felt insufficiently protected by the EIS as a whole.

In 1933, the Scottish Schoolmasters' Association (SSA) was formed in this way by men teachers who felt their status threatened by women teachers' pressure for equal salaries (Deroche-Drieux 1976, 33). Bolstered by a dual-membership arrangement with the National Association of Schoolmasters (NAS) in England and Wales, with which it eventually merged in 1976, the SSA seceded from the EIS in 1954, one year before the principle of equal pay for men and women was instituted as government policy. The number of members reported by the SSA has fluctuated considerably (*ibid.*, 59). Membership apparently approached 4 000 in 1956, but fell away to just over 2 000 in 1965 before rising again to the former figure in 1974. Ten years later, its membership was said to have been 2 500 (*ibid.*, 47;

Humes 1986, 137). Although the smallest of the three main Scottish associations, it has been the most militant, especially on questions of salaries.

The SSTA is a larger and more moderate organisation. It has a substantial minority following among teachers of academic subjects in secondary school, and its influence in Departmental consultation on educational matters has been relatively weighty (see chapters 4 and 18). Like the SSA, the SSTA began as a grouping within the EIS, perhaps embryonically in 1921 (Deroche-Drieux 1976, 35), but later as a distinct body of dissidents when, in 1944, a number of teachers from the 'elite' secondary schools formed a 'defence committee'. Their main concern was that the EIS policy of a common maximum salary for graduate and non-graduate teachers represented a threat to the recruitment of highly qualified graduates into the teaching profession, and therefore a threat to the quality of secondary education. They felt that the internal structure of the EIS gave too much say to non-graduate, women primary-school teachers.

Among the SSTA's founders were some of the leading headmasters, including Dewar and J.J. Robertson, and principal teachers like Gray, who became its first General Secretary. Like these three persons, many of its most prominent members were 'classics'. When the SSTA broke away to form a separate association in 1946, it numbered almost a quarter of all secondary teachers, or some 1900 members, in categories that spanned the range of secondary teachers' levels of qualification (*ibid.*, 42). Its membership grew slowly to just under 4000 in 1969, but then rose rapidly in the 1970s (*ibid.*, 46). In 1972, it had more members in Edinburgh than in either Glasgow or Lanarkshire (*ibid.*, 56). The SSTA's numbers declined to slightly under 7000 in 1984 (Humes 1986, 137), representing roughly the same percentage of secondary teachers as in 1946.

Despite the educational prestige of its leading members, and its relative strength in the only sector of the educational system in which it recruited, the SSTA, like the SSA, was long denied formal access to the Department's procedures of consultation and negotiation. However, Gray told us that the Department was always glad to receive the SSTA's memoranda. The EIS brought pressure to bear in the late 1940s in order to reinforce its monopoly once the SSTA had broken away, whilst Labour Secretaries of State tried to heal the breach between the two organisations (Munro and Ross 1985). Murrie told us that Henderson Stewart, the Education Minister in the subsequent Conservative Government, also tried to bring the two bodies together (see chapter 8). However, other evidence suggests that the Minister wanted to tap more freely the SSTA's advice on certification, but that Murrie thought this would be seen as tantamount to recognition, a thin end of the wedge that the SSTA might seek to drive home for salary-negotiation purposes (*ibid.*). Gray told us that the SSTA was indeed pressing for this, and that Murrie 'was really staving us off but at the same time anxious to do everything possible to maintain contact . . . he didn't want to put us down exactly'.

At first, the SSTA was kept out. Bryden confirmed that Murrie favoured the *status quo* but, he told us, when Arbuckle succeeded Murrie as Secretary in 1957, Arbuckle 'let the SSTA in'. The recognition of the SSTA for the purposes of educational consultation coincided with Brunton's reforms of the secondary curriculum and examinations. But it was another seven years before the SSTA was able to gain entry to the salary-negotiation machinery.

Equal pay for women and men, and a common maximum salary for graduate and non-graduate teachers, were focal points of teachers' politics in the 1940s and 1950s. The size of each salary award, and its distribution to a teaching force which was stratified by qualifications, and divided by sectors and by gender, emerged as contentious issues in the 1960s and 1970s. The salaries question pointed up differences of interest and of bargaining power amongst teachers themselves as they pressed collectively for public recognition of their professional status, and for the levels of reward they felt were commensurate with it. Equal pay for women came over a seven-year period from 1955 as part of overall government policy towards pay in the non-industrial public service. The EIS objective of a common maximum had been achieved on the first post-war scales, although separately for men and for women, and led to the breakaway of the SSTA in 1946. The common maximum for women, however, was abandoned by the Government in 1951 in order to encourage graduate recruitment. It was abandoned for men in 1955 because the equal-pay policy would have created difficulties in recruiting graduates, and would have been expensive, if all women could rise to the graduate men's maximum (SED 1956a, 68).

Our description of salary negotiations relies on the accounts given by two men who were centrally involved in the process. Gilbert Bryden was an EIS representative on the NJC from 1953 to 1961, when he became General Secretary of the EIS. He continued as one of the principal negotiators on behalf of teachers up to his retirement in 1974, serving on the NJC and on the bodies which succeeded it (see below). Allan Rodger was the Secretary of State's assessor on the NJC before he became Under-Secretary in 1959. Thereafter, he had no place in the formal machinery, but continued to discharge Departmental responsibilities for teacher affairs until he retired in 1963. The relationship between Bryden and Rodger was a crucial one. Trust between ostensible antagonists persisted in the midst of public conflicts over pay, and through years in which the professional status of teachers, and their participation in educational decision-making, were under active consideration (see chapter 12).

On the employers' side of the NJC, there were twelve members, of whom eight came from the Association of County Councils and four from the Counties of Cities Association. On the teachers' side, all twelve came from the EIS. In addition, as assessors, there were three directors of education and three local-authority officials. The Secretary of State appointed a chairman and an assessor. Bryden outlined the process by which salary claims were negotiated:

BRYDEN. The Institute's salaries committee produced proposals for the [triennial] salaries review . . . based on the views of a number of panels.
. . . For example, there was a panel representing male honours graduates, one representing female honours graduates, one representing male graduates, one representing female graduates, one representing Chapter Six men teachers (that is, teachers who are now called teachers of practical and aesthetic subjects), one representing Chapter Six women teachers and one representing non-graduate women teachers. . . . A Special General Meeting . . . then, in theory, produced the final salaries proposals which were sent to the National Joint Council. The proposals were almost invariably remitted to a negotiating committee . . . which had five on each side. If you had no agreement within the negotiating committee, the proposals went to the full National Joint Council, where, as often as not, agreement was reached. If agreement wasn't reached, they went to arbitration . . . [under an arbiter appointed by] the Lord President of the Court of Session . . . [whose] conclusion became the finding of the National Joint Council, and it was sent to the Secretary of State, just as an agreement . . . was. . . . The Secretary of State then published draft salaries regulations and everybody who was interested had the chance to make observations on the draft. . . . All these observations were processed in the Scottish Education Department, I suppose in consultation with the Treasury, and the joint Parliamentary Under-Secretary of State who was in charge of education affairs in Scotland invited the National Joint Council to meet him in St Andrew's House.

Q. As far as you know, was that the first point at which the Treasury might come in?

BRYDEN. I really know nothing about the extent to which the Treasury came in. . . . All that I know for certain is that every now and again a senior civil servant from St Andrew's House went to the Treasury and argued the case for Scottish teachers' salaries. This I think probably happened round about the time of the meeting with the Joint Parliamentary Under-Secretary of State.

Rodger's account of the process, however, suggests that the Treasury's position came into play via the Secretary of State's assessor at an early stage in the negotiation within the NJC:

RODGER. Now, I sat beside the chairman and the two sides faced one another. . . . Informally both had a good idea of what the opposite side's attitude was to be. Usually it was . . . the teachers' spokesman who spoke first. Obviously in such a complex field with the many qualifications that teachers have, he couldn't cover every detail. He would make broad general proposals, probably not much more than that, in his general view, salaries should go up on this occasion by around about ten per cent; I don't mean ten per cent for everybody, but taking that all over. The other side would say, 'Well, we have considered this, and we think that, bearing in mind the increases that have been given in other walks of life which are comparable to yours, that we would be prepared to accede [to] an all-round broad increase of six per cent'. . . . Other people from both sides would make speeches, and perhaps neither side would give way. If I had a general message from the Treasury, say, that the Government would not go beyond eight per cent, it was at this stage that I would announce it. Then the chairman might say, 'Well, could you go to separate rooms, and see whether either of you could move in the direction of the other?'

Bryden's and Rodger's descriptions diverge at this point. Bryden said the SED's assessor never voiced arguments:

BRYDEN. They never took any part in negotiations, and if, as frequently happened, the two sides separated in the course of discussions, the SED's assessor always left, went out, very often, and had a cup of tea with the chairman, who of course also left.

Rodger, on the other hand, recalled that he was more actively engaged in the proceedings:

RODGER. I was free to go into either of the rooms and listen to their talk, and I would perhaps say to the teachers, 'I don't think that you should pursue your ten per cent too far, you know'. I said, 'I know that Burnham[2] in England is going to give eight per cent; and . . . the Treasury will say, 'What's good enough in England, should satisfy Scotland', and therefore if you pursue beyond eight per cent, you are probably going to get the Secretary of State into difficulty, and yourselves into the difficulty that your claim won't be met'. So I would leave them and I would go and see the authorities' side and I would tell them . . . that they should be prepared to go the length of eight per cent. The two sides would meet and the teachers' spokesman might speak again and say . . . 'the lowest we will go is nine per cent'. And this kind of bargaining would go on and then perhaps they would reach agreement. . . . Then they started on the details . . . perhaps the spokesman for non-graduate women would say, 'As non-graduate women, we are the lowest paid of all, and therefore, if it is going to be . . . a variable figure of eight per cent on average, we are the ones that should get the most'. And you would probably get the honours graduates saying, 'Oh well, if there are differences at the moment, and you are at the bottom of the scale, it is because we are much better qualified than you, and therefore it should be proportional increases'. . . . The teachers' side had not always resolved their internal difficulties beforehand.

Q. But it was always that sequence, was it, with the global figure first, and then the cut of the cake second?

RODGER. I wouldn't like to say that that was invariably so. . . . Burnham in England may not yet have reached agreement. Even if the English figure was known, I perhaps was not at liberty to state the full length that Scotland might be prepared to go. This is a point on which I disagreed sometimes with the Treasury and sometimes with the Secretary of State. . . . I would sometimes have to announce a figure which was less than that to which the Government were prepared to go to. I used to argue with the Treasury that this was wrong.

Q. You were in fact advised by the Treasury as to what sort of bargaining strategy to adopt, and what sequence it was to be done in?

RODGER. Yes, to some extent. . . . A global sum was not *exactly* determined in the first place. The Treasury had a global sum in mind, but subsequent pressures may have caused them to revise it, normally upwards. . . . As assessor, I knew the supply position and I sometimes gently prompted the official side to go not for a flat increase or flat percentage but for an advantage to a group in specially short supply.[3]

We have so far seen something of the importance to Scotland of the Burnham negotiations in England and of the Treasury's overall financial control. Equal pay for women was another example of how, in the 1950s, national policy affected Scottish teachers' salaries. Moreover, the Treasury sometimes queried Scotland's costly policy that male teachers, even in primary schools, must be graduates, and Rodger himself wondered how this difference could be justified. Nevertheless, it continued, as did the different structure of qualifications for teaching in secondary schools. As long as the Goschen formula lasted, the proportionately higher salaries bill, as compared with the South, was met from within Scotland's share, which was not earmarked to particular categories of spending on education. But Bryden thought that, even after Goschen was abolished, as much as thirteen-eightieths of the corresponding English expenditure still went towards salaries in Scotland.

The Burnham settlements could be used tactically for Scottish purposes. Bryden said that he, 'had lots of confidence in Rodger in spite of the fact that we often differed quite radically'. He illustrated how their relationship came into play:

BRYDEN. If there was a prior English award, it influenced the award in Scotland. . . . Quite frequently the reverse took place and then we influenced the English settlement. . . . For a very long time, as long as negotiations were triennial, the two settlements were more or less coincidental. . . . It was not until 1963 that we got out of alignment. The going rate at that time was three per cent and the English settled for six per cent on the understanding that there would be nothing doing for a couple of years. About the same time, we made a tentative agreement on a similar basis. But before anything had been finalised, it occurred to me that if we could get six per cent on the understanding that the settlement would last for two years, we might be able to get nine per cent for three. I knew that Rodger was going to London and I had a pretty good idea that he was going to put our tentative agreement to the Treasury. So I telephoned him and asked him not to come to any final decision before I had had another word with him. He promised. I got the teachers' panel together and put my suggestion to them. They agreed. I got Rodger as soon as he returned from London. He accepted the idea and the thing was put through. So while England had six per cent for two years, we had nine per cent for three, which put us out of alignment and it was quite a while before we came back into alignment again.[4]

Rodger explained the advantage he saw in this proposal:

RODGER. This suggestion, if I remember rightly, appealed to me because, although he was asking for . . . more, he was more or less giving us the assurance that we weren't going to have a further claim for a considerable time, and I thought that it was probably cheap to buy him off in this way. I think that I agreed to that . . . and got the Secretary of State to agree.

An adverse expenditure climate developed in the 1960s and persisted thereafter. The salary settlement of 1961 marked a dramatic turning-point for relations between teachers and government and for the developing professional and trade-union consciousness of Scottish teachers. The Secretary of State's treatment of the teachers' salary claim helped precipitate what was, in effect, the first-ever Scottish teachers' strike. We note its main consequences in chapter 12. Bryden explained what happened to the NJC's recommendation:

BRYDEN. We had our triennial settlement in 1960, and in early 1961 we went back to the NJC for more. . . . We actually got an award of about eighteen per cent, which was a colossal percentage in those days. It was twelve-and-one-half per cent together with a great reduction in the length of the scale, and that came out to eighteen per cent . . . and the Secretary of State rejected this and substituted one of about fourteen-and-one-half per cent. . . . Some of the scales, instead of being shortened to about twelve years or something like that, were pushed back to something like sixteen, and it was also a very poor award to the non-graduate teachers. . . . This was one of the occasions when we were far ahead of the English, and I'm sure that the Scottish Education Department had the utmost difficulty in extracting the money for that big settlement from the Treasury, and eventually they were forced to trim, and trim, and trim, and trim, and they looked, I suppose, at the supply situation. The supply situation for non-graduates was rather better than the supply situation for honours graduates, and they just decided to cut it off, and it gave us an immense amount of trouble.

The negotiating machinery came under scrutiny in the early 1960s and was revised twice. The first change in the machinery had to do with domestic Scottish divisions of interest on the teachers' side and with the issue of interest-group representation.[5] The second change came in 1967 with the establishment of the Scottish Teachers' Salaries Committee (STSC). This was the result of the pressure of political and economic circumstances upon the determination of Scottish teachers' salaries. The STSC adopted a new English procedure, which was urged upon Scotland by the National Board for Prices and Incomes (NBPI) in 1966, by having the Secretary of State's representatives as full members on the management side. The STSC had twenty-one members on the teachers' side (sixteen EIS, three SSTA, and two SSA), and a total of fourteen on the management side, including the two officials (Hunter 1972, 262). James Clark, who was an assessor on the local-authority side of the STSC, thought this put an end to 'shadow boxing' and made it a more effective body. Bryden's view was similar:

BRYDEN. The change from the SJC to the STSC was initiated . . . largely as a result of pressure from the Institute . . . largely by me. The main reason being that, while the NJC had worked quite well as long as the Secretary of State accepted the findings of the NJC, in the early sixties he had begun to depart from that and to upset the findings of the SJC. It became intolerable to have negotiations that were just chucked into the waste-paper basket as soon as they were finished, and . . . it seemed to me better to have all the fights within the negotiating machinery and at the end come to a final conclusion, than to . . . have the conclusion upset by the Secretary of State. . . . If there was an agreement, he was bound by that agreement. . . . But if there was a disagreement and the matter went to arbitration, he was bound by the findings of the court of arbitration unless both Houses of Parliament resolved that national economic circumstances required that effect should not be given to the findings. The likely difficulty of getting both Houses to reject the findings of a court of arbitration no doubt represented a substantial restriction of the powers of the Secretary of State.

On the other hand, any such restriction must be seen in the context of stronger governmental pressure to control incomes and public spending.[6] Graham put it this way:

GRAHAM. If the Treasury wanted to exercise any sort of control at all over expenditure in education in Scotland, they had to take some account [of] what was proposed for teachers' salaries. . . . Once governments developed pay policies, whatever they might be, what happened to teachers had to be looked at in that context because, usually, what happened to teachers was related to what happened elsewhere in the public sector.

We asked Bryden whether he then found that financial and Treasury arguments were being invoked at an earlier stage than previously:

BRYDEN. I would have said that there wasn't any change at all as far as I could see. Not until the . . . autumn of 1974, [when] we were trying . . . to persuade the Government to give us a large chunk of the Houghton award before it came out. We had a colossal battle, and at that time we, I think, practically won . . . but the Secretary of State's representatives, on the instructions of the Government, of course, wouldn't agree. And we were sure that the majority of members of the authorities' panel were prepared to agree with us, and we challenged them. . . . And it was then revealed that, when the STSC was set up, there was an agreement within the management side of the panel that, while the authorities would be free to determine the distribution of any offer that they might make, the size of the offer was left, ultimately, to the discretion of the representative of the Secretary of State.

There was, in fact, nothing covert about the agreement to give the Secretary of State control over the total sum. This had been explicitly stated by Ross when the Scottish Grand Committee debated the Remuneration of Teachers (Scotland) Bill that brought in the new machinery. Now that Government, under the rate-support grant, was footing the major part of the salaries bill and more of local expenditure overall, it could no longer merely rubber-stamp a recommended salary award. Moreover, he argued, incomes policy had to be borne in mind (PD 1967a). Millan's view was that the 'concordat' on the management side 'put the whole thing on a much more rational basis':

MILLAN. The overall cost of the settlement was something which was decided and determined by the Government, rather than the local authorities. Now, I don't mean by that that we simply went along and said, 'We have decided right at the start of the negotiations that this is what it is going to be, and we are not going to listen to anything that you say to us'. But ultimately, if there was a difference of view, the Government view rather than the local-authority view prevailed. You were involved in the negotiations right from the start, and that really gave you more scope for influencing the course of the negotiations. Of course, the local authorities don't like that, because they would like more freedom to decide what they do themselves.

Q. Did the Treasury set the total amount available before negotiation began?

MILLAN. No. It's not really a question of what the Treasury as such wants or sets. . . . If one is talking about a period when there is an incomes policy, the Government has a view about incomes generally, and therefore the Government management representatives on that committee are actually putting the Government view. It is not a Treasury view in the sense that there is some kind of negotiation between the Department and the Treasury in which . . . you go to the Treasury and say, 'We want to offer ten', and they say 'No. You can only give five', and then you offer seven-and-one-half. Really we didn't work like that, because during these recent periods in which I have been involved, anyway, there has been an *overall* Government view, and the teachers, as well as other people, have fitted into that. Therefore, in the salary negotiations, the Department are not taking an independent line, in the sense that they are determining it simply as an individual Department; they are following a particular Government policy, and that's really applied, again, right up until the negotiations in 1979, where the settlement was very much in line with what the Government policy at that time was.

The extremely favourable Houghton salary award was implemented in Scotland in 1975, but it was made on the basis of an independent salary investigation conducted for Britain as a whole (CI 1974). Houghton looked not only at the immediate pay claim but at salary and career structures as well, and some have remarked upon the irony that the windfall it recommended came just at the moment when an oversupply of teachers was envisaged (Whiteside and Bernbaum 1979, 99). The Clegg award, at the end of the 1970s, was also generous, and was based upon another independent national enquiry into teachers' pay (SCPC 1980). Government's unpalatable experience with such outside reviews made it reluctant to concede another one in the mid-1980s unless it was linked to conditions of service.

We now consider the problem of teacher supply, and the Department's attempts to master it.

Problems of Supply

For some thirty years after 1945, the schools were chronically short of teachers as policies interacted with demographic changes and with pupils' decisions about staying on at school. Together, these factors produced levels of demand that the SED and the local authorities could only partially anticipate, understand or control. Demand was pushed up, first, by the raising of the school-leaving age to fifteen in 1947, and by the high birth rates of the late 1940s. This bulge of pupils progressed as a moving frontier of demand through the primary schools, and then through the secondary schools after 1959. Even before the O-grade was available in 1962, increasing proportions were staying on to post-compulsory schooling, and more did so thereafter. A second population bulge of longer duration originated after 1955, and began to make its way into the primaries in the early 1960s. The leaving age was raised again in 1973. On top of this, roughly one pupil in three in the 1970s stayed on for at least an extra year, and one in seven for two extra years (Gray *et al.*, 1983, 70, figure 5.1). In addition, revisions of the Schools Code had by 1956 reduced the maximum numbers of pupils to forty-five in primary classes, to forty in the first three years of secondary school, and to thirty in the post-compulsory years. There were strong pressures at all levels of the policy community to improve staffing standards even further. The effect this might have on the demand for teachers was difficult to estimate precisely, but the Departmental Supply Committee put the possible additional total at 3100 if the primary maximum were, for example, forty, and the secondary uniformly thirty (SED 1962f, para.73).

On the eve of the Second World War, there were some 29000 teachers in Scottish schools, of whom fewer than 13000 were graduates (SED 1956a, 62). Ten years later there were only about ten per cent more teachers. One-third of all teachers were men, and there was a pariah caste of some 900 teachers who were uncertificated. There was an estimated shortage in 1949 of some 2300. It was expected that, through the mid-1950s, normal wastage would remove upwards of 1200 teachers annually, and that the large increases in the number of classrooms being built would add several hundred more teachers per year to the requirement (SED 1951c, paras 7, 9, 12, 15 and 23). The numbers recruited and in service rose continuously but too slowly, and many deficiencies remained. Salaries and promotion prospects improved, although, at a number of points from the early 1960s onwards, teachers felt that their relative economic position and their conditions of service had worsened. By the time the number of primary pupils began to decline in 1974, there were about 52000 teachers in the schools (SED 1975a, 23-4, tables E and F). Secondary rolls were still growing, and the total teaching force reached 58000 in 1976-77 (SED 1979b, table 1c). But, with falling school rolls, the long era of overall teacher shortage was then supplanted by the unfamiliar and volatile politics of contraction. Between 1979 and 1985, the numbers of primary and secondary pupils shrank by twenty per cent and around eight per cent, respectively. The corresponding reductions in the numbers of teachers were around twenty per cent and around six per cent (CI 1986, appendix 2).

The teacher shortage decomposed into several discrete problems, with different characteristics and different possible remedies, and the moving frontier of pupil demand shifted the problem from one sector to another as time went on. An undersupply of teachers who were qualified under Chapters Four and Five had begun in 1936-37 (SED 1944a, 12, tables 3 and 4; 13), and the all-round wartime shortages were anything but temporary. Even when overall shortages had been overcome, there was still the chronic problem, stretching back over four decades, of the acute shortage of teachers in mathematics, science, and technical subjects. Another long-standing difficulty was the uneven geographical distribution of all types of teachers. This resisted remedial strategies and remained an affront both to egalitarian values and to the aspirations of local communities.

The Department spent about three decades after 1945 wrestling with the changing nature and extent of staffing deficiencies, and with geographical inequalities in staffing. Several schemes were adopted to recruit more teachers, both generally and in selected categories. Some training courses were shortened and there were large publicity campaigns to attract people to the training colleges. Through improved arrangements for pensions and retirement, retired teachers were induced back into service and older teachers encouraged to stay in service longer. Financial inducements were also offered to even out the area distribution of teachers.

These expedients strained against the rigidities of training and certification requirements, and against the dubious attractions of teaching in the industrial West. The Treasury was unwilling to allow costly or precedent-setting solutions such as full pay and pensions for retired teachers returning to service, though Murrie, the Advisory Council and others argued for them. Remedies were also hampered by general shortages of educated, and especially university-trained, people from amongst whom additional teachers might be drawn. In an era of educational expansion, the young teachers that were required had to be taken, until the mid-1960s, from the smaller age-groups of the 1930s and early 1940s. There were more attractive employment prospects available, especially for graduates, and a trend to earlier marriage took a large proportion of newly trained teachers out of service within a few years of entry.

To what extent could general scale increases help to overcome shortages, as the EIS contended? The Department's annual report for 1951 said that shortages had influenced the new salary scales (SED 1952a, 61). Bryden cited instances where better salaries helped, but he thought they were neither large enough nor relatively favourable for long enough, to enable one to judge their effects. Indeed, the Department's own Supply Committee had said this in 1957 (SED 1957b, para.34). Bryden recalled that Maclay, the Secretary of State, was reported to have thought that even a doubling of teachers' salaries would have improved the supply position only marginally. Graham thought that there was an upper limit to the inducement higher salaries could offer. He noted that a high proportion of the universities' output of arts graduates was already being absorbed into teaching. It was not until the post-Robbins expansion of higher education that there was a large increase in the graduate intake. But Rodger recalled that the immediate post-war deficiencies and the gloomy prognosis had, at an earlier time, made better salaries a possible solution:

RODGER. At that stage, of course, this situation was a gift to the teachers' negotiators on salaries . . . they said that the way to get more teachers is to give teachers increased salaries.

Q. Was their philosophy accepted by the Department?

RODGER. No. Only in part . . . how could anybody tell if you put the teachers' salaries up by £100 [or by £200] a year, how many more teachers you were going to get? . . . But we thought the problem was bigger than that, and we thought that many people were staying out of teaching, not on financial grounds only, but for other reasons.

Even as early as 1943, the Advisory Council's interim report on the Recruitment and Supply of Teachers spoke loudly for better salaries and salary scales as the crucial means for increasing the supply in order to meet eventual post-war demands (SED 1944a, appendix I). Perhaps the Department itself had to be circumspect and underplay the extent to which better pay was the answer, lest it be seen to be a lobby on behalf of teachers. However, in its annual reports it often acknowledged a link between remuneration and supply. On the other hand, in the mid-1950s it did not improve the salaries of junior-secondary teachers to stem the loss of staff and raise their morale, although they were given additional money when junior-secondaries presented for the O-grade in the 1960s.

Some of the special programmes that were put into effect offered specific inducements. The first of these was the Emergency Training Scheme. It was launched in 1945, in Scotland as well as in the South, to restore pre-war levels of staffing and to prepare for the first raising of the leaving age, to fifteen in 1947. A shortened period of training on reduced entrance requirements was offered to persons who had given national service in wartime. The Scheme had its main impact before 1950. When it ended in 1959, well over 4000 teachers had been trained under it. At the end of the 1940s, the numbers in normal training were better, but the best university graduates were less attracted to teaching than to other careers, and wastage was taking its toll of teachers. The shortage was estimated at just under 3000 in 1950 and was rising (SED 1951a, 54). New developments brought a sense of impending crisis: an expanding building programme, the higher leaving age, and a new Code which reduced the primary class maximum. The very high birth rate that began in 1947 was expected to start affecting the schools by 1952. Rodger describes the origin of the second major scheme:

RODGER. Miss [Margaret] Herbison was the junior Minister at this time. . . . She said, 'I wish that you people would try to think out some means of getting more teachers'. And Mackay Thomson asked me . . . if I could spend the weekend thinking about it . . . I hit on the idea . . . that another source of recruitment should be tapped: namely the persons who had probably always wanted to be teachers . . . but for economic or other reasons had not been able to, and who had probably drifted into other occupations altogether. . . . On the Monday morning I presented [Mackay Thomson] with my ideas, which he agreed with. We took them to Miss Herbison, she agreed with them; and that was the origin of the Special Recruitment Scheme.

Q. How far was cost a consideration in such *ad hoc* schemes?

RODGER. I wouldn't say that cost was the prime consideration. . . . Grants, at least in some cases, would have to be considerable. Nor could I really quantify the costs. . . . I had put forward my view to a meeting of the Secretariat and no one (somewhat to my surprise) regarded the cost as an insuperable obstacle. Possibly the need for more teachers made them swallow something that would not normally have been acceptable. Then Miss Herbison liked the scheme and chose to disregard the difficulty over costs. Presumably we had to get Treasury approval, but, strangely, I have no memory of that. I certainly don't remember any real disputes.

The Scheme became a crucial source of recruitment outside normal channels before its scope was restricted in 1972 to graduates and technical specialists. In 1970-71 it accounted for more than twenty per cent of the total intake into primary and secondary training in the colleges (SED 1972a, 30).

Special Recruitment had been hatched within the SED, but the Department went outside for advice on how to overcome the worst shortages amongst academic subject teachers, those in science and mathematics in secondary schools. There was a fifteen per cent deficiency in 1953 and it was expected to be nearly twice that within a few years (SED 1953b, appendix, table 9). A committee was appointed, chaired by Sir Edward Appleton, Principal of Edinburgh University. Two secondary-school head teachers served on it, but its composition was heavily weighted towards higher education and industry. It reported in 1955 (SED 1955c).

The Appleton Committee couched the problem in several wider considerations: an overall shortage of educated manpower, of mathematicians and scientists, and of teachers in general. The report recommended better promotion prospects, the upgrading of third-class honours subspecialists, and lower entry requirements for training. Its proposal for higher salary scales for mathematics and science teachers was particularly controversial amongst teachers. Appleton frankly advocated 'dilution' through the use of non-specialists and subspecialists for work above the level of their qualifications. But this was anathema to teachers who cherished the goal of a graduate profession. Murrie told us that he would have backed salary differentials had it not been for EIS opposition. Yet the EIS, in rejecting subject differentials, turned the Appleton report into a broader gain through the NJC. With the local authorities' co-operation, it secured scale rises for all secondary teachers.

Rodger, as the SED's assessor on Appleton, seems to have appreciated the teachers' point of view, and viewed the Appleton recommendation with some despair:

RODGER. None of the three teachers' bodies would wear this. . . . They said, 'If you want strikes on your hands, start that. . . . I put the point, I'm fairly sure, that it was creating invidious differences between teachers who, in their view, were in the same rank, and of the same qualification.

As the first bulge in the age-group approached secondary education, teacher supply was a growing concern. It was clear by 1957 that staff shortages would become acute in the early 1960s and would continue at least until 1967. The SED again sought support from outside for a reduction in the standards for admission to teacher training. The Department took the Advisory Council out of mothballs and gave it a remit under the chairmanship of the Principal of St Andrews University, T.M. Knox (see chapter 11). J.J. Robertson was vice-chairman and Rodger the SED's assessor. To the Department's disappointment, however, Knox was unable to persuade the teachers on the committee to accept dilution. The report, like Appleton's, put the problem in the context of a general shortage of educated manpower and the need to increase the size of the pool of able pupils from which graduate teachers could ultimately be drawn (SED 1959d). The Advisory Council urged full pay and pensions for retired teachers returning to service, but the Government rejected this because it was inconsistent with the principles of public-service superannuation. Knox successfully proposed improved salary scales and responsibility payments. But, in rejecting the recruitment of non-graduate men for teaching general subjects, the Advisory Council upheld one of the main principles of the Scottish teaching profession. It dashed the hopes of Rodger, whose view was supported among committee members only by Betty Harvie Anderson of Stirlingshire's Education Committee. It was probably not a measure of his desperation that he went to her hospital bedside to obtain her Note of Reservation. But the Department needed whatever support it could gather. In her Note, Anderson criticised the Council's rejection of dilution and the inflexibilities in the salary and promotion structures which it had left untouched. In view of Appleton's unwelcome suggestions and Rodger's own disillusion, it might seem odd that the SED had remitted the secondary staffing question to yet another non-Departmental committee under an independent chairman. Rodger's comment on this adds a further irony, for it suggests that the Department had not really expected a dramatic breakthrough:

Q. Was the Advisory Council report a better instrument than Appleton, with which the Department could do something about shortages?

RODGER. No. It gave certain recommendations which we could try to put into operation, but, in fact, these did not generally prove to be very effective. The truth of the matter is that the Department had faced and thought about the shortage of teachers for years. An outside body could contribute nothing that had not occurred to us. . . . It is extremely difficult for a body to produce new productive ideas in a field which has been thought over for years.

Q. Could you have predicted that in advance?

RODGER. I think that I would have predicted that in advance.

Why the Department had chosen to work through the Advisory Council we explain in chapter 11.

Compression of the length of training courses and the upgrading of third-class graduates were among the recommendations made by the Advisory Council. Graduate recruitment did indeed rise from the late 1950s on, although mathematics and science still lagged behind. The staffing deficiency in mathematics, for example, remained around the twenty per cent mark for many years. Other expedients that were used for all categories of teachers included the attraction of married women back to teaching, and the compression of courses for Chapter Five students into seven months. In 1959, the maximum salary of third-class honours graduates was raised to equivalence with that of better qualified teachers, and their status as specialised teachers was granted in the Regulations.

The numbers recruited and in service rose continuously, partly as a result of some of these measures. But improvements were slow, for it proved extremely difficult to provide the salaries, conditions and status which would make teaching careers attractive in a strongly competitive market for trained persons. Although graduate recruitment improved in the 1960s, teachers with ambitions for promoted posts faced a gloomy prospect. Policies for 'rationalising' secondary provision had reduced the number of schools from just under 900 in 1950 to under 500 in 1972, at which time it was expected to fall to 400 by 1980 (SED 1973b, paras 2.3 and 2.9). Whereas, in 1970, about twenty-five per cent of pupils were in schools with rolls of 900 or more, the SED expected this percentage to have at least doubled by 1974 (Brodie 1972, 38, table 1).

With fewer headships available in the 1960s, and with ROSLA approaching, teachers faced unsatisfactory promotion prospects in the large comprehensive schools that were rapidly becoming the norm. In 1971, the Department published its review of the structure of promoted posts (SED 1971b, 1971c). The SED acknowledged the need to provide a better career structure as a result of rising pupil numbers, curricular changes, larger schools, and new departures in pupil guidance and extra-curricular activities. About 1000 promoted posts would be added to the 8000 existing ones, establishing the new ranks of assistant head, assistant principal (subject), and principal and assistant principal (guidance). These were phased in over two years from 1972, with indicative complements for schools (SED 1972d). With a lead from the centre, the managerial spirit had worked its way towards the schools in two ways. The Secretary of State 'emphasised the need for authorities to develop a policy for staff management and training designed to secure that all teachers in their employment should see a clear path to the highest posts' (SED 1972a, 29). And colleges of education planned courses that were 'designed to equip promoted staff with the managerial and other skills' required by the new posts (*ibid.*, 31). In the following decade, however, the new structure of promoted posts did more to keep teachers in the schools than it did to convert them to managerialism. A Departmental review in 1984 found that the school subject departments retained much of their decision-making autonomy (SED 1984). Meanwhile, the Department had noted one other curricular implication of staffing policies. With the move of aspirant teachers into the senior vacancies created in the 1970s, local curriculum development was depleted (see chapter 14).

Problems of Distribution

Great regional disparities in staffing meant far worse pupil-teacher ratios in Glasgow, Lanarkshire, Renfrewshire and some other authorities, mostly in the industrial areas. In 1968, for example, there was one secondary teacher in the City of Aberdeen for every thirteen of its pupils, but only one teacher in Lanarkshire for every twenty-one pupils (SED 1969a, 37). The worse-off authorities had to put up with oversize classes. They hired large numbers of uncertificated teachers and left vacancies unfilled. On the other hand, the plentiful local supply of teachers-in-training in Aberdeen sustained the philosophy of Clark and his education committee that schools should be staffed generously and in accordance with the expressed needs of head teachers. This kept the city's schools amongst the best endowed in Scotland: Lady Tweedsmuir's 'delectable place for teachers'.

The uneven distribution of teachers was seen as a problem on both sides of the Border. From the mid-1950s, it was being addressed by the Ministry of Education (Pile 1979, 130). Meanwhile, Rodger sought ways to even out the differences in Scotland. The Department involved the local authorities and the EIS in a working party that was set up to consider voluntary self-restraint in hiring by the above-average authorities. However, the attempt came to nothing in 1957. Murrie told us that, with respect to the education authorities, the SED had 'not really any influence, except to appeal to their better feelings'. 'Human nature being what it is', he said, 'teachers prefer to live in Edinburgh to living in certain other parts of the country, which perhaps should be nameless'.

Nevertheless, the working party tried again in 1959 (SED 1960a, 73). George Gray commented upon its approach:

GRAY. I think it was very largely a failure. It drew out the figures of supply and demand and employment, and showed what were the needs of each particular education area, and how it was satisfying these needs, and where it could get the supply of teachers. . . . The whole idea was to provide a kind of index figure to which each local authority would agree to stick. . . . A formula was devised, but it was a formula which no central authority could enforce.

The scheme was established only after difficult negotiations with the EIS and the local-authority associations (SED 1961a, 77-8). It lasted from 1960 to 1964 and gained over 400 more teachers for the worst areas (SED 1966a, 59). This helped a bit, but not enough to make dramatic inroads on the imbalance. Millan told us it was ineffective. Echoing Murrie's remark, Gray, Bryden and Clark all argued that one major drawback was that teachers were simply not as mobile as the scheme would have required.

The change of government to Labour in 1964 gave a new political impetus to the Department's attempt to cope with maldistribution. Local authorities, however, opposed the introduction of special allowances for teachers in Glasgow and in other hard-pressed counties (Scotland 1969, 222-3). A Departmental Committee was convened to consider the question of inequitable distribution (CDTS 1966). It was chaired by Dame Jean Roberts, a former teacher who had been a prominent figure in Labour politics in Glasgow, where she had held the posts of City Treasurer and Lord Provost. In 1966, Roberts recommended that all registered teachers in designated schools should receive an extra annual payment of £100. Opinion was divided over the Roberts report but, when the scheme was established in 1968, over 3600 posts were allocated by quota to the worst staffed authorities. They, in turn, designated the schools which were to receive them. Lanarkshire got about thirty-five per cent of the posts, Glasgow more than thirty per cent, and Renfrewshire fifteen per cent (SED 1969a, 41).

These measures continued with modifications into the mid-1970s. The Department also kept up the pressure for voluntary restraint, and urged authorities to even out their internal distributions of teachers as well. Millan saw Roberts as a useful form of positive discrimination:

Q. Do you think the amount of money was large enough?

MILLAN. Perhaps you could always argue for more. If I may say so, the teaching profession wasn't absolutely united in this; it depended really as to whether you were going to get the extra [money] or whether you weren't. I remember that there was a lot of controversy about travelling allowances and so on, which I thought was a bit unfortunate and unnecessary. Of course the scheme was ultimately abandoned and the teachers' unions bear a lot of responsibility for that.

Departmental annual reports commented on the success of redistribution. Whilst pupil-teacher ratios were generally improving in the worst areas, during the first triennium of Roberts they were considerably better in the designated than in the non-designated ones (SED 1972a, 28, table E). On the other hand, a more precise analysis of movements of teachers produced a sceptical conclusion: the inducement effect was 'by no means strong', and the scheme 'may have been more successful in retaining existing staff than in attracting new staff' to designated schools (SED 1972d, vol.3, para.2.60).

Despite some improvement, in 1974 Lanarkshire still had the worst secondary-school pupil-teacher ratio at nineteen to one, whilst Aberdeen, at eleven-and-seven-tenths to one, remained the best (SED 1973b, 57-8; SED 1975a, 23-4). There was little to attract teachers away from the better-off areas. Clark said that 'teaching had a good reputation in the North-East' because it offered greater opportunities for graduates then did other careers, and was the major traditional outlet for educated persons there. Compared with Lanarkshire, a higher proportion of those going into higher education opted for teaching. Low pupil-teacher ratios and good conditions in the schools impressed trainees during their teaching practice and added to the attractiveness of remaining in their home area. Aberdeen exported teachers to other areas. But, Clark told us, many refused to go to Lanarkshire and the West, even if, as happened in the early 1970s, there were no immediate prospects of a job in Aberdeen.[7]

Thus the forces acting to reproduce area inequalities of staffing were stronger than the central measures adopted to overcome them. The SED itself lacked central mechanisms that could change the situation more than marginally. And other mechanisms at the national level, such as the GTC (see chapter 12), the ADES, and the two local-authority associations (see chapter 18), were unable to agree a national interest that superseded the interests of the individual local authorities. A further problem was that, until at least the end of the 1960s, the SED lacked precise intelligence about the problems of supply, demand and uneven distribution across education authorities and across schools. Without it, the Department could not develop a definition of staffing requirements that could underpin arguments for a distribution of teachers that was more equitable, and more economic.

Improving Departmental Information on Supply

Rodger's earlier remark about the SED's long period of thinking about supply was a reference to the work of the Departmental Committee on Supply which sat from 1950 to 1962. It had been established one year after the English Ministry of Education had set up an external advisory council on supply and training. The Departmental Committee produced four reports (SED 1951c, 1953b, 1957b, 1962f). Apart from the annual SED reports, these were the main public sources of detailed information about teacher supply in Scotland as a whole.

The Committee's chairman for its first three reports was Grainger-Stewart, a lawyer by training who, Rodger said, 'was not good at figures at all', but who was in the chair because he was Deputy Secretary. Rodger, who was good at figures, was a member of the Committee on Supply. He chaired it for its final report published in 1962, and he was also assessor to both Appleton and Knox. Thus he was the key person in the collection, analysis and dissemination of staffing information. Appleton praised his 'lucid surveys of statistical material' (SED 1955c, para.117), and Knox gave credit to his 'encyclopaedic knowledge of facts' and to his clarification of the issues (SED 1959b, para.100). On the other hand, despite Rodger's efforts, Sir Henry Wood doubted that the SED was seriously conscious of the teacher shortage until nearly 1960:

WOOD. They had a regular committee on supply . . . but I don't think there was any forward-looking policy that was relating current shortage to the extent that it might grow in the early 1960s; at least, I thought they were slow to face up to the question.

Q. How would you explain their slowness? Was it lack of statistics? Lack of antennae?

WOOD. I don't really know. I think there was too long a gap between the production of the statistics and serious consideration by anybody in the Department who could understand them all. The civil servants like Rodger were overworked and [had] too many areas of responsibility.[8]

Rodger himself emphasised that the Departmental Committee could only report its findings and illuminate problems. It could not propose solutions, which were for other bodies including the NJC and the colleges. But the Department's main adviser after 1958 on training and supply, the Scottish Council for the Training of Teachers (SCTT), struggled with inadequate information, and had only vague executive powers in relation to supply and recruitment (see chapter 12). Moreover, the Supply Committee's picture of the supply situation depended greatly on the collection of figures from outside sources such as college principals, directors of education, and university officials. Gray thought that only the Department could do this, but Rodger's description of the committee's approach shows that the Department itself had trouble:

RODGER. Now, there were two sides to trying to forecast the supply position regarding teachers: first of all, how many did Scotland need? and how many were we going to get? And the differences between these tells the shortage. Now, 'How many are you going to get?' I found this much the easier of the two sides, because teachers come out of the general population, and, if one found how many teachers there were in the various years, and what the population was eighteen or nineteen years before that – that shows the percentage that's coming out. . . . There can be side winds on that, which are very illustrative. We wrote to the universities, for example, asking how many people they had, and how many would be graduating in this year, that year, and so on. They gave us estimates. . . . Then we would elbow this first estimate in this, that, or the other direction, according to the side winds that blew. Now that is the supply. Now the question is: what's the demand? We wrote to the directors of education and asked, 'How many teachers are you going to need this year, that year, and so on?'. . . . I had a suspicion that we were getting inflated estimates from the directors. The directors were putting down what *they* thought *they* would like. . . . The final figure of how many they were going to employ . . . would be determined, in part, by what the local authority could afford. So I wrote a memorandum about this and sent it to the district inspectors, to point out to them what my misgivings were. The first year, we took the authorities' figures, because we had nothing better, but after the first year was over I had thought that there were possibilities of error. So I asked the district inspectors to get in touch with the directors, and be with them when they were making their estimates, and to ask . . . 'Are you not inflating this?'.

The Department clearly was struggling in the 1950s towards a greater central capability to manage resources. In part, this meant getting the district inspectors to look over the shoulders of directors of education, whose estimates Rodger sometimes distrusted.[9] But there was a limit to what could be achieved simply by means of improved intelligence. On the demand side, the committee was beholden to education authorities' estimates of want, and to the question-begging equation of want with need.

Nevertheless, the Department continued its attempts to forecast supply and demand, and to improve local-authority estimates. Its Committee on Supply ended, perhaps significantly, around the time Rodger retired in 1963, although he could not enlighten us on the reasons for its demise. This roughly coincided with the beginning of Graham's period as Secretary, which later saw a major change in analysis and policy-making concerning staffing.

Supply problems persisted in the 1960s, although the numbers entering teacher training, particularly graduates, showed signs of improvement. As we have seen, geographical inequalities in staffing also persisted. The difficulties it encountered in redistributing teachers were one reason the Department advanced for its overhaul of the system of staffing analysis and control in the late 1960s and early 1970s. In considering Roberts' proposal, the Department had become 'increasingly aware of the lack of adequate criteria for determining shortage' (Brodie 1972, 34). One consequence of this was that 'the absence of agreed standards has continued to hinder attempts to secure an even distribution of teachers' (SED 1973b, para.1.3). On the other hand, there were several other justifications for developing better criteria. These had to do with the transformation of secondary schooling that had occurred in the 1960s, and with the expected ending of overall teacher shortages owing to the improvement in supply and an expected decline in pupil numbers. The Department saw the need for a more refined method of analysis in order to understand the relationships between school organisation, curriculum development and staffing, and to avoid a wasteful oversupply of teachers (SED 1973c, paras 5 and 9).

Moreover, it had evidently decided that this intelligence capability should be developed as a Departmental function, for outside organisations like the SCTT, the GTC and the ADES had vested interests in supplying and staffing according to wants, and could not take a synoptic view. South of the Border, Anthony Crosland, the Minister of Education, had discontinued the National Advisory Council for the Supply and Training of Teachers after 1965, later saying, 'if the Department couldn't do that job, which was central to all its activities, it ought to pack up' (Boyle and Crosland 1971, 173). But the SED went further in the direction of central-government control of staffing. With ROSLA looming, the search for objective and uniform staffing standards and units of measurement led the SED away from its reliance on the estimates of demand that the local authorities themselves reported, and towards a highly sophisticated central determination of need. Improved quantification was an important part of the new approach. But its fundamental feature was neither objective nor statistical. Rather, it was the decision by the Department to replace local-authority judgements with a single national standard determined centrally. This standard was developed iteratively through statistical analysis of local staffing situations, and discussion with those locally involved. But, once determined, the national formula was to be applied to all schools.

The undertaking began with a pilot survey in 1967-68 of school organisation and staffing. It included a detailed study of organisation and staff deployment in forty-seven schools. The results appeared in a staffing memorandum, published by the Department in 1969, which brought to light many anomalies and discrepancies (SED 1969c). These were attributed to the apparent determination of school staffing levels 'not by objective standards but by a variety of fortuitous influences' (*ibid.*, para.2.6). Discrepancies in distribution were accompanied by variations in perception: Graham told us that, when they studied this first batch of schools, they found that 'two similar schools had quite different ideas of what their shortage was and it didn't correspond at all to the real situation'. The memorandum was accompanied by Circular 714, which urged both a new method of ascertaining staffing needs, and a more even distribution of teachers (SED 1969d). The full-scale Staffing Survey published in 1972 (SED 1972e) fed a theoretical model which derived staffing requirements from information and assumptions about such factors as school organisation, curriculum arrangements, and distributions of pupils across the years. Detailed calculations produced a basic set of standards which could be translated into pupil-teacher ratios and staffing complements for individual schools. To provide flexibility, the complements included a five per cent 'float' element.

The new system was published in the 'Red Book' (SED 1973b). The Department saw the new system as a better way of forecasting and planning teacher supply centrally and locally, but particularly as a means of gaining greater influence for the Secretary of State in an important area of his responsibility. Greater influence required better Departmental intelligence, but central government did not increase its influence solely because it improved its knowledge capability. A logical prerequisite to the SED's improved intelligence was its assertion of a right to determine a single national standard. This assertion succeeded through the failure or reluctance of those outside to challenge a redefinition that deprived teachers and local authorities of the power to define their own reality of need.

Clark thought this approach was probably initiated by Graham's thinking, and that it was attractive to Forsyth McGarrity, who later on became Senior Chief Inspector (1973-81). Some local authorities stood to gain from its redistributive emphasis. Others, like Aberdeen, were firmly opposed to such standardised national formulae because they removed from the local authorities some of their power to allocate resources, and transferred it to the centre. In 1986, the Main report on teachers' pay and conditions noted that, despite the theoretical freedom for education authorities to depart from Red Book standards, in practice there was little scope for them to do so. The standards were used by the Secretary of State in calculating local-authority expenditure for the rate-support grant. Unless it could find savings elsewhere in the local budget, the education authority had to adhere to the Red Book, particularly if it wished to avoid controversies that might arise if it were to reallocate staff between schools (CI 1986, para.8.48).

The standards laid down at the inception of the Red Book, when taken along with the expected developments of secondary education in the post-ROSLA years to 1977-78, pointed towards a requirement for thirty-two per cent more secondary teachers than the 20700 in post in 1971-72 (SED 1973c, para.18). Teachers were apprehensive about the implications of Red Book staffing as the prospect of contraction came into view in the mid-1970s. But they also realised that the idea of a national standard might help them in their campaign to improve their conditions of service. They sought to counter the precision of the Red Book with a contract specifying their own duties. Teachers' employers had customarily relied upon teachers' goodwill when asking them to undertake non-remunerative work. But, in the early 1970s, the effects of comprehensive reorganisation and ROSLA aggravated problems of building and staffing to a point where relations between teachers, the local authorities and the SED again broke down. A strike at Hawick High School, ironically the school that had launched Forsyth McGarrity into the Inspectorate, was taken up by Bryden and the EIS, and turned into a national demand for a teachers' contract (Seeley 1982). This 'contract' was to be a scheme of conditions of service that would set precise limits to workloads in terms of normal maximum class sizes and numbers of working hours. A work-to-rule paralleled long negotiations in the STSCC over the terms of the scheme. The Committee's proposal was put to a ballot in the EIS and the SSTA, and was approved against the opposition of a sizeable minority that included the more militant teachers (*TESS* 21 November 1975, 5 December 1975 and 12 December 1975).

The contract took effect early in 1976.[10] Although its relationship to Red Book standards was unclear, the Department maintained that the scheme's staffing implications were well within its own calculations of standards (Thorburn 1975). A *TESS* leader in 1976 said that a Red Book which had started life as 'only a mathematical model' had become 'McGarrity's totem pole . . . the symbol of the SED's statistical supremacy, an *éminence rouge* more powerful by far than . . . real-life experience' (*TESS* 26 March 1976). In a period of severe expenditure restraint and falling pupil numbers, inroads were made on the built-in 'flexibility factor' in staffing complements. The General Teaching Council reacted with hostility to a Departmental discussion paper on staffing in 1981 (SED 1981). The GTC saw it as recommending an erosion of standards and as central pressure for the closure of schools: 'The paper makes it clear that recommended staffing standards . . . have been subordinated to the financial provisions of the rate support grant formulae and that financial support will be available largely on the basis of a crude pupil/teacher ratio' (GTC 1981, 1).

Thus there was a dialectic at work here. The Department arrogated to itself the right to set a universal definition of local need. Teachers responded by demanding and achieving the application of a universal standard of local obligation. They saw it as a measure of employment protection now that shortages had come to an end (*TESS* 30 January 1976; Thorburn and Munro 1976). The net result was a new institutional constraint on relations between individual employers and teachers, and between individual teachers and pupils (see below).

Summary and Discussion

We saw in chapter 9 how the Department kept overall control of capital expenditure and exerted its influence earlier in the process of designing and building schools, whilst at the same time loosening some of its control of detail, and attempting to promote local capabilities. In salary negotiations and in school staffing, however, the picture is different. The Department retained and increased its control, and did not attempt to enhance local decision-making. This was particularly evident from the late 1960s. The Department's influence in pay negotiations was exerted sooner, more directly, and more heavily; and the local authorities' part was circumscribed. Beginning in the early 1970s, staffing levels were no longer left to local decision, but were subject to the SED's determination of standards. The centre's authority in both salaries and staffing was linked to the increasing share of locally incurred expenditure it bore. In addition, its authoritativeness on staffing matters stemmed from its intelligence-gathering and analytical capability, which nevertheless remained seriously deficient until the 1970s. The Department used arguments about efficiency and equity in moving towards methods of manpower planning in which more accurate ways of ascertaining supply and demand played a crucial part. In contrast to the SED's approach to the school-building programme, here there was no talk of devolution to the local level. Nor were outsiders to be relied upon for advice. There was also closer coordination within the Department between two crucial areas. The new Departmental Study Group on Secondary School Staffing was joined in 1970 by the Curriculum Study Group. H. F. Smith of the Inspectorate wrote at the time that 'the advantages of a close working relationship between the two groups are obvious' (Smith 1970). In chapter 14 we discuss some of the consequences of this relationship for the curriculum.

So far, the picture we have presented in this and the previous chapter is one of the Department ascendant, moving from an already high plateau to scale the higher peaks. In so doing, it was gathering powers to itself, denying them to others, and ridding itself of the encumbrance of detail. As far as it goes, this picture is not inaccurate, for it reflects changes that occurred within the Department and in the structure of its relations with others over resources. But there is a risk of caricature here, for two main reasons.

The first is that, although the SED was the 'centre of first instance' for the educational constituency outside St Andrew's House, the increase in central control did not accrue to it alone. The initiative for change in salary negotiation procedures, and for closer financial control, came from government policies that applied to the public sector as a whole and bore heavily upon pay settlements and upon local government expenditure. We do not argue that government economic policy was successful. But the attempt to implement it required the SED, like the Scottish Office itself, to act in many respects as the agent of a larger, central, British government on whose agenda financial stringency took precedence over education. This limited the scope for an Education Department to act on behalf of its clientèle, and it soured relationships, although the innovation of the Scottish expenditure block at the end of the 1970s gave the SED more room for arguing education's case. The enormous size of the education budget, nationally and

232

locally, made it a prime target for Chancellors, especially at a time when English public opinion was growing more sceptical of the claims of the education service upon the public purse. Thus a 'centre' wider than the SED was making its presence felt in ways which were, however, congruent with the SED's own approach to comprehending and controlling resources and policy. In this sense, whilst the Department was always constitutionally part of the wider government, the SED's control over Scottish education, and its ability to deny local claims, were now more firmly buttressed by that connection.

The second reason concerns the degree to which the Department could solve the problems with which its stronger capability was designed to deal. The lesson that the Department had learned from the long history of its endeavours to see that the schools were staffed adequately and evenly was that partnership offered a weak and unreliable means of central control. The better-off local education authorities resisted measures to reduce shortages and disparities. So too did the teachers, if such improvements meant dilution, or meant an attack upon the principle of parity in salaries which treated all subjects and all geographical areas alike within an otherwise finely differentiated system. The Advisory Council's rejection of dilution strengthened the Department's conviction that it could not depend upon outside advice in order to attack the problem of supply; although, as chapter 12 shows, the SED eventually gained a victory in the GTC on the question of non-graduate male teachers.

A new way of determining staffing requirements seemed, therefore, an attractive way for the Department to gain more leverage on supply, and perhaps on distribution in general. The Department based its management of resources not simply upon better intelligence about demand and supply, but also upon a rejection of the traditional concept of demand as 'want', in favour of a new concept of 'the adequately staffed school'. This deprived individual local authorities of the power to use their own criteria of need, which might vary from one school or local authority to the next. Empirical judgements made in terms of the new criteria were definitive, and the Department could make them potent by linking them to financial provision. But, despite this enhancement of its power, the Department persisted, not very successfully, with specific inducements to redirect teachers to difficult areas. Moreover, the solution to the worst of the supply problem arguably owed less to the SED's measures than to the ending of overall shortages as a result of demography.

The Department's new instruments could help it to manage the contraction of the teaching force and of teacher training after 1975. But a more centralised approach to analysis and problem-solving could not guarantee the smooth implementation of Departmental policy on resources as the politics of the education system became noisy. The Department had major battles on its hands in its attempts to close colleges of education (see chapter

12); and, in contrast to the DES, it shrank in the 1980s from more involvement in local policy for the closure of schools (Adler and Bondi forthcoming).

The teachers had welcomed the new structure of promoted posts that the Department introduced at the beginning of the 1970s in order to make teaching careers more attractive. But they were put on their guard by the new duties placed upon them to implement ROSLA, and by the Inspectorate's criticisms of the way they performed them (SED 1976b). The ending of shortages threatened teachers' careers, but teachers were far from unified in the stance they presented to their employers and to the Department. However, the 'management' side could take little comfort from teachers' disaggregation, for this made industrial relations more turbulent, and jeopardised the co-operation that the Department needed for the substantive educational changes that were envisaged at the end of the 1970s.

Thus the centre's power was limited by the fact that the educational outcomes the Department sought were influenced by the way the schools were staffed, and the ways teachers organised professionally and taught their pupils. The Department could not directly control these factors. There was much political work for it to do if it were to gain teachers' co-operation, for it came to see that questions of curriculum were partly dependent upon teachers, not only as resources but also as active partners. The teachers' role in educational change was recognised in their representation on the new fringe bodies of the 1960s (see chapters 13 and 14), and at the local level as well (see chapter 12). But teachers were left largely on their own in the implementation of ROSLA in the 1970s, with depressing results. The national Standard Grade development programme of the 1980s, following Munn and Dunning, involved teachers more directly. However, the pace and centrally led manner of curriculum development exacerbated bad industrial relations. The Inspectorate was determined to regain its influence within the Department and over the system, but it did not do its political work as well as it might, and classroom teachers realised that their participation gave them a powerful weapon. They used this successfully, and with greater unity, to press their claim for better pay and working conditions.

Meanwhile, the post-war generation of policy-makers had passed into retirement. It had handled many of the strains of disagreement across organisations by absorbing them within a shared educational outlook, and within a political culture based on trust. Within this culture, broad areas of disadvantage were widely regarded until the 1960s as morally acceptable. Women had yet to achieve equal pay, and the brunt of building and staffing difficulties was borne by junior-secondary schools, and schools in the West of Scotland. All three sectors were thought to deserve less (see part v). But this was beginning to change in the 1960s, and the policy issues that arose thereafter were thornier and more divisive. Their resolution required more trust, not less. But the relationships between teachers, the Department, and the education authorities were now conducted with a brittle formalism of style and procedure. All had an interest in achieving the certainty and stability that might be afforded by explicit sets of rules and elaborated mechanisms of representation. A new constitutionality supplemented the older relations of discretion and trust between the Department and outsiders. The change was exemplified by the Department's specification of the new national standard of staffing, and by the teachers' response which implicitly incorporated this standard in their case for a teachers' contract that specified their conditions of service.

This dialectic had implications for interpersonal relations at both local and national levels. Locally, contractualism began to supplement, if not to replace, interpersonally negotiated reciprocities between employers, teachers and pupils, laying the ground for the disputes of the 1980s. Nationally, the proliferation of positions on consultative and negotiating bodies threatened to limit the power of the Department, but only to the extent that the Department itself failed to manage the expanding patronage of the new system. How it attempted to do this is the subject of parts IV and V.

NOTES
1. Later in this chapter we discuss the changes in the machinery for salary negotiation that took place in the 1960s. By 1982, a further change abolished the STSCC and brought negotiations for pay and conditions together in a single body, the Scottish Joint Negotiating Committee (SJNC) (CI 1986, para.13.1).
2. The Burnham Committee, composed of representatives of the local education authorities and teachers, was set up in 1919 as the negotiating body for teachers' salary scales in England and Wales (Tropp 1957, ch.12). It was abolished by legislation in 1987.
3. In a subsequent communication (15 March 1987), Bryden elaborated his description of the negotiation process in order to identify details of the negotiations that he felt should have figured in an earlier edited version of Rodger's account. Bryden wrote: 'The proposals for a triennial review never took the form of a demand for a simple percentage increase. They were laid out in great detail in the form of salaries regulations, embodying the several scales, additional payments and responsibility elements. Similarly, the reply of the authorities' panel, if they were prepared to go some way to meet us, was in the same detailed format. The teachers' proposals were presented by the Convener of the Teachers' Panel and/or the General Secretary of the EIS. No other view was advanced, and this rule was strictly adhered to even in later years when the Teachers' Panel included representatives of the SSTA and the SSA. This was the form throughout the years [1953-74] when I attended the NJC and the STSC.' On receipt of this we restored a brief section of Rodger's description of these matters. The revised version, in our view, is not necessarily inconsistent with Bryden's description. On a second matter, Bryden had no recollection of Rodger's going to-and-fro between the teachers' and the local authorities' representatives. Bryden commented: 'Perhaps Rodger's description is of procedure during the earlier years and indicates a more relaxed and informal approach to salaries negotiations than developed in the fifties and subsequently'.
4. Bryden's figures differ slightly from the seven and ten per cent shown in the

235

report of the Prices and Incomes Board (NBPI 1966, para.26).

5. The SSA complained about the EIS monopoly of representation on the NJC, and won an action in the Court of Session against the Secretary of State, Michael Noble, on the grounds that the NJC was unrepresentative of teachers and therefore did not comply with the 1962 Education Act. When the education authorities and the teachers failed to agree on what should replace the NJC, Noble set up the Scottish Joint Council for Teachers' Salaries (SJC) in 1964. This included representatives of all three teachers' associations. The SSA, however, broke confidentiality by publicising to its membership the details of what went on at SJC meetings. It was subsequently expelled from the SJC by the new Labour Secretary of State, William Ross, at the end of 1964.

6. An indication of the new policy context was given by the NBPI. The Secretary of State had referred the 1966 award of thirteen per cent to the Board and asked it to consider whether the award put Scottish teachers into a fair relationship with English and Welsh teachers. The Board, however, cast a critical eye on the cosy arrangement whereby salary negotiators on both sides of the Border sought to keep average salary increases in line with each other without any fundamental appraisal of manpower resources or of the rationale for financial rewards. It urged the simultaneous negotiation of English and Scottish salaries. On the other hand, it thought that awards of similar size were a superficial and illogical solution which denied the differences in qualifications and training required in both countries, and in the structures and levels of salary scales. These differences, it said, had been emphasised in the evidence presented to it, and they made overall comparisons impossible. It noted, however, that such comparisons went against Government policy (NBPI 1966).

7. Clark did not appear to dissent from a paper which, he told us, McEwan had presented to the GTC in the 1960s. This related staffing deficiencies in the West to the imbalance in the provision of teacher-training facilities which favoured the East of Scotland. For until the 1960s, training in the West was concentrated at Jordanhill College and at the Roman Catholic Notre Dame College. Both were in Glasgow and together offered fewer places than the other colleges (SCTT 1961, appendix IV). It was only as a result of a Ministerial lead, and belated discussion in the SCTT, that facilities for primary-school training were increased, and it was only after long argument that their location was dispersed to new colleges which would benefit central Scotland and parts of the West outside Glasgow.

8. Rodger confirmed this. Between 1945 and 1954 he had an 'impossibly heavy time', as he was in charge of teacher training, salaries, and superannuation, and, for a time, building. The Department's establishment officer was also in charge of finance, and he kept Departmental staffing down. Rodger recalled that both his seconds-in-command on the buildings and salaries side were once simultaneously ill for six months, but that he failed to get additional help. After Murrie came in 1952, he made each of these branches into a division. Rodger then gave up buildings.

9. In 1955, the Department sought to change the nature, and method of processing, of education authorities' statistics (SED 1955a, 62). A year later, the Department commented on the variety of standards in use for estimating local staffing deficiencies, and thought that 'some may have underestimated their true needs' (SED 1956a, 77). The Departmental Supply Committee remarked in 1962 that, 'soon after the publication of the Third Report, Glasgow Education Authority changed the basis of calculating their needs, thereby increasing the number of posts and the shortage by 600 in 1957' (SED 1962f, 11).

10. The Main report in 1986 observed that there was considerable misunderstanding about the nature of teachers' contractual duties and about the relationship between the scheme of conditions (the 'contract') and the actual contract of employment (cɪ 1986, paras 5.26 to 5.50).

Sir William F. Arbuckle, Secretary, SED

Sir Norman W. Graham, Secretary, SED

John S. Brunton, HMSCI

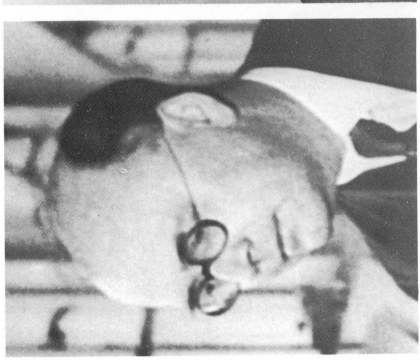

Allan G. Rodger, Under-Secretary, SED

The Rt Hon. Bruce Millan, MP, Secretary of State for Scotland

Gilbert S. Bryden, General Secretary, EIS

Sir John Mackay Thomson, Secretary, SED

Professor William McClelland, Executive Officer, NCTT

Sir William S. Murrie, Secretary, SED

Sir James J. Robertson, Rector, Aberdeen Grammar School

James R. Clark, Director of Education, Aberdeen

Dr David Dickson, HMSCI

John S. McEwan, Director of Education, Lanarkshire

Dr William McL. Dewar, Headmaster, George Heriot's School

Part IV

Schooling and Advice

We now move from our discussion of central government to consider various functions that lie closer to the practice of the schools: teachers, examinations, curriculum, and the organisation of the school system on selective or comprehensive lines. Our discussion of these in part II brought us to the point in the mid-1960s at which Brunton had thought that reform was coming to fruition. The new O-grade was rapidly reducing early leaving from senior-secondary courses, and both it and the Higher-grade were proving an effective means of curriculum reform. These changes had themselves required prior change in the organisation and role of the Inspectorate. The expansion they released itself triggered a further change in governance with the creation of a new Examination Board in the early 1960s, and this in turn contributed to the case for a new advisory body on curriculum.

At the end of part II, we saw how the role and chairmanship of the Consultative Committee on the Curriculum (CCC) were being contested within the SED, and the broader structure of advice decided. However, part III has shown that these events were not precipitated solely by educational reform and expansion, nor solely by Brunton's departure. They owed their origins also to the changing role of the SED in the wider structure of government, and especially to new thinking on the planning and management of resources. Government was increasingly coming to feel that these two functions were better done internally, and not by external advisory councils or committees. Another contributory factor, as we shall see, was the industrial action that teachers were now prepared to take in opposing Departmental policy.

Brunton said he had envisaged the CCC as 'a sort of Standing Advisory Council with a very broad responsibility for considering the curriculum in all its aspects', and as 'a relatively independent body giving powerful advice to the Secretary of State'. But the Advisory Council was not reconvened after 1961, and the CCC was constituted in 1965 with a remit that was narrower than Brunton had intended, and much narrower than the synoptic scope that the Sixth Advisory Council had won for itself with Tom Johnston's encouragement. Then, in 1966, the new and statutorily independent General Teaching Council was established. Thus, with the suspension of the Advisory Council, and the creation of the CCC, the Examination Board and the GTC, a new structure of advice had emerged. The advisory function was

243

now parcelled out to separate bodies, and was coordinated partly by the expedient of appointing certain members to more than one body, but mainly by the Department itself, through its assessors. Here was another aspect of the Inspectorate's changing role, and another occasion for questioning the independence of the advisory function. Integrating more fully at the top into the decision-making procedures of the Department, the Inspectorate was increasingly asked to orchestrate the disparate sources of outside advice as well.

Developments in England and Wales followed a different path. There, too, government thinking took its cue from its experience in resource management. But in the early 1960s, teachers and local authorities resisted attempts by the Ministry of Education to institute a Curriculum Study Group modelled on the Development Group of the Architects and Building Branch of the Ministry (Nisbet 1973, 19-27). Instead the Ministry (which became the Department of Education and Science in 1964) was forced to accept a new and concrete expression of partnership. The Schools Council, founded in 1964, was given statutory responsibility for advice and development on curriculum, teaching methods, and examinations. Teachers and local authorities each appointed their own members, as did the DES. Teachers were in the majority on all important committees (Lawton 1980, 23), but one commentator has observed that no one group had 'sufficient representation to persuade the Council to move in a direction which all other groups resisted' (Nisbet 1973, 51-2). The Schools Council lasted for two decades, until Sir Keith Joseph withdrew financial support.

In Scotland, the SED's control over the counterpart structures was much closer than in England. Nevertheless, the two educational systems were confronted in the 1960s by the same major issues: comprehensive reorganisation and ROSLA, the expansion of post-compulsory enrolments, the 'bulge' in the secondary-school population and, from 1968 onwards, growing difficulties over the procurement of resources to meet an expanded educational commitment. Thus three of our central themes recur in part IV. One is the relation between expansion and control. We argued in chapter 2 that a growing post-primary sector has posed continuing problems for the SED this century because it has put pressure on the Department to devolve functions to outsiders, prominent among whom have been many whose views the Department distrusted. How, and how successfully, did the Department manage the transition to the new structure of advice in the 1960s? How devolved was it, and how was it controlled?

Related to this, second, are questions concerning reciprocal influences between education and its governance. In the first half of the century, the disagreement between the Department and its outside critics over the separate development of secondary education had limited the ways in which the Department could organise the taking of advice. This structural limitation had in turn reinforced particular educational philosophies and practices, and especially the Department's dependence on incentives and controls that were external to pupils, teachers and schools. In rejecting the 1947 proposals of the Sixth Advisory Council for an internally assessed public examination at sixteen years, the Department had said, probably correctly, that teachers were not ready for it. But some had wanted it, and the Department did nothing to prepare others, for example by building on the experience of assessment that teachers had gained when running the Day School Certificate in the inter-war period, and the Leaving Certificate during the Second World War. Brunton told us that, in his view, teachers were still not ready for internal assessment when he introduced his O-grade reform in the early 1960s. Two decades after that, the arguments and practices in Scotland in the early 1980s were much the same, despite the attempt by the Dunning Committee (SED 1977b) to introduce a substantial element of internal assessment at all levels of national certification at sixteen years. In 1983 the Department described the Scottish Highers course as a situation of 'thoroughness and unrelieved formality', with external examinations as the principal target and conscientiousness the principal virtue (SED 1983b, para.3.16). In what ways, then, did the new structure of advice in the 1960s, and the methods by which it was controlled, have a distinctive influence on the educational thinking and practice that subsequently developed?

Then, third, there is the theme of inequality and its reproduction. We have discussed aspects of resource inequality in part III. But comprehensive reorganisation was driven by a belief that inequality in the distribution of resources and in access to opportunity were closely linked to social class, and to policies for curriculum, examinations and school organisation. How, then, did Scottish educational practice and philosophy, and the related governmental structures, influence the unfolding argument in Scotland over inequality, and influence the longer term impact of comprehensive reform?

The six chapters in part IV explore these themes. Chapter 12 examines the constitution and workings of the General Teaching Council. Chapter 13 looks at examinations and the Examination Board, and chapter 14 at curriculum and the Consultative Committee. All three of these chapters focus mainly on events after 1965 at the national level. In chapter 15 we retrace our steps chronologically to examine the origins and organisation of the selective system of secondary schooling between 1945 and 1965, and in chapter 16 we carry the story through comprehensive reorganisation to the mid-1970s and after. In these two chapters the emphasis is increasingly on the interplay between national and local policy, and between policy itself and actual provision in the schools. In this sense the two chapters are looking at the total secondary-education system in action, bringing together the different levels and areas of analysis discussed in earlier chapters. To set the scene for this, we first, in chapter 11, recapitulate the connections between the various areas of national educational policy in the post-war period. We also explain the demise of the Advisory Council, the body that had advised on policy for much of this period, and that occupied the policy space that the new structures of advice were eventually to command.

Eleven

Policy, Advice and Practice: an Overview

> . . . a man seldom judges right even in his own concerns, still less
> in those of the public, when he makes habitual use of no know-
> ledge but his own, or that of some single adviser.   J.S.Mill,
> quoted in a draft of the Secretary of State's speech for the opening
> of the Eighth, and last, Advisory Council[1]

> The Working Party is a body of people who agree with you and
> produce a report designed to achieve what you want. An Advisory
> Council is, in theory anyhow, a group of intelligent, experienced
> and interested people who will consider everything and arrive at
> a just and proper assessment of the situation.   Sir Henry Wood,
> Principal of Jordanhill College of Education 1949-71

Introduction

This chapter analyses the development of national policy for curriculum,
examinations and selection for secondary school, 1945-75. It considers the
Department's attitudes to expansion and progressivism, and points to continuities in policy before and after the Second World War. It also discusses
the uneasy relationship between the Department and the Advisory Council,
a relationship that was soured by the disputes over secondary-education
policy in the 1920s and 1940s, and strained thereafter by government's
continuing preoccupation with problems of resources. Both issues influenced the Department's decision to seek a new structure of advice in the
1960s to handle the problems that expansion posed. Another contributory
factor was the teachers' strike of 1961, a strike precipitated by a salary
dispute and by the Department's response to the increasingly urgent problem of teacher supply. In general, therefore, the chapter is intended to
integrate themes from the analysis in parts I, II and III, and to set the scene
for the new structures and policies that are analysed in the remainder of part
IV.

Continuity, Expansion and Change

As we saw in part II, the Advisory Council's report on *Secondary Education*
(1947) gave fresh impetus to progressive thinking and to hopes for expansion. It argued for *omnibus* schools and for a non-vocational, general
curriculum leading to national certification at sixteen years by means of
internal assessment with external moderation. But the SED either opposed

247

or ignored the Council's main proposals, and its own notion of reconstruction was conservative. Broadly it was to restore the system that by 1939 had already evolved to a point at which it could meet the main requirements of the Acts of 1945 and 1946. Mackay Thomson wanted to coordinate certification in Scotland with the changes that were being planned for the School Leaving Certificate in England and Wales. In other respects, however, Departmental policy from 1945 to roughly the mid-1950s continued the pre-war strategy we described in chapter 2. The outlines of this strategy were: a reduction in the number of small secondary schools; a shift in the basis of pupil promotion from stage to age, both in primary and secondary school; an insistence on a clear differentiation of types of secondary course, though not necessarily of secondary school, at twelve years; and a predominantly 'academic' course for all 'senior' secondary pupils, based on national certification at seventeen and eighteen years for entry to higher education. For the remaining seventy per cent or so of 'junior' secondary pupils there was, in effect, no national policy, except that there should be no national certificate for them, and that schools should do the best they could in the difficult circumstances bequeathed by war. In this sense the Department had only limited expectations of the potential effectiveness of the national system.

The general impression given by the Department's annual reports for the period up to 1952 is of a beleaguered and somewhat disdainful body that entertained at best only modest hopes of educating a resistant population by means of a decimated school system. The Sixth Advisory Council had wanted progressive, pupil-centred education both in primary and secondary school (SED 1946c, 1947b). The Department countered by delaying its response, and by outflanking the Council's proposals with its own examination reforms (see chapter 4). It also contested the progressive argument directly:

> Pupils to-day show less concentration and application than previously. In consequence, attainments in such subjects as require drill and revision if real proficiency is to be achieved are not so good as they used to be. . . . It might well be to the advantage of education if more emphasis were laid on the necessity for hard work, a term not at all synonymous with drudgery, and less on the immediately pleasurable activities of schooling. (SED 1951a, 13)

The Department held that 'the old standards [had] not yet been fully restored' in primary education (SED 1952a, 24), and that what was needed was not progressive methods, but an emphasis on the basic subjects and on the differentiation of pupils according to ability ('group methods') (Pringle 1985, ch.4). In secondary education it argued that age-promotion to secondary school, coupled with the raising of the school-leaving age in 1947, had exacerbated problems of control:

> Especially with pupils promoted solely on account of age, many of

whom are semi-literate, there are often other tendencies to counter besides ignorance; some of these pupils harbour feelings of resentment that they are still under tutelage and prevented from being wage earners. (SED 1951a, 16)

In the early 1950s, fewer than half the pupils leaving three-year ('junior') secondary courses had completed the course. The Department conceded that the fault lay partly in the educational system itself, and allowed that 'further efforts must be made to ensure that the junior-secondary course is an attractive and rewarding one, in order to induce pupils to stay on at school until they have completed it' (SED 1953a, 25). A similar problem in the five-year ('senior') secondary courses, however, was not blamed on the schools. Only a quarter of pupils selected for the five-year course at that time completed it. But the Department argued that the reasons for this resistance to schooling were 'social and economic, rather than educational'; pupils lacked application, youth employment was too lucrative, and parents behaved irresponsibly (*ibid.*). The Highers course was immune from criticism, the 'Holy of Holies' as Brunton described it to us (see chapter 15), or 'the Ark of the Covenant' in David Dickson's words.

The first stirrings of change within the Department were apparent by the early 1950s. With Mackay Thomson's departure from the Secretaryship in 1952, and with the growing influence of Arbuckle and Brunton under his successor Murrie, there was a change in the attitude towards change itself. The critique of a disordered society continued in the annual reports, and the problem of resources was a recurrent theme. But the Department was now beginning to argue that the school system could itself become more effective: pupil failure was 'too readily accepted as the inevitable consequence of existing conditions such as shortages of staff, changing social values and the distraction of outside interests' (SED 1955a, 30). Two years later, in 1956, the Department commented that 'reports from many areas tell of a lively and growing consciousness that secondary education cannot remain static but must move forward in accordance with a changing social and industrial pattern' (SED 1957a, 32).

All of the reports issued during Brunton's time as Senior Chief Inspector talk about change, both the need for change and the changes that were impending. Of these the most momentous was undoubtedly the introduction of the O-grade, for which planning began in the mid-1950s (see chapter 4). Introduced in 1962 as an essentially conservative measure, the O-grade was later to subvert the entire basis of post-war policy for examinations, curriculum and school organisation (see below). But it was originally intended, and it initially operated, as a means of bringing to fruition the wider policy for bipartite post-primary schooling that the Department had pursued since the late nineteenth century. Thus the reduction in the number of maintained and grant-aided secondary schools continued after 1945. By 1955 it had fallen from over 900 to around 800 (SED 1956a, 97). By 1965 it was something over 600 (SED 1966a, 33), and, by 1974, well under 500 (GSS 1976, 16). Over the same period, the number of secondary-school pupils more than doubled, to a little under 400000 (*ibid.*). The move towards promotion from primary school by age continued in the 1950s, and it came gradually to predominate. With fewer pupils falling behind in the annual promotion, heterogeneity of ability and attitude was a growing feature of the secondary-school intake. After 1945, therefore, the Department continued its drive towards increased pupil differentiation, that is, towards the provision of courses at levels of difficulty that were more finely adjusted to pupils' abilities. In the primary school, group methods were urged even when this meant that less able pupils nearing the end of their primary schooling would thereby be denied an effective preparation for the twelve-plus examination (SED 1956a, 11).

The principle of contest mobility had required that as many pupils as possible be given a chance to compete for as long as possible (see chapter 2). In effect, therefore, the primary schools were being asked to remove less able pupils from the contest at an earlier age. In secondary schools too the emphasis was on more and earlier differentiation (at fourteen years at the latest, rather than fifteen years). This was urged irrespective of the implications for pupils' coverage of the traditionally conceived broad curriculum, or for their access to full certificate courses that might qualify them for entry to higher education. Thus, here too, the principle of contest mobility was under attack:

> It has too often been accepted that all Certificate course pupils should initially follow in each subject a syllabus essentially designed to lead to presentation on the Higher grade. The intention has undoubtedly been to give as many pupils as possible the chance of obtaining Higher grade passes; in consequence, the decision to transfer pupils to a Lower grade section in any subject is normally postponed as long as possible. . . . This practice . . . [has] proved unsatisfactory. . . . We therefore strongly advocate that differentiation of syllabuses should take place as soon as the need for it becomes apparent. (SED 1959b, para.23)

Qualification for university in a broad range of subjects remained the official goal of the secondary course for very able pupils, though the Department wanted to differentiate these pupils too. In the 1940s Mackay Thomson and HMSCI Watson considered the introduction of a post-Higher S-grade, but postponed any change on the grounds that the standard would be too high for all but a very small minority.[2] In the late 1950s, however, the Department put a post-Higher examination back on the agenda, this time in the form of an A-grade (see chapter 13).

From 1945 to 1965, decisions on selection for secondary education were left, as before, to the local authorities (SED 1951b). At first, both national and local policy continued to rely on a clear-cut selection of pupils to different levels of secondary course at twelve years of age, and on external certification thereafter aimed at no more than one-third of the age-group. By the late 1950s, however, the Department was concerned over the high proportions of pupils that local authorities were admitting to senior-secondary courses, evidence again of central-local conflict over the contest-mobility principle (see chapter 2). The proportions in the early 1960s were approaching forty per cent of the transfer group, much higher than the proportions admitted to grammar schools in England and Wales. One of the last recommendations that the Department secured from the Eighth and final Advisory Council was that the local authorities collectively should reduce this figure (SED 1961b, para.85).

From the mid-1950s, curriculum development for senior-secondary courses was done through the revision of external examination syllabuses. Here again there was no scope for the progressive education recommended by the Advisory Council in 1947. For pupils on junior-secondary courses, however, there was still to be no national examination. But there was an attempt to state an educational philosophy for them in the 1955 Inspectorate memorandum *Junior Secondary Education* (SED 1955b). Ironically the memorandum drew heavily on the Advisory Council's 1947 critique of the effects of external examinations on liberal and progressive education.

However, even this recourse to progressivism was something of a temporary expedient, for the period from the mid-1950s also saw the beginnings of a different approach to junior-secondary education. This was to link it to post-school incentives that were analogous to the incentive that the Higher supplied to the pupils on certificate courses. For junior-secondary schools the main incentive was to be access to further education and to the prospect of a favoured training and job at a subprofessional level. The policy was not entirely new. Continuation classes for young school leavers had first been proposed in 1918, but little had been done at the time. The Sixth Advisory Council's report on secondary education had acknowledged a 'nascent vocational interest' in secondary pupils but had not centred its educational philosophy on it (SED 1947b, para.183). In the later 1950s, however, as further education began to expand, the Department increasingly pressed for what it called a new 'realism' in junior-secondary courses, and for more vocational education. *From School to Further Education* in 1963 recommended that junior-secondary education be based on the pupil's 'vocational impulse' (SED 1963b, para.55). Brunton chaired the working party that produced this report, and he always denied that he had wanted vocational education for fourteen- to sixteen-year-olds. Nevertheless, by the mid-1960s the educational philosophies of senior- and junior-secondary education were growing further apart, thus sharpening the implications of selection at twelve.

The term 'downward incrementalism' has been used to describe the process by which the external incentive of national certification, formerly offered only to an academic elite of pupils, was extended 'downwards' after the Second World War to larger proportions of the age-group through a series of piecemeal but incremental changes (Gray *et al.*, 1983, ch.4). The first such extension was the change in 1951 from a group-certificate to an individual-subject certificate. The second was the introduction of the O-grade in 1962. Brunton had intended to limit presentation for the O-grade to the most able thirty to thirty-five per cent of the age-group, and to set the minimum number of presentation subjects at three. His main purpose was to provide an 'intermediate' incentive (intermediate between the minimum leaving age and presentation of Highers in fifth year) which would persuade senior-secondary pupils to stay on at school. But the level of difficulty of the O-grade examination was set much lower than the Higher grade. This put the prospect of success in it within reach of considerably more than one-third of the age-group (*ibid.*). There could be no logical justification for restricting access to certificate courses to one-third of fourteen-year-olds, unless it were also possible to predict perfectly which pupils would stay on for a further two years and which would be successful. But such predictions were uncertain, and the O-grade thereby fuelled the support that teachers gave to the contest-mobility principle when they opened the doors of their certificate classes, and erred on the side of inclusion.

Three things happened. In the early 1960s, the proportions of pupils who stayed on and presented for the O-grade increased very rapidly; an attenuated academic curriculum spread from the Highers curriculum *via* the O-grade, thereby displacing Brunton's vocationally oriented courses; and presentations started to come not only from senior-secondary and *omnibus* schools, but also from former two- and three-year junior-secondary schools that started to 'grow' a fourth year. Thus the change in certification realised one of the major conditions that Archer identifies as a prerequisite of expansion, namely that the school system should not shunt a subset of pupils into dead-end tracks, but that its stages should be arranged end-on to allow sequential individual progress (see chapter 2). In 1951 Mackay Thomson had averted expansion when Scotland declined to follow England in introducing an examination equivalent to the O-level at sixteen years. But the expansion in the 1960s following the introduction of the Scottish O-grade had a major impact on school organisation, destabilising a feature that had been central to SED secondary-education policy throughout the century, namely the clear demarcation of certificate from non-certificate tracks in post-primary compulsory schooling.

A comment is appropriate here on the significance of these events for the correspondence theory of schooling and for the CCCS thesis of 'statist' schooling (see chapter 1). One does not have to look to continental structuralism or to American neo-Marxism for an interpretation of educational policy in Scotland in correspondence terms:

> The new dominie leathers them [the pupils] because he thinks that children ought to be disciplined so that they may be able to fight the battle of life. He does not see that by using authority he is doing the

very opposite of what he intends; he is making the child dependent on him, and for ever afterwards the child will lack initiative, lack self-confidence, lack originality.

What the new dominie does do is to turn out excellent wage-slaves. The discipline of the school gives each child an inner sense of inferiority, what the psychoanalysts call an inferiority complex. And the working-classes are suffering from a gigantic inferiority complex, otherwise they would not be content to remain wage-slaves. The fear that Duncan inspires in a boy will remain in that boy all his life. When he enters the workshop he will unconsciously identify the foreman with Duncan, and fear him and hate him. (Neill 1921, 16)

This was A. S. Neill (later of Summerhill school in England), writing from Forfar just after, not the Second World War, but the First, when the Department had also urged that rebellious youth be schooled to order (Fraser 1920, 30-1). As we have seen, Mackay Thomson and HMSCI Watson wanted a similar spell of repression after 1945. But what are we to make of the changes instigated by Brunton? Clearly there are two senses in which policy after 1955 could not be construed as an attempt to realise the progressivism of the Sixth Council. First, whatever Dickson said in *Junior Secondary Education* of 1955, the bipartite approach was fundamentally inimical to the Council's emphasis on the comprehensive school with a general curriculum as a locus of community. Second, the new O-grade examination at sixteen years was almost wholly external, leaving little professional initiative with the teachers. Whether or not Brunton genuinely believed that his reforms were implementations of Robertson's report (see chapter 5), they nevertheless constitute a fairly clear instance of 'statism' as we understand the CCCS use of this term: namely, the distortion of a progressive educational ideal by considerations of central control and meritocratic individualism (see chapter 1).

Furthermore, in Brunton's thinking on vocational education one can find a deeper continuity with the repressive stance of Mackay Thomson and Watson, and further support for the correspondence thesis. The Department wanted junior-secondary schools to provide 'social and character training' (SED 1957a, 32). Both Dickson's memorandum of 1955 and Brunton's report of 1963 asked schools to impress what the Department called a 'sense of reality' on junior-secondary pupils (SED 1962a, 47). This is what the French theorist and anthropologist Pierre Bourdieu has to say about the idea of a 'sense of reality':

Every established order tends to produce . . . the naturalization of its own arbitrariness. Of all the mechanisms tending to produce this effect, the most important and the best concealed is undoubtedly the dialectic of the objective chances and the agent's aspirations, out of which arises the *sense of limits* commonly called the *sense of reality*, i.e. the correspondence between the objective categories and the internalised categories, social structures and mental structures, which is the basis of the most ineradicable adherence to the established order. (Bourdieu 1977, 164, emphasis in original)[3]

Because the Department's main purpose for the national system was the production of university entrants, the 'objective chances' of junior-secondary pupils in respect of the system were nil, as Dickson frankly acknowledged (see chapter 15). There was no place here for misplaced pupil aspirations engendered by contest-mobility norms. This was the 'limit' or 'reality' of which the Department required pupils and teachers to have a sense. And Brunton sought to bring them to a sense of reality, to a sense of the 'objective categories' or 'social structures', by advancing this view of the 'mental structures' of junior-secondary pupils:

> As a general rule, they are not interested in academic learning and prefer physical activity to thinking; their mental activity is stimulated by real things and happenings in the physical world rather than by ideas and concepts. Though generalisations appeal less readily to them than to their abler fellows, they have nevertheless some ability to generalise from particular illustrations. The less their ability, the less well do they meet demands for sustained effort; they respond best to tasks which yield quick results, and most of them do not look far ahead. Generally, too, the less their ability, the less self-sufficient do they feel and the more dependent they are on the companionship and good opinion of their fellows. They like best to work in small groups or teams. (SED 1963b, para.14)

We could be listening in this passage to the colonial administrator's view of the African native. Bourdieu says of such classifications that they sustain power relations by securing their 'misrecognition'. In this case, of course, the problem facing Dickson and Brunton was that junior-secondary teachers and pupils had an all-too-developed sense of reality about their objective chances. That was why a majority of such pupils did not complete a three-year course, and why many of their teachers left for senior-secondary schools when given the opportunity.

Later, in part v, we analyse what we call the Scottish myth, the traditional orthodoxy of values and beliefs from which the Department's view of junior-secondary pupils was derived. This orthodoxy was ruptured by the expansion of O-grades, and by comprehensive reorganisation. For the Department to write in similar vein today about seven out of ten of Scottish children would be to divest itself of all moral authority. But what undermined the orthodoxy was neither a resistance to statist schooling by pupils or teachers, nor a rejection of the idea of education as schooling for academic certification and individual advancement. What undermined it, rather, was a wider and more sustained drive towards this very idea, inadvertently released by the Department when it introduced the O-grade, but led principally by schools themselves, and leaving former classifications of 'academic' and 'non-academic' pupils in moral, conceptual and statistical disarray.

However, at the very time that a synoptic review of educational purposes and values was needed, the public body that might have supplied it, and that had supplied it in the 1940s, was itself discontinued. It is to the reasons for this that we now turn.

The Structure of Advice

The Advisory Council had antagonised the Department by opposing its bipartite policy in the early 1920s, and again in 1947. But the policy had survived, and seemed, indeed, to be prospering in the early 1960s when the decision was finally made to discontinue the Council. Why, then, was the Council supplanted? Part of the answer is that memories are long, but the opportunities for action infrequent. The 1961 teachers' strike finally precipitated the change (see chapter 12). However, the Department had always doubted the value of the Council and, with time, changing circumstances had strengthened several aspects of the Department's case.

A number of arguments for a council had originally been advanced in the two decades before statutory provision was finally made in 1918. One argument was that a body was needed to aggregate Scottish opinion for a Department whose centre of gravity was London, not Edinburgh (Douglas and Jones 1903, 60-7). With the transfer of the bulk of the Department to Edinburgh by 1939, this argument no longer applied, though there were still some people after 1945 who maintained that the shortage of parliamentary time for Scottish affairs indicated the need for an alternative scrutinising and debating forum that was independent of the Department (PD 1956a). Another argument for a council had also weakened with time. This was that it should coordinate and standardise local-authority provision (Douglas and Jones 1903, 72-85; SRO 1917, 12 June 1917). But this consideration had lost some of its force even before the Council was established. The 1918 Act replaced the school boards by what were then thirty-eight *ad hoc* education authorities. Their number was eventually reduced to thirty-five and, in 1929, local responsibility for education was transferred to the *ad omnia* local authorities. These authorities consulted with the Department through their three national associations. Such consultations might themselves require coordination. From the Department's perspective, however, a weak advisory council would merely duplicate them, whereas a council that coordinated them effectively might well make them and itself too powerful.

If a council were largely superfluous to relations between London and Edinburgh, and between Edinburgh and the local authorities, might it not have a role to play in aggregating opinion more broadly across a variety of groups, including the local authorities and also their employees, the teachers? Struthers was Secretary of the SED when the original legislation was drafted. He doubted the value of a council, but several of the consider-

255

ations he had to weigh remained apposite throughout the Council's life. The new local authorities could negotiate with the Department more conveniently than the old school boards had done. The teachers' representatives already met the Department on occasion. Why should the Department give either sector a second channel of influence to the Department, or the opportunity to form coalitions at national level? Struthers also had his eye on the English Consultative Committee founded in 1900 (Selby-Bigge 1927, 203-6). In an internal Department memorandum he conceded that,

> there will be no doubt a great convenience in having important questions threshed out in the first place in the Advisory Council, if for no other reason but to give each party concerned an opportunity of understanding the other's view. (SRO 1917)

But he was emphatic that any council should have no executive powers and few opportunities for criticism:

> Its function would be not so much to criticise proposals already worked out by the officials of the Department, but to investigate matters referred to it by the Department, and to work out in definite detail concrete proposals for action which in turn would be examined by the Department's officials from the point of view of practicability and cost. (*ibid.*)

Struthers wanted a council to contain representatives of the universities and central institutions, together with 'people who had the confidence of the new authorities and also of the Teachers' associations' (*ibid.*). He felt that support from such a body would give the Department an additional authority for its policies. But he also thought that any council must be carefully controlled by the Department, for it would be open to manipulation by others. He wrote of the teachers:

> their object in urging their representation upon the Advisory Council is a purely professional one. The local education authorities . . . they regard as their natural enemies and they hope that with the support of the Department's representatives upon the Council . . . they may be able to improve their position *vis à vis* of the local authorities. (*ibid.*)

The 'professional' matters, in Struthers' sense of salaries and conditions, were eventually to be negotiated separately (see chapter 10). But there were other professional issues that might fall within a council's competence. Some, like teacher recruitment and training, were also clearly linked to the market position of teachers. But what of teachers' claims to professional status by virtue of their expertise in the 'mystery' of education, to use Murrie's phrase? Was this anything more than covert self-interest? Allan Rodger was central to the Department's dealings with teachers after 1945, and we shall see in the next chapter that he was sceptical of teachers' claim to a unique professional knowledge. If the claim were conceded, the case for the self-determination of teachers would be strengthened, and also the case for a council that gave independent advice to the Department.

The dispute in the 1920s over the future of secondary education had a lasting influence on the Department's attitudes to teacher professionalism. Craik, by this time an MP, deplored the new educational 'experts' – teachers, directors of education and college and university researchers – who were beginning to advance research-based arguments that higher proportions of the age-group than the Department's policy allowed were fitted by ability to take full secondary courses (Craik 1926). Such arguments only sustained the demands of the EIS for post-primary expansion through the intermediate certificate (see chapter 2). The Department rode out the Council's demand for the retention of the intermediate certificate (Young 1986, ch.2). But the various strands of the opposition, disillusioned with the Department's reining-in of the Second Council, then coalesced in a new institutional form in the Scottish Council for Research in Education (SCRE) (Wake 1984, ch.3).

The SCRE was founded in 1928 with support principally from the EIS, the local authorities and directors of education, the teacher-training colleges, and the universities. It is rightly renowned for its pioneering research studies of national intelligence (e.g. SCRE 1933, 1953). What is less well appreciated, however, is that the SCRE in its early years attempted to supply thinking, research and development across a range of educational issues that might otherwise have been dealt with by the Advisory Council and the Department, had relations there been better. 'Conscientious middle managers, disheartened by lack of direction', is the way the early membership of the SCRE has been characterised (Wake 1984, 92). Three years after the Council was founded, one of its leading figures, Professor William McClelland, launched it on the research study that was to lead to his 1942 recommendation that access to certificate-course work in Scotland be substantially expanded (McClelland 1942).

If this was disturbing for certain members of the Department, so also was the EIS argument that teachers' involvement in research was the hallmark of a true profession. In the 1920s and 1930s the SED stood apart from the SCRE, distrusting the motives and the progressive educational thinking of several of its leading figures. And well it might. Members of the SCRE regarded it as a growing point for a new partnership in education between teachers, the local authorities and higher education. Nourished by scientific and progressive thought, the partnership would promote teacher professionalism, in the sense of a research- and practitioner-based expertise, to a point where central state controls might be allowed to wither away. McClelland was appointed to the Sixth Advisory Council, and he wrote these ideas into its report on teacher training (SED 1946b). In it he proposed that teacher professionalism, in the sense of expertise, had developed to a point where teacher-training colleges should become autonomous institutes, independent both of the SED and of the universities, but with close relations to the SCRE (*ibid.*, paras 12 and 215). And, as a member of the Sixth Advisory Council's committee on secondary education, McClelland, together with Robertson, developed the case for teachers' control of an internally assessed national certificate at sixteen years. This was a proposal with expansionary implications that Mackay Thomson would not contemplate (see chapter 4).

Although both proposals were anathema to the Department, McClelland continued to argue for them from his position as Executive Officer of the National Committee for the Training of Teachers (NCTT), which he occupied from 1941 to 1959. Rodger told us that the Department was reluctant to consider any changes in the position of the teacher-training colleges as long as McClelland was in post. It was only with the reforms that followed McClelland's retiral that the Department brought the colleges into the process of curriculum development. Also, it is significant that Brunton chose to do the research and development work that led to the introduction of the O-grade, not through the SCRE, but directly in the schools. He told us that 'at that time the Research Council and the Department were scarcely speaking to each other, and to go to the Research Council would have been unthinkable in Departmental eyes. Rusk, the Director of the Council at that time, had no use for the Department and the Department had very little use for Rusk.'

At the very time, therefore, that the Department was debating the future of the Advisory Council in the 1950s, men like McClelland constituted a living warning to the Department of the influence that others could erect on the authority of expertise, and a living reminder of the difficulties that the Advisory Council's synoptic thinking had caused the Department in earlier decades.

Indeed, the indications are that the Department would have been happy enough to discontinue the Advisory Council in the early 1950s. A Seventh Council had met between 1947 and 1951, adding eleven reports to the thirteen bequeathed to the Department by its predecessor (Young 1986). The Department told the new Conservative Government in 1951 that the Council had given the Department more than enough work to be getting on with, and that there was no obvious new remit to give to the Council in a time of economic restraint. The Minister of State, Lord Home (1951-55), and the junior Minister, Henderson Stewart, accepted these arguments. In March 1952 an Order in Council allowed the Department to postpone the appointment of an Eighth Council (SI 1952).

Henderson Stewart, however, had been a member of the Sixth Council, and it was probably at his instigation that the Department issued its belated formal response to the Council's *Secondary Education* report (Robertson 1969c). He accepted the Council's suspension reluctantly, and insisted that it be reviewed annually. It was, in 1953 and again in 1954. Then, in 1955, he suggested to Murrie that a follow-up to the recommendations of the Appleton Committee on Teacher Supply (see chapter 10) might provide the occasion for reconvening the Council (SRO 1957a, 14 June 1955). However, this was just at the time that Brunton was setting up his own committee on the curriculum of the secondary school, choosing to use a Departmental working party, and not the Advisory Council, because he was 'determined it wasn't going to be a committee whose report would be pigeon-holed' (see chapter 4). Henderson Stewart did not press his case.

But the following year he did. The Labour Opposition had urged him in the House to reconvene the Council, arguing that the shortage of parliamentary time for Scottish educational affairs made regular review all the more necessary. They cited bursaries, and selection for secondary education as two contentious issues (PD 1956a, 1956b). Henderson Stewart in turn asked Murrie to consider three possible remits for a reconvened Council: fee-paying schools, comprehensive schools, and promotion tests (SRO 1957b, 8 November 1956).

The discussion within the Department saw difficulties both in the particular remits suggested by Henderson Stewart and also in the reconvening of the Council for any purpose whatsoever.[4] The remit on fee-paying seems to have been dismissed without much discussion, and for reasons that are not apparent in the surviving papers. The issues of comprehensive education and selection for secondary education were regarded as 'political' matters, first raised by the Opposition in the House, and therefore not suitable for resolution through the Council. Moreover, it was felt that the Sixth Council had already formulated the broad approach to these issues, and that too little time had since passed to evaluate the implementation of the Department's circulars on school organisation and promotion. Quite apart from the difficulty in finding suitable remits for a new Council, the fear was expressed that 'an omni-competent body might give advice on questions which had not been referred to them' (SRO 1957b, 19 November 1956). This had been the source of the Department's difficulties with the Sixth Council, though not with the Seventh Council of 1947 to 1951 which the Department had kept too busy (Young 1986, ch.10). But this tactic itself had led to more work for the Department, both in servicing the Council and in responding to its recommendations.

No-one in the Department in the mid-1950s seems to have thought the time was ripe for a new Council with a broad, aggregating and synoptic role that looked towards the 1960s. At one extreme was the view that the Council was constitutionally incapable of giving 'independent' advice precisely *because* the 1918 Act required that it consist of 'not less than two-thirds of members . . . qualified to represent the views of various bodies interested in education'. On this view, the most that a Council should be allowed was to be on hand to give unpublished advice to the Department at the Department's behest (SRO 1957a, 17 June 1955). At the other extreme was the view that a reconvened Council might prove useful in legitimating Departmental policy, but only if its remits and membership were carefully chosen. In essence the arguments had not changed ·since Struthers had rehearsed them forty years earlier.

Eventually three remits were chosen as a way of meeting Henderson

Stewart's request. These were on promotion from primary school, post-fourth-year examinations, and teacher supply. The topic of promotion was chosen not because of its implications for comprehensive schooling, but because of the Department's concern with senior-secondary school wastage and curricular reform. The Department wanted to reduce the proportion of the age-group transferred to secondary courses and to differentiate pupils earlier in secondary school. At the time the Department seems to have been contemplating a subsequent remit on comprehensive schooling (sro 1957c, 4 August 1958). Whether such a remit would have emerged can now be a matter only for conjecture. But it seems unlikely in view of the fact that, at a time when the Central Advisory Council in England was producing a succession of sociologically informed critiques of selection (ME 1954, 1959, 1963; des 1967), no comparable work was undertaken in Scotland either by the Department or the Advisory Council.

The examinations remit also reflected a long-standing Departmental interest in the introduction of a sixth-year A-level examination. This had led in 1957-58 to disagreements among members of Brunton's working party on the curriculum of the senior-secondary school. Some members feared the threat that a sixth-year A-level might pose to the fifth-year Higher (sed 1959b, para.120). The matter was referred to a special committee of the Advisory Council (sed 1960b) and a truce was agreed in the working party, presumably in order to preserve the unanimity of its report.

However, it was the problem of teacher supply that seems finally to have reconciled a reluctant Department to the Minister's wish to resuscitate the Council. This was the first remit to be given to the Eighth Council, and the only remit on which anyone in the Department thought that the Advisory Council might have a useful contribution to make. As the bulge in the age-group approached secondary education, the Department was increasingly concerned about supply. It was clear by 1957 that shortages would become acute in the early 1960s, and would continue at least until 1967. Faced with these immediate difficulties, officials were reluctant to open up the issues of selection and of the raising of the school-leaving age. The Department did not want 'perfectionist' recommendations which teacher shortages then obliged it to reject, as it had rejected many of the recommendations of the Sixth Council. It was persuaded instead to the view that 'for the next few years the limiting factor in what can be attempted in the educational field is the shortage of [school] staff' (sro 1957b, 14 November 1956).

To cope with the impending crisis, the Department wanted to reduce the standards required for admission to teacher training, and it was here that it thought that backing from the Advisory Council might help it ('Mr Henderson Stewart says that we must be careful not to suggest that the main job of the Council would be to lower standards. This will, however, be their main job' (sro 1957c, 17 January 1957)). To chair the Council the Department selected an Oxford-educated philosopher, T. M. (later Sir Malcolm) Knox, Principal of the University of St Andrews. Officials reported that Knox disliked McClelland's report on teacher training, 'because that report had envisaged that training colleges would become very important institutions rivalling on the education side the university departments themselves'. They recorded that he did not like Robertson's report on secondary education, 'which though well written, seemed to him to be egalitarianism run riot'. He was also reported as having a low regard for the training colleges, and no wish to give assistance through the Council to the teachers' case for a salary increase (s ro 1957b, 12 February 1957).

From the Department's point of view, however, things went badly. Knox was unable to persuade the teachers on the special committee of the Council to accept dilution. An official reported in May 1957 that,

> this teaching group is proving to be very firm in refusing to consider any concessions in regard to teaching qualifications, if these might be held to involve dilution in even the slightest degree. Rather surprisingly, Sir James Robertson, the Vice Chairman, seems to be as firmly resolved as any of his colleagues to prevent such concessions; for example he has opposed the recognition of teachers with third class Honours degrees as specialist teachers, even against the advice of the university representatives. So far, the teachers are the dominating influence on the Council; no non-teaching member has as yet made any strong influence to counter their narrow trades unionism. (s ro 1957d, 28-9 May 1957)

In the event, the Knox Committee did not deliver what the Department had wanted, and there disappeared the one argument that had commanded much support within the Department for the continuation of the Advisory Council. It was only in the area of teacher supply that the Department had looked to the Council, and had looked, not for new ideas, but for support for the predetermined policy of dilution. As Rodger told us, the Department had struggled with the shortage of teachers for years, and it doubted that an outside body would produce new thinking. In 1961 the junior Minister was advised by his officials that, in view of the other enquiries that were in hand, the Advisory Council should not be reconstituted. He seems to have agreed without demur (s ro 1961b, 11 and 17 August 1961), in effect terminating the Scottish Advisory Council some years before the decision to close its English counterpart.[5]

In spite of the Advisory Council, Rodger persisted with the policy of dilution, and the teachers in Glasgow struck. Shaken by the strike and by the growing power of teachers in England, the Department at first seemed to make major concessions, setting up the Wheatley Committee which led eventually to the General Teaching Council (g tc) (see chapter 12) and several smaller reviews (s ed 1962b, 1962c, 1962d, 1962e; s ed 1963c). Late in 1961 or early in 1962, it also established a Consultative Committee on Educational Matters (c cem) constituted on lines similar to those that the

English Schools Council was later to take. The CCEM was to act as 'a forum for discussion of general policy on educational matters, particularly those affecting curricula, examinations and school organisation' (SED 1963a, 78). It seems that the Association of Directors of Education and the main teachers' associations nominated their members to it, with no Departmental selection of nominees. Although it lacked executive functions, such a committee clearly had considerable potential, but whether or not it was intended only as a temporary expedient, we do not know. Certainly there was a potential for conflict with the new Examination Board (SCEEB), and with the Consultative Committee on the Curriculum (CCC). Moreover, teachers themselves were becoming more interested in the emergent GTC. When these new bodies were established, the fragmentation of the broader advisory function was completed. The CCEM lost its remit for curriculum and examinations and was renamed the 'Liaison Committee on Educational Matters'. It was given relatively trivial tasks and allowed to fade into obscurity in the early 1970s.[6]

Thus a moment passed in the early-to-mid-1960s when a new and institutionalised form of partnership might have emerged in Scotland much as it did in England. Thereafter, with the fragmentation of the advisory function, any future partnership in Scotland would be even more dependent on the Inspectorate. Brunton saw them 'drawing their net' over the whole of Scottish education (chapter 7). His successor, Dickson, used less predatory imagery:

> If the Scottish education system is going to work, it will only work providing there is a genuine, real, active partnership between the central government and its department, the local authorities, and the teachers; and I see us very much as a sort of catalyst bringing this cooperation into active being. (SCES 1968, Q.50)

Nevertheless, Dickson's Inspectorate was to claim for itself an authority to which no other group could aspire. 'The Inspectorate,' the Department told the Parliamentary Select Committee in 1968, 'are professional educationists with a width of view and a breadth of experience not shared by any other group in the Scottish educational world' (*ibid.*, 3). With only the Inspectorate to link the fragmented structures of advice, and to catalyse the separate parts of the national system, this claim would thereafter remain logically unassailable.

Destabilisation

The earlier part of this chapter has stressed the interdependence of the Department's policies for curriculum, examinations and school organisation. The extension of certification through the O-grade released an expanding demand for certification and for post-compulsory education, thereby destabilising these policies. Up to that point the extension of certification ('downward incrementalism') had been planned. Thereafter it was reactive,

reactive to rapid expansion, to comprehensive reorganisation and to the impending raising of the school-leaving age. In the later 1960s, schools were urged by the Department to drop the minimum number of O-grade presen-, tation subjects from three to one. Then, in 1973, the O-grade was 'banded': the pass/fail distinction was abandoned in favour of an award on the range A, B, C, D and E (D and E awards had previously been 'fails'). By the mid-1970s, some eighty per cent of pupils started O-grade work at fourteen years, and some seventy per cent presented for the examination, if only in one or two subjects. Many such pupils achieved only D and E awards which were still widely regarded as 'fails'. Truancy rates for fifteen- and sixteen-year-olds were high, especially among the one-third of 'non-certificate' pupils who did not take O-grade courses (Gray *et al.*, 1983, ch.11).

The SCEEB, the CCC and the GTC therefore began their work in the mid-1960s at the very time that the Department's overall policy was rapidly becoming a victim of its own success. If there were any prospect of maintaining clearly separate philosophies of senior- and junior-secondary education as the O-grade curriculum spread, it was further threatened by the return in 1964 of a Labour Government committed to comprehensive reorganisation. Here was a new factor. The expansion that was destabilising policy had also contributed to the fragmentation of the advisory function. If the various elements of advice were to be harmonised into broader policies, it could only be through the linking and catalytic role of the Inspectorate. But how could they play this role if their authority were challenged from above by the Labour Government and by their senior administrative colleagues? In the late 1950s the Department had envisaged that the broader questions of comprehensive education and ROSLA might be addressed by the Advisory Council in the early 1960s. But, after 1964, both issues were removed from the advisory agenda, principally because the professional consensus that the Department had moulded no longer obtained. ROSLA, Brunton told us, was decided against the views of all the major bodies in Scotland, including the Inspectorate; and there was little professional or Departmental support before 1965 for comprehensive reorganisation (see chapters 15 and 16).

As the Department's policies faltered in the mid-1960s, older controversies over the scale and form of post-primary provision were reactivated. What sort of provision should be made for the less able pupils who were now staying on in greater numbers? How many should take public examinations? Should these examinations be 'external' like the Higher and the O-grade, or essentially 'internal' like the inter-war Day School certificates, or the CSE Mode III that many teachers in England were beginning to develop? Should the Brunton philosophy of courses centred on the 'vocational impulse' form the basis of the curriculum, or should an attempt be made to adapt the elite tradition of general, non-vocational education to able and less able pupils alike?

Political and professional opinion were internally divided on these issues, and a demoralised Inspectorate at first found it difficult to control the centrifugal tendencies of the new advisory structure. For a time the CCC and the SCEEB pulled in different directions, and it required a major effort from the Inspectorate to contain this fragmentation and reinsert itself at the centre of a coordinated policy process. What emerged substantively from this effort was the final stage in the process of downward incrementalism: the endorsement by the Munn and Dunning Committees of a non-vocational secondary curriculum, and of certification for more or less everybody (SED 1977b, 1977c).

But Munn and Dunning were also innovative, signalling as they did a rejection of bipartism and vocationalism in favour of a broadly common curriculum, and a measure of internal assessment for pupils at all levels of national certification. The Dunning committee made an imaginative attempt to reconcile the provision of courses at varying levels of difficulty with the principle that the selection of pupils to these courses should be neither premature nor irrevocable. The Munn committee endorsed the principle of a liberal and humane curriculum for all pupils in compulsory schooling. In all these respects their thinking was closer to that of the Sixth Advisory Council than to Brunton's thinking. At the same time the measure of internal assessment they proposed was small, though possibly intended to grow, and the individual subject was confirmed as the basic unit of the curriculum, though with gestures towards integration. Both these principles were compromises with the existing body of educational experience and practice. So too, however, were the rejection of vocationalism, and the proposal to extend certification.

All in all, therefore, Munn and Dunning also represented a coherent and evolutionary response to the practices and demands of teachers that had accumulated over the previous fifteen years. But much of this coherence was subsequently lost in the selective implementation of the committees' proposals. Their impact was further dissipated as a result of continuing tensions between the Inspectorate and SED administrators, and between teachers and the Department as a whole. After 1977 the 'reality' of the system wavered uncertainly between a humane and comprehensive vision of the future and a powerful legacy from the past. Fitting the filter of correspondence theory over one's lens, the contours of the old bipartism could still be seen. So too could older styles of administrative control, and resistance to them. Nevertheless, vocationalism in the secondary-school curriculum, compulsory and post-compulsory, remained in disrepute until the early 1980s, when the growing assertiveness of a new government agency, the Manpower Services Commission, obliged the SED to reconsider its position.

NOTES

1. SRO (1957b). See Mill (1951, 448).
2. John Young drew this to our attention.
3. In the quotation we have substituted 'categories' for the translator's 'classes' in order to avoid confusion.
4. In this discussion we do not attribute views to individual officials (see chapter 3).
5. The other enquiries included the four that were set up in the aftermath of the 1961 teachers' strike (see chapter 12), and also the Robbins Committee on Higher Education in Great Britain (CHE 1963). We do not know whether William Ross reviewed this decision in 1964 when he became Secretary of State in the new Labour Government of that year. Certainly the Department had left open the possibility of a further Council by providing for the same in the 1962 Education (Scotland) Act. However, the Eighth Council had lent its support to bipartism and to the Department's attack on the generosity of the local authorities' admissions to senior-secondary courses (above). Neither stance was likely to commend such a body to the new Labour Government.
6. The working party that led to the establishment of the CCEM recommended that 'members of the committee representing the various associations should be appointed not by the Secretary of State but by their respective associations' (SED 1962b, 13). It also recommended that members could send substitute representatives. Whether these recommendations were adopted in the practices of the CCEM we are unable to confirm, though Sir James Robertson wrote that 'such a consultative committee was set up' (Robertson 1969b). Its inception is described in SED (1963a, 78), and its revised remit in SED (1970a, 101).

Twelve

Teachers and the General Teaching Council

[Graham] had great doubts, I think, at the beginning about the
GTC, but I remember he once said on the side to me . . . that he
was pleasantly surprised at what he regarded as the responsible
way in which the GTC was going about its business. That could be
interpreted in a variety of ways, I suppose.   Gilbert Bryden,
General Secretary of the EIS 1961-74

Introduction

From the late 1950s, the Department was increasingly aware that educational change would depend, not only on finding resources, but also on
gaining the co-operation of teachers. Brunton cultivated relationships with
them, and brought a number of them onto his working parties. In other
respects, however, teachers felt excluded from national and local decision-
making. William Campbell, General Secretary of the EIS (1952-60), contended that teachers' status would not improve unless their views were
taken into account by their 'partners' in central and local government
(*Scotsman* 15 September 1958). Except for the unique occasion of their
inclusion on Tom Johnston's committee on post-war school building (see
chapter 9), they were not consulted in the planning and design of schools,
and this they complained about, in their evidence to the Estimates Committee of Parliament in 1953, and again in 1961 (SC on Estimates 1953; 1961).
Joint consultation committees in the local authorities were often weak and
ineffective, and did not exist everywhere (SED 1962c, paras 46-7). In addition, teachers were disqualified by law from membership of local education
committees, unlike their English counterparts (SED 1962d). Beyond the
classroom, where they still remained in substantial control of practice,
salary negotiations provided the only regular occasions for teachers to be
represented in national decision-making. Yet teachers complained about
inadequate pay awards and about the workings of the negotiating machinery. Their suspicion of government deepened when attempts to achieve an
adequate supply seemed to be eroding standards of entry to the profession,
and over these the teachers had no control (SSTA 1957).

Coates (1972) has described the tactics used by teachers in England and
Wales in the 1960s to advance their interests and to gain more influence in
central decision-making. These included renewed efforts to achieve unity

266

amongst the teachers' associations and to win professional self-government. The attempt failed, but, starting in 1961, teachers engaged in militant national action in pursuit of both 'industrial' and 'professional' aims.

In Scotland too, the 1960s were turbulent years. Whilst Scottish teachers were organisationally less divided than their southern counterparts, unity was rarely achieved. Militancy erupted for the first time in 1961. Though largely confined to Glasgow, its national leverage was considerable. In this chapter we show how matters came to a head with a strike that catalysed changes in relationships between the profession, government and others. The most prominent innovation to which it led was the General Teaching Council (GTC), a professional body through which teachers hoped to gain a substantial degree of self-regulation and of influence over policy. Through the GTC, teachers expected to control the licensing of teachers and entry to training, and thus to control the gateways to the profession. But the Secretary of State's responsibility for education meant that he could not yield his right to regulate training and supply. Also, the colleges of education, and, in particular, their principals, retained a substantial degree of influence when the functions of the Scottish Council for the Training of Teachers (SCTT) were redistributed in the late 1960s. Furthermore, the GTC's powers over the registration and employment of teachers were limited in practice by the reluctance of the Secretary of State and some local-authority employers to enforce them strenuously when faced with shortages. As the Secretary of State's main adviser on training and supply, the GTC was intended to give teachers a greater say in national policy. But here, too, there were obstacles that prevented the GTC from establishing an influence on central policy that was something more than the influence that teachers exerted through other channels.

Teachers' Professionalism

In a lecture delivered sometime in the late 1950s or early 1960s, John Mackintosh, later Labour MP for Berwick and East Lothian, remarked on teachers' 'endless round of complaints about butchers who can afford better cars, [and] about lack of respect from children, parents, and the public' (Drucker 1982, 185). He linked these grievances to the absence of self-respect and unity in a profession whose status divisions harmed morale and interfered with its ability to speak with one voice on educational questions. 'Teaching, if nothing better offers', was what Mackintosh's university students told him when he asked about their intended occupation (PD 1967b). Mackintosh also scoffed at what he heard whilst visiting schools:

> The headmaster often pauses outside the classroom door and slips one the vital clue to the inmate – not, 'good teacher' or 'very interested in theatrical work' – but, 'this man has a second', 'only an ordinary MA,' or 'one of our few non-certificated teachers, I'm afraid'. (Drucker 1982, 185)

Teachers had long considered that improvements in their status were bound up with progression towards the cherished ideal of an all-graduate profession, or, failing that, with ensuring that all teachers held qualifications appropriate to their level and sector. Sir Henry Wood, the English-born Principal of Jordanhill College, remarked on this:

WOOD. The qualification issue has been pushed too far. In England if you go to a job in a secondary school, at least in my day, the headmaster said, 'What can you teach?' In Scotland he says, 'What are you qualified in?' And, you know, there is a subtle difference.

In their quest for recognition, teachers saw shorter training and lower entry requirements as retrograde steps. Professional recognition was essential to the improvement of their salaries and status, to the fulfilment of their ambition to regulate their corporate affairs, and to increasing their influence over policy. Teachers sought to participate in decisions about salaries and educational policy. In practice this gave a key role to the EIS, and later to other organisations, in representing teachers in the councils of the state (see chapter 10). Teachers were aggrieved when their voice went unheeded, or when the channels were blocked. For the right they asserted to a role in national decision-making rested on their claim to professional status, and the substantive educational outcomes of such decisions could, in turn, affect the strength of that claim.

Teachers' professionalism was grounded in their expertise as practitioners, which they gained through specific training, through the experience of classroom teaching, and through research-based knowledge of the process of education. This expertise, they thought, qualified them for more than the occupancy of seats round the negotiating table, and for more than the membership of consultative bodies. It supported a claim for partnership with the Department and the education authorities. Partnership involves the dispersion of authority and of control over resources to actors who are invested with some degree of autonomy and self-determination (see chapter 1). Teachers thought that to be acknowledged as partners would mean that their authority as experts was recognised as equivalent to authority derived from the political process. As the secret gardeners of the curriculum, they had long enjoyed a considerable degree of classroom autonomy. Whatever the place of this autonomy in wider systems of social control (Grace 1978, 1985), it was an essential component of their notion of professionalism. But professional status depended, further, upon their acquisition of occupational autonomy through control over their own corporate affairs, including recruitment, training, and forms of accountability. Recognition of their professionalism would not only increase their weight as participants in national decision-making, but would also reinforce their control over the content and process of education in the schools.

The Department had long understood the consequences of partnership for its own authority. It begrudged the recognition of teachers as professionals if to do so would constitute any loss of control. In its dealings with the Advisory Council between the Wars, it was reluctant to provide a platform for teachers to deploy expansionist arguments based on educational expertise, and fearful lest teachers use the Council to advance their own material interests. For the same reasons, it kept the SCRE at bay, and rejected McClelland's grand design for a training system that would underpin teachers' autonomy and expertise (see chapter 11). In the 1960s, however, it used the rhetoric of 'partnership' when appealing to consensus on the shared enterprise of public education (SCES 1968, Q.50). Likewise, it invoked 'professionalism' when enjoining on teachers an obligation to a service controlled from the centre.

Humes criticises professionalism as 'a rather shabby bargaining tactic used in the pursuit of different forms of self-interest' both by teachers and employers (Humes 1986, 139). He shares with Ozga and Lawn a view of the contradictory nature of professionalism (Ozga and Lawn 1981; Ozga 1985; Humes 1986, chs 2 and 7). Ozga and Lawn see professionalism as an ideology that has been used by the state to assert control, and used by teachers to assert their expertise-based interests against those of their employers or managers. They argue that professionalism should not be regarded as necessarily opposed to trade unionism. Teachers, as organised labour, might use strategies and form alliances to protect the ideals of professional autonomy and service against what they take to be governmental threats to the quality or availability of education. Ozga elsewhere points out that, as 'union' activities, strikes and the teachers' contract of service 'run counter to the ideology of professionalism as invoked by central and local government to obtain good behaviour from teachers' (Ozga 1985, 244). And she sees a further predicament for teachers. The scheme of conditions of service which Scottish teachers won in the 1970s may even run counter to a wider, client-related definition of professionalism espoused by teachers themselves, and by others. Ozga argues that the contract protects jobs in a declining market, but that adherence to it may sacrifice educational objectives as cuts are sought in other parts of the service, and in ways that affect its quality.

Rodger's sceptical view of professionalism reflects some of these tensions:

RODGER. Teachers in Scotland have always felt that they deserved high professional status. When they didn't get it, they asked themselves: 'What are the characteristics of a profession?' These are: a professional man or woman should have some body of knowledge that members of the public may be generally aware of, but which they don't know in the detail required by the expert. . . . The problem was that many teachers who were honours graduates were no different in their own subject from other honours graduates who may have gone elsewhere. . . . Therefore the only thing that teachers could fall back on as a mark of a profession was teacher training, and that is one of the reasons why teacher training, since 1920 or so, has become amongst teachers, a sort of sacred thing, since it's the way by which they mark themselves out as a profession.

But Rodger was not entirely sympathetic to teachers' claims to professional status, despite his own background in teaching and that of his father and brother, and despite the training that teachers underwent. There was 'a question mark in my mind', he told us. It was to be an important one in the deliberations of the Wheatley Committee which recommended the GTC, and on which Rodger represented the Department. He explained his philosophy of professionalism:

RODGER. I always considered that the Wheatley Committee was set up to deal with an issue which had perhaps come to a climax in the turmoil of 1961, but which . . . had simmered for fifteen years or more before that. . . . I remember . . . several times the EIS saying that they would like to be a professional body like the doctors. They wanted to have true professional status. . . . A professional man, to me . . . is an educated man. But, in addition to having a good general education, there is some specific field which he knows better than other well educated men. . . . A professional man has got professional attitudes to his work . . . he doesn't work by the hour; he doesn't work by time. . . . [He is] trying to do good to some members of the public. . . . Now, the teacher fails in one respect from qualifying because, does he have a professional body of knowledge which no one else possesses? . . . I doubt . . . whether the mere ability to teach . . . is something which is truly specific to the teachers. This is why I wonder whether the teacher is, in the full sense, a professional person. Further, the more they align themselves with the trade unions, and the more militant they become, the more they class themselves with artisans than with the professional groups.

Q. So it was presumptuous for the teachers to want to have a body to control the profession?

RODGER. No, I don't say that it was presumptuous, but you can make a logical case that he is not quite the professional man that the doctor is.

The 1961 Strike

The employment of uncertificated teachers was anathema to an occupational group which was concerned not only to shore up its economic position, but also to raise its standing in the public eye. Yet, in 1949, the education authorities were employing some 900 uncertificated teachers (SED 1951c, para.9), and the prospects of eliminating them from the education service were dim. Even when the supply of primary teachers improved, uncertificated teachers were still required at the secondary level. In 1961, their total number in all schools was nearly 2300, and was rising (SED 1962a, 12). For the badly-off authorities, like Lanarkshire, uncertificated teachers were indispensable if they were to avoid the worse fates of oversized classes and of an increase in part-time schooling. Likewise, any proposal to remedy the lack of male primary teachers by opening the three-year training course to men met implacable teacher hostility: such a measure would 'dilute' a profession which had ambitions to extend, not contract, the principle of graduation.

As we saw in chapter 10, the Knox Committee in 1959 had considered the admission of non-graduate men to training in order to ease the shortage. It had rejected this, despite strong pressure from the Department, because it 'would be bitterly opposed by the teaching profession' (SED 1959d, para.94). But, around the same time, the Department was reviewing the training system, including college-entrance and training standards, the nature of training, and certification. The National Committee for the Training of Teachers (NCTT) had gone, and with it William McClelland, who had been its Executive Officer since 1941. The Department now envisaged a fundamental and comprehensive revision of the much amended 1931 regulations (SED 1961a, 79). The SED's consultative memorandum put the non-graduate idea back on the agenda. The reaction of the teachers' organisations was all-important. In 1961, Gilbert Bryden was in his first year as General Secretary of the EIS:

BRYDEN. Over the years, in the fifties and earlier than that too, every now and again, you used to get a motion at an Annual General Meeting to the effect that a register of teachers should be set up . . . a register, of course, of properly qualified teachers; uncertificated teachers wouldn't be on that register and it would be impossible to employ them. . . . The SED was never very enthusiastic about it. . . . I don't think that the Institute felt very strongly about it either. . . . Sometime in 1960, the Scottish Education Department produced a paper . . . largely by Rodger . . . dealing with the supply of teachers, and in it they floated the idea that non-graduate men teachers for the primary school should be recruited more or less on the same basis as non-graduate women. Well, I knew about this idea; it had come up in one or two other places but had been rejected. . . . The Institute and the other teachers' bodies reacted very, very strongly against it, and there was a tremendous amount of unrest. Our Executive became so concerned that it called a meeting of representatives of the Institute, the SSTA and the SSA, to see if we could take common action. This was so unprecedented that it electrified the profession. Teachers began to hold what you might call ecumenical meetings in schools, and I began to receive letters advising us to set up a teachers' council. Well, I arranged a meeting with the Secretary of State in Dover House, of ourselves and representatives of the other two bodies, and we had a meeting with Mr Maclay. . . . [He] said that he appreciated our concern . . . and that he wouldn't come to any decision [about non-graduate men] without the fullest consultations, and so on and so forth; and he soft-soaped us in a big way, and the meeting came to an end with expressions of goodwill on all sides. In the meantime, however, our members in Glasgow had been sizzling away, and they suddenly decided that it was time they were having a strike. We thought at headquarters that a strike was a bit premature. . . . They thought that we hadn't really extracted anything of any importance from [Maclay] and in view of these circumstances they thought that they would continue with their strike. . . . Well, I went back to the Secretary of State and I told him about this, and he was very put-down. . . . Now, shortly after that, the Secretary of State rejected the proposals of the National Joint Council for the eighteen-and-one-half per cent increase . . . so that, of course, set the building alight and Glasgow had their strike.

More than 5 000 of Glasgow's 7 000 school teachers began a five-day strike on 8 May 1961 (*Glasgow Herald* 9 May 1961; McKenzie 1974, ch.2; De-roche-Drieux 1976, ch.III). The vast majority of those who came out were members of the Glasgow local association of the EIS, but they were joined by Glasgow members of both the SSA and the SSTA. Outside Glasgow, the only teachers who took part in the strike were SSA members in Lanarkshire, Renfrewshire and Ayrshire, who struck for one day.

In all three associations, it was branches in the west of Scotland that were the most militant. The first practical step had been taken in March, when a strike committee was formed at St Augustine's High School, Glasgow, under the leadership of Arthur Houston, an EIS member who had been a Labour Party candidate at the previous General Election (see chapter 17). Similar committees were soon formed at other schools. The officers and national executives of the teachers' associations were themselves at odds with the Secretary of State. But their political and financial support for a strike was limited, and at times seemed reluctantly given. Nevertheless, on the first day of the strike Bryden joined with Labour and Liberal MPs to address a standing-room-only meeting of teachers in the Kelvin Hall, Glasgow. A resolution was passed, by acclamation, calling for the resignation of the Secretary of State. But local militants were one step ahead. At an unofficial meeting on the following day, more than a thousand teachers overflowed the Central Halls in Glasgow to hear detailed proposals for a Scottish teachers' council. They urged the adoption of this objective upon the associations (*Glasgow Herald* 10 May 1961). The meeting was organised by Houston along with David Lambie. Although Lambie was on the management committee of the Glasgow EIS, the meeting did not have the support of the Institute. Lambie had sat on the Executive of the Scottish Council of the Labour Party, and, like Houston, had contested a Parliamentary seat.

Although the strike was brief and confined to Glasgow and a few neighbouring education authorities, Bryden thought that 'the Department was very much shaken'. He said that the strike 'had repercussions that went on for a long time . . . [and] the memory of it continued to shake them'. It gave the EIS considerable leverage to move the dispute into the arena of national politics. Bryden continued:

BRYDEN. One result of this was a debate in Parliament in the course of which Malcolm Macpherson [Labour, Stirling and Falkirk Burghs; Parliamentary Adviser to the EIS 1964-70] suggested that one of the reasons for the continuing teacher unrest was the fact that, whereas all the other professions had a substantial amount of control over entrance to the profession, professional discipline and so on, the teachers alone had none of this power. We made a lot of Macpherson's speech. For quite a while, we and the SED weren't on speaking terms; a most uncommon thing. . . . The President, R. J. Walker . . . thought that we should go up and see if we couldn't come to some sort of arrangement with the Government. So I rang up Stewart Aldridge [Assistant Secretary, SED, 1959-73] and asked him how the Department would react to an olive branch. He said they would react very well indeed. So . . . we put to [Maclay] the notion that teacher unrest was all about teacher grievances, lack of a teaching council, bad arrangements for negotiating salaries, and the lack of a widows' and orphans' pension scheme, and things like that. . . . And he agreed that it would be a good idea if a number of working parties were set up to discuss these matters. We said that we would like this kept secret until we had consulted our executive, because we had acted, of course, without the authority of our executive. So he agreed. We called our executive together. I explained what had happened, and asked them if they agreed that there should be this formal investigation with the implication, of course, that there would be no strikes for the time being. The executive accepted this with joy and alacrity.

Q. The Wheatley Committee on teachers' certification, plus four working parties, were set up at your initiative essentially?[1]

BRYDEN. Yes.

Q. Was that the first time you had that sort of very active response from the SED on issues such as this?

BRYDEN. I would say so, yes. I would attribute it to a variety of things. First of all to the colossal unrest. The unrest was produced by the combination of the notion of non-graduate men and the Secretary of State's rejection of the NJC salaries agreement. In the teaching profession, that's the best way to stir up unrest: have an educational issue and a bread-and-butter issue.

Q. The non-graduate men issue, was that a symbolic issue in some ways, in the sense that it was seen as undermining the Ordinary degree?

BRYDEN. Yes, very much so. . . . Lowering of the standards of entry to the profession. . . . One of the advantages of very seldom having a strike is that, when you do have a strike, it creates a stir. . . . But, you see, even before the strike, there had been a colossal amount of interest generated in Parliament and other places. And, on the other side, I think perhaps I had been building up a good relationship with Departmental officials. It was my first year as General Secretary, and I think perhaps there was a feeling that it was worth having a new start with a new General Secretary.

In the Department, teacher affairs were Rodger's responsibility as Under-Secretary, but his absence in Africa on a Colonial Office education mission for five months from January 1961 prevented him from dealing with the difficulties. As a result, he could not be clear on some details of the strike, but he agreed that it had been likely that two streams of discontent, on salaries and on uncertificated teachers, would come together at some time. He strongly favoured the admission of non-graduate men to primary teaching, and thought the 1960 proposal 'might well have' exacerbated the teachers' discontent:

Q. Would it have happened the same way if you had been here to deal with it?

RODGER. I have no doubt at all that, whatever the problems, Arbuckle in consultation with Aldridge, the Assistant Secretary, would have dealt with them every bit as well as I could have done.

Q. Did Aldridge have the same intimate knowledge of personalities? Possibly he had not won the same amount of trust as you had done.

RODGER. He didn't have as big a knowledge as I had, no. He hadn't had the time to develop an intimate knowledge of personalities . . . but I think the feelings and the troubles that were so prominent in my absence ran far too deep to have been overcome by just a feeling of trust.

In chapter 18 we consider, at greater length, the importance of trust between Rodger and Bryden for the relations between the SED and the EIS.

The Wheatley Report

The review of the training regulations was suspended when the Wheatley Committee was appointed by Maclay at the end of 1961. It reported in June 1963 to his successor, Michael Noble (SED 1963c). The Committee was chaired by the distinguished judge, Lord Wheatley, and its twenty-one members were drawn from many of the important interests, including the teachers' associations. In chapter 10 we saw how Bryden and Rodger got on amicably together in salary negotiations. On Wheatley they also met, but round a different table:

Q. Essentially Wheatley was a venue where the EIS bargained with the SED under the mediation of Lord Wheatley. Is that a fair representation of it?

BRYDEN. Pretty fair, yes. The education authorities' representatives, of course, took a very keen interest too. But you are right in saying that it was myself on one side and Rodger on the other. I think that's fair enough; with Wheatley doing his utmost to keep things going.

Also a member of Wheatley was John McEwan, Lanarkshire's Director of Education. He emphasised the part played by other members, including Douglas McIntosh and himself, who debated and aired a number of views. One, for instance, was McEwan's own idea of a nominated senate of the leading persons in Scottish education, 'not answerable to the groundlings, or to the militants at the hustings'. Rodger, too, thought others were important on the Committee. His main antagonist, he said, was not Bryden but J. A. C. Thomson of the ssa. Thomson was 'a militant and an extremist' whose 'extravagant claims on behalf of teachers . . . antagonised some of the Committee'.

Rodger said that Wheatley himself wanted to get an agreed report and thought this more important than getting the right report. The tone of the report suggests that the Committee found some of the arguments for a teachers' professional body less than convincing. These doubts, however, were overridden by more powerful considerations, including the wish to satisfy teachers' ambitions for higher status, the possible benefit to recruitment, and the need for co-operation in educational development. The 'agreed report' therefore proposed a General Teaching Council with substantial control over standards of entry to training, and with powers to register and to discipline teachers.

The 'right report', in the Department's eyes, might well have been one which devolved less power to a professional council than Wheatley did. Government's preoccupation with shortages made the 1960s an inauspicious time for it to relinquish its hold on standards of entry to training. On the one hand, Wheatley gave the Council the initiative to propose changes in the regulations governing entrance qualifications. On the other hand, the Committee inevitably deemed it impossible for the Secretary of State to abdicate his practical responsibility for teacher supply by giving up control entirely. It wished, however, to make it difficult for the Minister to make teacher-training regulations in the face of the Council's opposition or procrastination, or to reject its proposals. In those cases, Wheatley would have required him to use the 'affirmative-resolution' procedure, in which his policy would have to be debated and approved by Parliament, or even to bring forward a Bill.

Wood thought that Wheatley's proposed shift of power and initiative 'was obviously an embarrassment to the Department . . . and that was partly why it was so long in being implemented'.[2] Bryden agreed, saying that the sED's greatest objection was that a Council might restrict supply in order to boost salaries. In the event, Wheatley's affirmative-resolution proposal was rejected, and the Minister was required only to publish his reasons for rejecting GTC proposals. This was a crucial acknowledgement of the Secretary of State's ultimate power over supply and training. So, too, was the legislative provision for the Secretary of State, and not only the GTC, to initiate regulations. But, in most other respects, Wheatley's recommendations were enacted in 1965, and the GTC was inaugurated in the following year.

George Gray was the GTC's first Registrar. Elsewhere in our interview with him he expressed his disillusion with the Council, but here he explains its main functions:

GRAY. Now, what was envisaged by the Wheatley Committee was the maximum amount of control possible by the Council over content and the arrangement of training courses for teachers; a limited amount of control over what the colleges were doing; and then, centrally of course, the right to form a register of teachers, composed of those that were already certificated, those that would be approved by the colleges, and anybody who was acceptable by exceptional recognition; and lastly, of course, the right to deprive people of registration for various reasons, mainly misbehaviour. Now, this gave the control of certification, the award of certificates, the withdrawal of certificates, and, to a very large extent, the arrangements for the entry and the training of all kinds of persons in colleges, to the control of a Council. . . . The Secretary of State gave one very valuable concession in this respect, that he gave to the exceptions committee – the Committee on Exceptional Admission to the Register of the Council – full powers to accept or reject applications. He gave them disciplinary powers of a very high order, subject only to the control of the Lord President of the Court of Session.

The question of the Council's composition remained contentious for many years. Bryden told us that 'there was a great deal of bargaining about the proportion of teachers and non-teachers' in the deliberations of the Wheatley Committee. Rodger, on behalf of the Department, was reluctant to go as far as teachers wished. He explained how he had dug his heels in:

RODGER. I think that I was the person who prevented the teachers having a majority. I remember making a rather impassioned speech saying that I had hoped that an agreeable committee would reach agreeable conclusions, to which we could all subscribe. I saw a danger that there was something which might be made a recommendation, to which I could not subscribe. I said, 'I am in agreement with the teachers that the teachers should be in a majority . . . but I wish to include teachers of all kinds, whether they had been at a training college or not. I would include university professors of education as teachers; I would call all training-college staff teachers. . . .' And I said, 'Really, if the teaching body wants to have a high prestige in the public mind, it should associate itself with people who have a very high prestige. The general public are not going to give that prestige to any man or woman who happens to be teaching in the village school.'

The result was that 'teachers' had a twenty-five to nineteen majority, but only by stretching the definition of teacher to include four principals of education colleges. Consistent with this inclusion, Wheatley regarded teachers who staffed education colleges as eligible for election. Moreover, among the twenty-one elected primary, secondary, and further-education members, eleven were to be 'eminent teachers of standing', including head teachers and a principal of a further-education college. Among the appointed members, the Association of Directors would have three places, the universities four, and the two local-authority associations of the cities and the counties, two each. Wheatley proposed that the Secretary of State should nominate six persons, but this number was reduced to four in the Act establishing the GTC, in order to create places for representatives of the Church of Scotland and the Roman Catholic Church. Thus the Council was to have both elected and appointed members, but Wheatley did not wish members of either kind to act on the GTC as representatives of their sectoral categories:

> members should be thought of, and should think of themselves, as persons who hold office because their qualities and experience enable them to make a significant contribution. . . . They should exercise an independent judgment. . . . They should not be regarded, therefore, as delegates from, or representatives of, the particular institutions or bodies from which they are drawn. (*ibid.*, para.71)

This was becoming the SED's preferred formula for membership of public bodies, as we will see in the next two chapters on the Examination Board and the CCC. Wheatley attempted, nevertheless, to ensure that the GTC would be 'broadly based', and 'widely representative of the educational world' (*ibid.*, para.5). If the Council were thought to represent only the one sectoral interest, that of certificated teachers, its legitimacy would be compromised. So, too, would be its value to the Department as a mechanism for aggregating views on training, supply, and other issues of concern both to the profession and to the Department. For this, it was important to establish the Council as a body whose members would share a corporate identity that superseded their sectoral affiliations. The highly charged atmosphere of conflict in the 1960s made it advisable for the Department to be seen to be balancing the interests. However, the conflicts within the educational world made such a balance the more difficult to achieve, for they fuelled disagreements about the relevant constituencies and the correct proportions. Rivalry and suspicion amongst the teachers' associations made disputes over the GTC's composition and functions inescapable, and cast doubt upon its independence.

The General Teaching Council and its Problems

A GTC representative told the Select Committee on the Inspectorate in 1968 that the Council,

> has been living at rather a fierce rate from hand to mouth for eighteen months running fast to keep abreast of developments. In its very short history it has been thrown the tasks which other bodies have been bandying about for twenty years, and it has been in fact expected to throw up answers to these in eighteen months. (SCES 1968, Q.466)

The GTC was apprehensive of the poisoned chalice proffered by the Department. But, in any case, the Council did not have its problems to seek. The establishment of a register of teachers, which was the Council's main purpose, was seriously threatened when some teachers refused, on principle, to comply. The Council's inability to put a quick end to the employment of uncertificated teachers at a time of severe teacher shortage tested its authority from the start, and embroiled it in conflict. Dickson told us that the EIS offended the other associations by treating the GTC as a branch of itself. Wood thought that most teachers had no real idea of what the Council was about. He went on:

WOOD. There was tremendous anxiety among the teachers' organisations that the Council would become a sort of super teachers' union which would get to the Secretary of State . . . before they did.

The GTC, the Secretary of State and the teachers' organisations spent several years skirmishing over these issues (Inglis 1970, 1972; Hunter 1972, 271-6; Deroche-Drieux 1976, ch.4). This strained the GTC, interfered with its advisory role, and dissipated the idealism of Wheatley. But, bearing in mind the issue that led to its inception, it is ironic that, within a matter of months, the GTC had approved the Department's proposal for primary training for non-graduate men. Perhaps this is an indication of the Department's influence on the composition and membership of the Council. On the other hand, Bryden told us that the EIS had come close to abandoning its resistance to non-graduate men shortly before, at an Annual General Meeting. However, once the GTC had approved the new policy, Ross delayed its implementation rather than risk losing EIS support for the new Council (Deroche-Drieux 1976, 256).

The Department's officials on the GTC played an important part by communicating Departmental requests and views to the Council, informing it and shaping its agenda. This enabled the SED to seize an early initiative and promote its own aims, at least at the outset. At other times, however, the Department came under heavy pressure from the teachers' interests, especially over the vexed questions of registration and of the employment of unregistered and uncertificated teachers. It was not illegal for local authorities to employ such staff, and many did so extensively. An outraged SSTA made its support for registration, and later, its co-operation over the reform of the GTC, contingent upon firm government action to eliminate uncertificated teachers. But shortages were uppermost in the mind of the Secretary of State. Only after a protracted series of proposals and counterproposals did he arrange a compromise, amending the Schools Code to eliminate uncertificated primary and secondary teachers by 1968 and 1973 respectively. This was implemented through a machinery of reference panels that was itself a matter of further controversy (see chapter 18).

There were other instances of conflict in which the separate teachers' organisations appeared to dominate the GTC's operations. The Minister's relations with the SSTA were severely strained when he dragged his feet over the SSTA's claim that Lanarkshire was breaking the law by continuing to employ uncertificated primary teachers after 1968. The SSA, which had no members on the Council, constantly sniped at the GTC. It supported those certificated teachers who refused to register, and argued in favour of nominated representation of teachers' organisations, rather than election by educational sectors. The press campaign mounted by the EIS to promote registration was more visible than the GTC's own efforts. On one rare occasion, in March 1970, the three associations united to get the GTC to concede the principle of consultation with the teachers' organisations on major policy matters (GTC 1971, 116). But the GTC appeared to be as much a battlefield for internecine squabbling, as it was a professional body enhancing the corporate status of teachers.

As the junior Minister with responsibility for education, Bruce Millan was disillusioned with the GTC. Bryden thought that Millan himself would not have conceded the amendment to the Code which eliminated uncertificated teachers. Our conversation with Millan brought to light his sense of frustration over the GTC's 'wholly unrealistic demands for the immediate dismissal of every uncertificated teacher'. He continued:

MILLAN. It got bound up with a whole lot of different issues, including issues of teacher politics. There was a time during all of this controversy when, I must confess, I thought that the best thing to do would be to abandon the whole idea. . . . I inherited that situation and, of course, in any case, it was Willie Ross' responsibility, and not mine as an Under-Secretary. But it took up an immense amount of time . . . to the detriment of [my] doing other more useful things. And, as I said, there was certainly a point at which I think that it would have been perfectly reasonable to say to the profession, 'Well, this was something that was introduced at the professionals' request, and it was something to improve the status of the profession, and if you don't really want it, or you can't persuade a large number of your professional colleagues that it is a good thing, then I think that we should give up the whole idea'. . . . We didn't do it; we persevered. And we took a lot of abuse for doing that. But it is now working, I think, very well indeed. . . . There was no question of my not being enthusiastic about it. I simply got a bit fed up with the teachers, for whose benefit it was meant to be, complaining about it. . . . If they couldn't agree amongst themselves, then it was unclear, at some points, why I should be working so hard to give them all these benefits.

But it was the attitude of the Secretary of State, William Ross, that was crucial. A former teacher and an EIS member, Ross' concessions at several critical points helped to keep the GTC going when the teachers' organisations threatened to withdraw their support. Several of our interviewees agreed that it required an act of political will to set up and sustain the Council in such a turbulent atmosphere. Graham recalled that Ross' teaching background quickened his interest in it. Bryden gave some of the credit to Graham, whom he thought 'pretty helpful with the GTC'. He thought Graham 'a fairly strong man, and there needed to be a strong man at the Department while the GTC trouble was going on'. But he reserved most praise for Ross, who, he said, had more to do with its inception than any other person. Dickson and Wood confirmed that Ross remained firm in the face of doubts, although they differed slightly in their explanations:

Q. Would it have survived without Ross' active support?

DICKSON. No, I don't think so. I think there was a time when it could easily have been allowed to collapse.

Q. Did Ross save it by increasing teacher representation on it?

DICKSON. No, by simply refusing to give in, so to speak, when there was all the opposition to it that there was, and all the grumbling that went on. He could quite easily have said, 'Oh well, if this is the way people feel, we can fold it up'. It would have been a pity to fold it up, and it would have left us with some difficult problems; for instance, it had relieved the Inspectorate of its commitments in the certification of teachers, which was becoming a very large and time-consuming operation.

This was Wood's view:

WOOD. It certainly would have foundered but for Willie Ross, who was determined that this Council which he established was going to succeed. One of the ways that he assured its future was to change its composition so that teachers were in the majority, and in my opinion this has meant that it has really become an organ of the EIS.

The change in composition occurred after the 1969 Review of the GTC (SSS 1969). On the enlarged Council of forty-nine which took office in 1971, places were given to twenty-six teachers elected from the separate sectoral constituencies. The requirement that a proportion of teachers' places be filled by head teachers was abolished. We asked Bryden:

Q. Why did Ross increase the teacher representation?

BRYDEN. Because we asked him to . . . because so many people, including our own members, were making a fuss about the impotence of the GTC, and we were trying to improve its effectiveness and also its image.

Dickson, we recall, had noted the EIS' proprietary attitude towards the GTC before 1970. This attitude was perhaps to be expected, as EIS members filled all but one of the elected seats on the first GTC. Although Wood remarked on the same attitude after 1970, in fact SSTA members by then had five seats, and were to hold eight in 1974. In any case, Wood, Gray and Dickson had nothing favourable to tell us about the elective aspect of the GTC. Wood said, 'it doesn't seem to me to be the way to get wisdom'. Gray went further and criticised the nominated interests as well:

GRAY. The fact of the matter is that, to a very large extent, the Council has not attracted enough persons of quality. . . . The members who are *really* interested are the teachers, the principals, and the employing authorities (directors and councillors). The others, who give their services as representatives of 'interested' bodies, have a poor attendance record owing to pressure of business. Even the councillors are too busy to attend as they should. The university members – one or two of them have been outstandingly good, but the others indifferent. So decision-making, planning, formulation of educational ideas, are largely the work of teachers and principals. . . . Now, the teacher members are elected in a national election because they have become known *in the work of their associations*, and they come very often, normally in fact, primed with policy which they repeat parrot-fashion, and which is not their own original thinking. . . . Perhaps people are elected simply because they are names that are known, and very often the best brains in the profession have had nothing to do with teacher politics and are unknown as a consequence.

Indeed, the EIS, and later the SSTA, supported lists of official candidates (Deroche-Drieux 1976, 285-7). Deroche-Drieux observes that 'the teachers' representatives seem sometimes to have been the instruments of the professional associations, serving the policies of their association more than the interests of the categories which they should have represented' (*ibid.*, 273, our translation; see also Robertson 1986). But the politicisation of the GTC by the teachers' organisations was accompanied by apathy amongst the teacher electorate, possibly in reaction to the turmoil of the first Council, and to its evident lack of autonomous powers. Whereas some eighty per cent of teachers voted in the first GTC elections in 1966, only thirty-six per cent voted in 1970, and only about one-third at subsequent quadrennial elections.

The GTC and Teacher Training

Despite the changes in the GTC's composition as a result of the 1969 review, the Council was unsuccessful in its bid to gain more control of college-entrance qualifications and training. It already had executive power over teacher registration and discipline. Its role thereafter in advising on, and controlling, supply and training remained limited to the exertion of pressure upon the SED and the colleges. But the Department continued to consult (or ignore) the EIS, the SSTA, the principals and the directors, as it had always done. The GTC might add its voice to the chorus. But, because it was more a colony of its constituent interests than it was their aggregator, the Council could only double the parts, neither enriching the polyphony nor performing solo. It could make little distinctive contribution to the relationship between government, teachers and the training system. The ground had already been occupied by interests and prominent persons whose governmental connections were better established, and who were less dependent upon the GTC than it was on them.

Only a few years earlier, the colleges of education had gained a considerable measure of freedom from detailed control by a central body. This happened in 1958 when the SCTT replaced the NCTT and its Central Executive Committee, which McClelland had chaired. Such loosening of control was consistent with Brunton's desire to devolve Inspectorate responsibilities, and to gain the colleges' support in his development of the curriculum. However, Gray was certain that it was Rodger who was largely responsible for the change (see chapter 5).[3] Thereafter, the Department itself had more overall control of the training system, and directly supervised the colleges' financial estimates. But, in the days of educational expansion and teacher shortage in the late 1950s and 1960s, it held the colleges on a loose rein.

The SCTT was mainly a coordinating body whose primary function was intended to be that of advising on national policies relating to teacher training. Under the 1958 regulations, this function redounded to the advantage of the college principals. McClelland had earlier convened the college directors (later called principals), along with the SED assessors, as a committee that met regularly, outside the structure of the NCTT, to discuss ideas and to communicate opinion to the Department. Osborne (1979, 74) notes that a Committee of Principals had existed since 1923. Wood, however, credited McClelland with its invention, and remarked that, by the mid-1950s, 'it had got some kind of reputation' as a body to be consulted. Rodger said that this group of training-college directors and SED assessors in effect ran the whole training system, concerting views and coordinating the colleges. When the SCTT took over, the Committee of Principals (CP) was formalised within the SCTT as a statutory body to which the Council could refer business. The effect was that the CP could formulate the SCTT's advice to the Secretary of State and to the colleges. Wood thought that 'in the eyes of some teachers and the EIS it perhaps got too powerful'. Gray said that J. J. Robertson, the SCTT's Chairman, complained to Arbuckle that the CP was given too much power to go its own way. Gray told us that he himself shared this view. Over the years, the principals of the large colleges took the chair of the CP in turns. Therefore, Gray argued, without an independent chairman, or members who were not principals, it was too easy for them to aggrandise their colleges to the detriment of the whole. Although Gray held the CP responsible for the lack of unity in the training system, Rodger rated the CP very highly. As assessors on the SCTT, he and other SED officials always attended the CP's meetings (SCTT 1961, 1964, 1967). For most of the first two years of the SCTT, these were, in fact, formally described as meetings of 'Principals and Assessors'.

When the SCTT was wound up, and its functions were reallocated to the SED, the GTC and the colleges, the CP was relocated under a virtually functionless Joint Committee of Colleges (JCC) which was established as an umbrella organisation, sharing the GTC's secretariat.[4] Under the JCC, the CP remained an important link between the Department and the training system. However, Osborne considers that the CP 'collectively has insignificant influence compared with that of its members', and that it makes little contribution to educational policy (Osborne 1979, 74-5). The college principals themselves were given four seats on the GTC and played a leading part, filling the posts of chairman and vice-chairman, and convening several of its standing committees. Although Dickson told us that he did not think they had any undue influence in the GTC's first three years, Gray disagreed. The GTC, as the teachers' professional body, could not exercise control over the training system against the wishes of the colleges. Well might William Inglis, Principal of Moray House College, write:

> The risks of conflict between the Council and the colleges are minimal . . . partly because the colleges themselves have representatives [sic] on the Council. . . . The bodies represented on the [college] governing bodies are virtually the same as those on the Council. (Inglis 1972, 20)

The GTC's Visitation Committee is illustrative here. It could visit colleges, recommend changes of courses, and complain to the Secretary of State if a college refused to accept its recommendations. However, its convener reported in 1974 that Inglis' statement had not yet been put to the test. The Visitation Committee had done little work, and had acted cautiously with only exploratory visits in its first five years (GTC 1974, 2). Perhaps this is not too surprising, as the first convener of the Visitation Committee was a principal himself, Sir Henry Wood of Jordanhill College. And, in fact, this minimal exercise of its function was entirely in keeping with Wheatley's stipulation that the GTC should keep off the colleges' patch (SED 1963c, paras 116-19). But, if the GTC could not press too heavily upon the colleges in the salad days when training and higher education were expanding, neither could it defend them when the chips were down and the existence of some colleges was threatened (Cope 1978). Wood offered a rueful comment on the implications of the changes that began in 1958, and that were confirmed with the advent of the GTC:

WOOD. The SED now dealt with colleges one by one. . . . This made no difference until very recent times. . . . In the 1960s the colleges could obtain more or less any funds they needed. . . . The system of controls did not matter much. . . . As soon as things became tight in the early 1970s, partly because of recession but mainly because of the apparent ending of teacher shortage . . . the colleges were left naked, without any national body to take an overview and stand up to SED. . . . The colleges could therefore be picked off one by one.

The GTC and Advice on Teacher Supply and Training

Wood's remark about 'an overview' leads directly to the question of the performance of the GTC in giving advice to the Secretary of State on teacher supply and training. We asked Rodger what was envisaged:

Q. In the discussion on the Wheatley Committee, did people expect the GTC to play an advisory role? When the Minister was defending the failure to convene the Advisory Council in the early 1960s, he told the House that the advisory function, as far as teaching was concerned, was going to be built into the GTC.[5]

RODGER. Yes. I think something like that was said.

Q. Was it a prime consideration in the minds of the Committee, or was the advisory function of secondary importance?

R ODGER. I would say narrower conditions concerning the government of the teaching profession were the prime consideration. The advisory function was not forgotten, but I would say that it was secondary to the other.

Before the GTC, central government had had several sources of advice on supply (see chapter 10) and on training. Among them were the Appleton Committee in the mid-1950s, and the Advisory Council. The Council had reported on these topics in 1944 (SED 1944b) and in 1946 (SED 1946b). The latter was a major report that reflected McClelland's ideas on teacher autonomy (see chapter 11). As the NCTT's Executive Officer, McClelland, in concert with the training-college directors, played a key part in communicating ideas from the colleges to the Department. The Department, meanwhile, had established its own Supply Committee in 1950. When the SCTT took over from the NCTT in 1958, the new regulations gave the Scottish Council a broad but vague license to advise the Secretary of State on training, and to assist him in relation to recruitment. This enhanced the status of the SCTT, and of the college principals in particular.[6] The SCTT itself thought that its duties were well defined in regard to training, but were unclear as to supply and recruitment (SCTT 1964, 117). Nonetheless, it was asked to perform its advisory role from the start, when the junior Minister, Niall Macpherson, urged it to consider the creation of a new college to meet an anticipated rise in demand for places on training courses (SCTT 1961, 14-15). To do this, the SCTT needed figures on teacher supply. These could come only from Rodger and the Department. Whilst the SCTT in the next few years sought data from schools in order to obtain an accurate estimate of future demand, it relied mainly on the SED's statistics and awaited the Departmental Supply Committee's fourth report, due in 1962, to clarify the picture. The SCTT, Gray told us, found the Department very free with the statistical information, 'but we couldn't readily get it for ourselves and organise it', and its interpretation was 'notoriously difficult'.

The GTC was later to labour under similar difficulties. The Wheatley Committee thought it essential that the GTC be informed on questions of supply in order to perform its functions, including that of advising the Secretary of State. Wheatley wanted the Departmental Committee on Supply to be transformed into a joint committee appointed by the SED and the GTC (SED 1963c, paras 151-2). This did not happen, but the Council set up its own Supply Committee in 1967, chaired by David Stimpson, Principal of Dundee College. It did this in response to Departmental pressure to broaden the basis of entry to the profession by admitting men to the Diploma course, and also by instituting a four-year college associateship course for secondary teachers. Such an associateship had been recommended earlier by the principals and the SCTT. The GTC agreed to admit men to the Diploma, and its Supply Committee then concentrated upon the supply implications of the raising of the school-leaving age, expected in 1970. It considered ways of expanding recruitment for secondary teaching without the controversial associateship,[7] but eventually the GTC recommended that ROSLA be deferred. The Supply Committee also considered ways of coping with an expected surplus of primary recruits, and advocated improved staffing levels (GTC 1971, 21-2, 55-6, 66-7).

The Council, and especially perhaps some of its non-teacher members, recognised the importance of the statistical foundation to its recommendations. Indeed the establishment of the Supply Committee itself apparently owed something to the Council's fear that the teachers' wish for a postponement of ROSLA would become GTC policy before a proper statistical analysis of supply was available (*ibid.*, 24-5). But the Committee, like the SCTT before it, had to acquire its data on teacher supply from the Department. McEwan, by then a member of the GTC, put it this way:

McEWAN. One felt that the GTC was very, very dependent on the Secretary of State's staff for its administrative work . . . particularly statistics of teacher-supply, teacher-distribution; and, of course, the Scottish Education Department were using computer resources which made them very, very much better able to produce what was required in the way of information than we could ever have been in the Council itself.

Gray expressed the GTC's indebtedness to the SED for the information 'which formed the only data available to the Council in the first years of [its] life' (GTC 1970). He told us that it was a 'grave defect' for the GTC to be asked to 'animadvert on supply to the Secretary of State, when in fact it has to ask the Secretary of State for the figures'. Having got the data, however, it was some three years before the GTC was in a position to make its recommendations on supply. This was done only after the report had been referred for comment to the teachers' associations, a procedure which was voted in a motion which Stimpson opposed (GTC 1971, 100).

Bruce Millan's view was that the controversies over registration and over uncertificated teachers prevented the GTC from taking the initiative and fulfilling its intended advisory role in the early years. On the other hand, it is arguable that there was no specialist advisory vacuum to be filled by a teachers' council. In chapter 10 we quoted Rodger's scepticism about the ability of outside bodies to come up with anything new on a matter over which the SED itself had agonised for a long time. The Departmental Committee on Supply included outsiders, and was a fact-gathering, forecasting, and analytical body which did not make policy recommendations. It had fed the external committees who were to do the latter, but it also provided the basis for the Department's own policy advice to the Minister. The 1962 report was its last. Rodger retired in the following year, but the routine administrative collection of information, its inclusion in SED annual reports, and its dissemination to organisations like the EIS, continued as before.

In the event, the advisory function on teacher supply was not hived off to an outside body, for in the late 1960s the Department itself was developing a firmer analytical grip on supply and staffing with the surveying and modelling techniques that resulted in the 'Red Book' (see chapter 10). The Department emphasised its wish to secure a more equitable allocation of teachers to schools, but it also looked to future possibilities of contraction in the training system. One of the justifications the Department put forward for more accurate knowledge of supply and demand was to '[avoid] the personal hardship and the waste of human resources that would be entailed if the supply of teachers were to increase at a rate that could not be readily absorbed or afforded by the system' (SED 1973c, para.9). By the mid-1970s, it appeared likely that the supply could indeed be neither absorbed nor afforded for many years to come. Government plans to reduce the intake to the colleges in 1976 angered the GTC, which found that its 'special position as standing adviser on supply had been ignored' (GTC 1976, 1). Two years later, following Millan's proposal to close some colleges, the Council's chairman, James Scotland, reported the GTC's involvement in 'lengthy, tortuous and often distressing debates on teacher supply'; and the Council was yet to establish its claim to consultation in the 'border territory' of staffing standards. Thus, twelve years after its inception, the GTC was still complaining that 'our main handicap has been inadequate statistical advice on which to found our recommendations. With ready and full cooperation from the Department, we have managed to achieve a substantial improvement' (Scotland 1978).

Millan did not succeed in closing education colleges, largely because the Labour Government's precarious parliamentary majority temporarily increased the influence of individual backbench MPs on central government's decisions (Cope 1978). But closure remained on the agenda after the change to a Conservative Government in 1979. In March 1980, the GTC objected to the large reduction in college entry which the Department proposed. Nevertheless, the Council acknowledged the need for reductions. It considered three alternatives: proportionate misery all round; disproportionate cuts to keep the smaller colleges open; and closure of some colleges. 'With great reluctance', it advised the third option. The GTC couched its advice in general language, but urged that Strathclyde Region be favoured because of teacher-recruitment problems in Lanarkshire and Glasgow. It pointed to the needs of Catholic schools in the West, and to the slower population decline in Grampian Region; and it plumped for the retention and development of the larger colleges (GTC 1980a, 86-9). The Secretary of State's decision in August was in line with much of this thinking. But his proposal to close Hamilton College in Lanarkshire drew a strong protest from the GTC, which complained that the Secretary of State 'had not fully accepted its advice'. They very much regretted that he 'did not issue a discussion paper before taking his decisions on the future of individual

Colleges' (GTC 1980b, 132).

Reflecting on those years in our interview in 1980, Millan showed some impatience with the way in which the GTC's advice depended at bottom upon the consent of its influential constituent groups. His remarks hint at the effect such consent had on the authority of the GTC's advisory voice:

MILLAN. The GTC has now recently, apparently, decided that it would be a good idea to close some of the colleges of education. . . . First of all the colleges and everybody else that doesn't want them to close, say that this is an outrageous proposal – scandalous, etc. etc. – and that's perfectly understandable perhaps. The second thing is that a whole lot of people say that this is, in any case, nothing to do with the GTC, they are not entitled to advise us on this. That makes you say, 'Well, what are they entitled to advise us on?' It was apparently all right for the GTC, when I originally thought that it would be a good idea to close a few colleges, to make the strongest of representations to me, including personal representations, that this would be a disastrous thing to do. The teachers and others thought that that was a legitimate role for the GTC at the time. But they are now recommending that they should be closed, and everyone is calling into question whether they have any right to say anything about the colleges at all.

Beneath its intramural quarrels and its extramural clashes with the Secretary of State, what was the common denominator in the GTC's policy stance? Gray and Wood were in no doubt that it continued the traditional Scottish emphasis on qualifications for teaching, and failed to formulate fresh ideas. Here is Gray:

GRAY. There is a lack of original thought among the teachers. It is supplied by the principals, and the animus against colleges of education dies very hard. . . . To be fair, I don't think it has ever been borne in on the minds of electors that perhaps the GTC has a role to play in leading educational thought.

Wood developed the point:

WOOD. The whole system . . . has been dominated by the great hierarchy of qualifications . . . and the GTC has really just perpetuated this. . . . It hasn't any innovatory sort of ethos or philosophy or power, it's merely changing the old system of qualifications for this, that and the other. . . . This is bound to be the attitude you get within the GTC – the system's all right, we are just here as sort of guardians to see that nobody gets in that shouldn't get in. . . . I went to a meeting in McClelland's office in 1948 and the Senior Chief Inspector was laying down the qualifications for ordinary graduates to teach things like history and geography in secondary school under article 39, and I protested that this was far too academic . . . and Godfrey Thomson said, 'Well, I said this when I came here in 1925 but it is still going on'.

Discussion

The founding of the GTC as a body to control the teaching profession and advise the Minister was a concession to a rising teacher assertiveness that the SED could not afford to ignore. It wanted to enlist the co-operation of teachers in the developments that were envisaged for the 1960s. In the aftermath of the 1961 strike, the price to be paid was some concession to teachers' aspirations to be consulted more regularly, and to have their professional status recognised. The working parties of 1961 bore fruit (SED 1963a, 78-9), although much of it was never to ripen. Legislation in 1963 improved widows' pensions. It also allowed teachers to serve on local-authority education committees, whilst the reorganisation of local government, some ten years later, strengthened this representation by requiring education committees to include two teachers. We cannot say how far the recommended procedural improvements to joint consultation between teachers and employers were implemented.[8] At the national level, as we saw in chapter 11, the new Consultative Committee on Educational Matters (CCEM) soon was displaced by the more functionally specific bodies for advice on examinations and curriculum that were set up in the mid-1960s, and on which teachers sat (see chapters 13 and 14). But the prize that teachers most eagerly sought was a council, an organisation which would elevate their public- and self-esteem, and which would also increase the voice of the profession in educational decision-making. Teachers wished to emulate doctors and others who had powers to regulate their affairs and to license practitioners, and whose status the teachers thought was linked to these responsibilities. The Department acquiesced in this wish. But, in acknowledging teachers' professionalism, it also saw an advantage accruing to itself and to the local authorities: 'an increase in the prestige of teaching as a profession is bound to help recruitment' (SED 1963c, para.59).

Here, of course, was a dilemma. The Department could not lightly accede to the teachers' desire for professional self-regulation if it meant relinquishing its own right to control standards of entry to teacher training and therefore, in the end, to determine the size of the teaching force. This the Department would not do, and, in the event, did not do. For, in any compromise it made with teachers' claims, it still had to hold its responsibility to the public interest above its desire to satisfy the interests of the profession. That public interest, as Wheatley saw it, was not so much in protection against charlatans, for Parliament had taken care of that for quite some time, but in having sufficient teachers in the schools. This was also the local authorities' interest, but only individually, not collectively. The hard-pressed among them would benefit if a GTC eventually attracted sufficient teachers into the national pool to solve their own problems locally. But, until that time, uncertificated teachers would still be needed. The Department had long resisted the blandishments of the teachers' associations to foreclose the possibility of uncertificated, and therefore 'unprofessional' teachers, serving in the classroom. But other interests on a GTC might also press to exclude the uncertificated.

Not only were the local authorities represented in the GTC, but so too were the colleges of education. The training they were providing was of great importance to a professional council. But Wheatley warned the GTC against close supervision of the colleges, and gave it few real powers to do so. For the colleges had been on a liberating track since the late 1950s, as part of a bargain struck between them and the SED. The colleges' prestige and autonomy was boosted in preparation for the role the Department wished them to play in national educational developments. Whilst it was not for the GTC to set aside that bargain by riding the colleges hard, the Secretary of State tightened his control of their finances. In addition, legislation in 1969 gave him the power to close colleges, and, in 1976, the power to discontinue a college course and to alter the number of students they could admit (Thorburn 1976).

The GTC was a microcosm of the fragmented educational system at large, and merely brought its tensions under one roof. The GTC harboured several conflicting interests which could not easily be reconciled in matters of supply and training (Humes 1986, 152-3). The central-local conflict was one, the employer-employee conflict a second (see chapter 10), and the haves-and-have-nots a third. And there were other lines of cleavage too. The colleges' common interest was fractured when closures were mooted. College lecturers resisted attempts to make them register with the GTC, and were growing more assertive of their interests. These they saw as separate from those of principals and promoted staff, and sometimes as opposed to them. The most serious divisions, however, were amongst the teachers themselves, where the campaign for a professional body had started. They were riven by sectoral and associational divisions, and there was no necessary unity between 'eminent heads' and ordinary classroom teachers.

We are not assuming that all cleavages necessarily produce conflict, nor that conflicting groups cannot reconcile purposes and form alliances, if only temporarily and tactically. Certainly they did on many occasions in the GTC. But, whilst the Council originated in a Departmental bid for peace, it was not well constituted to promote the reconciliation that peace required. Wheatley tried to harmonise two objectives. One of them was the ambition of the teachers' associations for direct participation in the policy centre. The other was expressed in Wheatley's prophylactic injunction that elected and appointed members should ignore their associational identities and speak as individuals (SED 1963c, para.71). Whilst Wheatley eschewed the representation of teachers' associations on the GTC, it implicitly recognised the importance of a balanced, broadly representative composition, and envisaged 'a powerful Council, which we hope would develop into a body of great prestige and act as a main source of ideas and initiative over a wide field of matters of concern to the teaching profession' (*ibid.*, para.65). For the GTC to speak with an authoritative professional voice, it would require both a more deeply rooted unity outside than it enjoyed, and more support both from its professional constituency and from the Department. The Department hitherto had preferred to pick and choose the teachers with whom it would work. Some of the positions on the GTC would be filled in ways that were unlikely to produce members of whom the Department disapproved. But others would be filled by teachers who were not beholden to the Department, and whom the Department had never had the opportunity to approve. With only a limited power of patronage over the GTC, the Department was reluctant to concede it too much.

Nevertheless, for a Department that was running short of ideas and time on teacher supply, some enhancement of the status of teachers was attractive as an eleventh-hour solution to the Department's most intractable problem. Higher status might attract more teachers, even though the Department doubted the validity of the teachers' claim to be professionals. And, by placing classroom teachers in the same category as college principals, Departmental influence over the teachers' associations might be extended, especially if teachers accepted the Department's claim that this pairing enhanced teachers' status. For most teachers, however, the GTC was an irrelevance, and it was a nuisance when it came to registering. Eventually they turned out in higher proportions to ballot in the affairs of their associations than they did for elections to the GTC.

The GTC's advisory capability seized up under the pressure of its conflicting internal interests, and under the weight of the issues that the Department forced on it before it could aggregate a sense of the profession, and of itself as a Council. It had executive functions to perform in the system of probation and in registering teachers, and it wielded important powers of exceptional recognition. In this sense, it had a *raison d'être* which the Department found useful in its load-shedding effort. And it also had the protection, for a time, of the Labour Secretary of State. But, registration itself was highly contentious, absorbing much of the Council's energies in its early years, and strewing rocks in its path. There was little chance that it could initiate advice, or deliver it confidently when asked. On many of the important professional issues, the Department sought its answers within itself, or through other channels. This it found more reliable than recourse to a body on which the elected representatives of teachers held a majority. For, as there were many 'matters of concern to the teaching profession', in Wheatley's words, so, too, were there many sources of advice. A somewhat disillusioned, but anonymous, nominated member of the first GTC observed in 1974:

> One difficulty seems to be that the various problems of the educational world are handled by so many different bodies – the Scottish Education Department, the Scottish Teachers' Salaries Committee, the Consultative Committee on the Curriculum, the SCE Examination Board. The GTC is only one of these. (GTC 1974, 3)

We discuss two of the others in chapters 13 and 14.

NOTES

1. The four working parties considered (1) consultation between the SED and teachers' associations on questions relating to curricula, examinations, and school organisation (SED 1962b) (2) education authorities' procedures for appointing teachers, for tenure, and for consultation with teachers on buildings, curricula, and organisation (SED 1962c) (3) the appointment of teachers to education committees in local authorities (SED 1962d) (4) pensions for dependents of deceased teachers (SED 1962e).

2. Although the Labour Party might have been committed to a GTC before the 1964 General Election, as Graham and Millan thought, it was not in the Party's Scottish manifesto (Labour Party, n.d.). Nevertheless, the Teaching Council (Scotland) Bill was introduced in December 1964, only two months after the Labour Government took over from the Conservatives. The Scottish Grand Committee debated the principle of the Bill in February 1965. Michael Noble, the Conservative former Secretary of State, confirmed that the DES had been displeased that Wheatley conceded so much. He hinted that the Bill's departure from the report was the price of DES acquiescence (PD 1965b). The DES had reason to be concerned. It was in the midst of resisting a similar demand for a council in England and Wales. A Teachers' Registration Council had existed there from 1912 to 1949. It had no power of control over entry to the profession. In 1959, the Minister rejected a proposal for a council with such power. Shortly after the GTC was established in Scotland in 1965, Crosland, the Education Minister, refused a request for an official working party to consider a new proposal, on the grounds that he could not lose control over entry standards during a time of teacher shortage. In 1969, teachers found the new Minister, Edward Short, more sympathetic. His working party suggested powers along the lines of Wheatley, but proposed that teachers be not elected, but appointed, to the council by their associations. Teachers were divided over Short's recommendations. Labour left office in 1970, and in the following year the NUT turned down the proposal (Coates 1972, 52-7; Gosden 1972, 256-61; Gould 1973; Fenwick and McBride 1981, 189-90).

3. Rodger told us that he had many informal talks about the future of the training system with college principals and with university friends. Inspectors sounded out the directors of education and the EIS. Rodger and Pringle, the Senior Chief Inspector, visited Scotsmen who were professors of education in English universities to get their opinion on the suitability for Scotland of the English institutes of education. When Brunton replaced Pringle, Brunton discussed the training system with Rodger. But Rodger recalled that it was he himself who had drafted a memorandum for Murrie that recommended a reorganised training system along the lines of the one that eventually was established. Murrie then interrogated all the senior people in the Department about Rodger's memorandum.

4. There is, however, some evidence that the SED in 1966 unsuccessfully opposed Wheatley's proposal that a JCC be established, on the grounds that it was not essential to the efficient functioning of the training system (GTC 1971, 12). In the GTC, 'Professor Nisbet, supported by Professor Adams, represented the need for some such corporate and statutory body which would, for example, obviate the possibility of the Council reaching a wrong conclusion where the real nature of the problem was not known: the advisory capacities of the Committee of Principals had been fully utilised by the Scottish Council for the Training of Teachers' (*ibid.*).

5. Our question was slightly inaccurate. What Ross said was, 'the Advisory Council . . . is a body which will disappear in the growth and development of the new Teaching Council' (PD 1965a).

6. The regulations said that the SCTT 'may at any time, and shall when consulted by the Secretary of State, advise the Secretary of State on any problem' to do with training (SI 1958a, reg.36; see also SED 1958c, para.35). However, the draft regulations published in February 1958 had not given the SCTT any power of initiative (SI 1958b, reg.38; see also SED 1958d, para.34). Rodger could not explain why the Council's powers were strengthened as a result of consultations with interested parties on the draft regulations. However, he thought it was sensible: 'If it was to be a body with some reality of power, and something to do, they shouldn't only answer questions put to them, but they should have the right to raise questions, if questions are worth raising. It is one way, a good way, of upgrading a body.'

7. The associateship was opposed by teacher-members of the GTC as 'dilutionary', and was ultimately rejected by the Council after some friction between principals, directors and teachers.

8. The last circular issued under Arbuckle's name before he retired as SED Secretary exhorted education authorities to review their practices with a view to implementing the recommendations about teachers' membership and about joint consultation (SED 1963d).

Thirteen

Certification and the Examination Board

The risk . . . was that the Department, as a result of no longer
controlling the examination which the great majority of pupils
would take, would largely lose effective control of the curriculum
of most pupils under sixteen, which might come in practice to be
dictated by the examination board. Minute of HMSCI Gilbert
Watson's views, 1947[1]

Introduction

Watson's advice was heeded in 1947 when the SED decided not to accept the
Advisory Council's proposals for an examination board. But the introduction of the O-grade examination in 1962 threatened to place an intolerable
burden on the Inspectorate unless it were able to devolve its examination
functions. The Education (Scotland) Act (1963) provided for the foundation of the Scottish Certificate of Education Examination Board (SCEEB).
It was appointed in 1964 and took over formal responsibility for the conduct
of the SCE examinations from the SED in January 1965. In this chapter we
look first at the powers of the Board and at the various controls, formal and
informal, to which it was subject. Thereafter, the bulk of the chapter shows
how the Board formulated policy and reacted to change, especially to the
rapid spread of presentations for the O-grade examination in the later
1960s, and to the impending raising of the school-leaving age. We show how
the policy of 'downward incrementalism' (see chapter 11) was further
developed, and how it excluded the option of an internally assessed examination for less able sixteen-year-olds. Our examples mainly concern provision for the final two years of compulsory schooling, but we also look briefly
at policy for a post-Higher examination for the sixth year. More generally,
the chapter illustrates some of the ways in which policy and practice were
influenced by the negotiation of the problems that expansion posed for
governmental control and for doctrines of representation.

Powers

The composition, powers and functions of the Board were formally established by the 1963 Act and the regulations made under it. They were broadly
along the lines recommended by the Advisory Council in 1960 (SED 1960b,
paras 79-83) at Brunton's instigation (see chapter 4). This is how the Board

described its own composition in 1971 :

> The Board consists of thirty-eight members appointed by the Secretary of State – namely a Chairman, and thirty-three members appointed from persons nominated by various bodies representing educational interests – the universities, associations representing local authorities, governing bodies of central institutions and colleges of education, the Association of Directors of Education and teacher organisations, and four members who have experience in industry or have other qualifications which in the opinion of the Secretary of State make them suitable for appointment to the Board.
>
> The Secretary of State may also appoint one or more of his officers to be an assessor or assessors sitting with the Board. . . .
>
> The Board is in the main a policy-making body and its executive functions are exercised through committees, panels, examining teams and its permanent staff. (SCEEB 1971, 6)

The main functions of the Board were:

> to advise the Secretary of State on such matters relating to examinations for pupils receiving secondary education as he may from time to time refer to them or as the Board think fit; and . . . to conduct the examinations each year for the Scottish Certificate of Education. (SI 1963, para.5)

Thus the Board was a statutory body with both executive and advisory functions, and it could advise the Secretary of State on its own initiative. Nevertheless, the Secretary of State retained formal authority over it. He had to approve conditions for the examinations, and the regulations allowed him 'after consultation with the Board [to] give such directions as to the discharge by the Board of their functions as appear[ed] to him to be expedient'. He also had the power to fund the Board, to fix the level of any local-authority contributions, and to appoint members from among persons nominated by the bodies listed in the quotation above.

These powers also gave the Secretary of State several channels of influence: through control of finance; through his right to pick and choose suitable people, or at least to veto unsuitable ones; and through the persuasion that his assessors might exercise at meetings. In 1970 there were four assessors on the Board, two administrators and two inspectors. Each assessor was 'entitled to attend and speak at meetings of the Board and of committees, subcommittees and subject panels but [was] not entitled to vote except at meetings of any committee or subcommittee or subject panel of which he [had] been appointed a member' (*ibid.*). Subject panels assisted the Examinations Committee of the Board in the conduct of the examination. Normally they had six members, of whom three were teachers and one an HMI. The Board itself decided that members of the Board were ineligible for panel membership.

The influence that the Secretary of State derived from his formal powers depended in part on the way his officials played their roles, and on the response of individual Board members. Such influence can be regarded as formal and legitimate, in that the Secretary of State's formal powers indicated the channels through which his influence would operate (e.g. appointments and assessorships). But much still depended on the readiness of Board members to make common cause with Departmental policy, especially in instances where the Secretary of State's formal powers and obligations were less clear, or where precedents had yet to be made. One problematic area, which we deal with mainly in the next chapter, was the relationship between examination policy and policy for the curriculum. The two were closely connected. But at what point was the Board obliged to defer to the CCC or directly to the Secretary of State? Indeed, what discretion did the Secretary of State have to develop policies independently of the Board? And to what extent was he, and indeed the Board itself, obliged to take account of the views of the 'nominating bodies' whose members sat on the Board? These were questions on which the Act and regulations were vague, and where precedents were lacking.[2] But there was much to play for. If the Department were to influence examination policy at a time of rapid expansion and change, formal mechanisms alone would be insufficient. New rules of the game would have to be developed by the players themselves, and the selection of players restricted to those who could be trusted to play the game in the right spirit.

We look first at how the nominating bodies were represented on the Board.

Representation and Control

The concept of 'representation' is crucial to all theories of indirect (i.e. non-face-to-face) democracy. It also has fairly obvious implications for pluralism and corporatism. If groups' interests are well represented through fringe bodies, then a pluralist interpretation of such bodies is strengthened. If, however, the representation of groups is cosmetic, or partial, or manipulated in some way, then a corporatist interpretation of fringe bodies gains in credibility. Following Birch (1971), Holden (1974, 30) points out that the idea of representation has several, overlapping meanings, but no single 'essential' one. He distinguishes three meanings in particular: first, the representative as the agent or spokesman of a principal; second, the representative as a person sharing some of the characteristics of a class of persons; and third, the representative as a person who symbolises or 'stands for' some class or other. But he also emphasises the ramifications of the term, saying that 'there are many different theories or doctrines of representation' (*ibid.*).

In this chapter our interest in representation is twofold. First, the SCEEB, along with the CCC and the GTC, was claimed to give different groups representation in the structures of educational governance. But what did this mean in practice? Second, there is the question of professional expertise, of Murrie's 'mystery' of education. How were expert contributions to decision-making to be reconciled with the representation of interest groups, expert or otherwise, and with the official's authority as the agent of the Crown-in-Parliament? What interpretations, then, did the Department and the major interest groups give to the different meanings of 'representation'? And how were the views of educational professionals reconciled with the dictates of Ministers, and with other demands? As a first approximation, we can say that the outside interest groups asserted the representativeness of fringe bodies in the first two of Holden's senses, and especially in the first (the representative as the agent or spokesman of a principal). The Department, on the other hand, tended to assert the last two meanings, and especially the third (the representative as symbolic of a class). Later, in part v, we analyse the sociological basis of the Department's attempt to reconcile the competing doctrines of representation with each other, and with the two exigencies of political authority (the Crown-in-Parliament) and expert knowledge. Its attempt at reconciliation had concrete effects on educational policy and practice, and we illustrate examples of such effects in this chapter.

In exploring the question of representation, we must first look at the procedures by which appointments were made to the Board and its subject panels, and also at the capacity in which members then spoke and acted. Brunton told us that 'one of the purposes behind the establishment of the Examination Board was to bring the universities (and other relevant outside agencies) into the examination business and into the whole school process'. We asked him:

Q. Was there any intention that membership of the Examination Board should be on a representative basis rather than an individual basis?

BRUNTON. Oh yes. This was from the outset a representative body, with representatives from the universities, from the colleges of education, the central institutions, the teachers and headmasters and from industry and commerce and the Inspectorate. Who the representatives should be, of course, was a matter for the universities and the other bodies themselves.

Brunton went so far as to say that the Secretary of State in 1964 had appointed only the Chairman of the Board, Sir David Anderson, and not the other members. But documentary evidence shows that this cannot have been the case.[3] One informant told us that the Chairman had advised the Department on whom to select from among the nominees, but he also confirmed that Brunton had wanted a 'representative' Board. Only the Departmental papers are likely now to resolve this question. But it is possible that they will reveal a vigorous discussion within the Department, leading eventually to a compromise between the principle of Departmental selection and the principle of group nomination. The latter, it will be recalled, had probably been conceded in 1962 to the short-lived Consultative Committee on Educational Matters (see chapter 11). Rodger remembered that he was consulted on the question:

RODGER. The general feeling [was] that, democracy being what it was, we jolly well had to let the bodies choose their own people, although I remember also a certain disgust with that to some extent, because, no doubt about it, our experience was that often the teaching bodies chose a person or persons other than those that we would have chosen.

Q. And yet Brunton told us that he had wanted the Examination Board to be a representative body in the strong sense of 'representative'. That is to say: they would choose their own members, and there wasn't to be Departmental scrutiny of the lists.

RODGER. Possibly. . . . I would have said that both Brunton and Arbuckle were very much in on this, and probably very much in agreement on this; but I would have thought that the final decision on this would have been a decision between them. . . . I think that both of them, in their hearts, would have wanted to choose the people, but that they would have found it politic to do the other thing.

As we shall see, it is fairly certain that the Board members, other than those members nominated directly by the Secretary of State, were appointed by a combination of nomination *and* selection. Nevertheless, when members were listed in the Board's publications they were sometimes grouped into named nominating sectors including one for 'teachers' representatives'; and in 1971 the Board made this claim for its status:

> The Board serves as a forum for discussion, with *the views of the different bodies concerned* given expression through the widely based membership of the Board and through the submission of observations in the course of formal consultation. As a national body . . . the Board has a responsibility to the public as a whole which implies detachment in judgement as well as accountability in administration. (SCEEB 1971, 16, our emphasis)

A year later, when the Board announced its controversial decision to 'band' the O-grade (in effect removing the pass/fail distinction), it said that its consultation was 'representative of all the main educational interests in Scotland' (see note 5 below).

Thus, what Brunton said he wanted of the Board, and what the Board said it did, sounded very much like 'representation' in all three of Holden's senses. The Board was presented as something more than the executive agent of the central authority; it was also an arena within which policy differences between groups, differences in their goals and values, were to be acknowledged, negotiated and then resolved into a common policy. But the Act and regulations had indicated neither for nor against this view. How, in fact, did events unfold?

William Dewar was appointed to the Board in 1964 and became Chairman of its Examinations Committee. As headmaster of an Edinburgh school, he had worked closely with Brunton for some years (see chapter 4). He told us that he thought that Brunton himself had had a major influence on the first appointments to the Board. He also described how appointments were made to the twenty or so subject panels of the Board, and he offered a different view on the question of representation:

DEWAR. The Department had the tremendous problem . . . of starting to select the people they wanted to be involved. They couldn't just take every Tom, Dick or Harry. Brunton himself had been very shrewd. He had watched what had happened in the Advisory Council and watched what happened in the working parties. He kept his ear to the ground. He knew which of his inspectors were to be trusted. (There were some whose judgement was faulty or courage lacking.) Brunton had been busy on this and, for the purposes of setting up the Board, what the SED asked local authorities to do, and what they asked professional organisations to do, was to nominate several people from whom some might be invited to join as members: not to nominate them, as it were, directly to the Board, but to nominate them as possible candidates. And this enabled the Department to select in the light of its own information. . . . There is no doubt that the choice of the people who would be on the Board was very largely his. That is my interpretation of what happened. I think it was all to the good.

Q. By what criteria were appointments made to the panels?

DEWAR. What we did in the first instance was to have an inspector as the convener of the individual subject panel until we got things going. To that end the Department gave me, or rather there came to the Board from the Department, a list of over 300 teachers and others from whom the personnel might be chosen to constitute the panels. We wanted people who were themselves good teachers and had reliable judgement; basically the test was that they had, in fact, got good certificate results and were recommended by the Inspectorate. It was left to me as Convener of the Examinations Committee to make the selection in order to try to ensure the involvement of people from all over Scotland. . . . I have always been keenly aware of the situation of the fellows and the women who are away out on the periphery of Scotland 'in the provinces', and we felt that it would be a tremendous boost to morale, as well as spreading the work and the interest, if we could try to ensure that, over the whole picture, people were involved from all over Scotland.

Q. Given the extraordinary concentration of education problems in the West doesn't this have a disadvantage that the sorts of problems that, for example were being experienced in Glasgow, don't get the sort of representation . . .

DEWAR. [interjecting] Wait a minute; what are the problems?

Q. Well, I am wondering about any aspect of curriculum affected by comprehensive reorganisation, teacher shortages or whatever.

DEWAR. Yes. But this would not affect the work of the panels. . . . It's the panels we're dealing with at the moment, not the Committees of the

Board. . . . The subject panels had a very limited remit.

Q. So that's why representation of teachers is . . .

DEWAR. [interjecting] Let's watch this word 'representation'. What we were endeavouring to ensure was that, in respect of this work of assessing papers and evolving new syllabuses and so on, we should go all round the country. Now this did not prevent any part of the country from making representation. This didn't mean that we said, 'All right, there's nobody coming from Glasgow'. Moreover, we were also choosing from the universities, the central institutions, the colleges of education, and so on.

Q. Well, how big would the influence of the schools be on the three committees of the Board?

DEWAR. Nil, *qua* schools. . . . They were asked to come onto the Board as individuals.

Dewar, then, selected the subject-panel members according to his own two criteria of 'good certificate results' and geographical representativeness over the whole 'picture' of Scotland. In later chapters we discuss how this picture of Scotland was composed, and the substantial influence that it had on policy and practice. As to the Board itself, Dewar held that its members sat, not in a representative capacity, but 'as individuals'. This was the view that the Department itself preferred with respect both to the Board and the CCC, though, to our knowledge, it has been publicly stated only in relation to the latter.[4] The doctrine of 'individual' membership, however, did not extend to the Secretary of State's assessors on the Board. Graham, for example, told us that the Inspectorate did not sit 'as individuals'. They were officially described in 1968 as sitting 'in their own right', but this hardly clarified the basis of their authority since it was distinguished both from sitting 'as the representatives of the Secretary of State' and from sitting 'as experts' (SCES 1968, 7).

Much of the time, no doubt, there was little at issue here. James Clark was a member of the Board from 1967 to 1975. This was what he had to say about his own status on the Board, and that of the Inspectorate:

CLARK. At no time did I feel that I was putting forward, either on the CCC or the Exam Board, a view of the Association of Directors, unless, on a particular issue, there had been discussion at the Association of Directors, and a decision made by the Association as to whether they were for or against something. When that happened, I invariably indicated that the Association of Directors had discussed this particular matter and that the view of the Association was such and such; and I can't think, off hand, of an occasion when I as an individual basically differed from the view of the Association. I might have given different importance to different aspects of it.

Q. Were such comments admissible? Were you allowed to say that the view of your Association was this?

CLARK. On the few occasions that it happened, the answer is 'Yes', and

I did.

Q. What does the formula mean, that people 'sit as individuals'?

CLARK. Well, for ninety to ninety-five per cent of the time, the contribution that you are making to the discussions on these boards is, in fact, your own personal contribution. You don't know the view of the Association.

Clark thought, however, that the Inspectorate's position was sometimes ambiguous, and that the ambiguity could be exploited as a source of influence. He also thought that assessors very often had 'power without responsibility':

CLARK. Inspectors, sometimes, were actual members of working parties or boards or what have you, and on other occasions they were there as assessors. Now, if they were there as assessors, technically, as I saw it, they were there to answer questions, if asked; this is really the position of an assessor. If they are members, then they make their contribution. What I did not know, ever, was whether an inspector was putting forward a view as an individual, or an Inspectorate point of view, while sitting as an individual member of a committee. What I did know was that somebody like myself spoke as an individual, except on the rare occasions when an issue came up which had been discussed by the Association, and I made it clear that the Association's view was such and such, that I had participated in that discussion; and, if I differed from it in any way, I said so.

The Association of Directors (ADES), however, had a firm view on the Department's control of appointments:

CLARK. I recall a discussion in the Association of Directors when we had to put forward a director for membership of the Exam Board. We did this and the Department asked us to put forward, I think, three names from whom one was to be chosen; and the Association was very annoyed at this, because they felt, as an Association, that they were in a better position to say which director might be on the Exam Board than somebody in the Department choosing among three on criteria that were unknown to the directors themselves.

In 1961 the EIS had welcomed the Board 'as part of the movement towards greater professional autonomy' (*SEJ* 15 December 1961). Two years later, however, it complained that the Department had now reduced the proportion of teacher representation proposed for the Board (*SEJ* 27 September 1963). And, like the ADES, the EIS found itself at odds with the Department over appointments. In Bryden's view, the issue was never resolved:

BRYDEN. Our attitude was that a member of the Institute was always a member of the Institute and was a representative of the Institute wherever he was. Not all of our members agreed with that, but still the bulk of them did, especially if they were appointed through me and not by the Department going out and picking up somebody, taking out somebody from a school. . . . I don't know that we ever really forced the Department to concede that, when there was a member of the Institute who was appointed to such a body, he was there directly appointed by ourselves, representing our views and our views only. I don't think that they ever conceded that, except in the more obvious cases, formally, but now and again they adopted expedients in order to get round both their scruples and our objections.

Q. You suggested that the attitude of the EIS to representation on the Examination Board was rather different from your attitude to representation on the CCC, and, I think, you were implying that the idea of representation is rather stronger in the case of the Examination Board than of the CCC.

BRYDEN. Teachers are directly represented on the Examination Board, but not on the CCC.

Q. Dewar's view was that people were nominated by the teachers' associations, and an element of selection then took place.

BRYDEN. That is arguable.

Q. Would you say that we are talking here about two different perceptions of a situation which is essentially ambiguous or unresolved anyway? It seems to me that this is an area of negotiation between the various parties. On the one hand, authoritative bodies like the Board and the CCC are anxious to have a broad spectrum of representative opinion with a small 'r' It's a recognition of the realities of power and influence and the exigencies of communication. But at the same time they are reluctant to accept the degree of control that would go with according real rights of representation to the various parties.

BRYDEN. Yes, I think I would agree with that. . . . Mind you, it depends a little bit on the fashion of the time. I think there are times when it is more fashionable to regard members of a trade union, if you like, or another body, as having a right to represent the views of their parent body and to report back, and to try to influence the body on which they are sitting to adopt the views of the parent body. And there are other times when that is much less fashionable. But I would say that the SED is generally opposed to the idea of a body like the Institute having too much power over a Departmental body, such as it might have if it does too much reporting back.

Examination Policy for ROSLA: CSE Mode III

Clark told us that the Association of Directors did not have a collective view on examination policy. But the EIS did. In the 1960s, in anticipation of ROSLA, it pressed for a major extension of national certification to less able pupils (EIS 1966b). By the late 1960s, if not earlier, the EIS wanted any new or modified certificate to incorporate some internal elements along the lines of the Certificate of Secondary Education (CSE) Mode III (Currie 1970). Teachers in England had played a major part in developing the CSE for pupils who would find O-level courses too difficult. Mode III of the CSE examination, in particular, gave teachers a role both in providing courses, and in assessing pupils for certification. In Scotland, however, the SSTA, of which Dewar was a founding member, did not want the SCE O-grade to be adapted for the 'ROSLA pupils'. The SSTA argued instead for a purely school- and LEA-based certificate, if indeed there were to be one at all. How was the new machinery of advice and consultation used to address this issue, and how did the 'representativeness' of the Board influence the policy and practice that developed? We look first at Scottish thinking on the CSE Mode III, and then at the two further steps in the policy of 'downward incrementalism' that this period saw: the reduction of the informal minimum number of SCE presentation subjects from three to one; and the decision in 1972 to abandon the pass/fail distinction and to 'band' the O-grade.

We asked Brunton whether it was intended that the Board should initiate advice, or merely give advice when the Secretary of State called for it. His answer implied a more active monitoring role for the subject panels than Dewar perhaps had been prepared to allow (see above):

BRUNTON. The intention was clearly that it [the Board] should initiate advice if it thought fit to do so. It was dealing with the examination, after all, and it ought to be seeing, through its scrutiny of scripts and all the rest of it – its consideration of papers and syllabuses – what was needed in the schools, and what were the requirements of bodies which recruited from the schools.

Initiation, however, was rare. We asked Dewar to instance occasions when the Board had initiated advice rather than given it in response to a request coming from the Department:

DEWAR. I can't think of one off-hand, but we have to bear in mind that there was a tendency from the very beginning (I am not sure that it is there in black and white) for the Secretary of State to adopt the attitude, 'You will advise me when I seek advice'.

It was not there in black and white; the Board did have the power to initiate advice. We put the same question to Graham:

Q. Do you recall any case when the Board came to the Secretary of State saying, 'Look, you really ought to be apprised of this, or to think about that'? Or was the advice purely to your own dictation?

GRAHAM. Off-hand my recollection would be the same as Dr Dewar's, that it wasn't that advice wasn't given but . . . it tended in practice to be an informal exchange and not a set-piece exercise.

And this, indeed, was how policy on CSE Mode III was developed. Sir Henry Wood was a member of the Board from its inception until 1967. He thought that it had been 'dominated throughout most of its life by Dewar and McIntosh . . . carrying out their philosophies: Dewar's notion of what went on in the secondary school and McIntosh's notion of what examining was all about'. Douglas McIntosh himself was a Board member from 1964 to 1977. Clark agreed with Wood's assessment, though with one qualification:

CLARK. I think that we've got to be quite fair here. Whether we like it or not, the Exam Board, until the O-grade banding (you can look on that as a watershed), but the Exam Board in its earlier days certainly, was a vehicle for producing certificates for secondary pupils who had stayed on beyond the then leaving age and which led to successful presentation. To that extent, what Dewar and McIntosh contributed to the Exam Board was in line with that broad function; they were bringing their knowledge and expertise to the Exam Board in that way. It could be said, and I wouldn't disagree with it, that in certain aspects of the exam situation, Douglas McIntosh, as a member of the Board, had more first-hand knowledge than most, if not all, of the members; and therefore it was right and proper that he should make that available to the Board when they were discussing issues. Similarly, Dewar, but perhaps not to the same extent, because there were other secondary heads there.

Dewar told us how he became involved in the evaluation of the CSE in the mid-1960s:

DEWAR. As Convener of the Examinations Committee I went down to England with Ian Urquhart, as the Director of the Board, and HMCI Neville Fullwood from the Department to look at CSE. . . . We brought back a very full report, a copy of which is in the hands of the Board but, formally, the report is the property of the Department.

Q. Why was Fullwood on that party going to England, and why was the report lodged with the SED? Was this not a matter solely for the Board?

DEWAR. No. As a matter of fact we were sent down by the SED. Fullwood was an SED assessor on the Board. The Board itself was not looking into CSE at that time. It was the Department that wanted us to be brought into this survey at that early stage. The Board at that time, however, was under continuous pressure, it was not severe but it was continuous pressure from, I think, the EIS and certain members of the EIS, to go over willy-nilly to certificates for everybody. But the Board did not have an instruction from the Secretary of State, and in fact I found myself under pressure, as Convener of the Examinations Committee, to consider instituting something of this kind. But I was not convinced of either the advisability or the practicability of such a development. . . . What failed to impress us were the safeguards against misuse. . . . On Mode III (which is essentially internal examinations with external moderation), here we took the view that there was a certain amount, I wouldn't put it any stronger (after all we had merely a quick sample to go on), a certain amount of teaching directly towards the examination paper.

Q. And would that have mattered?

DEWAR. I think this brings us to the basic question. The real question here is, 'What does the Certificate certify?' If it is certifying that this particular child, given a very restricted area on which to work, and given pleasant circumstances, and pleasant conditions, plus firm direction, did well, if that is what it's going to certify, then let's say so. But let's not pretend

303

that this is something comparable with a highly academic certificate.

Q. The feeling was, then, that the possibility of national examinations comprehending the entire age-group wasn't on, as far as you're concerned?

DEWAR. It's never been on. . . .

Q. Were you not getting pressure from teachers on the subject panels for something like CSE?

DEWAR. No. . . . None at all. I cannot recollect a single occasion. We were very careful about the subject panels. I chose them from the very beginning.

In explaining its decision in 1963 to reduce the proportion of Board places proposed for the EIS, the Department had apparently told the EIS that teachers would be substantially involved in the detailed work of the Board through the subject panels (*SEJ* 27 September 1963). In practice, the criteria by which Dewar defined the good teacher, and interpreted the concept of 'representation', resulted in appointments to the subject panels that did not transmit upwards to the Board any significant pressure for internal assessment or for the certification of larger proportions of the age-group. In chapter 17, as part of a wider discussion of how eminent educationists have been defined and recruited, we identify the types of teachers that Dewar selected from the list the Department had supplied. They were highly unrepresentative of Scottish secondary teachers as a whole, the majority of the appointees coming from pre-twentieth-century schools mainly in the East and North. This composition nevertheless corresponded well with Dewar's own understanding of Scottish schools and community, and with the symbolic importance of the 'provinces' to him. Meanwhile, the Board allowed the Department to dispense with the niceties of formal consultation and advice over the CSE. Here, too, Dewar played a significant role by falling in with the small group that the Department sent to England.

Thus three factors explain why a formal review of internal assessment and teacher-led curriculum development failed to materialise in Scotland in the 1960s, even though there were powerful trends in this direction in England and Wales. One factor was the manipulation of the Board by the Department, and the Board's acquiescence in this. A second was the Department's influence over appointments, both to the Board and, in conjunction with Dewar, to its subject panels as well. The third factor was much less explicit, but no less powerful for that. It concerned shared assumptions about the criteria for recognising good teachers, good schooling, and the identity of the Scottish educational system that was 'out there' waiting to be represented to, and on, the Board. We will not attempt to decide the relative importance of each of these three factors here, partly because they overlapped and reinforced each other, as we show in part v. In Clark's view, however, the failure of CSE Mode III to reach the national policy-agenda then had a decisive effect on local practice:

CLARK. I thought a lot about CSE Mode III, apart altogether from the Exam Board; and one of the difficulties, I think, was that, if anything was going to be done on this, it seemed to me that, in Scotland, it had to be done nationally; that, for example, it would have been a very long, uphill battle for any one local authority to decide to do it. . . . We had experience of local certificates. For example, at one time we had a local secondary certificate in Aberdeen, and these had considerable credibility in the local situation. But, of course, they were really of very little use to anybody outside. . . . But I think that, for CSE Mode III in Scotland, there would have to be a national decision to go ahead with it. At no time, when I was a member of the Board, was this discussed. Nor do I think, in particular, that the professional representatives were ready for it.

Q. You said that the directors of education always invited their counterparts from England to their meetings. Were you aware of it yourselves as directors through contacts such as this?

CLARK. Oh yes. In fact, not only myself, but quite a number of my colleagues, from time to time, were visiting areas and schools in England, where we discussed aspects of this, and I'm sure that it seemed to many of us – although we never came together and made any recommendation about it – that there were possibilities here that should be explored.

Q. But the Association was never active in it?

CLARK. No. You see, this was another thing: I suppose that when the Exam Board was set up, you now had a national board that was responsible for examinations and certificates. In a sense, previous local initiatives tended to wither away.

Clark also thought that the founding of the CCC had a similarly enervating effect on curricular developments at local level, and this despite the fact that Graham had wanted a reformed Inspectorate and Department to stimulate local initiatives (see chapter 14). We asked Graham about the Department's review of CSE:

Q. The report was actually a report to the SED rather than a report of the Examination Board. Would this be an example of the Secretary of State's inviting the Examination Board to give advice?

GRAHAM. Well, it wasn't strictly the Examination Board giving advice, because it was, as I think you said, a three-man committee. . . . Most people would agree that it was only sensible to take a hard look at what was happening south of the Border, which these three very experienced people did, and reported on what they found.

Q. Why must you choose to act that way rather than through a formal report by the Board to the Secretary of State?

GRAHAM. I suppose we thought . . . it would be useful for the senior member of the Inspectorate most concerned to take part in this.

Q. Is this an indication that the Department was still actively interested in examination policy and felt that it wasn't getting sufficient information through the normal channels?

GRAHAM. Well, CSE raised a really wide question beyond the strict business of examinations, because, as I well remember Dr Dewar pointing out to me on more than one occasion, a great deal of the entry arrangements into technical education hinged on the O-grade, and we would have been liable to put a good deal of that at risk either by scrubbing the O-grade or introducing an alternative examination on any large scale.

This was the final judgement of one of our informants on the Department's review of the CSE: 'You see, this is insidious. . . . You pick the persons that you want so that they will give you the answer that you want, and you say, "Oh, but the Examination Board was represented". That's in your document and it's true, but it was represented in the way that you wanted it to be represented.' We asked this informant whether there had been any formal definition of the term 'representative' in the dealings of the Board, or whether it was a matter of usage alone. He thought it was a question of usage, adding, 'And you see, it takes somebody who has been partially trained by Machiavelli to know the difference. This is the joy of the whole process.'

Downward Incrementalism

The orchestrated resistance to internal assessment in effect killed the CSE Mode III option in the 1960s, though such courses were later to be developed by two of the larger education authorities created by local-government reorganisation in 1975. Meanwhile, some solution had still to be found to the two problems of the expansion of O-grade presentations and of the approach of ROSLA. On the first problem, neither Bruce Millan, who became junior Minister in 1966, nor his Senior Chief Inspector, David Dickson, felt that there was much they could do. Dickson said they did not attempt to persuade head teachers or directors to try to damp down demand for the O-grade: 'We didn't get time. . . . We became involved in comprehensive education too quickly'. And this was Millan's view:

MILLAN. I think if you have an examination which is not a group examination but is done on an individual-subject basis, the pressure will come anyway from the parents and the pupils themselves, as well as from the schools. I don't think that you could stop that happening. In other words, whatever the theoretical arguments were, you couldn't keep the O-grade examination on the basis that it was only for the top thirty per cent of the pupils. . . . But it doesn't follow that, from that, you say, 'Well, everybody should take some kind of examination'. That is, I think, another argument, but I think that it is unrealistic to expect that we could contain it to a particular group of pupils, particularly under the comprehensive system. You may not wish to encourage the 'going for the O-grades at all costs', as it were, to the detriment of other things, but you won't prevent that happening on a considerable scale.

Q. Were you personally in favour of the idea of people just taking the one O-grade, if they could get the one?

MILLAN. I'm not against that, no. You say, 'personally in favour of that'. The system is geared to allow that to happen, it is not done on a group basis, therefore one must allow that to happen. What I am not in favour of is organising the schools so that the only thing that counts at the end of the day is whether you get an accumulation of O-grades. . . .

Q. Did you regard examination policy as part-and-parcel of a general policy to offer incentives to pupils, who, through comprehensive reorganisation, were getting the opportunities that they hadn't had before; in order to provide, if you like, accessible incentives to encourage them to stay at school and take examinations? Was this part of a general policy for education?

MILLAN. Yes. I think that it is inevitably part of it. You can always say, well, that you don't want the whole school to be geared to the examination system (and I certainly believe that very strongly). . . . Now, for a whole lot of pupils, the comprehensive system opened up the opportunities for taking examinations which they wouldn't have otherwise had, getting certificates, etc. at the end of the day, and that is inevitable, and it ought to happen. Provided that it doesn't happen to the detriment of the school curriculum generally, I think that is a good thing.

On the Board itself, however, Dewar was actively opposed to the incrementalist drift in presentation policy:

DEWAR. We were in effect really concerned about people being encouraged to stay on who could with advantage stay on. This was the expression we adopted, 'with advantage', and we thought primarily of the advantage to them. But Bruce Millan at that time was plugging the advantage to business. . . . The big problem arose over those pupils who were potentially borderline. It's all very well to say, 'Right, this group are non-SCE'. But what about those who fall into the middle? There is a huge no-man's land there; and the middle, incidentally, is where we find the majority, isn't it?. . . . Now this is the great difficulty. The Department had said, after the O-grade was introduced, 'If a pupil is likely to get even one O-grade, he should be presented'. . . . I have many contacts up and down Scotland. Bear in mind that I had been up and down Scotland in my professional career. I had been President of the Headmasters' Association, and I was in constant contact with a fair number of knowledgeable and experienced people including Bill Anderson, for example, up in Inverness [Rector of Inverness High School 1968-83]. Accordingly, at the time when I was attempting to find an alternative to what they were going to do to the O-grade, I wrote to about seven people altogether up and down Scotland, whom I knew to be balanced in their outlook, and I found that, at the same time as they were replying to my queries, they were voicing to me spontaneously opposition to the idea that we must give a certificate to everybody.

Clark confirmed Dewar's account of the Department's attitude:

Q. Were you conscious, on the Board, of pressure from the Department to give everyone O-grades, of a view that, if pupils could get one, then they should be put in for it?

CLARK. Yes. I don't think that there was any doubt about that.

But the pressure was also coming, Clark thought, from a general change in teachers' attitudes, a change which penetrated the Board and began to divide it as ROSLA approached, and as the case for an easier examination at sixteen became more urgent. Should the O-grade be banded? Or should a CSE-type solution be sought?

CLARK. The representatives of the profession on the Examination Board, for whatever reason, were pretty certain that the profession was not ready, or going to accept CSE Mode III, and while Dewar was undoubtedly against it, I can think of, at that time, no member of the teaching profession who was on the Board who was advocating it as a way out. In fact, looking back, I have the distinct impression that particularly the teaching representatives – and probably the others, in the main, went along with this – were much more anxious to find ways and means of [having] nationally recognised pieces of paper which were, rather, an extension of what was then provided, than anything else. . . . In broad terms the EIS had the biggest single influence on the introduction of banding.

With the approach of ROSLA the Board convened, in 1968 and 1970, two national conferences, or folk-moots (to borrow Kogan's phrase), of the Scottish educational world (SCEEB 1968, 1970). Still, however, the Department argued for the limitation of national certification to about half of the age-group (SCEEB 1970, 13-18). However, the main EIS speaker at the 1970 Conference wanted much more: a national certificate for the majority of pupils, in the award of which the internal assessment by the school would count for thirty to forty per cent of the final mark. The speaker explicitly contrasted the EIS position with that of the SSTA, and warned that, if the EIS requirement were not met, ROSLA would lead to disruption by pupils (Currie 1970). Dewar was also a principal speaker at the 1970 Conference, but on the Board he was finding himself under increasing pressure:

DEWAR. I fought tooth and nail against this new subdivision of O-grade. In fact my opposition must have been unique in its insistence. There are no fewer than six occasions in that minute of the Examination Committee in which my dissent was recorded, and I was in the chair at the time!

Clark and Graham confirmed Dewar's opposition to banding. Clark told us, too, that he and another Board member, Hugh Fairlie (Director of Education, Renfrewshire 1964-75), were also opposed to banding. Between the lines of the public announcement of O-grade banding in 1972, one can sense the disagreement among the members of the Board.[5] Indeed, opposition on the Board to the banding policy was sufficiently vigorous for the Board to recommend what was eventually to become the Dunning review of certification and assessment (SED 1977b):

CLARK. I was involved in that [recommendation]. In fact, I was not only in favour of it, but I actually proposed the motion in the Exam Board which led to the recommendation, although it's not recorded in the minutes (they didn't record the proposers). I remember after our debate on the banding of O-grades, oddly enough, Hugh Fairlie and I discussing whether or not notice of motion should be submitted to get this whole thing looked at, and, we hoped, ultimately, put on a sounder basis. At any rate, this was an example of the Exam Board initiating advice to the Secretary of State.

Q. Can you actually think of any more examples?

CLARK. I can't.

Dunning eventually recommended a system of national certification at sixteen years for nearly all pupils, based on three overlapping levels of presentation. The overlap was intended to obviate the premature selection of pupils to courses of different levels of difficulty. Pupils were to have been allowed to present different subjects at different levels, and there was to have been a substantial component of internal assessment at each level. In 1983, the Conservative Government gave final approval to the implementation of a single national certificate for nearly all pupils at sixteen years, but with internal assessment only at Foundation (i.e. lowest) level. Earlier, however, in 1979, Bruce Millan as Labour Secretary of State, had rejected Dunning's proposals, preferring instead the continuation of the existing O-grade system, with some modifications, and with more emphasis on less able pupils (Kirk 1982, ch.5):

MILLAN. Why I am rather against the idea of certification for all, is that I think that a lot of that is more to do with motivating the teachers than with motivating the pupils, frankly; that if they don't have a certificate to work to, they don't quite know what to do with their pupils, that's really a lot of the argument there. I think that if you work towards a system where you are giving certificates which, in educational terms, are not really terribly valuable, you are rather liable to disillusion the pupils, because they find that they have got something which is valueless, in terms of their further employment. . . . What I think one ought not to do, is to go for a system which tries to solve this problem by giving certificates that really aren't worth very much at the end of the day, and which will have the danger, the great danger, that you really will be beginning to categorise pupils again. I think that if you take Munn and Dunning together, you see, with the three types of courses, and the three grades of certificates, you really can have a three-tier school, in fact. I mean, if all went wrong, that is what you would finish up with. . . . But it seemed to me that Munn and Dunning, taken together, were so complicated . . . it would only be exceptional schools with exceptional teachers that could actually cope, and produce the results that Munn and Dunning wanted. And a lot of other schools would not be able to cope because it is too complicated, too difficult; and then you might get the three-tier system instead of the two-tier system operating within the school. This was my worry about Munn and Dunning, which is why I took the view that I did: that the important thing is to try and develop the courses for the less academically inclined pupil, in the first instance; that is the glaring deficiency of the comprehensive school at the minute.

A Post-Higher Examination

We have concentrated so far on policy for certification in fourth year (though, of course, the O-grade was also intended to play a part in fifth and sixth years as well). However, the Department's preference for a style of directive informality in its relations with the Board was not confined to the issue of the O-grade. It is also apparent in policy for the Higher and post-Higher examinations. In these areas, too, the views of teachers and the practices of the schools constrained the development of Departmental policy, and were in turn constrained by it. But, in the area of post-compulsory provision, there was also an additional factor in the shape of the university presence.

For decades, many of the senior officials in the Department had trodden a path from a Scottish first degree to a second first degree in Oxford. They included Craik, Struthers, Mackay Thomson, HMSCI Watson, HMSCI Pringle, Murrie and Arbuckle. In the mid-1930s, Mackay Thomson had argued for more specialisation in the fifth and sixth years, in order to increase the number of Oxford and Cambridge entrance scholarships gained by Scottish school leavers (Lloyd 1979). Then, in the 1940s, he and Watson suggested a scholarship-level examination for the sixth year, though they did not press their case at the time. Brunton, in the 1950s, did not let the matter die. But he was unable to achieve unanimity on a post-Higher A-level in his working party on the curriculum of the senior-secondary school (SED 1959b, para.120). Instead, he swiftly remitted the question to a special committee of the Advisory Council on which he himself was a Departmental assessor. In 1960, the committee recommended the introduction of a post-Higher, Advanced-grade, examination for the sixth year. But it also asked for the retention of the Higher-grade as a qualification for university entrance (SED 1960b). Late in 1961, the Secretary of State accepted this recommendation (*SEJ* 15 December 1961). Dewar was a member both of the working party and of the Advisory Council committee:

DEWAR. The committee [of the Advisory Council] states quite clearly that no endeavour should be made to make it [the A-grade] something that the universities would use for giving exemptions either from the first year entirely or from the first-year examination. They were quite adamant about that, and we [on the Board] were quite adamant about that. We started from the point that we did not wish this to be thought of as being something that was available only for subjects recognised by, or professed in, the universities. Now this was terribly, terribly important. And that's why we made that point right at the very beginning. And, as time went on, our thinking on this became even clearer and we became quite firm. Unhappily the Department, without consulting us, proceeded to set up its own subject panels, to take the advice of the universities, and drew up papers which, if they were successfully tackled, were to give exemption from first year. They sent them out to the schools for comment, and the schools would have *nothing whatever* to do with them. I remember my excellent head of technical department . . . Jimmy Robertson . . . the forenoon when the Department's specimen papers had been sent out he asked to see me. He came in, and I knew from the wiggle of his nose that Jimmy was angry as you can make them! He said, 'Sir, you didn't tell me you were going to send out papers. *This is terrible*', he said, 'this is going to get them right into the second year. You can't possibly do it. *It's not on*'. . . . The Department now apparently wanted an Advanced-grade that could be used to give exemption, for example, from first-year university or from the preliminary pharmaceutical requirement. This was the novel element. To me, the most mysterious thing of all, as I have said to you, was the fact that our chairman, Sir David Anderson, was apparently not told.

We asked David Dickson about Dewar's comments:

DICKSON. Well, in the first place, the Inspectorate did not approach this from the point of view of what would gain exemption from anything in the universities. It had reference, really, to methods of teaching a sixth-year class, and our main aim was, somehow or another, to introduce an examination which would lead to the kind of teaching which is most likely to benefit a lad when he goes to university and has to work on his own. It would consist of practically no class teaching in the sense of the teacher pumping the pupil full of material, but much rather of work which the pupil did on his own, and thereby prepared himself to work on his own, as he would at university. It was more a method of working that we were after.

Q. Why was the academic standard of these specimen papers set so high?

DICKSON. Well, it was meant to be in advance of the Higher-grade, otherwise there wasn't much point to it, we thought. The Higher-grade takes a student into First Ordinary classes in university, and therefore this would have to aim at something beyond First Ordinary. Maybe it aimed too high, but I'm not so sure.

Q. Well supposing it had gone through, would the consequence of that have been ultimately a question mark over the four-year Honours degree?

DICKSON. Well, this depends on what you do. When I went to university fifty years ago, I missed out First Ordinary Latin and went straight into Second Ordinary Latin, which was regarded as a second-year class. This was the kind of thing that was in our minds. It's not a new practice, by any means, in the Scottish university. Having done Second Ordinary, you then took life a little bit more easily in the second year of your four-year graduation course, and spent time with Professor Taylor and Professor

311

Grierson and people like that. And other people, of course, like Murrie, did the same thing, only they did their Honours degree in three years.

Thus what the Department had in mind was the type of fast-lane education that had started off many of its own senior officials. In 1964, however, the new Labour Government was unlikely to give priority to such an A-level and, with the additional opposition of teachers like Dewar, the Department decided not to press the matter. It withdrew its papers, and the development of the post-Higher examination was thereafter formally done by the Examination Board. When it emerged in 1968 as the Certificate of Sixth Year Studies (CSYS), the syllabus and examination were something of a compromise. On the one hand, the Board and the Secretary of State denied to the CSYS the status of a formal qualification. This placated the teachers who feared the threat to the Higher-grade. It also allowed the Board to claim that it was promoting a liberal ethic of 'study for its own sake' on behalf of all sixth-year pupils, and not just those bound for university. On the other hand, the Board made the conditions for entry to CSYS courses so high that only an able minority in sixth year could meet them. Also, the Board preserved the principle of certification by means of the written, terminal, external examination in all the academic subjects of major interest to the universities. This seemed to disregard much of what the Advisory Council had said about the need to reduce the emphasis on external examinations in the schools (McPherson and Neave 1976). We separately asked Dewar, Brunton and Dickson about this:

DEWAR. The proposal of internal testing plus external moderation was introducing a principle that we did not feel we had thoroughly examined ourselves. We were not dismissing it as being something we would never touch, though basically we were against it. We felt that this savoured too much of an examination of the old type, that was our first point. Our second point was that, until we had studied this, we were not going to be able to see where external moderation would lead us.

Dewar's caution reflected a legacy of decades, a legacy in which the Department's concern for control had denied to teachers an examination framework within which they could accumulate a convincing body of alternative pedagogic experience. It was also a framework, therefore, that would leave the Department itself unconvinced of the case for change. This emerged clearly from our discussion with Brunton:

Q. The Board says it is interested in the practice of internal assessment and external moderation. This was something which was originally strongly recommended by the 1947 report of the Advisory Council.

BRUNTON. Yes, I agree.

Q. It's a mode of assessment which would have been appropriate, for example, for Sixth Year Studies, which is intended to be a very diverse curriculum with a good deal of initiative coming from teachers and pupils. And yet one has seen little other than written, terminal examinations

312

coming out of the Board.

BRUNTON. There was no chance of the [Sixth] Advisory Council's recommendation being adopted at the time when it was made. Something of this kind had already been tried. Before the War a certificate awarded to fifteen-year-old leavers, called the Day School Certificate (Higher), had been based very largely on internal assessment, with moderation by the Inspectorate. And, during the War, the Leaving Certificate examinations had been conducted on a somewhat similar basis, moderation in this case being in the hands of local committees of teachers, with inspectors as chairmen. In neither case had there been much success. The schools were not ready for a radical change of the kind suggested, and the teachers certainly did not want it. Neither did the universities and colleges, or those in charge of professional entry. . . . In framing the Sixth Year examination, the Board had in mind, at least to some extent, the possibility that the new certificate might be of interest to the universities; and there was, at that time, no evidence that the universities would look with favour on anything but a formal, written examination, though a good deal of flexibility of syllabuses was allowed.

Dickson told us that he was disappointed with the way the CSYS had worked out. We asked him:

Q. Do you think that a different mode of assessment would have helped it?

DICKSON. I think it would.

Q. Would you have got the universities to accept it?

DICKSON. Well, I didn't care tuppence whether the universities accepted it or not.

Q. But could you have got teachers to accept it?

DICKSON. Without the universities? That's another point. That is the main disappointment that one has had.

Discussion

Policy for the sixth year exhibits several features commonly ascribed to pluralist systems of government. One is that no party got what it had originally wanted; and a second is that practice interacted with policy, with incremental but disjointed results. The Department was unable to institute an examination that would reproduce its own kind. The universities did not get a formally recognised means of selection that would assist them in managing entry in a period of expanding student demand. Nor were they wholly successful in transferring first-year university work to the schools' sixth year. Those teachers who wanted greater school-based control of assessment were disappointed; but so too were those who wanted an external examination that would give them better control of their sixth-year pupils. All in all, each party got a little of the change it wanted, but had in the main to accept a compromise.

A third pluralist feature was that the resultant incrementation of policy left the existing system fundamentally unchanged. Teachers were almost wholly successful in preserving the formal status of the Higher-grade as the terminal school examination. In this two considerations seem to have weighed, both with roots in the axis of contest-mobility and localism that had opposed the Department in earlier generations. This axis emphasised the importance of provision that was accessible by virtue of being generous and available locally (see chapters 2 and 11). The Jimmy Robertsons of the educational world rejected an A-level that would have reduced the university's accessibility, were the new examination ever to displace the Higher-grade, a development which the Inspectorate thought might happen after a decade. Nor was a sixth-year examination allowed to displace provision for university entry in fifth year. Here what was stressed, in particular, was the viability of the small country school that was not large enough to sustain a sixth year. It was argued that country schools would lose many of their pupils, were an over-rigorous definition of a 'completed education' to require pupils to stay on longer at school. The Eighth Advisory Council argued that the importance of country schools was such that the resultant problem would be 'national' in character. Dewar signed this report (SED 1960b), and one detects behind its arguments his concern for the 'fellows and women away out on the periphery of Scotland, "in the provinces"'.[6]

The interest of this position is that it parallels the argument that was made before the First World War about the national importance of the parish school. Anderson (1983a, 158) points out that, although the nineteenth-century argument may have overestimated the role of parish schools in giving poor boys access to educational opportunity, the fact of their existence delayed the imposition of a university matriculation standard, and thereby helped to keep the universities accessible. The defence of the country school in the 1960s had similar consequences. It remained possible thereafter for pupils to enter university from the fifth year with Highers qualifications completed at around seventeen years. As post-compulsory provision expanded in the 1960s, and as recession deepened in the 1970s, so this option was taken up more frequently, especially by pupils in Glasgow. When the Department again mooted the introduction of an A-level in the early 1980s, it found that about half the entry direct from school to degree-level courses in west-central Scotland had left school from fifth year. Elsewhere in Scotland the comparable proportion was about a tenth (McPherson 1984b). Since the rejection of the A-level in the early 1960s, patterns of transition from post-compulsory schooling, and the various provisions made for it, had diversified regionally to a point where a standardising national reform could be imposed only with great difficulty. In the early 1980s, a post-Higher examination was rejected yet again. Thus policy and practice developed in an incremental but disjointed way, and in this sense, also, the outcomes were pluralistically determined.

The foundation of the Examination Board itself, however, was less a concession to pluralism than a concession to expansion. Watson's warning of 1947 was heeded when the new O-grade examination finally obliged the Department to establish the Board. The Secretary of State took powers of direction over the Board, and created a powerful channel of influence through his assessors. He also contended that his assessors remain his representatives in the first of Holden's senses (as spokesmen or agents of himself as principal). They were to retain the authority of their office, whereas members from the nominating constituencies were to abrogate their representative identity and become 'private' individuals with 'personal' views. The relegation of non-Departmental members to this reduced status was a matter of practice rather than of law, and it had few implications when Board members and assessors were broadly agreed on substantive policies. But both the EIS and the ADES contested one of its procedural implications. This was the right that the Department claimed to select Board members from among those nominated. How great an influence this gave the Department we cannot say, but we presume it implied something more than a purely procedural assertion of the Department's authority. At any rate, the first members of the Board did not object publicly and collectively to the Department's continuing initiative over the A-level, nor to its use of a single Board member and a single Board official for the purpose of evaluating the CSE. In its early years the Board was deferential and responsive. One presumes this was, at least in part, a consequence of the Department's influence on the process of nomination and selection.

This presumption is strengthened by the evidence of increasing misgivings among Board members as ROSLA loomed. They had been appointed at the time that Brunton's bipartite policy was apparently approaching its fulfilment. But all this changed with the change of government to Labour in 1964, with comprehensive reorganisation, and with the expansion of O-grade presentations. It was one thing to collude with the Department to exclude the CSE, and with it the proposal for a nationally recognised certificate for the less able. It was quite another thing to defer to the Department if that meant conceding the certification of the majority of pupils in comprehensive schools by means of a 'banded' O-grade. This resistance could be broken of course, both by an immediate instruction from the Secretary of State, and later by replacing the objectors at the end of their terms of office with appointees who held different views. Certainly there is evidence of a marked change by the mid-1970s in the types of appointments made to the Board and its subject panels (see chapter 17). But, in 1965, national policy had been based on the bipartite principle for so long that it would not have been easy for the Department, had it wished, to find trusted individuals who could propound alternative philosophies of practice with the confidence of proven experience.

Here was a crisis of values and symbols. The good teacher had hitherto been defined as the teacher who produced good certificate results. As we shall see (see chapter 17), this definition tended to favour teachers from schools outside west-central Scotland, and from schools with socially advantaged pupil intakes. Until ROSLA in 1973, moreover, good teachers were recognised, not by the criterion of what they had achieved for all their pupils by the end of their compulsory education, but by what they had achieved for the minority of their pupils who had elected to enter post-compulsory schooling, and who had been selected for certificate presentation. Such teachers symbolised to the Department all that the Department believed to be best about the Scottish educational tradition. And what was true of the good teacher was even more true of the senior members of the Inspectorate at the time.

The appointment of the Dunning Committee was therefore something more than a political concession to a disaffected body of opinion, articulated by Dewar, Fairlie and Clark, that had unexpectedly retained some influence for itself on a new fringe body following a change in political control. It also marked the final, belated and grudging recognition by the Department of the legitimacy of the question that the Sixth Advisory Council had addressed in its 1947 report *Secondary Education*: namely, how are the purposes of an elite secondary education to be restated when secondary education is made the right of all? The Department evaded this issue in the 1940s. But, by the early 1970s, it was clear that it would require an extended effort at consultative repair to achieve an agreed answer that would not undermine an Inspectorate whose authority was rooted in a *mystery* that had itself been defined in terms of the bipartite system. And it would take even longer to build up a body of alternative educational practice that would carry conviction either with teachers or with the Department. A comment of Dickson's captures this well: 'If a course doesn't have an examination and a certificate at the end of it, then it hasn't got an awful lot of chance of being accepted'.

NOTES

1. SRO (1950, 18 July).
2. Neither the Act nor the regulations referred to curriculum. But the Act empowered the Board to 'advise on . . . matters relating to examinations'. A generous interpretation of this clause might take it to subsume the syllabuses of examination subjects. The Act placed no restriction on the power of the Secretary of State to make whatever provision for examinations he himself wished. The legislation did not clarify whether members of the Board sat 'as individuals' or as representatives of their nominating bodies, if any. It might be argued that the latter intention is implied in clause 9(1) of the regulations. This required that not less than one-third of the Board's Finance Committee should be appointed 'from among persons nominated by the associations recognised as representing the interests of the education authorities'. It is difficult to see what purpose this provision had other than to promote the representation of the education authorities, in the first of Holden's senses (below, in this chapter). On the other hand, the representatives of the Secretary of State who sat as

assessors to the Board were allowed by regulation 7 to nominate substitutes to participate in Board meetings. This power did not extend to the Board members themselves. Although the regulations did not explicitly preclude substitutions, these arrangements do not suggest that those who framed the legislation intended that Board members should sit as representatives of their nominating associations. But we cannot finally say whether or not these obscurities were intended.

3. For example, the following is recorded in the minutes of the meeting of 5 May 1964 of the Scottish Council for the Training of Teachers (SCTT): 'In a letter of 22nd April 1964 the Scottish Education Department had intimated that from among persons nominated by Governing Bodies of Colleges of Education the Secretary of State had appointed Mr Scotland, Principal of Aberdeen College of Education, and Mr Wood, Principal of Jordanhill College of Education, to be members of the [Examination] Board for a period of three years' (SCTT 1964, 439).

4. See note 2 and also chapter 14.

5. 'The changes proposed result from consideration which the Board has for some years been giving to the future role of the Ordinary grade examination. In 1970 at a Conference arranged by the Board and representative of all the main educational interests in Scotland the problem was fully discussed. Thereafter the Board reviewed the various issues involved and consulted the Secretary of State in the matter. On his suggestion the Board considered the possibility of substituting a system of rankings for the present pass/fail system and this was approved by the Board in June of this year' (SCEEB 1972a). 'The invitation by the Secretary of State to consider the substitution of a system of grades in place of the present pass/fail system was accepted by the Board: the possible merits of such a development were recognised as were the countervailing problems it could create. After taking all known considerations into account the Board came to the conclusion that the balance of advantage lay with this new proposal.' (SCEEB 1972b).

6. 'In Scotland, before the growth of large urban and industrial areas, the typical community was the small provincial town, in which the educational provision beyond the primary stage was made in the small local academy or secondary department. Although radical changes have come about both in the size and in the character of many Scottish towns, that educational provision has continued to be made in the same typical way. If the Higher grade were discontinued, the "top" of the small senior secondary school would be so diminished in numbers that it would no longer be economic. We are convinced that this drastic diminution would occur even if another and a more demanding examination were instituted at a later stage in the school. The problems which would arise would therefore be nationwide in their incidence' (SED 1960b, para.15). See also Robertson (1966) who talks of 'powerful resistance' to the demotion of the Higher-grade springing 'from everyone's concern about the grave effect of such a change in the fortunes of those small senior secondary schools in which Scotland abounds'.

Fourteen

Curriculum and the Consultative Committee

We have always tended . . . to have rather more control of things
in the schools than the DES insisted on, and I have very often been
told by the DES that we were very sensible.   David Dickson,
HMSCI 1966-69

Introduction

The Consultative Committee on the Curriculum (CCC) was established in
1965. In the same year the new Labour Government issued its circulars on
comprehensive reorganisation, and the Examination Board took over from
the Inspectorate responsibility for the conduct of the SCE examination.
Brunton was in his final year as Senior Chief Inspector, but Graham had
been in post for less than two years, and still had some eight years to go as
head of the Department.

As we have seen, Brunton's plans for the CCC began to clarify as he
thought through the wider consequences of the new examination system
and of other innovations he had mobilised. He told us he had wanted 'some
body . . . on which all these different interests would be represented, which
would have a general oversight of the curriculum, and which would be at
least a relatively independent body of real authority giving powerful advice
to the Secretary of State' (see chapter 4). The evidence suggests that the
Department may have been on course for this objective in the early 1960s.
In 1962, one of the working parties set up after the 1961 strike reported on
consultation between the teachers' associations and the SED (SED 1962b).
Brunton was a full member of the working party, and its unanimous recommendations for a new Consultative Committee on Educational Matters
(CCEM – see chapter 11) incorporated two proposals that were consistent
with a 'strong' view of partnership: any party would be able to initiate
meetings and items of business (*ibid.*, para.27); and the members representing the teachers' associations would be appointed by their respective
associations, and not by the Secretary of State (*ibid.*, para.34). These
provisions were explicitly intended to create 'scope for more topics to be
brought under consultation at the initiative of the [teachers'] associations'
(*ibid.*, para.8). The remit would cover 'curricula, examinations and school
organisation', and would overarch the new Examination Board.[1]

We cannot tell from this document alone where Brunton had envisaged

318

that such a body might fit into the overall structure of advice. Nothing is said about the role of the Advisory Council, though the report does endorse the mechanism of the Departmental working party constituted along the lines of those chaired by Brunton (*ibid.*, paras 12, 13 and 15). Brunton had not been a strong supporter in the 1950s of an advisory-council approach, and, as we have seen, he made it his business to get the right people appointed to national bodies, insofar as he was able. Nor is it yet clear whether Graham's arrival in the Department in 1964 influenced the discussion. One presumes it did. In the event, the ccc that emerged in 1965 embodied neither the specific proposals made by the 1962 ccem working party, nor the scope and independence that Brunton told us he had wanted.

What is more, to the consternation of Brunton and many others, Graham himself took the chair of the ccc. We have seen in Part iii that Graham thought it his job to ensure that the changes associated with the reorganisation of central-local financial arrangements in the 1950s drew the Inspectorate towards the administration, and the Department itself towards the mainstream of the Scottish Office. Graham worked hard at procuring resources and reducing costs, and he furthered the integration of the Inspectorate into a single Departmental hierarchy for decision-making (see chapter 7). To make that decision-making effective, he attempted to clear the decks at the centre, and to devolve tasks that he considered properly 'local' to the local authorities and to other agencies (see chapter 9).

Graham saw himself as following through on a thrust of change that had begun in the 1950s and that was directed primarily at the management of resources. But, within this general reorganisation, several points of control over curriculum were also candidates for relocation. When we suggested to Graham in our interview that the changed position of the Inspectorate in the Department might be seen as a move towards centralisation, he demurred:

GRAHAM. Well, it was the integration of the Department.

Q. You wouldn't agree that, when a central Inspectorate provides a curriculum function, it relieves the local authorities of the need to develop strong advisorates?

GRAHAM. No, it was designed to stimulate it, to put more emphasis on it.

A stronger local-authority presence in curriculum was to develop in some areas after local government reorganisation in 1975, but much still came from the centre. In particular, once Graham had retired, the ccc left the course on which he had set it. No-one doubts that Graham was an effective Secretary, or that he was a shaping influence in the formative years of the ccc. By the end of the 1970s, however, the ccc itself confessed that it was not properly geared into the activities of the regional authorities (SED 1980b, para.70). Moreover, critics within the Department attacked both the ccc and the Inspectorate for the very features that Graham had wished to purge. The Rayner review of 1979 thought the ccc too large, unwieldy and inefficient (SED 1980c, 3); and a resurgent Inspectorate, working partly through the ccc, was later criticised in the Rendle review both for its initiation of policy independently of administrators in the Department, and also for its failure to devolve tasks to local authorities and to extant fringe bodies (so 1981, paras 4.38-4.46 and 8.2-8.12). In 1986, a further Departmental review, the Crawley review, criticised the ccc again for poor articulation with the regional education authorities (sed 1986, paras 5.5-5.8). Crawley also thought the ccc neglectful of questions of resources and teacher co-operation when framing its policies, and he argued for retrenchment, in its funding, staffing, committee structure and level of activity (*ibid.*).

The form that the ccc took under Graham, and the changes that followed his retiral, are two themes of this chapter. It is partly a story of the swing of the pendulum between Inspectorate and administration. But it would be a mistake to represent the first fifteen years of the ccc solely as a failing attempt by administrators to contain resilient professionals and a proliferating structure of committees. We can also see in the events of the period a continuing attempt by central government to respond to the pressures that expansion was placing on it, by searching for new ways of mobilising advice and support at the fringes of central government and beyond. Unlike the Advisory Council, the ccc was not a statutory body. It was established as a purely advisory committee charged with the general oversight of the curriculum, and with no executive functions. By 1977, however, it had acquired its own budget and a major executive role in all areas of curriculum development, intersecting both with the colleges of education and the Examination Board. These changes in the ccc at first promised to increase the system's capacity for 'top-down', centrally initiated curriculum development (so 1981, para.4.42). But they also had implications for wider judgements about partnership, pluralism and corporatism. By the end of the 1970s, advisory and executive functions were more closely integrated with each other across broader reaches of the system than had been the case under the Advisory Councils; many more people and agencies participated in the executive and advisory process, through fringe bodies; and there were also signs of increased activity 'beyond the fringe' by educationists working on government development programmes that were only indirectly accountable to the ccc or the Examination Board (ccc 1984, paras 6, 7 and 27-31).

The wider implications of these changes are discussed mainly in Part v. In this chapter we look first at the diverse influences that brought the control of the curriculum to the fore in the early 1960s. Thereafter we examine the founding of the ccc itself, its formal status in the machinery of government, its membership and chairmanship, and the role that it claimed for itself. We also examine two continuing problems that it faced: the relation of curriculum advice to curriculum development; and its own relationships with the Examination Board.

In exploring these issues we illustrate the impact of expansion on governmental structures, and the influence of these structures, in turn, on the substance of the curriculum and on the philosophies prescribed for it. Continuing features of the Scottish curriculum over this period were its use of the subject as the main curriculum unit; its emphasis on the 'academic' to the exclusion of the social, vocational and aesthetic; and the relatively low discretion that it allowed to teachers, or to pupils, to initiate their own topics and methods of learning. There was also a persistent dualism in priorities and philosophy. On the one hand, with comprehensive reorganisation and the continuing effects of 'downward incrementalism', there was a concern to explicate for a majority of pupils the general education that had originally been conceived for a small elite. On the other hand, there was also a reluctance to examine the philosophy and practices of elite education, especially as manifested in the Highers curriculum. Instead there was a continuing feeling that priority for curriculum development lay 'at the bottom end', among less able pupils. Was this positive discrimination? Or was it a subtle reproduction of an older bipartite philosophy? Munn and Dunning, and in particular Dunning, attempted to break this dualism with their recommendations for a comprehensive restructuring of curriculum and certification for all pupils. However, Bruce Millan decided in 1979 to retain the SCE O-grade. It was only with the return of the Conservative Government later that year that first approval was given to an essentially wholesale reform for all pupils, though even then the proposals for internal assessment were largely confined to the 'bottom end'.

The character of the curriculum owes much to the way in which the question of control was handled during this period. We look first at how the issue of control reached the agenda, and at how government itself responded.

Curriculum Becomes Overtly Political

Resources apart, the SED influenced the school curriculum in the twenty years following the 1945 Act mainly through the Schools (Scotland) Code, the SLC (later SCE) examination syllabuses, and various memoranda and surveys promoted by the Inspectorate. It is difficult to say how much curriculum development was initiated by the schools themselves, though in all probability little was done by schools teaching mainly certificate courses. There were no locally employed inspectors, of course, like there were in England, and it was not until the late 1960s that the Scottish local authorities began to employ advisers in any numbers, or to develop curriculum-resource centres for teachers.

However, in England and Scotland alike, the early 1960s saw the emergence of arguments for a greater effort at curriculum development, and for a national structure to sustain it. In both countries, broadly four sorts of influence were at work. First, there were factors arising from examination policy and from pupils' and schools' responses to it. Pursuing greater and earlier 'vertical' differentiation of pupils by ability, the SED in 1959 had relaxed the requirement that prescribed subjects be studied at certain stages of certificate courses. The district inspector retained the right to require a school to alter courses that neglected 'some essential element of secondary education', and the Department insisted that 'general' education be not compromised (SED 1959b, paras 19 and 20). Nevertheless, the change gave more scope to schools, whether they used it or not, to vary courses in examinable subjects, and to offer further courses in non-examinable subjects or topics. Rising enrolments underlined the case for greater flexibility of curriculum. As more pupils stayed on to take O-grades, countervailing pressures were created. For the less able pupils who stayed on and did only a part-certificate course, new curricula were required for their non-certificate work in third and fourth years. However, the provision of such courses was itself made more difficult by expansion. The pupil demand for certification inflated. As the less able acquired some certification, so the more able took more (Gray *et al.*, 1983, ch.5). Schools continued to concentrate their resources on certificate presentation. Moreover, timetabling for non-certificate work, which often required blocks of time, was impeded by the priority that schools gave to the certificate.

Thus, by the mid-1960s, continuing expansion provided a solution: more pupils would be caught in the net of the certificate curriculum. But this solution, in its turn, promised further problems. Continuing expansion meant more post-compulsory pupils, and more pupils taking more certificate courses. This would make the position of entirely non-certificate pupils increasingly invidious as they came to be outnumbered by certificate pupils. A failure to develop courses for non-certificate pupils would exacerbate the problem. For certificate pupils, certificate inflation would pose problems of 'balance', both among the examined courses, and between the examined courses and the non-examined. As we have seen, the Labour Government of 1964-70 encouraged the development of non-certificate courses. But it also encouraged the spread of certification, thereby disrupting much of its curricular planning for ROSLA.

A second influence, to which expansion gave added weight, was the continuing argument over professional autonomy following the 1961 strikes. In England teachers won substantial and direct representation on the Schools Council. They also gained considerable control over assessment for the new Certificate of Secondary Education (CSE) that was introduced in 1963 for less able pupils. *Unpopular Education* argues that government was obliged to concede control to the teachers if teachers in their turn were to contain disorder in the schools, and prevent the wider decay of social democracy of which this disorder was symptomatic (CCCS 1981, chs 4 and 5). But it would be difficult to sustain this argument for Scotland. As we saw in chapter 11, the SED had clearly wished to school pupils to order in the 1940s and 1950s. But the Department eventually made fewer concessions to teachers' autonomy. Nevertheless, the Department was shaken by the 1961 strike and, with parliamentary criticism of Brunton's *modus operandi* as HMSCI (PD 1964), control of the curriculum was a public issue in the dying days of the Conservative Government in 1964.

A third influence on the political salience of curricular issues was the changing framework of education for fifteen-to eighteen-year-olds. Two aspects of this change were ROSLA and the growth of further education. If expansion and issues of professional autonomy put curriculum on the agenda in the early 1960s, the decision to implement the raising of the school-leaving age, announced by the Conservative Government in 1964, guaranteed that it would stay there. For teachers in most types of school there was now no escaping the prospect of having to teach fourteen- or fifteen-year-olds who would be taking no certificate courses. The bulge in the birth-rate was straining the secondary system, and many teachers doubted that schools would be given sufficient additional resources to implement ROSLA. When ROSLA eventually came in 1973, delayed by two years because of post-devaluation cuts in public spending, the majority of Scottish teachers were against it (CCCS 1981, 196). Indeed, from the time it was announced, the EIS had warned of the disruption that ROSLA portended.

But what were the 'ROSLA pupils' to be offered? National policy for certification in the 1960s (as distinct from the actual practice of schools, over which formal policy had a weakening hold) precluded certification for more than half of the age-group at most; and CSE Mode III had been kept off the national policy agenda in Scotland (see chapter 13). Brunton had advocated a curriculum for academically less able pupils centred on the 'vocational impulse', and this offered one possible answer to the problem of motivating ROSLA pupils. But Brunton's thinking had the taint about it of the bipartite system that was being dismantled after 1964. Moreover, vigorous growth in further-education provision had started in the late 1950s. Thus, if they pursued a vocational solution too enthusiastically, schools might cede to the colleges control of curriculum for older pupils. Whilst continuing to press for an extension of national certification, the EIS in 1966 opted for a non-vocational curriculum based on 'a good general education', and for a 'ROSLA year' taught entirely at school (EIS 1966b). Eventually the Institute was to achieve its demands, more or less, and later still the Munn Committee was to legitimate them (SED 1977c). But in the mid-1960s they constituted, not so much a solution to the 'ROSLA problem', as a set of limits within which a solution had to be sought.

These were not the only influences on the political importance of curriculum. Teachers began to advance the claims of new subjects, and there were pressures, too, from outside education. Britain's flagging industrial performance prompted demands from industry for better craft and technical education. In the post-Sputnik age, there was also pressure for more, and more practical, science and mathematics in the school curriculum, and for a

323

better place for science and technology in higher education. The Scottish Council (Development and Industry) consolidated these demands in the Toothill report on the Scottish economy (sc(DI) 1961). It pressed *inter alia* for a sixth-year A-grade examination, and for more specialisation in scientific and technical subjects in certificate courses at school. It also renewed the Appleton Committee's abortive recommendation for teacher salary-differentials in favour of mathematics and science subjects (see chapter 10). Brunton, of course had already given an impetus to curricular reform in mathematics and science, and one detects the coordinating hand of Brunton in the fact that the sc(DI) recommendations faithfully reproduced the sED's general policies for secondary education. The new Labour Government made access to science a feature of its general programme for equalising educational opportunity, and a science lobby continued to press its own claims (csp 1968; cmrst 1968). Thus a further source of tension was the resultant demand for more science, more specialisation and, in effect, for more teachers, and more expensive teachers, for able pupils.

The Early Location and Character of the ccc

From the point of view of the sED administration in the early 1960s, there were strong arguments for locating the new body close to the centre. Much was already at risk. Concessions had been made to teachers and local authorities in the aftermath of the 1961 strike. Moreover, some sort of statutorily independent council for teachers was now in the offing, and a new Examination Board had yet to prove whether or not it would readily fall in with the Department's views. Also, there was a growing Departmental scepticism of the value of extra-Departmental advice, whether on specialised fronts like buildings and teacher supply, or on the broader fronts of primary and secondary education as a whole. Administration and Inspectorate alike believed that outside contributions would be effective only if the individual contributors were carefully chosen, and their advice closely integrated with official thinking and practice. The Department did not want synoptic thinking from other bodies' nominees. To place an effective body, or an effective individual, too far from the centre would be to risk another McClelland (see chapter 11). There was also a lesson to be drawn from Brunton's era: namely, that when the mobilisation of an outside network of institutions was managed through the Senior Chief Inspector, this could tip the balance of influence within the Department too much in the Inspectorate's favour. On the other hand, an active network that was not controlled from the Department raised the old spectre of proliferating sectional and local demands that were uncoordinated, expensive and socially inefficient. Every subject would want a place in the sun.

As always, the problem for the Department was how it could respond to an area of increasing priority without, on the one hand, greatly increasing its own numbers or, on the other hand, conceding a measure of control to outsiders in the course of enlisting their help. What was happening in England could not be ignored. Professional autonomy was in the air, and it carried north of the Tweed. Whilst normative arguments against central government's control of the curriculum had never been supported so strongly in Scotland, especially where certificate courses were involved, such arguments were nevertheless made, and were reinforced by the English example.[2]

In the event, the Department repudiated the substantial concessions to consultation with teachers and local authorities that it had made in the immediate aftermath of the 1961 strike. In particular, there was the embarrassment of the Consultative Committee on Educational Matters (CCEM). Its remit included the curriculum, and its non-Departmental members were, we believe, directly nominated by outsiders (see chapter 11). Whilst the Department might want to claw back some of these concessions, it could not afford to exclude altogether the EIS and west of Scotland interests that had promoted the 1961 strike, and that had so patently failed to break through into national councils under Arbuckle and Brunton. Moreover, the 1964 election made a former Ayrshire teacher, William Ross, Secretary of State for Scotland, giving the West and the EIS a greater say in whatever advisory structure replaced the Advisory Council. Ross, we were told, was on first-name terms with many senior members of the EIS.

Furthermore, some measure of decentralisation, if only cosmetic, was necessary to protect the Secretary of State during a period of rapid change. However 'promotional' the Department might want to be in leading curriculum development, there were advantages in its denying its seal of approval to innovations until some other body had won public consent to them. The starting point for curriculum change should at least appear to be at some distance from the Minister, especially in areas like religious education and sex education that were sensitive for the preponderantly Labour-voting Catholic minority. Now that Graham was determined to integrate the Inspectorate more closely with Departmental decision-making, and now that inspectors were having to swallow in silence a policy of comprehensive reorganisation that at least some found unpalatable (see chapters 15 to 17), the argument for retaining some locus of advice that was seen to be independent of the Department could not lightly be dismissed. Moreover, such advice would have to be 'representative', in some shape or form, if consent were to be presented as national.

The constitution that was given to the CCC in 1965 tried to balance these considerations. The instability of this compromise helps explain some of the features of the CCC's early practice, and also the stresses and changes to which it later became subject. On the one hand, the CCC was firmly located at the centre. The twenty-five members of the committee included four inspectors and two administrators from the Department itself, nine teachers, of whom four were from the industrial West, and eight members from further and higher education. There was only one director of education, and only one member from industry and commerce. The remit was:

> to maintain a general oversight over the school curriculum, both primary and secondary; to draw the attention of the Secretary of State to any aspect of the curriculum, whether general or particular, which seems to call for consideration by specialist bodies; and to comment on the recommendations made by any working party appointed by the Secretary of State on its advice. The aim is to keep the school curriculum under continuous review. (SED 1969b, 5)

On the other hand, the authority and power of the CCC were severely limited in several ways. The remit itself was restricted to education at school. It did not set out the relationship of the CCC's 'general oversight' to advice coming from the Examination Board. Nor was the CCC given the quasi-independent, corporate identity that the Examination Board had from statute, or that other educational bodies take from their status as companies limited by guarantee. Instead, the Secretary of State simply announced by circular letter that he was inviting individuals to 'advise him on the development of the curriculum of primary and secondary schools' (*ibid.*). Furthermore, members of the CCC were neither directly nominated, nor selected by the Secretary of State from among those put forward by nominating bodies (as with the SCEEB). They were simply 'appointed as individuals, for their personal knowledge and experience, rather than as representatives of particular organisations' (*ibid.*). Each CCC was to be appointed for a fixed term of three years. More important, it was to be given no executive powers, no budget and no staff of its own, being serviced instead by Departmental officials. The intention was that development work would initially be done by *ad hoc* Departmental committees and groups. These were to report their findings to the CCC, and to seek its blessing. Outsiders were to sit on these committees and groups, some of which were already in existence in 1965. But the committees and groups were commissioned by the Department and, in the early years, were mostly chaired by the Inspectorate.

In these ways, then, the Secretary of State sought to divorce himself from the early stages of curriculum innovation and to keep his new body of advisers well away from the control of executive functions, whilst at the same time giving it a general competence over curriculum, admitting influential opinion to his counsels, and linking advice to action.

In describing his original intentions for the CCC, Brunton mentioned to us 'intense opposition from certain members of the administration' (see chapter 4). However, it is fairly certain that neither Inspectorate nor administration wanted to admit teachers or others to a full advisory and executive partnership. Brunton said of the Schools Council in England:

BRUNTON. This was a very large organisation with a very large infrastructure, and it did not seem to me that anything of that kind was necessary in Scotland, because we were smaller and much more intimate, and the various parts of the educational system were much more closely in touch with each other.

During his time as Senior Chief Inspector (1966-69), Dickson spoke and wrote about the Department's search for a new partnership (SCES 1968, Q.50; Dickson 1969). But his emphasis was rather different when we asked him why the CCC was not originally given direct responsibility for the working groups and committees that did the executive work:

DICKSON. Well, the CCC is a consultative committee only, and this would really involve the CCC in a great deal of permanent executive work rather than consultative work.

Q. What's undesirable about that?

DICKSON. Maybe they didn't want the CCC to be too powerful in its own right.

Q. Was it also perhaps taking fright at the vision of the Schools Council pattern?

DICKSON. Well, we didn't want a Schools Council. That was quite clear, and we wouldn't have one.

Q. The feeling was what? That it was too unwieldy?

DICKSON. Too large, too complicated, too difficult to run.

Q. Was the feeling also that it limited the Secretary of State's influence too much?

DICKSON. I don't think that we would have admitted that, but that feeling may have been present. . . . We have always tended, as you know well enough, to have rather more control of things in the schools than the DES insisted on, and I have very often been told by the DES that we were very sensible.

Dickson and Graham together gave a similar, though more guarded, account of their attitude towards the Schools Council in their oral evidence to the 1968 Parliamentary Select Committee on the Inspectorate (SCES 1968, Qs 82-95). On this matter at least, inspectors and administrators seemed to have been at one, and at one also with the leader of the major teachers' union. Bryden also told the 1968 Select Committee that the EIS had not wanted a formal structure like the Schools Council, preferring the type of contact he had established with persons like Brunton and Rodger (*ibid.*, Qs 319 and 341; see also chapter 18).

Why then had administrators in the Department opposed the founding of a new curriculum body? We can only guess, but the probability is that the administration could not see how a compromise could be struck between the conflicting considerations, described above, that would not confirm the Inspectorate in the relative independence that Brunton had won for it. In 1968 Graham had explained the origins of the CCC in the need to manage, aggregate and rationalise the curricular innovations that had begun under Brunton:

GRAHAM. The origin of this . . . was the realisation that everybody felt that particular subjects of the curriculum could stand overhauling. . . . Some of this has started *ad hoc,* notably on mathematics and science. . . . Then we began to feel there were some dangers in too much *ad hoc*ing and that we had no means of looking at the balance of the curriculum as a whole. There is always a risk of the subject specialists becoming too obsessed with the importance of their own particular subject and demanding or postulating amounts of school time that just cannot be there if a balance is to be held. This was really one of the dominant considerations in leading us to the conclusion that there ought to be some over-all body [*ibid.,* qs 82-3].

Thus 'balance' for Graham did not express a developed educational philosophy, though the Munn Committee was later to attach one to the idea. Rather, it was something that was to be 'held' between competing subject constituencies. Graham wanted a structure to contain proliferation and to rein in the Inspectorate. But could the latter be achieved along with the former? The arrangements for the new CCC required the Inspectorate to act as a link between advice and action, between policy for curriculum and policy for certification, and between centre and periphery. The compromises could be made to work only by giving the Inspectorate a ubiquitous if ambiguous role. It is this, one imagines, that explains Graham's controversial decision to take the chair of the CCC himself. When the 1968 Select Committee pressed Graham on this, he explained it, not in terms of policies, but, unusually for him (see chapter 3), in terms of personalities:

GRAHAM. I think to be quite frank that if there had been anyone with the time outside who seemed to us eminently equipped to do this, we should have appointed someone. I do not think there is any real significance in this. I think it has been very useful to the Office. We have hitherto avoided the situation altogether which I think sometimes arose in the days when we had an Advisory Council in that the committee proposed and the Secretary of State disposed [*ibid.,* q.83].

When we asked him to elaborate, he commented:

GRAHAM. I don't remember any view having been taken when I came into the formative stage of this as to how it should be chaired. There was a very definite view that we should try to avoid the situation which had arisen with the old Advisory Council which had formulated views which had then been rejected by the Secretary of State. The idea that the Secretary should take the chair, I think, largely, sprang from that. It was a means of avoiding, as far as one could, any risk of conflict, and it was also a convenient device in that the Secretary of the Department was not a professional educationist, and there was no risk of the committee being dominated from the chair. Conceivably that could have happened had it been chaired by a professional educationist from outside.

Q. There was a feeling that this had happened with the old Advisory Council?

GRAHAM. Well, undoubtedly Sir James Robertson, I've always understood, had a strong influence on the old Advisory Council. The alternative would have been to have somebody from the Inspectorate in the chair, which might have produced the reaction that the committee was dominated by the Inspectorate, which we were all anxious not to see.

Dickson told us 'there were a lot of eyebrows raised' when Graham took the ccc chair. He also doubted Graham's view that no sufficiently eminent lay educationist was available as an alternative, saying 'I think we could have found somebody'. But Robertson, by now retired, had blotted his copybook on the Knox Committee when he refused to accept dilution of standards for admission to teaching (see chapter 11). The Department was clearly resolved that neither the Inspectorate, nor a person of Robertson's eminence, should have determinate influence in the new structure.

It remained for the Department to explain and justify the new arrangements to the wider world. Many of Brunton's network of outsiders found positions somewhere in the new structure (see chapter 17), and some, like Dewar on the Examination Board, could be irritatingly independent. But they had lost their channel of influence through the Senior Chief Inspector. Dickson and his Inspectorate colleagues clearly had a major part to play in promoting links with the new structures. But the Inspectorate's new role had been acquired at the cost of its absorption into a decision-making hierarchy with Graham at its head. The Examination Board had a measure of formal independence, and its members had been appointed under the previous, Conservative, Government. But was the ccc to be anything more than a pretext for the Department to continue to advise itself whilst appearing to admit the views of outsiders, or anything more than a means of putting the Inspectorate to new tasks in a period of unpalatable policy change? Such doubts were expressed to the 1968 Select Committee on the Inspectorate by one of Brunton's former allies in the reorganisation of the colleges of education, W. B. Inglis (Principal, Moray House College of Education 1951-66):

INGLIS. This growing power of the HMI has been accompanied by the decline of the Advisory Council on Education to such an extent that it has not met since 1961. We have no independent body that is not influenced deeply and profoundly by our HMIs looking at Scottish education at the present time, nor had we such a body when we were facing the problems of comprehensive secondary education and raising the school-leaving age. . . . While this [the ccc] is a body that has of course many other interests represented than the HMI, it is a matter of some surprise to me to find that the chairman of that body should be the Secretary of the Scottish Education Department. This seems to me to be an unusual arrangement. The effect of all this is that we find the HMI committing themselves in these published reports to policies that may be overturned by a change of government [*ibid.*, Q.273-4].

Brunton himself dismissed Inglis' criticisms, when we raised them, invoking instead the traditional claim that the Department led because it was expected to do so:

BRUNTON. Inglis was expressing his view some twelve or thirteen years after things happened, and it is often very possible with hindsight to suggest that things might have been arranged differently. I must say that I never experienced the difficulty that he was apparently aware of, nor, so far as I know, did any other member of the Inspectorate. Back in 1955, when I became s c I, the teachers were crying out to s E D to give them a lead, and if I had not tried to do it I believe, frankly, that no lead would have been given.

Nevertheless, the 1968 critique seems to have struck home for, in the following year, the c c c's first triennial report attempted to present the new advisory arrangements not as discontinuous, but as an unremarkable, evolutionary development leading from the Sixth Advisory Council (1942-46), through Brunton's working parties of the 1950s, to the c c c in 1965. Even so, the c c c's claim to a place in an unbroken advisory line of succession could not be authenticated without some rewriting of the history of advice. Its first triennial report referred to Ritchie's report on *Primary Education* (s E D 1946d), and also to Robertson's report on *Secondary Education* (s E D 1947b). But it conspicuously omitted to mention another of the Sixth Council's major reports, that in which McClelland had argued the case for a relaxation of Departmental control over teachers (s E D 1946d; see also chapter 11). Referring to Ritchie's and Robertson's reports, the c c c said, 'These reports . . . were the first produced by a body constituted on lines which have since become familiar, for the members of the Council were drawn from schools, universities, training colleges, education authorities and the Department'. The c c c also claimed that 'the Advisory Council confined itself to the general and did not enter upon the particular' (s E D 1969b, 8).

'Not so', was Robertson's riposte in 1969, in one of a series of articles in which he, Dewar and Inglis attacked the reorganisation of advice:

ROBERTSON. Not so: the Department supplied the Secretary and the Assistant Secretary to the council, but it had neither member nor assessor on it. . . . The next paragraph of the first [c c c] report tells us that 'the advisory council confined itself to the general and did not enter upon the particular'. What does this mean? Of the 120 pages of the *Report on Primary Education* (1946) fifty are devoted to the subjects of the curriculum; of the 150 pages of the *Report on Secondary Education* (1947) seventy are similarly devoted to the curriculum. What does emerge by negative inference from this report on the first triennium is that s E D shows no disposition whatever to return to a council which is really representative, in the sense that its members are in the main chosen by the interests concerned [Robertson 1969b].[3]

But, on this last point, Brunton and Graham would probably have agreed. Indeed, the first triennial report of the c c c cleverly and correctly claims

Brunton's first major working party (on the curriculum of the senior-secondary school; see chapter 4) as 'the kind which is now accepted as the normal pattern'. Here the CCC emphasised, of course, not Brunton's careful selection of individuals, but the fact that this working party had brought together 'a widely representative and experienced group of educationists' (SED 1969b, 8). In fact the group was not representative of Scottish teachers; nor were the teachers who subsequently became involved in the various committees of the CCC, especially in its first decade (see chapter 17). Nevertheless, the CCC urged that 'all the partners in the education system must be involved locally as well as nationally', and it thanked those who had 'made a reality of the idea of partnership which the Committee embodies' (*ibid.*, 6). Subsequently, the Scottish Office presented the committees of the CCC to the general public as 'representative of practising teachers', and it described the members of a major CCC committee as 'representing a wide variety of educational, industrial and community interests' (SO 1977).

The CCC under Graham

Graham himself told us that the CCC mostly 'worked as a unit, and ideas developed in discussion'. He had, nevertheless, thought it worth his while to chair the CCC and, on one occasion in 1972, had threatened to resign the chair when he objected to the way the discussion was going. We discussed his chairmanship with him:

Q. Isn't one consequence of having the CCC chaired by the Secretary that it would be difficult to consider policies – or react indeed to Ministerial policies – adversely?

GRAHAM. I can only say that I don't remember any difficulties of this sort. The essential function of the chairman was to conduct the business and keep the committee moving, and not to express educational views.

Q. Who initiates business in the CCC?

GRAHAM. Anybody. Any member.

Q. Was it within the remit of the CCC to ask the broader question of the viability of ROSLA?

GRAHAM. It wasn't within its remit, because that wasn't what it was set up to do. Raising the school-leaving age was decided by Ministers as a matter of policy, just as comprehensive reorganisation was decided as a matter of policy.

Q. This was a much tighter remit than the remit that Brunton would have wanted for it originally.

GRAHAM. I have no idea what Brunton would have wanted for it originally.

Brunton, it will be recalled (see chapter 4), had told us:

BRUNTON. I thought of it, if you like, as a sort of standing advisory council with a very broad responsibility for considering the curriculum in all its aspects. The 'normal' Advisory Council was not a continuing body. A new Council was appointed from time to time and given a remit to consider particular questions.

Q. Whereas your envisaged C C C would have had a continuous life and initiated its own problems?

BRUNTON. Yes.

Dickson confirmed that Brunton had argued within the Department for a C C C along these lines, and he told us that he had 'always assumed' that Graham had taken the chair in order to ensure that the C C C's views 'had a real channel into the administration'. He also thought that Graham could easily distance the Department from the C C C's advice, should he so wish, by having the C C C set up its own committees. When we put Brunton's model to them, Clark and Dewar also agreed that this was their recollection of how Brunton had envisaged the C C C. Brunton himself told us that he thought the C C C had developed 'to some extent at least, as a Departmental committee, partly because the Secretary of the Department, who is not an educationist, is its chairman'. He also said that he doubted 'the effectiveness of its advice on such major problems as those posed by the raising of the leaving age or the development of comprehensive education'. In the 1950s, by contrast, opinion within the Department had seen both of these issues as candidates for discussion by a new Advisory Council (see chapter 11).

James Clark was a member of the second C C C (1968-71). We asked him about Graham's chairmanship:

CLARK. I think if the C C C had been a body with an independent chairman, some of the discussions, inevitably, would have taken a different course. I think that Sir Norman Graham, by virtue of his position, was conscious of government and political policy; was very conscious of the resource angle; and (and I'm not being critical of him here) inevitably, I think, because he knew of these, in a sense, he had a different opinion of what the C C C should be recommending, than might have been the case had there been a completely independent chairman, who was going to report, from a body, on a specific educational issue. . . . I think that with C C C proposals, having Norman Graham there, knowing the political and financial background, it was much less likely that there would not be Departmental or Secretary of State support for whatever came forward from the C C C.

Dickson agreed with us that the C C C had initially dealt with 'relatively simple and straightforward things', but thought the benefit to the C C C of its exercising influence through the chair was worth the price of silence on the educational implications of major policy issues.

Even within the circumscribed remit allowed by Graham, the first two Committees (1965-68 and 1968-71) showed little inclination to fulfil the formal purpose of the C C C by developing thinking on broad areas of curriculum. Eventually, of course, a committee of the C C C under James Munn was to elaborate principles for a 'balanced' education for fourteen- to sixteen-year-olds (S E D 1977c). But Munn's committee started its work only after Graham had retired, and in circumstances to which we will shortly come. Graham did not think it was his own job to express 'educational views' from the chair of the ccc, and he lacked a professional background in education. Perhaps these were contributory factors. But if so, they were not the only ones. Graham may or may not have valued general educational thinking. But he did value resource management, and there is good evidence that the Department viewed curriculum balance in the 1960s, not so much as a problem of philosophy, as of resources. The Department was making a major effort on the Staffing Survey (see chapter 10). From this perspective, there was little purpose in curricular prescriptions that would only founder on the inequities of the distribution of teachers between schools and between authorities (sed 1969a, 36-9; sed 1975a, 9).

Nor did Graham want the ccc itself to absorb excessive resources, and this too inhibited the development of synoptic thinking. Graham wanted less *ad hoc*ing, but he was equally clear that the solution was not to 'shadow' every area of the curriculum with a subject committee and an associated development activity. That way inefficiency lay, and the creation of permanent new bureaucracies. Thus the first ccc had only one committee to deal with the whole of primary education, the argument being that a sector that had recently been reviewed (sed 1965b) had a lower claim on committee resources. Curriculum review, in other words, was seen as a finite activity. The Department did accept that it must support some of the development work that followed reviews, and four curriculum-development centres for science, mathematics, English and modern languages, were created in the colleges between 1967 and 1971. But, under Graham, it was never accepted that all subjects should have committees, or that there should be a development centre corresponding to each subject committee. Moreover, Graham also regarded the work of the development centres as finite. By 1973 he was asking, waspishly, whether the time had not now come to close them down, or at least to consolidate them into a single national centre. In 1986, Crawley took a similar line (sed 1986).

As mentioned, the first two cccs did not manage the central committees nor the development centres. Thus subject committee was separate from development centre, and the ccc from both. This loose articulation must have made it difficult for information on the curriculum to flow from the schools to ccc members on a systematic and comprehensive basis. By contrast, members of the Examination Board could systematically monitor the examined curriculum through the routine work of the Board's subject panels. Comparable information on curriculum could flow to the ccc only through the Inspectorate. Thus a general review of curriculum would always require a special effort, and priority treatment from both Secretary and Senior Chief Inspector. We raised this with David Dickson:

Q. How seriously did the ccc try to take its remit to review the whole curriculum in its early years? One's impression is that it operated very much on a subject basis.

DICKSON. Yes, I think this is fair. I think it would have been too much to expect it to do the whole curriculum at the start of its career.

Q. Do you not think it needed a different intelligence service?

DICKSON. It would have had to be set up in an entirely different kind of way. This is becoming almost an Advisory Council type of consideration.

Q. Where was the information coming from?

DICKSON. The information about what was going on in the schools came from the Inspectorate.

Q. How useful was the Statistics Branch of the SED?

DICKSON. At that stage it was just beginning to develop.

And this was how the second CCC described its attempts to review the whole curriculum, fully six years after the decisive move towards comprehensive reorganisation:

> As a first step in looking at the shape of the secondary curriculum as a whole a sub-committee of members was set up. . . . The conclusion of the sub-committee was that it was too early to consider the shape and balance of the curriculum generally since individual subjects had not all received the same degree of attention from the point of view of curricular reform. (SED 1972b, 5 and 6)

Of course, in a world of changing knowledge, piecemeal curriculum development could never have brought all subjects to a comparable point of development, if there is such a thing, at any one time. If this were always to be a pre-condition to overall review, that review would never take place. Why did it?

The CCC and the Examination Board

This brings us to what was, perhaps, the single most important problem faced by the CCC under Graham, and to the key to the changes in the CCC's structure, functions and ambitions that rapidly followed his retiral. By the late 1960s, the school system was feeling the expansionist consequences of the 1955 decision to introduce the O-grade examination. The issues of overexamination, curriculum balance and course difficulty were growing in importance. The O-grade had been designed for the most able thirty per cent or so of pupils. Now that it was being attempted by half the age-group, a majority of examinees was failing all or a majority of its examinations (Gray *et al.*, 1983, ch.5). The same trends that exacerbated these problems, however, tilted the balance of influence over curriculum further in favour of the Examination Board, and away from the CCC. The initial intention had been that the CCC should not, for the most part, concern itself with certificate pupils. But, in 1964, such pupils had still been expected to constitute only about a third of the third-year, secondary-school population. Graham put it like this:

GRAHAM. That, I would accept, was a legitimate function, a proper function, of the CCC, to look at the curriculum at the top end of the school. But, as you know, in the formative years they concentrated to a great extent on the curriculum at the lower end of the secondary school.

But, by the time the first CCC issued its Report in 1969, doubts were setting in, and there was friction with the Examination Board:

> In the higher classes of secondary schools the content of the curriculum is in practice largely shaped by the syllabuses for the examination for the Scottish Certificate of Education issued by the Scottish Certificate of Education Examination Board. . . .
>
> The Consultative Committee's interests are wider than those of the Board and the Committee recognised that it bears the prime responsibility for advice on the content of school courses. But there are curricular questions in which the Examination Board is directly concerned and a strict demarcation is not possible. Broad questions affecting the secondary curriculum, for example, the introduction of new subjects or groups of subjects, should be for the Curriculum Committee to consider in the first instance. On the other hand, it is the Board's duty to consider initially all questions arising on existing examinations. The Examination Board accepts that in general the external examinations should reflect and be based upon the work of the schools and should not dictate it. The measure of common membership between the Examination Board and the Consultative Committee helps to ensure that each body is kept in touch with those activities of the other which concerns it. (SED 1969b, 5 and 11)

We asked Graham about this interpretation:

Q. I'm wondering about the sentence, 'It's the Board's duty to consider initially all questions arising on existing examinations'. Looking at the Statute and regulations, I couldn't see that interpretation . . . there is no reference to whether or not the Board had the power to initiate examinations where that would involve the initiation of a new curriculum in a secondary school. Am I right and, if so, was this an understanding that was reached between the CCC and the Board in informal discussion at some point after the regulations were drawn up?

GRAHAM. The passage you read seemed to me to be trying to say that, where the CCC had not operated, which at that time was true of considerable areas of the existing curriculum, it was for the Board to cope with the situation that we had, and to set whatever examination in, say, Higher English, seemed to them appropriate, given the curriculum as it had been. If you come now to some subject that was not in the existing curriculum – I remember, for example, pressure for an examination in geology – this doctrine meant that it was for the CCC to consider whether and to what extent geology was an appropriate subject in the school curriculum, and then, in the light of what the CCC concluded and what response there was from the schools, it was for the Board to construct an appropriate examination in geology.

As it happened, Dewar had raised this very instance in our earlier interview with him:

DEWAR. One particular connection where this difficulty became prominent was in my endeavour to have a paper instituted in geology. . . . As far as I was concerned geology was something that was on the doorstep of the children up in the Highland rural secondary schools. . . . Now this should have been something for the Board itself to decide. . . . I pleaded from the very beginning – oddly enough I was just reading a minute last evening on this . . . for a clarification of where the CCC influence and scope ended and where ours began; and I think one of the reasons . . . why I did not get a positive and firm answer was that the Board was there by law. . . . The Board was instituted by the 1963 Act and, if the terms of that Act were observed, there was no doubt in my mind that *we* had the responsibility. Now the CCC was not set up directly from an Act. It is, if you like, an offshoot to reflect the Secretary of State's power to make regulations and report. It stems indirectly from an Act, and I could never get a definition of the areas of responsibility. In fact, there are minutes of meetings between ourselves and the Department on this and other matters. I of course was present at all of them as Convener of the Examinations Committee. At a certain meeting I had the particular purpose of seeking the definition. . . . Projected developments should never, in my opinion, have been put to a subordinate body like the CCC. They should not have had power to stop us from getting on with the job but they were doing it.

Graham himself dismissed Dewar's interpretation:

GRAHAM. Subordinate to whom?

Q. Dewar is making the point that the Board was established by statute, and, I think, he was drawing the inference from that, that in some sense it was superordinate.

GRAHAM. Not to the Secretary of State. . . . The Secretary of State just set it [the CCC] up. The Secretary of State could get his advice wherever he liked surely. No Secretary of State would have accepted that he was subordinate in any way to the Examination Board.

It remains unclear, however, whether the CCC was subordinate to the Examination Board in matters in which the Secretary of State was not directly involved. One presumes that much depended on what the CCC was saying on particular issues, and on how closely, in consequence, the Secretary of State wished his authority to be associated with the body that was saying it. How had James Clark seen this issue?

Q. You occupied an interesting position, because you were on both the CCC and the Examination Board.

CLARK. Yes. . . . My view was that once the CCC had been established, it seemed to me that if a request was made to the Exam Board for a new examination, as in geology, that, in courtesy, the Exam Board should have immediately remitted that to the CCC.

Q. And that was the view that you took in the Board as well, was it?

CLARK. This was my view, yes.

Q. In that case, you differed from Dewar's interpretation.

CLARK. Yes.

Q. How did the Exam Board divide on this issue? Was Dewar alone?

CLARK. Oh no, I don't think so, not by any manner of means.

Q. It had a statutorily defined competence?

CLARK. Yes, I agree with you that that is important. It was competent for the Exam Board to do this.

Geology may only have been one subject, but it focused the constitutional issue, and acted as an irritant out of all proportion to its importance. Here is Graham:

GRAHAM. It would be unreal for the Examination Board, quite apart from the physical load that they would be imposing on themselves and those who work for them, to go on endlessly proliferating subjects just because some school in some part of Scotland, or some teacher fancied an examination and would like to put his pupils in for an examination in some subject that nobody had thought of before.

If nothing more, geology was a reminder to the SED that members of the Examination Board could be inconveniently independent, as indeed people like Dewar and Clark were also proving in their resistance to the proposal favoured by the Secretary of State for banding the O-grade. But the fundamental problem for the CCC was that the expansion of certification was eroding its area of undisputed competence, and was rapidly overturning curricular initiatives to which it had lent its diminishing authority. These initiatives included schemes for curriculum centred on Brunton's 'vocational impulse'; Ruthven's attempts to preserve a non-examined area of curriculum for certificate and non-certificate pupils alike (SED 1967b); and attempts to develop and timetable integrated courses, and also new courses, for ROSLA pupils (SED 1966c). The CCC had championed each of these, and in each case the initiative had soon faltered (SED 1975a, 9), thereby weakening the authority of the CCC and of the Inspectorate presence behind it.

Bruce Millan was junior Minister at the time, with responsibility for education:

MILLAN. You see, we were accused at that time – going back to the raising of the school-leaving age – of having done no work on courses for the fourth year, and so on. This was quite untrue, because . . . the Inspectorate (I think it actually was a subcommittee of the CCC, or at least issued under the auspices of the CCC) issued guidance on suggestions for courses for the raising of the school-leaving age [SED 1966c]. I remember that the inspectors had innumerable meetings with directors, principal teachers, and subject advisers, and so on . . . but to get the thinking down to the school level to people who are actually going to have to do it, is really very difficult.

We asked Graham:

Q. To what extent could the Board have done anything about the explosion of O-grade presentations? Was this discussed between the CCC and the Board?

GRAHAM. No. The CCC did not concern itself with examinations.

And we asked Clark how the CCC reacted:

Q. Was there an awareness on the CCC in the late 1960s that things like the Ruthven proposal, and the paper on the raising of the school-leaving age, were just going to be pushed out by the O-grade explosion?

CLARK. Yes.

Q. How did you handle the sense of powerlessness that this implied?

CLARK. I was involved, in the Exam Board, in the discussion about O-grade banding and so on, which I opposed. But the CCC as such didn't make representations to the Exam Board about this. The feeling of, if you like, helplessness was much more at the local level. . . . I was not involved, as a member of the CCC, in making any representations to the Exam Board. I did speak in the Exam Board – as did Hugh Fairlie [Director of Education, Renfrewshire 1964-75] – about the extension of the O-grade, and particularly when the proposal for banding was put up, which I thought was deplorable.

Concern over the diminishing authority of the CCC led in 1970 to the appointment of a CCC working party on *The Communication and Implementation of Aims in Secondary Education*. Its conclusion was pessimistic:

> At the levels of Directors, Advisers and Headteachers (but certainly at no lower level), [the CCC's] work was recognised, without perhaps having undue weight attached to it. As the national curriculum advisory body, the Committee had failed to make any impact further down the school, its triennial report was unknown and it tended to be identified either as an agency of the Department or as yet another outside body imposing demands on the profession without proper consultation. . . . Not surprisingly in view of its highly developed system of communications the Examination Board emerged as the leading communicator in the field, although it was asserted that communication took place in one direction only. It was generally accepted as the major determinant in curriculum change, and as one whose decisive voice cast further doubt on the functions of the Consultative Committee. (CCC 1974, 6-7)

On the Threshold of Change

It was early in 1974 that the CCC heard its subcommittee's confirmation that CCC influence was approaching a nadir. What should be done? Within the Scottish Office, the role of the Inspectorate had come under critical scrutiny (see chapter 7). Outside, the Examination Board was more bullish than ever. It was continuing to insist on its right to introduce a geology examination, and it was pressing the Secretary of State to set up a major review of certification policy in third and fourth year. If that review were established, and if it were eventually to adopt the EIS proposal for near-universal certification, the marginalisation of the CCC would be completed, and the hold of the Inspectorate further weakened.

There were, broadly, three ways in which the CCC could act to increase its influence. One was to accede to the EIS demand for the direct representation of teachers on the CCC and on its infrastructure of committees. Bryden had not wanted a Schools Council in Scotland. His successor as General Secretary of the EIS was John Pollock, an Ayrshire teacher and election agent for William Ross. Pollock was a CCC member from 1968 to 1976. He argued on the CCC that stronger teacher representation and more consultation would make it more effective. Neither the Chairman, nor the rest of the CCC as a whole, seems to have supported him.

A second alternative was to build stronger links to the local authorities, and thence to the schools. But, in his last year as chairman of the CCC, Graham resisted the argument that curriculum development by the new regional authorities that were shortly to be created might best be promoted by changing the 'top-down' structure of the CCC. Nor could the Inspectorate have been happy at the further erosion of their power that was implied by the prospect of larger local authorities with an active involvement in curriculum.

The third solution, and the one which was adopted, was to give the CCC itself an executive capacity, a job of work to do. In many people's view, Dewar's for example and Dickson's, its purely advisory function was a weakness. Graham had wanted to keep advice separate from execution, linking them through the CCC chair. However, a CCC subcommittee that he had asked to examine the curriculum development centres concluded after his retiral that they should be made directly responsible to the CCC.

The emergence of the Munn Committee in the same year was also a response to the growing dominance of the Examination Board. As we have seen, the second CCC (1968-71) showed little inclination to address general curricular problems. Nor did the third CCC until early in 1974 when it considered a paper from its Central Committee on Science (SCCMSTE 1975). Did the paper's proposals for more science simply require a reaffirmation of the disregarded Ruthven report; or was a broader review of third and fourth years necessary? What tipped the decision in favour of a general review was the news that Clark, Fairlie and others on the Examination Board were likely to succeed in their demand for a general review of certification and assessment. At all costs, the CCC argued, it must influence that review. Initially the CCC envisaged a short exercise, lasting a matter of months, to feed into the deliberations of the committee on certification. But a small and hasty exercise could easily have been swept aside by a more powerful review body. The Munn Committee on curriculum was given a standing similar to that of the Dunning Committee on assessment, and a similarly broad remit. Munn remained a committee of the CCC, whilst Dunning was detached from the Board. But the two memberships were overlapped, and in this way the Department began to reassert an influence over curriculum that had all but slipped away.

The Department and the Inspectorate reserved for themselves the major contribution to the development programme that followed the Munn and Dunning reports, adopting what the CCC was to describe in 1984 as 'a leadership role with the CCC and other national bodies as partners' (CCC 1984, 3). But the leaders got too far ahead of their other partners, the teachers. The burden of curriculum development the teachers were asked to carry within the national programme was a major factor in precipitating the longest-ever period of industrial action by teachers. Late in 1986 there was a question mark over the future of the Standard Grade examination that had been developed from the Munn and Dunning reports and examined for the first time in that year. The wheel had turned full circle in the twenty-five years since the strike of 1961.

Summary and Discussion

The political salience of curriculum issues increased in the 1960s, and comprehensive reorganisation posed fundamental questions concerning what should be taught, at what level of difficulty, to which pupils, and in what manner. The need for practical answers that could be made to work in the schools became even more urgent with the approach of ROSLA. In the CCC, Scotland established a national body that was intended to keep the whole school curriculum under continuous review, and to promote its development. In its first decade, however, the CCC had only a marginal impact on what the schools taught, and it shrank from synoptic review and prescription. When competition from the Examination Board eventually obliged it to prescribe, it gave a seal of philosophical approval to existing practice and, with one exception, made only marginal suggestions for change.[4] The exception was that the academically derived, non-vocational, subject-based curriculum that had emerged from the downward incrementation of certification since the 1950s, was now recommended for extension to all pupils in the new context of assessment for all.

The expansion of certification was one reason, perhaps the major reason, why the Examination Board made the running on curriculum after 1965. But the way the CCC was constituted was a contributory factor, and one which, arguably, left its imprint on the educational philosophy at which the CCC belatedly arrived. In constituting the CCC, the Department struck a compromise between two considerations, one new and one old. The newer consideration was the representation of teachers on advisory bodies that were located close to the executive functions of the administration and Inspectorate. Some concession in this direction had been forced on the Department by the turbulence of the early 1960s, but it was still anxious not to give away too much. The older consideration was that curriculum change should be Departmentally led. The teachers' 'penetration of the centre' had proved less decisive than had for a time seemed likely in the early 1960s (see chapters 11 and 12). Nevertheless, the Department still wished to keep teachers' contributions individual rather than corporate, advisory rather than executive, and well distanced from the central mechanisms of curriculum development and control. It would be a bonus if the activities of the new advisory body on curriculum were accepted as representative of teachers' interests.

Other than the Inspectorate and the national certificate, however, the main central mechanism for curriculum development in 1965 was nothing more than a piecemeal and underdeveloped collection of *ad hoc* committees, run separately by the Department. Graham wanted less *ad hoc*ing, but no fundamental change either in the nature of these committees, or in the scale of their activity. He did not want subject-constituencies to grow, or to acquire new or larger committees at the centre that might promote their separate subjects in proliferating and competitive development. Over at the Examination Board, every certificated subject was managed by a panel that was in turn responsible to the Board. But the ccc under Graham lacked an organisational infrastructure that could provide an analogous monitoring function across the curriculum. There was, of course, the Inspectorate. But the influence of the Inspectorate was contracting with the expansion of certification. Departmental administrators hoped to recapture the ground they had lost to Brunton. And the authority of the Inspectorate was itself still rooted in subject-expertise. All in all, the ccc in the first decade was not a configuration that was likely to produce the new and synoptic curricular thinking that would answer the questions posed by comprehensive reorganisation and rosla.

If the Department under Graham were suspicious of professional self-aggrandisement at the centre, whether by teachers or inspectors, what of initiatives at the level of the local authority and the school? Here, too, events in and around the Examination Board were important. Clark, we recall, thought that only the Examination Board, of the agencies then extant, could provide the wider context required for the development of local curricular initiatives along the lines of cse Mode iii. But the internal, teacher-led, assessment that characterised this mode of certification was never considered by the Board, for a variety of reasons (see chapter 13).

That said, aspects of the ccc's structure and location may also have inhibited local initiatives. As the Department began to learn from its survey of staffing (see chapter 10), it arguably gave resource considerations priority over issues of curriculum content, philosophy and method. The local authorities had not responded as the Department would have wished to its attempts in the 1960s to reduce area staffing disparities. Why then encourage curricular thinking that would shift the initiative to the local authorities and the schools? To allow favoured schools and authorities to establish their own staffing needs in the light of a locally determined curricular philosophy could well have sharpened area staffing disparities, especially if that philosophy increased the individual teachers' role in assessment and certification, and thereby increased the case for more teachers. Indeed, when CSE Mode III did develop in some areas of Scotland from the mid-1970s on, the prime movers were two of the new regional authorities with staffing standards well above the national average. Moreover, an Inspectorate that was anxious to regain its influence over the curriculum produced a number of local and national evaluations in the early 1970s that were highly critical of teachers' and authorities' responses to the curricular challenge of ROSLA. The unspoken assertion of this critique was the need for a strong Inspectorate lead, but Clark, in particular, criticised the Inspectorate for misrepresenting the record of his own education authority.[5] The Inspectorate argued also that the substantial expansion of promoted posts in 1974 had absorbed the energies and ambitions of teachers who had previously been active in local curriculum development (SED 1975a, 9). Clark told us that the creation of the new national fringe bodies in the 1960s had had similar effects, drawing attention and action towards the centre, and away from the school and classroom.

Precisely what Graham's influence was, as chairman of the CCC, we cannot say. But we do know that staffing and resource considerations were his main concern as Secretary, that he communicated these concerns regularly to the CCC, and that, in Clark's view at least, the chair had a significant influence on the direction of discussions. In the late 1950s Departmental officials had mooted, but deferred, the possibility of a remit to the Advisory Council on comprehensive schools. Graham himself was clear, however, that comprehensive reorganisation and ROSLA had been decided in the 1960s as matters of national policy, and were not for discussion by advisory bodies. In the early 1970s, he resisted an internal attempt on the CCC to strengthen the representation of teachers along the lines of the Schools Council in England. And he was also unsympathetic to an internal attempt to get the CCC to restructure itself so as to promote greater curricular initiatives by the new regional authorities after 1975. Synoptic review and educational philosophising rose in the CCC's priorities only when its declining authority was threatened by the prospect of a separate, national review of certification that might confirm the Examination Board in its new-found role. This also was the point at which the Department restructured the CCC, giving it direct authority over the curriculum development service, a budget of its own, and a new committee structure that shadowed the curriculum more comprehensively than Graham had allowed (Humes 1986, ch.5).

We are unable to say how the Department handled the implications of the restructuring for its own control of the CCC. But it may be of some significance that the restructuring was effected only after Graham's retiral, and under his 'stop-gap' successor, Martin Fearn, whom Dewar told us was a weak chairman. What can be said, however, is that the restructured CCC, allied to the development programme that followed the Munn and Dunning reports, gave the Inspectorate fresh scope for its activities, and fuelled administrative resentment of professionally initiated educational developments that were careless of resource implications (see chapter 7). In 1979, the Scottish Office offered up the CCC for a Rayner scrutiny, and later made its case to Peter Rendle, the retired Scottish Office administrator who reviewed the Inspectorate in 1980-81. Deep cuts in the Inspectorate were proposed (SO 1981, para.14.5 p to v).

The threat was evaded only because of a new and unexpected factor. The new Conservative Government of 1979 was the first of its party to show an active Ministerial interest in Scottish educational policy (see chapter 8). In offering support for new Government initiatives in the sixteen-to-nineteen area, the Inspectorate was keen to win assurances of continuing Ministerial support for Inspectorate-led development towards the new Standard Grade Certificate at sixteen years. The Inspectorate was in a strong position, essentially because the Government had to do something about youth unemployment when the British youth labour-market collapsed in the early 1980s. But here the mediation of British policies by the Scottish Office was a factor. The British solution to recession was sought through education and training. In England, the Manpower Services Commission (MSC) became a major competitor of the DES in central provision for these functions. But, in Scotland, the threat that the MSC posed to the territorial competence of the Scottish Office produced the 1983 *Action Plan* from the SED (SED 1983a; Donaldson 1986). The Plan gave the SED a major influence over all education and training for young persons between sixteen and eighteen years (the upper limit of eighteen was later dropped). The allegiance of Scottish Ministers and officials to the Scottish tier of government proved stronger than administrators' hostility to the aggrandisement of education professionals (Allen 1984; Raffe 1984b). Despite recession, the expansion of provision continued, giving the Inspectorate some respite from attack. But the respite was only temporary. The teachers' industrial action that started in 1984 was commonly attributed to Inspectorate misjudgements over the pace of development towards the implementation of the Standard Grade. The message for the Inspectorate was clear, if by now familiar. What gave it a new edge, however, was the appointment late in 1986 of John MacKay as junior Minister with responsibility for education. MacKay was formerly a teacher, and was reputed to have something less than unreserved admiration for an Inspectorate that had at one time inspected him.

Finally, we may comment briefly on some of the implications of this chapter for other accounts of educational policy-making. We mentioned that the CCCS group treated the growth of CSE Mode III in England in the 1960s as a consequence of concessions that the state was obliged to make to a profession whose function it saw as that of containing social disorder in, and through, the schools (cccs 1981, 124). The threat of disorder was feared no less in Scotland, and teachers were no less influential at the centre, where they won the GTC. Yet CSE Mode III, and the prospect of similar courses in the future, appeared in Scotland only from the mid-1970s on, and then as a result of initiatives by the new regional education authorities. In other words, the scale, nature and timing of changes in British curricular practice were mediated by governmental structures and processes. In Scotland contradictions and instabilities within the central government of education did more to influence curricular stability and change than did some wider threat of social disorder. Also important was the growth of national fringe bodies. These offered a new arena for teacher activity and ambition and, in Clark's view, contributed to a withering of local teacher initiatives. This is not to deny that the Department's curricular thinking in the 1940s and 1950s could be described as statist (see chapter 11). Nor is it to suggest that the practical outcomes of reforms after 1965 give the statist thesis no purchase. It is, however, to give some support to Salter and Tapper's argument that educational policy formation is increasingly encapsulated within a governmental setting, and mediated by it (see chapter 1).

Archer, too, is helpful here (by 'internal initiation' in the following passage she means change initiated by teachers):

> Professional Associations in centralized systems have much less freedom to respond directly to community or student demands. Thus their internal initiation is heavily constrained by the traditional academic definition of instruction enshrined in official examinations. This means that the changes they can introduce are those broadly compatible with it, and these innovations thus tend to be matters of concern to the profession but of indifference to the polity. In brief this has spelt academicization in both teaching and research, a concentration on pure knowledge which, while politically uncontentious, canalized expansion in one direction alone. In consequence the main effect of Internal Initiation was a prolongation of studies: more and more pupils were pushed upwards into academic options, a situation which Bourdieu has likened to everyone being treated as an apprentice professor rather than as a professional apprentice. As a process mediating between education and society, Internal Initiation was a force for the intellectualization of demand rather than a response to stated requirements in centralized systems. (Archer 1982, 29-30)

This general statement applies rather well to the development of the Scottish secondary curriculum since comprehensive reorganisation. External certification continued to inhibit the development of alternative bodies of educational practice that might carry conviction with Scottish teachers, despite their efforts at initiation, and despite the example of their English counterparts. The Scottish polity remained broadly indifferent to curricular issues (see chapter 16), though this was true, the cccs group argue, of the English polity as well (see chapter 1). Another characteristic that Archer deduces from centralised styles of control is also apposite. This is the concern of the central authority to achieve local control by specifying in great detail the conditions of local practice. A case in point is the modularisation, under the Action Plan, of much of the Scottish post-sixteen curriculum into forty-hour units defined largely from the centre.

Tinged though it was by statism, centralisation and encapsulation, Scottish curriculum development in the 1960s and 1970s can, nevertheless, also be described as pluralist. The curriculum was a piecemeal and disjointed product of conflicts between, on the one hand, the facilities and constraints inherent in certification and, on the other, a variety of national and local philosophies and practices. As a policy process this conforms in three respects to Kogan's understanding of pluralism. First, school practice was a powerful determinant of policy, even though the nature of the changes produced by 'internal initiation' was constrained by the 'traditional academic definition of instruction enshrined in official examinations'. Second, some change did increment, but disjointedly so. Third, in Munn and Dunning the attempt was made to impose rationality after the event and, in Kogan's analysis, the retrospective imposition of rationality is also a feature of pluralism. Nevertheless, the educational reality that emerged from this attempt in the 1980s departed from the original intentions of the reform, and was itself contested.

NOTES
1. 'It would still be appropriate for the Department and for the associations to bring under discussion . . . general matters relating to the Scottish Certificate of Education, including educational trends revealed by examination results, etc.' (sed 1962b, para.33).
2. See Sir Henry Wood's oral evidence to the 1968 Select Committee on the Inspectorate (sces 1968, q.219). Also, the first ccc stated: 'neither the Secretary of State nor the Scottish Education Department, has any direct responsibility for the school curriculum. Education authorities (and other bodies who manage schools), acting with the advice of the heads of their schools and their teachers, decide what shall, or shall not, be taught in their schools (subject to the statutory requirements for the provision of instruction in religion) and it is for them to decide whether or not to accept any advice which is offered to them' (sed 1969b, 5). Sir James Munn, chairman of the ccc, advanced similar arguments about curriculum development in 1985 (Munn 1985).
3. In fact, local-authority and director-of-education members of the Sixth Council were appointed without nomination, though the teachers' associations were invited to submit nominations (sro 1957b, 4 January 1957).
4. A member of the Munn Committee has described the Munn/Dunning exercise as an attempt to ensure 'that the lines of future development would be dictated by a professional consensus', and by 'what teachers can be persuaded to accept' (Kirk 1982, 92 and 105). Antecedents of the curriculum recommended by Munn are to be found in the proposals made by the scre in 1931 (scre 1931),

by the Sixth Advisory Council (SED 1947b), and by the 'Ruthven' Committee of the CCC (SED 1967b). Darling (1978), McIntyre (1978) and Drever *et al.* (1983) provide a critique of Munn and Dunning, and Kirk (1978, 1982) an explanation and defence. Brown and Munn (1985) and Simpson (1986) describe some subsequent developments in practice.

5. See the 1976 review of ROSLA (SED 1976b), and also the Inspectorate's criticisms of Aberdeen (SED 1975b) and Lanarkshire (SED 1977e). Clark told us that he had very strong feelings about the report: 'I think that the Aberdeen report was not a fair reflection. . . . I said so. I wrote to the Department about it, and I got a brief acknowledgement of my letter, and nothing further. . . . I think there should be a forum in which they [the Inspectorate] have to defend, and, if need be, produce evidence for what they say'.

Fifteen

Selective and Comprehensive Schooling 1945–65

I think there is a lot of misunderstanding about this, and a lot of
myth as well. People seem to think that before Circular 600 [in
1965] we had a pretty-well comprehensive system in Scotland
anyway. This is just utterly untrue. We had a selective system in
Scotland, as they did south of the Border.   Bruce Millan, Secretary of State for Scotland 1976-79

Introduction

In the organisation of secondary schooling after 1945, and in its later
reorganisation along comprehensive lines, we see much of the policy process
in action. Schools were a point of 'service delivery', and the distribution of
resources to them was influenced by the various national and local factors
reviewed earlier. These included the boundaries and standing of education
relative to other policy areas; Ministerial priorities and style; relations
between politicians, officials and educationists, both nationally and locally;
and relations between the central and local authorities themselves. But
schools are more than mere sites for the onward transmission of resources.
They, and the communities they serve, compete with each other for resources and status, and most seek to influence the mechanisms of resource
distribution to their own advantage. Schools are also a point where policy
and practice meet, and where differing aims are contested. In their school
and classroom practice, teachers may oppose or misinterpret directives and
advice coming from outside, or else transmute them; and so too may pupils,
sometimes through classroom confrontation, but more often through the
expedient of withdrawal, either as truants or as early leavers. As we said in
chapter 2, one of the main motors of policy change throughout the twentieth
century has been the stubborn refusal of pupils to start on courses thought
proper to their intellectual level, and to complete the courses they started.

 As a major issue, perhaps the major educational issue of the period after
1945, selective and comprehensive schooling is a proving-ground for
theories of educational policy-making. Kogan (1975, 231-3) and Archer
(1979, 589-95) find in comprehensive reorganisation in England a pluralist
and indeterminate interplay between policy and practice, centre and
periphery. The Centre for Contemporary Cultural Studies group regard
comprehensive schooling as a further instance of the capitulation of the left

to the ideology and practice of 'statist' schooling (CCCS 1981, 127-9). 'Correspondence' theorists emphasise the contribution made by intelligence testing and selection to the legitimation of ideologies of leadership and social inequality that favoured capitalism (Bowles and Gintis 1976, ch.4).

What light does Scottish experience throw on these issues? And what do we learn about policy-making in Scotland from the history of its school organisation? These are the themes of this chapter and the next. In this chapter we first of all set the scene by analysing the pre-1945 inheritance of schools and ideas. Then, taking our examples initially from Fife, we show how this inheritance influenced the local authorities' construction of a new system of universal, bipartite secondary education. The story then moves back to the national level, where we examine the failure of the SED's attempts to reform junior-secondary schooling. Finally, we explore this failure at local level, and show the emerging criticism of the bipartite policy in Aberdeen and Lanarkshire. The concluding discussion assesses the implications of these events for models of policy, before the narrative continues in the next chapter with the national emergence of the move for comprehensive reform.

The Inheritance of Institutions and Ideas

When the school-leaving age was raised to fifteen years in 1947, there were over 900 public secondary schools in Scotland. Some thirty of these were grant-aided by central government; they selected their pupils, and almost all charged fees. A number of local-authority schools also charged fees, or had primary departments that did so. They also selected their pupils, often giving preferential admission to pupils from the primary department. In the early 1960s, they numbered around twenty. The remaining public schools were fully maintained by the local authority, charging no fees. Altogether some 200 of the public secondary schools, including all of the grant-aided and local-authority fee-paying schools, offered six-year certificate courses. Outwith the four cities, many six-year schools also accepted pupils for non-certificate courses, and, in this sense, were not fully selective. There were also a number of private secondary schools, but only about ten were of any consequence. Figures for the mid-1960s indicate that the private sector served less than two per cent of the Scottish school population, whilst the grant-aided and local-authority fee-paying schools served about five per cent. All in all, fee-paying was more common in the cities before comprehensive reorganisation. It was especially common in Edinburgh, where fee-paying pupils in state schools constituted a quarter of pupils aged twelve, but a much higher proportion of those in post-compulsory schooling.[1] Edinburgh was exceptional but, as the capital city, and the city in which Scottish Office officials educated their own children, it was an important exception.

The post-1945 secondary system originated in several distinct stages of development that have since continued to influence school provision and policy. Two of these stages were already completed before the First World War, but the third only followed the legislation of 1945. Few new secondary schools were founded or designated between the Wars, though some efforts were made to supply deficiencies in denominational (Catholic) provision (Fitzpatrick 1986, ch.5).

Of particular importance to our story are the sixty or so 'first-generation' schools that had been recognised by the Department as secondary schools by the turn of the century.[2] Many were of early foundation, and many of high prestige. They reflected a pattern of pre-industrial provision that had failed to adapt to urbanisation; Clydeside schools and city schools were not well represented among them. Nearly all of these schools have survived. Between 1945 and 1965, all were selective in some measure, and something under half of them charged fees, either as grant-aided or local-authority schools. After reorganisation, the large majority became six-year comprehensive schools, fully maintained by the local authority. We shall see in later chapters that this first generation of schools has had a continuing influence on the thinking of the educational policy community, and on recruitment to it.

The second generation of schools operating after 1945 had taken its modern form in the first decade of this century when the Department designated approximately 200 schools as 'Higher Grade'. The Department intended these schools to supply the gaps in post-primary provision that had resulted from the nineteenth-century shift of population to the towns and cities. For a time the Department did not want them to offer a full Leaving Certificate curriculum, and it anticipated that they would, on average, attract pupils of lower social status than the first-generation schools (Anderson 1983a, 223-51). However, some local authorities, and especially Glasgow, did want their Higher Grade schools to grow into full secondary schools (Roxburgh 1971, ch.7). Later, in 1923, all Higher Grade schools that offered five-year courses were formally assimilated to full secondary status. After 1945, there were about 120 survivors that offered full certificate courses. Few charged fees.

None of these first- or second-generation schools was Catholic. Before 1918, Catholic schools received central-government grants. After 1918, the responsibility for virtually all Catholic schools was transferred to the new local authorities. This transfer, together with some additions between 1918 and 1939, gave Scotland a public sector of some 200 schools offering senior-secondary (Highers) courses at the time of the 1945 Act.

With some minor variations in number, these 200 or so schools were the only non-private schools offering five- and six-year senior-secondary courses between 1945 and 1965. When Circular 600 announced reform in 1965, it was thereby setting itself to reorganise a system in which the large majority of schools in the prestigious, senior-secondary sector had been securely in

place for at least half a century, winning the support of their local communities, building their reputations, and seeing their former pupils rise to
important positions. Twenty years after comprehensive reorganisation,
nearly all the first- and second-generation schools had become comprehensive. But they still had pupil intakes that were socially privileged, had higher
average levels of examination attainment (McPherson and Willms 1986),
and were eagerly sought after by parents (Adler 1986). Thus policy and
practice after 1945 must be understood against the background of a stratified
configuration of schools that had been shaped much earlier by the Department, and that had taken root in the life of neighbourhood, community and
profession.

After 1945, the 700 or so schools that did not offer senior-secondary
courses were commonly called junior-secondary schools, though the name
had no official standing and embraced a variety of types (SED 1952a, 27).
The junior-secondary schools had developed from the various non-secondary, post-primary institutions that the SED had encouraged through the
uncompromising bipartism of Circular 44 (see chapter 2). Especially in
populous areas, they existed as three-year schools, not because there were
insufficient pupils in the area to sustain post-compulsory certificate-course
work in economically sized units, but because policy explicitly required
them to provide an education that was shorter and different in kind.

In more scattered areas, however, the denial of six-year status to junior-
secondary schools was more a matter of resources, and less a direct consequence of the bipartite philosophy. Such schools were the only secondary
schools in their respective areas, and were often of long standing. They
normally accepted potential Highers pupils for the early years of their
secondary course, and they therefore had comprehensive intakes. They
could not provide full Highers courses, primarily because of the SED's policy
in scattered areas of centralising senior-secondary provision. School centralisation was linked to the policy of bipartism, of course, but where the
policies conflicted in scattered areas, centralisation had priority. Thus many
large towns, and many small towns and villages with their hinterland areas,
centralised all secondary provision, both for certificate and other courses, in
the one school, variously described as '*omnibus*' or 'comprehensive'. This
description was also applied to schools of this type that were fed by additional certificate pupils coming from outlying areas, usually after two years
of secondary education in local, short-course schools. In some areas, certificate pupils from outlying areas were fed into a central, senior-secondary
school that offered only certificate courses. Either way, however, the question was eventually to arise: was not the central-feeder arrangement already
comprehensive? Benn and Simon's answer was that it depended on whether
parents had a genuine choice of schools when their child reached the point
of transfer to the central, receiver school, commonly around the age of
fourteen. If so, the arrangement was comprehensive. If not, and especially

if selection were involved, the arrangement was not comprehensive (Benn and Simon 1972, 60).

The central-feeder model was not confined before 1965 to sparsely populated areas and to town-and-village settlements. It was also used in several of the relatively populous areas outside the four cities where there were sizeable Catholic minorities. Lanarkshire, Renfrewshire and Ayrshire all contain examples. In such areas, the education authority had, in effect, to provide for two separate school populations. Moreover, in some places Catholics opted for single-sex education. This further increased the number of subgroups for which provision had to be made. Localism played a part here as well. A community might not be large enough to support a six-year school; the cost of small classes in the post-compulsory stages, and especially in the sixth year, was often prohibitive. But it could argue for a local two- or three-year school, both to give focus to the community, and to save its younger secondary pupils an arduous daily journey. Later, when O-grade courses were introduced in the early 1960s and the trend towards staying-on at school began to accelerate, the case for retaining a local school was strengthened in cases where it could grow a fourth year and offer certificate courses to sizeable numbers of pupils.

The SED had been defeated by the forces of localism in the 1890s, and had struggled thereafter to rein in what it saw as the inefficient proliferation of small schools. By 1944 it had not had much success. The number of primary and secondary schools was much the same as it had been in 1918, although catering for a somewhat smaller school population. What had changed by 1944, however, was the underlying conflict between the Department and its critics over the relation of schooling to the social order. Localism remained strong, but the allied argument for an open form of secondary schooling was no longer vigorously prosecuted. At some point after the furore over Circular 44 in the early 1920s, the Department regained the advantage in its ideological battle to establish the bipartite, social-efficiency model of schooling as the legitimate descendant of the Scottish democratic tradition. More work would be required before one could put a date to the decisive shift in the balance of advantage. But, by the 1930s, the argument seems to have been less about whether there should be selective promotion to certificate courses at an early age, and more about the efficiency and the equity of the selection procedure, and the proportions that should be given an opportunity. Craik in the 1920s thought the proportion should be limited to between five and ten per cent (Craik 1926). Some of the new 'educational experts', whom he deplored, thought more. A renewed assault on selection and differentiation was to come from the Sixth Advisory Council when it recommended the *omnibus* school as 'the natural way for a democracy to order the post-primary education of a given area' (SED 1947b, para.164). But even the Council believed that, by the age of twelve, pupils differed so much in academic potential that they should be streamed for all academic work, whatever type of school they were in (*ibid.*, paras 185-90).

The contribution of the mental-testing movement to the shifting climate of opinion in the inter-war period is a matter of some dispute. To form a view we must briefly look further afield because, if the continued rumblings of the parochial schools issue were domestic, debates about intelligence testing were international. So, too, was the progressive movement in education, and leading Scottish educationists were simultaneously involved in both. Correspondence theories of education in England and the USA have understood the spread of mental testing broadly as a response of state bureaucracy to problems of social control posed by the internal contradictions of capitalism. There are various strands in the argument, all of them emphasising the interests of the state, or of an elite group or class working through the state, in removing issues of social purpose and social justice from the political agenda. Mental testing, and related scientific theories of mind, are seen as widely credited, though actually spurious, means to this end. Thus attention is drawn to the way in which intelligence testing could be used to transfer control of selection decisions from the teacher, or the parent, to the administrator or the psychologist. At the same time, it is argued, the theory of intelligence 'individualised' success and failure, diverting attention from between-group inequities in provision, and also from the culturally relative definitions of merit that favoured some groups more than others. In this context the origin of mental testing in the Victorian and Edwardian eugenics movement is seen as germane, a movement that feared that an excessively fertile, but innately inferior working class would swamp its social superiors (Torrance 1981).

A common view of the period is that the practice and ideology of mental testing came to dominate English education between the two World Wars, and largely explain the survival of the grammar school thereafter (Pedley 1963, 43; Benn and Simon 1972, ch.2). Recent scholarship has cast some doubt on this, however, emphasising the incomplete and patchy adoption of mental testing by the English local authorities during the inter-war period. Sutherland argues that selection in favour of elite groups survived precisely because English decision-making was decentralised and the penetration of intelligence testing only partial. Indeed, in her account the history of mental testing exemplifies the decentralised and pluralist character of the English system (Sutherland 1984, chs 9 and 10).

Paterson (1975, 1983) has applied a correspondence interpretation of mental testing to Scotland between the Wars. But, in Scotland too, the thesis is hindered by the fact that only a minority of Scottish education authorities had incorporated intelligence tests in their promotion procedures by the mid-1930s.[3] So varied were these procedures, that McClelland could say of them in 1935 that there were thirty-five Scottish local authorities and thirty-five different ways of tackling the problem (McClelland 1936, 58). Nor was the SED enthusiastic about intelligence testing. The evidence is far from complete but, if anything, it seems as though the Department in the inter-war period did rather less to understand intelligence tests and promote their use than did the Board of Education in England.

Sutherland (1976, 153) attributes much of the Board's inactivity to the effects of the Depression. No doubt the economic situation had a similarly inhibiting effect in Scotland. But other factors were also at work. The Department kept its distance from the investigations of national intelligence conducted by the Scottish Council for Research in Education (SCRE), and also from the development of tests of intelligence supervised by Professor Godfrey Thomson at Moray House College. On several counts, the Department was suspicious of the SCRE and of the leading figures associated with it, among them Thomson, McClelland and Boyd.[4] The Council represented a new alliance of teachers, local-authority directors and other figures in the world of school and higher education, and a new alliance also of scientific and progressive thought (Bell 1975, 1986; Wake 1984). New claims to professional autonomy were gathering there, and new pressures for expansion. Thomson (1929, 219) and McClelland both argued that Scotland should provide secondary education (in the sense of Leaving Certificate courses) for a higher proportion of the age-group than the Department envisaged. In McClelland's hands, the group test of intelligence became a powerful weapon in the argument. In 1932, he began the research that was to be published ten years later as *Selection for Secondary Education* (McClelland 1942). His conclusion was that senior-secondary education should be offered to between twenty-five and thirty per cent of pupils. But he also emphasised that this was an underestimate insofar as it assumed no amelioration in adverse social conditions, nor in the attractiveness of the senior-secondary curriculum (*ibid.*, 214).

Selection After 1945

In the 1930s McClelland criticised external examinations for distorting education (McClelland 1936, 174), and this critique was forcefully restated by the Sixth Advisory Council of which he was a member. In 1947, the Council recommended an internal examination at sixteen years, with external standardisation, intended for pupils in both senior- and junior-secondary schools (SED 1947b, ch.8; Young 1986, 279-94). Ironically, however, it emerged from our discussions with Allan Rodger and David Dickson that McClelland's own work on selection contributed to the failure to implement the Council's progressive proposals:

RODGER. There is no doubt that McClelland's book *Selection for Secondary Education* had a big effect on *many* Scottish authorities, whether the director of education had been a student of Boyd, McClelland, Thomson or of none of them.

We asked Dickson:

Q. What about the Council's recommendations for a complete change in the examination structure? The introduction of the common examination at sixteen years. Were these ever on?

DICKSON. No. I don't think so. You see, the influence of the 'seventy-fifth percentile' on people was very, very strong indeed, and this was so counter to that.

Q. Why was it so strong?

DICKSON. Because it worked, in the sense that it provided a practical way of dividing children, after the age of twelve, and getting on with their secondary education.

A. S. Brockie was Director of Education for Midlothian from 1938 to 1957. David Walker joined him in 1941, becoming Assistant Director in 1942.

WALKER. Brockie was very keen on altering the system of transfer from primary to secondary education, because Midlothian still had this old system of a qualifying examination where those who passed went into academic courses, and those who didn't might go into advanced divisions [of primary schools]; but I think the feeling was that they were just filling in their time until it was time to leave school, at that time the age of fourteen. So, when the McClelland report was published in 1942, Brockie saw this as a way of getting things stirred up over this question, and it was then that I devised this 'promotion' test, as they called it, a transfer battery of two intelligence tests, a test in English, a test in arithmetic, and teachers' estimates scaled in English and arithmetic. . . . And [Midlothian] was probably the first area in Scotland which had really applied the McClelland scheme, in full force, as an operative scheme.

Q. Did you do that without reference to the other authorities or to the Advisory Council at that stage?

WALKER. Yes. Just Midlothian. All these authorities were very independent in their way of transferring children from primary to secondary education.

Q. How much contact did you have with McClelland over the development of it?

WALKER. A fair amount. . . .

Q. Was the problem seen as the problem of the advanced divisions of the primary school, or seen as the problem of the able, working-class pupil who wasn't in fact performing well on the qualifying examination, as it was being administered?

WALKER. I think the first, probably, was the major thing. The second one did arise to some extent, but it was a relatively minor problem at that time, to my recollection. . . . I think his [Brockie's] idea was to stir up the primary-to-secondary transfer situation, and it certainly did this. . . . [The test was given to] all pupils in primary seven, which is the last year of the primary school, and my foggy recollection is that we also said that any pupils in primary six who were over a certain age had to be put up. In the old days they would just sit there and go into primary seven in the following year, even though they were thirteen years of age. But with this thing we started to operate the clean-cut. . . .

Q. And what proportion were you aiming to promote?

WALKER. We followed McClelland's cut-off [of] . . . twenty-five per cent, but there was an appeal mechanism. . . .

Q. Did you have twenty-five per cent of places available?

WALKER. Oh yes. Oh, there was no difficulty about that, no difficulty, and never has been in any of the places where I have been. This idea that there is or was a limited number of places being competed for, is wrong; and, actually, in Scotland as a whole, the history is that the percentage of people put in academic courses went from twenty-five to twenty-eight, thirty, thirty-five, forty, in some areas. So it wasn't a case of places, it was a case of where to fix the border-line.

Q. What was the view of the SED?

WALKER. Well, I can't read the minds of the SED, especially at that time. . . . My impression is that the Department were very sympathetic. There were one or two people in the Department then who were Edinburgh BEds.[5] Allan Rodger was one . . . I remember he was very sympathetic. . . . [Also, the Advisory Council heard about the Midlothian scheme. They] put this recommendation about two intelligence tests and teachers' scaled estimates and so on in as an appendix to the report [SED 1947b, Appendix 4]. The SED . . . issued Circular 108 in 1947 recommending a battery with two intelligence tests and scaled estimates and so on, and this was adopted by practically the whole of Scotland, in the subsequent years. . . .

Q. That is an indication that an SED circular is perhaps necessary to get local authorities to act in concert one with another?

WALKER. Yes.

Fife

In 1944, Walker moved to Fife to become Depute Director of Education. The Director, Douglas McIntosh (1944-66), was a leading figure in Scottish mental testing after 1945. He had assisted McClelland in the Dundee investigation, and McClelland in turn had sponsored him for the Fife post. In 1948, McIntosh published a popularising version of McClelland's research aimed especially at local-authority administrators (McIntosh 1948), and he remained a vigorous apologist for meritocratic selection based on tests of intelligence and attainment. He was a member of the Seventh and Eighth Advisory Councils, and was associated with the 1961 report of the Advisory Council on transfer procedures from primary school (SED 1961b). He also conducted his own research in Fife on transfer procedures (McIntosh 1959), and promoted similar work through the SCRE, of which he was President from 1960 to 1972. Walker later served under him as Director of the SCRE 1958-70. The political balance of the Fife Education Committee fluctuated in the 1940s and 1950s,[6] but it seems always to have accepted the meritocratic rationale, and to have supported McIntosh's preference for selective schooling:

WALKER. Fife, as you know, has always had a reputation for being well ahead. Gregor McGregor, the Director [1919-41], away back in the 1920s, he was one of the first to apply American tests of achievement in a Scottish county. And that inheritance did continue, and Douglas McIntosh was very much of the same type of mentality, so that in a way the climate in Fife was even more favourable than it was in Midlothian, to change, and try new ideas. And they had a very good set of people in the Education Committee in the days when I went there. . . . There was John Sneddon who was a Labour member [1929-64], and a really first-class man; a miner, who worked perpetual night shifts so as to keep himself free to attend education committees and other meetings during the day; a man who I would say was absolutely incorruptible, the old type of Labour man who had got to the top because he had a message . . . and his aim in education was to see that all working-class children got a chance. Of course his son [Tom Sneddon] became the chairman of the GTC [in 1975]. . . . You could always depend on John Sneddon to help you, support you, in any proposal that would help to further education in Fife. A second one was John Allan of Dunfermline [Education Committee Chairman 1955-64], who was a more urbane type of statesman. . . . He was a Labour man too. . . . There were of course some of the Moderate party who were always looking at the rates and trying to keep the expenditure down, but there was quite a body amongst the Moderates who could be helpful in the Education Committee.[7] And you got some very intelligent and good discussions in the Education Committee. McIntosh always used to try to arrange the Education Committee agenda so that there was at least one thing on a really educational level that could be discussed.

Q. Could you give an instance?

WALKER. Well, this whole question of transfer from primary to secondary education, you would get this, not people arguing about what's an intelligence test or so on, but what is the purpose of secondary education? Do we want all able children to do academic courses? And one way we used to express it in the Education Committee was, 'If you put all your able children into academic courses, where are you going to get intelligent plumbers?' And, after discussing it in the Education Committee, we came to the conclusion that it was better for a future plumber to go into an academic course, even if it was only for three years, to really stretch his mind. . . .

Q. Did the Committee, for example, set the percentage of places that it wanted to develop in academic secondary courses?

WALKER. There was a small subcommittee, composed of so many Education Committee members and so many teachers, and of course staffed by the administration, at which all appeals came up. It was called the transfer committee, and the members were the ones who would fix the percentage of passes, depending on advice that they got from the administration.

Circular 206 of 1951 (SED 1951b) left decisions on school organisation to the local authorities. Rodger told us that 'while the Conservative Government did not particularly favour comprehensive schools, neither did they go against them. The instructions that we got from Ministers were: "Let an authority do what it thinks best in the local circumstances"'. We asked Walker what happened in Fife:

WALKER. Well, at that time it was for a certain number of selective academic schools. . . . and this was one thing that the Education Committee used to discuss at times. I was in favour of comprehensive schools. McIntosh was in favour of selective schools, but he didn't mind at all if I came into the debate supporting comprehensive education; and the Committee used to think that this was great fun, to hear the Director advocating selective schools and the Depute Director advocating comprehensive schools. . . .

Q. Did your view of comprehensive education go as far as mixed-ability teaching?

WALKER. No. . . . My idea of comprehensive schools – I think this was the prevalent idea at that time – was that all the children of a given area were taught in the same school, but I was thinking of courses suited to the ability and aptitude of the people within the school. . . . Adam in Kirkcaldy High School [Rector 1948-71] used to tell us that it was more difficult to transfer a child from one course to another inside a school than it was to transfer a child from one school to another. . . . It was a thought, that you didn't just solve a problem of comprehensive education by putting them all in the one building. And there was one other school in Fife which had always been regarded as a comprehensive school, but, when you actually got in to the school, you discovered that it had really two completely different sections, the academic one and the junior-secondary one, and they had separate staffs, almost separate buildings, and so on. So it was really two schools in the one campus, though it was called one school and was regarded as comprehensive.

Q. Was morale in junior-secondary schools at that time good or bad?

WALKER. Varied. In some excellent. Viewforth School in Kirkcaldy, under Donald Mackay [Headteacher 1919-48] . . . [he] was a first class headmaster, and the morale in that school was very high. There were others . . . where the morale was not high at all.

Q. Was there felt to be an educational purpose for junior-secondaries in the way that there was for the senior-secondaries?

WALKER. In this particular school in Kirkcaldy, yes. . . . In some of the others where the morale was low, I just don't know whether the people had got this idea of purpose. You had the feeling sometimes that the headmaster of one of these schools was a . . . failed academic; he had missed his line. He was on the line of promotion, and he felt that he had to go into a junior-secondary school in order to move up the next step to a senior-secondary school, but never managed the next move. But these were only few.

National Policy

That these difficulties were not peculiar to Fife emerges from Brunton's analysis of junior-secondary education across Scotland as a whole:

BRUNTON. The problem of the junior-secondary school was, in kind, if not in degree, similar to the problem of the senior-secondary school. The courses provided were, in far too many cases, little more than watered-down versions of the somewhat academic courses which had been found inappropriate for many pupils in senior-secondary schools. . . . Even in these practical fields the teaching was all too often unimaginative. As a result, the pupils were bored and uninterested, and saw little purpose in their education. Moreover, the buildings were often old, drab and rather poorly equipped, and many of the teachers had had little more than a minimal preparation for secondary-school work. Most teachers with Honours degrees who had received full training for secondary-school work wanted to teach in senior-secondary schools. The committee of inspectors appointed to consider these problems presented in 1955 a pretty good report on junior-secondary education [SED, 1955b] which at the time aroused a good deal of interest and did inspire some schools to try to make improvements.

Rodger gave the credit for the report to Dickson, whom he described as 'one of the best, most fundamental and most practical thinkers that the Department has had in recent times. Despite his own high level of scholarship he had a real understanding of the interests and needs of ungifted pupils.' Dickson did not, however, query the fundamental distinction between 'academic' and 'non-academic' education which gave junior-secondary schools their own, residual, identity:

DICKSON. What was never quite clear, what nobody has ever really settled, to my mind anyway, is what difference you are going to make between the children once you've decided that some of them should take a full academic-type secondary course and that others should have a different kind of course; what difference do you make in the treatment of them? This is what we were trying to suggest in the junior-secondary report, and we did it, of course, by looking at the junior-secondary pupils in isolation from the others. You know, we said, 'Well, let's forget about the academic people; they are being well enough catered for'. Whether they were or not is really another matter.

Q. So the committee of inspectors was working within the prevailing structure?

DICKSON. Yes indeed. This is fair. . . . The advantage that one saw in certain of the old junior-secondary schools, dealing particularly with the disadvantaged type of child (you know, living in poorish housing conditions and so on) – the junior-secondary school could, and some of them did, become quite specialised in dealing with the particular difficulties of that kind of child, educational difficulties in the broadest possible sense of the word 'educational'; not concerned merely with school subjects and examination passes but the social-education side.

The thrust of Dickson's 1955 report was that junior-secondary schools should abandon an academic and didactic approach in favour of the progressive methods recommended by the Advisory Council in 1947, instilling a sense of 'reality' into pupils, and training their characters (see chapter 11). But the schools' response was disappointing:

DICKSON. This report didn't have the effect that one would have hoped for. . . . The one big difficulty was to get the teaching profession to accord a sort of equality of prestige to the junior-secondary school. Most teachers tended to look on them as inferior places, as indeed everybody else did, including the children. . . . What one had hoped for was that junior-secondary schools might have got working, over a period of years, and would have developed some end-piece of paper which wouldn't necessarily have been based on written examinations at all, or on written external examinations.

Q. On the other hand, the local authorities were providing certification for the junior-secondary schools.

DICKSON. Yes, this had a very limited success because people kept complaining that it wasn't a Scottish Education Department certificate.

Dickson told us that the Department did not consider improving salaries in junior-secondary schools in the 1950s to stem the loss of staff and improve their status. But junior-secondary schools were later allowed to present for the new O-grade, which brought additional payments. In permitting this, the Department seems to have been torn between a desire to improve morale and earnings in this sector, and a fear that the new examination would displace a progressive junior-secondary alternative (SED 1962a, ch.2). Dickson also told us that he had hoped that the junior-secondary curriculum might eventually build up to parity of prestige, and six-year status, unencumbered by an external examination. But, by the early 1960s, the prospect of this was receding.

In England, the growing concern over the status of the secondary-modern schools prompted the appointment in 1961 of the Newsom Committee of the Central Advisory Council (ME 1963). But the mode and thrust of the response in Scotland was quite different. The Department adopted a working-party approach, setting up a committee under Brunton which reported in 1963. In England, the Newsom Committee made the social deprivation of secondary-modern schools a major theme of its three-hundred page report, and also of its research. In Scotland, by contrast, the Brunton Committee reported no research in its eighty-four pages, and it dealt with the theme of social deprivation obliquely, and in just one paragraph. There it acknowledged that 'discipline and general problems of behaviour have overshadowed much of the work attempted in schools' (SED 1963b, para.20). Whilst some of the blame was attached to factors beyond the schools' control, schools themselves were also castigated for perpetuating the academic tradition, and for overestimating their pupils' mental and personal capacities (see chapter 11). This was how Brunton described his Committee's work to us:

BRUNTON. What the Committee did was to follow on from the Inspectorate report on junior-secondary education [SED 1955b] and to have its consequences examined. . . . We had had a good deal of success in building bridges between the senior-secondary school and further and higher education and employment. I wanted to construct similar bridges, at appropriate levels, for the junior-secondary school. . . . You must understand that the Leaving Certificate was traditionally the Holy of Holies of Scottish education. Teachers, and indeed the public at large, understood this examination, and changes in it were a matter of public interest and understanding, and could meet with fairly ready acceptance. Consequent changes in the curriculum could also be accepted, provided they did not fundamentally alter the examination, regarded as the gateway to the universities and to success in the professions. This was not the case with the junior-secondary school . . . [where] we didn't think that a national examination was a good idea. For one thing, there had been a sort of national examination before the [Second World] War and it had not been very successful. Also, if you impose a national examination on the schools, then you tend to introduce rigidity into the curriculum and into teachers' practices. Moreover, the post-war junior-secondary school contained many pupils who in earlier days had been retarded [held back] in the primary school, and we thought that a general examination would be very difficult to standardise and would have an inhibiting effect. The problem of the junior-secondary school was very largely a local one with respect to employment and so on, whereas the problem of the senior-secondary school was much broader, even national, in character.

The arguments for and against national certification might have indicated the solution of a CSE-type of examination. Brunton told us that his committee considered this option at the time that the CSE was evolving in England, but rejected it.

The response to the Brunton report was no better than the earlier response to Dickson's:

BRUNTON. Teachers and the public did not understand, or misconceived, the recommendations of the Brunton report. Secondary education and the teacher-training system were deeply rooted in the subject tradition, and they did not understand a proposed system developing out of a 'vocational impulse' or, if you like, a 'centre of interest' round which would be grouped the various subjects, the practical or 'vocational' core being used to develop proficiency in the pupil's English, mathematics, science, social studies, etc., the pupil's whole education being developed round something which would arouse his interest and give some direction and purpose to what he was learning. . . . The Committee chose to emphasise the 'vocational impulse' because one of the main preoccupations of the pupils was the jobs, chiefly in local industry and commerce, to which they would go on leaving school, and it was of great importance to the pupils, and to the nation, that their resources of knowledge and of skill should be developed to the full. The success of the type of education advocated was proved in the schools where new courses were introduced, but these schools were unfortunately few in number. . . .

Q. Is it a fair conclusion to say that, in the case of the junior-secondary report and the Brunton report, the Inspectorate was taking more of an initiative, ploughing a lone furrow, and failing to carry teachers with them?

BRUNTON. That's true to some extent, I suppose, though the lack of immediate success in the junior-secondary school was due in part also to the attitude of some education authorities; and . . . many of the suggestions foundered on difficulties with other bodies, such as the Factories Inspectorate, on difficulties in providing really suitable accommodation, and on the unwillingness of politicians to allow pupils below the statutory leaving age to receive part of their education outwith the schools, in further-education colleges.

George Gray gave us a similar view, pointing in addition to the opposition of the teachers' associations, and highlighting succinctly the failure of Scottish educational culture to evolve a moral alternative to academic education:

Q. One of the implications of the Brunton report would have been an expanded role for the further-education colleges in the education of the older adolescent. The other implication would have been a much greater recognition of the technician and the craftsman. Both of these were, as I understand it, opposed by the teachers' associations.

GRAY. Oh yes, to a very large extent.

Q. Is this why the Brunton report was never implemented?

GRAY. To many Scottish parents the fact that a boy or girl is being given a technical or domestic or commercial course is *ipso facto* a declaration that the pupil has no academic ability. Resistance is automatic. Second, I think there is a national prejudice against vocational education, quite misplaced, but real. It leads to the pupil's falling between two stools. The 'non-academic' emerges as neither 'academic' nor 'practical'; he either goes into a dead-end job or he has to have the guts to take tertiary education courses. Then, third, whatever Brunton said or did not say, many teachers (and the associations to some extent) were deeply suspicious that further-education personnel would be asked to teach fifteen-year-olds in further-education wings. Many of those were, of course, not trained to the point of eligibility for certification. And finally the cost factor involved was felt to be excessive.

361

Aberdeen

The local authority in Aberdeen was Labour-controlled for most of the thirty years after 1945. Clark went there as Assistant Director in 1945, becoming Depute Director in 1946, and Director ten years later:

CLARK. We had no new senior-secondaries built in the post-war period. They were already there. . . . Approximately twenty-four or twenty-five per cent of the youngsters were going to these schools at that time from the primary. . . . The issue was never raised between 1945 and 1965, of building a new senior-secondary school in Aberdeen. . . . I think – and this is only speculation – that if Aberdeen had had to increase its senior-secondary intake between 1945 and 1965, I think there would have been serious consideration, particularly in the early part, given to some form of multilateral school, as in the Advisory Council's secondary report.

Q. How was the norm of twenty-five per cent arrived at?

CLARK. In the initial post-war discussions in the Education Committee, up to about 1948, about the right percentage, we had the advice of people on the Committee in those days, like Dr Norman Walker, who was Reader in Education in Aberdeen [and a member of Council of the SCRE 1929-60], and latterly John Graham, who was Professor of Divinity and later Lord Provost. We had a fair proportion of people as Committee members who were knowledgeable about the educational thinking of the day.

Q. Were people like Norman Walker following McClelland?

CLARK. Oh, I think they were unduly influenced by McClelland. . . . I think this figure of twenty or twenty-five per cent loomed large in those days, and was in a sense never really seriously questioned by the lay members of the Committee against the combined educational knowledge, if you like, of the members of the Committee like Dr Norman Walker; and I am bound to say that the officials and their thinking and background were pretty much in tune with this. . . . Plus all these boys going to Gordon's [Robert Gordon's College, a grant-aided school], which really was a big factor in the situation, I think.

Q. Did you get guidance from the Inspectorate on this at all?

CLARK. It was left entirely to the Education Committee. . . . The man who was the longest serving convener of the Aberdeen Education Committee post-war was Colin McIver [1952-66]. He was a great junior-secondary man; he had been a junior-secondary head. McIver was a great believer that, for quite a number of youngsters, although they might eventually go on to higher education, the initial start to secondary education could be better in a sympathetic junior-secondary school, from which . . . there were opportunities at almost every stage to transfer.

Q. Isn't it true that very few people actually took advantage of those opportunities?

CLARK. Not nearly as many as we would have liked. Yes, I would agree.

Q. What was McIver's reaction to the 1955 junior-secondary report?

CLARK. He was very pro the report.

Q. Could you describe what happened in the Committee?

CLARK. McIver had the opportunity, with me, of discussing . . . the junior-secondary report with David Dickson, because we had David Dickson in Aberdeen on quite a number of occasions to talk to heads, to secondary teachers, to talk to people like McIver; which he did very willingly, he was delighted, and he was a great help. McIver as Convener then approved and encouraged every suggestion that was put up, to improve, in terms of the report, what could be done in secondary schools. In the Education Committee, on this matter, he was very positive.

Q. How far do you think implementation went in Aberdeen?

CLARK. As in all of the authorities, it was variable.

Q. How alive was McIver to the wastage from the senior-secondary course, which was an aspect of the criticism of the old senior-secondary?

CLARK. Well, McIver was more critical of the senior-secondaries and their wastage, than he was of, if you like, the junior-secondaries and the opportunity that they *could* give, though it wasn't accepted to the extent that he would have liked.

Q. To some people, the problem of wastage meant that they should have a comprehensive system and do away with selection altogether. You're saying that McIver was actually wedded to the bipartite system?

CLARK. No. I think that the point that I'm making is rather different: that there were those in the Labour Party who felt that the old [junior-]secondary schools, as distinct from the senior-secondary schools, were not doing the kind of job that they wanted them to do, whereas McIver thought that for certain youngsters, they certainly were. But I never heard McIver say at any time that he was against the comprehensive approach, but he did accept that there would be differentiation. I think, in all fairness, one has to think of the climate of the times. In the fifties and the early sixties, there wasn't the same push to think in terms of comprehensives as a possible alternative, as there was later on. . . . I think that local politicians – certainly those that discussed the matter with me in the fifties – were much more concerned as to whether or not the ideas that were being put forward south of the Border at that time, were going to find favour on the Scottish scene. . . . If you go back to the agendas of Labour Party Conferences in the fifties, I'm sure that you will see motions about comprehensive education and so on. These Labour Party Conferences were UK conferences, and people from Aberdeen and the Scottish Labour Party were going to them. They were hearing these discussions. On the whole the local Labour Party politicians who heard these discussions, I don't think were particularly impressed, at that time, with comprehensive education as a possibility. . . . I can recall, for example, a discussion with some of the Labour Party politicians at that time, after a Labour Party Conference, and the thing that they came away with

... was that there were boroughs and authorities in England where the percentage of youngsters who had started a grammar-school course, was one-third to a half, or thereby, of the percentage that got into senior-secondaries in Aberdeen. . . . McIver was not particularly interested in comprehensive education as an alternative to the Aberdeen system in the fifties; but the point that I was trying to make earlier was that neither, really, was anybody else to any great extent in the fifties, and the appearance of the young Turks was, in a sense, coincidental with the change, and, obviously, emphasised by them.

The principal 'young Turks' were four Labour councillors who were coming to the forefront of Aberdeen politics in the early 1960s: Robert Hughes, James Lamond, Robert Middleton and John Smith.[8] Middleton told us that he was the first person in Aberdeen politics to question the accuracy of the transfer procedure and the sanctity of the twenty-five per cent limit to senior-secondary school places. Clark thought this less than fair to McIver, who 'wasn't all that thirled [wedded] to exam results', but he confirmed the sea-change in political mood:

CLARK. In the early 1960s, although the Committee remained Labour controlled throughout that period, there were changes in personnel on the Committee, and there came onto the Committee at that time, in 1962 or 1963, a small number of members who were obviously keen on the idea of comprehensive education . . . and they in fact brought the matter to a formal discussion by the Committee when one of them, who actually became Under-Secretary of State, Bob Hughes, put forward a notice of a motion that the Committee should consider the whole issue of comprehensive education and what it would mean in Aberdeen terms. This was some considerable time before Circular 600 came out.

Clark's response to Hughes' motion was a twenty-seven-page proposal for the reorganisation of Aberdeen's secondary schools on a two-tier basis. We return to it in the following chapter.

Lanarkshire

We asked McEwan about his authority's policy:

McEWAN. The Committee was very evenly balanced originally, in 1945, as far as I recall. Certainly there was a Conservative or a Moderate chairman of the Education Committee when I was appointed, but then, shortly after that, the next election changed the complexion to Labour as far as the Education Committee was concerned . . . I think that from the next election after that it was really definitely a left-wing council all the way through to 1975.[9]

Q. What do you think was the source of these men's warmth of feeling towards education? Was it Fabian Socialism?

McEWAN. I don't think that they were intellectual socialists, in the main. They were gut-reaction socialists, more moved by feelings about social injustice than theory. In some cases it was just family tradition.

Q. What sort of families? Miners?

McEWAN. Miners, a lot of miners, of course. Steel workers, people who had handled employees, spokesmen for the employees, very often conscious of the fact that the employees were very often not very articulate; who felt that the employee element in society must be made more articulate. . . . We always had people who believed in education for education's sake, right through to the end, whatever the spring from which this welled up inside them. The slight blight is not, perhaps, that ideologues took over from idealists, but that there came a climate of recurring financial trouble, the stringency in respect of spending and so on, and, from time to time, worry about the danger to election success from great increases in rates if we were allowed to spend; and this had a dampening effect on enthusiasm for spending money. . . .

Q. What was the county's policy on the provision of places in the senior-secondary courses? What determined the number of places that were available?

McEWAN. We had a special creaming for a place like Hamilton Academy and certain other schools, St Patrick's High School and various others. We creamed off twenty per cent of the age-group to that type of school. Otherwise, we were accepting thirty or thirty-three per cent for certificate courses, and we included, of course, every pupil actually on the percentile mark, and that made the percentage of the age-group up to two points more, very often.

Q. How were those two figures, thirty per cent and twenty per cent, arrived at?

McEWAN. Of the age-group. They were based on McClelland. . . .

Q. Was there a feeling amongst members that it should have been higher?

McEWAN. Not a great feeling, no.

Q. What was the basic structure of secondary-school organisation that was contained in the proposals for building before the 1960s?

McEWAN. A combination of four-year schools and six-year schools was quite common, though the all-through school had its place.

Q. Did you have, as it were, an *ad hoc* policy for each school, or was there an overall policy for the county?

McEWAN. It was generally a case of an *ad hoc* decision for each school based on the circumstances of each area. For the new town of East Kilbride, however, there was an overall policy, originally, to provide several four-year schools feeding one senior high school. . . . Bishopbriggs was designed to be four-year in the first instance, and six-year, possibly, to follow, depending on the population build-up. Some of the others were originally built, quite definitely, as non-certificate, junior-secondary schools, replacements for very, very bad buildings, or relief schools for other schools in the area that were grossly overcrowded.

Q. Was there any plan which would, in the long-term, have made the existing older academies, the prestigious academies of the county, into comprehensive schools in the sense that they would accept all pupils from the area?

McEWAN. Not until the 1965 debate that we're talking about.

Q. How strong was the attachment of local Labour feeling to these older academies? In somewhere like Fife, one gets the sense that they were very proud of them. Was there the same attachment in Lanarkshire?

McEWAN. In many cases, yes. People were fond of Lanark Grammar School, an *omnibus* school. People were fond of Dalziel High School, which was a selective school, but which didn't have the same academic prestige in some minds, perhaps, as Hamilton Academy, which was even more highly selective. In the area of Hamilton, people were very attached to St John's Grammar School, a four-year school, which lost its very best pupils to Hamilton Academy all along the line. It always did. But people were still very fond of St John's Grammar School.

Q. Would local opinion have been behind a policy that was based on the retention of these six-year selective schools, but with a broadening of the bases of their recruitment by feeding them with four-year schools, with transfers across at the age of fourteen?

McEWAN. Some local opinion would have been favourable to such a scheme. You got local feeling in different ways. The one of which you were most generally conscious, as time passed, was the feeling that was engendered every year by the selection procedure for pupils at twelve plus, where disappointed parents became very vocal and got a lot of support from councillors. Councillors came to recognise that pupils' disappointment was a very hurtful thing, although at first they had welcomed the selection system as a means of recognising *merit* as opposed to influence or social standing, and often discounted some of the parents' concern as mere overprotection. Then they came to question the validity of the selection procedure, and you had to write a report showing whether selection proved to be justified four or five years later by certificate results. The resulting reports always seemed to provide fair confirmation of the validity of the selection procedure, but this did not quieten all criticism, especially when it became fashionable to argue that the results were favourable only because the system was 'self-validating'. . . . We questioned it [the transfer scheme] in Lanarkshire ultimately . . . largely because it was being manipulated. We were satisfied that some teachers were coaching . . . that some teachers were giving their pupils extra time on what is supposed to be a timed test. Of course this was all done 'to benefit their pupils'.

Discussion

A number of writers have commented on the divided attitudes of the Labour Party in England towards the issues of selection and comprehensive reorganisation (e.g. Banks 1955; Parkinson 1970; Barker 1972; Benn and Simon 1972; Fenwick 1976). Less work has been done on the Labour Party in Scotland, but here too there was ambivalence and division. When framing the 1945 legislation, Tom Johnston had reluctantly conceded the retention of grant-aided schools, and of fee-paying in those local-authority schools that charged fees.[10] Johnston's successor was generally ineffective. He was replaced in 1947 by Woodburn who, like the Attlee government in general, gave less priority to education than to housing and redevelopment. We have found no evidence in the surviving files to indicate that the Scottish Office Ministers in the Labour administrations of 1945-51 did anything to promote the Advisory Council's arguments for the comprehensive school. The abolition of selection for secondary school became Labour Party policy in 1951, and some Scottish Labour MPs thereafter argued the case in parliamentary debate. Overall, however, there was little Scottish pressure on the Labour leadership in the 1950s for comprehensive reform (Mackenzie 1967).

The evidence from Aberdeen, Fife and Lanarkshire helps to explain the attitude in Scotland. It indicates that there were strong attachments to the local academies and to the meritocratic and bipartite system of schooling of which, for decades, they had been a part. The system was based on equality of access to privileged courses that were more generously provided in Scotland than in England, and on a gradually expanding basis. Expansion itself, however, was eventually to help to undermine confidence in the system. As higher proportions of successive age-groups were selected for senior-secondary courses, so the number of dissatisfied 'borderline' cases was statistically bound to increase. Moreover, an expanding senior-secondary sector continued to drain junior-secondary schools of resources, teachers and esteem. In 1947, the Advisory Council conceded that junior-secondary education was an experiment as yet untried. But by the early 1960s it had become apparent, to use the words of an Education Committee Chairman in Fife, that 'a junior-secondary school was a junior-secondary school'.

Various commentators point to the thrall in which intelligence testing held politicians and educationists alike in England. Was this also true of the immediate post-war period in Scotland? Broadly, yes. McClelland reigned, and politician deferred to professional in each of the authorities we have examined. There is evidence that the senior-secondary policy made some inroads on social-class inequalities of access to certification between 1945 and 1965 (Gray *et al.*, 1983, ch.12), and evidence also that the Scottish system at the time gave more weight to ability, as measured by intelligence tests, than the system in the USA (Hope 1984, ch.3). But the fact remains that, throughout this period, middle-class pupils (i.e. pupils with non-manual fathers) were disproportionately represented in senior-secondary courses, and especially in their upper stages (Gray *et al.*, 1983, ch.12). Nevertheless, it would be premature to move to an interpretation of testing in this period primarily in correspondence terms. For one thing, the prime movers in Scottish mental testing were all paid-up educational progressives who opposed the bipartism of Circular 44. It is true that some critics have seen in the progressive movement itself the hidden hand of capitalist social control at work,[11] and it is also true that certainly Thomson (Sharp 1980), and possibly also McClelland, made little public fuss in the 1940s and 1950s over the ways in which testing was used. But they had seen the bipartite policy, and Victorian meritocratic individualism, long predate their work on intelligence. Also, both men in the 1930s had wanted access to the university ladder to be made more generous and more equitable. For a time in the 1950s it seemed as though universal secondary education was achieving this.

If it is not self-evident that the leading Scottish figures in mental testing intended their work to sustain capitalist social relations, what can be said about the unintended consequences of their work, and about the things that others did in the name of their ideas? A preliminary point here is that the development of mental testing in Scotland up to 1946 looks very much like an instance of a pluralist education system in action. The origins of the movement were international, British and Scottish. The experts disagreed amongst themselves about the nature of intelligence and about the best uses of intelligence tests. Boyd, for example, valued them primarily for individual and diagnostic purposes, and as an aid to remedying difficulties in individual learning (Bell 1986, ch.6). Much of the early development work was done locally by academics, school teachers and administrators, and they formed their own national organisation, the SCRE, partly in order to help their investigations. Even then, however, there was only a piecemeal response from the Scottish local authorities and none, initially, from the SED. It was left to the SCRE to evaluate the variety of local-authority practice and to recommend the best aggregation from it. This work, in its turn, was endorsed by the Advisory Council, and the eventual role of central government was merely to sanction and generalise by circular a body of practice that had originated at various local points in the system some two decades before that.

Why did the SED eventually move on testing? Arguably the answer lies in the systematisation of post-primary provision that was required after 1945, and in the Department's continuing attempt to apply the principle of promotion by age rather than stage (see chapter 2). Before the legislation of 1944-46 (or perhaps before the 1936 Act), the 'ragged edge' of post-primary schooling between eleven and fourteen was not an offence to formal individual rights. But this is what it became once the right of all pupils to secondary education was formally recognised. For Brockie and Dickson, McClelland's scheme offered a practical way of applying a universal clean-cut to a population of primary-school pupils among whom were many who were not in the school class, or stage, appropriate to their age. Whether this helped or hindered the working-class child was a secondary consideration, as were McClelland's other purposes in promoting testing. In Griffith's terms (Griffith 1966), the Department's intervention was administrative and regulatory, rather than promotional. Thereafter, the Department left questions of transfer at twelve mainly to the local authorities. As far as the Department was concerned, they continued to transfer too many pupils to senior-secondary courses, and to do it too late. But it was only towards the end of the 1950s, when the 'bulge' in the age-group was approaching secondary school, that the Department attempted to regulate this situation again by asking the local authorities to reduce the proportions of pupils entering senior-secondary courses (SED 1962a, ch.2).

One may therefore extend to Scotland Salter and Tapper's conclusion that 'the almost universal employment of intelligence testing in the secondary school selection process *after* 1945 was a direct consequence of how the 1944 Education Act was implemented rather than any dramatic change in the character of capitalism as a result of the war years' (Salter and Tapper 1981, 146, emphasis in original). What is more dubious is that the intention in Scotland was to 'protect' the senior-secondary, or grammar school from mainly lower-class incursions. This is the motive that Salter and Tapper discern in England (*ibid.*, ch.7). In Scotland, however, the retention of fee-paying in some local-authority schools already provided a protection if, indeed, protection were necessary. But it is doubtful if it were either needed or desired. There were proportionately more senior-secondary places available in Scotland than there were grammar-school places in England, and most Scottish local authorities expanded their provision as time passed. In the *omnibus* schools, moreover, access to senior-secondary courses remained firmly under the control of teachers.

Nevertheless, it could be argued that reference to the consequences of testing, and reference to the motives of its originators, is to miss the point that the mental-testing movement legitimated the bipartite policy by giving it scientific respectability. Thus, it might be said that, even when tests were not used, or were used only as one of a battery of instruments for selection, capitalist hegemony was reinforced by an underlying philosophy of relatively immutable individual differences in ability. This argument is necessarily vaguer, referring as it does to climates of opinion or similar ideas, and it does not sit easily with the Department's scepticism about the new educational science. But it is not without force. It receives support, for example, from the sort of thing that Brunton's Committee said about the mentalities and dispositions of non-academic pupils (see chapter 11). Also, the influence of the climate of ideas can be seen in the specific instances of the Education Committees in Fife, Aberdeen and Lanarkshire, each of which left the concept of intelligence unquestioned, and to the professionals, for some twenty years.

But ideologies that deceive can cut both ways. Was the Department deceived too? Did it sincerely believe that only twenty-five per cent or

369

thirty-five per cent of children were academic? If not, the decision to introduce the O-grade, taken in 1955, is incomprehensible. McIntosh warned of the inflationary implications of the O-grade during Advisory Council discussions in 1959 (sro 1961a, fourth meeting), but he was ignored. Later, when it was too late for the Department to go into reverse, he and Walker published a paper showing that a two-year O-grade course set at a standard where one-third of the age-group would succeed, could expect to enrol at least half of the age-group in its early stages (McIntosh and Walker 1970). The O-grade, in other words, set a short fuse under the bipartism on which the Department's policy had been based for decades. What is more probable, therefore, is that Brunton, the Department and much of the wider policy community were caught in the thrall, not of intelligence testing, but of bipartism. Thus it never occurred to them that a 'natural' division into academic and non-academic pupils at twelve years might be undone between fourteen and sixteen years. The most plausible conclusion is that Brunton shared the Department's preoccupation with stemming wastage from senior-secondary courses, introducing the O-grade for that purpose (see chapters 4 and 5). In doing this, he simply made a mistake, a mistake which the Department could have avoided had it understood better the logic of McClelland's work on selection. But the Department was not talking to the scre at the time (see chapter 11), nor to McClelland.

How the bipartite philosophy had come to exercise its hold on the policy community is a theme of chapter 17. By the early 1960s, however, this hold was being weakened from below by the generous promotion policies of the local authorities, and from above by the Department itself, as it brought in the O-grade in an attempt to counter the wastage that arose from this generosity. The issue began to stir politically. Senior-secondary expansion meant that inequalities of provision between junior- and senior-secondary schools, and courses, grew starker; and also that more parents were touched by the failure of their borderline children to gain access to this privileged provision. Some teachers manipulated the transfer procedure in order that their pupils stay in the contest for mobility. The demand for equality of opportunity for access to privilege began to harden into a stronger demand, namely for equality of treatment as such. As the 'bulge' of pupils approached secondary schooling, and as the secondary-school building programme got under way, the issue assumed a concrete, pressing and local form. New schools were required, and replacement buildings for old schools, prestigious and non-prestigious alike. Where were they to be built? What courses were they to offer? And, most important of all, which children were to be allowed through their doors?

NOTES
1. Benn and Simon (1972, 199). Changes in school organisation after 1945 make

it appropriate to give only order-of-magnitude figures in this paragraph, though a number of precise figures for the mid-1960s can be found in Highet (1969), on which we have drawn here.

2. Details of the classification used here may be found in McPherson and Willms (1986).

3. The evidence on the exact number is inconclusive. Wade (1939, 143), on whom Paterson (1975) relies, reported that twelve authorities had used intelligence tests in 1933 as part of the promotion procedure. However Hartog (1937, 20-3) identified only four local authorities that used intelligence tests in 1935 to select pupils 'to a higher grade or a different kind of education'. Three of these authorities had current or past Directors of Education who were prominent in applied psychometric research, namely, Ayr (W. A. Hepburn, Director 1927-44), Fife (Gregor McGregor 1919-41), and Wigtownshire (William McClelland 1919-21). The fourth authority was Bute. Hepburn, McGregor and McClelland were all active in the affairs of the Scottish Council for Research in Education.

4. Thomson is the villain of Paterson's thesis, but Bell (1975) has shown that Thomson himself had little interest in servicing administrators' needs, nationally or locally. Thomson supported (streamed) comprehensive schools (Thomson 1929, 209), and Sharp has speculated that his retreat from public issues in later life is attributable to his mixed feelings over the use of group intelligence tests, developed under him at Moray House College, to help administer a bipartite secondary-school system (Sharp 1980). J. J. Robertson thought Thomson a major influence on many of the progressive recommenda-tions that he, Robertson, wrote into the *Secondary Education* report of the Sixth Council (see chapter 4) (Robertson 1964). Robertson himself had been a student of William Boyd at Glasgow. Outside Scotland, Boyd is possibly best known as author of *The History of Western Education* (Boyd 1921). He was head of the Department of Education at Glasgow University, serving there as Lecturer and Reader from 1907 to 1946. Bell writes: 'William Boyd . . . made probably the greatest and most varied mark on Scottish education of any departmental head of education in any University. He considerably developed the study of educational history, and with [Alexander] Darroch [Professor of Education at Edinburgh University 1903-24], he established strong links between Scotland, the New Education Fellowship and the world of Dewey. He was also involved in the child guidance movement and was instrumental in setting up the first Scottish child guidance clinic, while his enthusiasm for diagnostic testing first awoke the interest of the Educational Institute in modern educational research. . . . Yet all he achieved was achieved without the political power and influence of a chair and often in the face of opposition from a university hierarchy which viewed him with much ideological suspicion. . . . Suspicion of his personal politics (his social work among the unemployed of Clydebank and his outspoken views on their plight had given him a quite undeserved reputation as a Marxist) appears to have been a major reason why he was never elevated' (Bell 1983, 159 and 165). The New Education Fellow-ship was one of the principal fora of progressive educational thinking in the inter-war period. Bell (1986) draws attention to the diversity of thinking and practice among leading figures in Scottish psychometrics, and the involvement of a number of them in the progressive movement.

5. Provision for the Bachelor of Education degree was made in the second decade of this century, though the pace and direction of its subsequent development differed between the four universities. In the main, however, the degrees were

founded 'to communicate the old historical/philosophical and the new American/German experimental ideas to the intellectually most aware and/or the most ambitious of Scottish teachers' (Bell 1986, 246; see also Bell 1983).

6. The chair of the Education Committee was held as follows: 1937-48, Labour; 1948-55, Independent; 1955-70, Labour; 1970-71, Independent; 1971-78, Labour. The chair did not automatically change with changes in overall political control in the County. For example, Labour strengthened its position in 1952 but did not displace the Independent Chairman, who was regarded as 'progressive' in educational thinking. Again, Labour lost control in 1967, but its Committee Chairman remained in post. We are indebted to Lesley Gow and Sir George Sharp for this information.

7. 'Moderate' and 'Progressive' parties representing the 'independent right' at local-authority level survived in some areas until the mid-1970s (Harvie 1981a, 113).

8. These four were all aged around thirty years when they began to make their mark in Labour Party politics in Aberdeen. Robert Hughes served as a councillor from 1962 to 1970 and convened first the Health and Welfare Committee and then the Social Work Committee. He chaired the Aberdeen City Labour Party from 1961 to 1969 before becoming Member of Parliament for Aberdeen North in 1970. He was a junior Minister in the Scottish Office in 1974-75. James Lamond was a councillor from 1959 to 1971, and became Lord Provost at the end of that period. From 1970 he represented an English constituency (Oldham East, later Oldham Central and Royston) in Parliament. Robert Middleton came onto Aberdeen City Council in 1961, and was Convener of its Education Committee from 1966 to 1969. He joined the Scottish Council of the Labour Party in 1978, and from 1979 led the Labour group on Grampian Regional Council. He stood unsuccessfully for Parliament at several general elections. John Smith was first elected an Aberdeen councillor in 1963, and served on the Education Committee from 1969 to 1975. He was Lord Provost from 1971 to 1975, when he left the new Aberdeen District Council shortly after the reorganisation of local government. As Lord Kirkhill, he then served as Minister of State in the Scottish Office from 1975 to 1978.

9. From 1955 to 1975, a single Labour councillor, William Bell, was Chairman of the Lanarkshire Education Committee.

10. Lloyd describes Mackay Thomson's role in the decision to retain fee-paying. The Secretary opposed Johnston and Westwood, the junior Minister, maintaining that corporation fee-paying schools were popular as a social meeting-ground. This view complemented the Conservative argument that no child was debarred from secondary education merely because a place had been bought by a child of less promise. Although Labour wanted to abolish fee-paying, Johnston and Westwood gave way lest abolition upset the cities and increase the rates (Lloyd 1979, ch.9).

11. See, for example, Katz (1971, ch.3, especially 118-20). Hamilton (1985) indicates lines for future research in Scotland.

Sixteen

Comprehensive Reorganisation

> The Labour Party has never really thought out the implications of comprehensive education and the result is that the residual ideas of the previous dispensation survive, uninspected. R.F. Mackenzie, Headmaster in Fife 1957-68, and in Aberdeen 1968-74[1]

Introduction: Whose Decision?

The Ministry of Education's Circular 10/65 of 1965 stated a preference for the all-through, eleven to eighteen, comprehensive school, but it also endorsed five other ways in which secondary schooling might be organised on a non-selective basis. Circular 600, issued in the same year by the SED, prescribed only one final form of organisation. This was the six-year, all-through, fixed-catchment, comprehensive school for twelve- to eighteen-year-olds. The Circular did, however, concede that some variant of a two-tier system might be an unavoidable interim arrangement, especially in scattered areas (SED 1965b, paras 10 and 11). Despite these differences, both systems had nevertheless decided at the same time to abolish selective transfer, and to do this by the same means, i.e. by circular not legislation. This indicates that there was a single decision for Great Britain as a whole, a decision which Bell and colleagues (1974, 101) argue had been taken 'more than a decade before the issue of the circulars . . . by the Labour Party operating at a United Kingdom level'. It was this decision, they say, that was eventually applied to Scotland, and it was the Labour Party in England that had earlier made the pace, not the Scottish Council of the Labour Party (*ibid.*, 98). We have no direct evidence as to how matters were coordinated in 1964-65 between the Secretary of State for Scotland, the Minister of Education, and their respective Departments. However, Bell and colleagues infer from a comparison of the two circulars that the Scottish circular was not written by English Ministers, nor by officials at the DES. And they conclude that 'both systems, once the major policy decision had been made, were allowed to "get on with it"' (*ibid.*, 103). We put their conclusion to Norman Graham, who was Secretary of the SED at this time. His only comment was, 'Well, I would not expect anything else, that once the major policy decision was made, both Departments got on with it'. Neither William Ross nor Judith Hart, the Scottish Ministers involved in the decision, gave us interviews. However, it seems that the contents of Circular 600 were primarily a Scottish matter, though the decision to issue it was not.

Bruce Millan replaced Hart as junior Minister in April 1966. He could not tell us about Ministerial decisions before he took office. But, with Clark's account of the Aberdeen Labour Party in mind (see chapter 15), we asked him a more general question on the autonomy of the Scottish policy:

Q. To what extent did you regard it as an English issue that was imported north of the Border?

MILLAN. Not at all as the importation of an English issue. I think there is a lot of misunderstanding about this, and a lot of myth as well. People seem to think that before Circular 600 . . . we had a pretty-well comprehensive system in Scotland anyway. That is just utterly untrue. We had a selective system in Scotland, as they did south of the Border, and the arguments about the ending of selection and the rest were exactly the same in Scotland as they were in England, and views were as passionately held in Labour Party circles in Scotland as they were in England. . . . I think I would accept that there really were better chances of, as it were, working your way through the system in Scotland than there were in England. But . . . you really were working a multilateral system. In fact, there was a very complicated system of schools: there were old junior-secondaries, there were some new four-year schools that had followed the introduction of the O-grade, and there were schools transferring [pupils to Highers courses in other schools] at all sorts of particular times. . . . But there was a more genuine disposition in Scotland towards changing it to the comprehensive system than there was in England. The arguments about selection, in other words, I think had been largely won in Scotland by the time we sent out our circular. . . . Of course, there were a number of schools in the Highlands, and elsewhere, where there was something very much more approaching what one would call a comprehensive school, and it was perhaps for that reason that we had less hostility towards the idea in Scotland than they had in certain areas of England, and indeed, far from hostility, a general acceptance of the idea. But the system was basically selective for the vast majority of pupils, and two-thirds at least of the pupils were going to schools which didn't even pretend to be comprehensive, and of the other third, the number which were genuinely comprehensive must have been really quite a small proportion. So you really had basically a selective system.

Millan's estimate here is supported by official figures. In 1965, only twenty per cent of secondary schools, containing thirty-four per cent of secondary pupils, were already six-year schools having a comprehensive first-year intake. A further fifteen per cent of schools, containing a further thirteen per cent of pupils, were short-course schools, but with a comprehensive first-year intake. To our knowledge, none of these six-year or short-course comprehensive schools organised its first year on mixed-ability lines. All other schools had selective entries (SED 1966a, 33).

But, if the system were basically selective, was the argument against selection won to the extent that Millan asserts? And how did its winning shape the system of schools that emerged from reorganisation, and shape the type of education they offered? This chapter addresses these questions, looking at the way in which the comprehensive policy was developed and applied in central-local transactions. The narrative moves between Ministers, administrators and inspectors on the one hand, and directors, councillors and teachers on the other. It draws its examples mainly from events in Lanarkshire, Renfrewshire, Glasgow and Aberdeen. The discussion at the end of the chapter summarises the evidence in the light of some of our wider themes.

How Lanarkshire Got All-Through Schools

As we saw in the previous chapter, Lanarkshire had a 'left-wing' administration throughout virtually all of John McEwan's period as Director of Education. Yet, in 1965, only five of its seventy-six schools were six-year comprehensives, and only a further five were short-course schools with a comprehensive first year. The remaining sixty-six schools were selective, eleven as senior-secondary (six-year, certificate) schools, and the rest as junior-secondaries. Seven of the junior-secondaries offered courses for the O-grade. McEwan himself was openly dismissive of the case for comprehensive reorganisation, blaming English sociologists and Scottish ideologues for its currency. He told his committee that, 'although considerations of class consciousness and social apartheid may be a major issue in England . . . they are much less important in Scotland and in Lanarkshire' (McEwan 1965a, 1680). In his discussion with us he enlarged on this view:

McEwan. I think there's an awful lot of rubbish written in England based on calculating how many pupils from manual homes make this or that stage in education . . . I think that it's very trivial and biased and un-academic, even though it is done by some academics. . . . I think that you should treat human beings as you find them, rather than bother about their origins; and your ability is your ability, rather than something to be seen in the context of what your father did.

Q. Do you see this as something that is peculiarly English?
McEwan. Yes.
Q. It doesn't exist north of the Border?
McEwan. Not much bother with it up here.
Q. In Lanarkshire, how far was there an awareness of the wastage problem, the problem of able children leaving school before they have reached the level that their ability would otherwise have taken them to?

McEwan. There wasn't a great deal of worry about that on behalf of the pupils, largely because I think we felt that those who left school at say fifteen or sixteen, but who had the ability to go on to eighteen, were probably doing themselves no harm at all by going into whatever they were going into. They were getting good jobs, and their education was not necessarily finished because they happened to have left school. . . . Early leaving is not necessarily synonymous with wastage.

375

In the next chapter, we return to these views of McEwan's as part of our wider discussion of the egalitarian ideology in Scotland. We asked him how, in late 1964 and early 1965, he had begun to frame his advice on reorganisation:

McEWAN. I was always very conscious of the fact that highly qualified staff were very few in numbers in the county, and you couldn't have a quick increase in the number of Honours graduates in mathematics for example. Therefore we hadn't to have a great number of senior-secondary schools. We had to have a small number, even on a comprehensive basis. I was much impressed by the fact that in the county, before reorganisation, the schools with the greatest prestige, apart from the highly selective ones, were schools that had about 100 pupils in the fifth year, good, able, Scottish group-leaving-certificate types of pupil. And in order to have 100 of these in the fifth year, assuming twenty-five per cent of an age-group could measure up to this standard, you would have to start off with 400 in the first year; and therefore you were committed to 400 in each of the first four years (on a sixteen-year-old school-leaving-age basis) plus the 100 in the fifth year, plus half of that, say, in the sixth year. So logistics meant that, to have an all-through school of the desired standing and strength at the top, you must put up with this very, very large school, with 1600 or 1700 pupils. . . . My first memorandum on secondary-school reorganisation [in February 1965: McEwan 1965a] . . . didn't come down in favour of any one particular form of organisation or type of school, but listed a very large number of considerations which should be taken into account in planning any reorganisation – staff economy, size of school, primary/secondary transition, choice of course, subject-option flexibility, the sophistication of older adolescents, the raising of the school-leaving age, transition to the world of work etc. – and mentioned all the varied types of school (and their merits and disadvantages) that were under discussion at the time: the 'all-through' secondary, the Leicester Plan,[2] junior-high/senior-high schools, sixth-form colleges, the intermediate or middle school/senior-high school arrangement, the college high school or college of arts and crafts etc. The [Schools and Schemes] Subcommittee seemed interested, and I was congratulated on this document; and a sub-subcommittee was given a remit to consider sample areas of the County and report on the various alternative forms of organisation which appeared possible in these areas. This sub-subcommittee did not in fact condescend on any form of organisation for any area but seemed at their meetings to accept that this pattern of middle or intermediate schools, leaving at age fourteen to a senior-high school for some pupils and a college of arts and crafts for others, would adequately fit in with needs and considerations. In the end, after a month or so of meetings looking at sample areas, I wrote what I hoped might be accepted as reasonable conclusions from the committee's deliberations [McEwan 1965b]. In that document I suggested that the all-through school would suit

in some areas (meaning the less populated areas), in some the Leicester
Plan might be appropriate, while in others a suitable pattern would be that
of three-year middle schools for ages eleven to fourteen (P7, S1 and S2),
leading to a senior-high school for S3-S6, with attendance at a college of arts
and crafts as an alternative to the senior-high school. Accompanying
diagrams in fact showed pupils in *all* areas having access to a college of arts
and crafts from age fourteen, either in their own area or in another. I
pointed out that these plans would all eliminate selection at twelve-plus; the
incorporation of P7 in the middle school would ease transition from primary
to secondary schooling; the senior-high schools, with older pupils only,
could develop more easily an atmosphere suited to older adolescents; and
colleges of arts and crafts would provide continuity from secondary to
further education.

McEwan told us that the sub-subcommittee 'accepted this memorandum
as a proper approach to the many problems inherent in the review of
secondary education and as a basis for decisions on points of detail'. We
asked him:

Q. Was this policy based on an acceptance of the senior-secondary
academic curriculum and on Brunton's *From School to Further Education*?
Were you working within the framework of these two?

McEwan. Definitely the Brunton report was one of the things at the
back of my mind in advocating colleges of arts and crafts as a follow-on to
middle schools from age fourteen.

Q. What happened when it came to the full Committee?

McEwan. What happened was that the subcommittee had the minutes
of the sub-subcommittee and the two memoranda on their agenda at a
special meeting. But, without any preliminaries, the Chairman of the
Education Committee read out a motion, which was passed with virtually no
discussion, insisting on the all-through school as the ultimate in all areas.
Anything else [was] to be merely an interim arrangement [LCC 1965].
There was no preliminary discussion of the memoranda or of the minutes of
the sub-subcommittee dealing with the matter. . . . I was later given to
understand the emphasis on the all-through school had come from a
County Labour Party meeting not confined to county councillors (as the
group was).

Q. Was that the first time that this sort of County meeting had influenced
things in that way?

McEwan. I don't know. . . . I think that there were occasional meetings
of this kind, about which one seldom heard. But I doubt very much if there
were more than just this one that really influenced a major decision in
education.

Q. Would that reflect Judith Hart's influence as well?

McEwan. I don't know.

Judith Hart was elected MP for Lanark in 1959, and was junior Minister responsible for education from 1964 to 1966, when Bruce Millan succeeded her. Another local M P who may have been influential was Margaret Herbison, Labour member for Lanarkshire North. Herbison had been an important influence on the Labour Party's adoption in 1951 of a policy of comprehensive reorganisation. (chapter 8; Barker 1972, ch.5). Her political agent, a member of the Lanarkshire Education Committee, was later reported as having said to McEwan at the time of reorganisation that 'comprehensive education was the county policy and if he wouldn't implement it [they] . . . would get another director of education' (Thorburn 1985). McEwan was clearly surprised by the sudden hardening of the local Labour Party's support for the all-through school. When the crucial motion was passed, he and the sub-subcommittee were asked 'to examine the implications of the policy now formulated' (L C C 1965, 1663), no small task in a county wherein sixty-five of the seventy-six secondary schools had no fifth or sixth year.

There are indications from other areas too that local Labour-group meetings attempted to enjoin the all-through policy on Labour members of education committees.[3] Nevertheless, by April 1966, many authorities, urban and rural, had submitted schemes based to some degree on alternatives to the all-through model.[4]

Central-Local Negotiations

The S E D had managed to reduce the number of secondary schools by about a third in the twenty years after the 1945 Act. But the school system still embodied much of the organisational heterogeneity that Craik and Struthers had struggled to contain (see chapter 2). Comprehensive reorganisation gave the Department a fresh opportunity to standardise local provision. David Dickson told us that he wrote the Department's survey of secondary-school provision published in its annual report for 1965:

D I C K S O N. What I was anxious to show in that report was the enormous variety of organisation which existed and which had developed naturally without any pushing by anybody. It had all arisen from local circumstances. Sometimes only because there happened to be in existence a building of a certain size in a certain place. I was astonished myself at the variety I found.

In his survey, Dickson had complained that geography, local history and local jealousy had all had an influence, and that too often the pattern of an area 'ha[d] simply grown over the years without any overall plan to control it'. He had hoped that Circular 600 would correct this situation (S E D 1966a, 37-8). But how were the Department and the new Labour Government to cut back this variegated growth, especially now that the education authorities' first responses to Circular 600 threatened to feed it? We discussed Labour's strategy with Bruce Millan:

Q. Circular 600 left a lot of scope for negotiation. The availability of teachers, the disposition, size and age of buildings, and the demographic characteristics of the area are all allowed to be arguments that an authority might use to modify the implementation of the all-through policy. At the same time, when the question was put to the vote in local education committees, there was sometimes an absolute insistence on the all-through comprehensive. At a local level a strong party line was followed, and committees became political.

MILLAN. Well, I think that I might put it rather differently. . . . Of course, one had to take account of the local circumstances . . . but there was a general preference for the six-year school. Now I conducted a lot of these negotiations myself with authorities . . . I think that they were meant to put in their proposals almost by the time I took over, I suppose in April 1966. In fact, the detailed implementation of proposals took a very considerable time, and I had discussions with most authorities about them. . . . On the whole, authorities made up their own minds in that particular direction. It wasn't a question of Government's having to put pressure on them; they decided, looking at their own circumstances, that this was the best thing to do, and it happened to coincide with our view. Where our views didn't coincide, I had discussions with the authorities, and on the whole, we persuaded them that they should go for six-year schools.

Q. Well, in a sense, there was pressure, because it was clear that there was going to be no further building money for schools that weren't six-year schools in areas where they were considered appropriate.

MILLAN. Well, that is not really quite true. You see, there was never a separate programme of building anyway for comprehensive reorganisation. In a sense, it is almost the other way about. Many authorities said, 'Well, we want to go six-year, but you are not going to give us the money to build new six-year schools'. And we said, 'No, we can't do that, but there is a very big school-building programme which we are providing for the additional pupils because of the raising of the school-leaving age, and within that, if you act sensibly, you can actually make a lot of progress towards your six-year comprehensive schools simultaneously' [SED 1966d]. Most of them in fact did do that. I think that directors generally were in favour of the comprehensive system. . . . Now, I am not saying that they were all in favour of doing it in a particular way. Obviously that would be too much to hope for, perhaps unhealthy. But they were basically in favour of comprehensive reorganisation, even in areas where they had education committees whom you would think would be instinctively or politically against it. I could mention examples, but I won't, where a director was strongly pro-comprehensive in a very strongly Tory area. Secondly, I think even in Tory areas, the education committees were basically in favour of it as well. This was the difference between Scotland and England. It didn't become a party-political issue at local level. I'm not saying that there weren't odd arguments. But you didn't have, in Scotland, the kind of situations that eventually led to the attempt at compulsory reorganisation in England, where local authorities, strictly for political reasons, were standing out against the Government. I honestly didn't have any arguments like that with the education authorities. In fact, I would say that there were some Tory-controlled authorities that were among the more enthusiastic about reorganisation. . . . I didn't have a great series of political rows about reorganisation. The exception to that was, of course, the issue of fee-paying, particularly in Edinburgh, on which we eventually legislated. . . . [The negotiations] were very hard work, and they went on for a long period, but I found the discussions extremely rewarding, because there was a general consensus of view, normally. . . . I think that the county with which I had the longest discussions on this was probably Renfrewshire, because they were actually in process of establishing a junior-high and senior-high system when the circular came out. . . . We inherited a situation in which a lot of the schools had already been built or were actually in the building, and that makes life very difficult. There were special problems in parts of Renfrewshire, and then there was the problem about having separate Catholic schools, which always makes planning much more difficult in terms of numbers in particular areas. So there was a very complicated set-up there. . . . The junior-high/senior-high idea I think had also attracted Dr McIntosh of Fife [Director of Education 1944-66]. He, I suppose, along with Mr Fairlie of Renfrewshire [Director of Education 1964-75], was one of the leading advocates of that; it had all sorts of problems, including whether the transfer should be at the end of S2 or S4. . . .

Q. In Fife I think you had a Labour-controlled Committee, whereas in Renfrewshire you had an Independent Committee.

MILLAN. Yes. But Mr Robertson, I think it was, who was the Chairman of the Education Committee in Renfrewshire, was actually in favour of comprehensive reorganisation. I had no political difficulty with him. Mr Devlin . . . in Fife . . . was a good and strong chairman there. Dr McIntosh, of course, was a very strong Director indeed. . . . The trouble about the junior-high/senior-high system is that you finished up with, as it were, too many schools of too small a size. . . . It was a lot easier when you were starting from scratch, and you were providing for roofs-over-heads for ROSLA. You built six-year schools and you closed down some others anyway, because they were old, or whatever, and you got the result that you were looking for. But, if you were in the middle of a building programme or had just completed a building programme on a two-tier system, then you inherited a much more complicated problem. I never took the view that I was going to force solutions down their throats that would be educationally undesirable, for example, by having a so-called six-year school in three different bits which were two miles apart or something. That happened a lot in England, and I don't say it didn't happen at all in Scotland, but it certainly did not happen because I forced it on the authority. I tried to avoid that kind of solution . . . and that is why, at the end of the day, certainly by the 1970s, we didn't have a system with nothing but six-year schools, or anything like it.

Young (1971) has provided a detailed case-study of the negotiations in Renfrewshire, based on private and public documents and also on interviews with a number of the leading figures, including Millan himself. He shows how Fairlie, the Director, had brought the 'two-tier' system with him from Fife where he had worked under McIntosh. McIntosh had advocated the system in the early 1960s (McIntosh 1962), and had planned a number of schools to this blueprint before his abrupt resignation in 1966. Fairlie, however, had a 'strong hold' over the Renfrewshire committee (Young 1971, 45), and the plan to which he started to build in September 1964 provided for only two all-through schools. He justified the two-tier model as a compromise between the selective and comprehensive systems, a compromise which embodied, in his words, 'progressive selection' or 'less rigid selection' at a later age (*ibid.*, 15-16). Young finds that 'no one on the Committee pursued a particular form of reorganisation from a sense of political commitment' (*ibid.*, 46); the Labour members were in a minority; they accepted the two-tier system; they did not function as a group; and they were sometimes divided by inter-community suspicions. Young concludes that 'such party politics as existed was played at County Council level' (*ibid.*, 47). Millan himself drafted the letter rejecting Renfrew's proposals some months after the March 1966 election had returned Labour with a larger parliamentary majority. Young writes that Millan found the committee 'reasonable' (*ibid.*, 49), ready to abolish fee-paying in its schools, and willing to reconsider the case for all-through schools. Even so, the negotiations took two years and nine months and resulted, even then, in compromise. It was only after 1975, when Renfrew was reconstituted within the Labour-controlled Strathclyde Region, that an all-through policy for the whole area was adopted (McKechin 1976).

One other study, by Laing (1984), illuminates important aspects of the central-local negotiation of reorganisation, in this case in Glasgow. Laing shows how the Labour majority-group delayed the abolition of its selective, fee-paying schools principally because its many Catholic supporters feared the consequences for the Catholic schools of this type, and especially for St Mungo's Academy. At one time, St Mungo's was the main state, selective secondary-school for Catholics in Glasgow and north Lanarkshire. To turn it and other selective Catholic schools into territorial comprehensives appeared to threaten a group that already considered itself underprivileged, and to threaten also the distinctive denominational character of Catholic education. At this time, in Laing's view, 'the Labour Party in Glasgow demonstrated a confusion of conflicting and competing views which militated against a coherent policy' (*ibid.*, 78). Labour lost control locally in 1968, and Glasgow joined with Edinburgh in resisting the abolition of fee-paying and selection. Ross and Millan failed to shift them by negotiation and had to legislate instead. Labour regained control of Glasgow in 1971, by which time the Conservative Government that was returned in 1970 had rescinded Circular 600 and restored to local authorities the power to charge fees. Gordon Campbell and Hector Monro were, respectively, the Scottish Secretary of State and the junior Minister (1971-74) responsible for education. They thought of forcing Glasgow to continue selective provision. But they were advised against intervention by their officials, partly on the grounds that the city's selective schools undermined the authority's comprehensive policy towards which it had worked for over twenty-five years.

When the Labour Government left office in 1970, much remained to be done. Between 1965 and 1970, the 300 non-certificate, four-year schools in Scotland had been halved in number. But the number of four-year schools offering O-grades had fallen only slightly, to 138. The number of six-year comprehensives was approaching 200, but 53 education-authority senior-secondary schools remained, together with 29 grant-aided schools.[5] The system that confronted Campbell and Monro in 1970 was still far from comprehensive. Had the decision on forms of school organisation been solely one for central government, or had Campbell given higher priority to the issue (*ibid.*, 103), it would clearly have been reversible. In the event, in March 1973, Campbell accepted Glasgow's decision to abolish its selective and fee-paying provision. When Labour returned to office in 1974, eighty-five per cent of Scottish secondary pupils were in six-year comprehensive schools.

Middle Schools

The case of middle schools also illustrates limits to the power of the centre. Circular 600 suggested that 'there may well be room for experiment in a few areas with a system of "middle schools", taking pupils from age nine or ten to age fourteen' (SED 1965c, para.12). McEwan, as we saw, was keen to try this in Lanarkshire, and so too were several other directors in their own areas. There was also support from the Secretary of the SED:

GRAHAM. We would have liked to see some experiments – and they would have been experiments, because the thing didn't exist – with the middle school, which had considerable attractions from the point of view of economy of resources in those areas where the all-through school didn't exist. It would have, for example, facilitated dealing with the difficult problem of the top. . . . There were undoubtedly areas where, if there had been middle schools, it would have been easier to produce a really effective top school, a fourth-to-sixth-year school, in those areas where there wasn't a strong tradition to stay on at school, and only a relatively small proportion of the age-group staying on. But, as you said, there was very strong opposition from the profession which is, I suppose, partly conservatism – the new animal – and partly a concern that they were going to divide the profession. There was, at that time possibly more than there is now, a

382

feeling that anybody should have the opportunity to teach the top end of the school. This, in the last analysis, was what really mattered. . . . In one or two areas where tentative ideas of this kind were put forward it was quite clear that there was a good deal of opposition.

Clark confirmed that this had been the case in Aberdeen:

CLARK. The middle-school issue was raised as a possible way of meeting the comprehensive situation. The Committee's lack of enthusiasm for it meant that there were no prolonged negotiations with the teachers' associations on it because they just weren't all that interested.

As we have seen, McEwan in Lanarkshire also had an unsympathetic Committee. In Edinburgh, by contrast, a proposal for a three-tier system of comprehensive schools in the Leith and Portobello districts was part of the City's plan to retain its selective fee-paying schools. But opposition from the EIS was decisive, and neither the Director, George Reith (1961-71), nor the Senior Chief Inspector of Schools, David Dickson, was able to move them:

DICKSON. There was very little support for this type of organisation. To me, disappointingly little. I tried to encourage more of it personally, because I thought it was worth experimenting with. There were two authorities who seriously considered middle schools to solve problems in particular parts of their areas, Edinburgh and Stirlingshire. But in neither area did the final solutions involve a real middle-school organisation.[6]

Q. How much help could you give George Reith in his discussions with the EIS?

DICKSON. Well, we were doing our best with the EIS privately quite apart from George Reith. The difficulty lay of course in the field of teachers' qualifications. You could not have run a middle-school system without stretching the regulations, or using them rather unorthodoxly. The difficulty . . . was whether they were going to have teachers teaching pupils of secondary-school age, who did not have an Article 39 qualification.[7]

Bryden confirmed this account of the EIS position:

BRYDEN. Funnily enough, our primary chaps were quite prepared to accept the idea of middle schools. . . . But, rather to my surprise, our secondary members opposed it, and so the Institute generally stamped on it.

Neighbourhood Schools in Aberdeen

Circular 600 wanted young people to spend 'the formative years of early adolescence in schools where the pupils represent a fuller cross section of the community' (SED 1965c, para.5). But it did not say which community it had in mind, the local neighbourhood, the town or city, or Scotland as a whole. This did not matter very much in respect of the one-quarter or so of pupils in Scotland who lived in places where there was only ever likely to be one secondary school to attend. But for many pupils living in localities served by more than one school, and especially for the one-third of pupils living in the four major cities, there were marked differences between the social characteristics of particular neighbourhoods. The Circular recommended the 'school providing a full range of courses for all pupils from a particular district who would attend it throughout their secondary career' (*ibid.*, para.10). It also said that 'all pupils from a particular primary school [should] proceed in normal circumstances to the same secondary school for at least the first two years of their secondary education' (*ibid.*, para.13). Fixing catchments in this way was bound to widen the social mix of the average secondary school, simply because it removed the social differentiation consequent upon selection at twelve. But, beyond that, its effects were uncertain, and depended upon the extent of the residential segregation of the social classes in each locality, on the idiosyncrasies of the school-catchment map, and on the determination of politicians and officials to redraw it.

We did not ask Millan how far considerations of social mix had figured in his evaluation of the education authorities' proposals for reorganisation. What can be said is that, ten years later in the mid-1970s, there were still wide variations in social-class composition between comprehensive schools in each of the four cities, though this variation was subsequently somewhat reduced; outside the cities the social-class composition of school catchments was less variable (McPherson and Willms 1987). Research on the construction and maintenance of Scottish school-catchment areas is meagre, but the available evidence shows that the resolute local defence of privilege has contributed to the differentiation of city schools along social-class lines (McKechin 1979; Laing 1984; Petch 1986). James Clark was our only source of information on the question of catchments, and his account, to which we come shortly, provided some pointers to the importance of the issue in the developing debate in Aberdeen.

As we explained in the previous chapter, most of Scotland's six-year (certificate) schools in 1965 dated from before the First World War. Aberdeen was no exception with its Academy, High School and Grammar School, and with Robert Gordon's College, a grant-aided school. For the first twenty years after 1945, the building need in Aberdeen was for new junior-secondary schools, and not, in the City's view, for an additional six-year school. But, by the early 1960s, the bulge in the secondary-school population, and the upturn in post-compulsory enrolments consequent upon the new O-grade, made rebuilding and relocation an urgent necessity. A decision was taken to move the Academy from its cramped location in the city centre to an expanding suburb of mainly private housing at Hazlehead. Then, as Clark told us (see chapter 15), Councillor Hughes put comprehensive reorganisation on the agenda. The Academy's impending move focused the debate on two questions with city-wide implications. What sort of school should be housed in the new buildings? And should its catchment as a neighbourhood school include pupils from the adjacent council-house areas of Mastrick and Summerhill, the edge of which was only five minutes walk from the new Hazlehead site across a pleasant open dell?

CLARK. It was seen by most members of the Committee in the early 1960s (perhaps 1964-ish or thereby, 1964-65) that comprehensive education must be considered . . . as an alternative to the existing system. And I think that, certainly on the Labour side, there was fairly general agreement on this. Secondly, I think initially, despite the agreement that it was a major issue that must be discussed, there was no unanimity as to what the implications of this might be. In other words, members saw the ultimate implementation of the comprehensive idea in a variety of different ways. Thirdly, I think that it would be fair to say that, whatever else happened, following a positive decision on comprehensive education, the one thing that it did mean – and those who thought about it were unanimous on this – was the elimination of selection at the end of the primary school. This was the big factor. . . . Fourthly, it gradually emerged that, whatever the system was, whether it was all-through, or whether it was some kind of break, it was desirable that an attempt be made to have equality of provision throughout the City, and, consequently, the main implication of this for Aberdeen was what was to be the new status of the existing senior secondaries . . . Hazlehead in particular, but also the Grammar School and the High.

Q. Hazlehead in particular just because the building issue had crystallised earlier?

CLARK. In particular, that's right. Now, these were fairly clear. As the debate developed, there was a rising tide of opinion, led in particular by Bob Hughes and John Smith – I would say these two in particular, but almost to the same extent by Bob Middleton – that all-through must be the answer [see chapter 15, note 8]. Now, at this stage, I was aware of the fact that – and in fact I knew what was going on, because members talked to me about it – there was a lot of discussion in the Labour Party as to what the party line was to be here; and, ultimately of course, it came down on the all-through. It was at that stage, I think, or round about that time, that the very important issues of social mix, allocation of catchment areas, possible variation in the types of comprehensive school because of the differences in social mix and for other factors, really came to the surface.

Following Hughes' motion, Clark presented his first proposals for reorganisation to the Committee in December 1964 (Clark 1964). His report accepted the prevailing critique of intelligence testing and accepted also that the new O-grade had invalidated previous arrangements for selective transfer at twelve years (see chapter 15). But it also warned against the 'unthinking acceptance' of a 'foreign point of view' derived from English experience, that was inappropriate to Scotland's 'different educational heritage'. Clark therefore proposed that all Aberdeen pupils should transfer at twelve on a non-selective basis to a neighbourhood junior-high school. There would be broad-band setting on entry, based on primary teachers' estimates and a verbal-reasoning test. At the end of second year, parents would 'have the option of having their children transferred to the senior-secondary schools, after receiving educational guidance'. Though technically senior-high schools under the new arrangement, the Grammar School, High School and Academy would retain their names: 'there is merit in preserving something of traditional value to Aberdonians'. The junior-high schools would offer only O-grade and vocationally oriented ('Brunton') courses, but there would be a further transfer at the end of fourth year.

Clark's two-tier proposal corresponded closely to 'scheme three' of the five schemes proposed under the English circular. Benn and Simon thought 'scheme three' was 'by far the most complicated and controversial'. Transfer to the senior-high school at fourteen might sometimes be based on 'free' parental choice, with no restrictions imposed by the availability of places in the upper school, or else it might be 'guided' in ways that were implicitly or explicitly selective (Benn and Simon 1972, 60-3). Clark's scheme was never to be tested by experience. On paper it gave choice firmly to the parents, but it asked the guidance to act as 'an essential brake on those parents who would seek the status symbol of attendance at one of our excellent senior secondaries for their children, irrespective of their needs' (Clark 1964, 19).

The Committee cannot have been fully satisfied with Clark's proposals because, six weeks later, he produced a further report on the implications for Aberdeen of a one-tier system. He argued against such a move on the grounds of size, availability of buildings, lack of social mix, and uncertainties over the age of transfer from primary school. And he also suggested that only a senior-high school could support a sixth year of a size that could provide courses for the Advanced-grade that the SED was then promoting (see chapter 13): 'this is an important problem for we cannot allow our justifiable concern for the average or below average to prejudice the emergence of our abler boys and girls as fully qualified people' (Clark 1965, 4).

The argument continued, certainly until March 1966, when Clark debated the merits of his two-tier proposals at a local teach-in (*SEJ* 4 March 1966). But the arrival of Circular 600 six months earlier had deprived him of an important source of support:

CLARK. The initial proposal . . . would have meant a quicker transfer to comprehensive education. . . . Inspectors who were involved in that consideration gave it as their professional private opinion that this was a starter and, indeed, some of them commended it without qualification. Some of them did this before Circular 600. I never found a single member of the Inspectorate who voiced an opinion on that particular proposal after the issue of Circular 600.

Q. I think I understand what you're saying.

CLARK. I'm being extremely tactful here. I'm not saying that my own Committee was wrong in deciding against this interim proposal. I'm not saying they were wrong in going for the all-through comprehensive programme and all that entailed in the way of building and other provision by a certain date. What I am saying, at this point in time, is that, as far as professional education is concerned, as voiced by certain members of the Inspectorate, this seemed to be quashed after the political edict. . . .

Q. The wind was blowing pretty hard with Circular 600 and ROSLA in the offing. Whereas (this is hypothesis) Brunton would have stood against it, Dickson was prepared to bend with it.

CLARK. I would agree with that, because there were inspectors who read my first report and who commended it privately, and I got no support from the Inspectorate whatsoever during the discussions on the possible introduction of comprehensive education. I think that, if John Brunton had agreed with what I put forward originally, and I think that he probably would have done, he would have taken a rather different line.

Q. Another difference, of course, would be that Dickson had Graham as his Secretary, and he did not have Murrie-Arbuckle backing.

CLARK. This is true. And I think that different senior chief inspectors were conscious, to a different degree, of the thinking of their political masters.

Q. Can you elaborate on that?

CLARK. Well, quite frankly, as far as I know – and I'm speaking from the outside – I think that Circular 600 was much more a political document than an educational one about a major educational development, and I think that a strong Inspectorate would have had a greater influence on the contents of Circular 600.

Q. Can you tell us how you handled the catchment-area question?

CLARK. This was important, and there were a lot of discussions as to how it could be done, but there was little doubt in the minds of the members of the Committee at that time, that they didn't want anything artificial, if they could possibly avoid it. And I remember suggesting to the Convener, at that time, that one of the considerations really had to be, I thought, an endeavour to link up a certain number of primaries, normally three or four, with a secondary, to try to make a unit, and as far as possible have the selection of the primaries, where there was the possibility of a primary going to one school or another, taking into account, at that stage, the effect that the allocation of that particular primary might have on the social mix of the two schools concerned. . . . But this didn't, and couldn't, in a city like Aberdeen, solve the problem of social mix, in the sense that, even although this was done, there were schools that had greater proportions of certain types of youngsters than others. . . . We were aiming at having ten comprehensives in Aberdeen of a maximum of about 1200 pupils each. We reckoned that, if we couldn't have a perfect social mix, there were sound educational advantages in having increased linkages between a secondary and a small group of primaries. . . . Taking into account the fact that the Committee did not want bussing and transporting and this kind of thing, once that's established, it seemed to me, from the educational point of view, that any artificial break-up of an area was less worthy of consideration than linking particular primary schools with a secondary.

Q. Could I ask how your idea of social mix was defined in operation? Was it in terms of housing types?

CLARK. Broadly.

Q. Did you find that the existing deployment of the different types in the city gave you much scope for movement?

CLARK. It didn't. As an educationist, I have been critical of aspects of the housing policy since the early post-war years. You see, if you look at an area like Northfield, where, when it was established first of all, you had virtually all council housing, with a population of roughly 12000 – something like the size of a town like Elgin – you're not really going to get much of a social mix for any comprehensive school serving an area of that kind.

Q. How easy did you find it to carry the Convener of the Education Committee with you in this? What sort of discussion was there?

CLARK. There was quite a lot of discussion in the Committee, but there was no division at the end of the day. Once the issue had been fully discussed and the difficulties of the placement in the city of council and private housing were considered, there was no division at the end of the day, but [the view was that] the recommendation that we had considered – the allocation of primary schools to a secondary – was, on balance, the best decision to make. . . .

Q. This must have meant that other people would have had a go at drawing lines on maps, and that kind of thing.

CLARK. That's right.

Q. And what about the contentious area between Summerhill and the Mastrick area, and Hazlehead?

CLARK. The short answer is: the Committee decides. The issue was put quite clearly to the Committee. The primary catchment area was the important one in this context, and there were arguments *pro* and *con* by various members of the Committee, depending on their particular outlook. But this really was a matter of Committee decision.

Q. Do you agree with the suggestion that the commitment to all-through schools was rushed through because of the symbolic importance of Hazlehead, plus the political need for an irrevocable commitment before the party lost power?

CLARK. I agree with you that I think that certain members thought that way. I think it would also be fair to say that, at that point in time, there were certain members of the Labour Party who, pretty quickly, came round to the view that the only answer was the all-through comprehensive, and they were anxious that the decision be made, a commitment be made, to all-through comprehensives right away, almost whatever the consequences were.

Q. Why did they think that? You're suggesting a divided party.

CLARK. Knowing the individuals, I think that there were variations among the various members of the Labour Party as to what was the best thing to do. I think that they ultimately got unanimity on the basic principle, that there should be comprehensive education, however they were going to define it or implement it. And, as you say, this came before Circular 600. But I think that among the Labour Party, there were those who felt, almost from the beginning, if not from the beginning, that the only answer was all-through comprehensives. If I may just add to that, I think some of them may have regretted the commitment to that kind of decision, in principle, before they had thoroughly explored the consequential issues such as social mix. . . . In private conversation quite a number of the leading members of the Labour Party, then and since, have said to me that they were sorry that they didn't accept the first plan. . . .

Q. Were they after opportunities for the old type of grammar education for their children, on the assumption that all schools would become like the Grammar and the Academy? When social mix was really presented to them in the terms of the hard, concrete fact of which primary schools would feed into which secondary schools they didn't like the implications. Is that too simple an interpretation?

CLARK. You are not the first person who has said that.

Q. Andrew Walls [Labour member of Aberdeen Education Committee 1971-74] makes the point that the city has been Labour-controlled for a long period, but that the education they want for their children is after the traditional, academic, selective fashion.[8]

CLARK. A fair number of Labour councillors have been educated at [Robert] Gordon's College.

Clark's testimony, of course, is the view of just one man, albeit one who was centrally involved. A similar view of the Labour record in Aberdeen, but from a somewhat different vantage point, is to be found in R. F. Mackenzie's account of his headship of Summerhill Academy, the school that served the Mastrick and Summerhill estates (Mackenzie n.d.). Mackenzie was appointed in 1968 and suspended, though in effect sacked, in 1974. He regarded Clark as 'a man of conservative educational principles' (*ibid.*, 94-5), and thought his Education Committee similar:

> The Labour members of Aberdeen Education Committee failed to defend the comprehensive revolution because their ideas on education came from their own upbringing in establishment-controlled schools. (*ibid.*, 34)
>
> The Labour Party has never really thought out the implications of comprehensive education and the result is that the residual ideas of the previous dispensation survive, uninspected. Aberdeen Education Committee were keen that no vital changes should be made in North-East of Scotland education. (*ibid.*, 98)

Summerhill is a microcosm of the issues and individuals discussed in this

389

chapter. The school had been opened by Sir James Robertson in 1965 as a junior-secondary school. In Mackenzie's view its first head had valued the Scottish tradition of academic advancement and strict discipline, and had wanted to show that his pupils 'were every bit as good as the pupils at Aberdeen Grammar School or Aberdeen Girls High School' (*ibid.*, 13). The third of the 'elite schools of the old dispensation' (*ibid.*, 34) was Aberdeen Academy, and Norman Walker (see chapter 15) persuaded the Education Committee to give the name 'Academy' to Summerhill, along with all the City's new comprehensives, when it was reopened as a comprehensive on Mackenzie's arrival. The Secretary of State, William Ross, spoke at the reopening, and he seems to have drawn on the critique of academic external examinations that Robertson and the Advisory Council had developed in their *Secondary Education* report of 1947.[9] Mackenzie was already known for his progressive views on examinations and discipline. As the head of a junior-secondary school in Fife, he had earlier brushed with Douglas McIntosh (see chapter 15) and with his Labour-controlled committee over these issues (Mackenzie 1970, 63, 83-4, 125 and 137-9). Robertson had publicly supported him at the time (Robertson 1969d, 226), but history was rapidly to repeat itself in Aberdeen. Mackenzie failed to win the support of sufficient staff and parents for his progressive approach to curriculum and discipline. Conservative councillors helped turn events in the school into a local *cause célèbre*. With regionalisation and new elections approaching, support in the Committee drained away, despite Clark's protracted attempts to negotiate the issues between the parties. Mackenzie felt that Labour councillors, MPs and Ministers had deserted him and Summerhill. He saw this desertion as symptomatic of a wider Labour reluctance to reform the content and practice of education, and to substitute education as community for education as meritocratic social selection (Mackenzie n.d., *passim*). In this respect his analysis of his own situation in Aberdeen had much in common with the critique of the Labour Party's support for 'statist' schooling offered by the CCCS group in *Unpopular Education* (see chapter 1, above).

Selection Within Secondary School

We asked Millan about the meritocratic view:

Q. Our impression is that many saw comprehensive reorganisation in the 1960s as an opening-up of the opportunity of certification that previously had led to university or whatever, to a wider proportion of the age-group, and saw it in terms of an equalisation of educational and employment opportunities, in rather instrumental terms.

MILLAN. Yes. I think that it is a fair representation. As I say, it is not a unanimous view. It is the difficulty of expressing success in meaningful terms, except through examination passes. How do you prove that you have turned out pupils from a school that are better educated and have had more value in their education, in terms which are non-quantitative? I don't know how you do it, actually; how you measure it. So, I think that it is very easy to look at the examination successes and say that that shows that the system is working, but it is not enough.

Millan himself volunteered that the reorganisation of externals had occupied more of his energies than the reform of the curriculum, and the shaping of practices and relationships within the school:

MILLAN. Most of the discussions then [before 1970] were about how you would get the system operating in terms of buildings, and how you would adjust pupil entry and zoning. There was less discussion about what happened within the schools. Now, a good deal of that did go on, but what happens inside a school is, in a sense, more difficult to influence, and takes longer than the catchment areas and the rest. That is all very complicated and very difficult, and sometimes very controversial. . . . The inspectors were putting a lot of guidance or influence in these particular areas. But I would say that, up until 1970, we hadn't made as much progress with that area as I would have liked. You see, not everybody was sold on the idea. The sort of argument that you got was, 'mixed-ability teaching is all right, but please exclude my particular subject'.

The policy for mixed-ability teaching marked a sharp break with previous policy and practice, and was introduced as David Dickson was taking over from Brunton as Senior Chief Inspector:

Q. Brunton himself wanted an acknowledgement of the legitimacy of setting arrangements [i.e. the grouping of pupils by ability in each subject] in Circular 600, as I understand it?

DICKSON. Yes, I think that's true. Yes. . . .

Q. Subsequently the Department was very anxious to put under people's noses examples of successful mixed-ability teaching, and to emphasise the needs of the less able pupils. Is that correct?

DICKSON. I think so. Yes. We tended to recommend particularly a broad banding of some sort, as an initial step if nothing else; it might prove to be the final step. If, as an initial step away from the older ways of rigid division at twelve plus, you start off comprehensive schools with streams, from the word go, this seemed to us quite a contradiction in terms.

One source told us non-attributably that the early drafts of Circular 600 had explicitly permitted the continuation of setting or streaming. There was no such allowance in the final draft of Circular 600, but the main recommendations for mixed-ability organisation were not issued until Circular 614 of 1966 (SED 1966b). We asked Millan how easy it had been to persuade the Inspectorate of the advisability of mixed-ability teaching:

MILLAN. I don't think that they needed much persuasion.

Q. Did you spend a long time with David Dickson over this issue?

MILLAN. Not persuading him, if that's what you mean. . . . I am not aware that it ever arose with me that I was asking them to do things which they found professionally objectionable. . . . Their view on this was basically the same as the directors, and the education committees and the general public : that selection had proved to be undesirable ; that one should abolish selection ; that one should discourage selection under another heading by splitting everybody up in a comprehensive school. But they also knew my view which was that, while I wanted that to be done, and as rapidly as possible, I was not asking people to do things which were educationally impossible, and I was willing to allow for the fact that you have to persuade teachers as well, the people who are actually doing the thing at the chalk face. . . . I think that the way the system works is that you take a view which you may discuss with the Inspectorate and others, and that would be outlined in the circulars you are sending out on these important issues from time to time. And then the Inspectorate would work within that circular in persuading people along these lines. But, at the end of the day, the Inspectorate doesn't have the power over an individual school to say that they have to organise the school in this particular way ; that isn't the way that the system works.

The documentary and oral evidence broadly confirm Millan's account. The annual reports of the Department for the years 1966 to 1970 encouraged schools to adopt mixed-ability practices. But the tone was always tentative, as it also was when Dickson addressed a conference of teachers in 1969, saying of the common course, 'I am not going to tell you the answer to all the problems. We just don't know' (*SEJ* 13 June 1969). This was also the tenor of Inspectorate advice on the ground, as McEwan recollected it :

McEWAN. There was more peddling of the idea of a common course among senior teachers, not just the youngsters but some rectors and the Inspectorate, than among the members of the Committee. This was something that was developing in teacher thinking rather than in Labour Party or political thinking. . . . I'm not much enamoured of the idea myself. I can't really see the point of promoting the idea of consultation with the primary school, and extracting all the good advice and guidance that you can get from primary-school teachers, if you are going to ignore it the moment the child arrives in the secondary school, and put him in a mixed-ability group on the basis of a clean slate, ostensibly ignoring what you have learned about his capacity. . . .

Q. Did you feel that people like Dickson and his local inspectors were pushing the common-course idea in Lanarkshire?

McEWAN. I never had it peddled to me. One got the impression that the schools were, perhaps, looking over their shoulders at things that had been hinted or suggested, perhaps, by some inspectors. I didn't think, myself, that there was any strong push to have the common course as a matter of policy from the Inspectorate. But some headteachers seemed definitely inclined to move in this direction.

Clark's recollection of events in Aberdeen was similar :

CLARK. Once the Committee had committed itself to the all-through comprehensive policy, I was asked to consult the teaching staff on a variety of issues: the implications of this for social education, the implications of this decision in curricular terms and methodology, and this included mixed ability. And these were thrashed out at a long series of meetings between representatives of the teaching staff, including the heads, and myself. . . . We did recommend that we would start by having mixed-ability grouping in S1 and S2. . . .

Q. Did you find that the Inspectorate was also taking a lead in guiding you in this direction?

CLARK. I think the honest answer to that is, 'Not very strongly'. The Inspectorate knew what was going on, the kind of discussions that I was having; and my impression is that they were perfectly happy to allow us to carry on in this way. And, as far as mixed-ability teaching is concerned, we obviously came up with the result that they would have wanted if they were following SED policy.

Q. What was the effect of the withdrawal of Circular 600 in 1970 when the Government changed hands? Was the ship set on a course that it couldn't veer from at that stage?

CLARK. Yes. . . .

Q. Do you have any comments on why this innovation was apparently so rapidly accepted?

CLARK. Well, this is . . . an illustration of something that I feel is very important: that in educational matters, if those concerned are fully consulted, if communication is good, if issues are argued out, if there is a solid base of that kind for change and experimental work, you find that many teachers are prepared to make a real go of something. I do not believe, and I think this is one of the reasons why teachers are called 'conservative' at certain times and in certain ways – I do not believe that you can, willy-nilly, impose major changes on a group of professional people. You've got to work at it, and for it.

Under the Conservative Government of 1970-74, the Inspectorate's public position on mixed-ability teaching became yet more permissive. An HMI report in 1972 concluded, 'it is no longer reasonable, if it ever was so, to believe or expect that there is a single, uniform, demonstrably superior solution appropriate to the needs and circumstances of all schools at all times' (SED 1972c, para.76). But the report found that most schools had, in fact, adopted some form of mixed-ability organisation in their first two years (*ibid.*, paras 12-14); and it echoed Clark's and McEwan's accounts in concluding that 'experiments with new forms of organisation and with the common course have clearly for the most part resulted from the initiative of headteachers . . .' (*ibid.*, para.74). Millan, who with Ross and Hart initiated the change to mixed ability, was in broad agreement:

MILLAN. What happens inside the individual school is not under the control of the Minister in any direct way. He can influence it and guide it, but he doesn't go in there and tell the headmaster how to run his school. We don't have that kind of system in the UK, although there are other countries, as I understand it, with a very much more centralised system where you have curriculums, and indeed timetables, which are centrally organised. . . . Normally in these countries, as I understand it, that is done on the basis of long periods of discussion and negotiation. But, once the decision has been made, then it is applied everywhere in exactly the same way. But our system doesn't operate just like that.

Did Millan think, then, that comprehensive reorganisation had achieved its purpose?

MILLAN. Obviously there isn't any point in just shifting the selective system back a couple of years. The idea was to look at the individual capacities of individual children and not to slot them into academic and non-academic categories. . . . Now, of course, that raises immense problems of school organisation which we haven't solved to this day. And we have just had the Munn and Dunning reports and of course we know that we haven't got a system in our comprehensive schools that relates equally favourably to every individual pupil.

Discussion

By comparison with England and Wales, Scotland started reorganisation in 1965 with more schools that were comprehensive in an *omnibus* sense, and, in the following ten years, pursued a narrower range of organisational options, and brought them closer to completion. Nevertheless, although the change was decisive, the evidence of this chapter does not alter the received view that comprehensive reorganisation in Scotland was a British policy applied to Scotland, with little Scottish impetus before the early 1960s. There were, of course, various domestic considerations that made implementation easier, but they were not the main precipitating factors. The pre-1965 *omnibus* schools were rigidly streamed, and had been adopted by many authorities, especially in rural areas, for reasons more of resource than of reform. Glasgow, it is true, opted to build only comprehensive schools after 1945. But in practice this was mainly a policy for large council-housing estates. The selective senior-secondaries were left intact. Fees were retained in a number of them in 1945, and, twenty years later, the issue of fees was to delay the implementation of reorganisation. By then Glasgow was admitting forty per cent of its transfer pupils to selective (certificate) courses. There, and elsewhere in Scotland, expansion had contradictory effects. It persuaded many that Scotland did not need comprehensive reorganisation. But it also increased dissatisfaction with selection, because more pupils were now rejected at the borderline (see chapter 15).

The abolition of selection at twelve years was one thing, but its elimination from secondary education was quite another. Even Circular 600 did not advocate that. Indeed, many thought the Circular consistent with the differentiation of provision according to pupil ability, and this is reflected in the education authorities' first plans for reorganisation, submitted early in 1966. When we put this to Millan, he said that he thought the directors we interviewed were possibly not representative. But, representative or not, McIntosh of Fife, McEwan of Lanarkshire, and Clark of Aberdeen were all influential, and all proposed to reorganise, at least initially and some finally, on a basis that was wholly or partly two-tier ('scheme three' of the English Circular 10/65). It is difficult to find a director who initially volunteered an all-through blueprint for the populous areas of a major education authority: not Reith in Edinburgh, nor Fairlie in Renfrewshire, nor Bain in Glasgow (Laing 1984, 57). Cameron in Dunbartonshire was mentioned to us as a supporter of the all-through comprehensive, but even there the initial proposals for Clydebank were two-tier. Midlothian may have been an exception. Inspectorate opinion is largely unknown. Brunton, we were told, supported comprehensives, but had reservations about a mixed-ability first year. Moreover, the whole thrust of S E D policy while he was Senior Chief Inspector was towards a greater differentiation of course provision earlier in secondary school.[10] The glimpse that we have of Inspectorate advice in Aberdeen in the early months of 1965 shows support for Clark's two-tier proposals. The E I S was opposed to fee-paying, but was uncommitted on selection and the all-through comprehensive (*SEJ* 1 June 1962). As far as professional educational opinion was concerned, therefore, one must treat with some scepticism Millan's claim that, on the eve of Circular 600, the arguments about selection had largely been won.

Nor had they been entirely won within the Labour Party itself. In Scotland, a lead came in the 1950s from prominent Scottish M Ps such as Ross and Herbison, and, by the early 1960s in Fife and Aberdeen, the issue was being promoted by a new generation of councillors less thirled to the ideology of an expanding meritocracy. But Labour councillors in many localities were reluctant to place the party line above their loyalty to the local academy, and there were some antagonisms between Labour committee members representing different areas. Both circumstances impeded the development of consistent policies against selection.

Scotland was not unusual in this respect. In England, also, some Labour authorities were reluctant to reorganise, both before and after 1965 (Pattison 1980). What was more common in Scotland, however, was a match between the political complexion of the central and local authority, and this, as much as anything else, explains why reorganisation proceeded more decisively in Scotland than it did south of the Border. The policy took time to organise, and perhaps was less easy to promote when the Labour Government had a parliamentary majority of only six. Nevertheless, as the Lanarkshire example shows, an education committee could be brought into line even in these circumstances. But many were not, until the March 1966

General Election had strengthened Labour's hand. Millan found the subsequent negotiations hard and time-consuming, but he was not obliged to negotiate with political opponents as often as were his counterparts in England.

Size also may have been a factor here. Millan had to deal with only thirty-five authorities, and he had a larger Schools Inspectorate to advise him, relative to England. There the Minister of Education, Anthony Crosland, either did not have, or had not allowed himself, sufficient resources to keep pace with the education authorities' responses to Circular 10/65 (Boyle and Crosland 1971, 191). It may even be, as Benn and Simon have argued, that Crosland was also hampered by the DES policy 'to get as much agreement as possible by pursuing a consensus line . . . [and] a strategy of an accelerated rate of growth for comprehensives within a bipartite structure' (Benn and Simon 1972, 86 and 87). Benn and Simon believe that the English Ministers 'had no choice but to rely on the DES for a great deal of policy implementation' (*ibid.*, 85). But we have come across no suggestion either that the Labour Government in Scotland depended overmuch on its officials, or that it was frustrated by them. Indeed the evidence on reorganisation in Glasgow indicates the reverse.

To suggest, as we do, that the pace was made from the centre in Scotland, is not, however, to argue for the thesis of Scottish centralisation, except perhaps in the sense that Millan and Ross had a more effective Department at their disposal than Crosland and Short, and possibly a more compliant one. In Scotland, no less than in England, the local authority could frustrate central government. Millan could shift Renfrewshire only so far. When the Scottish administration was opposed on the issue of fees, as it was by Edinburgh and by Glasgow after 1968, it was obliged to turn to legislation. When the Labour administration in Glasgow confronted the Conservative Government, Campbell and Monro backed down. The decisive factor in each instance was not the power of the central department, but whether or not the Government had political allies in the local authority. In this respect Scottish reorganisation was no different from reorganisation in England. There too, the majority of authorities that started to reorganise by 1970 were Labour-controlled at the time (Litt and Parkinson 1979, 114).

There are further parallels. Reviewing a number of case studies of reorganisation in England, Ribbins and Brown have found that, with the exception of the Catholic Church, non-political groups such as parents, teachers and education officials were not important initiators of change: 'In the great majority of cases the demand for reorganization entered the system through the agency of the local political party' (Ribbins and Brown 1979, 190).[11] But, they warn, 'the argument that the pace of reorganization has depended on the political colour of the controlling party locally needs to be used with some care' (*ibid.*, 191). As in Scotland, they found a range of opinion within each party, with the views of one or two individuals often being decisive.

And they also found Conservative-controlled authorities, especially in rural areas, that were prepared to accept comprehensive schemes. Here, again, Scotland was similar.

One difference, however, between England and Scotland seems to have been that the parliamentary party did more to stimulate the local political demand in Scotland, and to shape the form it took. Ribbins and Brown found in England that a report by the chief education officer usually formed the basis for the authority's final decision on the form of organisation to be adopted. By contrast, in a number of instances in Scotland, the director's initial proposals were overruled locally, or were substantially modified in subsequent central-local negotiation. It may also be that the Scottish Ministers themselves were more directly involved in local negotiations than their English counterparts.

Two further contrasts with England merit a comment. Ribbins and Brown report few cases in England of major teacher influence on the form of reorganisation adopted locally. But the opposition of Scottish teachers to the middle-school model seems to have been decisive both locally and nationally. Second, compared with the DES, the SED may have done more to promote mixed-ability teaching in the first two secondary years. But the Department's impact was limited, and what strikes one most about the comparison with England here is the restricted ability of a 'power-dependent' centre to effect changes in school organisation and practice when local support was lacking. In this respect one is looking, on both sides of the Border, at pluralist systems in action.

Conversely, one is also struck by the power of the Scottish centre, when supported by the local authority, to implement decisive and uniform organisational change. Millan and Dickson both emphasised the complexity of the local inheritance of buildings and organisational forms in 1965. Yet ten years after a decision to adopt the all-through form (which in Renfrewshire was not until regionalisation in 1975), short-course schools had virtually disappeared from all Scottish authorities, other than those serving remote areas. The speed, universality and uniformity of this change casts doubt on the thesis, advanced especially by Archer (1979, 583-95), that organisational variety in schooling (in her terms a lack of uniformity and systematisation – see chapter 2, note 5 above) tends to sustain a weak central authority, and *vice versa*. Much also depended in the Scottish case, and perhaps decisively so, on the conjunction of political allegiance between centre and periphery.

Is this, then, the final conclusion to be drawn from Scotland's experience of reform, that the political process can reshape the institutional inheritance? It may seem unconvincing in the light of the ambivalence and conflict that characterised the everyday politics of reorganisation, and in the light of subsequent doubts about its achievement. But we must understand the character and achievement of the reform against the backdrop of the six decades of selective post-primary schooling that had gone before. A stratified school system had become part of the taken-for-granted world of generations of pupils, teachers and parents. As we shall see in the next chapter, it had also bred a policy community that would reproduce that system for future generations. In conjunction with a worsening economic climate, these constraints meant that reorganisation could not be effected overnight. It was not until the mid-1970s that the majority of pupils started their secondary education in the type of comprehensive school the Labour Government recommended. Until then, the evidence is that social-class inequalities in educational attainment had remained more or less stable. But thereafter they changed. As selection was abolished, the social-class gap in attainment started to decline, and so too did social-class differences between the pupil intakes to secondary schools. There followed substantial improvements in the educational attainment of working-class boys and girls (McPherson and Willms 1987).[12] But a process of social equalisation that had been politically initiated could also be undone politically. Through the Assisted Places Scheme of 1981, the Conservative Government restored state support to the grant-aided schools, most of which eventually became wholly private. At the same time, parents were given the statutory right to choose their child's school. The net gains in pupil intake tended to accrue to the first- and second-generation schools, and thereby threatened to return many of the third-generation schools to the inferior position that their antecedents had occupied under the bipartite system.

NOTES

1. Mackenzie (n.d., 98).
2. This was a two-tier system. Before ROSLA in 1973, 'in order to ensure that at least two years were spent in the upper of the two tiers, the transfer age was fixed at fourteen: those who voluntarily chose to go on to the upper school undertook to stay at least two years' (Fairbairn 1980, 1).
3. On a Labour group meeting in Renfrew in 1966, see Young (1971, 49). For evidence of similar meetings in Aberdeen and Fife, to which we cannot attach precise dates, we rely on non-attributable information from two of our interviewees.
4. The *SEJ* reported on 10 June 1966 that 'most authorities favour the junior and senior high school system under which certificate pupils may transfer from a four-year junior high school at the end of their second or fourth year'. It continued, 'but this is not really a very happy compromise with the principles of comprehensive education; all it does is defer for two years the selection and segregation of pupils of different levels of ability which comprehensive education is primarily intended to avoid'. For specific areas see reports in the *SEJ* for Aberdeenshire (1966, 223 and 236), Dunbartonshire (1966, 575), Edinburgh (1966, 270) and Glasgow (1966, 1189). Evidence for Aberdeen, Lanarkshire and Renfrewshire is presented elsewhere in the chapter.
5. Figures from SED 1966a, 33, table A; and SED 1971b, table 4 [4].
6. No middle school was established in Edinburgh, and only two in Grangemouth.
7. Article 39 allowed qualified, graduate primary-school teachers to teach, in the

lower years of secondary school, a subject they had studied for at least two years at university.

8. 'I think that basically most of our Labour Party folk were essentially conservative when it came to education ; what they really wanted was a greater access of the same sort of opportunities as had been represented by the senior secondary schools of the old system' (Walls 1975).

9. Compare Mackenzie (n.d., 35) with SED (1947b, para.233 and appendix III).

10. Some of the annual reports issued during the period of Brunton's influence sniped at comprehensive schools (see SED 1954a, 28 ; 1956a, 27 ; 1962a, 41), but this may reflect the influence of Conservative Ministers.

11. A fuller summary of research on comprehensive reorganisation in England, together with a discussion of its implications for models of policy-making, can be found in James (1980).

12. The evidence on the stability of social-class inequalities in attainment up to the mid-1970s (Gray *et al.*, 1983, ch.12) is framed in terms of the Registrar-General's classification of social class. McPherson and Willms (1987) base their conclusions on a composite measure of socio-economic status.

Part V

The Policy Community

Seventeen

The Kirriemuir Career[1]

The process of identity formation and the process of social reproduction are one and the same. . . . we can understand personal
identity and social structure not as distinct states of being but as
elements of a single process of becoming. . . .   Philip Abrams
(1982, 262)

They [Arbuckle and Rodger] were the kind of individuals whom
you could talk to. You could have gone on holiday with that kind
of person. . . . But I had excellent relations with a lot of the other
members of the Scottish Education Department in the days when
I was to-ing and fro-ing there.   J. S. McEwan, Director of Education for Lanarkshire 1950-75

Introduction

The making of Scottish educational policy has seen a striking continuity of
relationships among a small group of educationists and officials. But there
have also been changes in the size and composition of this group, in the
nature and diversity of its beliefs, and in the interweaving of its governmental and non-governmental membership. Between the Wars the group was
small, and the Department kept its progressive members in particular at
arm's length. This began to change in the mid-1950s, and by the early 1960s
there was a growing body of like-minded men, for they were mostly men,
whom the Department was involving in the shaping, promotion and implementation of its bipartite philosophy. Two events in the first half of the
1960s, however, were to weaken the influence of this group and the basis of
community within it. One was the 1961 teachers' strike which exposed its
tenuous articulation with rank and file teacher opinion, especially in the
industrial West. The other was the return in 1964 of a Labour Government
committed to the ending of selection at twelve. For a time at least, the drive
towards comprehensive reorganisation was to achieve by central political
intervention what a progressive Advisory Council in the 1920s, and again in
the 1940s, had failed to achieve by argument alone, namely a reduction in
the priority given to the academic elite relative to the rest of the school
population. This ruptured the community of beliefs and values within the
policy community at the very time that its relations with government were
themselves being restructured. What followed was a period of moral and

conceptual disarray accompanied, as we have seen, by organisational tension and conflict; in short, a breakdown of consensus which presaged an elaborate effort at consultative repair, beginning at the time of ROSLA in 1973 and extending into the 1980s.

We have already suggested one reason for the importance of a policy community: educational expansion required the Department to share the increased burden and diversity of its work with outsiders, including members of national fringe bodies, and local-authority officials. There was also a contribution to be made to the definition and legitimation of educational goals. The possibility of education as a public, interpersonal system presupposes some ordering of values and related goals, whether through rational choice, bargaining, coercion, or the habitual continuation of unexamined practice. But the legislation of 1944-46 defined educational goals only in broadest outline, and could never, in any case, have specified all areas of their application and realisation. This is because legislators cannot know all eventualities or local circumstances; they cannot be expert in everything; and there is no social science that will infallibly guide the translation of goals into outcomes.

Thus deference and trust have a major part to play. If it is to happen at all, policy action cannot wait on perfect knowledge, nor on exhaustive consultation; the policy community must be trusted by those outside. This requirement is partly offset by electoral, legal and other procedural forms of accountability, and also by the admission of interest groups and experts to the formulation and implementation of policy. Their inclusion in the advisory process helps in turn to explain the importance of deference and trust within the policy community. Neither group-interest nor professional expertise is logically compatible with the vertical line of accountability linking central-government officials through Ministers to the Crown in Parliament. Parliamentary sovereignty can concede neither to interest groups nor to professionals. Both must be trusted to defer. Both, in turn, must trust that their deference does not compromise their professional or representational obligations. Similar considerations apply within local government, and to relations between central and local government.

Collective action across the policy community therefore required that its members understand and accommodate this logical incompatibility. The professional experts in the Inspectorate were required to tolerate the ambiguity of their allegiance, to the Crown and to their *mystery* (see chapters 6 and 7). A similar tolerance was required of members of some fringe bodies. On the one hand, such bodies were understood as the places where government would negotiate with interest groups. On the other hand, on some fringe bodies, government denied a 'representative' identity to individual members drawn from these groups. Members had also to accept ambiguity in the role of government assessors (see chapters 13 and 14). For their own part, central-government administrators had to take educational expertise at least partly on trust, the expertise both of the Inspectorate and of educationists from outside.

Compounding these logical difficulties, which only trust could solve, were other conflicts that had arisen contingently, such as that between the ccc and the Examination Board. In its management of the resultant problems, central government had considerable scope for discretion when defining, interpreting and suspending the rules of the game, and when presenting a selective public account (see chapter 14). In consequence, one of government's criteria, when it chose outside collaborators, was that they could be trusted to know when they and others might properly break the rules. And this put a high, though paradoxical, premium on the moral standing of recruits to the community, and on their sympathy with the Department's aims.

Communities have their own moral systems of value and belief, their own procedures for recognising or excluding members, and their own internal relationships of trust and deference. The anthropology of the policy community was itself an influence on policy and its outcomes. Overlapping political and civil society as it did, its members mediated civil inputs to the political machine, and the outputs from it. By examining the recruitment of policy-makers, and the basis of community among them, we may hope to grasp some of the ways in which societal values were selected and ordered; how the basis in knowledge for their application was recognised as valid and sufficient; and how certain policies, rather than others, were the practical outcome.

In what follows, we first describe the 'Scottish myth', a traditional and popular view that has been taken of the egalitarian nature of Scottish society and of its realisation through the school system. This view was linked to issues of national identity, and it provided an ontological basis for a community of values and beliefs. It was, nevertheless, deeply rooted in pre-industrial experience. We then show how the careers of nationally recognised teachers like Dewar, Robertson and recruits to the Inspectorate, were atypically structured so as to confirm for them the validity of this view, and their own careers as its exemplification. Thus they were thrice identified to the Department as trustworthy: by virtue of their values; by virtue of their experience; and, until the 1960s, when the Inspectorate finally lost its freehold on the Secretaryship, by virtue of the close approximation of their values and experience to those obtaining at the top of the Department. An analysis of appointments, from the mid-1950s onwards, to the Advisory Council and to other national bodies then shows that such careers, though highly unrepresentative of those of Scottish teachers, were nevertheless the norm among policy-makers with a background in education. The myth was thereby inserted at the centre of the advisory process. The following two chapters then broaden the analysis to consider the workings of the policy community in relation to the major associations and pressure groups (chapter 18), and the Department's methods for managing public opinion (chapter 19).

The Scottish Myth

In 1969, Norman Graham, then Secretary of the SED, and John Bennett, David Dickson's successor as Senior Chief Inspector, were questioned by the Commission on the Constitution under Lord Kilbrandon. The Commission had been asked to review the case for a Scottish Assembly:

KILBRANDON. Would you say there is in Scotland the general feeling that the Scottish system of education is far superior to the English?

GRAHAM. I think that is probably so.

KILBRANDON. Do you think it is justifiable?

GRAHAM. I would not myself attempt to judge this. It is very difficult to establish criteria by which to measure, and I think the performance will vary just as much within a country as between countries.

KILBRANDON. But if it is so difficult to judge, what do you think gives rise to this myth, or is it just a general feeling of 'Wha's like us'?

GRAHAM. There is undoubtedly an historical justification for it. I am not myself an historian of Scottish education, but there is no doubt that in time past public education made earlier and greater progress in Scotland. There must be some significance in the fact that a public school in Scotland means a public school, whereas in England it means a private school. . . .

KILBRANDON. But supposing an intelligent foreigner were to say to you: 'You have I believe a different system of education in Scotland than in England?' and you would say yes. He would then say, 'What are the principal distinct differences?'?

GRAHAM. The main differences now are, first in terms of organisation, that we divide between primary and secondary education a year later than at present in England and Wales . . . that in the secondary schools virtually all our teachers of academic subjects are university graduates; that in the examination system the final school examinations are in practice a year earlier than they are in England and Wales, and the curriculum is more general, less specialised. Then in the university sector . . . the degree structure is in some faculties substantially different. . . .

BENNETT. I think Mr Graham has mentioned the salient points. I would simply add I think that they are reflections of our national characteristics. We have an interest in the common man, therefore we have an interest in a broad education. Our education is not nearly so specialised [CC 1970, Qs 729-33].

Directly or indirectly, this exchange touches on a number of the features of Scottish education discussed in chapter 2. These include institutional features, like the broader Highers course and Ordinary degree, and underlying cultural features such as the pride in education, in a public and national system, and in their links to an egalitarian national identity. Kilbrandon talked of 'myth', and two of the logical features of myth are also evident here. First, myth is rooted in history, and its correspondence to a present reality is problematic. It is neither to be uncritically dismissed nor uncritically accepted, as Graham's response to Kilbrandon well illustrates. Second, myth is simultaneously expressive and explanatory. It is about hearts and minds. It asserts identity, celebrates values, and explains the world through them: 'we have an interest in the common man, *therefore* we have an interest in a broad education'. Logically, myths may be expressive and true, or expressive and false. Either way, they may influence what people do.[2]

Myths are typically expressed through stories, the stories both of history and fiction. But, as we saw with Brunton in part II, action, history and fiction are not always easy to separate, and sometimes feed each other. Until recently, the main historical story about Scottish education has told of the gradual implementation of the Knoxian plan for a national educational system to serve the godly commonwealth. The main literary fiction has been the celebration of the 'lad o' pairts', archetypically in Maclaren's story of that name (Maclaren 1895), but in many other novels, poems and songs as well (Anderson 1985a). The two heroes in Maclaren's story are Geordie Howe, the son of an impoverished Perthshire widow, and Domsie the master or dominie of the parish school. Domsie prepares Geordie for entry to Edinburgh University where he covers himself in academic distinction, outshining 'all thae academy boys'. Exhausted by his years of study, however, he dies before he can fulfil his role's highest destiny of entry to the Christian ministry.

Geordie's career illustrates two separate strands of Scottish egalitarianism: a solidary, collectivist strand, and an individualist one (McPherson 1973). Opportunity was open to Geordie, however poor his circumstances. The local school educated him and many others like him: 'seven ministers, four school-masters, four doctors, one professor and three civil service men had been sent out by the auld schule in Domsie's time, besides many that "had given themselves to mercantile pursuits"' (Maclaren 1895, 9). A local farmer supported Geordie financially, and the whole community rejoiced in his success, and took credit from it. At university, too, Geordie's friendships were made across diverse social ranks in a 'commonwealth of letters' that took a distinctively Scottish form. Its members coalesced in a democracy of intellect, at sympathy both with each other and with the varied ranks from which they had risen. Thus the myth offered a reconciliation of two potentially conflicting ideals of society. One stressed individual advance upwards through society's ranks to positions of leadership. The other stressed harmony across its ranks.

Between the poles of history and fiction spanned by the myth, there were other forms of discourse: reviews, polemic, reminiscence, and especially biography and autobiography. In living and reflecting on their lives, people measured themselves and their fellows against these heroes and values.

Thus life came to imitate literature, and literature, life. The identities of persons in a variety of educated occupations were thereby engaged in a culture that was neither fact nor fiction, but a creation of their own that reinterpreted tradition.

Craik, the son of a minister, and the first Secretary of the Department (1885-1904), matched the tradition only in part. But his successor, Struthers (1904-21), did so more nearly. Morgan (1929) celebrated Struthers as one of the great 'makers' of Scottish education along with Craik. Struthers had got his secondary education as a pupil teacher under his own Domsie, in Morgan's words, 'a splendid example of the old parochial type who prepared many pupils for distinguished careers in all walks of life' (*ibid.*, 231-2). Morgan wrote of Struthers that 'No-one has done more in recent times to realise the ideals of the early educational reformers' (*ibid.*, 241). In turn, it was Struthers himself who sanctioned one of the most explicit celebrations of the Knoxian ideal, in Circular 44 of 1921:

> The force of public opinion is strong enough to ensure the maintenance of the immemorial Scottish tradition that, subject to the over-riding condition of intellectual fitness, no child, whatever his home circumstances, shall be debarred access to the Secondary School and the University by lack of opportunity. There is abundant evidence that . . . the liberality of Education Authorities has brought Scotland nearer to the ideal than she has been at any previous period in her educational history. (SED 1921, para.4; see also Weighand 1974, 84-6)

This celebration, however, was for a purpose, for it was Circular 44 that confirmed the imposition of the Department's bipartite philosophy on the development of secondary education under the 1918 Education Act. The Department at the time was engaged in a protracted battle with outside opinion over their custody of the immemorial tradition. Its fulfilment, the Department argued, lay in the social efficiency of selection at twelve and the subsequent sponsorship of merit through bursaries (see chapter 2). 'After all', the Circular continued,

> there is no denying the fact that in every country only a relatively small percentage of the population will be endowed by nature with the mental equipment which they must possess if they are to profit by Secondary School or University study. A frank recognition of this truth is essential if a proper organization is to be established. . . .This implies, wherever practicable, an entirely separate organization even in subjects which are common to the Secondary and to the non-Secondary group. (SED 1921)

Opponents resisted the 'separate organisation' of bipartism, arguing the threat to community solidarity and to what we have called in chapter 2 the principle of 'contest mobility', the principle by which opportunity is kept open for as many as possible, and for as long in the school career as possible. Both parties, in other words, appealed to different strands in the tradition, the Department to the national promotion of individual merit, its opponents to the solidarity of the local community. Both strands, as we have said, were to be found in Maclaren's story of the lad o' pairts.

Like history, biography and much fiction, therefore, the myth emerges as a reconstruction of the past for present purposes. A corollary is that its content and emphasis may change. Anderson (1985a) has pointed to the way in which the emphasis on the national system declined as the English came gradually to accept for themselves, and therefore for Scotland too, that the state had a proper role in secondary education. Other elements also received less attention after the First World War, among them a student-centred and disputatious pedagogy, a system of assessment that was anti-pathetic to external examination, and a set of school and university institutions that were peculiarly adapted to the poverty of the nation and the height of its educational ambitions (McPherson 1972, 1973, 1983). All were held to shape what, in the philosophical idealism of the day, was represented as a national character at once fiercely egalitarian, intellectual, disputatious and ambitious. Walter Elliot, Secretary of State for Scotland from 1936 to 1938, talked of its 'democratic intellectualism' (Elliot 1932, 63). Several of these elements were to resurface in the thinking of the Sixth Advisory Council, and later still in George Davie's evocation of the nineteenth-century Scottish university in *The Democratic Intellect* (Davie 1961; see also Davie 1986).

After Circular 44, however, the argument had focused increasingly on the narrower issue of opportunity. If bipartism and sponsorship were to be the new order, could not the older collectivist strand be preserved by substantially enlarging the proportion of pupils selected at twelve years or thereby, for subsequent sponsorship? Between the Wars, the configuration of forces around the SCRE pursued this argument with vigour. They helped to bequeath to Scotland after 1945 a secondary system, which, though bipartite and selective, preserved various elements of the earlier 'contest' model (McPherson 1973), and was more accessible than that in England (see chapter 15). Two of our interviewees, McIntosh and Walker, themselves contributed to research that showed that the provision of selective, senior-secondary courses after 1945 in Scotland was so generous that the working-class Scottish pupil had as good a chance of entry to them as the middle-class child in England had of entry to a grammar school (Douglas *et al.*, 1966). Nevertheless, McClelland had written in 1935 that the 'central and unbroken strand in our long educational tradition is the recognition of the right of the clever child, from whatever social class he may come, to the highest and best education the country has to offer' (McClelland 1935); and this was acknowledgement, if only implicit, that the other strands in the tradition were broken or for the time being lost.

As several writers have pointed out, the enduring elements of the myth could be pressed to the service of arguments either conservative or radical.

Anderson (1985a) shows how the social mobility of individual Scots by means of education was variously interpreted in the nineteenth century both as a refutation and as a confirmation of the view that Scottish society was class-stratified. And McCrone, Bechhofer and Kendrick (1982) have this to say about that quintessential expression of Scottish egalitarianism, Robert Burns' 'a man's a man for a' that':

> Burns seems to strip away differences which are essentially social. In spite of these . . . Burns is saying, people are equal. . . . He is calling, not for a levelling down of riches, but for a proper, that is, *moral*, appreciation, of 'the man o' independent mind'.(*ibid.*, 132)

Such a call, the authors argue, is essentially conservative: 'If man is primordially equal, social structural inequalities do not matter, so nothing needs to be done' (*ibid.*, 131).

Two other features of the myth are apposite. First, it placed the locus of social identity in the village and small town, not in the city, and especially not in the Clydeside conurbation with Glasgow at its centre. 'The myth', McCrone and colleagues write, 'describes putative conditions in the typical pre-capitalist and pre-industrial community, rural or urban. Social identity is one of community, not of class' (*ibid.*, 135). Second, by the beginning of this century, if not earlier, the source of social identity was linked to morality and leadership (see Anderson 1985a, 97). In 1918, a Glasgow philosopher, Hector Hetherington, co-authored a 'contribution to the philosophy of civic society'. In this he traced the origins of civic virtue and leadership to the individual's solidary commitment to his local neighbourhood. Such commitment, he argued, was more characteristic of the small community than of the socially problematic forms of the city. He added that:

> it is a notable and instructive fact that Scotland and Ireland with their distinctively national traditions and institutions have furnished political and intellectual leaders to the Empire in numbers out of all proportion to their populations. . . . And it is quite possible that, if the analysis of origin were pursued further, certain areas within Scotland . . . might be found to be more productive of leaders than others and these areas precisely those in which the breath of local life blows most strongly. (Muirhead and Hetherington 1918, 168-9)

Thirty years later, Hetherington returned to this theme when he made a case for the leadership of Scottish democracy by an elite comprising the landed interest, the Church and education. If this paradox illustrated the continuing ambivalence of the myth, so too did his argument that the path to social renewal lay through tradition (the quoted passage survives only in reported speech):

> Rural depopulation, the concentration of the vast mass of their people in Glasgow and in the narrow lands between Clyde and Forth . . . these were matters . . . which gave them pause. But . . . under the leadership

which they saw moving in Scotland . . . they were in better heart . . . to attack that situation and . . . he [Hetherington] believed that one of the best grounds for confidence was that the Scottish tradition had never been allowed to die. In country school houses, in country mansions such as he knew when he was a boy, and in the recruitment from these to the schools and churches of their expanding cities there had been a noble assurance that the best part of life lay . . . in spiritual values. . . . As these things were defended so was served the cause of democracy. . . . (*SEJ* 14 November 1947)

By this time, Hetherington had become Principal of Glasgow University. He was later to work closely with Brunton, and the EIS, to whom he had addressed these sentiments, had just made him an Honorary Fellow. Teachers, too, honoured the myth and its figures.

A classic by first training, Hetherington linked his argument to the classical culture of Greece and imperial Rome. This was common at a time of British imperial ambition (Campbell 1968). So, also, was the cultural recoil from the city and industrial forms. Wiener (1981) has discussed the English search for national reassurance in rural gentility. But, in Scotland, hope was invested to a greater degree in the public education system: 'We have a tradition of sound education in Scotland. . . . It is our substitute for the English tradition of gentility' (Bridie and Maclaren 1949, 5).

James Bridie, who wrote this, was a product and chronicler of an Edwardian university culture that exercised considerable influence on Scottish thought and politics in the 1930s and 1940s. As a student, Bridie was a friend of Walter Elliot, and these two products of the independent school, Glasgow Academy, dominated the clubbish literary life of the Glasgow University Union. Bridie, though not at that time Elliot, was active in its politics. Also active at Glasgow in the same years was Tom Johnston, sponsor of Keir Hardie in a Rectorial election. Hetherington and Johnston both sat in Henry Jones' Moral Philosophy class. Hetherington's biography of Jones relates that it was conducted on the broad and disputatious lines of tradition, and also that its members were 'for the most part of very modest means and had to make their way in the world by hard work and in a country where university honours are prized'. Eventually they would supply 'the leaders of national life in the succeeding generation' (Hetherington 1924, 72 and ch.4). Hetherington's biographer represents him as an industrious lad o' pairts moving, as a student, in a homespun social circle that overlapped but little with the 'high indifference' of the Academy-dominated Union of Bridie and Elliot. Later, however, he was to become close friends with them (Illingworth 1971, 1-11).[3]

Harvie has described reformist 'middle-opinion' in Scotland in the 1930s as made up of writers, architects, planners, industrialists, professionals and politicians, whose 'predominantly academic and professional leadership overlapped with one another and with moderate nationalistic politics' (Harvie 1981b, 6). Diverse though it was in social origin and party-political allegiance, the generation of students from the decades immediately before and after the First World War was subsequently to make common cause in pressing a Scottish case in British politics. One element in this case was their shared understanding of Scotland's past, a past that they felt they had experienced in the forms of their own education, and a past that they made available to a wider public through biography, essays, lectures, fiction, journalism, and politics itself. The shared symbolic space of parish, academy, Scotland and Empire, a shared background in classical studies, and a university culture wherein 'a pre-1914 Oxonian would have found himself thoroughly at home' (Coote 1965, 35), all shaped a sense of common identity that subsequently helped to hold a range of political opinion to a nationalistically tinged programme of reform. In 1935, for example, Tom Johnston helped found the Saltire Society, dedicated to the regeneration of Scottish life and culture. Among its members were Johnston, Hetherington, Bridie and Elliot, and also several school teachers who were later to become members of the Sixth Advisory Council. One of these was J. J. Robertson, the author of the Council's *Secondary Education* report.[4]

The Reproduction of the Myth

Ten of the thirteen men who gave attributable interviews had a professional background in education. With some differences of emphasis, the majority of them described the post-1945 Scottish system as nationally distinctive and socially open, and many identified their own career with that of the lad o' pairts. They included Gray, Walker, Dewar, and also David Dickson, whom we may take as an example.

Dickson told us that he had been a bursar, or scholarship boy, at Morrison's Academy, Crieff, where he had known William Dewar, another bursar. Like Dewar, Dickson took a first in classics at Edinburgh University. He then taught for a period at the Royal High School in Edinburgh, entering the Inspectorate in 1940. Teachers of classics who followed him at the High School included Peter Thompson, a founding member of the SSTA, and two close colleagues of Brunton's, HMI James Shanks (see chapter 4) and George Gray (see chapters 5 and 12). We asked Dickson how he would characterise the Scottish educational system:

DICKSON. I think that the Scottish system, more than others with which I have a certain amount of acquaintance, sets out deliberately, and on the whole, successfully, to ensure that people from humbler homes can get a full secondary education and move on to university thereafter.

Q. The lad o' pairts?

DICKSON. The lad o' pairts if you like, only a little lower down the scale than I tend to place the lad o' pairts, whom I regard as a man who becomes a Professor of Philosophy ultimately.

Q. The lad o' pairts, is that your own experience?

DICKSON. Yes, indeed, and the experience of a very considerable number of people. I remember once entertaining a group of Russian educationists . . . along with a group of eight of my own colleagues. It transpired in the course of questioning that, of the eight, I think seven were of what could be called working-class origin. This impressed the Russians so much that they decided that we had chosen them deliberately, for that reason; but frankly we hadn't. This kind of thing happens more readily in Scotland than anywhere that I know; much more readily, for instance, than it does in England. That's one of the features of Scottish education which pleases me. In general, I think, we have always tended to value hard work more than many educational systems have done.

Dickson told us that he broadly subscribed to George Davie's view of Scottish education in *The Democratic Intellect* (Davie 1961), though he was 'not so sure that it is as true now as it once was'. He also thought that the directors of education, and his colleagues in the Department would share his views on the characteristics of the Scottish system. Allan Rodger certainly did:

RODGER. I would say that the democratic tradition is the most powerful historical influence in modern Scottish education. You see, if you go right back to John Knox's *Book of Discipline* of 1560, he envisaged a school in every parish. He envisaged that the best pupils of these schools should go to a more centralised secondary school; the best of these should go to the universities. In short, he was really talking about promotion by merit, a meritocracy, from as early as 1560. Everybody went to school. They got the same chance; equality of opportunity; if you had the ability, you rose. I think that this was a remarkably democratic tradition to be spelt out as early at 1560. It was a long, long time till it was implemented, and indeed, in some respects, it wasn't fully implemented till the 1918 and the 1945 Acts, but it had its influence all along in Scotland. I think that one of the strengths, for example, in the nineteenth century . . . was that when you went to your smaller towns – Inverness, Montrose, Dumfries, or the like – you had got schools which were virtually comprehensive schools; the whole population went there. Well, this seems to me to be entirely in keeping with the tradition set in 1560 by Knox. A lot of these schools were absolutely first-rate schools. Sometimes a town outgrew its school, and developed a second one, which might not be a full secondary school but only a junior-secondary school. But the Knox democratic system was seen at its best in a town which was small enough to have its one secondary school completely comprehensive, taking in everybody. Montrose is a good example; Arbroath is another; Brechin is another, though things may have changed in these towns in recent years. . . . In places like Dumfries, Montrose, and so on, all grades of society were mixed up together in the one classroom. It was possible in a village to get the laird's son and the ploughman's son to sit side by side competing against one another. Again there is an absence of social barrier.

Q. How far did your colleagues in the Department share your understanding of these characteristics?

RODGER. Well, I think that I would definitely say Arbuckle. Arbuckle was quite fond of quoting the *Book of Discipline*. He could even quote you the words, which is more than I can do. I think that Brunton was pretty well aware of this democratic tradition. . . . I wouldn't like to speak about the younger fellows, whom I don't really know, but I think that what I have said about the characteristics of Scottish education would represent the fairly generally accepted view amongst the older members, my contemporaries and those that were ten to fifteen years younger.

Rodger's younger colleagues reached retirement in the 1970s, at about the same time as Graham, Arbuckle's successor as Secretary. Graham's account of his view of the tradition, and of his colleagues' views of it, was consistent with Rodger's. Arbuckle's predecessor, Murrie, said, 'I think it was something in our blood, but I don't think we thought much about it'.

Bruce Millan, as we have seen, was well enough aware of the mythical component of the democratic tradition. In an earlier interview, too, given in 1966, he had thought the democratic claim a partial, if fading, reality:

MILLAN. I think there is a stronger democratic tradition in Scottish education; I think this is genuine. I think that perhaps we tend to overemphasise it now and believe that equality of opportunity has gone further in Scotland, substantially further than it has in England. I think that was true at one time; it's perhaps not quite as true nowadays, but I still think there is a stronger democratic tradition. . . . in the sense that there has been a stronger tradition in Scotland than in England of the boy from a modest background using education as the opportunity of improving his way in life. The lad o' pairts in the Highlands, for example, is a much stronger tradition in Scotland than I think probably anything that there is in England similarly [Millan 1973].

These beliefs were grounded in objective experience in several ways. First, relative to other countries, the overall national system emerges well on indicators of egalitarianism, especially in the first half of the century (Douglas *et al.*, 1966; Hope 1984, ch.3). One consequence was that a higher proportion of students at Scottish universities in the inter-war years were from working-class origins than was the case in England. It is true that, in both countries, such students were under-represented in the older professional faculties such as medicine and law. Nevertheless, the early careers of elite Scottish educationists passed through settings in which working-class success through education was relatively salient. The proportion of working-class students was highest in the arts faculties, followed by science and then the professional faculties. But more graduate teachers were recruited from the faculties of arts than from either of the others. Moreover, from each type of faculty, it was the graduates of working-class origin who were more likely to train as teachers. Training was compulsory, and the training colleges were therefore more homogeneously working-class than the universities. Thus Scottish recruits to teaching had already begun to encounter more instances of working-class success among their immediate peers than had other Scottish students or, for that matter, recruits to teaching in England.[5]

Once trained, the aspirant to the Scottish teaching elite tended to follow a different career-path from that of his fellow teachers. This path led through social and geographical settings that could reinforce a sense of an egalitarian system that had already been absorbed from the culture, and that was beginning to harden with the validation of immediate experience. The clue to this path emerged from two interviews, one that Robertson gave in a television interview with Esmond Wright in 1962, and the other our own interview with Dewar:

WRIGHT. Let's look at your own career. It started in Kilmarnock?

ROBERTSON. In Kilmarnock, a coeducational school, then moved to Glasgow, a little while in Hutcheson's Grammar School; and then . . . a sixth year in the High School. . . .

WRIGHT. You're omitting to mention the fact that you were first bursar in the Glasgow University Bursary. . . . Until you retired three years ago you were Rector of Aberdeen Grammar School. . . . Before that you were Rector of the Royal High in Edinburgh; before that you were Rector of Falkirk High School for nine years; before that you were Rector of Fort William Senior Secondary.

ROBERTSON. Well . . . when I trained after the First World War, I started in Glasgow; and Dr William Boyd, wise counsellor as well as a great teacher, said to us 'Now get out of Glasgow. Glasgow is so big, the schools are so big, that of necessity promotion will come very late, be very slow. Get out of Glasgow.' I got out of Glasgow. I quickly got promotion as a principal teacher. I tried that out in two schools and then I applied for a smaller school, in the Highlands. . . . Fort William was a typical small-town school, the one which is repeated almost endlessly in the pattern of Scottish life. It had a wide range of ability, it had quite a wide social and economic range, and a school like that was a very good apprenticeship. The same in a measure was true of Falkirk High School, though it was more highly selective. In Aberdeen Grammar School the selection, intellectually, was not too rigorous. There was a certain selection socially – it was a fee-paying school – but we had a great variety of types and many levels of ability. . . .

WRIGHT. This movement is still somewhat unusual, surely, in the experience of Glasgow?

ROBERTSON. It's bound to be. You see, there are no small schools. . . .

WRIGHT. Wouldn't you describe your own career as that of a lad o' pairts?

ROBERTSON. . . . I suppose, in a sense, yes. . . .

WRIGHT. Should not a great deal more attention be paid to the bursary today?

ROBERTSON. Yes I think it's a pity that the availability of public money has, in certain areas of the country, caused a waning of interest in this competitive effort by the best boys and girls [Robertson and Wright 1962].

And this is how Dewar described his early career:

DEWAR. I myself had been a bursar [at Morrison's Academy, Crieff]. . . . Many a 'lad o' pairts' wanted to go into teaching . . . the tremendous advantage that I had over most teachers in Scotland [was that] I served in four different areas and I knew my own country town of Crieff as well. . . . I was unemployed for about two months when I came out [of teacher training] in 1929. . . . A post appeared in Aberdeen. . . . The Grammar School was a local-authority fee-paying school. There were bursaries. . . . After three and a half years there I went as Senior Classics Master to Dumfries Academy, which was quite a contrast; from a city and large port to a relatively small town of about 36000 inhabitants with one senior-secondary school . . . [in] a sprawling county, but with several well formed, almost independent communities, Annan, Langholm, Lockerbie, Beattock, Moffat. . . . Each of these towns had its own identity. In each there was a three-year secondary school, comprehensive in the sense that, in Moffat for example, all the children from the primary schools round about Moffat . . . came to that school. Nobody was sent to Dumfries in the very first year. But at the end of year three those who were judged fit . . . were transferred. . . . But, as usual, I think there was a tendency to put more people into the senior-secondary certificate course at the beginning than was justified by the results. . . . In a place like Dumfries the discipline was very easy, the children were almost docile. . . . We had children who were eager, very eager indeed, and we had them from a variety of homes. There was no question of class distinction, none whatever, although Dumfries Academy had its own primary department, and this was, and still is, a common thing in Scotland. We hear, incidentally, if I may go off slightly at a tangent, far too little about this practice in Scotland, of having the whole of the child's education in one school, and it is not confined to the grant-aided schools. You get it, for example, in Kirriemuir, if you want a present example. There's any number up and down Scotland, and we hear very little of it.

Q. Largely rural schools?

DEWAR. Provincial, I prefer to use the expression 'provincial'.

Q. What's the distinction?

DEWAR. I think of 'rural' as embracing a very large number of very small schools, and there are very many such in Scotland. Whereas for me 'provincial schools' are larger without being large absolutely, and they serve a wider area. That's the distinction I make.

Q. Provinces with respect to Glasgow and Edinburgh?

DEWAR. These are urban areas, big urban areas. Suppose you go out into

Angus. Now that's a province.

Dewar added, 'I have always been keenly aware of the situation of the fellows and the women who are away out on the periphery of Scotland in the provinces!'. After Dumfries, Dewar moved to Greenock Academy and thence to George Heriot's School, Edinburgh. He emphasised to us that, at all his schools, poor boys had, like himself, received bursaries. He also said that he had no doubt that the system he had known was accessible, both geographically and to a wide social spectrum.

Robertson and Dewar between them named eleven six-year secondary schools where they had been pupils or senior teachers. At the time of their association with them, all had been either burgh schools (mostly fee-paying) or city schools (all fee-paying). With the exception of Fort William, a 'good apprenticeship', all had been among the 'first-generation' secondary schools of the nineteenth century or earlier (see chapter 15). There was no mention of a school that was non-selective and non-fee-paying in 1945, and no mention of a school founded in the twentieth century.[6] Robertson saw the school at Fort William as 'typical', and 'repeated almost endlessly in the pattern of Scottish life'. When Dewar searched for examples, he turned to Angus and to the small town of Kirriemuir. The 'provinces' were prominent in his mental representation of the country.

There is here, we suggest, a symbolic axis that parallels the axis of careers that were traced through the historical heartland of the pre-industrial educational system. One might say that this symbolic world is bounded by Angus, standing for the East and North, and with Kirriemuir at its heart; by Dumfries in the South; and, in the West, by a Glasgow academy, perhaps the Academy. We may call it the 'Kirriemuir career', after the popular Kailyard author J. M. Barrie.[7] Barrie was educated at Webster's High School, Kirriemuir and at Forfar Academy, both in Angus, and thereafter at Dumfries Academy and Glasgow Academy. This pattern was not entirely fortuitous, because he attended the Glasgow and Dumfries schools whilst lodging with his teacher brother who went to a classics post at Glasgow Academy, and thence to Dumfries and promotion to the Inspectorate. Barrie deprecated Glasgow, and he articulated for his contemporaries the solidaristic values of the small town, its academy and the lad o' pairts (e.g. Barrie 1938, 88-9, 98, 166, 194). His contemporaries recognised that the education-authority schools of the city had no place on the symbolic map, and no place either on the career path of the ambitious teacher ('get out of Glasgow'). Preferment lay through the sixty or so prestigious secondary schools of the pre-industrial system. There were only a dozen of these in the four cities. For the ambitious lad o' pairts, therefore, the career frontier lay, not in the West, but in the East, North or South; not in the city and the future, but in the parish and the past.

This flight from the city and from the state-school foundations of the twentieth century gave a further basis in immediate experience to the belief of elite teachers in egalitarianism. The residential segregation of social groups was most pronounced in the cities, and there the school systems were most sharply differentiated, both by function and by social class. Elsewhere, secondary schools were more likely to be *omnibus* and to contain a cross-section of the local population (SED 1947b, ch.7). It can be shown that, much later, in the 1970s, social class had a greater influence on the attainment of city pupils than it had on pupils outside the cities, or in areas with an *omnibus* tradition; and there is good reason to think that this was a long-standing pattern.[8] What is certain is that the sparsely populated areas of Scotland had much higher rates of post-compulsory enrolment after the Second World War than the industrial areas of the West.[9] Thus the path of the Kirriemuir career did not confront elite teachers with the worst examples that Scotland could furnish of the impact of social class on educational provision and attainment. The selective character of the schools and classes in which they taught will have been a further protection from these aspects of Scottish reality.[10]

It is an open question whether such teachers could be expected to have known that the educational world they experienced was selectively structured. In principle they could, and no doubt many did, despite the persuasive message embedded in their culture and experience. Dewar, for example, was well aware of the social divide in Greenock during his time there, and he acted on this knowledge (see chapter 4). But, perhaps for others, knowing was one thing, heeding another. Moreover, the symbolic world of the Kirriemuir career was not only descriptive and explanatory; it was a moral world as well. To perceive the reality of this world in moral terms was to leave intact one's belief in the integrity of the national system and of the solidary Scottish community. Educational failure was explained instead in terms of the moral failings of the individual. This was the dark side of the myth and the basis of the 'symbolic violence' (Bourdieu 1977, 190-7) endured by generations of pupils who were measured against the lad o' pairts and found wanting (Neill, 1921; Gow and McPherson, 1980). Brunton attributed character deficiencies to junior-secondary pupils (see chapter 11), and a similar attribution even penetrated Scottish educational research in the 1950s, leading it to underestimate the impact of social class on educational attainment in senior-secondary courses.[11] Gray, Dewar, Dickson and Rodger all emphasised the hard work and dedication that the tradition expected of the lad o' pairts.

The moral dimension of the myth had a spatial aspect that, again, direct experience might confirm. It concerned west-central Scotland and the reasons for its apparently lower level of educational attainment. Glasgow and Lanarkshire will serve as examples. Lanarkshire, in particular, had one of the lowest rates of post-compulsory enrolment in Scotland.[12] It also had a director of education whose attitude to social rank echoed Burns' 'for a' that' ('I think that you should treat human beings as you find them, rather than bother about their origins' – see chapter 16). McEwan told us that he and his Education Committee had not regarded early leaving from senior-secondary courses as wastage, because the pupils concerned were entering good jobs and, possibly also, continuing their education by an alternative route through further education. Rodger, however, deprecated this, and contrasted it with cultural attitudes elsewhere in the country:

RODGER. Going back some years to the days when Pringle was the Senior Chief Inspector, he told me that, after service in various areas, he felt that there was a better spirit in the North than he met in the South-East centred on Edinburgh, or the South-West centred on Glasgow. He had been chief inspector in the North before he became Senior Chief Inspector. I feel that the spirit of hard work is certainly not to be found very markedly in the Clydeside area; and I would say that that was true even when I was an inspector before the War. It is true today, judging from the reports that I am hearing from my grandchildren, as well as from modern inspectors.

Q. Why do you think this spirit is not found there?

RODGER. I think that if you wanted to rise in the world, and if there was no great industry, you had to become professional; you had to do well at school. Glasgow was industrialised, and the way to get on in Glasgow was to excel in your craft. Of course, it requires a very high ability to become a top-class engineer, but I think that, at one time, a very large number of Glasgow people felt assured of a good artisan job, and didn't need to look anywhere else. You know, the areas in Scotland that produce the highest numbers of university students (in proportion to population) were Shetland and Orkney, simply because there were few jobs. So I think that there is a big relationship between the ease of getting work and the thought of trying to enter the professions.

This view is also evident in the annual reports of the Department in the 1940s and early 1950s, for example in the report for 1954:

> According to a number of reports, the pupils in some of the larger cities in the industrial belt are more difficult to interest, less inclined to work hard, and less amenable to discipline than pupils in the rural areas. It may well be that the latter are less assailed by distractions and more conscious of their membership of a close-knit community. (SED 1955a, 23)

We shall suggest in the next chapter that this attitude also influenced the Department's conception of its own role in central-local relations in the west of Scotland. It was an attitude that was reinforced, not only by area variations in early leaving, but also by the lower rates of entry in the West to post-Higher work in the sixth year. In trying to develop the sixth year, the Department had had in mind the type of education that had in the past sponsored many of its own senior officials (see chapter 13). A local culture that could not respond to these developments ran the risk of being seen from Edinburgh as a culture that did not understand or value the nature of professions and of leadership. Few of its products penetrated the upper levels of the Department. And, we suspect, fewer still within the Department argued that the culture and organisation of schooling in the West represented a different, but equally valid, response to the experience of industrialism.

Appointments and Sponsorship

We may now gather together the several strands of our argument to show how the membership of the policy community was constituted. First, expansion obliged the Department to involve outsiders in the formulation, promotion and implementation of its policies. Second, the making of policy placed a premium on the trustworthiness of the new men; and this was reinforced by the novelty of Brunton's undertaking, and by the risks that Murrie and Arbuckle ran in backing Brunton's working parties against internal opposition from administrative colleagues. It was also necessitated by the logical contradictions inherent in democracy's attempt to reconcile the authority of the Crown in Parliament with the exigencies of expertise, and of accountability to groups and localities. Third, the basis of morality, and therefore of trust, was the Scottish myth. Fourth, the Kirriemuir career tended to bring to professional eminence in education men who fulfilled the myth and subscribed to its explanations and values. This was also the basis on which appointments to the Inspectorate were commonly made, and on which the Inspectorate itself commonly recommended individuals for national appointments.

Thus one finds that the path taken by Dewar and Robertson had earlier been trodden by a high proportion of recruits to the Inspectorate from school teaching. We do not have the data to map each career step, but we have been able to identify the schools in which appointees were teaching at the time of their appointment to the Inspectorate. The sixty-six first-generation secondary schools (see chapter 15) were the principal springboard. These mainly comprised burgh secondary schools, like Dumfries Academy which produced Brunton, together with a small number of city fee-paying schools. These included Aberdeen Grammar School, where Mackay Thomson had taught, Glasgow's Academy and High School, and the Royal High School, Edinburgh, which produced Dickson and several others of his generation. These first-generation schools constituted less than one-third of the secondary-school sector during the inter-war period, and less than one-tenth in the twenty years after 1945. Nevertheless, during the inter-war period, they produced fifty-six per cent of recruits to the Inspectorate from school teaching. Their dominance continued at the same level in the twenty years after 1945, but weakened thereafter. Most of the remaining recruits to the Inspectorate from school teaching were supplied by the second generation of schools. These schools had been designated Higher Grade schools mainly between 1900 and 1908, and had acquired full secondary status in the

1920s. They were intended to supply the gaps in the first generation of provision. There were more of them, therefore, and their distribution over different types of community was less unrepresentative (McPherson and Willms 1986). Between 1918 and 1965, they supplied around one-third of Inspectorate recruits from school teaching, but this proportion is low relative to the fraction that these schools comprised of the secondary sector after 1923, which was always well over half.

Between 1923 and the early 1960s, few six-year secondary schools were founded or designated. The first- and second-generation schools founded before the First World War therefore constituted the backbone of the Scottish selective, senior-secondary sector between 1923 and 1965. It was in this sector that the majority of recruits from school teaching to the Schools Inspectorate up to 1965 had gained most of their professional experience. The contribution of the rest of the Scottish school system to Inspectorate recruitment was minimal, partly, of course, because inspectors were required to examine for the Leaving Certificate until 1965. Before then, there were hardly any appointments from primary schools, junior-secondary schools, or Catholic schools, secondary or otherwise, despite the fact that, in 1945 say, such schools comprised nine out of ten of all schools. The number of appointments made from schools in west-central Scotland was also low, relative to the size of the school population there. One further consequence of this pattern of recruitment should be noted, and that is the tendency to appoint from schools that served populations of above-average socio-economic status: three-quarters of HMI appointments from schools between 1945 and 1965 were from schools that were advantaged in this way. Between 1965 and 1983, however, the proportion fell to the half that could be expected on the basis of chance alone.[13]

The foregoing analysis helps explain why Brunton should turn especially to staff in the prestigious first generation of secondary schools in his search for teachers who could be trusted, and who would be persuasive to the Department. Dewar is an example. Throughout Brunton's period as Senior Chief Inspector (1955-66), Dewar was centrally involved in the HMSCI's development of national policy for curriculum and certification, and his national involvement continued after Brunton's retiral. Dewar had gone to Dumfries Academy in 1932, the year Brunton left his own post at Dumfries Academy to join the Inspectorate, and only eight years after Barrie had publicly woven webs of egalitarian fancy around the pupils of the school. Later, Dewar sat on Brunton's working party of 1955-59 that developed proposals for the introduction of the O-grade (see chapter 4). Three of the four teachers on the working party were from first-generation schools, and the fourth was from a private girls school in Edinburgh. Dewar was appointed a governor of Moray House College, and was then elected chairman of the governors. The College nominated him to the newly formed Scottish Council for the Training of Teachers (SCTT) that in 1959 took over from the

National Committee for the Training of Teachers (NCTT) (see chapter 12). Of the eight secondary teachers on the SCTT, six were from first-generation schools. One consequence of this pattern of appointment was that there was only one teacher from a west of Scotland school. A second was that there were no women. A third was the preponderance of 'classics'. George Gray, the first secretary of the SCTT, and himself a classic from Edinburgh's Royal High School, told us, 'I remember one occasion in the Scottish Council for the Training of Teachers, when a very important document was being produced on behalf of the Council, and there were ten people around the table, and eight of them were Honours classics'. Dewar was also appointed to two of the three 'special' committees set up by the Advisory Council 1957-61 (see chapter 11). The three teachers on the Council itself were all from first-generation schools; so too were most of the additional teachers appointed, like Dewar, to the special committees.[14]

Thus, like the inspectors, the secondary teachers who helped to make national policy in the later 1950s were almost exclusively representative, by position, and also, largely, by previous professional experience, of deeply traditional and socially privileged areas of the school system. The Kirriemuir career contributed to this pattern of appointment, as perhaps did the nominations made by the teachers' associations. But there is no doubt that the Department itself welcomed the pattern and helped maintain it. In 1972, a higher proportion of unionised teachers in Edinburgh were members of the SSTA than in Glasgow, Lanarkshire or Ayrshire (Deroche-Drieux 1976, 56). The Department increased the status of the SSTA in order to promote the influence of teachers like Dewar and Gray (see chapters 10 and 18). It also retained a firm control over appointments to national committees. Where this was resisted, the Department had the last word.

Brunton's successor, Dickson, enlarged on the influence of the Inspectorate. We asked him if he agreed that Brunton had exercised control over national appointments:

DICKSON. Yes, I think so. He retained it in the Department's hands. . . .

Q. How would you estimate the influence of the Inspectorate here? They probably have wider contacts and know more people than any other single agency; they are consulted officially or unofficially by local authorities on their own external appointments.

DICKSON. Unofficially.

Q. This must give the Inspectorate a great deal of influence at all levels of the system, though an intangible influence.

DICKSON. This is true. I think the influence of the Inspectorate in that kind of way has been greater than their influence in their formal and official aspect.

Q. What does a person have to do to bring himself to the attention of the Inspectorate?

DICKSON. You mean, 'How does a man impress the inspector as a probably useful member of a working party, as a potential adviser'?

Q. Or collaborator.

DICKSON. I think he must, in the first place, be efficient at his job. That is what the Inspectorate is good at estimating. Thereafter, he must be the kind of person who will obviously get on with other people on a committee. I would imagine that any inspector would tend to be 'agin' the sort of person who, unless he has his own way on a committee, will resign. We've had experience of that kind of thing. It leads to nothing and nowhere. You must have the kind of person who will disagree on a committee but remain a member of it, and do his best to influence his colleagues.

The appointment of teachers to the subject panels of the Examination Board in the mid-1960s gives some indication of the consequences of the Inspectorate's application of these criteria. As we saw in chapter 13, the appointments were made by Dewar using a list supplied by the Inspectorate. Again, the first-generation schools predominated. They supplied half of Dewar's first appointees even though they comprised only about a sixth of the schools which presented pupils for SCE examinations at the time. Again this meant that the schools from which panel members were drawn were, for the most part, located in socially privileged neighbourhoods. Four-fifths of the teachers appointed by Dewar came from schools that served neighbourhoods of above-average socio-economic status. This pattern, however, weakened in later appointments to the panels. On the Board itself, four of the nine teachers that joined Dewar in 1964 came from first-generation schools, and only one from a school founded after 1918.[15]

Similar influences are apparent in the appointments made to the committees and working parties of the CCC. On the Committee itself, headteachers from second- and third-generation secondary schools in the west of Scotland began, for the first time, to appear in numbers on a national committee. This no doubt reflected the continuing repercussions of the 1961 teachers' strike, and the change in the political control of patronage that came with the appointment of a Labour Secretary of State for Scotland in 1964. But, in the appointments made to the CCC's infrastructure of working parties and committees, the predominance of the first-generation schools continued. The CCC was intended as much to complement as to overlap the Examination Board, and much of its early work concerned curriculum for less able pupils (see chapter 14). All secondary schools therefore had an interest in the CCC, whether or not they presented pupils for the SCE. In 1965, there were over 600 secondary schools, of which the 66 first-generation schools constituted about one-ninth. Nevertheless, they supplied thirty-five per cent of the teachers appointed under the first CCC (1965-68), and forty-one per cent of those appointed under the second (1968-71). Thus, the number of teachers they contributed to the infrastructure of the CCC was three to four times higher than might be expected.[16] Clark, who served on the CCC from 1971 to 1980, was sure that such appointments reflected Inspectorate judgements, and not those of the local authority:

CLARK. I don't think that there is any doubt about it at all that the Inspectorate had considerable influence in these matters. They got out and about, and they did hear of teachers and heads and so on – and probably saw them – who ran certain types of schools, or did certain types of things, or who were particularly interested in and knowledgeable about certain aspects of the curriculum or whatever. And, undoubtedly, a lot of these people, rightly, were appointed to the CCC. But ultimate decisions were made, undoubtedly, within the Department.

We have not been able to extend our quantitative analysis of recruitment to senior positions in the colleges of education, nor to senior local-authority administrators. Instead, we must rely here on a comment by Allan Rodger which suggests that they shared a background that was similar to that we have just described:

RODGER. I would say that inspectors of schools, assistant directors of education and directors of education, and training-college staff all tended to be drawn from the best of teachers. These were three groups that were all endeavouring to get the best that they could out of the teaching profession; and you might find that one particular man would be on a leet for the Inspectorate, but could equally easily have been on the leet for a director-ship or for an assistant directorship, or for a training-college post. There-fore, one could really say that these three groups got off to an equal start. They were the best that could be got from the profession. But they didn't finish up equal. It's very much my opinion that inspectors grew in their jobs; that directors might grow, or might not; and that training-college people deteriorated in their posts, except for the principals.

The Department allowed the principals considerable influence, both on the SCTT and later on the GTC (see chapter 12); and perhaps it was with the principals in mind that Rodger added this comment:

RODGER. The tradition in the Department, as far as I knew it, because I can't speak of it of the time before I was an Assistant Secretary, was: ride the training colleges on as light a rein as possible. . . . Our Inspectorate . . . were recruited from the same kind of people as were the college lecturers, therefore it would have been rather *infra dig* for people who were more or less their equals to be in any way superior to them.

At the local level, the influence of the Inspectorate over appointments seems to have varied between authorities. Inglis, the Principal of Moray House College, criticised what he considered to be undue Inspectorate influence when he gave evidence to the Select Committee on the Inspecto-rate in 1968:

INGLIS. There seems to me to be great dangers inherent in the situation where the inspector has a large hand in making policy . . . and then has the opportunity of advising the education authority about the . . . promotion of a head teacher. Is he not almost inevitably looking for the head teacher who carries out with diligence the proposals . . . prepared by his colleagues [s c e s 1968, q.298]?

It emerged from the committee's enquiries that Glasgow always consulted the Department about appointments to head teacher (*ibid.*, q.291). It seems that the Inspectorate there were working with the Directorate to break a method of appointment that was sensitive to political canvassing by the candidates, and which gave little opportunity to younger teachers and to teachers from outside Glasgow.[17] McEwan told us that he often consulted the Inspectorate about applicants from outwith Lanarkshire for senior school positions, and sometimes about local applicants too. And he agreed that this enhanced Inspectorate influence over the schools:

McEwan. Oh, there is bound to have been some of that. I mean, teachers would look over their shoulder at anybody who had a possible influence on their promotion – anybody would whether they were teachers or not – and, naturally enough, only a fool would ignore recommendations about a principal teachership, for example, from the inspector of modern languages.

But it may be that the Inspectorate generally played a more interventionist part in certain west of Scotland authorities than they did elsewhere; for example, they were unusually active in planning Glasgow's school building (see chapter 9). The Director of Education for Edinburgh told the 1968 Select Committee on the Inspectorate that Edinburgh rarely consulted the Inspectorate on appointments (*ibid.*, q.294). McIntosh was dismissive of their knowledge of Fife, or influence in it (*ibid.*, qs 228, 232 and 238). As to Aberdeen, Clark had this to say:

Clark. Quite frankly, we did not, in Aberdeen, rely to any extent, particularly latterly, on the views of members of the Inspectorate. . . . The Advisorate, obviously, in a sense, took over. They knew all the people, whereas the Inspectorate didn't necessarily know all of the people . . . but district inspectors at that level also varied very much, and there were district inspectors whom I would have discussed appointments with. . . . There were others that I wouldn't have bothered about. So we are talking about the quality of the man. . . . I cannot recall any member of committee ever asking at . . . a staffing interview, 'Did the local inspectors have any comments to make?'

Those Who Were Not Called

Clark was discussing appointments to posts that were located, as it were, towards the boundary of the policy community, possibly even outside it. We have not attempted to define or locate this boundary precisely, and, in any case, it may be that a different metaphor would serve better, concentric circles of influence and prestige perhaps. We can, however, identify some of those persons who were clearly beyond the pale of the community. When an analysis of the Kirriemuir career was first published several years ago, it elicited the following response from Tom O'Hagan, then a primary-school head teacher in the North-East of Scotland:

O'HAGAN. You have done a great deal to help me understand the attitudes and perspective of my late parents who were teachers in Glasgow from 1945 until about 1972. . . . Their allegiances were to Glasgow and Ireland rather than Scotland. Among their attitudes to education, which were shared with their Catholic teaching colleagues were: sardonic opinions on almost every pronouncement emanating from any Scottish educational body; indifference to any educational developments taking place outside Glasgow; a profound sense of being constantly sold out in pay negotiations by the 'genteel' teachers from the provinces; and contempt for anyone who went outside Glasgow for promotion – such promotions didn't really count. The people they held in regard, whose opinions they listened to, were unsung contemporary labourers at the chalk face. The Inspectorate were regarded as upstart counter-jumpers and anything which issued from the SED fell on deaf ears. I came to interpret these attitudes in two ways. The huge cynicism over all things administrative I took to be the standard posture for teachers. The disregard for everything outside Glasgow I understood to be a kind of urban arrogance which saw all things outside the city as hick. It never dawned on me that it could have been Scotland that could have cold-shouldered Glasgow into this position. I . . . taught a few years in primary schools in Glasgow . . . and, rather surprisingly, washed up here . . . as a country dominie, last of a dwindling breed. Hardly a Kirriemuir Career, but being a headteacher and therefore invited along to meetings attended by people in charge of larger establishments, I am in a fair position to view the budding of some potential Kirriemuir Careers. More interestingly, I am able to make a comparison between the attitudes of my parents and the attitudes of my present colleagues. For me, in accordance with the parental attitudes on which I was raised, coming here was a cop out, hardly to be taken seriously. Yet, in marked contrast to my feelings, I found my colleagues here steeped in the lore of traditional Scottish educational values, enormously self-important, given to orotund and reverberating speeches of the type which you feel are intended for the ears of an eager nation. Knowing Strathclyde, the direct unpompous manner, and the more complex social problems . . . I had to blink back my amazement at the omniscient and omnipotent postures of those people whom I considered to be, like me, very much on the sidelines, i.e. outside Glasgow. . . . Even those who come from or have worked in Glasgow are quick to relegate the importance of the city and contribute to the provincial pomposity, because they are in the midst of a Kirriemuir Career and Glasgow has no place in this. . . . Those who get out of Glasgow are quick to forget it, and Glasgow forgets them.

Paul Willis (1977, 3) has talked of an 'element of self-damnation in the taking on of subordinate roles in Western capitalism'. He had in mind, in in particular, pupils who resisted the cultural values implicit in their schooling. By asserting alternatives, Willis argued, they voluntarily but unwittingly embraced the very identity that would subsequently enslave them. The cynicism and indifference towards educational administration described in the passage above, and the hostility to provincial gentility, suggest a similar element of self-damnation among their teachers. Resistance, too, could result. The man who mobilised the 'unsung labourers' in the 1961 teachers' strike, Arthur Houston, was a teacher in a Glasgow Catholic school. He had entered teaching, not through the conventional induction, but as a mid-career entrant from the ranks of the Royal Navy, retrained under the Special Recruitment Scheme. He had strong links with the Labour Party, and he operated outside the formal structures of his association, the EIS (McKenzie 1974, ch.2).[18] Thus, the conflict that broke the 'no-strike' orthodoxy of professionalism among teachers, and that led eventually to the reorganisation of the structure of advice, was finally precipitated by an individual whose own career had evaded the established processes of identity formation and social control.

Myth and Tradition in England

We continue our discussion of the Scottish policy community in the next chapter, where we look at the EIS and other pressure groups. But we end this one on a comparative note. It is true that there were links between the Kirriemuir career and the private sector of Scottish schools, but what we have identified here is primarily a Scottish *public-school* establishment, in the usual sense of the term 'public'. The idea of a British public-school establishment, in the English sense of 'public-school', is familiar enough. But it tends to characterise smaller and more exclusive elites who share little in common with the generality of those involved in particular areas of policy and service delivery (Boyd 1973). In England, therefore, there may be less of a basis for community among members of a national policy collectivity. Kogan, for example, writes of English education:

> The same group of DES officials, local authority association officials, chief officers and councillors may face each other over decades in determining policy. Yet the group is not closed, let alone an elite. They do not have the main characteristics of a closed system, of socio-economic class, of recruitment, or of social integration. Both the Permanent Secretary at the centre and the head of a village school have authority. But they have different educational backgrounds. Even where there is consistency of background or continuity of contact, there is little social communication. (Kogan 1975, 235)

In Scotland, by contrast, there was a common basis of recruitment in the Kirriemuir career, and an ontological basis for 'social integration' and 'social communication' in the Scottish myth. Perhaps, too, the difference between England and Scotland was partly a matter of size, for Kogan does attach considerable weight to the operation in England of 'powerful cultural and social networks established within some local education authorities' (Kogan 1978, 128). Certainly, size was a factor that Graham thought important in Scotland:

GRAHAM. It was a much more closely integrated system. I mean, if we wanted to discuss the problems of raising the school-leaving age, or the problems of staffing in secondary schools, we could get all of the directors of education or virtually all of them . . . in Hamilton College of Education or out at Middleton Hall for a couple of days, and thrash the whole thing out, both formally in sessions and informally over dinner and in a bar afterwards, which as a technique is quite inconceivable in the English situation.

Size may also have affected role structures, at least in central government:

DICKSON. At one time I had three big jobs on. In England they would have had at least four inspectors doing what I was doing, because they had enough numbers to provide specialists.

Q. How would they have managed the relationship between the Inspectorate and the administration in the DES?

DICKSON. I am not aware that they ever transferred people from the Inspectorate to the administration. . . . I would be inclined to think that there was less natural and easy liaison between the administration and the Inspectorate in England than here. Numbers have a great deal to do with it of course.

But not only numbers. Wood, it will be recalled, worked both in Scotland and England:

WOOD. The English have never believed in education and . . . the Oxbridge civil servant despised what he called the public elementary school. Now this has never been as bad in Scotland, as you know. This attitude exists, but it has never been as fierce in Scotland as it was in the South.

Overall, one should not exaggerate the national differences here. Both countries had their public-school elites, though in different senses of the term. Physically, moreover, Scotland is not a small country. If the Scottish policy community were small, it was partly because central government itself limited the plurality of groups that were admitted to it. In its policies towards schools and local authorities, central government worked consistently over the years to reduce the number of agencies with which it had to deal. Also, though Scotland had its distinctive myth, its appeals to myth were not distinctive. Benn and Simon (1972, 50-1) draw attention to the part such appeals have played in arguments about comprehensive education in England. Following Clarke (1940), they also point to exactly the same process of selective reinterpretation that is apparent in Scotland: 'to invoke "tradition", as if it were a single and autonomous factor is to overlook that there have always been at least three "traditions" in English education'

(Benn and Simon 1972, 51).[19]

The Scottish myth has typically been the cry of a people under attack, the affirmation of a culture threatened by economic, social and political change. What has become increasingly apparent in the last twenty years is that there is also a British tradition, or myth, that would yield to the type of analysis conducted in this chapter. In this case, as Fenwick (1985, 137) has suggested, 'the language of the myth is the language of "partnership" '.[20]

NOTES

1. Parts of this chapter are based on an earlier publication (McPherson 1983). We are grateful to Doug Willms for his indispensable contribution to some of the new statistical analyses on which we draw in this revision.

2. The suggestion is not, however, that myths are sufficiently precise to indicate a single course of action, or a single test of their truth. Much depends on how, in practice, they are interpreted. For a discussion and illustration of how one may engage the expressive and empirical claims of myth, see Gray *et al.* (1983), especially chs 16 and 17.

3. Illingworth's (1971) biography of Hetherington is a good example of the interpretation of an individual's life in terms of the myth, even though some of the facts fit the fiction less than perfectly (McPherson 1983, 221-2).

4. See Saltire Society (1948). Munro, an ex-President of the EIS and member of the Sixth Advisory Council, was active in the affairs of the Saltire Society (see Saltire Society 1941). So too was the Rector of Dollar Academy, Harry Bell, a member of the Eighth Advisory Council, and credited with an initiating role in the Sixth Council (Lloyd 1984, 106-7).

5. Systematic Scottish evidence for the first half of the century is not available, but relevant indications can be found in the following: Kelsall (1954, 1957), McDonald (1964), McPherson and Atherton (1970), Kelly (1976) and especially Mercer and Forsyth (1975). For England and Wales, see Floud and Scott (1956). As in England, women teachers in Scotland may on average have had higher social origins than men teachers. But most women who married were required to stop work, and spinster teachers taught mainly in the less prestigious primary sector, or, if in the secondary sector, found it difficult to get promotion (Cruickshank 1970; Fewell 1984). The greater importance of the public sector in Scotland, together with the training requirement, will probably have resulted, in Scotland, in less social-class differentiation of male teachers by school sector than Floud and Scott report for England and Wales.

6. Strictly speaking, George Heriot's School falls outwith the operational definition of a first-generation school, given towards the beginning of chapter 15. This is somewhat anomalous, however, because the school was founded in the seventeenth century and was remodelled as a fee-paying school in 1885 (Anderson 1983a, ch.5). In 1901, however, the Department did not recognise it as a secondary school under the Minute of 27 April 1899.

7. Brewer's (1981, 623) describes the Kailyard School as a 'school of writers flourishing in the 1890s, who took their subjects from Scottish humble life. It included Ian Maclaren, J.J.Bell, S.R.Crockett, and J.M.Barrie. The name is from the motto – "There grows a bonnie brier bush in our Kailyard" – used by Maclaren for his *Beside the Bonnie Brier Bush* (1895)'. The influence of the School continued well into the twentieth century. Many hold it principally responsible for a widespread and nostalgic sentimentalisation of Scottish life that diverted attention from its harsher aspect.

8. See Gray *et al.* (1983, ch.14); and McPherson and Willms (1986). Willms (1986) reviews research from several countries that shows that the proportion of higher social-class pupils in a school is positively associated with higher attainment for pupils of both higher and lower social class in that school. This effect is also found in Scotland (McPherson and Willms 1986), and provides a further reason for believing that the Kirriemuir career presented teachers with more frequent 'objective', i.e. experiential, evidence for the success of working-class pupils, than was to be encountered in other schools.

9. SED (1965a, 14). See also the annual reports of the SED from 1951 onwards beginning with SED (1952a).

10. Selection will have reduced the salience of the lower average attainment of lower social-class pupils in three ways. First, the majority of such pupils were selected out of senior-secondary schools and courses at the transfer stage, or shortly after (Gray *et al.*, 1983, ch.12). Second, a similar, but more voluntary process of selection took place at the minimum school-leaving age (*ibid.*). The third reason concerns the feeder-receiver school configurations which were common outside the cities (see chapter 15), and here we have to rely on evidence from the 1970s alone. It shows that the pupils who transferred from the feeder school to the receiver school for certificate work, tended to have a higher mean attainment than their counterparts who had attended only the receiver school. This was especially true of lower social-class pupils (McIver 1981). The net effect of all these processes was, we infer, that the lower social-class members of the senior (i.e. older) certificate classes were, on average, unusually able, and tended to do well. By the late 1950s, among pupils completing Highers courses, there was virtually no association between attainment and social class (Gray *et al.*, 1983, fig.12.2). Many teachers who taught mainly the senior classes of senior-secondary courses were thus confronted by further experiential evidence that social class was no barrier to attainment in Scotland.

11. See Macpherson (1958, especially 42, 74 and 77). He thought it an 'inescapable' conclusion that 'character plays a most important role in determining whether a pupil stays on course or drops out. Perseverance, conscientiousness, and the will to do well are factors which count. . . . Unless we are prepared to take measures to improve pupils' characters and attitudes, a most difficult task, it would seem that not all of the potential ability in an age-group could be realised in practice.' By contrast, the view associated with Brunton (see chapter 11) was that the task was not all that 'difficult'. The inadequacy of the Highers course, and unresolved systemic problems of difficulty and motivation, were held to be responsible for failures of individual motivation (SED 1959b, para.27-8): 'Once real interest has been aroused, the pupils themselves will lead the way'. The Macpherson study actually scaled down its estimates of the size of wastage on the grounds that pupils with motivational deficiencies who left school at fifteen years had only limited prospects of success in the Highers examination. Since Brunton, however, and especially since the Munn report (SED 1977c), official policy has been to treat motivation as a factor endogenous to the school system.

12. See the annual reports of the SED from 1951 onwards, beginning with SED (1952a). In 1955, for example, only Dundee, Glasgow, and two small counties had post-compulsory enrolment rates as low. The Lanarkshire rate in that year was twenty-two per cent, compared with a national average for all non-private schools of twenty-nine per cent (SED 1956a, table 28).

13. The socio-economic status of neighbourhoods is measured here by a proxy variable describing the average socio-economic status of each school's pupil

intake in the period 1974-76, by which time the vast majority of education-authority maintained schools had non-selective intakes. For further details of the measure, see McPherson and Willms (1986). Details of the schools in which appointees to the Inspectorate held posts at the time of their appointment are taken from Bone (1967), supplemented by a list kindly supplied by the SED. It should be noted that the numbers of serving teachers appointed directly from schools to the Inspectorate began to decline in the 1960s. At the same time there was an increase in the members appointed from various types of college.

14. For details of the appointments to the Advisory Council and the NCTT see respectively *SEJ* (22 February 1957) and *SEJ* (27 March 1959). These appointments can be compared with those made by Tom Johnston to the Sixth Advisory Council in 1942. Of the seven teachers appointed, only two were from the West. On the other hand, only three were from first-generation secondary schools, whilst two were from junior-secondary schools, one from a Catholic school founded in 1923, and one from an infant school. Two appointees were women. To some degree, of course, appointments reflect the nature of the work that the committee in question must undertake. Nevertheless, the appointments made in the 1950s were more traditional than those made in 1942. Presumably this reflects political influence in part (see also chapter 11), and also a Departmental insurance policy against the risk inherent in the admission of teachers to the locus of decision-making at the centre.

15. SED (1965a, table 1) shows that there were 381 schools providing SCE courses at the beginning of 1964. (It is not clear whether some of these provided only the early stages of such courses, but these will, in any case, have been in a minority.) Thus, the sixty-six first-generation schools were considerably overrepresented in panel appointments. For the definition of neighbourhood socio-economic status see note 13. The percentage of panel members supplied by the first-generation schools fell from fifty-two per cent in 1965 to twenty-eight per cent by 1970. But, ten years later, it was still at that figure, even though the first-generation schools by that time constituted only fourteen per cent of the 470 secondary schools. The overrepresentation of first-generation schools in panel appointments had thus declined, but was still not negligible. Details of membership of the panels of the Examination Board in 1970 and after are published in the annual reports of the Board, beginning with SCEEB (1971). We are grateful to the Board for supplying us with details of panel memberships 1965-69.

16. Details of appointments to various committees and working parties under the CCC may be found in SED (1969b, 1972b, 1975c, 1980b and 1983c).

17. Personal communication from a former HMI based at one time in Glasgow. McKenzie (1974, 106) reports that, 'so far as I can ascertain, all Headmasters in Corporation [City] schools have served as teachers in Glasgow'. The one known exception was the Rector of Glasgow High School.

18. In commenting upon a draft of this chapter, Gilbert Bryden cast doubt upon Houston's importance in the 1961 strike. By contrast, McKenzie argues that 'Mr Arthur Houston and his colleagues in St Augustine's Secondary School played a crucial role in stimulating "grass-roots" involvement in EIS affairs. . . . At no time did he have direct consultation with the leadership of the Local Association. . . . However, he had a vital informal contact in the person of Mr David Lambie, an ex-Chairman and Member of the Committee of Management . . . who like Mr Houston, was very active in Scottish Labour Party politics' (McKenzie 1974, 18, 21). Lambie became Chairman of the Scottish Labour Party in 1964, and was elected MP for Ayrshire Central in 1970. From 1967 to

1970, he was chief negotiator for the EIS in the Scottish Teachers' Salaries Committee. McKenzie emphasises that support for industrial action in Glasgow was by no means confined to Glasgow Catholic schools (*ibid.*, 20).

19. 'The first of these is the ruling-class tradition of education, the academic tradition invoking the classically orientated "liberal arts" and closely associated with professions which themselves are conservative in organization. The second is the vigorous tradition reaching back through nonconformity to the Protestant reformation, and forward to the middle-class reformers of the nineteenth century who were concerned to promote the teaching of science and re-volutionize traditional education both at secondary school and university. The third is the tradition of instruction for the working class, provided for them by their betters. It is this last, Clarke urged, that must be brought to the surface and transformed' (Benn and Simon 1972, 51). See also Clarke (1940).

20. Fenwick argues that R. A. Butler's attempts to construct a parliamentary coalition of sufficient strength to pass the 1944 Education Bill helped create 'the myth of an education system from which politics was banished and under which questions of administration – resources, timing – were paramount'. He writes, 'The myth of partnership most closely corresponded to reality at the time of the passage of the Education Act, 1944, not only in political rhetoric but in the considered legislative intentions of the President of the Board of Education and his officials'. But he also argues that 'over the last forty years the reality of an exclusive partnership in educational government has been so eroded that the myth is no longer sustainable'. His use of the term 'myth' is identical to ours: 'By myth I here mean a story which is about both the way the world is *and* the way it ought to be – history *and* doctrine and therefore a powerful guide to action by precedent while it remains widely believed' (Fenwick 1985, 137-9, his emphases).

Eighteen

Government, Individuals and Pressure Groups

I remember that Sir William Arbuckle retired at the same time as
the Under-Secretary Mr Rodger retired. We felt that this indicated a big change in the Department. . . . I remember speaking
about this once at a dinner and saying that we were going to have
no more Arbuckles and no more Rodgers in the Department. We
all agreed that this was something that was to be very much deplored.   Gilbert Bryden, General Secretary of the EIS 1961-74[1]

Introduction

The policy community was the community of individuals who mattered, and
it was also the forum in which the interests of groups were represented,
reconciled or rebuffed. We now examine the workings of the community in
relation to the major formal groupings of teachers, local authorities and
officials. How did they interact with each other, with the Department, with
local and national politicians, and with Westminster? Who trusted whom?
Who respected whom? In what ways were the relations between the various
bodies dependent on the relations between individuals? And what were the
outcomes, in the realisation of sectional goals, in the merging of interests
that were ostensibly separate, and in the shaping of common goals and
policies? This chapter illustrates two main themes: relations between the
Department and the major pressure groups; and relations between groups
and individuals in the exertion of influence on the Department. In the
following chapter we add the evidence from earlier chapters to what we
learn here about the politics of pressure groups, and the successes and
failures they had.

For oral evidence, we rely here mainly on Clark, McEwan and Bryden,
and in particular on Rodger. From 1945 to 1963, as Assistant Secretary and
Under-Secretary, Rodger was an important arbiter of the Department's
attitude to virtually all the bodies that counted, and to many of the individuals. Hence his assessments were important, no matter whether they were
right or wrong. In the 1950s, his contacts were every bit as extensive as those
that Brunton was striving to develop. Through these Rodger was able to
promote and inhibit both individuals and ideas, filtering, shaping and, in
other ways also, 'aggregating' the opinions that eventually emerged as
policy. It is probable that his influence within the Department was not

confined to the policy areas for which he had formal responsibility as Under-Secretary. He was also the Departmental authority on educational psychology, statistics and selection, and he told us that Arbuckle regularly consulted him on schooling and curriculum.

Career and Role

In the previous chapter, Rodger said that senior appointees in education were recruited from the 'same kind of people' as the Inspectorate. We start this chapter with Rodger's account of his own early career and of some of the people who influenced him. It testifies to a face-to-face community sharing a common student background that, for some, led later to professional educational study. The roles its members came to fill were structurally proximate, one to another, in that careers could traverse them. We learn of the importance of sponsorship. We learn also how Rodger's responsibilities after 1945 brought him into regular contact with incumbents of positions throughout the system whom he had already encountered in the compass of his own career. The structuring of his formal role, the way he played it, and his effectiveness in it, all owed something to his earlier contacts and experience. Our analysis of Brunton's time as Senior Chief Inspector has already suggested that we should consider roles in the light of the biographies of their incumbents, and not merely as static locations in a formal organisational plan. Rodger's account reinforces this view:

RODGER. While a student [of Mathematics] at [Edinburgh] University, I knew and became friendly with a number of persons in other departments, with whom I afterwards worked. For example, I knew Arbuckle, who was doing History; A. B. Taylor, who became an Inspector of English [1933-48], and later Registrar General of Scotland; Alec Law, who became an inspector [1939-67]; and, in my first year of the [B Ed] degree in Education, a classmate with whom I was friendly, Robert Macdonald, became a colleague in the Inspectorate [1930-62]. He finished as a chief inspector of schools. . . . I started off in teaching in 1925, and I wanted as much experience in as short a time as possible. My father, being a headmaster in Fife, knew Gregor McGregor, the Director of Education in Fife [1919-41]. He had always taken an interest in my career; and I simply went to him and said, 'I want to get the maximum experience in the minimum of time'. So he put me to a school where I got a certain amount of work in all four subjects, mathematics, physics, chemistry, and geography [Viewforth School, Kirkcaldy]. . . . Then, in my fourth year of teaching, I was asked by Professor Godfrey Thomson, who was by now Professor at Edinburgh, to become one of his lecturers. . . . Administration, at that stage, did not really enter my thoughts all that much. It entered my thoughts, rather accidentally, much later. . . . I was singularly lucky to have had both McClelland and Godfrey Thomson as heads of the Education Department [of Edinburgh University]. . . . I would say that, during my career, McClelland and

Thomson have been two of the biggest influences in Scottish education, and I always regarded myself as singularly fortunate to have had this close contact with them both. . . . I would probably put Thomson's as the sharpest intellect that I have ever come up against.

Q. And yet possibly, in the long-run, it was McClelland who had more influence.

RODGER. Perhaps in Scotland, yes. He was very much more Scottish than Thomson, and therefore he had more influence in Scotland. He was brought up in, and understood, the Scottish system better since he had also served it in several capacities. . . . After serving as a teacher he was the first Director of Education in Wigtownshire [1919-21]. Thus he had a wide Scottish background; therefore, he was more able to be influential in Scotland than Thomson. Furthermore, McClelland occupied administrative posts. His post as Professor of Education at St Andrews was coupled with that of Director of Studies in Dundee Training College, which was an administrative post. . . . St Andrews established only the diploma stage of the BEd degree, and anyone who took the diploma there and wished to complete the degree had to go elsewhere. Douglas McIntosh took the diploma in St Andrews but the degree in Edinburgh, under Thomson. I think that some of what you say, though true, was accidental. McClelland had extreme loyalty to his best students, and to those who worked with him. Indeed, I would have said – and it's about the only criticism that I would pass on McClelland, in his later days, at any rate – that, if two or three people were in for an appointment, and if he was influential in determining who should be appointed, he was not always, in my opinion, an impartial judge. He tended to favour the persons with whom he had worked. . . . Thomson similarly occupied a combined post in Edinburgh. . . . But it just so happened that, with the possible exception of myself, who was a lecturer under Thomson, none of his former students ever worked with him as closely as Douglas McIntosh. It may interest you to know that, when McIntosh first introduced intelligence and scholastic tests into his promotion examinations for secondary schools in Fife, he came to Edinburgh to get the tests. In fact, I made them, though they were made under Thomson's auspices. . . . After I had been in Moray House for six years, Thomson said, 'Rodger, I don't see a post arising on my side which you can get in reasonable time', and added, 'I think that you've now served a long-enough apprenticeship, that you should really be going into something much bigger'. He said, 'You keep your eyes open, and I'll keep my eyes open for anything', and he said, 'I'll do all I can to get you whatever post you want'. . . . The Professorship of Psychology in Belfast, the Professorship of Education in Swansea, the Depute Director of Education in Edinburgh, the head of the Psychology Department in Jordanhill College, and a post in the Inspectorate, all fell vacant simultaneously, and I went in for them all.

Rodger was appointed to the Inspectorate in 1935, but was soon seconded to the administrative side of the Department, which he joined formally in 1945. He remained an administrator for the rest of his career, but retained many of his earlier contacts:

RODGER. The Senior Chief Inspector was usually no expert in the theory of education or psychology (especially in their modern psychometric developments). They weren't trained in that particular field, and, therefore, the Senior Chief Inspector often asked for help from some other member of the Inspectorate who was a specialist in that line. That happened to me. I was asked by the Senior Chief Inspector of those days to do the educational psychology work of the training colleges. . . . Furthermore, the fact that I was in Thomson's team meant that I was having contact with university people in the other universities who were on the education and psychology sides. I sometimes met, too, their chief students; so that, in a sense, all of the BEds all over the country were persons that I had a chance to know. Later, after I became an Assistant Secretary in 1945, I was assessor on all training-college committees, and so got to the people in that world. Also, the Secretariat had two or three meetings a year with the Association of Directors of Education, and thus I met the directors, whom of course I also met when dealing with problems in their area.

We turn now to the way Rodger put this background to use in the service of the Department, and helped to orchestrate the Department's relations with outside individuals and groups.

Teachers' Associations

Bryden told the 1968 Select Committee on the Inspectorate that the EIS regretted the departure of Arbuckle and Rodger because the Institute wanted to see at the top of the SED a 'substantial representation of people who have been through the mill themselves [as] . . . teachers' (SCES 1968, Q.319):

Q. My impression from your evidence to that Committee is that the Institute officially was pretty well satisfied with relationships with the Inspectorate.

BRYDEN. I wrote all the evidence for that largely out of my own experience. I thought highly of the Inspectorate myself, so that what you see there is largely my view. One or two of my members . . . thought I had been too kind to the Inspectorate. I remember a former Secretary of the Department coming round to express his appreciation. I had never met him, but it was Sir John Mackay Thomson.

As General Secretary of the EIS, Bryden found himself in 1961 standing somewhere between a membership that was becoming impatient for change, and a Department with whom he could deal (see chapters 10 and 12). He told us that he 'got on very well' with Brunton and met him frequently (see chapter 5). He also trusted the Inspectorate's judgement of people: 'I sometimes consulted the Inspectorate about people myself. If I wanted to know about a particular person for a particular reason, I have sometimes rung up the Senior Chief and asked him to get a report.' Brunton, for his part, told us that 'many matters which are now often blown up into matters of confrontation were settled by the Secretary of the EIS and myself over a cup of coffee'. In such relations personal trust was clearly essential, no more so, perhaps, than over the negotiation of salaries, where a quiet word from Rodger on the Treasury position could influence the point at which the EIS decided to settle (see chapter 10). The Department's dealings with the large majority of Scottish teachers hinged on such trust. Bryden told us that, before the 1961 strike, he had been 'building up a good relationship with Departmental officials', and that he found himself carried somewhat reluctantly into industrial action. Initially Bryden negotiated with another official because Rodger himself was abroad when the strike began (see chapter 12). Rodger told us: 'my wife got fed up with the 'phone ringing, with Arbuckle or some other asking when I would be home'. But home he came to involve himself in the resolution of the dispute. By 1963, if not earlier, the auld alliance between Bryden and Rodger was again in operation, producing a salary award that gave Scottish teachers more than those in England, though spread over a longer period (see chapter 10). Bryden liked the award, and he told us that he had 'lots of confidence' in Rodger, in spite of the fact that they 'often differed quite radically'. How did Rodger regard Bryden?

RODGER. I always found Bryden a very reasonable man. My own personal relationships with Bryden were always good. . . . He has always treated me very much as a friend, and has done so since I retired. There have been about three occasions, since I retired, when the EIS has wanted to make representations to the Secretary or to the Secretary of State, and he has written to me and told me the facts and what they wanted to write. . . . In all of the cases I have said that they shouldn't write the proposed letter at all, and they took my advice. But it does show the relationship between him and me that, even after I retired, that's the kind of thing that he would consult me about.

We asked Rodger how he ranked the influence of the EIS, relative to other associations, on the Department's thinking on educational matters:

RODGER. I think that I would say that the Association of Directors topped the list; the teachers' associations would probably come next; the Committee of Principals would probably come next; and the association of education authorities would almost certainly come last. But in all groups there were individuals of high prestige with us, and their views counted. . . . [We probably met] the EIS eight to ten times a year, leaving salaries out of account; SSA . . . once a year; SSTA maybe three or four times a year. Our meetings with these bodies were sometimes sought by us, sometimes by them; sometimes on *ad hoc* issues, sometimes for a more general talk. Now, the differences in the estimates that I'm giving you are not just a function

. . . of our estimate of the importance of these bodies; it was rather a function of the width of the bodies. You see it didn't matter whether an educational issue referred to infant, junior, junior-secondary or senior-secondary school problems, EIS were in it, whereas the SSTA only comes in on secondary points.

Q. Would you say that the quality of the thinking that was coming out of the SSTA, and the quality of the people in it, was superior to that of the EIS, and more of the quality and type of thinking to which the Department could agree?

RODGER. Yes, I think that that is on the whole true. I think it's inevitable. . . . The SSTA really began as a body to try to fight for better conditions for the secondary teacher, particularly the Honours graduates. Now, I would say that I have always found the EIS to be a good, gentlemanly, mannerly body. Their delegation would come up to the Department; they would state their view, which was often contrary to your own, very strongly, but they always behaved very well. I think, however, that there was something in the SSTA's contention that they [the EIS] were dominated by a non-graduate group. Their delegation, when they came up, would probably include a number of non-graduate women who had never seen beyond the infant department or the lower range of the primary school since they themselves were students, whereas the SSTA were secondary teachers who were graduates and Honours graduates. Therefore, I'm sure, Brunton would find them more in line with himself and his line of thinking.

We asked Bryden about the SSTA and about the attitude of the Department's Secretaries:

BRYDEN. There is no doubt that every now and again we missed, in our membership, the chaps who had gone into the SSTA. It was very regrettable that some of the very good chaps who were in the SSTA weren't in the Institute, because of their weight and assistance. . . . You asked about the response of the SED under the three Secretaries. We found Murrie . . . very good. Murrie was a good EIS man. I don't know whether he liked us, but he felt that the best policy from his point of view was to deal with the body that he knew about. . . . Arbuckle was a pro-SSTA man. Murrie kept the SSTA out, but one of the first things that Arbuckle did was to let the SSTA in. . . . Before his time the SED didn't consult the SSTA. As soon as he became Secretary they did.[2] This is on purely educational matters of course. . . . It may be significant that, when Arbuckle was about to retire, somebody in the Executive proposed that we should give Arbuckle a dinner; and somebody said, 'Well, why give Arbuckle a dinner? We have never given the Secretary of the Department a dinner before'. And somebody else said, 'Well, during Arbuckle's time there have been a great number of beneficial changes'. And a very shrewd member of the Executive stood up and said, 'Yes, all obtained in spite of Arbuckle'. And I think perhaps there is some truth in that. . . . An interesting character, Graham, most interesting bloke. In some respects very sympathetic, very open with his information, very frank, also very difficult to shake – at least that was certainly the impression that he gave. I'm sure he was difficult to shake, but if you got his sympathy, very helpful. How did we press policies? Well, I suppose mainly through the SED. The SED was normally – particularly during my time, and during my predecessor's time – the body that we looked to for furthering our aims. If we succeeded in converting the SED, we felt that we had gained our point. And my predecessor used to regard the Secretary of the SED as Head of the House. If we were unsuccessful with the SED, we sometimes went direct to Members of Parliament, and sometimes direct to Ministers.

Q. Did you distinguish between the administrative side and the Inspectorate? Did you find that there were some avenues that were more conducive to pressure than others?

BRYDEN. I wouldn't like to say. They were certainly individuals who were much more sympathetic than others, but obviously that's not the sort of thing that I could talk about. We also, of course, every now and again, pressed policies on the local authorities. Sometimes we did that through the directors of education, and sometimes we did it direct through the authorities themselves. Clearly, if we were concerned with salaries and conditions of service, we pressed that through the appropriate bodies: the STSC, the STSCC. Nowadays – not very much in my time, but I should imagine very much now – we would exert pressure through the STUC. Every now and again we might have an opportunity of meeting a Parliamentary Select Committee. . . . The best example of that that I can think of at the moment was when we met the Select Committee on the Inspectorate. In my time, at least, we saw the SED frequently. Not necessarily the Secretary. We only saw the Secretary when it was a really important big meeting, but there were a lot of other meetings in which we would see one of the Under-Secretaries or perhaps an Assistant Secretary. I myself could see the Secretary at any time I wanted . . . about a dozen times a year, maybe more than that. There was never an occasion when I asked to see the Secretary and was refused. We saw Ministers whenever we wanted to see Ministers. These things develop, you know. I think my predecessor was pretty content to see the Department alone. He didn't very often press for meetings with Ministers. During the 1960s we certainly saw Ministers far more frequently.

Q. Do you think that the business of teachers' associations became more political in the 1960s?

BRYDEN. It depends what you mean by 'political'. In the sense that we saw Ministers and Members of Parliament, whereas previously our contacts had nearly always been with the civil servants; if that would make it more 'political', then the answer is yes.

Q. Why did your strategy change?

BRYDEN. I think perhaps because of the way in which things developed

439

as soon as I took over [in 1961]. You see, I took over at a time of great excitement, and at a time of great excitement you tend to meet Ministers because they become a bit sensitive to what you are doing; and I think that I and my immediate colleagues became more accustomed to speaking to Ministers than the earlier people had been. We began to develop quite an elaborate parliamentary liaison system round about the turn of the decade. We appointed a couple of parliamentary advisers, and the fact that we had naturally took us to Westminster more often. . . . To begin with we had a Labour Member and a Conservative Member, and after a bit with the Liberal revival we had three; and then, when the Liberals lapsed, we reverted to two. I understand my successors changed the system. They no longer have parliamentary advisers. I don't know why. Perhaps they were becoming a little bit less fashionable. Anyway, I found it a very helpful thing. We used to have a regular meeting with members of all the parties, usually some time in November. . . .

Q. Do you think it is easier for the Institute to influence a Labour Government than it is to influence a Conservative Government, in that the links between teachers and the Labour Party are probably stronger than the links with the Conservative Party, in terms of contact and experience?

BRYDEN. I would say not. Not in my experience. Let me put it this way: I found it just as easy or just as difficult to influence the administrations in which there were Conservative Secretaries of State: Maclay, Michael Noble, Gordon Campbell.

Q. Did you find any difference on purely educational issues, as distinct from salaries and conditions issues?

BRYDEN. I wouldn't say so. Generally my experience was that I would rather deal with a Conservative Government than a Labour Government. . . . On the whole I found them more responsive. But, as I say, there was nothing much to choose between them.

We pressed Bryden on this point, asking him about one of the major areas of disagreement between the EIS and the Department, already touched on in chapters 10 and 12:

BRYDEN. They were terribly complacent about the employment of uncertificated teachers. And that I would say was . . . one of the greatest differences between ourselves and the SED for a very very long period. . . . The power to prevent the employment of an uncertificated teacher . . . was introduced by Willie Ross in an amendment to the Code.

Q. At your instigation?

BRYDEN. Yes. In 1968 the Code was amended to take account of a stop-gap arrangement called reference panels; and the amendment contained a clause which, in effect, restricted the employment of unregistered teachers to a period ending on 31 July 1973.

Q. Do you think you would have got that sort of amendment from a Secretary of State who hadn't been a teacher himself?

BRYDEN. Oh, I wouldn't like to say one way or the other. . . . I don't know that it was because he himself had been a teacher. I wouldn't like to say that. I don't think we would have got it from Bruce Millan, if you like, but we might have got it from Hector Monro. . . . It finally took effect, I think, while Hector Monro was in charge of education.

The restriction of uncertificated teachers was imposed when the end of the overall shortage was in sight and, indeed, when there threatened an equally embarrassing surplus. Bryden's account of his dealings with the Department on this well illustrates the rules of the game that circumscribed the area within which he and the Department agreed to differ:

BRYDEN. I think, in spite of that complacency, that the SED tackled the question of getting hold of statistics and studying the problem much more effectively than they ever did in England. Then you come to the extraordinary question of how it is that, all of a sudden, you got teacher unemployment. Somewhere about the early 1970s we were invited to come along to a meeting at St Andrew's House, in which I think it was the Senior Chief Inspector who outlined to us what appeared to be the trends of teacher supply and demand over the next few years. And, to everyone's astonishment, he produced figures which indicated that the teacher shortage was coming to an end. I asked for a copy of his statement, together with diagrams and all the rest of it, and they refused to give me a copy. They said that they had no objection to the rest of us taking notes, but they wouldn't give us any figures.

Q. Did you try to press them to release this information?

BRYDEN. Well, I tried to press them to give me more information, without any success. I suppose if I had been really bloody-minded I could have written to the papers about it, but we were there, as I say, on a quasi-confidential basis.

Q. Would it have been possible to get a question in Parliament?

BRYDEN. Yes it would. Yes, I imagine it would, though you can't always get an answer to a question in Parliament.

Q. Is that a technique that you have used, though?

BRYDEN. Oh, if I am invited by the SED to go to a meeting and it's explained to me that it is on a confidential or a quasi-confidential basis, I obviously wouldn't do anything to upset it.

Q. Yes, I understand that. But in general, using a Parliamentary Question as a technique to evoke public interest?

BRYDEN. I very seldom found that it was necessary, as I always had so much access to Members of Parliament and Ministers and so on.

Q. You mentioned that you might have written to the press about it. Do you think the press does have a role in shaping significant public opinion on such issues?

BRYDEN. I wouldn't know whether I would like to put it in that way, but certainly if I had wanted to, I could have scared the pants off the SED by getting it to the press. The SED is very sensitive to unfavourable reports on a thing like that appearing in the press.

We asked Bryden what issues his members thought important, and how successful the Institute had been:

BRYDEN. It was first of all the bread-and-butter issues. Obviously, conditions and salaries are important to members. . . . But they were also very much concerned by the quantity and the quality of teachers. That's one of the reasons why, if you really want to get the teachers buzzing like an upset skep of bees, the thing to do is to combine two issues, a bread-and-butter issue and an educational issue. It's an absolutely infallible recipe. Quite interested in the training of teachers, very interested in in-service training. . . . Defence of members was always an important issue. In fact, I would think that the majority of members think that the defence of members is the main reason for their belonging to a professional organisation. Methods of teaching: they didn't very often make that an important issue within the Institute. They regarded that as a more private matter. And there you see the general issues.

Bryden's assessment of the Institute's success in pressing bread-and-butter issues is given in chapter 10. Other, more 'educational', issues also had a bread-and-butter aspect, for example, the EIS opposition to middle schools, discussed in chapter 16. Bryden's comment on this illustrated the Institute's role in aggregating conflicting teacher interests:

BRYDEN. Funnily enough, our primary chaps were quite prepared to accept the idea of middle schools. I don't know whether some of them thought that it might make it easier for ordinary graduates, that it might be a particularly appropriate place for ordinary graduates. But rather to my surprise our secondary members opposed it, and so the Institute generally stamped on it. One of the more effective arguments, I think, was that it was really an organisational issue; there wasn't much in the way of educational theory behind it.

Q. Were there similar considerations behind what I take to be EIS opposition to the proposal coming from the DES that, with the raising of the school-leaving age, the final year might be spent in further education rather than in secondary school?

BRYDEN. I don't know. I could never understand it myself. I always thought that it was quite a good idea, but other people opposed it violently. I think our people opposed it on doctrinal grounds. . . . If you're raising the school-leaving age the pupils must stay at school. There is a fundamental difference between school and further education. I think that was the way they argued.

These were instances of successful opposition to initiatives arising from elsewhere. Bryden also mentioned occasions of successful initiation: policy on the SCE O-grade (see chapter 13), and the new Bachelor of Education degree introduced following a recommendation of the Robbins Committee on Higher Education in 1963 (CHE 1963).[3] But not all Institute initiatives were successful:

BRYDEN. We were unsuccessful, in spite of very heavy pressure on our part, in getting the Government to agree to set up area education committees. Now the area education committee was an attempt to overcome the disadvantages of large regions that were set up under the reorganisation of local government. . . . We actually got the Opposition – this must have been 1973 or 1974 – we got the Opposition to table amendments to the Local Government (Scotland) Bill that was going through, but they didn't press them very hard.

In Bryden's overall assessment of EIS influence, incremental change featured along with give-and-take:

BRYDEN. When I became General Secretary, my President was R. J. Walker. . . . Walker in his Presidential address in June 1961 outlined what he called his decalogue, in which he put forward ten points which he considered of major importance for the teaching profession, ten changes that he wanted introduced, things like the GTC, widows' and orphans' pensions, the appointment of teachers to education committees, and that sort of thing.[4] Well, when I was about to retire I had to write a speech to deliver at my final dinner, and I looked out R. J. Walker's decalogue; and, as I had suspected, about two things in the decalogue, I think, were no longer relevant because we had ceased to think in that particular way, but practically all the rest had been achieved. . . . The lesson that I learned is that, if you've been a reasonably good pressure-group, provided what you are pressing for is something that is achievable and something that's not all too unreasonable, if you keep going, in the long run, you eventually get it, but you've got to keep pegging away and, of course, you've got to be ready to press hard at the right time. And it's always worth bearing in mind, though I've little doubt that our own people would never bear it in mind, the Spanish proverb, 'Get what you want and pay for it'. And I think there was a marvellous example of that in the GTC. The GTC was set up to keep out the non-graduate male teachers. We got the GTC and, as a result of getting the GTC, we got the non-graduate male teachers.

The Local Authorities

Rodger said that he thought that the local-authority associations had least influence on the educational thinking of the Department. One reason was that they were divided among themselves and dominated by the largest authority:

RODGER. [Before regionalisation in 1975] there used to be two [local-authority associations] . . . the cities and the counties. We would have to see them both, and they often spoke with different voices. I hardly remember them saying the same thing on anything. . . . For example, take the Counties of Cities, which formed one association: well, Edinburgh, Aberdeen and Glasgow were on that. Glasgow were all in favour of the counties with riches throwing some of their riches into Glasgow; but Aberdeen and Edinburgh, who had the riches, were by no means anxious to throw any of the riches into Glasgow. . . . I don't know how it was that they always seemed to think differently, but they did. Of course the Association of Counties of Cities, to give it its proper name, was dominated by Glasgow, and as far as education was concerned, Glasgow thought in terms of schools of 1000 and 2000 pupils, or even more. The problems that arose in Glasgow were these problems, and their answers were determined by these conditions. Their views seemed to overwhelm the other city areas.

The Inspectorate disliked the political influence on teacher appointments in Glasgow (see chapter 17), and thought little of the authority's ability to coordinate housing development with school building (see chapter 9). But it emerged from our discussion with Clark that there was a second reason for the lack of local-authority influence:

CLARK. The two main local-authority associations, the Association of County Councils and the Association of Counties of Cities, were different in their approaches to education. When an educational matter was discussed by the Association of Counties of Cities, the four directors of the four cities came together, and, if need be, we each put forward our own individual point of view. The Association of County Councils, on the other hand, had three directors from the thirty-one counties, advising them on educational matters. So, to some extent it depended on which three directors were advising the county councils. And there was this kind of difference. It was often said that the city directors were in an advantageous position, because each city director could, if need be, put forward his own individual point of view, whereas this was virtually impossible through the County Councils' Association. When we came to the Association of Directors, we were all, of course, on a similar basis. But, since both the local-authority associations as well as the Directors' Association were often, most times, asked for comment, some of our county colleagues, from time to time, felt that the city directors had rather more influence than the county ones. But it's because of this combined machinery.

The implication of these arrangements for the Department's attitude to the local authorities emerges clearly enough from a comment of Rodger's:

RODGER. The local authorities, they would come last. You see, when we saw them, we knew that we were either seeing persons who didn't know education, or who were simply spouting the views of their directors, so we're better taking that direct from the Association of Directors.

Clark gave us an example from his dealings with Graham:

CLARK. I think that he was astonished that there should be any form of opposition to the setting-up of school councils. There was a meeting at St Andrew's House, which he chaired in 1972 or 1973, when representatives of the Counties of Cities and the Association of County Councils met to discuss whether or not there should be school councils, what kind of councils they should be, whether this proposal should be included in the Bill. I remember that one of the directors there who was from the County Councils' Association that day was Hugh Fairlie, and both he and I spoke strongly against the idea. Norman Graham was astonished that there should be any opposition to this. I won't go into the pros and cons of this at the moment, but the combined local-authority associations had no effect on that decision whatsoever. We were left very much with the impression, whether it was right or wrong, that this was something which was going ahead irrespective of the consultation.[5]

Rodger told us that, 'when a subject was strongly political, an association (or more likely persons thereon) might have views different from their directors', and this directs attention to the relationships between individual directors and councillors. On resource issues, directors did not always have matters their own way. For example, immediately after the Second World War, housing was a higher political priority in Glasgow than school building. But Clark was adamant that a good director could secure the requisite resources if he worked at relations with the authority's leading officials and politicians. On educational issues, however, the director's influence was perhaps more easily secured. The history of selective schooling after 1945 has already illustrated the way in which councillors for a long period were ready to defer to the professional judgement of their directors (see chapter 15). McIntosh, Clark and McEwan had all enjoyed the support of their chairmen, at least until the national impulse began to stir local opposition to selection. Here McEwan expands on the reception of Dickson's *Junior Secondary Education* report (SED 1955b – see chapter 15). His comments illustrate the limited political input to policy-making at local level that prevailed for much of the post-war period, thereby restricting the input at the national level too:

McEWAN. [Councillors] tended to assume that this [Dickson's report] was an agreed thing that had been handed down, and that, if the director of education didn't seem to be drawing attention to something that was tending in the wrong direction, then it not only came from on high, but was suitable for Lanarkshire, and the job was to get on with it. . . . You met the councillors daily, and you heard them talking in the smoke room, and in the committee. You had chairmen that you knew very well. And, generally speaking, you knew the kind of thing that they were expecting, although they wouldn't formulate it. Formulation of policy is something that the officials do; that is, putting it in words and being precise about it. But, in any such formulation of plans or policy, what's in the councillors' minds definitely would have to be taken fully into account. . . . What I've often said is that the official needs the councillors as his eyes and ears, and that this is an underestimated role of the councillor. He should get far more credit for his representative function than for his deliberative function. That is where he is immensely useful if he is a good councillor, in drawing your attention as an official in the central office to things in his area that you would have noticed if you had been out there recently, but that you didn't notice because you weren't out there recently. There was only one director at a time and two or three deputes, but over 100 councillors. And you can rely on their judgement, more or less, according to who they are, and act accordingly. . . . You felt that, if they had problems, they weren't going to stand up on a platform and make a great fuss locally, because the simplest thing to do was to come in and see the director of education and assume that something could be done. If there was nothing that could be done, they would be told why nothing could be done. If there was anything that could be done that wasn't quite what they wanted, then they would discuss with you whether that was the best thing that you could do; but it was all very quietly done, and they would then say, 'All right, I will do my best to put that across'. They chose this function not so much of formulating policy, as of defending policy, usually of course determined by themselves, in committee, though formulated perhaps, by the director of education.

In McEwan's case this mutuality could extend to national salary negotiations:

McEwan. Before there was an STSC, what happened was that a Lanarkshire member of the County Councils' Association, a very forceful one, used to come and say, 'Here are the draft salary proposals. (I shouldn't let you know, but here they are.) What do you think of them?' And I would say, 'Well, I think that they are ungenerous', or, 'I think that that's unfair to the Honours graduate', or something like that, if this was the view that I took. And, so far as I am aware, he would go and argue on these lines, if he was at least half inclined to the same view himself. He would reinforce his views with anything that he thought was useful in what I had contributed to his thinking. But I was not in a position, theoretically, to know what was happening in the committee.

Comprehensive reorganisation in Lanarkshire saw the Education Committee abruptly reject McEwan's advice (see chapter 16). Up to that point, however, his experience can probably be generalised quite widely, and certainly to Aberdeen:

Clark. I would think that, as Director, I was failing as a professional, if I didn't know the area better than any single councillor; know the needs of the schools and what was required; try to see developments in the long-term perspective; and I think that this is what the average councillor would expect of a director of education. . . . There were quite a number of occasions, over the years, when I indicated as clearly as I could to the Committee that they should not do something, because of the effect that this would have on the schools, or group of schools, or whatever. . . . I think that it's very important that a director has the confidence of his convener, and that the convener is prepared to discuss with the director, prior to and after meetings, how matters should be presented, what the implications are, and so on. This doesn't mean to say that the director and the convener should always think alike.

Q. Is it a correct interpretation of this relationship that a continuing initiative, month to month, comes from the director? That he depends on his convener, first of all to give a sense of what he can get through the committee, and then, indeed, to get it through and explain it to the larger constituency – the parents, the voters who eventually have to live with the result? Is this what you thought?

CLARK. Yes.

Q. Putting it very crudely, what we are saying is that it was a function of the politicians to facilitate, and to legitimate to wider constituencies, an impulse or policy that was coming primarily from the directorate?

CLARK. And approved by the politicians, after they were convinced that this was a sound thing to do.

These conclusions can be generalised beyond Lanarkshire and Aberdeen. In their study of chief education officers in England, Kogan and van der Eyken (1973, 13) said,

> strong though central authority might be . . . and cogent though the power of ruling groups of local councillors undoubtedly is, the main axis of authority in education lies between the Chief Officer of an LEA and the heads of schools and colleges.

We read this conclusion to Rodger:

RODGER. If you are talking about educational practice, what education means, how it should be conducted, and so on, the main powers lie with the director of education or his assistants and the teachers, particularly the head teachers. The inspector, however, comes into this quite strongly. . . . If we are talking about the bigger aspects of education – should we have comprehensive schools or not? – then I think that the politics of central government comes very heavily into it. So, if it is administration, then I don't agree with Kogan. If it's grass-roots education, I'm inclined to agree with Kogan, but I would bring the inspectors into it too.

Q. Perhaps more so in Scotland than in England?

RODGER. I would not like to be dogmatic about that. . . . The layman, either the politician or the local politician, they play their part, though I don't think that it is a very decisive part. But then you come down to people like us in the Department, and the directors of education in the authorities. Well, I think that the administrators, both in local authorities and in central authority, are more important than the persons who are supposed to be their bosses, be they Ministers or the local councillors.

Directors of Education

'They were very important as a group, and many of them as individuals':

447

this was Brunton's assessment of the directors. Dickson regarded them as the key link between the Department and the local authority, and he told us that, in many authorities, the Inspectorate did not deal regularly with the education committee chairman. The Department had consulted the Association of Directors from time to time during the inter-war period, and in 1945 had established a regular liaison with the Association (ADES n.d., 12-17). Rodger thought the directors the single most important outside group:

RODGER. I think I would say that we rated them as a consultative body more highly than any other. The Department's Secretariat had from two to five meetings a year with the Association of Directors, and either side could place items of its choice on the agenda.

Q. Would you say they were more influential than the teachers' associations?

RODGER. Probably they were, in our hearts, yes. You see, while we could never admit this publicly, I think that we probably all felt that, when we were meeting the directors of education, we were meeting a more informed body than the EIS.

It was also a much smaller body. Between 1919 and 1975, only 147 appointments were made to the directorships of Scotland's thirty-five education authorities, giving an average tenure of over ten years per appointment. Only 135 individuals were involved, nine of whom held two appointments successively, and two of whom held three. Twenty authorities were directed by only two persons each in the period 1946-75, including all the major west of Scotland authorities with the exception of Dunbartonshire (which, nevertheless, had only two directors between 1932 and 1973). Amazingly, all but two authorities, both small, were served by the same director for over half the period 1945-75. McEwan (1950-75) and Clark (1956-75) were therefore not untypical in this respect. At any annual meeting of the Association in this period, they would have found that well over half of the directors were unchanged from fifteen years previously. The longest serving was H. Stewart Mackintosh, who became Director for Wigtownshire in 1931, for Aberdeen City in 1939, and for Glasgow in 1944 where he remained until 1968. But there were others who served for over thirty years, and many who served for twenty or more.[6]

Clearly the quality of the directors' contribution would depend on a small number of individuals. Equally, however, there was opportunity here for individuals to build reputation and influence on a stable base of regular contact with their fellow directors and with a small number of senior inspectors and administrators in the SED. Few, however, seem to have done so. Clark thought that the number of nationally influential directors in his time was only between six and ten. Many authorities, he suggested, were too small to offer their directors much opportunity, and some of the larger authorities were too burdened:

CLARK. I think it fair to say that this small group [of influential directors] were associated with some of the cities and some of the larger counties. I think that it was more difficult for somebody from a small county to have this kind of opportunity and, perhaps, make this kind of impact. . . . I think that some of them from the smaller counties didn't have the width of day-to-day experience in handling a whole variety of problems, or certainly not on the fairly large scale that those of us in the bigger areas had. . . . One would assume that the more experienced and better of those in the smaller areas who wanted to, came into the larger areas and had this kind of opportunity then.

We asked Rodger which directors carried most weight with the Department, and he answered in terms both of the individuals and of the qualities he valued in a director. To take the latter first:

RODGER. I remember, rather idly one night, putting down the names of the directors of education who were, in my view, in the running for what you might call the top place. I put down the attributes that I would expect in a good director, marking them all. . . . Although I cannot now remember them all exactly, the qualities I thought important were probably as follows: (1) ability to get on with the education committee (2) ability to influence and persuade them (3) ability to get on with headmasters (4) repute among teachers in the area (5) general soundness of educational views (i.e., whether they agreed with mine!!) (6) knowledge of modern education, including educo- and psychometrics (7) power – in regard to (5) and (6) – to influence the Association of Directors (8) ability to see problems of his own area (9) having seen the problems, to get priorities right (10) having seen the problems, to get things done (11) attitude to, and respect in, the SED. Then, having listed the qualities, I made a list in order of merit (as I thought) of the top half dozen or so of the directors. I think I might have given a top place ten marks, second place six, third place four, fourth place three, fifth place two, and sixth place one. I found that [Alec] Young [Director of Education, Aberdeenshire, 1945-68] had no tens, but so many sixes that he certainly led in total, quite substantially.

This exercise was evidently a diversion, but a diversion, nevertheless, that was indicative of a tendency to look to psychometrics for the measure of the man. Further clues to the basis of directorate influence emerged from Rodger's enumeration of the individual directors who had the Department's attention:

RODGER. Looking back to the pre-war days I would say . . . R. M. Allardyce [Glasgow 1929-44], Gregor McGregor of Fife [1919-41], and the Lanarkshire man . . . R. C. T. Mair [1924-45] . . . [also] John Morrison in Aberdeenshire [1928-45]. . . . Mind you, I don't quite know whether Allardyce was so highly thought of, or heeded, because he was Allardyce or because he was Director of Education for Glasgow. In a country the size of Scotland, you cannot ignore one-fifth, which is Glasgow. . . . Then coming to the post-war period: William Hepburn who was, first, Director in

449

Ayrshire [1927-44], then of Lanarkshire [1945-50]; he was very important.
. . . And James B. Frizell in Edinburgh [Edinburgh 1933-61]. . . . His
strength lay in his high prestige amongst his other directors. . . . He was
largely instrumental in founding the Association of Directors. . . . He did
very much work for the directors. For example, when the directors felt that
their salaries should go up, and they wanted someone to come up to the
Department to press this point, Frizell was usually their negotiator. In this
way, and in others, he built up quite a reputation with the directors of
education.[7] But nobody, including Frizell, would claim that he was an
educationist. But he was successful, very soon, in getting a depute, Alec
Young, who was first-class. Alec Young took over all of the educational
side, and Frizell simply administered the office. When Alec Young went to
Aberdeenshire [Director 1945-68], he was succeeded by George Reith
[later Director of Edinburgh 1961-72], and he took over all of the educational side. . . . George Reith was very good. . . . He stood in high regard
with us. . . . Douglas McIntosh came into the picture [Fife 1944-66]. There
was a time when we paid a great deal of attention to a man called David
Howat [Inverness 1937-43; Perth 1943-55], who then went to become head
of the Dundee Training College. . . . Now he was a man of, we thought, very
sound common sense, and a man of very great intellectual gifts. Then James
Clark of Aberdeen came along [1956-75]. He was very important. There
was a time when John Crawford – first Kirkcudbright [1932-46], then
Renfrewshire [1946-64] – was important. He carried a very great weight
amongst the directors themselves. Then, in more recent times, Thomas
G. Henderson in Midlothian [1957-75]. . . . H. Stewart Mackintosh could
not be ignored, as he was Director of Glasgow. Stewart Mackintosh didn't
carry great weight because he was Stewart Mackintosh, but because he was
Director of Education of Glasgow. But he had his points. He was a great
humanitarian who influenced the Department's thinking on matters like
youth clubs, the education of the handicapped, and such like. . . . John
McEwan came into the picture [Lanarkshire 1950-75]. He followed
Hepburn in Lanarkshire.

Rodger bracketed McEwan with Mackintosh as directors who had not
made much of a mark nationally, but who nevertheless commanded attention because of the size of their authorities. The one other director that
Rodger mentioned was Lachlan Young (Berwickshire, 1947-55; Perth and
Kinross, 1955-75).

The twelve directors singled out by Rodger were among the sixty-six
whose tenure overlapped the period 1945 to 1964, the period of Rodger's
seniority in the Department's administration. From Rodger's enumeration
we can infer that Clark was right to suggest that the influential directors
were associated with the larger authorities, although clearly this alone was
no guarantee of influence. Clark seems also to have been right about the link
between influence and career mobility. Nine of the sixty-six directors in this

period held more than one directorship. Rodger mentioned five of these nine as influential (fifty-six per cent), compared with only seven of the remaining fifty-seven (twelve per cent). Mobility was not a certain indicator of influence; but immobility identified the non-influential directors, other than some of those, like Clark himself, who remained in the one post in a large authority.

Rodger's list also throws light on the importance he attached to 'a knowledge of modern education' (see above). Fifteen of the sixty-six directors held the degree of B Ed, Ed B or M Ed. Bell (1986, 246) writes that this degree was introduced in order to 'communicate the old historical/philosophical and the new American/German experimental ideas to the intellectually most aware and/or the most ambitious of Scottish teachers'. Eight of the fifteen directors who held the degree figured in Rodger's top twelve, compared with only four of the fifty-one directors who lacked a degree-level professional qualification in education. This alone does not show a causal link. It is possible, for example, that the acquisition of a second degree is merely an indicator of ability or ambition. But this seems unlikely in view of the fact that twelve directors held another type of second degree, in law, but that only three of them were singled out by Rodger: Frizell, who built his influence through the A DES; Lachlan Young who also held the B Ed; and John McEwan. Other explanations are possible,[8] but the most probable one is that offered by Rodger himself: namely that a director was more likely to acquire Rodger's respect if he had a professional training in human measurement. Eight of the twelve most influential directors had such a background, and no doubt this contributed to the formation of the professional consensus of the period, though the link between the B Ed/Ed B and belief in the group intelligence test should be neither assumed nor exaggerated (see chapter 15).

Another striking feature of the list of twelve is the underrepresentation of directors from the west-central authorities which contain half of Scotland's population. This is partly because there were fewer authorities in the West. On the other hand, they were all populous and should, by rights, have produced more than four directors of note. Here we should bear in mind that Rodger's judgement of directorate performance in the West of Scotland may have been influenced by his hostility to the priority that West of Scotland Labour politicians gave to housing over education. Recalling the 1940s, Rodger said that 'the biggest battles took place in Glasgow' where the local authority 'had very much the same attitude as Ministers'. He also conceded that 'McEwan had a difficult committee. . . . There were clamant housing needs in Lanarkshire as well as in Glasgow'; and he judged that Dunbartonshire and Lanarkshire 'were the two counties whose politics bedevilled things more than in any other county in the country'. Rodger told us that, in tackling this, 'the biggest ally we [the S ED] had was Stewart Mackintosh in Glasgow, because the biggest blunders were made in Glasgow'. He went on:

RODGER. I would give a great deal of credit for getting Glasgow out of the mess to Brunton, when he was District Inspector in Glasgow. . . . A really energetic, go-ahead, forward-looking inspector, and a non-assertive . . . director, that was the situation for years after the War in Glasgow. It was always our inspector who got things done. To be fair to Stewart Mackintosh . . . he suffered from being overwhelmed by a multitude of problems. Himself a humanitarian, he gave less time to major planning problems that involved cold statistics than he should.

For a quarter of a century Mackintosh and McEwan were responsible for education in Scotland's two largest authorities, containing one-third of the population. Any final assessment of the balance of influence in central-local relations cannot avoid a judgement on the performance in post of these two men. We ourselves cannot attempt this judgement, except to repeat that Rodger's estimation was clearly influenced by his own involvement in the difficulties to which he alluded. It can be said, however, that these difficulties had a substantial influence on Rodger's and Brunton's belief in the need for a promotional central authority; and they can have done little to mitigate Rodger's criticism of the educational values of the West (see chapter 17).

Thus a picture emerges of a Departmental view of west-central Scotland as a culture that neither valued education in the traditional Scottish way, nor was competent itself to develop it. Beset by social problems, bedevilled by 'politics', the West had fewer leading schools, produced fewer leading teachers, and made less of an impact on the Association of Directors, or on the Department itself. In these ways disadvantage compounded disadvantage. Viewed within the moral framework of the myth, the West neither succeeded nor deserved to succeed. It did not field a ball-winning team of directors. It was left to others to make the running, and to take whatever advantage there was to be had from their individual standing with the Department.

But what, finally, was the collective standing of the ADES with the Department? And, if it truly was the most important outside group, which policies bear testimony to its power? We asked Clark about the Association's influence:

CLARK. I may be prejudiced here, but I have the strong impression that over the whole period of the thirty years after the [Second World] War, the Association of Directors probably carried more weight with the SED than any other single body. . . . About ten directors . . . met on average about once a term with the Department, as a liaison committee, and issues raised there were important for all of us. . . . Normally it [the committee] consisted of. . . . the President, Vice-President [and] Secretary at the time, plus others who served on the liaison committee for a period. But we always tried to ensure that cities, the larger counties and the rural counties were all represented by one or two people. . . . This was the committee where the directors' representatives and the Department's top officials came face to face across the table, and the atmosphere was normally very good. Both sides were generally looking for responses from the other side, and this was important. It was the committee where we, as directors, felt that we had the best opportunity of raising something with the Department at an early stage; to get Departmental reaction, to perhaps put in a word of warning about something cropping up, and the like. . . . The matters discussed at the liaison committee almost invariably were initiated in part by the Department and in part by the Association. And, again inevitably, some of the matters raised by the Association were, in a sense, the first shots in something that was going to build up and be quite important, and which ultimately resulted in Departmental decision and in, perhaps, a circular. And I think this is fairly true of the whole period. There was this joint collaboration at the liaison-committee stage. I would say again that this particular liaison committee operated for most of the time on a pretty satisfactory basis. We covered a lot of ground at these meetings in the Department. It was usually chaired by the Permanent Secretary, and he brought in all his specialists, as required, for every item. It was not a question of a small group just saying, 'All right, we'll look at this and come back with something at the next meeting'. . . . This was really the forum, the place where we could be quite frank across the table, and were quite frank across the table, and I think that this was beneficial to both sides.

When, however, we explored with Clark the outcomes of the influence exerted by directors through the ADES/SED liaison committee, and we did this at length, few concrete examples came to mind. The ADES for example opposed ROSLA unsuccessfully, and was only cursorily consulted over Circular 600 on comprehensive reorganisation. Teachers' salaries figured infrequently. Clark remembered only discussions of the reform of the negotiating machinery in the 1960s, and of the implications of salary awards for supply and distribution. He did recall that the Department had tried to use the liaison committee to press the directors of well staffed authorities to co-operate on the redistribution of teachers to less favoured areas. But he also said that he himself had resisted this pressure. Discussions in the liaison committee were not strictly confined to matters of central-local relations, nor to purely administrative concerns. Curriculum, for example, was considered, though less frequently after the founding of the CCC, and then mainly in response to CCC publications and initiatives. Clark did instance drama in secondary schools as an example of a topic that the CCC took up in response to an ADES suggestion (CCC 1977). However, he could not think of a more important policy outcome that had resulted from an ADES initiative. Rodger, too, had difficulty in thinking of examples:

Q. Can you think of issues where the thinking of the Department was materially changed as a result of representations, either positive ones or negative ones, from these bodies?

RODGER. Well, at the moment I don't remember anywhere the Department's views were altered. But I do remember cases when our views were strongly reinforced by the directors. I think the directors of education's views and those of the Department tended to coincide about how the training colleges ought to be reorganised [see chapter 12], but they certainly put forward a very strong viewpoint on that. They also put forward strong viewpoints on examinations too, when we first determined that the Leaving Certificate should not be a group certificate but should be awarded on a subject basis [see chapter 4]. They were very strong on that. They were not necessarily decisive, because that was how our own views were going to go anyway; but these are issues on which I remember they put forward strong views.

We must now discuss the ways in which this extraordinary harmony was achieved.

NOTES
1. Oral evidence to the 1968 Select Committee on the Inspectorate (SCES 1968, Q.319).
2. However, the SSTA had apparently been invited to nominate members to the Seventh Advisory Council (SRO 1957b, unsigned minute on the history of the Advisory Council).
3. This should not be confused with the degree of the same name introduced at the beginning of the century (see chapter 15, note 5). The name of the older degree was changed to Master of Education when the newer degree was brought in. The latter offered initial teacher training concurrently with a first-degree course.
4. The ten demands were: free negotiation of salaries and other conditions of service without dictation by the Secretary of State or the Scottish Education Department, the new machinery to include powers for retrospective payment when necessary; a superannuation scheme which included provision for pensions for widows, orphans and dependants; salaries with family allowances; no withdrawal of pension from retired teachers returning to service; pensions geared to the cost-of-living index; an appointments system independent of extramural influence (this to include a reexamination of the security of tenure of the teacher, and especially of the headmaster, in the performance of his duties); full consultation with headmasters on the building and reconstruction of schools; teachers' rights to membership of education committees, and subcommittees dealing with educational (or scholastic) matters; a major voice in determining qualifications for admission to courses in colleges of education; and complete control of the profession itself through the establishment of a register, entry on it alone giving entitlement to teach in Scotland (*SEJ* 16 June 1961).
5. 'School councils were required by the Local Government (Scotland) Act of 1973, began to be formed in 1975, and by 1977 there were 302 school councils established and actively serving all 3669 state schools throughout Scotland. They were required to discharge "such functions of management and supervision" of schools as each education authority should determine and their membership was to include teachers, parents, at least one person interested in the promotion of religious education, and, in certain circumstances, representatives of further education and the community' (Macbeth, MacKenzie and

Breckenridge 1980, 9).

6. We are grateful to Mr Ian Flett of the Association of Directors of Education in Scotland, for supplying us with details of all directors of education 1918-75. Mr Flett is currently writing a history of the ADES since 1945.

7. 'Stability . . . came in November 1935, with the appointment to the Secretaryship of that remarkable man, James B. Frizell of Edinburgh, who held the post with distinction for no less than twenty-five years. During the major part of that time he discharged the duties now shared by the Secretary, the Assistant Secretary, and the Treasurer, and no praise can be too high for the efficiency with which he did so. His great administrative ability and his boundless energy were devoted freely to our service, and there is no doubt whatever that he did more for this Association than any other man has done' (ADES n.d., 10). It was Frizell who persuaded the Department in 1936 to consult corporately with the Association of Directors of Education. The Association had come into conflict with the Department over Circular 44 in the early 1920s (see chapter 2), and consultation thereafter had been intermittent (*ibid.*, 12-17). In chapter 9 we touched on Frizell's involvement at a national level over the question of school buildings.

8. For example, it may be that holders of the BEd were more likely to benefit from patronage of the type that Rodger said was exercised by McClelland and Thomson (above), and to have done so irrespective of their actual performance. For evidence on this, and an extensive analysis of the careers of those who took the degree, see Bell (1986, chs 8 and 9).

Nineteen

Consultation, Corporatism and Control

I remember he [Murrie] came to lunch once and spoke at the end of the meal, and quoted, in his own defence, the lines of Burns which ended up 'What's *done* we partly may compute, but know not what's *resisted*'. . . . When Murrie had resisted something it was normally resisted in silence.   Gilbert Bryden, General Secretary of the EIS 1961-74

Introduction

Burns links the enigmatic influence of pressure groups to the wider problem of the empirical analysis of power that we raised in chapter 1. Rodger and Clark both thought that the directors of education were the most influential group in Scottish education. Yet neither man could attribute a major policy change to the directors, and both thought that the directors were powerless to resist a major political initiative like the raising of the school-leaving age in 1973. Similarly, Bryden and Clark told us that governmental consultation over comprehensive reorganisation was merely formal.

The point is not, however, that pressure groups have not initiated change. On the evidence of chapters 12 and 18, the EIS, for example, clearly has done so. But what was also important was the context that pressure groups provided for governmental activity, restraining it here and helping it there. This context was essentially ambivalent. When they aggregated their members' demands, pressure groups could simplify the outside world with which government had to deal. This function was, in turn, linked to influence. The Association of Counties of Cities was relatively unsuccessful in aggregating opinion, and failed in consequence to command Rodger's respect. By consulting with pressure groups the Department, for its part, sought to inhibit the development of conflict and to achieve support for its own policies.

Relationships such as these are not easy to study. Because overt conflict was infrequent, there were few occasions when choices were made between publicly formulated alternatives. Moreover, even when conflict and choice were in evidence, the issues and participants had already been determined in some degree by the exercise of power. These considerations pose evident difficulties for an analysis of power based on the empirical evidence of what people thought and did. They indicate, too, that we must examine the cultural categories that framed the discourse of consultation, and consider the shaping of the governmental institutions through which that consultation was effected.

In the first half of this chapter we catalogue the techniques that the SED used in its efforts to shape policy issues and outcomes. In doing this, we draw on examples from earlier chapters, as well as fresh evidence, mainly from Rodger. Thereafter, we broaden the discussion of consultation to consider the Scottish educational policy community in the wider context of policy communities in British government. Pluralist interpretations of policy communities emphasise their multiplicity, their indispensability to government, and their independence of it. Corporatist interpretations assert that government has considerable influence over the constitution of such communities, and over the issues they affect.

A further comment is needed here on the concept of aggregation. 'The main systematic difficulty', Kogan wrote in his 1975 study of interest groups in education, 'was not in tracing the main policies . . . nor in tracing the actions of the interest groups. It was rather in determining relationships between interest groups; in seeing who impacted on whom and with what effect; in identifying those who made the decisions; *in short, the process of policy formation*' (Kogan 1975, 21, our emphasis). And towards the end of the study he concluded, 'It is not clear how the aggregation of practice takes place. . . . The DES denies it has the power to aggregate or lead yet it plainly does so' (*ibid.*, 238). And plainly the SED does as well. But, if aggregation is what stops people being 'all over the place' (see preface), it also describes a process that is much more diffuse than administrative or Ministerial fiat, though potentially as powerful.

Most commentators agree that the DES plays an important role in the formation of policy. Kogan's conclusion is that aggregation is done imperfectly and reactively by a few political leaders and 'determined officials', mainly at the centre. Salter and Tapper, however, ascribe a more systematically manipulative role to DES officials than Kogan can accept. As we saw in chapter 1, they are particularly severe on the recourse of pluralist explanations to the idea of 'the climate of opinion' as a way of explaining how disaggregated priorities and practices are shaped into policies. Rather, they see the DES as systematically attempting to disseminate an ideology that serves its own, bureaucratic, interest. But their argument relies mainly on inferences from public policy-documents and similar sources, as, indeed, do most analyses of DES activity, and they have little to say about the details of DES transactions. More recently, Broadfoot has suggested that the DES lacks the 'bureaucratic apparatus' to implement the responsibilities for which it is formally accountable. She, too, draws attention to the need for empirical studies of contemporary policy that relate the micro-politics of interpersonal relations to the macro-politics of the central authority's attempts at policy formation.[1] But there are currently few such studies extant.[2]

Methods of Control

One 'determined official' whose evidence throws light on the role of central government is Allan Rodger. Through his evidence in particular, we are able to catalogue some of the tactics by which the Department shaped the climate of opinion, both what was 'in the air', and what was drawn from it to inspire policy. Superficially, these tactics can be divided into interpersonal procedures to do with the control of individuals, and structural procedures to do with the control of organisations. Such a distinction cannot be pressed too far, however, because the value of a body to the Department could depend on the types of individuals who served on it. Conversely, the value the s E D accorded to individuals could depend on the group or body for whom they spoke.

The fortunes of the ss t A illustrate how the Department might enhance the standing of a body if it liked the individuals concerned. Murrie and Henderson Stewart both preferred that the Department deal only with the E I S. But Arbuckle 'let the s s t A in'; the standing of the prime-movers in the ss t A was too high, and their educational views and values too consonant with those of the Department, for them to remain always on the outside.

Another example of the promotion of preferred individuals by means of the corporate enhancement of their group can be found in the fortunes of the principals of the teacher-training colleges (after 1958, colleges of education). Many of the principals sat on the Committee of Principals (c P) (see chapter 12). The Department salvaged the c P from the demise in 1958 of the National Committee for the Training of Teachers (N c t t), and enhanced its power within the body that succeeded the N c t t, the Scottish Council for the Training of Teachers (s c t t). Later the c P was preserved alongside the General Teaching Council (G t c) when that body replaced the s c t t in 1966. Why did the c P survive these structural changes? The answer is that the Department, and Rodger in particular, found themselves in sympathy with the college principals who sat on the c P; not so much with McClelland (Principal of Dundee College 1925-41), but certainly with Inglis for one. Inglis was Principal of Moray House College from 1951 to 1966. Along with Rodger, he wanted to end McClelland's domination of the N c t t and to win greater freedom for the individual colleges. Rodger told us that he regarded Inglis as a major figure and 'in all respects an excellent educational thinker' who was influential 'in all educational quarters, including the Department'. Rodger also told us that, if anything, the Department thought even more highly of Wood who was Principal of Jordanhill College from 1949 to 1971. Coming from England, Wood was critical on educational grounds of the rigidity of Scottish teaching qualifications. Rodger was critical of them on resource grounds; they gave the teachers' unions considerable negotiating strength at a time when the staffing demands of secondary schools would have been greatly eased by greater flexibility of qualification. Rodger told us: 'probably of all the men that I have worked with in the educational world, I have found that my views were closer to those of Wood than to those of anyone else. I have always liked Wood.' Hence, when the scтт replaced the NCTT in 1958, its status was enhanced. The NCTT could not initiate advice, but the scтт could. Rodger explained this as follows:

RODGER. If it was to be a body with some reality of power, and something to do, they shouldn't only answer questions put to them, but they should have the right to raise questions, if questions are worth raising. It is one way, a good way, of upgrading a body.

We asked Rodger about the role of the cp:

RODGER. My impression is that we [the Department] would say to McClelland, as chairman of the Committee of Principals, that the Committee should reach a conclusion which should be put forward by him to the NCTT – so long, at least, as McClelland remained in office. . . .

Q. Would this have happened under J. J. Robertson's chairmanship of the scтт [1959-61]?

RODGER. I would think so. I don't think that J. J. R. would have objected to that.

In other words, if the Department were confident of the views of the individuals who were likely to be involved, it might tailor the existence and powers of a body accordingly. Thus the cp was retained when the scтт was replaced by the GTC. The cp was where the principals sounded out the views of their colleagues (Osborne 1979). As principals, several cp members would also sit on the GTC, the statutory body that was intended to secure the professional autonomy of teachers, though this also had required that Rodger secure a definition of 'teacher' that was broad enough to encompass college principals (see chapter 12).

If corporate recognition and corporate aggrandisement were two techniques of aggregation, what other means did the Department use to control bodies? Most obviously, there was the termination of bodies that were awkward, and the creation of new ones. The main example here is the reorganisation of the advisory structure described in part IV. This replaced a potentially synoptic Advisory Council with a segmented array of bodies, each with a restricted remit, coordinated mainly through the Inspectorate. As we have emphasised, however, the Sixth Advisory Council had achieved its integrated structure only through the intervention of the Secretary of State for Scotland and through the chairmanship of Hamilton Fyfe (see chapter 4). The Department had given only limited remits to the Second to Fifth Councils that met between the Wars, and, after 1950, it set itself to disaggregate the advisory process again. The Eighth Council was deliberately structured so as to prevent its tendering synoptic advice or setting its own remits. The segmentation of the new structure of advice after 1965 could therefore be regarded as the final step of a process, beginning after the Sixth Council, whereby the Department returned to the precept of 'divide and rule' that it had followed ever since its difficulties with the First Council in the early 1920s (see chapters 2 and 11). A further aspect of aggregation by government, therefore, was its disaggregation of structures through which a counter-politics might emerge.

As we have said, it was mainly the Inspectorate that linked the elements of this revised structure, though some administrators were also involved. A further link was provided by the expedient of multiple memberships. Clark is a case in point, sitting on various bodies, including the STSC, GTC, CCC, SCEEB and ADES. But this was not a tactic that could be extensively used. It put a premium on members' understandings of when, and with whom, they should observe the confidentiality of each body's proceedings. It required members to accommodate the conflicting and ambiguous demands that were sometimes imposed on them by the structural incompatibilities of the bodies concerned. And, above all, it presupposed an overall sympathy with the Department's policies. Were these conditions not met, the Department might achieve co-operation from individuals on one body only at the cost of deferring to the same individuals on another. The viability of administrative structures was thus a function of the issues and individuals concerned. A recent example is Sir James Munn's chairmanship of the CCC and of the MSC (Scotland).

Especially with a non-statutory body like the CCC, it was relatively easy for the Department to redefine powers and membership according to circumstance. It will be recalled that the CCC's abortive predecessor, the Consultative Committee on Educational Matters, was simply allowed to wither away in the late 1960s or early 1970s. Statutory bodies, however, were more difficult to change, and so too were bodies that had executive responsibilities. The reform of the GTC needed political will and scarce parliamentary time. Much could be done, however, through Statutory Instruments. The 1952 change in the regulations for the Advisory Council made it possible for the Department after 1961 simply to neglect to reconstitute it (though the 1962 Education (Scotland) Act provided for a Council). But, even where a body was statutorily constituted, had the power to initiate advice, and had executive responsibilities, the Department might still circumvent formal procedures. It bypassed the Examination Board when it took advice from Urquhart, Dewar and Fullwood on the CSE Mode III (see chapter 13), and it bypassed the GTC when deciding on college-of-education closures in 1980 (see chapter 12).

Rather than circumvent a body from which it might get an unwelcome or untimely response, the Department might pass an issue between bodies until a preferred option resulted. Rodger could not get the Knox Committee to legitimate the non-graduate male teacher. But the issue was eventually put to the GTC, which obliged (see chapters 11 and 12). Interpassing was also a feature of the Department's attempts to introduce an A-level. The Department failed to get agreement for an A-level from Brunton's 1959 working party. Rather than see the issue threaten the unanimity of his report, Brunton slipped it to a 'special committee' of the Advisory Council, to which he was an assessor. He then looped round to take the favourable recommendation the committee passed back to him, and fed it out to his Inspectorate to continue the offensive by issuing specimen papers for a sixth-year examination. When the defence of Scottish teachers held firm, the recommendation was smuggled to the back row of the Examination Board. There it was shielded whilst Dewar feinted with the CSYS, and waited for the Department line to regroup, pick up the A-level, and run with it again (see chapter 13). The ability of the Department to get bodies into the right place at the right time gave it a policy stamina that none could match.

So far we have been concerned mainly with the structure of bodies and the remits they received. What about the appointees and their arguments? We have already discussed the ways in which teachers of high standing and sound views were culturally defined. The Kirriemuir career produced the type of teacher who could be invited into the councils of the state as representative of the best in teaching, but without that invitation's compromising the values on which Departmental authority was based. Intentionally or otherwise, a large part of Scotland's cultural, educational and political experience was thereby discounted, or else discounted itself by rejecting provincial gentility and the wisdom from the East. All this happened before the Department came to consider particular committee memberships. The culturally received definition of good teaching was such as to underrepresent among the 'good' teachers women, Catholics, the industrial West, and teachers in predominantly working-class schools. These tendencies were reinforced by the Department's preference for the SSTA, whose membership in the late 1950s was located mainly in schools outside the Clydeside conurbation.

The process of appointment to national bodies was sometimes disputed between the Department and outside groups, especially after the 1961 strike. For the Seventh Advisory Council, local-authority and directorate representatives were chosen directly, but the teachers' associations nominated appointees from among whom the Department made its selection. The expedient of group nomination followed by Departmental selection seems to have been more widely used for the Eighth and final Council (1957-61), and thereafter for the Examination Board. It was a compromise between the interests of the Department and those of outside groups. But it left the Department with virtually total control of appointments to those bodies whose membership categories were not statutorily prescribed. What was true of Brunton's working parties remained true, for example, of their manifold CCC descendants. Moreover, the Department attempted to apply the doctrine of individual, as distinct from corporate, representation to the membership of some statutory bodies like the Examination Board, as well as to that of non-statutory ones. This expedient allowed the Department to say that various interest groups participated in the process of aggregation, but relieved that process from the expectation that it reconcile incompatible views these groups might hold.

Departmental control of appointments was self-evidently important in the case of non-statutory bodies. But it was also a factor in the dealings of statutory ones. When the policy climate changed in the mid-1960s, the Department had difficulties with the Examination Board, and it took some years to change the type of teacher appointed to it. Again, the direct election of teacher representatives to the GTC limited the proportion of appointments that the Department could influence and the resultant scope that the Department allowed the Council. In choosing appointees, the Department, as Dickson said, was looking for good committee men who would 'obviously get on with other people and not resign over disagreements' (see chapter 17). But, even when a strong spokesman for group interests slipped through, other appointees might neutralise the consequences. Rodger gave us examples:

RODGER. In the Knox Committee, one of the teacher representatives gave a very trades-unionist talk about things that they would tolerate and things that they wouldn't tolerate, and about how uncertificated teachers could not be tolerated in schools, and so on, and so on, and so on. Now, one of our members . . . was a trade-union leader, F. Donachy [one-time chairman of the General Council of the STUC]. He said, with very great firmness, after the teacher had spoken, that he had spent a great part of his life at trade-union meetings, and that he had never heard such narrow-minded, militant trade unionism spoken as by the teacher who had just spoken, which shut him up for a few days. . . . So you see, there is a case where Donachy, who didn't know enough about the subject to make a positive contribution, nevertheless could come along with a sharp criticism that was very, very useful. . . . Having served on the like of the Appleton Committee, the Knox Committee and the Wheatley Committee, my view is that the intelligent, interested outsider can sometimes bring a very welcome breath of fresh air. There were some teacher arguments, for example, which were downed very heavily by David Raphael [then Professor of Social and Political Theory and Institutions, Glasgow University] in the Wheatley Committee. Now there was an example of Raphael, an outsider – if I can call him an outsider; although a Professor, he was not within the 'narrow' teaching profession – who spoke vigorously. I would say that he voiced a good, intelligent, man-in-the-street point of view against some of the sheer silly selfishnesses of the teachers.

Where outsiders did not produce a neutralising argument, there was usually a Departmental assessor to hand though, again, their right to speak might be contested, and officials themselves might vary in their interpretation of the role. Rodger, as we have said, helped to broaden the Wheatley Committee's definition of 'teacher' to a point at which school teachers would not have a majority on the GTC. For reasons he could not explain, Rodger was a full member of Wheatley, and not just an assessor. But he added, 'I think I have had equal influence either way'. Rodger also said of the SED assessors on the NCTT, 'If they expressed a point of view, that was certainly heeded, very much heeded. If the committee were suggesting something and they didn't like it, and said so, they [the committee] would probably not go ahead.'

The fortunes of the GTC exemplify several other aspects of control. One is the Strasbourg-goose tactic. The Department remitted to the GTC one of its most intractable problems, namely to persuade teachers to accept the admission of non-graduate males to teacher training. This was only one of a number of issues with which it stuffed the fledgling body, leaving it little room to spread its own wings. A further factor was that the GTC was almost entirely dependent on the Department for its information on teacher supply. One reason why the Department was uneasy over the NCTT under McClelland was that the NCTT collated and controlled significant intelligence on teachers in training. Similarly, until the 1970s, the Department had little alternative but to use local authorities' own judgements of need when estimating the national teacher shortage. Thereafter, however, the Department developed its own intelligence capability to the point where it was in control of the production and distribution of authoritative intelligence on supply and demand. In previous decades, other agencies had sometimes produced their own assessments of staffing, nationally and locally. But the Department's Red Book of 1973 (SED 1973b) was firmly in the public domain, and its basis in evidence was never seriously challenged once the Department had established its right to determine a single national yardstick for the measurement of local need (see chapter 10). Thus, it was the Department that controlled the manner and timing of the release of intelligence, who would receive it, how confidential it would be, and how detailed in its description of local circumstance.

The production of information is a function of organisations' attempts to comprehend and control their external environment, and a function of the public accountability enjoined on them. We have seen, however, that, for much of our period, the directors of education mediated local political inputs, and the inputs of the local authorities at the national level (see chapter 18). Especially during the years of Conservative Government from 1951 to 1964, the use of educationists to represent local political interests had the added attraction to the Department that it filtered out opposition opinion. When the reconstitution of the Advisory Council was being considered in 1956, a Departmental official advised Murrie that the two-stage procedure of nomination followed by selection should be applied to all constituencies, including the local authorities, on the grounds that,

> This would give us greater freedom of manoeuvre and would avoid the possibility of our being faced with the difficulty of each association

nominating a Labour member from the West of Scotland, as might easily happen. (s ro 1957b, 20 December 1956)

Under a Conservative government, therefore, the axis of influence tilted further towards the East. Politically influenced appointments flowed gently into the eastward course that had been cut for more than a century by the Kirriemuir career. There would be little here to muddy the representation of a provincial, Protestant Scotland that was carried downstream to the decision-makers in Edinburgh.

With little coming from the localities, therefore, the main political pressure towards public accountability was transmitted through the national political process. This pressure should not be underestimated. As Rodger said, 'the e is was always powerful enough and influential enough to get some m p to express their point of view either in the House, or by letter to a Minister'. He told us that, when he was Assistant Secretary with responsibilities for buildings and for teacher supply and salaries, he had, once a day for a month, estimated the amount of 'defensive' work he had done. The proportion was seventy per cent. At the same time, however, at least some of the political pressure exerted through Westminster was shaped by the Department. Chapter 8 saw Rodger orchestrating the contributions of m ps to debates in the Scottish Grand Committee. He also turned the planted Parliamentary Question to the Department's own advantage by including the Department's view of the 'guts of the question' in the answer, even though it was not strictly called for. It would be too much to claim from this that officials scripted the parliamentary input. The tactics Rodger described may have been used only occasionally. What is more difficult to ignore, however, are his judgements that few, if any, ideas arose from parliamentary debate; that their quality was 'desperately poor'; that fewer than half of the Scottish m ps were present at the Estimates Debate at any one time; and that fewer than one-third of Scottish m ps were sufficiently interested in education or resource questions, and informed about them, to make a contribution that the Department might think important.

Kogan (1975, 1978) describes an impoverished parliamentary input to policy-making for English education, and this judgement seems to have at least as much force for Scotland (see chapter 8). The main significance of the parliamentary mechanism was that it allowed outsiders to press the Department into consultation. However, the main work of consultation was done, not in Westminster, but in Scotland, and not by politicians, but by educationists and Departmental officials. Nor was consultation wholly, or even largely, a matter of formal discussion between duly constituted groups. This aspect was important in its own right, but important also for the informal opportunities it afforded. Moreover, formal consultation often embraced informal networks that themselves had no point of formal contact with the Department. For example, when formulating its 1958 reform of the teacher-training colleges, the Department consulted widely with Scotsmen, mainly with a background in the BEd (see chapter 18), who had attained influential positions in university departments of education in England. We asked Rodger about the importance of informal contacts:

RODGER. I was trying to tell you how I worked when I had to make up my mind on what form the training system should take. I had the job of actually formulating the initial proposals before they went to Murrie and ultimately to the public. I would say that the things that crystallised thoughts in my mind were not so much formal talks here and there, but informal talks with colleagues such as Murrie, Arbuckle, Brunton, and members of the Inspectorate; with the principals of the training colleges; with people in the universities, both in Scotland and in England. What I am saying about training colleges could well be said about other subjects too. In my memory of the kind of work that happened in all sorts of educational fields with which I was concerned, informal talks, perhaps over lunch, or in somebody's staff room, were important, although perhaps not officially given the cognisance of the talks that went on over the council table. A lot of discussion went on in the Department, you know, amongst the Departmental leaders.

If there were formal consultation thereafter, the task of producing the final aggregation of views still lay with the Department:

RODGER. Now, any one of these bodies might have made a suggestion which appealed to us. Sometimes a suggestion which was made by one body ran contrary to the suggestion made by another, and there was a cancelling out. But all that I can really say is: the starting-off point, the first published document, was our cock-shy, sent to the world to criticise; and the final was what we finally determined after hearing all their views.

What we see here is the counterpart in the informal arena of one of the principal changes that the Department made after 1945 in its formal relations with the local authorities: namely, getting Departmental influence into the process of policy formation at an earlier stage. 'There was increasing feeling from the end of the War', Rodger told us, 'that the Department should exercise less authority, delegate more, let its constituent bodies be more responsible'. Described like this, the intention sounds like an attempt to move from an 'administrative' model of partnership (in which the local authorities were regarded as agents of the Department – 'its constituent bodies') to a model in which the 'agent' was also treated as a 'principal', or 'author' of actions in its own right (see chapter 1). What occasioned this move, however, at least as far as the important area of buildings was concerned, was the Department's wish to avoid the conflicts that could arise when an authority had developed its plans to an advanced stage without consulting the Department. Rodger described the Department's new relationship with the local authorities as follows:

RODGER. We were trying to give the authorities less feeling of control, by getting collaboration at an early stage, rather than exercising control after they had gone far in preparing a job. Well, this same feeling persisted, and was stronger still, with the colleges. We felt, certainly I felt, that here we were dealing with personnel who were important in their own right; you couldn't override them. Therefore we did not want to devise a system whereby we were very much in control, or indeed to put anybody under very close control.

Formal consultation, in other words, was to be a fairly late stage in the overall process of aggregation. Its functions were as much defensive and cosmetic as anything else:

RODGER. We felt very strongly that we could not afford to ignore these bodies. Now, one of the reasons is that, first of all, by hearing them – that's important – then by taking into account what they said – that's also important – either of these can be useful to the Secretary of State as a defence against what he did, because he could say, 'Well, I only did this after consulting'; or better still, 'After consulting and paying heed to . . .'.

One possible advantage that lay with Rodger was his involvement in salaries and resources. We pressed him on whether these responsibilities lent added weight to his views and dealings in other areas, with the EIS for example:

RODGER. There is certainly that possibility. I can see somebody thinking: I had better not antagonise Rodger, because he is on the salary business. But, if there was ever such a thought, it never obtruded itself in any way to my notice. I never thought of it. I think that I can honestly say that I was on good terms with Bryden and Sellar[3] on all matters.

Q. You were never conscious that this was an element that you could use?

RODGER. No. It is an element that I wouldn't use anyway; I wouldn't want to.

Q. You would be determined to keep the salaries issue quite separate?

RODGER. Yes. I would think that it is verging on bribery and corruption to mix up these two things.

Similarly, Rodger insisted that he 'saw no connection' between the way the Department allocated building resources, and the educational policies it wished to promote. None of our interviewees suggested to us that they had felt inhibited in the educational views they could express to Departmental officials by the Department's influence over salaries and other resources.

Buildings and salary scales have as much to do with collective, as with individual, advantage. However, a teacher's individual interests are more directly affected by his or her own appointment and preferment. This was an aspect of resource-distribution where Departmental influence was considerable, and where opinions were shaped accordingly. Dickson thought 'the influence of the Inspectorate in that kind of way ha[d] been greater than their influence in their formal and official aspect' (chapter 17). The Kirriemuir career gave a traditional complexion to the Inspectorate. In their turn, traditional values were diffused by Inspectorate influence over appointments to national committees, and to education posts in some local authorities. There is, however, a further connection to be made here. The growth of national committee work, especially from the mid-1960s onwards, provided a larger and more visible arena of performance. A very rough estimate might be that about 200 teachers were involved in such committees by 1970, and a somewhat smaller number of schools. This would compare with only a handful of teachers and schools in the 1950s. Clark thought that, with the advent of the CCC, much curricular activity had moved from a local-authority to a national setting. Membership of a national committee thereby became an important stepping-stone for local promotion, whilst performance in the committee gave the ubiquitous Inspectorate additional evidence of a teacher's suitability for further advancement.

Meanwhile, changes at local level in school organisation and staffing added to the growing importance of the national arena. Until the mid-1960s, only the performance of teachers in the 200 or so schools offering full certificate courses might in principle be assessed against a single, national standard. Teachers in some 700 junior-secondary schools, falling to around 400 by the early 1960s, could not be so assessed. By the mid-1970s, however, more or less all of the 450 secondary schools had been drawn into a national domain of assessment. Moreover, the reduction in the number of secondary schools meant that increased comparability was possible at a local level also, where schools could now operate as a collectivity. For example, Walker told us that the Fife authority before the mid-1960s had convened meetings with the Directorate only for the heads of certificate-course schools: 'We didn't have the same arrangement with the junior-secondary schools because there were about forty or fifty junior-secondary schools in the county at that time and it would have been just a mass meeting'. But, in most authorities, the continuing reduction in the number of secondary schools now made it practicable for one or two teachers from each school to meet face-to-face on matters of common concern.

Comprehensive reorganisation, moreover, eventually led to an increase in the number of promoted posts within each school (see chapter 10). In the typical comprehensive school in the mid-1970s, there might be some ten teachers in posts with a recognised element of managerial responsibility. Quantification should be taken here with a pinch of salt, but the change can be expressed by contrasting the 200 or so head teachers of certificate-course schools before 1965 with the 2000 teachers that there were ten years later at, or above, the level of assistant head teacher; a change from one per cent of secondary posts in the mid-1960s to eight per cent at the second date.[4] Thus, the link between national committee work and local promotion prospects gave the Inspectorate a second line of influence over appointments. Aspirants to promoted posts, and performance in post, were more visible. They could be judged against criteria embodied by the Inspectorate in the framework for national committee work. And these criteria could be more widely applied because of the reduction in the number of schools, the increase in national committee work, and the spread of certification. The contraction of opportunities for promotion that accompanied falling school rolls was later to reinforce the importance for individual promotion of participation in the national arena.

Often the ability to set the criteria was, in effect, the ability to choose the person. It was an ability, therefore, that the Department was always concerned to monopolise. It was most effectively exercised when potential candidates could be persuaded to evaluate their own worth in the light of criteria favoured by the Department:

RODGER. I will tell you an interesting point about J. J. Robertson and myself. When Boyd retired from the headship of the Education Department in Glasgow University, Glasgow wondered whom they would appoint, and they made up their mind to approach J. J. Robertson, and did. This demonstrates the high opinion in which he was held. So they asked J. J. Robertson to be Professor of Education in Glasgow; and J. J. Robertson asked me if he should take the post. I said that I would like a wee while to think about that. On the following day I met him again, and I said, 'Well, my recommendation is: don't'. He said, 'Why?' And I said, 'On the side of philosophy of education, and on the side of being able to express that philosophy magnificently, there can be few people better equipped than you'. Then I added: 'A very modern side of education which your colleagues, the professors in other British universities, would probably be stressing would be the psychological background of education, in terms of modern psychology. They might stress modern statistical work, on which a sort of science of education and psychology was being based.' Then I said, 'You don't have that background, and therefore you might possibly feel yourself at a disadvantage and feel uncomfortable in the company of some of the people who would be really your colleagues in other universities, men whom you would meet as joint examiners'. He thought that this was decisive, and this was why he didn't take the post of Professor in Glasgow.

The eventual appointee had a formal postgraduate training in educational measurement, and was in fact to make a distinguished 'humanist' contribution. But Robertson's loss of confidence, if that is what it was, has an almost tragic significance. Arguably denied consideration for the chair of the CCC (see chapter 14), Robertson had earlier denied to himself another chair from which he might have taught the educational philosophy that had underpinned the work of the Sixth Council. What gives Robertson's decision an added significance is that we find him, towards the end of his life, writing about education and the ontology of myth. In doing this, he drew on the insights of nineteenth-century sociology that writers like Bernstein (1967) were beginning to popularise, and he attempted to develop from them a philosophy of education that could meet the changing needs of Scotland in the 1970s (Robertson 1970). What a university chair would have added to the scope and public impact of this endeavour one can only speculate.

Rodger himself did not think there was anything in the view, when we put it to him, that the Department's reorganisation of advice in the 1960s had been designed to guard against structures that could be dominated by a major outsider like Robertson or McClelland. He said, 'I think that on the whole we tended to welcome any really big person who emerged'. His preferred explanation, like Brunton's, was that the revised advisory structure had emerged piecemeal from the exigencies of certification reform, and from the 1961 strike. But he also said that his own preference was to maintain a piecemeal or disjointed element in any subsequent shaping:

RODGER. I don't think that I would be in favour of endeavouring to maintain a continuity of general advice. For one thing, the people who were on the Advisory Council from 1942 to 1947 wouldn't live for ever; you have got to keep changing them. Well, if you keep changing them, are you just going to have changes arising through changes of personnel, rather than through changes of philosophy? Should the broad, general consideration which the Advisory Council gave to major subjects in those years not be sufficient to keep you going for quite a period, during which there is a period of consolidation? Is consolidation following on general thought not almost a necessary sequel? Further, the Department, by reading letters and articles in good newspapers or periodicals (e.g. *The Times Educational Supplement*), through its meetings with directors of education and the EIS, and through inspectorial contacts with forward-thinking people in the schools, does in fact have a continuity of advice, a continuous knowledge of 'what is in the air'.

These are the views of an official who spent the last twelve years of his career serving a Conservative government. Bruce Millan, on the other hand, is a former Labour Minister whose two periods of office followed Rodger's retiral and the replacement of the Advisory Council with the new structure of advice. Yet his views in many respects run parallel to Rodger's:

MILLAN. I think that if you are appointing advisory bodies, you should try and appoint the best people to them, and not just appoint, say, the teacher-politicians, who, although they may be very good teacher-politicians, may not be terribly good educationists. Now, there is a problem about this: if you have got a committee, and you need eight teachers or something, there is no point in appointing seven members of SSTA and one member of EIS, because that doesn't represent the balance of the teaching organisations' memberships. So you would try to have some regard to their respective memberships but not in any strictly arithmetical way; but you have to have that in mind, because it is quite unrealistic not to have that in mind. But nevertheless, you try to get the right people to do the right job, and not simply allow the organisations to nominate whoever is on the executive or whatever it is at the minute.

Q. How would you know who were the right people to do the right job?

MILLAN. Well, sometimes you actually do know them personally, because Scotland is a fairly small country, and you may know something of them; their personal reputation and so on. But then, I think that you are very much relying on your inspectors particularly, and your administrators' advice. You may have people who have been on other committees who have performed particularly well. There may be people who may have done something quite interesting in their own schools and so on. There are different ways of finding out. Of course, they have got to be good at working on a committee. . . . Now on the question of fragmentation of advice: Well, there is no lack of advice; that comes from everywhere. That is not the problem. I don't think that it would actually help very much to try and put all these bodies together. I think that you would get something that would be completely unwieldy, and which would only then set up about fifteen different subcommittees, anyway; so, in a sense, you would get perhaps something like the present structure. . . . There is a tendency to split everything up anyway, so if you put everything together, I'm not sure, at the end of the day, that that helps very much. I think the problem, in Scottish education, on many of these matters – particularly when they are politically sensitive, or when you come up against the particular views of, say, the teacher unions – is that, because you have to consult so many different people, there are tremendous opportunities for delay and obstruction and difficulties of ever getting a consensus on anything. Now that means, I think, that the decision-making isn't as quick as it ought to be, and that it probably isn't as effective as it ought to be, because there is this great process of consultation. . . . And I think the difficulty doesn't just apply in education. It is even worse in the Health Service, for example . . . because there the Ministers are ultimately supposed to be executively responsible for running the service. The Health Boards are agents of the Minister, so he is directly responsible in the way that, if you are Minister of Education for Scotland, you are not directly responsible for running the schools; you have the local authorities and all of the rest of it. . . .

Q. Was it worse when you had thirty-five education authorities?

MILLAN. No, I don't think that that makes any difference, because I think that the different interests are the same whether they are operating through thirty-five or eight. You have still got the teacher unions; you have got the colleges; you have got the local authorities and so on. . . . It might, theoretically, be able to give you a more coherent local-authority view than you would have had before. I am not sure whether that has actually made a great deal of improvement in the situation.

Millan told us that he doubted the value to a Minister of parliamentary debate on education. We asked him where, then, he thought the system got its ideas:

MILLAN. The ideas tend to come from within the system itself; that is really what it amounts to. We have been talking about the Inspectorate, the Department, and the various consultative bodies, and the rest of it, and in a way it is a fairly closed kind of system, if you like. I think that that is probably highly undesirable, but that is the way in which it operates; and there isn't in Scotland, as far as I am aware, any independent source of educational thinking which is of great influence on what is actually happening in practice. . . .

Q. Isn't there a particular danger that Scotland, as you say, is a small community, more of a face-to-face community, that appointments to committees are very often based upon the personal knowledge of the inspectors; that there isn't the pluralism, there isn't the criticism that you would have in a system such as England?

MILLAN. Well, I'm not sure that the English experience is any better than ours. I think in many respects it is less favourable than ours. But if you are saying that it would be very good to have a whole lot of independent people saying interesting things and producing interesting ideas about the Scottish educational system, then I must agree with you.

Q. That is what the Advisory Council did, amongst other things.

MILLAN. Well, I don't remember the resuscitation of the Advisory Council's being a great issue, in the period that we are talking about up to 1970. But I would be open to persuasion that perhaps we ought to have some kind of general body giving, as it were, general advice, and producing general thinking. But I think there is a tendency in a whole lot of areas in Scotland – not just in education – for academic and other work not to make much influence on what actually happens in terms of policy. I think that this is not just an educational problem.

Q. Why do you think that is?

MILLAN. I suppose that the links, somehow or other, are not precise enough between the Ministers and the other people working in their field. It may be, of course, that because the Secretary of State is responsible for so many different things, he is not able to devote sufficient of his energy at a time to particular problems. I was Secretary of State for three years. As well as education I had health, agriculture, fisheries, industry, housing, local government and a lot of other things to look after. If I had been Secretary of State for Education in England, or some other Minister with responsibility for only one particular subject, I think I certainly would have wished to have some kind of independent advice available, formally or informally, in a way which is difficult to achieve effectively in Scotland, either because it isn't available or, more probably, because the pressures on the Secretary of State make it more difficult for him to find the time to take advantage of what *is* available. This has implications of course in the arguments about devolution for Scotland.

Discussion

The term 'policy community' denotes a set of persons and groups which stretches across the divide between government and outside interests, and which is directly involved in the making and implementation of policy. It is generally agreed that policy communities are a characteristic feature of British governmental life, and that they raise serious questions about the role of Parliament, political parties, and the Cabinet in a system which is, formally, an elective democracy. But there is disagreement over how precisely they should be described, and over their wider significance. Some writers regard them as contributing to a fragmentation of public policy-making. Others see them as providing at least some order and regularity in a pluralistic system of bargaining. Still others interpret their importance in terms of a wider shift towards corporatism.[5] What, then, is the significance of the educational policy community in Scotland?

We have suggested that educational expansion has combined with governmental change to shift the SED, since the early 1950s, from a predominantly regulatory mode to a predominantly promotional one. This, in turn, has increased the Department's dependence on outsiders, to help it with its work, to bring it local and expert knowledge, and to articulate its relations with the groups who would experience change, or lead change. The Department's 'power-dependence' opened central-local relations to the politics of negotiation (see chapter 9). The negotiated compliance of teachers was also indispensable to the Department. Between 1945 and 1975, say, every group in Scottish education discussed hitherto, including the Department itself, had successes and failures, not only in proposing new lines of action, but also in opposing initiatives taken by others. In this respect, pluralism was a feature of the policy process, and partnership a fair description.

There are, however, two qualifications that should immediately be made to this conclusion, both of which, to judge from the literature, apply not only to the educational policy community in Scotland, but to other policy communities as well. First, the issues that were determined by negotiation within the policy community were only of limited scope. 'Grand' issues that were largely determined outside included comprehensive reorganisation, ROSLA in 1973, the administrative reorganisations of finance in 1958 and of local government in 1975, and the scale of public expenditure. Second, central government itself played an important constitutive role in the activities of the policy community. It had a major, though never total, influence over the access of groups and individuals, the agenda of issues, and the rules of the negotiating game, including timing, confidentiality and doctrines of representation. Rodger's evidence is a reminder of the institutional stamina of central government, and of the extensive repertoire of controls that it can use to promote some policies and inhibit others.

This, then, is a picture of contained, pluralist decision-making on ordinary issues, but decision-making that was manipulated by central government, if not covertly, then at least to a greater degree than is implied in the official accounts of the consultative process in Scotland. Perhaps, also, it was a pluralism that was somewhat better aggregated in Scotland than in England and Wales. Could one usefully call this corporatism? The distinction between pluralism and corporatism turns largely on the degree of conflict or consensus in the relations between groups and government. In broad terms, pluralism holds that a dispersed array of groups presses demands on government, whilst corporatism holds that selected groups collaborate with government in formulating and implementing policy. But, in chapter 1, we noted the close resemblance between the more systematic variant of pluralism, and 'societal' corporatism. Both forms lie somewhere between the poles of dispersed pluralism and 'state' corporatism, and both differ in kind from anarchy and from direct rule by the state. However, writers disagree about the precise criteria on which differences between these 'middle' forms can be drawn, and about how to interpret the evidence. Schmitter (1982, 265) remarks that corporatism 'is clearly not something a polity has or does not have'.

The evidence we have presented on Scottish educational policy-making testifies to characteristics found both in pluralism and corporatism. But our reservations about the extent of pluralism in the system do not lead us to unequivocally corporatist conclusions. Crouch (1985, 86) advises 'great care before labelling an individual piece of behaviour as corporatist. . . a few instances of co-operative national industrial relations bear the same relation to neo-corporatism as a single swallow does to summer'. But how many swallows make a summer? The problem is not numerical but is one of convention, of how systemic patterns are to be recognised.

'Partnership' is a candidate for such a pattern. We have argued that partnership connotes some dispersal of power away from the centre and towards groups that have scope to determine their own priorities. In this sense it resembles pluralism. From a different perspective, partnership resembles corporatism in the exclusiveness of its relationships, in its assumption that mutual interests outweigh the partners' separate or conflicting interests, and in the sharing of authority. The policy community was constituted from amongst the categories of the educational partnership in order to transform consensus into decision, and decision into action. Its affinity with corporatism cannot be ignored.

However, one crucial test is success. Grant observes: 'What corporatism offers is the possibility of arriving at *effective* bargains, in the sense that they can be secured and implemented, rather than being simply talked about in the hope that changes in the behaviour of the discussants will follow' (Grant 1985b, 21, his emphasis). Evidence of governmental attempts at manipulating policy-making is not enough. If such manipulation were incipiently corporatist, it was a corporatism that was not very well realised in the case of the educational policy community in Scotland. From government's point of view, the demands of teachers were not well controlled after the 1950s. Here the dangers of a corporatist strategy were evident. By coopting teachers from among those whose values and careers were most consonant with those of its own officials, the Department risked emphasising the gap that separated governmental interests from those of the classroom teacher. By drawing eminent teachers towards the centre, it risked drawing them away from their classroom colleagues whom they were alleged to represent. By involving teachers in its own activities, it risked an impossible burden, unless it could at the same time mobilise the periphery. Instead, in the 1960s, teachers themselves began to mobilise, but more for industrial action than for educational change.

The EIS enjoyed a virtual monopoly of teachers' interest-representation on policy issues until the 1960s, when Arbuckle 'let the SSTA in'. This widened the consultative network and formally acknowledged the plurality of the teacher interest. But the EIS retained its vast numerical preponderance, and the number of organisations representing teachers remained small. Even so, the reliability of the 'good, gentlemanly, mannerly' EIS as a bargaining partner for government was found wanting in the early 1960s, when teachers' resistance stiffened against the Department's attempt to 'dilute' the profession. The EIS leadership learned that it could not easily contain a militant membership, and the association as a whole learned that much could be gained through conflict with government (see chapter 12).

Amongst the education-authority interests, it was the directors who took precedence as government's most reliable negotiating partner, whilst the local-authority associations did not share a common outlook. Rodger said that the associations had little knowledge of education to offer the SED, and so were bypassed in favour of the directors. The ADES bargained some policies with the SED in the 'frank' and 'beneficial' atmosphere of the liaison committee, but there was much that passed it by. Moreover, as the failure of teacher redistribution illustrates, the Department could not depend upon the directors collectively to implement important policies. Nor did corporatist solutions play a significant part in the SED's promotional approach to the problems of school building. Here what mattered most was the relationship between on the one hand, the Department's administrators and district inspectors, and on the other, the individual education authority and its director.

Perhaps after Brunton the Department was still trying to perfect and extend a corporatist strategy. Equally, however, it was surely apparent by the end of the 1960s that there were limits to what government could hope to achieve solely through manipulation of the educational policy community, at least as it then was constituted. For one thing, the policy community was too inconsequential. Its issue-scope, as we have said, was limited. It neither initiated any of the major changes mentioned earlier, nor supported them. Nor had its stance on these issues been a decisive influence. More-over, this limitation in issue-scope was just one aspect of a segmentation among policy communities that further limited their utility to government. Education, industry, housing and social services, all tended to operate as separate communities. From government's point of view, some of the greater 'policy messes' had resulted from this segmentation: school building in Glasgow, for example, and the failure of Brunton's attempts to link school, further education and industrial training.

Nor could government expect the educational policy community to correct this situation by quickly enlarging its substantive scope. The restricted and highly specialised expertise of the Schools' Inspectorate in the early 1960s was one reminder, to any administrator bent on change, of the extent to which knowledge and concern about young people was to be found outwith the confines of the educational world, as it then was defined. To raise a different sort of person to eminence in the policy community would take decades, for it would require a transformation in the criteria of professional success and in related patterns of appointment and promotion. The Inspectorate, for example, began to recruit substantially from colleges of education and further education only in the 1960s, and it took fifteen years before the new men were able to influence policy from the top. Set against this timetable for change, and the dependencies it would entail, including administrative dependence on the Inspectorate, other instruments of control were also attractive. Corporate management, the reorganisation of local government into larger units, and attempts to improve the planning and management of public expenditure, all are indicative of administrative impatience with the limitations of segmented and professionally permeated policy communities as instruments of policy. The recourse to these administrative expedients itself has implications for the corporatist thesis, and we comment on some of these in our final chapter. But they suggest that government was far from satisfied with what could be achieved through policy communities alone, at least as they were traditionally defined and organised.

Of course, the attempt to improve administrative control in the 1960s was occasioned by general governmental considerations, and was not primarily a consequence of government's dissatisfaction with education and its governance. Nevertheless, education was always something more than just another service delivered by government on the advice of a policy community. It was also a large and growing component of public expenditure. Furthermore, as correspondence theory reminds one, it had to do with the hearts and minds of young citizens. It helped to shape their wants, and their understanding of their interests and desserts. Thus, the ideology of the educational policy community had implications for the ways in which goods and services were distributed in other policy areas, even though the policy communities themselves may have had few direct dealings with each other.

So far, our discussion of aggregation has left the question of interests to one side. Has government habitually chosen to aggregate in the interests of some group or groups? Alternatively, has there been a bias in the process of aggregation, even though government may not have chosen the bias, and may have played only a contributory role in the aggregating process? Our evidence throws more light on the second possibility than on the first, and it is evidence that indicates that ideological aspects of the educational policy community had a significance that was somewhat wider than its service-delivery function alone. Chapter 17 has shown how the Scottish myth sustained a common sense of identity both within the policy community, and between it and the wider world of education. In doing this, however, it can also be argued to have sustained inequities between groups, including social classes, and to have constrained government's understanding of the extent to which these could be changed. The myth offered to the policy community a morally and empirically persuasive view of schooling and its possibilities. Moreover, the interests of each of the major parties within the policy community were served by some aspect of this view. The argument that Scottish arrangements reflected national character allowed the Scottish Office administration to deflect Treasury criticism of the financial benefit to Scotland of the Goschen formula. It sustained university arguments for the importance of generous admission to the three-year General degree, and also for the consequent need for a fourth year for the completion of Honours. The extra year, in its turn, allowed honours-graduate teachers to justify the higher salaries they received by comparison with their English counterparts (fewer of whom, however, were professionally trained). It was from the elite of honours-graduate teachers that the bulk of the Inspectorate was recruited. This was a large body, relative to Her Majesty's Inspectors of Schools in England, and one, therefore, that had a particular interest in the case for a national, Scottish system. Moreover, its own professional authority rested on the supposition that its members were among that system's finest product.

However, it is not logically necessary to invoke interests to explain beliefs, even when interests are consonant with beliefs and do not make them uncomfortable. In general, we are suggesting, the experience of provincial, Protestant, professional, Scotland offered few challenges to the currency of the myth or to the potency of its symbolic elements, among them the general curriculum, the common school, and the lad o' pairts. Nevertheless, as we have said, the myth discounted the experience of major groups in the population. Intentionally or otherwise, assent to the myth, or to elements therein, sustained this institutional bias.

The institutional bias of the myth derived in part from its criteria of success and moral probity. Pupils' success, and the professional teacher-expertise related to it, were defined in terms of certificate examinations. But only a minority of schools before 1965 presented pupils for certificate examinations. Catholics, cities, and working-class neighbourhoods were less well served than their counterpart groups. Among the certificate schools, those serving predominantly middle-class catchments will have produced better certificate results on average. Two reasons for this have little, if anything, to do with the quality of their teaching. Middle-class pupils tend to do better than working-class pupils, whatever type of school they are in. Also, pupils of all backgrounds tend to do better the more middle-class are their fellow pupils (McPherson and Willms 1986). Thus, the ambitious teacher might be drawn away from the city school, the working-class school, and the Glasgow school in particular, not just because such schools were large and promotions there infrequent, nor just because the job might be more satisfying elsewhere. A further factor was that teachers who moved to schools with more favoured pupil intakes would find that the examination attainment of their new pupils would more often sustain any claim, they, the teachers, might make to be good teachers on the objective criterion of examination results. If the ambitious teachers were also good teachers, that is, good at producing learning gains for pupils of all types of social background or ability, then their departure was a real loss to the less favoured schools and pupils they had left behind. At its starkest this loss can be seen in the area distribution of staffing shortages up to the 1970s. The most depleted schools tended to be Catholic, or predominantly working-class, or junior-secondary, or located in the west of Scotland. These inequalities are also apparent in the composition of the group of schools from which teachers were appointed to the subject panels of the Examination Board in the mid-1960s. 'Normal' expectation would be that half of the schools would serve neighbourhoods of below-average socio-economic status, and that just under half would be located in the West (i.e. in what was later to become Strathclyde Region). In fact, only one-fifth of panel teachers were from schools of below-average socio-economic status, and only one-third were from schools in the West (see chapter 17). But the myth offered an explanation for these spatial- and social-class inequalities in terms of the moral failings of the groups and individuals involved. Thus, the evidence of distributional inequality did not seriously embarrass the myth's egalitarian claims, and more especially so because it could rightly be claimed that pupil and teacher quality were judged by a universal criterion of certificate performance. Such judgements in turn reinforced the view that schooling could only ever have small effects for the large majority of pupils. In these ways, therefore, the myth was institutionally biased, and constituted a third dimension of power in the sense identified by Lukes (1974).

The bias inherent in the myth relieves one of the need to posit a sustained conspiracy by individual government officials to help explain the evident fact that Scottish education reproduced inequalities that were neither rational nor fair. What is most striking is that inequalities that were irrational and unjust arose from decisions that were, in their own terms, reasonable, objective and universalistic. Perhaps the main argument against conscious conspiracy is that there was no need for one; events themselves could be trusted to conspire.[6] Individual officials may or may not have been so motivated, but we ourselves can go no further in judging this than is allowed by the evidence already presented.

In one respect, however, to soften a judgement of conscious conspiracy to one of culpable complacency is still not to go far enough. It is true that our own argument has emphasised the active role of government in shaping the policy community and its beliefs. But we have also suggested that this was often done in an attempt to improve the tools of government, and to surmount the logical incompatibilities inherent in the attempts of representative democracy to inform its policies with knowledge. Such situations allowed of a variety of motives, and the culpability of the official may simply have been that, on occasion, he gave a higher priority to making the machinery of government work than he did to the policies it processed. In one sense, this conclusion renders the institutional bias more sinister because more deeply embedded among competing priorities. But, precisely because the bias was a matter of priority, it was also open to change. It was not intractable, as comprehensive reorganisation showed. On the other hand, the political impetus for reorganisation in Scotland came mainly from England where it was informed by the sociological critique of selection. That no such critique developed in Scotland is largely attributable to the hold of the myth on the perception and imagination of the policy community. It is fruitless to speculate whether the processes of Scottish civil society would have weakened the hold of the myth had it not been for English political influence. Without English influence, there would have been no myth; or it would, at least, have been very different.

There is a further reason, too, for doubting the inevitability of the institutional bias, and the conscious conspiracy of officials in maintaining it. The myth had countervailing effects. Scottish working-class pupils had better access to education than their English counterparts, even though social-class relativities in educational attainment within Scotland may have been similar to those in England. Again, the myth's emphasis on the viability of the small country school had the unintended effect of maintaining a relationship between school and higher education that was more beneficial to the interest of urban working-class pupils than the proto-compulsory sixth-year that the Department wanted (see chapter 13). Growing numbers of students in the 1970s entered higher education from the fifth year. To be sure, we have in the A-level issue an instance of officials pursuing an elitist policy over decades. But it is also an instance of the continuing frustration of elitism by the rural slant of the egalitarian ideology. The internal consistency of ideologies is no more to be assumed, therefore, than the inevitability of their effects. The latter require empirical testing, and one test that can be applied is the evidence, reported in chapters 16 and 17, on the extent to which the political egalitarianism of the 1960s changed the incipiently corporatist composition of the policy community and the social inequities of the system it delivered.

NOTES
1. 'The reality [of central government's role in education] is considerably more complex than any simple conspiracy theory would suggest with different sorts of interests and different levels of concern combining to produce a pattern of power-relations which is dominated by the informal processes of personal negotiation. To illuminate these processes detailed empirical studies of the political and administrative relationships between the different branches of the DES itself are required. Further . . . it is the normative assumptions on which such interaction is based that are the real source of power albeit unremarked and unopposed since they carry the power to determine selectively the way in which issues are discussed and the solutions proposed. How this influence is exerted – through participation in key committees in particular – also requires detailed study if we are fully to understand the process of policy-making' (Broadfoot 1986, 61).
2. One example, however, is Maclure's (1984) study of post-war school building in England and Wales. He shows how the building programme was devised and executed by a network of central and local administrators, educationists, architects and manufacturers. They sponsored each other's movements into key positions, created organisations, and formed alliances that were crucial to innovation. Many of the official papers of this period are not yet publicly available. However, Maclure's access to papers for the earlier years, and to many of the persons involved, allows him to cast light upon the importance of interpersonal relationships in the policy process. It also helps to point up the close connection between spatial design, curriculum, and pedagogy. Another study that relates micro- to macro-politics is Ranson's (1985a) article on policy-making for sixteen- to nineteen-year olds. He argues that there was a broad consensus in the DES over policy objectives. Underlying this, however, 'formidable clashes of interest emerged between the sectoral traditions of Schools and Further Education Branches over departmental strategy' (*ibid.*, 58). Conflict 'escalated up the Department, involving Ministers, who were constrained to take sides' (*ibid.*, 59). Ranson illustrates these divisions with anonymous quotations from DES officials. Outside the field of education, Heclo and Wildavsky's (1974) book on the Whitehall 'village', centred on the Treasury, is the best-known study of a British policy community at work.
3. A. M. Sellar, Deputy Town Clerk of Edinburgh, Joint Secretary of the NJC (see chapter 10), and principal spokesman for the education authorities in national salary negotiations in the 1950s and 1960s.
4. Calculated from SED (1966a, table 19) and GSS (1977, table 24).
5. Among the main general sources on policy communities are Richardson and Jordan (1979) and Jordan (1981). They describe the close relationships between groups and government in Britain, and they search for a reformulation of pluralism. They go beyond earlier British discussions of pressure-group politics in which descriptions of policy communities can also be found (e.g. Eckstein 1960; Self and Storing 1962). Examples of more recent studies of policy communities in different fields are Richardson, Jordan, and Kimber (1978), Hogwood (1979), and Dunleavy (1981a). Rhodes discusses policy communities at length, defining them as 'networks characterised by stability of relationships, continuity of restricted membership, vertical interdependence based on shared service delivery responsibilities, and insulation from other

networks and invariably to [sic] the general public (including Parliament). . . .
They are highly integrated' (Rhodes 1985a, 15). Rhodes also uses a more
encompassing 'network' model to discuss intergovernmental relations (Rhodes
1985a, 1986a, 1986b; Wistow and Rhodes 1987). Sharpe (1985) and Laffin
(1986) distinguish between policy communities and professional communities
in various policy fields, whilst Dunleavy (1981a) discusses the role of professional communities in 'ideological corporatism'. Jordan (1981) explores the
differences between policy communities, 'iron triangles', and 'issue networks'.
These are related terms that have been used in studying American politics, but
Cohen (1982) uses the issue-network concept to analyse the role of inspectors
in English policy and practice concerning educational opportunity for ethnic
groups. Recent writings on 'quangos' (e.g. Barker 1982; Raab 1982a) touch on
the part played by these non-departmental or 'fringe' bodies in the networks of
public policy-making. Jordan (1981) finds evidence for 'institutionalised
pluralism' in the role of advisory committees and appointed bodies in non-
economic fields. He rejects corporatist descriptions of British policy-making,
but Rhodes discusses 'quangos', and the policy communities to which they
relate, in terms of corporatism (R. Rhodes 1981, 4-5 and 120). However,
Rhodes' frustration both with the ambiguity of corporatist theory, and with the
rigid characteristics of corporatism as specified by Schmitter, has led him to
regard 'the equivalence of meso-corporatism and policy networks [as] more
apparent than real at present' (Wistow and Rhodes 1987, 38). But he is
reluctant to exclude corporatism as a candidate explanation of relationships
within central-local policy communities and networks, although he does not
consider the strategies of aggregation and control to be uniquely corporatist
(Rhodes 1985a, 1985b, 1986a, 1986b).

6. Our conclusions here are similar to those reached by Lodge and Blackstone
(1982) in their review of DES attitudes to social and educational inequality.
Their main argument is that a shared Departmental attitude contributed to the
reproduction of educational inequality by displacing redistributive policies by
other priorities: 'The DES does have an ideology of change, perhaps best
described as "evolutionary pragmatism". . . . [It] is informed by three things –
managerial efficiency, expansionism and consensus – none of which is necessarily conducive to change (in the sense of a radical redress of inequality)' (*ibid.*,
37). Lawton's conclusions on the role of DES in curriculum policy are also
apposite: 'HMIS and civil servants, sharing similar social and educational
backgrounds, tend to make the same kind of assumptions, and tend to possess
similar beliefs, ideologies and obsolete theories. It is likely that DES policy,
where it exists at all, is the result of that kind of "common sense" set of shared
assumptions rather than a carefully formulated theoretical viewpoint' (Lawton
1980, 28-9).

Twenty

Conclusion

> It is very difficult to describe all this. . . . the system does change,
> and change significantly, but it can't be done by administrative or
> Ministerial fiat, you know. It just doesn't work like that.   Bruce
> Millan, Secretary of State for Scotland 1976-79

Introduction

The received account of Scottish education describes it as a centralised
system, relative to England, in which the constituent parts traditionally look
to the centre for a lead. We have taken issue with this view on two main
grounds. First, we have argued that Scottish institutions, including the
centre itself, have considerable centrifugal potential. The occasions when
people have been persuaded to take their lead from the centre represent an
achievement over considerable odds, though always at the cost of some
limitation on the range of policies that can be pursued. The received account
itself contributes to this achievement by suggesting that the order it describes is natural, and that the centre lies only in Scotland.

The other problem with the centralisation thesis is that it does not explain
very much. Whilst it may account reasonably well for the unproductive
decade ending in the mid-1950s, it cannot explain a number of the major
developments that followed. The SED's thinking in the late 1950s and early
1960s, for example, gave no hint of the fact that, fifteen years later, it would
stand committed to a system of comprehensive, non-vocational secondary
education, with certification for virtually all sixteen-year-olds by means of a
single national certificate. Nor, towards the end of the 1980s, has one any
great confidence that this will still be the order of affairs a further fifteen
years hence. Many of the major changes in policy and provision since 1945
have originated outwith the Scottish centre, and often in the face of its initial
indifference or opposition. Educational expansion, universal national certification, and comprehensive schooling are examples. Equally, many of the
Department's own initiatives did not progress beyond the stage of early
consultation; those that progressed did not always succeed; and long-standing policies were sometimes knocked off course. In the 1970s, for example,
the Department was obliged to abandon the view, that it had taken from the
beginning of the century, that a substantial part of the curriculum in post-primary schooling should be vocationally related. By the mid-1980s, however,

481

it was moving back towards this position, again under pressure from outside. Thus any characterisation of the system as centralised would have to allow that it was talking about a centralisation that was often ineffective, at least as far as the management of change was concerned. The utility of such a description must be in some doubt, especially when it leads to the paradoxical characterisation of a centre that is so powerful that it lacks the power to effect the limited decentralisation it sometimes seeks.

Can we, then, characterise the making of Scottish educational policy as pluralist? Several sorts of evidence might be mustered in support of a pluralist thesis. In part I we pointed to an historical diversity of institutional forms and educational beliefs that bequeathed a potential for pluralism to Scottish education after 1945. In parts II and III we disaggregated the institutional structure of 'the centre' and explored the conflicts of interest and belief that occurred between individuals, between departments, and between functional groups, particularly Inspectorate and administration. Then, in part IV, more detailed studies have led us to characterise the making of certain selected policies as pluralist. Overall, moreover, we have observed that all the major formal groups since 1945 have had successes and failures both in proposing and opposing policies, and that the effect has been to take the system in a direction that no one group could be said originally to have wanted. The claim that the development of the system in the 1960s and 1970s followed the course set by Advisory Council in 1947 is but one example of rationality imposed after the event.

However, these arguments and evidence are not in themselves a conclusive demonstration of a pluralist system. Naively stated, the pluralist thesis is more easily satisfied than any alternative. It is easy enough to find examples of the frustration or satisfaction of the demands of any group, and easy enough, therefore, to conclude that the policy world is messy, indeterminate, and responsive to a variety of demands. Equally, however, even within a single policy field like education, it is not too difficult to find instances of state *dirigisme* that indicate centralisation, instances of collusion between government and interest groups that indicate corporatism, and instances of shared authority that indicate partnership. But single instances are not enough, especially when there are counter-examples to hand.

Then, also, there is a problem of generalisability. Abstract models like pluralism and corporatism can easily harden into a reified view of the social order that exaggerates its inevitability and its constraining effects on individuals. Clearly, we have been dealing in this book with institutions that must be called 'social' or 'structural' by virtue of the fact that they antedated and outlasted particular individuals, and influenced their actions thereby. But we have only been able to explain the functioning, reproduction and change of these institutions by acknowledging the biographies of the individuals involved, the issues they addressed, and the legacy of their predecessors. The SED's structure and relationships in 1945 were still informed by educational disputes of the later Victorian and Edwardian eras, and they began to change in the 1950s in part because education was asked to address new issues. The careers of Brunton and Rodger illustrate how formal governmental roles owed their viability in part to the contacts and experience their incumbents brought to them, in Rodger's case from the scientific and progressive movement in education, and in Brunton's from his wartime experience of administration. Equally, the viability of the structure of governance in this period also owed much to the shared values, beliefs, and experience of the Kirriemuir career. It provided a moral purpose for education and a common grounding for individual identity. It simplified the 'reality' of Scotland that policy-makers perceived, and thereby shaped the policies that emerged. Personal identity and social structure were not 'distinct states of being' but were, in Abrams' words, 'elements of a single process of becoming'.

How, then, is one to generalise beyond the time and place of this configuration of individuals, institutions and issues? This question arises whether or not one regards our account as history, or as social theory, or both. And it is especially pertinent from the standpoint of the late 1980s. Much of our evidence has been supplied by attributable and informed testimonies that are firmly in the public domain. This has brought the better evidenced part of our analysis to a close in the mid-1970s by which time few of our informants were publicly active. Emphasising historical continuities as we have, we would be surprised if our analysis were wholly irrelevant to what came after. Equally, however, there have been major changes, even discontinuities, in British experience since the mid-1970s which must be acknowledged in any account of how the system works.

Recent Changes

Perhaps the main motors of change acting on education have been the decline in the birthrate, economic recession, and the fact that government and governed alike are older, and in some ways wiser. A further factor, as far as Scotland is concerned, is nationalist resurgence. This lasted sufficiently long to maintain a separate Scottish element in the policy response to the 1970s. It has been kept alive in the 1980s by the argument that the Conservative Government lacks the legitimacy of a significant number of parliamentary seats in Scotland. For its part, the Government may well regard the direction of Scottish educational policy in the 1980s as one that the rest of Britain should follow, and one therefore that should not be put at risk by disturbing the relative autonomy of the Scottish policy process.

The fact of demographic decline is incontestable, though its implications for the scale of educational provision are not, especially in the post-compulsory sector. Nor is the impact of the recession on education, real enough as it is, wholly discontinuous with earlier experience. Viewed against events since 1918, the years of greatest educational expansion, say from 1958 to the mid-1970s, appear as a brief and untypical episode. Moreover, even in this brief period, overall shortages and area disparities in provision continued to shape central government's thinking on how it should organise itself and its relations with the local authorities. The oil crisis of 1973 underlined the message of the 1968 retrenchment in public spending, namely, that it was becoming increasingly difficult to meet the costs of educational expansion. Even so, there is a sense in which the years of expansion did not end in the early 1970s. The recession challenged the orthodox equation of education with economic growth, and it occasioned arguments for a different type of education, differently delivered. But, whilst there were arguments about emphasis and cost, there was no serious proposal to roll back the advances made since 1945 in the institutional structure of provision.

Indeed, the recession posed a crisis for education precisely because more education, and not less, was seen as a means to tackle its causes and consequences. Recession has influenced educational policy in a number of ways. It has, first of all, led pupils and students to make demands of educational provision that the system has not been suited to fulfil. In the 1950s and 1960s, a major problem for secondary schools was that the majority of able pupils were leaving school at the minimum leaving age. In the 1970s and 1980s, the problem was that an increasing number of less able pupils were not leaving at this age. Not for the first time was reform to be occasioned by the stubborn refusal of pupils to conform to systemic expectations. However, changed provision could not be financed incrementally because of the limits that were imposed on public spending. A redistribution of expenditure was required and, if necessary, new mechanisms for effecting it.

A further effect of recession has, of course, been the successive cuts in public spending: the cash limits on expenditure first imposed in 1976; the penal application of cuts in the rate-support grant beginning in the early 1980s; and rate-capping a year or two later. Because these moves have coincided with demographic decline, they do not necessarily imply an over-all reduction in *per capita* resources for education, although there have been reductions in particular spending areas. Nor, as we have said, is government concern for efficiency new. What is new, especially since 1979, is the Conservative Government's determination to impose public-spending decisions on the local authorities, and to dispense if necessary with consultation and persuasion. Thus, the new and assertive stance of central government can be seen as a move away, not only from the pluralism of partnership, but also from incipiently corporatist attempts to shape the partners' spending priorities to its own ends. These strategies have been replaced by increased central direction of finance, by attempts to constrain the local authority by broadening its accountability locally, and by increasing local 'consumer' choice.

Central-government assertiveness is also more visible in education policy itself, though how directly this results from the recession is less clear. Since the mid-1970s, the DES has been more promotional in the shaping of policies for examinations, curriculum, and standards. It has, in effect, moved towards a Scottish model by locating a larger proportion of its Schools Inspectorate at the centre, by withdrawing its support from the Schools Council, by unifying the national examination at sixteen, and by proposing to assume control of non-university higher education. In both countries, moreover, there have been attempts to reduce the influence of teachers and education authorities by increasing the local influence of parents. In England, parents have greater representation on the governing bodies of schools, and in both countries they have acquired a limited right to choose their child's school. This policy has been widely understood as an attempt to undermine the comprehensive secondary-school policies of Labour-controlled local authorities, and again, therefore, as an attack on the traditional partnership. The increased use of centrally funded educational initiatives, such as the Assisted Places Scheme, is similarly understood, as are proposals to allow state schools to leave the control of the local authorities.

The Conservative Government, however, prefers to portray its intervention in pluralist terms, as the attempt to break a duopoly of influence enjoyed by teachers and education authorities both nationally and locally. By enfranchising parents and encouraging industry to participate in educational provision, the Government claims to be taking important steps on the road to a restructured partnership, south of the Border at least (Ranson 1985b). Nevertheless, in Scotland and England alike, major central initiatives have been taken through the agency of the MSC. In its activities relating to young people, the MSC has developed into a powerful instrument of centrally led innovation for education and training from the later compulsory stages onwards. As such, the MSC reflects a growing central government mistrust both of the central-local partnership principle and of the capacity of the DES to initiate.

Nobody disputes that the centre has become more active in education since the mid-1970s. But the nature and significance of this change are debatable. Is it mainly a matter of political assertiveness? If so, what are the parts played by politicians, by officials and by their various departments? Alternatively, is increased central activity an indication of a more fundamental institutional shift in the locus of power? As to the roles of the various UK departments, especially those in England, the significance of our own study is mainly heuristic. Our evidence suggests that the assumption that there is a single departmental centre to an educational system has, if anything, become more misleading since 1945 rather than less. The institutional isolation of the SED has been eroded by factors that will also have borne on DES. Perhaps, through the medium of the Scottish Office, they have been focused rather more effectively on central educational administration in

Scotland than was possible in England. Certainly, one sign of DES isolation was the rise of the MSC.

On the roles of politicians and officials, the Scottish experience perhaps has more to contribute. The political accountability of the central administration of education has been weaker in Scotland than in England, leaving correspondingly more scope to Scottish officials, whether or not they chose to use it. Until the mid-1950s they chose not to, nor did their Ministers encourage them. Thereafter they became more promotional. But they were drawn into this stance with some reluctance, and initially only to compensate for failure: the failure of the local authorities to plan buildings and distribute teachers; and the failure of the selective school system to retain its able pupils. In the 1960s, the spread of national certification beyond the types of school and pupil originally envisaged by the Department, drew the Department further into a promotional role, again with some reluctance, and again as a result of failure. On this occasion it was the failure to devise a system of certification that could be contained within the favoured sector of the bipartite system.

Thus, increased central activity in Scotland began almost two decades before the onset of recession, and cannot be explained by recession alone. On the other hand, the new promotionalism initially addressed problems that were not dissimilar to those of the recession to come, problems of the shortage and maldistribution of resources, and of the underutilisation and misdirection of talent. In other words, the Scottish evidence suggests that there is a danger of exaggerating the discontinuities, both of external challenge and policy response, that the 1970s brought. There is also a danger of exaggerating the implications of the new promotionalism for political accountability and partnership. We have seen, for example, that Labour Ministers in Scotland were well served by their officials in the 1960s and 1970s when dismantling selection and fee-paying in the maintained sector. More generally, as the Department became more promotional, so it found itself accountable in wider fields than did the 'sleepy hollow' of the 1940s.

If much of the change that was apparent in the 1980s originated before the recession, and even before the period of increasing political assertion, can it be better understood in terms of some institutional, or 'morphogenetic', change in government, schooling, or both? As one looks at events since 1945, perhaps three changes call for an initial comment: the extension of the scope of schooling; the increasing proportion of educational expenditure borne by central government; and central government's increasingly promotional stance. Each has mixed implications for the power of the SED.

First, then, schooling has increased its scope. More pupils are involved for longer. This arises from the increase in voluntary enrolments and from the statutory extensions of the period of compulsion. More recently, the two-year Youth Training Scheme, allied to prospective changes in social-welfare policy, has begun to extend elements of compulsion to eighteen years. Also, as the frontier of compulsion has advanced, so the emphasis on differentiated provision (i.e. streaming and allied practices) has declined, first for eight- to twelve-year-olds, and later for twelve- to fourteen-year-olds. Especially since Dunning in 1977, the issue is now disputed for four-teen- to sixteen-year-olds. An accompanying change has been the extension of the goals of secondary education, beyond the narrowly academic for more able pupils, and beyond the narrowly vocational for less able pupils. This, too, has entailed a reduced emphasis on differentiated provision, essentially by assimilating less able pupils to the type of curriculum previously reserved for the able minority. Political argument since the mid-1970s has sometimes questioned schooling's reduced emphasis on differentiation. But the extension of the institutional scope of schooling has not been seriously challenged.

The extended scope of schooling might seem to imply an extension in the power of the central Department. In one respect, however, it has severely reduced governmental options. Because the extension of scope has been accompanied by a reduction in differentiation (i.e. a greater equality of provision), it has reduced the moral degrees of freedom government enjoys. It is less easy now for the Department, should it so wish, to distribute scarce resources differentially by tolerating a raw deal for women teachers, or for schools in the West, or for less able pupils, or for poorer neighbourhoods. Deepening resource constraints emphasise the dilemma government has faced with the loss of a unifying ideology to legitimate differential provision. An increasing emphasis on managerial efficiency in the use of resources is as much a response to this ideological loss as a response to recession. So too are attempts to establish the principle of consumer choice as an alternative basis for the selective allocation of scarce resources. Both responses were in evidence in Scotland in the 1980s, though the latter owed much to English influence on Scottish educational policy, and little to the preference of the SED itself (Adler, Petch and Tweedie 1987).

The emphasis on managerial efficiency is also, of course, a response to education's increasing share of national expenditure up to the mid-1970s, and to the increasing proportion of that share borne by central government up to that time. This is the second change of importance, but again one with mixed implications. On the one hand, the Department has continued to increase its financial control. On the other hand, it has found itself more constrained by controls exercised by an increasingly federal Scottish Office, itself acting within a managerial regime imposed by the Treasury and the Cabinet. The Inspectorate, in particular, has lost autonomy, and has found its expense-generating activities subject to repeated scrutiny.

Nevertheless, the Department, as we have said, has moved from a regulatory to a promotional stance. This is the third change of consequence. The Department is better organised to initiate and guide change, and readier to attempt it. This has required it to reorganise internally, to develop a network of national non-Departmental bodies, and to support moves towards larger and more powerful local authorities. Indeed, it supported this aspect of partnership from the outset, welcoming the *ad hoc* authorities that replaced the School Boards in 1918, and the *ad omnia* authorities that replaced them in 1929. After 1945, however, the Department continued to doubt the competence of local government, its ability to plan for education in the broader local setting, and its willingness to act in concert, for example over the distribution of teachers. In the 1960s, the Department's strategy was to argue for larger education authorities. Its hope was that it could devolve to them much more of the detail of finance and planning, whilst exercising controls that were more effective, but less demanding of the Department's time. In building, the control of borrowing for capital expenditure became more important. In staffing, the new mechanism was a centrally determined standard of local staffing needs. Allied to this were moves, as Rodger put it, to get the Department's influence in earlier, with both the local authorities and the non-Departmental bodies.

Again, however, the implications of the Department's promotionalism are not straightforward. In Strathclyde Region, the Department got a larger local authority than it had wanted, and one that might easily take a yard from any inch the centre let out. If this made the SED think twice about encouraging local initiative, so too did the constraints on spending that central government began to impose, with increasing severity, shortly after regionalisation. However, though far from trivial, these limits to the Department's ability to exploit the new arrangements were only contingent or circumstantial. Other limitations were more fundamental. A promotional stance implied a greater dependence on the outside agencies through which the Department would work. But, if they were to be given a longer leash, there would need to be a greater consensus than hitherto over the direction in which they were pulling. Such a consensus was no longer provided by the Scottish myth and the Kirriemuir career. Instead, the Department became yet more dependent on the potential of national certification to supply a universal motivation for pupils and teachers, and to reconcile conflicting educational purposes. Any limit to this potential was a limit to the power of the Department to meet its enhanced commitment; hence, one might argue, the protracted attempt to reconstruct a consensus after 1974 in the negotiation and development of the Standard Grade. Hence, too, the growing emphasis on implanting management techniques and organisation at all levels of the system as a way of fostering common understandings.

One further aspect of the Department's promotionalism may be mentioned. The number of secondary schools was reduced, average school size was increased, and provision became more standard. A trend towards larger and more standardised units of service delivery has not been confined to the educational sector of social policy. In part, it is a consequence of a general attempt to manage public expenditure better. In education, this has seen a halving in the number of secondary schools since 1945 and, from the 1970s, the determination of their staffing entitlement by a single national formula. Comprehensive reorganisation and the spread of the certificated curriculum have strengthened these trends. Again, however, their implications are mixed. On the one hand, larger and more standardised units may be more easily managed from the centre. On the other hand, they may enhance the collective awareness of teachers and their own possibilities for common action. Witness the negotiation of the national teachers' contract in 1975, and the question of its renegotiation after the industrial dispute in the schools some ten years later.

Schooling, then, has extended its institutional and normative scope, reduced the differentiation of its provision, and delivered its product in larger and more standardised units. The central authority has become more promotional and has increased its control of expenditure. Yet, as we say, none of these changes points unambiguously to an increase in the power of the Department to effect the changes it seeks throughout the system. Such an ability, it may be recalled (chapter 2, note 5), was Archer's criterion of centralisation. How, then, are these changes to be construed?

One way that might be tried is in terms of the two models of pluralism distinguished in chapter 1. One model is characterised by the mutual orientation of participants to a single system wherein groups' interests are negotiated at national level. The other model is characterised by the dispersion of centres of decision-making, and by the relative weakness of mutual orientations among the principal agents, so much so that the notion of a single national system might itself be disputed. Now, there is a sense in which both models were in evidence up to the 1960s, the former especially in the area of senior-secondary education, the latter in the lower-status areas of junior-secondary and further education. The national system was normatively articulated around the myth of the lad o' pairts, and this ideology, together with the Kirriemuir career, shaped the interests it served. There were large areas of lower-status education, however, that it did not touch, and could not mobilise. Schooling started to extend its scope in the early 1960s, however, and to incorporate, in the national system, schools, pupils and teachers that had hitherto been of lesser account. New agencies of change were created, and mutual orientations among all agencies increased. One might say, in other words, that areas of dispersed pluralism were displaced by a pluralism that was increasingly coordinated. This mutual articulation of participants is close to what Archer means by the term 'systematisation' and, as she says, it is to be analytically distinguished from centralisation. Such a trend would not imply that the centre necessarily gets its own way, but only that the stakes are higher. There is the possibility of effecting extensive change, but there is also the possibility of meeting extensive opposition.

Change in a Wider Perspective

To say this, however, is still to leave much unsaid about the stability of any emergent change, and about its implications in the longer term. Here a wider historical perspective is useful. We have represented the emergence of the modern system of public education in Scotland in terms of a continuing conflict between an 'open' and a 'closed' social ideal, played out against a backdrop of urbanisation and social-class differentiation. Central government has periodically attempted to systematise the resultant structures in the light of its own ideas of social and governmental efficiency, but has been hampered for extended periods by economic recession. On occasions the conflict has visibly shaken the Department, in the last decades of the nineteenth century, again in the 1920s, and in the 1960s once again. Is there any reason to think that this latest occasion will remain the last?

The conflict between the open and the closed ideal has been fought most keenly at the moving frontier of new provision. From the 1880s to the 1920s, it was contested for twelve- to fourteen-year-olds; and in the 1950s and 1960s, for fourteen- to sixteen-year-olds. Its subsequent shift to the sixteen- to eighteen-year stage would probably have continued whether or not recession and youth unemployment had deepened. But the pace of change has quickened. Since the early 1960s, policy and provision for sixteen- to eighteen-year-olds have recapitulated in a mere twenty years a process of systematisation that had earlier taken many decades more to unfold in relation to post-primary schooling. The quickening pace of change is possibly to be explained by the fact that government itself is learning how to systematise and promote. It is older and, in some respects wiser.

If the conflict has rolled through to the gates of higher education, what are the implications for the less dispersed model that may now be emerging in its wake in the secondary sector? How stable is the new configuration, and how different from the old? First of all, it may be doubted whether a national certificate can adequately adjudicate values and supply incentives now that certification is universal. The motivating power of the certificate depended upon its scarcity and singularity (the 'Holy of Holies'). Logically it cannot serve the universal and plural purposes envisaged under the Standard Grade reform. Moreover, now that the conflict over forms of provision has moved to the post-compulsory period, there is a greater potential for conflict between the Department and the one sector of public education not directly accountable to it, namely the universities. A century ago, the Department harnessed to its own purposes the power of the universities over certification and the distribution of life chances. Its subsequent use of this power depended on a national consensus over the unitary purpose of certification, namely to serve the lad o' pairts. In the contemporary context of universal certification this consensus can no longer be assumed. This is not to deny that lower levels of certification have achieved a social value in the 1970s and 1980s by virtue of their use by employers. For the most part, however, employers are less concerned with the specific contents and skills attested by certificates, than they are with their holders' positions in an overall hierarchy of attainment. Whether that hierarchy would cohere without a link between certification and higher education is doubtful. Witness the repeated failure of attempts to certificate junior-secondary school leavers with locally awarded certificates. Again, if the M S C's training schemes were to become a major means of distributing access to differentially favoured jobs and training, the potential of the Standard Grade to motivate pupils and teachers could be severely reduced, unless, of course, the Standard Grade itself screened access to different types of M S C scheme. Control of certification is thus a central issue.

Demands for vocational relevance in the secondary curriculum highlight the dilemma posed by the plurality of demands on certification at sixteen. The S E D's increased dependence on certification as a means of control in the 1960s and 1970s contributed to the displacement of vocational alternatives. So, too, did the concessions that teachers won in gaining admission to the C C C, in excluding further-education colleges from a significant role in secondary education, and in securing Munn's endorsement for a subject-based, non-vocational curriculum. It was not surprising, therefore, that Scotland did not initially participate in the M S C's moves to reintroduce vocational education with its Technical and Vocational Education Initiative (T V E I) of 1983. That decision was subsequently reversed, and T V E I is now to sit alongside Standard Grade. Early indications suggest that it might well be assimilated to the existing philosophy of general education, and might not radically change the structure of the curriculum. If T V E I is not assimilated, however, it would entail either an extension of the plurality of purposes that a universal school certificate must comprehend, or else greater differentiation of provision in the later compulsory stages, and more selection of pupils. Thus there is potential here for a return to something like the old bipartism beginning, not at twelve, but at fourteen years.

As school rolls fall, changes in the institutional organisation of schooling could hasten such a return. The pre-1965 senior-secondary sector (the first- and second-generation schools) served communities where the demand for post-compulsory schooling tended to be high. Now almost entirely comprehensive, the schools in this sector have tended to maintain higher rolls than otherwise because their post-compulsory enrolments have tended to remain high relative to other schools. There has been better provision, especially for fifth and sixth year. In urban areas this advantage has attracted pupils from other catchments. Certificate examination results have also tended to be better for pupils of all abilities in the older schools, and links to higher education stronger in consequence. Such schools are less likely, therefore, to be open to change than the third-generation schools, i.e. those that developed their post-compulsory provision only after 1965. Many such schools are at risk of reverting in effect to four-year status.

The emerging differentiation of schools by community is not new. It goes back to the nineteenth-century failure to adapt the public system to the urbanisation of the population, to the differentiation of school and community by social class, and to the shift of the population to the West. It also owes something to the Department's thinking, at the beginning of this century, on the educability of local communities and the level of school provision they merited. Nevertheless, the effects of two decades of comprehensive reorganisation cannot be discounted. The salaries, conditions and roles of teachers are more standardised, and are likely to breed resistance to differential treatment for schools, for levels of pupil ability, and for areas of curriculum. This has been the thrust of teacher politics at national level since 1918 at least. Local communities, too, have a greater expectation of formal parity of provision, which is one reason why neither the SED nor the local authorities have been quick to grasp the nettle of secondary-school closure. Also, the Standard Grade, a national certificate for all pupils, is itself one outcome of the comprehensive drive towards parity of provision and esteem, and it further institutionalises a norm of universalism in provision.

The Corporatist Thesis

In the argument so far we have distinguished between the increased political assertiveness of governments' policies for education, and a wider process of institutional change. The increase in political assertiveness started in the 1960s and strengthened in the 1970s, whereas the processes of systematisation and standardisation began earlier, and had yet deeper historical roots. We have tentatively described this institutional change in terms of the displacement of a dispersed pluralism by a pluralism of a more coordinated or systematic character; and we have argued that its implications for the power of the centre are mixed. It has probably reduced the potential of dispersed agencies to sustain local change and variety, and it has increased the potential of central government to effect the changes it seeks throughout the system. But this enhancement of the central potential is limited in a number of ways. These include the enhanced potential of other groups to resist change; the reduction in the variety of moral options available to the centre; and the wider governmental scrutiny to which the educational centre is now exposed. Thus a more coordinated pluralism might, on occasion, multiply the consequences of increased central political assertion, and thereby effect widespread change. But the very fact of increased political assertiveness is itself an indication that the central authority remains dissatisfied with the direction and governability of the changing system. This is precisely what some pluralist writers assert. But it is this very prospect of ungovernability that leads corporatist writers to suggest that pluralism's inherent instability and lack of adaptive capacity oblige government to improve its strategies of control. It is to this and other contentions of corporatist theory that we now turn.

The previous chapter has already assessed the significance of the Department's manipulation of individuals and bodies in the policy community. Our conclusion was that the Department's attempts to perfect this aspect of corporatism between the mid-1950s and the mid-1970s made it increasingly conscious of the limits to this strategy, especially for a Department that was becoming more promotional and more subject to changes in political control. The scope of the policy community was too limited, its links to other policy communities too tenuous, its constitution too traditional, its pace of reconstitution too slow, and its dependence on the centre too great. A succession of financial and administrative changes, starting in 1958, testify to government's attempts to find better means of non-executant promotion and control, and means that did not give the Inspectorate and other professional educationists their head.

But what has been the impact on the educational policy community of changes since the early 1970s? One view might be that the policy community was a temporary creation of a period of transition, from dispersed to coordinated pluralism, or from Departmental autocracy towards a more complex system of corporatist bargaining. Another possibility is that the generation that was raised in the inter-war years, and that moved into positions of leadership in the 1950s and 1960s, shared a set of beliefs and experiences that made possible a community of policy-makers, but that this 'assumptive world' was historically unique to that generation, and will not be repeated among subsequent leaders. A third view is that the importance of the policy community has diminished, and that it was a creation of the brief years of expansion, receding with recession as the influence of the Treasury increased. Indeed, several British developments since the mid-1970s suggest that government can, in principle, displace its partners by direct rule, or override them through law (Ranson 1985b). This implies the attrition of the trust that underpinned the legislative settlement of the mid-1940s.

Whilst each of these possibilities is plausible, we do not think that, individually or collectively, they indicate the end of the educational policy community in Scotland. Our first reason for saying this is deductive. We have argued that the policy community has been necessary to the solution of practical problems posed by logical contradictions, and discontinuities in the theory of representative democracy. We believe that this theory still informs British politics and administration, though we acknowledge that we may be wrong. Nevertheless, because we believe this, and because we do not see evidence of new solutions to these contradictions we infer that a policy community still functions, in some shape or form, and to some purpose or other.

Furthermore, a number of the structural changes that we have discerned since the mid-1960s might be seen as predisposing or supporting conditions for a new form of policy community in the 1980s and after. These conditions include the reduction in the number of secondary schools; the post-1965 presumption, increasingly realised in practice, that all schools are equal parts of a national system; and the increased standardisation of secondary provision. They also include the creation of management structures within each school; the spread of certification providing national criteria for the evaluation of schools, managers and teachers; the presence of the Inspectorate at the increasing number of points of articulation in the system; and the Inspectorate's omnipresence in the development and implementation of certificate reform at sixteen years. The relative decline in teachers' salaries, and the diminished prospects of promotion since the restructuring of the early 1970s, have also increased the importance of the national arena, and this will be maintained in the longer term by the contraction of the secondary-school sector, and by the introduction of short-term contracts in several sectors.

But what form of policy community might be sustained by these conditions? How does one interpret the extension and standardisation of an arena of national activity over which government exercises considerable patronage and control? Perhaps this 'designer pluralism' is corporatism by another name. Again, however, this would be a judgement that elided the system's potential for corporatism with its achievement. Nor is this potential solely corporatist. Extension and standardisation also have a diversifying potential insofar as they were intended to reach schools, communities and groups that had previously been accorded an inferior status in the national system. Thus the hold of the Kirriemuir schools over the membership and thinking of the policy community weakened in the 1970s, thereby undermining the social basis of the assumptive world that senior members of the Inspectorate shared with influential educationists outside. Within government, too, the process of diversification was extended. Recruitment to senior administrative positions had long since been detached from a traditional Inspectorate route. Now the Inspectorate was itself diversifying as it recruited new inspectors from colleges of education and further education. The widening governmental context for education in the 1970s brought further variety to the backgrounds and assumptions of those involved in shaping educational policy.

To sustain a corporatist interpretation of these changes, one would have to show that the enlarged and diversified group now influencing decisions shared an identity of purpose, with government and across it. We have established how this happened in the case of the Kirriemuir career. But we have no evidence of comparable status for the last decade. Humes (1986) argues that the 'leadership class' in Scottish education is united in self-serving submission to patronage and power. But he gives little attention to the substance of policies and, like us, he lacks direct evidence on policy-makers' beliefs and intentions in recent years.

Conclusion

Judging from the outside, however, we doubt that the policy community has found a new identity of purpose and belief to replace the waning Kirriemuir career. The indications point, instead, to conflict, diversity and change; to a painstakingly constructed consensus that yet proved too fragile to sustain the implementation of new policies; to forced departures in policy whose progenitors hoped to build consensus on their way. The protracted consultations by Munn and Dunning did not produce a policy for certification that was persuasive either to politicians or to administrators in central government. In the course of their further development and early implementation, the committees' proposals were greatly altered. Later, teachers proved to be unreliable instruments for translating policy into practice. They saw the implementation of Standard Grade as less a bargained process than an imposition, and, through long and bitter industrial action, they forced the Department, as well as pupils, to pay a heavy price for it. Nor was the principle of general education sufficiently well supported to resist the vocationalism of the MSC. In the post-compulsory sector the SED launched the Action Plan, not because there was agreement throughout education on what should be done, but because there was no agreement (Mack 1984). To be a member of the policy community after 1975 was not, we surmise, to embrace a corporate purpose and identity. The task, rather, was to accommodate the changes and discontinuities of principle that were a growing feature of the educational policy world. This is not to deny that the new vocationalism and the new managerialism constitute attempts at ideological reconstruction. But the new vocationalism is contested, and what is significant about the ideology of educationists as managers is its silence on questions of value. In the present, variegated, context of educational politics, to affirm values is to highlight dissensus, and thereby to put the basis for collective action at risk.

Thus, it is in the Action Plan, at the moving frontier of new provision, that we find policy in its ideologically most evasive form. Like the earlier Munn and Dunning reviews, the Action Plan was precipitated by competition between government agencies. Had the SED not acted, it would have conceded to the MSC significant and growing control over the post-compulsory curriculum in Scotland. At the same time, the Department's own control relied heavily on an SCE examination that was generalist in philosophy and ill-suited to the abilities of the majority of pupils in post-compulsory schooling. But the Department could not reform the SCE examination to head off the MSC without alienating the universities, whose recognition of it for admissions purposes gave the SCE its standing. The solution that the Department adopted was ingenious precisely because it managed not to formulate for decision the perennial questions of value that were at issue here: namely, what part of the curriculum should be vocationally related, and at what point in a stratified and selective system of education should it be situated? In the early 1960s the policy community could have delivered agreed an-

495

swers in no time at all, but not in the early 1980s.

The core of the Action Plan was the modularisation of the post-compulsory curriculum under a new national certificate awarded by a body that was ultimately controlled by the SED. In theory, modules could be acquired by any consumer, in any number and order, in any institution, and for any purpose. To an economy-minded Government devoted to a philosophy of limited state intervention, the attractions of modularisation were, first, that it made for efficient service delivery and, second, that it obviated the need for an explicit and public resolution of conflicting priorities. Modules were to make all things possible.

In practice, of course, there was a variety of institutional constraints on individuals' access to modules, deriving especially from the demands of employers and other selectors. One that soon became apparent was the refusal of the universities to countenance swift and radical change in the SCE. The Department did not press the issue, nor the proposal to unify all post-compulsory certification under a single examining body. Meanwhile, in the Scottish Tertiary Education Advisory Council (STEAC) which reported in 1985, the Department had helped to appoint a body that was prepared to recommend that ultimate funding responsibility for the Scottish universities be passed from the DES to the SED. Had this happened, the SED could have exerted more pressure on the universities to support its certification policies. In the event, a weaker form of devolution of control over the universities was decided. It gave the Secretary of State for Scotland a formal but limited role in a new funding body for all UK universities. What significance this change has for the Department's leverage over the Scottish universities remains to be seen. We speculate, however, that the SED urgently wishes to change the Scottish universities' attitude to its reforms of post-compulsory certification so as to allow it to mount a more coherent response to the incursions of the MSC. It may also wish to acquire from the Industry Department for Scotland formal responsibility over the activities of the MSC in Scotland, at least insofar as they relate to young people.

The SED had a further and equally urgent reason to seek control of the Scottish universities. This is because the Department faces a major loss of influence in non-university higher education from the late 1980s onwards, when the size of the school-leaving groups available for higher education start to decline. The cuts in university finance in the early 1980s led to considerable expansion in the non-university sector of higher education controlled by the Department, including the transfer of Napier College in Edinburgh from local-authority control to the status of a central institution under the SED. Nevertheless, the universities have continued to attract the more able students, on average, than other institutions of higher education. If, in the 1990s, the universities return their *de facto* admissions requirements to their pre-1981 levels in order to maintain student numbers that are planned in a British rather than a Scottish context, there could be a major contraction in the colleges controlled by the Department. This would directly undermine the Department's policies for further education, and weaken its control of the school curriculum before and after sixteen.

It is true that these conflicts have yet to be resolved, and true also that there are in Scotland perhaps fewer institutional impediments to a corporatist resolution than there are elsewhere in Britain. We have in mind here the relative ease with which Ministerial and departmental responsibilities for education, training and industry could be realigned within the Scottish Office. Also, there are signs that the ideology of Scottish egalitarianism is being refurbished in support of better articulation between the Standard Grade, the National Certificate and entry to higher education. If this or other arguments were to press the universities into recognising the new qualifications for admissions purposes, the SED would be greatly strengthened in its dealings with other bodies in central and local government. But this lies in the future, and we cannot say whether any government would allow a Scottish settlement of the place of vocational education and training in the curriculum to proceed irrespective of its implications for arrangements in England and Wales. Nor, from the arguments we have considered, is it obvious that a corporatist settlement of the issue would necessarily benefit dominant producer groups and militate against the interests of the disadvantaged.

Our argument so far suggests that a corporatist interpretation of the past decade would have to be one that did not assume the same degree of ideological unity that characterised the policy community until the 1970s. Such an interpretation might be developed along several lines. One would be to argue that the issues that have divided the policy community in recent years are trivial by comparison with the assumptions that unite it; that it is, for example, agreed on the principle of compulsion, on the extension of the scope of schooling, and on the extension and standardisation of national certification. In such an analysis, policy disputes over purposes could then be represented as a function of inter-agency disputes over the control of an extending national system. How vocational and non-vocational education were accommodated would be less important than the universal grading of pupils and students that carried with it the message that their ultimate station in life was a proper reflection of their individual worth.

A second line of argument would be that the extension and coordination of the national system that we have described was less important for what it was than for what it displaced; that a system, for example, in which an expanding policy community spent well over ten years talking about Munn and Dunning, was a system that had a diminishing potential to develop alternative ideas and practices, or to respond to new demands. Such arguments could, in turn, be linked to the demise of institutions, like the Advisory Council and an independent research council, where alternative thinking might coalesce, and also to the de-skilling that is implicit in the notion of teachers as managers of curriculum packages that others have produced.

A third approach would be to argue that the spread of certification had reduced the functional importance of the ideological unity of the policy community. Here the contrast would be between a bipartite system, where purposes were coordinated by explicit collective consent to the moral imperatives of the Scottish myth, and a comprehensive system, where the work of selecting pupils to different levels and types of course was done by a system of universal certification that left moral judgements implicit. Such an interpretation is attractive because it would accommodate both the intensity of current competition for the control of the principles of national certification, and the otherwise paradoxical fact that both the Munn and Dunning development programme and the Action Plan have avoided explicit discussion of what those principles were.

The array of corporatist arguments presents a sombre picture, though not a wholly convincing one. First, they are not easy to reconcile with the evidence that the reorganisation of the school system, initiated in the 1960s and completed in the 1970s, thereafter delivered education on a more equitable basis. A system in which disadvantaged pupils in the past decade have significantly improved their qualifications, relative to advantaged pupils, cannot be wholly explained by theories that stress the institutional bias of corporatism. Nor can one in which female pupils and Catholic pupils on average outperform their counterparts. These features, it is true, are in part the fruits of an earlier political assertion that acquired much of its impetus from outwith the Scottish policy world. But they do indicate that the aspirations of social democracy in the 1950s and 1960s were not wholly unrealistic. Moreover, our analysis suggests that a corporatist settlement along the lines just outlined would itself be vulnerable to the very conflicts and instabilities that had prompted its emergence. For a government to maintain stable policies in these circumstances without recourse to political assertion would, we suggest, require a policy world that had much of the material and ideological coherence of the Kirriemuir career. That such a world is emerging, or will shortly emerge, seems to us less probable than a scenario of continuing conflict over educational opportunities and purposes, settled as often by compromise or by explicit political assertion, as by corporatist collusion or deception. That political assertion matters is a lesson that was learned in the 1960s, and learned again in the 1980s. Its application in the 1960s to the open ideal, and in the 1980s to the closed ideal, have been matters of political preference. But, either way, the implications for human agency are far from pessimistic.

Is This How It Really Is?

Finally, a comment is necessary on the logical status of our conclusions. We opened this book with a practising politician talking about his difficulty in explaining how the educational system worked. We close it acknowledging our own. No doubt we could have helped ourselves by producing better evidence and clearer arguments. But the fact that we share our difficulty with someone who had familiarised himself with the system for a total of nine years as Minister indicates that the problem of understanding the system is common to politics and *academe* alike, and is not simply a consequence of limited information or of a misplaced attempt on our part to 'turn familiar events into theoretical fodder'. It is the familiar itself that is problematic, both for practice and for theory, and it is the problem of the familiar that makes the arbitration of competing explanations difficult, and intrinsically political.

The assumptive world of the educational policy community was deeply persuasive to those who shared in it. It ordered their understanding of the nature of Scotland and the schools that served it, and it did this by ordering their sense of themselves and the service they could give. Their socialisation to a common identity was part of a wider process of sorting and selection by which the policy community was constituted, making the world of practice possible, and with it the reproduction of a social order. Without a sense of self within a common order, the world of immediate experience lay 'beyond validation and understanding'. By entering into this sense, one became 'busy, but blind'. In other words, Silver's statement of the problem of history and theory (see chapter 1) applies no less to the everyday world of policy and practice than to the attempts of *academe* to explain that world. People constructed histories and theories of the world in order that they could act in it and on it, and respond to the ways that it acted on them. These representations of the world structured the ways in which it was experienced. But they were, nevertheless, arbitrary. They were highly selective, being blind to much, leaving much unseen. Also, they were inescapably evaluative.

We have found it helpful to characterise these representations of the world as myths, as stories that people tell about themselves to celebrate values and explain experience. The main story we have analysed is that of a democratic society that looked to great men at the centre to implement an egalitarian system of national education. But the same type of analysis applies no less to the idea of the educational system as the product of partners in a common enterprise. In both the centralisation and the partnership models, we find a symbiosis of fact and value, a theory supported by data it has helped to create, and a tradition constructed through the selective reinterpretation of the past. The same is broadly true, we think, of the higher-order stories told by pluralist and corporatist theory. What ultimately makes the arbitration of all these explanations difficult is not paucity of evidence, nor conceptual overload, but the disputed nature of the reality that the theories claim to represent, and the value judgements that inevitably they incorporate.

There was, after all, a dark side to the Scottish myth. Being selective and arbitrary, its construction of social reality was constructive for some, but destructive for others. This is evident enough of a representation of Scotland that excluded Glasgow, or of a representation of true 'pairts' that excluded seven pupils out of ten. It is perhaps less evident in the way that other constructs were built into the social order, those, for example, of 'teacher', 'education', 'expert', 'professional', 'policy' and 'practice'. Nevertheless, the dominant definitions of all of these were disputed at some point in the four decades we have reviewed. So, also, was the notion of representation itself, the notion through which the constructs of the social order were articulated with the formal procedures of representative democracy. We see this articulation as crucial to the resolution of disputes over the familiar. Judging whether or not a group is representative requires a prior judgement about the reality of the society that awaits representation. It is no accident, therefore, that the idea of 'representation' has reference both to political procedures and to social explanation. The adequacy of procedures for political accountability is, we think, intimately related to the adequacy of social accounts.

Most people in education in the past decade have felt the ground of the familiar shifting under their feet. To them at least, sociology's assertion of the contingent and arbitrary nature of the everyday will be plausible and also, we think, welcome, because one's understanding of how it really was no longer serves one well in understanding how it really is. What many people will find more difficult to accept, however, are the apparent implications of this position for social explanation and political practice. If all that social explanation can offer is an assertion of the irreconcilability of discrete experience, one is left only with coercion or deception as the basis for social order, or else with no order at all.

We do not, however, think that these are the only possibilities. With two of our colleagues we have elsewhere offered an alternative view (Gray *et al.*, 1983, ch.17), and we will not repeat our reasons in detail here. The heart of the argument, however, is the affinity we have remarked between representation as political procedure and representation as explanation and portrayal. An adequate social account is constructed only through attempts to open one's eyes to all groups and experience. Similarly, democratic accountability leaves no-one out of account. Social explanation and political accountability share the norm of universality, and this can be achieved only through procedural agreements. It is these agreements that make possible non-arbitrary empirical representations of reality, but that also guarantee their endless negotiability. To argue this is not to say that common definitions cannot be agreed as a preliminary to empirical evaluation, nor, conversely, to say that social accounts are value-free. Nor, in particular, is it to assume that governments always behave rationally and accountably. Indeed, there are powerful reasons why they often do not. But it is to argue that, in a society where a government's *claim* to legitimacy is that it is behaving rationally and accountably, a set of procedural rules can in principle be identified for the negotiation of disputes about what is happening in the world. The dialogue of this book is a small part of the wider dialogue indicated by this argument.

To seek explanations, as we have done, from those who took decisions, is part of the cure for ignorance. But it is also to risk a special sort of ignorance, for the policy community was structured in ways that filtered and refracted its sense of Scotland's experience, and systematically misrepresented it thereby. Its shared sense of the world, its common sense, was morally contestable and descriptively incomplete. To say this is not to impute wilful distortion to individuals, nor to arrogate to *academe* an unbridled authority to adjudicate conflicting values or conflicting claims about reality. It is simply to recognise that the norms of social science and the norms of representative democracy share the common enterprise of improving the public account. By this criterion the dialogue of the educational policy community in Scotland was deficient. Its sense of the familiar was partial, and was achieved at the cost of that other, wider, familiarity that universality entails. The essential point to grasp, however, is that the policy community's own account of the world, sustained though it was through myth, could be rationally engaged by means of the very terms on which the community's claim to legitimacy was based. The democratic intellect logically required that the common sense of the policy community be fed by a sense that was more authentically common, in that it had survived a wider critical scrutiny than was allowed by the procedures for accountability then extant.

Where a department never explains, and is never obliged to explain, the prospects for explanation and accountability are bleak. But, where a department or a government has to explain in order to govern, there is at least a prospect of improvement in explanation and in governability alike. History and myth, policy and practice: the democratic intellect was all of these, and is so still.

Appendix 1

Persons Interviewed

We list only the main positions that are relevant to this book.

Attributable Interviews

Brunton, John S. HMSCI 1955-66; previously Assistant Secretary, SED. CCC; NCTT; SCEEB; SCRE; SCTT; ACES Committee on the Post-Fourth Year Examination Structure in Scotland; ACES Committee on Transfer from Primary to Secondary Education; GTC Working Party on the Training of Graduates for Secondary Education; Working Party on Consultation between the Teachers' Associations and the Scottish Education Department on Educational Matters; Working Party on the Curriculum of the Senior Secondary School; Working Party on the Linkage of Secondary and Further Education (the Brunton report). Interviewed by the authors, August 1976.

Bryden, Gilbert S. General Secretary, EIS 1961-74. NJC; SCRE; STSC; Committee on the Teaching Profession in Scotland (the Wheatley report); Committee on the Supply of Teachers in Scotland; Committee on the Distribution of Teachers in Scotland (the Roberts report); Working Party on Pensions for Widows, Widowers, Children and other Dependents of Teachers in Scotland. Interviewed by the authors, May 1977.

Clark, James R. Director of Education, Aberdeen 1956-75. ADES; CCC; GTC; SCEEB; SCRE; SCTT; STSC; Committee on the Teaching Profession in Scotland (the Wheatley report); Committee on Truancy and Indiscipline in Schools in Scotland (the Pack report). Interviewed by the authors, May 1977.

Cunningham, Sir Charles C. Secretary, SHD 1948-57. Interviewed by Anthony Seldon, May 1980.

Dewar, Dr William McL. Headmaster, George Heriot's School 1947-70. Governor, Moray House College of Education; SCEEB; SCRE; SCTT; SSTA; ACES Committee on the Post-Fourth Year Examination Structure in Scotland; ACES Committee on Transfer from Primary to Secondary Education; Working Party on the Curriculum of the Senior Secondary School. Interviewed by the authors, June 1976.

Dickson, Dr David HMSCI 1966-69. CCC; GTC; SCEEB; SCRE; Junior Secondary report; Working Party on the Linkage of Secondary and Further Education (the Brunton report); Working Party on Appointments to Teaching Posts, Conditions of Tenure of these Posts, and Arrangements for Consultation between Education Authorities and Teachers. Interviewed by the authors, June 1977.

Graham, Sir Norman W. Secretary, SED 1964-73. CCC. Interviewed by the authors, May 1977.

Gray, George D. Registrar, GTC 1966-72; previously Secretary, SCTT. SCRE; SSTA; GTC Working Party on the Training of Graduates for Secondary Education; Committee on the Supply of Teachers in Scotland. Interviewed by the authors, October 1976.

McEwan, John S. Director of Education, Lanarkshire 1950-75. GTC; SCTT; ACES Committee on the Post-Fourth Year Examination Structure in Scotland; ACES Committee on Transfer from Primary to Secondary Education; Committee on the Teaching Profession in Scotland (the Wheatley report). Interviewed by the authors, August 1977.

Millan, The Rt Hon. Bruce, MP Secretary of State for Scotland 1976-79; previously Parliamentary Under-Secretary of State for Scotland, and Minister of State, Scottish Office. Interviewed by the authors, March 1980; interviewed by Robert Bell, October 1973.

Murrie, Sir William S. Secretary, SED 1952-57; later Permanent Under-Secretary of State, Scottish Office. Interviewed by the authors, January 1977.

Robertson, Sir James J. Rector, Aberdeen Grammar School 1942-59. ACES; EIS; SCRE; SSTA; SCTT; ACES Committee on Measures to Improve the Supply of Teachers in Scotland (the Knox report); ACES Committee on the Post-Fourth Year Examination Structure in Scotland; ACES Committee on Transfer from Primary to Secondary Education. Interviewed by Esmond Wright, April 1962.

Rodger, Allan G. Under-Secretary, SED 1959-63; previously HMI, and Assistant Secretary, SED. NCTT; SCTT; ACES Committee on Measures to Improve the Supply of Teachers in Scotland (the Knox report); Committee on the Supply of Teachers of Mathematics and Science in Scotland (the Appleton report); Committee on the Supply of Teachers in Scotland; Committee on the Teaching Profession in Scotland (the Wheatley report); Ministry of Works Committee on School Buildings for Scotland. Interviewed by the authors, December 1977.

Walker, Dr David D. Director, SCRE 1958-70; previously Depute Director of Education, Fife. Interviewed by the authors, September 1976.

Wood, Sir Henry P. Principal, Jordanhill College of Education 1949-71. CP; GTC; NCTT; SCEEB; SCTT; ACES Committee on Measures to Improve the Supply of Teachers in Scotland (the Knox report); GTC Working Party on the Training of Graduates for Secondary Education; Committee on the Supply of Teachers of Mathematics and Science in Scotland (the Appleton report); Committee on the Teaching Profession in Scotland (the Wheatley report). Interviewed by the authors, September 1976

Appendix 1

Unattributable Interviews Conducted by the Authors

Dunning, Joseph Principal, Napier College of Commerce and Technology 1963-81. SCRE; Committee to Review Assessment in the Third and Fourth Years of Secondary Education in Scotland (the Dunning report). Interviewed October 1983.

Eadie, Alexander, MP Chairman, Fife Education Committee 1963-65. SCRE. Interviewed August 1977.

Fletcher, Sir Alexander MacP., MP Parliamentary Under-Secretary of State, Scottish Office 1979-83. Interviewed December 1983.

McIntosh, Dr Douglas M. Principal, Moray House College of Education 1966-74; previously Director of Education, Fife. CCC; CP; SCEEB; SCRE; SCTT; ACES Committee on Measures to Improve the Supply of Teachers in Scotland (the Knox report); ACES Committee on the Post-Fourth Year Examination Structure in Scotland; ACES Committee on Transfer from Primary to Secondary Education; Committee on the Teaching Profession in Scotland (the Wheatley report). Interviewed June 1977.

Macintosh, Farquhar Rector, Royal High School (Edinburgh) 1972 to the present. Governor, Jordanhill College of Education; SCEEB. Interviewed October 1983.

Middleton, Robert Convener, Aberdeen Education Committee 1966-69. Interviewed June 1977.

Morris, J. G. (Ian) HMCI 1973-83. SCRE. Interviewed February 1984.

Munn, Sir James Rector, Cathkin High School 1970-83; later Chairman, MSC (Scotland). CCC; Committee on the Structure of the Curriculum in the Third and Fourth Years of the Scottish Secondary School (the Munn report). Interviewed November 1983.

Nisbet, John D. Professor of Education, Aberdeen University 1963 to the present. CCC; GTC; SCRE. Interviewed November 1983.

Reith, Dr George Director of Education, Edinburgh 1961-72. CCC; SCEEB; SCRE. Interviewed November 1976.

Robertson, David G. Director of Education, Tayside 1975 to the present; previously Director of Education, Dundee. SCRE. Interviewed December 1983.

Walls, The Rev. Professor Andrew F. Aberdeen Education Committee 1971-74. Interviewed June 1977.

Appendix 2

Abbreviations

ACE: Advisory Council on Education
ACES: Advisory Council on Education in Scotland
ADES: Association of Directors of Education in Scotland
AEAS: Association of Education Authorities in Scotland
BE: Board of Education
BOAPAH: British Oral Archive of Political and Administrative History
CC: Commission on the Constitution
CCC: Consultative Committee on the Curriculum
CCCS: Centre for Contemporary Cultural Studies
CCEM: Consultative Committee on Educational Matters
CCES: Committee of Council on Education in Scotland
CCS: Committee on the Civil Service
CDTS: Committee on the Distribution of Teachers in Scotland
CES: Centre for Educational Sociology
CHE: Committee on Higher Education
CI: Committee of Inquiry
CLASP: Consortium of Local Authorities Special Programme
CLGF: Committee on Local Government Finance
CMRST: Committee on Manpower Resources for Science and Technology
COSLA: Convention of Scottish Local Authorities
CP: Committee of Principals
CPCMM: Committee of Privy Counsellors on Ministerial Memoirs
CSA: Committee on Scottish Administration
CSE: Certificate of Secondary Education
CSP: Council for Scientific Policy
CSYS: Certificate of Sixth Year Studies
DAFS: Department of Agriculture and Fisheries for Scotland
DCOSA: Departmental Committee on Section 2 of the Official Secrets Act
      1911
DES: Department of Education and Science
EIS: Educational Institute of Scotland
GCE: General Certificate of Education
GSS: Government Statistical Service
GTC: General Teaching Council
HMCI: His/Her Majesty's Chief Inspector
HMI: His/Her Majesty's Inspector
HMSCI: His/Her Majesty's Senior Chief Inspector
HMSO: His/Her Majesty's Stationery Office
HO: Home Office
HORSA: Hutting Operation for the Raising of the School-Leaving Age
IDS: Industry Department for Scotland
JCC: Joint Committee of Colleges

505

LCC: Lanarkshire County Council
LEA: Local Education Authority
LPSC: Labour Party Scottish Council
ME: Ministry of Education
MHLG: Ministry of Housing and Local Government
MSC: Manpower Services Commission
MW: Ministry of Works
NAS: National Association of Schoolmasters
NBPI: National Board for Prices and Incomes
NCTT: National Committee for the Training of Teachers
NJC: National Joint Council
OECD: Organisation for Economic Co-operation and Development
P1, P2 etc.: first year of primary school, second year etc.
PD: Parliamentary Debates
PESC: Public Expenditure Survey Committee
RCLGS: Royal Commission on Local Government in Scotland
RCSA: Royal Commission on Scottish Affairs
RIPA: Royal Institute of Public Administration
ROSLA: Raising of the School-Leaving Age
SC: Select Committee
SCCMSTE: Scottish Central Committee for Mathematics, Science and Technical Education
s1, s2 etc.: first year of secondary school, second year etc.
SC(DI): Scottish Council (Development and Industry)
SCDS: Scottish Curriculum Development Service
SCE: Scottish Certificate of Education
SCEEB: Scottish Certificate of Education Examination Board
SCES: Select Committee on Education and Science
SCI: Senior Chief Inspector
SCPC: Standing Commission on Pay Comparability
SCRE: Scottish Council for Research in Education
SCSA: Select Committee on Scottish Affairs
SCTT: Scottish Council for the Training of Teachers
SDA: Scottish Development Agency
SDD: Scottish Development Department
SED: Scottish Education Department
SEJ: Scottish Educational Journal
SEPD: Scottish Economic Planning Department
SERC: Scottish Education Reform Committee
SHD: Scottish Home Department
SHHD: Scottish Home and Health Department
SI: Statutory Instruments
SIO: Scottish Information Office
SJC: Scottish Joint Council for Teachers' Salaries
SJNC: Scottish Joint Negotiating Committee
SLC: Scottish Leaving Certificate
SO: Scottish Office
SOMS: Scottish Office Management Services
SRO: Scottish Record Office
SSA: Scottish Schoolmasters' Association
SSRC: Social Science Research Council
SSS: Secretary of State for Scotland

SSTA: Scottish Secondary Teachers' Association
STEAC: Scottish Tertiary Education Advisory Council
STSC: Scottish Teachers' Salaries Committee
STSCC: Scottish Teachers' Service Conditions Committee
STUC: Scottish Trades Union Congress
SWSG: Social Work Services Group
TES: Times Educational Supplement
TESS: Times Educational Supplement (Scotland)
TVEI: Technical and Vocational Education Initiative
UGC: University Grants Committee
WO: Welsh Office
YTS: Youth Training Scheme

References

A list of abbreviations, including those used in the text to indicate authorship, is given in appendix 2.

Abrams, P. (1982) *Historical Sociology*, Shepton Mallet, Open Books.

Addison, P. (1975) *The Road to 1945*, London, Jonathan Cape.

Adler, M. E. (1986) *Parental choice in education: A study of Section 1 of the Education (Scotland) Act 1981*, final report to the Economic and Social Research Council on Project E00230036.

Adler, M. E. & Bondi, E. (forthcoming) 'Delegation and community participation: An alternative approach to the problems created by falling primary school rolls', in L. Bondi & M. H. Matthews (eds), *Education and Society: Studies in the Politics, Sociology and Geography of Education*, Beckenham, Croom Helm.

Adler, M. E., Petch, A. & Tweedie, J. (1987) 'The origins and impact of the Parents' Charter', in D. McCrone (ed.), *The Scottish Government Yearbook 1987*, Edinburgh, Unit for the Study of Government in Scotland.

Ahier, J. (1983) 'History and sociology of educational policy', in J. Ahier & M. Flude (eds), *Contemporary Education Policy*, London, Croom Helm.

Aldrich, R. & Leighton, P. (1985) *Education: Time for a New Act?*, Bedford Way Papers 23, London, University of London Institute of Education.

Allen, C. H. (1979) 'The study of Scottish politics: A bibliographical sermon', in H. M. Drucker & N. L. Drucker (eds), *The Scottish Government Yearbook 1980*, Edinburgh, Paul Harris.

Allen, D. (1984) 'Sixteen-to-eighteens in Scotland: An Action Plan', unpublished dissertation presented in part fulfilment of the M Ed degree, University of Edinburgh.

Anderson, P. (1980) *Arguments Within English Marxism*, London, Verso.

Anderson, R. (1983a) *Education and Opportunity in Victorian Scotland: Schools and Universities*, Oxford, Clarendon Press.

Anderson, R. (1983b) 'Education and the state in nineteenth century Scotland', *Economic History Review*, vol. XXXVI, 4, November, 518-34.

Anderson, R. (1985a) 'In search of the "Lad of Parts": The mythical history of Scottish education', *History Workshop*, no. 19, 82-104.

Anderson, R. (1985b) 'Scottish secondary schools and Scottish society in the nineteenth century', *Past and Present*, no. 109, 176-203.

Anderson, R. (1985c) 'Education and society in modern Scotland: A comparative perspective', *History of Education Quarterly*, vol. 25, no. 4, 459-81.

Anderson, R. (1986) 'Sociology and history: M. S. Archer's *The Social Origins of Educational Systems*', *Archives Européenes de Sociologie*, vol. XXVII, no. 1, 149-61.

Anderson, R. (1987) 'Democracy and intellect', *Cencrastus*, no. 25, Spring, 3-4.

Apple, M. W. (1982a) *Education and Power*, London, Routledge & Kegan Paul.

References

Apple, M. W. (1982b) *Cultural and Economic Reproduction in Education: Essays on Class, Ideology and the State*, London, Routledge & Kegan Paul.

Archer, M. S. (1979) *The Social Origins of Educational Systems*, Beverly Hills & London, Sage.

Archer, M. S. (1980) 'Sociology and comparative education: A reply to Edmund King', *Comparative Education*, vol.16, no.2, June, 179-85.

Archer, M. S. (1981) 'Educational politics: A model for their analysis', in P. Broadfoot, C. Brock & W. Tulasiewicz (eds), *Politics and Educational Change: An International Survey*, London, Croom Helm.

Archer, M. S. (1982) 'The theoretical problem of educational expansion', in M. S. Archer (ed.), *The Sociology of Educational Expansion: Take-off, Growth and Inflation in Educational Systems*, Beverly Hills & London, Sage.

Archer, M. S. (1983) 'Process without system', *Archives Européenes de Sociologie*, vol.xxiv, no.1, 196-221.

Archer, M. S. (1984) *The Social Origins of Educational Systems* (University edition), London, Beverly Hills & New Delhi, Sage.

Association of Directors of Education in Scotland (ADES) (1947) 'A special conference of the Association of Directors of Education in Scotland at the Playfair Hostel, Edinburgh, during the weekend from Friday 21st to Monday 24th March, 1947', unpublished mimeograph.

Association of Directors of Education in Scotland (n.d., about 1971) *The First Twenty-Five Years 1920-1945*, Edinburgh, ADES.

Association of Education Authorities in Scotland (AEAS) (1925a) 'Minute of Meeting of the Executive Committee 16 March 1921, and Appendix: Letter to the Secretary, Scottish Universities Entrance Board', in AEAS, *Minutes of Meetings May 1919 to May 1922*, Edinburgh, the Edinburgh Press.

Association of Education Authorities in Scotland (1925b) 'Minute of Meeting of the Executive Committee 15 March 1922', in AEAS, *Minutes of Meetings May 1919 to May 1922*, Edinburgh, the Edinburgh Press.

Bachrach, P. (1967) *The Theory of Democratic Elitism: A Critique*, Boston, Little, Brown & Co.

Bachrach, P. & Baratz, M. S. (1962) 'Two faces of power', *American Political Science Review*, vol.LVI, no.4, 947-52.

Bachrach, P. & Baratz, M. S. (1970) *Power and Poverty: Theory and Practice*, New York, Oxford University Press.

Banks, O. (1955) *Parity and Prestige in English Secondary Education: A Study in Educational Sociology*, London, Routledge & Kegan Paul.

Barker, A. (ed.) (1982) *Quangos in Britain: Government and the Networks of Public Policy-Making*, London, Macmillan.

Barker, R. (1972) *Education and Politics 1900-1951: A Study of the Labour Party*, Oxford, Clarendon Press.

Barnett, J. (1982) *Inside the Treasury*, London, Andre Deutsch.

Baron, S., Finn, D., Grant, N., Green, M. & Johnston, R. (1982) 'Silver foils: A reply', *British Journal of Sociology of Education*, vol.3, no.2, 189-97.

Barrie, J. M. (1938) *M'Connachie and J. M. B.*, London, Peter Davies.

Belford, A. J. (1946) *Centenary Handbook of the Educational Institute of Scotland*, Edinburgh, Educational Institute of Scotland.

Bell, R. E. (1975) 'Godfrey Thomson and Scottish education', paper presented at a conference of the British Educational Research Association, University of Stirling, unpublished mimeograph.

Bell, R. E. (1981) 'Institutions of educational government', Unit 8 of Course E200, *Contemporary Issues in Education*, Milton Keynes, Open University Press.

Bell, R. E. (1983) 'The education departments in the Scottish universities', in

References

W. M. Humes & H. M. Paterson (eds), *Scottish Culture and Scottish Education 1800-1980*, Edinburgh, John Donald.

Bell, R. E. (1986) 'Educational studies in the Scottish universities, 1870-1970', unpublished PhD thesis, Open University.

Bell, R. E., Fowler, G. & Little, K. (eds) (1973) *Education in Great Britain and Ireland: A Source Book*, London, Routledge & Kegan Paul.

Bell, R. E. & Grant, N. (1977) *Patterns of Education in the British Isles*, London, George Allen & Unwin.

Bell, R. E., MacKenzie, M. & Ozga, J. T. (1974) 'United Kingdom', Unit 4 of Course E221, *Decision Making in British Education Systems*, Milton Keynes, Open University Press.

Bell, R. E. & Prescott, W. (eds) (1975) *The Schools Council: A Second Look*, London, Ward Lock Educational.

Benn, C. & Simon, B. (1972) *Half Way There: Report on the British Comprehensive School Reform*, 2nd edn, Harmondsworth, Penguin.

Bernstein, B. (1967) 'Open schools, open society?', *New Society*, September 14.

Birch, A. H. (1971) *Representation*, London, Pall Mall.

Birnbaum, P. (1982) 'The state versus corporatism', *Politics and Society*, vol.11, no.4, 477-501.

Board of Education (BE) (1943) *Curriculum and Examinations in Secondary Schools: Report of the Committee of the Secondary Schools Examination Council*, London, HMSO (the Norwood report).

Bogdanor, V. (1979) 'Power and participation', *Oxford Review of Education*, vol.5, no.2, 157-68.

Boli, J., Ramirez, F. O. & Meyer, J. W. (1985) 'Explaining the origins and expansion of mass education', *Comparative Education Review*, vol.29, no.2, 145-70.

Bone, T. R. (ed.) (1967) *Studies in the History of Scottish Education 1872-1939*, London, University of London Press.

Bone, T. R. (1968) *School Inspection in Scotland 1840-1966*, London, University of London Press.

Bourdieu, P. (1977) (translator, R. Nice) *Outline of a Theory of Practice*, Cambridge, Cambridge University Press.

Bourdieu, P. & Passeron, J. C. (1970) *La Réproduction*, Paris, Les Editions de Minuit.

Bowles, S. & Gintis, H. (1976) *Schooling in Capitalist America: Educational Reform and the Contradictions of Economic Life*, London, Routledge & Kegan Paul.

Boyd, D. (1973) *Elites and Their Education*, Slough, NFER.

Boyd, W. (1921) *The History of Western Education*, London, Black.

Boyle, E. & Crosland, A. (1971) in conversation with M. Kogan, *The Politics of Education*, Harmondsworth, Penguin.

Boyle, L. (1966) *Equalisation and the Future of Local Government Finance*, Edinburgh & London, Oliver & Boyd.

Braverman, H. (1974) *Labor and Monopoly Capital*, New York, Monthly Review Press.

Brewer's (1981) *Dictionary of Phrase and Fable*, London, Cassell.

Briault, E. W. H. (1976) 'A distributed system of educational administration: An international viewpoint', *International Review of Education*, vol.XXII, no.4, 429-39.

Bridie, J. (1939) *One Way of Living*, London, Constable.

Bridie, J. & McLaren, M. (1949) *A Small Stir: Letters on the English*, London, Hollis & Carter.

References

Broadfoot, P. (1980) 'Assessment, curriculum and control in the changing pattern of central-local relations', *Local Government Studies*, vol.6, no.6, 57-68.

Broadfoot, P. (1986) 'Power relations and English education: The changing role of central government', *Journal of Education Policy*, vol.1, no.1, 53-62.

Brodie, A. W. (1972) 'Central manpower planning in Scottish secondary education', in Central Statistical Office, *Social Trends*, no.3, London, HMSO.

Brown, R. G. S. & Steel, D. R. (1979) *The Administrative Process in Britain*, 2nd edn, London, Methuen.

Brown, S. & Munn, P. (eds) (1985) *The Changing Face of Education 14 to 16: Curriculum and Assessment*, Windsor, NFER-Nelson.

Browne, S. (1983) Letter to the Editor, *The Times*, 21 September, 13.

Burns, J. H. (1960) 'The Scottish Committees of the House of Commons, 1948-59', *Political Studies*, vol.VIII, no.3, 272-96.

Bush, T. & Kogan, M. (1982) *Directors of Education*, London, George Allen & Unwin.

Butler, R. A. (1971) *The Art of the Possible*, London, Hamish Hamilton.

Byrne, E. M. (1974) *Planning and Educational Inequality: A Study of the Rationale of Resource-Allocation*, Slough, NFER.

Campbell, F. (1968) 'Latin and the elite tradition in education', *British Journal of Sociology*, vol.19, no.3, 308-25, reprinted in P. W. Musgrave (ed.) (1970) *Sociology, History and Education*, London, Methuen.

Campbell, R. H. (1979) 'The committee of ex-Secretaries of State for Scotland and industrial policy, 1941-1945', *Scottish Industrial History*, vol.2, nos 2 & 3, 1-10.

Campbell of Croy, Lord (1978) 'The Office of Secretary of State for Scotland', tape recording in *Scotland's Record*, Edinburgh, National Library of Scotland.

Cawson, A. (1978) 'Pluralism, corporatism and the role of the state', *Government and Opposition*, vol.13, no.2, 178-98.

Cawson, A. (1982) *Corporatism and Welfare: Social Policy and State Intervention in Britain*, London, Heinemann.

Cawson, A. (1985a) 'Corporatism and local politics', in W. Grant (ed.), *The Political Economy of Corporatism*, London, Macmillan.

Cawson, A. (ed.) (1985b) *Organized Interests and the State: Studies in Meso-Corporatism*, London, Sage.

Cawson, A. (1985c) 'Conclusion: Some implications for state theory', in A. Cawson (ed.), *Organized Interests and the State: Studies in Meso-Corporatism*, London, Sage.

Centre for Contemporary Cultural Studies (CCCS) (1981) *Unpopular Education: Schooling and Social Democracy in England since 1944*, London, Hutchinson.

Chapman, R. (1970) *The Higher Civil Service in Britain*, London, Constable.

The Civil Service Yearbook (various dates) London, HMSO (issued from 1985 by the Cabinet Office; 1982-84 by the Manpower and Personnel Office; 1974-81 by the Civil Service Department; before 1974 titled *The British Imperial Calendar and Civil Service List*).

Clark, J. R. (1964) *Memorandum on Comprehensive Secondary Schools*, report to the Education Committee of the Corporation of the City of Aberdeen, 31 December 1964, unpublished mimeograph (Aberdeen University Library).

Clark, J. R. (1965) *Memorandum on Comprehensive Secondary Schools: Appendix on a One-Tier System*, report to the Education Committee of the Corporation of the City of Aberdeen, 16 February 1965, unpublished mimeograph (Aberdeen University Library).

Clarke, F. (1940) *Education and Social Change: An English Interpretation*, London, Sheldon Press.

511

References

Coates, R. D. (1972) *Teachers' Unions and Interest Group Politics: A Study in the Behaviour of Organised Teachers in England and Wales*, Cambridge, Cambridge University Press.

Cohen, G. (1982) 'Issue networks in the analysis of inter-governmental relations: The role of inspectors at central and local government levels in furthering equal opportunity in education for ethnic minorities', *Policy and Politics*, vol.10, no.2, 217-37.

Collins, R. (1975) *Conflict Sociology: Toward an Explanatory Science*, London, Academic Press.

Collins, R. (1979) *The Credential Society: An Historical Sociology of Education and Stratification*, New York, Academic Press.

Commission on the Constitution (cc) (1970) *Minutes of Evidence II*, London, HMSO.

Committee of Council on Education in Scotland (cces) (1902) *Report with Appendix, 1901-1902*, London, HMSO, Cd 1109.

Committee of Council on Education in Scotland (1913) *Report 1912-1913*, London, HMSO, Cd 6726.

Committee of Council on Education in Scotland (1920) *Return: Showing State-Aided Day Schools with Statistics Relating Thereto, for 1918-1919*, London, HMSO.

Committee of Inquiry (ci) (1974) *Report into the pay of Non-University Teachers*, London, HMSO, Cmnd 5848 (the Houghton report).

Committee of Inquiry (1986) *Report into the pay and conditions of service of school teachers in Scotland*, Edinburgh, HMSO, Cmnd 9893 (the Main report).

Committee of Privy Counsellors on Ministerial Memoirs (cpcmm) (1976) *Report*, London, HMSO, Cmnd 6386 (the Radcliffe report).

Committee on Higher Education (che) (1963) *Report*, London, HMSO, Cmnd 2154 (the Robbins report).

Committee on Local Government Finance (clgf) (1976) *Report*, London, HMSO, Cmnd 6453 (the Layfield report).

Committee on Manpower Resources for Science and Technology (cmrst) (1968) *The Flow into Employment of Scientists, Engineers and Technologists*, London, HMSO, Cmnd 3760 (the Swann report).

Committee on Scottish Administration (csa) (1937) *Report*, Edinburgh, HMSO, Cmnd 5563 (the Gilmour report).

Committee on the Civil Service (ccs) (1968) *Report*, London, HMSO, Cmnd 3638 (the Fulton report).

Committee on the Distribution of Teachers in Scotland (cdts) (1966) *Measures to secure a more equitable distribution of teachers in Scotland*, Edinburgh, HMSO (the Roberts report).

Connolly, W. E. (ed.) (1969) *The Bias of Pluralism*, New York, Atherton Press.

Consultative Committee on the Curriculum (ccc) (1974) 'Communication and implementation of aims in secondary school', unpublished mimeograph.

Consultative Committee on the Curriculum (1977) *Drama in Scottish Schools: A Discussion Document*, Edinburgh, HMSO.

Consultative Committee on the Curriculum (1984) 'Draft proposal for changes in the substructure of the Consultative Committee on the Curriculum' (enclosure to ccc 84/22), unpublished mimeograph.

Coote, C. (1965) *A Companion of Honour*, London, Collins.

Cope, E. (1978) 'Consultation or confrontation? The campaign to save the Scottish colleges of education', in H. M. Drucker & M. G. Clarke (eds), *The Scottish Government Yearbook 1978*, Edinburgh, Paul Harris.

512

References

Corr, H. (1983) 'The sexual division of labour in the Scottish teaching profession, 1872-1914', in W. M. Humes & H. M. Paterson (eds), *Scottish Culture and Scottish Education 1800-1980*, Edinburgh, John Donald.

Council for Scientific Policy (CSP) (1968) *Enquiry into the Flow of Candidates in Science and Technology into Higher Education*, London, HMSO, Cmnd 3541 (the Dainton report).

Craik, H. (1926) 'The education fight and the nation', *National Review*, April, as quoted in G. Stewart, *The Story of Scottish Education*, London, Pitman, 1927, 153-5.

Crossman, R. (1975) *The Diaries of a Cabinet Minister, Volume One: Minister of Housing 1964-66*, London, Hamish Hamilton & Jonathan Cape.

Crouch, C. (1982) *The Politics of Industrial Relations*, 2nd edn, London, Fontana.

Crouch, C. (1983) 'Pluralism and the new corporatism: A rejoinder', *Political Studies*, vol. XXXI, no. 3, 452-60.

Crouch, C. (1985) 'Corporatism in industrial relations: A formal model', in W. Grant (ed.), *The Political Economy of Corporatism*, London, Macmillan.

Crowther-Hunt, Lord (1980) 'Mandarins and ministers', *Parliamentary Affairs*, vol. XXXIII, no. 4, 373-99.

Cruickshank, M. (1970) *A History of the Training of Teachers in Scotland*, Edinburgh, Scottish Council for Research in Education.

Cumming, C. E. (1971) *Studies in Educational Costs*, Edinburgh & London, Scottish Academic Press.

Cunningham, C. (1980) Interview with Anthony Seldon, 29 May, London, British Oral Archive of Political and Administrative History, British Library of Political and Economic Science, London School of Economics and Political Science.

Curle, A. (1949) 'Sir George Macdonald', in L. Wickham Legg (ed.), *Dictionary of National Biography 1931-1940*, London, Oxford University Press.

Currie, N. (1970) 'Examination requirements for the sixteen year old: impact on the Ordinary Grade of raising the school leaving age', in Scottish Certificate of Education Examination Board (SCEEB), *Report of Conference on Examinations, March 1970*, Edinburgh, SCEEB.

Dahl, R. A. (1956) *A Preface to Democratic Theory*, Chicago, University of Chicago Press.

Dahl, R. A. (1958) 'A critique of the ruling-elite model', *American Political Science Review*, vol. LII, no. 2, 463-9.

Dahl, R. A. (1961) *Who Governs?: Democracy and Power in an American City*, New Haven, Yale University Press.

Dahl, R. A. (1982) *Dilemmas of Pluralist Democracy: Autonomy vs. Control*, New Haven, Yale University Press.

Dale, R. (1982) 'Education and the capitalist state: Contributions and contradictions', in M. W. Apple (ed.), *Cultural and Economic Reproduction in Education: Essays on Class, Ideology and the State*, London, Routledge & Kegan Paul.

Dale, R. (1983) 'The political sociology of education', *British Journal of Sociology of Education*, vol. 4, no. 2, 185-202.

Darling, J. (1978) 'Philosophy of education and the Munn report', *Scottish Educational Review*, vol. 10, no. 2, 25-32.

Davie, G. E. (1961) *The Democratic Intellect: Scotland and her Universities in the Nineteenth Century*, Edinburgh, Edinburgh University Press.

Davie, G. E. (1986) *The Crisis of the Democratic Intellect: The Problem of Generalism and Specialisation in Twentieth-Century Scotland*, Edinburgh,

Polygon.

Davies, B. (1982) 'Sociology and the sociology of education', in A. Hartnett (ed.), *The Social Sciences in Educational Studies: A Selective Guide to the Literature*, London, Heinemann.

Davies, B. (1983) Review of *Education and Power* and *Cultural and Economic Reproduction in Education* by M. W. Apple (both London, Routledge & Kegan Paul), *British Journal of Sociology of Education*, vol.4, no.2, 177-84.

Dealy, M. B. (1945) *Catholic Schools in Scotland*, Washington, DC, Catholic University of America Press.

Department of Education and Science (DES) (1965) *The Organisation of Secondary Education*, London, DES (Circular 10/65).

Department of Education and Science (1967) *Children and their Primary Schools*, a report of the Central Advisory Council for Education (CACE) (England), London, HMSO (the Plowden report).

Department of Education and Science, and Welsh Office (WO) (1977) *A New Partnership for Our Schools*, London, HMSO (the Taylor report).

Departmental Committee on Section 2 of the Official Secrets Act 1911 (DCOSA) (1972) *Report*, Volume 1, London, HMSO, Cmnd 5104 (the Franks report).

Deroche-Drieux, M-E. (1976) *Les Associations Professionelles d'Enseignants en Ecosse 1930-1975*, doctoral thesis, 3rd cycle, University of Strasbourg II.

Dexter, L. A. (1970) *Elite and Specialized Interviewing*, Evanston, Illinois, Northwestern University Press.

Dickson, A. (1980) 'Class and nationalism in Scotland', in R. Parsler (ed.), *Capitalism, Class and Politics in Scotland*, London, Gower.

Dickson, D. (1969) 'Planning for change', in J. Nisbet and G. Kirk (eds), *Scottish Education Looks Ahead*, Edinburgh, W. & R. Chambers.

Dobie, T. (1967) 'The Scottish leaving certificate 1888-1908', in T. R. Bone (ed.), *Studies in the History of Scottish Education 1872-1939*, London, University of London Press.

Donaldson, G. (1960a) *Scotland: Church and Nation through Sixteen Centuries*, London, SCM Press.

Donaldson, G. (1960b) *The Scottish Reformation*, Cambridge, Cambridge University Press.

Donaldson, G. (1969) 'Scottish devolution: The historical background', in J. N. Wolfe (ed.), *Government and Nationalism in Scotland*, Edinburgh, Edinburgh University Press.

Donaldson, J. T. (1986) 'Scottish education: The 16+ Development Programme', *Educational Management and Administration*, no.14, 9-15.

Douglas, C. M. & Jones, H. (1903) *Scottish Education Reform*, Glasgow, James Maclehose & Sons.

Douglas, J. W. B. (1964) *The Home and the School: A Study of Ability and Attainment in the Primary School*, London, Macgibbon & Kee.

Douglas, J. W. B., Ross, J. M., Maxwell, S. M. M. & Walker, D. A. (1966) 'Differences in test score and in the gaining of selective places for Scottish children and those in England and Wales', *British Journal of Educational Psychology*, vol.36, no.2, 150-7.

Downs, A. (1967) *Inside Bureaucracy*, Boston, Little, Brown & Co.

Drever, E., Munn, P., McIntyre, A. & Mitchell, R. (1983) '"Framework for decision" – or "business as usual"?', *Scottish Educational Review*, vol.15, no.2, 83-91.

Drucker, H. M. (1979) 'The political parties', in D. I. MacKay (ed.), *Scotland: The Framework for Change*, Edinburgh, Paul Harris.

References

Drucker, H. M. (ed.) (1982) *John P. Mackintosh on Scotland*, London, Longman.
Drucker, H. M. & Kellas, J. G. (1985) 'The Scottish Affairs Committee', in
G. Drewry (ed.), *The New Select Committees: A Study of the 1979 Reforms*,
Oxford, Clarendon Press.
Dunleavy, P. (1981a) 'Professions and policy change: Notes towards a model of
ideological corporatism', *Public Administration Bulletin*, no.36, 3-16.
Dunleavy, P. (1981b) *The Politics of Mass Housing in Britain, 1945-1975: A Study
of Corporate Power and Professional Influence in the Welfare State*, Oxford,
Clarendon Press.
Eckstein, H. (1960), *Pressure Group Politics: The Case of the British Medical
Association*, London, George Allen & Unwin.
Educational Institute of Scotland (EIS) (1963) 'Anatomy of an Examination
Board', *Scottish Educational Journal*, vol.XLVI, no.39.
Educational Institute of Scotland (1966a) *H. M. Inspectorate in the Sixties*,
Edinburgh, EIS.
Educational Institute of Scotland (1966b) *Towards 1970*, Edinburgh, EIS.
Educational Institute of Scotland (1975) 'Parliamentary representation: Back-
ground to the appointment of parliamentary advisers', Edinburgh, EIS,
mimeograph, January.
Edwards, G. E. (1972) 'The Scottish Grand Committee, 1958 to 1970', *Parliamen-
tary Affairs*, vol.XXV, no.4, 303-25.
Elliot, W. (1932) 'The Scottish heritage in politics', in His Grace the Duke of Atholl
and others, *A Scotsman's Heritage*, London, Alexander Maclehose & Co.
Englefield, D. (ed.) (1984) *Commons Select Committees: Catalysts for Progress?*,
London, Longman.
Fairbairn, A. N. (ed.) (1980) *The Leicestershire Plan*, London, Heinemann.
Fenwick, I. G. K. (1976) *The Comprehensive School 1944-1970: The Politics of
Secondary School Reorganization*, London, Methuen.
Fenwick, K. (1985) 'Changing roles in the government of education', *British Journal
of Educational Studies*, vol.XXXIII, no.2, 135-47.
Fenwick, K. & McBride, P. (1981) *The Government of Education in Britain*,
Oxford, Martin Robertson.
Fewell, J. (1984) 'Women school teachers and gender in Scotland between the
wars', unpublished dissertation presented in part fulfilment of the MEd degree,
University of Edinburgh.
Findlay, I. R. (1973) *Education in Scotland*, Newton Abbot, David & Charles.
Finn, M. E. (1983) 'Social efficiency, progressivism and secondary education in
Scotland, 1885-1905', in W. M. Humes & H. M. Paterson, (eds), *Scottish
Culture and Scottish Education 1800-1980*, Edinburgh, John Donald.
Fitzpatrick, T. A. (1986) *Catholic Secondary Education in South-West Scotland
before 1972: Its Contribution to the Change in Status of the Catholic Community
of the Area*, Aberdeen, Aberdeen University Press.
Floud, J. E. & Scott, W. (1956) 'Recruitment to teaching in England and Wales', in
A. H. Halsey, J. Floud & C. A. Anderson (eds), *Education, Economy and
Society: A Reader in the Sociology of Education*, New York, Free Press.
Floud, J. E., Halsey, A. H. & Martin, F. M. (1956) *Social Class and Educational
Opportunity*, London, Heinemann.
Forsyth, J. P. & Dockrell, W. B. (1979) *Curriculum and Assessment: The Response
to Munn and Dunning – a Pre-Publication Survey*, Edinburgh, SCRE.
Fowler, G. (1974) 'Central government of education 1: Policy formation', Unit 2 of
Course E221, *Decision-Making in British Education*, Milton Keynes, Open
University Press.

References

Fowler, G. (1975) 'DES, Ministers and curriculum', in R. E. Bell & W. Prescott (eds), *The Schools Council: A Second Look*, London, Ward Lock Educational.

Fowler, G., Morris, V. & Ozga, J. (1973) *Decision-Making in British Education*, London, Heinemann.

Fraser, D. M. (1920) 'General report on the schools in the Western Division of Scotland', in His Majesty's Chief Inspectors of Schools in Scotland, *General Reports for the Year 1919*, appended to the Committee of Council on Education in Scotland, *Report 1919-1920*, London, HMSO, Cmd 782.

Fritzell, C. (1987) 'On the concept of relative autonomy in educational theory', *British Journal of Sociology of Education*, vol.8, no.1, 23-35.

Fry, G. K. (1969) *Statesmen in Disguise: The Changing Role of the Administrative Class of the British Home Civil Service 1853-1966*, London, Macmillan.

Fry, G. K. (1984) 'The attack on the civil service and the response of the insiders', *Parliamentary Affairs*, vol.XXXVII, no.4, 353-63.

Fry, G. K. (1985) *The Changing Civil Service*, London, George Allen & Unwin.

General Teaching Council (GTC) (1970) *Report on the Supply of Teachers*, May, Edinburgh, GTC.

General Teaching Council (1971) *Minutes of Meetings of Council*, vol.1, March 1966 to January 1971, Edinburgh, GTC.

General Teaching Council (1974) *GTC News*, no.5, October.

General Teaching Council (1976) *GTC News*, no.9, October.

General Teaching Council (1980a) *Minute of the Sixth Meeting of the Fourth General Teaching Council for Scotland*, vol.4, 1980/6, 5 March.

General Teaching Council (1980b) *Minute of the Eighth Meeting of the Fourth General Teaching Council for Scotland*, vol.4, 1980/8, 1 October.

General Teaching Council (1981) 'Supply Committee Discussion Paper: Staffing Standards in Primary and Secondary Schools', 3 February, in *Minute of the Tenth Meeting of the Fourth General Teaching Council for Scotland*, vol.4, 1981/10, 4 March.

Gethins, M., Morgan, C., Ozga, J. & Woolfe, R. (1979) 'The Welsh Office, the Scottish Education Department and the Northern Ireland Office: Central or devolved control of education?', Unit 3 of course E222, *The Control of Education in Britain*, Milton Keynes, Open University Press.

Gibson, J. S. (1985) *The Thistle and the Crown: A History of the Scottish Office*, Edinburgh, HMSO.

Giddens, A. (1984) *The Constitution of Society*, Cambridge, Polity Press.

Gillett, E. (1983) *Investment in the Environment*, Aberdeen, Aberdeen University Press.

Glass, D. V. (ed.) (1954) *Social Mobility in Britain*, London, Routledge & Kegan Paul.

Gosden, P. H. J. H. (1972) *The Evolution of a Profession*, Oxford, Basil Blackwell.

Gosden, P. H. J. H. (1976) *Education and the Second World War*, London, Methuen.

Gould, Sir R. (1973) 'The teaching profession', in D. E. Lomax (ed.), *The Education of Teachers in Britain*, London, John Wiley & Sons.

Government Statistical Service (GSS) (1976) *Scottish Educational Statistics 1974*, London, HMSO.

Government Statistical Service (1977) *Schools Pupils Teachers 1974-75: Scottish Educational Statistics, Special Edition*, Edinburgh, HMSO.

Gow, L. & McPherson, A. F. (1980) *Tell Them From Me: Scottish School Leavers Write about School and Life Afterwards*, Aberdeen, Aberdeen University Press.

Grace, G. (1978) *Teachers, Ideology and Control: A Study in Urban Education*, London, Routledge & Kegan Paul.

References

Grace, G. (1985) 'Judging teachers: The social and political contexts of teacher evaluation', *British Journal of Sociology of Education*, vol.6, no.1, 3-16.

Graham, N. W. (1965) 'The administration of education in Scotland', *Public Administration*, vol.43, no.3, 299-311.

Graham, N. W. & Bennett, J. (1971) 'Visit to Ontario, Canada and to USA', in *Bulletin – Curriculum Study Group* (later *Inspectorate Bulletin*), no.4, January, 1-3.

Grant, J. (1876) *History of the Burgh and Parish Schools of Scotland, Volume 1* (only one volume published), London & Glasgow, Collins.

Grant, W. (ed.) (1985a) *The Political Economy of Corporatism*, London, Macmillan.

Grant, W. (1985b) 'Introduction', in W. Grant, (ed.) *The Political Economy of Corporatism*, London, Macmillan.

Gray, J. M., McPherson, A. F. & Raffe, D. (1983) *Reconstructions of Secondary Education: Theory, Myth and Practice since the War*, London, Routledge & Kegan Paul.

Greenwood, J. & Wilson, D. (1984) *Public Administration in Britain*, London, George Allen & Unwin.

Griffith, J. A. G. (1966) *Central Departments and Local Authorities*, London, George Allen & Unwin.

Halsey, A. H. (ed.) (1972) *Trends in British Society since 1900: A Guide to the Changing Social Structure of Britain*, London, Macmillan.

Halsey, A. H. & Crewe, I. M. (1969) 'Social Survey of the Civil Service', in *The Civil Service, vol.3(1), Surveys and Investigations, Evidence submitted to the Committee under the Chairmanship of Lord Fulton 1966-1968*, London, HMSO.

Halsey, A. H., Floud, J. & Anderson, C. A. (1961) *Education, Economy and Society: A Reader in the Sociology of Education*, New York, Free Press.

Halsey, A. H., Heath, A. F. & Ridge, J. M. (1980) *Origins and Destinations: Family, Class and Education in Modern Britain*, Oxford, Clarendon Press.

Hamilton, D. (1985) 'Progressivism re-considered', *History Workshop*, no.20, 195-8.

Hanham, H. J. (1969) 'The development of the Scottish Office', in J. N. Wolfe (ed.), *Government and Nationalism in Scotland*, Edinburgh, Edinburgh University Press.

Hargreaves, A. (1982) 'Resistance and relative autonomy theories: Problems of distortion and incoherence in recent Marxist analyses of education', *British Journal of Sociology of Education*, vol.3, no.2, 107-26.

Hargreaves, A. (1983) 'The politics of administrative convenience: The case of middle schools', in J. Ahier & M. Flude (eds), *Contemporary Education Policy*, London, Croom Helm.

Hargreaves, A. & Hammersley, M. (1982) 'CCCS Gas! Politics and science in the work of the Centre for Contemporary Cultural Studies', *Oxford Review of Education*, vol.8, no.2, 139-44.

Harris, K. (1982) *Teachers and Classes: A Marxist Analysis*, London, Routledge & Kegan Paul.

Harrison, R. J. (1980) *Pluralism and Corporatism: The Political Evolution of Modern Democracies*, London, George Allen & Unwin.

Hartog, P. (1937) *A Conspectus of Examinations in Great Britain and Northern Ireland*, London, Macmillan.

Harvie, C. (1977) *Scotland and Nationalism: Scottish Society and Politics, 1707-1977*, London, George Allen & Unwin.

Harvie, C. (1981a) *No Gods and Precious Few Heroes: Scotland 1914-1980*, London, Edward Arnold.

Harvie, C. (1981b) 'Labour and Scottish government: The age of Tom Johnston',
The Bulletin of Scottish Politics, no.2, 1-20.

Harvie, C. (1981c) 'Socialist and patriot', *Times Educational Supplement (Scotland)*, 30 October, 19.

Headlam, M. (1937) 'Sir John Struthers', in J. Weaver (ed.), *Dictionary of National
Biography 1922-1930*, London, Oxford University Press.

Heald, D. (1980a) 'Scotland's public expenditure "needs"', in H. M. Drucker &
N. L. Drucker (eds), *The Scottish Government Yearbook 1981*. Edinburgh,
Paul Harris.

Heald, D. (1980b) *Financing Devolution within the United Kingdom: A Study of the
Lessons from Failure*, Research Monograph no.32, Canberra, Australian
National University, Centre for Research on Federal Financial Relations.

Heald, D. (1980c) 'Territorial equity and public finances: Concepts and confusion',
Studies in Public Policy No. 75, Glasgow, University of Strathclyde, Centre for
the Study of Public Policy.

Heald, D. (1982) 'Local authorities', in M. Cuthbert (ed.), *Government Spending
in Scotland: A Critical Appraisal*, Edinburgh, Paul Harris.

Heclo, H. & Wildavsky, A. (1974) *The Private Government of Public Money:
Community and Policy inside British Politics*, London, Macmillan.

Hetherington, H. J. W. (1924) *The Life and Letters of Sir Henry Jones*, London,
Hodder & Stoughton.

Highet, J. (1969) *A School of One's Choice: A Sociological Study of the Fee-paying
Schools of Scotland*, London & Glasgow, Blackie & Son.

Hodges, L. (1983) 'The spy who came out in the open', *The Times*, 14 September, 10.

Hogwood, B. W. (1979) 'Analysing industrial policy: A multi-perspective approach',
Public Administration Bulletin, no.29, 18-42.

Holden, B. (1974) *The Nature of Democracy*, London, Thomas Nelson.

Hope, K. (1984) *As Others See Us: Schooling and Social Mobility in Scotland and
the United States*, Cambridge, Cambridge University Press.

Houston, R. (1982) 'The literacy myth?: Illiteracy in Scotland 1630-1760', *Past and
Present*, no.96, August, 81-102.

Houston, R. (1985) *Scottish Literacy and the Scottish Identity: Illiteracy and Society
in Scotland and Northern England 1600-1800*, Cambridge, Cambridge
University Press.

Humes, W. M. (1986) *The Leadership Class in Scottish Education*, Edinburgh, John
Donald.

Humes, W. M. and Paterson, H. M. (eds) (1983) *Scottish Culture and Scottish
Education 1800-1980*, Edinburgh, John Donald.

Hunter, F. (1953) *Community Power Structure: A Study of Decision Makers*,
Chapel Hill, NC, University of North Carolina Press.

Hunter, S. L. (1972) *The Scottish Educational System*, 2nd edn, Oxford, Pergamon
Press.

Illingworth, C. (1971) *University Statesman: Sir Hector Hetherington*, Glasgow &
London, George Outram.

Inglis, W. B. (1970) 'The General Teaching Council for Scotland', *British Journal of
Educational Studies*, vol. XVIII, no.1, 56-68.

Inglis, W. B. (1972) *Towards a Self-Governing Teaching Profession*, Edinburgh,
Moray House College of Education.

Jackson, P. M. (1979) 'Financial control and responsibility', in D. I. MacKay (ed.),
Scotland: The Framework for Change, Edinburgh, Paul Harris.

James, P. H. (1980) *The Reorganization of Secondary Education*, Windsor, NFER.

Jencks, C. S., Smith, M., Acland, H., Bane, M. J., Cohen, D., Gintis, H.,
Heyns, B. & Michelson, S. (1973) *Inequality: A Reassessment of the Effect of*

Family and Schooling in America, London, Allen Lane.

Johnston, T. (1952) *Memories*, London, Collins.

Jordan, A. G. (1981) 'Iron triangles, woolly corporatism and elastic nets: Images of the policy process', *Journal of Public Policy*, vol.1, part 1, 95-123.

Jordan, A. G. (1983) 'Corporatism: The unity and the utility of the concept?', Strathclyde Papers on Government and Politics, no.13, Glasgow, University of Strathclyde, Department of Politics.

Karabel, J. & Halsey, A. H. (eds) (1977) *Power and Ideology in Education*, New York, Oxford University Press.

Katz, M. B. (1971) *Class, Bureaucracy and Schools: The Illusion of Educational Change in America*, New York, Praeger.

Keating, M. (1975) 'The role of the Scottish MP in the Scottish political system, in the United Kingdom political system and in the relationship between the two', unpublished Ph D thesis, Council for National Academic Awards.

Keating, M. (1976) 'Administrative devolution in practice: The Secretary of State for Scotland and the Scottish Office', *Public Administration*, vol.54, no.2, 133-45.

Keating, M. & Midwinter A. (1983) *The Government of Scotland*, Edinburgh, Mainstream.

Kellas, J. G. (1968) *Modern Scotland: The Nation Since 1870*, London, Pall Mall Press.

Kellas, J. G. (1984) *The Scottish Political System*, 3rd edn, Cambridge, Cambridge University Press.

Kelly, A. (1976) 'Family background, subject specialisation and occupational recruitment of Scottish university students: Some patterns and trends', *Higher Education*, vol.5, no.2, 177-88.

Kelsall, R. K. (1954) 'Self-recruitment in four professions', in D. Glass (ed.), *Social Mobility in Britain*, London, Routledge & Kegan Paul.

Kelsall, R. K. (1957) *Applications for Admission to Universities*, London, Association of Universities of the British Commonwealth.

Kennedy, G. (ed.) (1976) *The Radical Approach: Papers on an Independent Scotland*, Edinburgh, Palingenesis Press.

King, E. (1979) '*The Social Origins of Educational Systems* by M. S. Archer (1979): A review', *Comparative Education*, vol.15, no.3, October, 350-2.

King, E. (1980) 'Prescription or partnership in comparative studies of education', *Comparative Education*, vol.16, no.2, June, 185-95.

Kirk, G. (1978) 'Philosophy of education and the Munn report: A rejoinder', *Scottish Educational Review*, vol.10, no.2, 33-6.

Kirk, G. (1982) *Curriculum and Assessment in the Scottish Secondary School: A Study of the Munn and Dunning Reports*, London, Ward Lock Educational.

Knox, H. M. (1953) *Two Hundred and Fifty Years of Scottish Education 1696-1946*, Edinburgh, Oliver & Boyd.

Kogan, M. (1973) 'The Plowden Committee on Primary Education', in R. Chapman (ed.), *The Role of Commissions in Policy-Making*, London, George Allen & Unwin.

Kogan, M. (1975) *Educational Policy-Making*, London, George Allen & Unwin.

Kogan, M. (1978) *The Politics of Educational Change*, Manchester, Manchester University Press.

Kogan, M. (1979) 'Different frameworks for educational policy making and analysis', *Educational Analysis*, vol.1, no.2, 5-14.

Kogan, M. (1981) 'Education in "hard times"', in C. Hood & M. Wright (eds), *Big Government in Hard Times*, Oxford, Martin Robertson.

Kogan, M. (1982) 'Changes in perspective', *Times Educational Supplement*, 15

January, 4.

Kogan, M. (1983a) 'The central-local government relationship: A comparison between the education and the health services', *Local Government Studies*, vol.9, no.1, 65-85.

Kogan, M. (1983b) 'The case of education', in K. Young (ed.), *National Interests and Local Government*, London, Heinemann.

Kogan, M. & Packwood, T. (1974) *Advisory Councils and Committees in Education*, London, Routledge & Kegan Paul.

Kogan, M. & van der Eyken, W. (1973) *County Hall*, Harmondsworth, Penguin.

Labour Party (n.d., about 1964) *Signposts for Scotland*, London, the Labour Party.

Labour Party Scottish Council (LPSC) (1941) *Plan for Post-War Scotland*, Glasgow.

Labour Party Scottish Council (n.d., about 1955) *Statement on Policy for Scottish Education*, Glasgow.

Laffin, M. (1986) 'Professional communities and policy communities in central-local relations', in M. S. Goldsmith (ed.), *New Research in Central-Local Relations*, London, Gower.

Laing, A. (1984) *'Sursum semper*: A socio-historical study of educational policy-making in Glasgow following the issue of Circular 600', unpublished dissertation presented in part fulfilment of the M Ed degree, University of Edinburgh.

Lanarkshire County Council (LCC) (1965) *Minute of Meeting of Education (Schools and Schemes) Committee of 27 May 1965*, 7 July.

Lawn, M. & Ozga, J. (1986) 'Unequal partners: Teachers under indirect rule', *British Journal of Sociology of Education*, vol.7, no.2, 225-38.

Lawrence, B. (1972) *The Administration of Education in Britain*, London, Batsford.

Lawton, D. (1980) *The Politics of the School Curriculum*, London, Routledge & Kegan Paul.

Lehmbruch, G. (1982) 'Introduction: Neo-corporatism in comparative perspective', in G. Lehmbruch & P. C. Schmitter (eds), *Patterns of Corporatist Policy-Making*, Beverly Hills & London, Sage.

Lehmbruch, G. & Schmitter, P. C. (eds) (1982) *Patterns of Corporatist Policy-Making*, Beverly Hills & London, Sage.

Lightfoot, M. (1983) 'The new interrogators', *Times Educational Supplement*, 27 May, 6.

Litt, E. & Parkinson, M. (1979) *US and U K Educational Policy: A Decade of Reform*, New York, Praeger.

Lloyd, J. M. (1979) 'The Scottish school system and the second world war', unpublished PH D thesis, University of Stirling.

Lloyd, J. M. (1984) 'Tom Johnston's parliament on education: The birth of the Sixth Advisory Council on Education in Scotland, 1942-43', *Scottish Educational Review*, vol.16, no.2, 104-15.

Lodge, P. & Blackstone, T. (1982) *Educational Policy and Educational Inequality*, Oxford, Martin Robertson.

Lowi, T. J. (1979) *The End of Liberalism: The Second Republic of the United States*, New York, W. W. Norton.

Lukes, S. (1974) *Power: A Radical View*, London, Macmillan.

Macbeth, A. (1983) 'The government of Scottish education: Partnership or compromise?', in D. McCrone (ed.), *The Scottish Government Yearbook 1984*, Edinburgh, Unit for the Study of Government in Scotland.

Macbeth, A., MacKenzie, M. & Breckenridge, I. (1980) *School Councils: Policy-Making, Participation or Irrelevance?*, Edinburgh, SED & HMSO.

McClelland, W. (1935) 'Distinctive features of Scottish education', *The New Era in Home and School*, vol.16, no.7, 172-4.

McClelland, W. (1936) in P. Monroe (ed.), *Conference on Examinations*, New

York, Bureau of Publications, Teachers College, Columbia University, 57-9.

McClelland, W. (1942) *Selection for Secondary Education*, London, University of London Press.

McCormick, K. (1986) 'The search for corporatist structures in British higher technological education: The creation of the National Advisory Council on Education in Industry and Commerce (NACEIC) in 1948', *British Journal of the Sociology of Education*, vol.7, no.3, 293-317.

McCrone, D., Bechhofer, F. & Kendrick, S. (1982) 'Egalitarianism and social inequality in Scotland', in D. Robbins (ed.), *Rethinking Social Inequality*, London, Gower.

McCrone, G. (1969) *Regional Policy in Britain*, London, George Allen & Unwin.

McCrone, G. (1985) 'The role of government', in R. Saville (ed.), *The Economic Development of Modern Scotland 1950-1980*, Edinburgh, John Donald.

McCrone, G. & Randall, J. (1985) 'The Scottish Development Agency', in R. Saville (ed.), *The Economic Development of Modern Scotland 1950-1980*, Edinburgh, John Donald.

Macdonald, G. (1937) 'Sir Henry Craik', in J. Weaver (ed.), *Dictionary of National Biography 1922-1930*, Oxford, Oxford University Press.

Macdonald, M. & Redpath A. (1979) 'The Scottish Office 1954-79', in H. M. Drucker & N. L. Drucker (eds), *The Scottish Government Yearbook 1980*, Edinburgh, Paul Harris.

McDonald, I. J. (1964) 'Educational opportunity at university level in Scotland', unpublished dissertation presented in part fulfilment of the BEd degree, University of Glasgow.

McEwan, J. S. (1965a) 'The nature and organisation of secondary education: A review of current and possible developments', Appendix 1 to the *Minute of Meeting of the Education Committee of the County Council of Lanarkshire, 7 July 1965, 1664-1686*, February.

McEwan, J. S. (1965b) 'The organisation of secondary education', Appendix 2 to the *Minute of Meeting of the Education Committee of the County Council of Lanarkshire, 7 July 1965, 1664-1686*, May.

McIntosh, D. M. (1948) *Promotion from Primary to Secondary Education*, London, University of London Press.

McIntosh, D. M. (1959) *Educational Guidance and the Pool of Ability*, London, University of London Press.

McIntosh, D. M. (1962) 'The junior and senior high school', *Scottish Educational Journal*, 19 October, 764.

McIntosh, D. M. & Walker, D. A. (1970) 'The O-grade of the Scottish Certificate of Education', *British Journal of Educational Psychology*, vol.40, no.2, 179-99.

McIntyre, D. (ed.) (1978) *A Critique of the Munn and Dunning Reports*, University of Stirling, Department of Education.

McIver, J. (1981) 'Are pupils in four-year schools disadvantaged?' *Collaborative Research Newsletter*, no.8, 21-6, Edinburgh, CES.

Mack, D. W. (1984) 'An action plan for Scottish education', *Journal for Further and Higher Education in Scotland*, vol.9, no.1, 2-7.

Mackay, D. I. (1969) *Geographical Mobility and the Brain Drain: A Case Study of Aberdeen University Graduates, 1860-1960*, London, George Allen & Unwin.

McKechin, W. (1976) 'Consultation in Renfrewshire', *Times Educational Supplement (Scotland)*, 21 May, 19.

McKechin, W. (1979) *A School in Eastwood Park: A Case Study in Local Authority Decision Making and Public Participation*, Paisley, Paisley College of Technology Local Government Unit.

McKenzie, D. W. (1974) 'The Glasgow EIS', unpublished dissertation presented in part fulfilment of the MEd degree, University of Glasgow.

MacKenzie, M. (1967) 'The road to the circulars: A study of the evolution of Labour Party policy with regard to the comprehensive school', *Scottish Educational Studies*, vol.1, no.1, 25-33.

Mackenzie, R. F. (1970) *State School*, Harmondsworth, Penguin.

Mackenzie, R. F. (n.d., 1976) *The Unbowed Head: Events at Summerhill Academy 1968-74*, Edinburgh, Edinburgh University Student Publications Board.

Mackie, J. D. (1960) *A History of the Scottish Reformation*, Edinburgh, Church of Scotland Youth Committee.

Mackintosh, J. P. (1968) *The British Cabinet*, 2nd edn, London, Methuen.

Mackintosh, M. (1962) *Education in Scotland: Yesterday and Today*, Glasgow, Robert Gibson & Sons.

Maclaren, I. (1895) *Beside the Bonnie Brier Bush*, 4th edn, London, Hodder & Stoughton.

MacLean, C. (1976a) 'Inspectorate 76', *Times Educational Supplement (Scotland)*, 30 January, 19.

MacLean, C. (1976b) 'Inspectorate 76', *Times Educational Supplement (Scotland)*, 6 February, 25.

MacLean, C. (1976c) 'Inspectorate 76', *Times Educational Supplement (Scotland)*, 13 February, 24.

Maclure, S. (1984) *Educational Development and School Building: Aspects of Public Policy 1945-73*, London, Longman.

McNay, I. & Ozga, J. (eds) (1985) *Policy-Making in Education: The Breakdown of Consensus*, Oxford, Pergamon Press.

McPherson, A. F. (1972) 'The generally educated Scot: An old ideal in a changing university structure', Unit 15 of Course E282, *School and Society*, Bletchley, Open University Press.

McPherson, A. F. (1973) 'Selections and survivals: A sociology of the ancient Scottish universities', in R. Brown (ed.), *Knowledge, Education and Cultural Change: Papers in the Sociology of Education*, London, Tavistock.

McPherson, A. F. (1983) 'An angle on the geist: Persistence and change in the Scottish educational tradition', in W. M. Humes & H. M. Paterson (eds), *Scottish Culture and Scottish Education 1800-1980*, Edinburgh, John Donald.

McPherson, A. F. (1984a) 'An episode in the control of research', in W. B. Dockrell (ed.), *An Attitude of Mind: Twenty-Five Years of Educational Research in Scotland*, Edinburgh, SCRE.

McPherson, A. F. (1984b) 'Post-compulsory schooling: The sixth year', in D. Raffe (ed.), *Fourteen to Eighteen: The Changing Pattern of Schooling in Scotland*, Aberdeen, Aberdeen University Press.

McPherson, A. F. & Atherton, G. (1970) 'Graduate teachers in Scotland: A sociological analysis of recruitment in teaching amongst recent graduates of the four ancient Scottish universities', *Scottish Educational Studies*, vol.2, no.1, 35-55.

McPherson, A. F. & Neave, G. R. (1976) *The Scottish Sixth: A Sociological Evaluation of Sixth Year Studies and the Changing Relationship between School and University in Scotland*, Slough, NFER.

McPherson, A. F. & Willms, J. D. (1986) 'Certification, class conflict, religion and community: A socio-historical explanation of the effectiveness of contemporary schools', in A. C. Kerckhoff (ed.), *Research in Sociology of Education and Socialization*, vol.6, Greenwich, Connecticut, JAI Press.

McPherson, A. F. & Willms, J. D. (1987) 'Equalisation and improvement: Some effects of comprehensive reorganisation in Scotland', *Sociology*, vol.21, no.4, 509-39.

Macpherson, J. S. (1958) *Eleven-Year-Olds Grow Up*, London, University of London Press.

Margolis, M. (1979) *Viable Democracy*, London, Macmillan.

Marsden, W. E. (1982) 'Historical studies and the sociology of education', in A. Hartnett (ed.), *The Social Sciences in Educational Studies: A Selective Guide to the Literature*, London, Heinemann.

Martin, R. M. (1983a) 'Pluralism and the new corporatism', *Political Studies*, vol.XXXI, no.1, 86-102.

Martin, R. M. (1983b) 'Pluralism and the new corporatism: A reply', *Political Studies*, vol.XXXI, no.3, 461-2.

Marwick, A. (1964) 'Middle opinion in the thirties: Planning, progress and political "agreement"', *English Historical Review*, vol.LXXIX, no.311, 285-98.

Maxwell, J. (1969) *Sixteen Years On: A Follow-up of the 1947 Scottish Survey*, London, University of London Press.

Mee, A. J. (1964) 'Recent developments in science teaching in Scotland', *Advancement of Science*, vol.XXI, no.89, 65-72.

Mercer, G. & Forsyth, D. J. C. (1975) 'Some aspects of recruitment to schoolteaching among university graduates in Scotland, 1860-1955', *British Journal of Educational Studies*, vol.XXIII, no.1, February, 58-77.

Michael, J. (1982) *The Politics of Secrecy*, Harmondsworth, Penguin.

Middlemas, K. (1979) *Politics in Industrial Society: The Experience of the British System Since 1911*, London, Andre Deutsch.

Midwinter, A. (1984) *The Politics of Local Spending*, Edinburgh, Mainstream.

Mill, J. S. (1951) 'Representative government', in J. S. Mill, *Utilitarianism, Liberty and Representative Government*, New York, Dutton.

Millan, B. (1973) Interviewed by R. E. Bell in the radio broadcast 'London Scottish -4' for the Open University course E221, *Decision-making in British Education Systems*, recorded 25 October 1973, tape number TLN43FW004.

Mills, C. W. (1956) *The Power Elite*, New York, Oxford University Press.

Mills, C. W. (1970) *The Sociological Imagination*, Harmondsworth, Penguin.

Milne, Sir D. (1957) *The Scottish Office and Other Scottish Government Departments*, London, George Allen & Unwin.

Ministry of Education (ME) (1954) *Early Leaving: A Report of the Central Advisory Council for Education (England)*, London, HMSO.

Ministry of Education (1959) *15 to 18: A Report of the Central Advisory Council for Education (England)*, London, HMSO (the Crowther report).

Ministry of Education (1963) *Half Our Future: A Report of the Central Advisory Council for Education (England)*, London, HMSO (the Newsom report).

Ministry of Housing and Local Government (MHLG) (1957) *Local Government Finance (England and Wales)*, London, HMSO, Cmnd 209.

Ministry of Works (MW) (1945) *School Buildings for Scotland: Post-War Building Studies No. 21*, London, HMSO.

Mitchell, J. (1985) 'Educational administration in late nineteenth and early twentieth century Scotland', unpublished typescript available from the author.

Monroe, P. (ed.) (1936) *Conference on Examinations*, New York, Bureau of Publications, Teachers College, Columbia University.

Morgan, A. (1927) *Rise and Progress of Scottish Education*, London, Oliver & Boyd.

Morgan, A. (1929) *Makers of Scottish Education*, London, Longmans, Green.

Morris, J. G. (1976) 'Innovation and development in the Scottish educational system', *Scottish Educational Studies*, vol.8, no.2, 67-74.

References

Moyser, G. & Wagstaffe, M. (eds) (1987) *Research Methods for Elite Studies*, London, George Allen & Unwin.

Muirhead, J. H. & Hetherington, H. J. W. (1918) *Social Purpose: A Contribution to the Philosophy of Civic Society*, London, George Allen & Unwin.

Munn, Sir James (1985) 'The Scottish experience', unpublished address to the *Times Educational Supplement* Conference on Secondary Education, 21 November.

Munro, N. & Ross, D. (1985) 'Union's big freeze-out', *Times Educational Supplement (Scotland)*, 11 January, 5.

Munro, R. (Lord Alness) (n.d.) *Looking Back: Fugitive Writings and Sayings*, London, Thomas Nelson.

Nash, R. (1984) 'On two critiques of the Marxist sociology of education', *British Journal of Sociology of Education*, vol.5, no.1, 19-31.

National Board for Prices and Incomes (NBPI) (1966) *Report No. 15: Scottish Teachers' Salaries*, London, HMSO, Cmnd 3005.

Neill, A. S. (1921) *A Dominie in Doubt*, London, Herbert Jenkins.

Newman, O. (1981) *The Challenge of Corporatism*, London, Macmillan.

Nisbet, J. (ed.) (1969) *Scottish Education Looks Ahead*, Edinburgh, W. & R. Chambers.

Nisbet, J. (1973) 'The Schools Council, United Kingdom' in *Case Studies of Educational Innovation: At the Central Level*, vol.1, Paris, OECD.

Niskanen, W. A. (1971) *Bureaucracy and Representative Government*, Chicago, Aldine.

Nordlinger, E. A. (1981) *On the Autonomy of the Democratic State*, Cambridge, Mass., Harvard University Press.

O'Connor, M. (1983) 'The Inspectorate that wasn't afraid to be inspected', *The Guardian*, 30 August, 11.

Osborne, G. S. (1966) *Scottish and English Schools: A Comparative Survey of the Past Fifty Years*, Pittsburgh, University of Pittsburgh Press.

Osborne, G. S. (1968) *Change in Scottish Education*, London, Longmans.

Osborne, G. S. (1979) 'Information Paper 3: The Committee of Principals of Scottish colleges of education', *Scottish Educational Review*, vol.11, no.1, 74-7.

Ozga, J. T. (1985) 'Teacher contracts and teacher "professionalism": The Educational Institute of Scotland', in M. Lawn (ed.), *The Politics of Teacher Unionism: International Perspectives*, London, Croom Helm.

Ozga, J. T. & Lawn, M. (1981) *Teachers, Professionalism and Class: A Study of Organized Teachers*, London, Falmer.

Parkinson, M. (1970) *The Labour Party and the Organization of Secondary Education 1918-1965*, London, Routledge & Kegan Paul.

Parkinson, M. (1982) 'Politics and policy-making in education', in A. Hartnett (ed.), *The Social Sciences in Educational Studies*, London, Heinemann Educational.

Parliamentary Debates (PD) (1956a) House of Commons Official Report, Fifth Series, Session 1955-56, vol.558, cols 1170-86, 29 October 1956.

Parliamentary Debates (1956b) House of Commons Official Report, Fifth Series, Session 1955-56, vol.558, cols 1200-5, 30 October 1956.

Parliamentary Debates (1957a) House of Commons Official Report, Fifth Series, Session 1956-57, vol.564, col.1083, 12 February 1957.

Parliamentary Debates (1957b) House of Commons Official Report, Fifth Series, Session 1957-58, vol.580, col.227, 17 December 1957.

Parliamentary Debates (1957c) House of Commons Official Report, Fifth Series, Session 1957-58, vol.580, col.239, 17 December 1957.

References

Parliamentary Debates (1958a) House of Commons Official Report, Scottish Standing Committee, Session 1957-58, vol.IV, cols 374 and 376, 25 March 1958.

Parliamentary Debates (1958b) House of Commons Official Report, Scottish Standing Committee, Session 1957-58, vol.IV, col.194, 13 March 1958.

Parliamentary Debates (1958c) House of Commons Official Report, Scottish Standing Committee, Session 1957-58, vol.IV, col.208, 13 March 1958.

Parliamentary Debates (1961) House of Commons Official Report, Fifth Series, Session 1960-61, vol.640, col.687, 11 May 1961.

Parliamentary Debates (1964) House of Commons Official Report, Standing Committees, Session 1963-64, vol.VI, Scottish Grand Committee, The Brunton Report, col.49, 17 March 1964.

Parliamentary Debates (1965a) House of Commons Official Report, Standing Committees, Session 1964-65, vol.V, Scottish Grand Committee, Teaching Council (Scotland) Bill (Consideration of Principle), col.8, 2 February 1965.

Parliamentary Debates (1965b) House of Commons Official Report, Standing Committees, Session 1964-65, vol.V, Scottish Grand Committee, Teaching Council (Scotland) Bill (Consideration of Principle), col.98, 4 February 1965.

Parliamentary Debates (1967a) House of Commons Official Report, Standing Committees, Session 1966-67, vol.XII, Scottish Grand Committee, Remuneration of Teachers (Scotland) Bill (Consideration of Principle), cols 6-7, 7 February 1967.

Parliamentary Debates (1967b) House of Commons Official Report, Fifth Series, Session 1966-67, vol.749, cols 1322-3, 3 July 1967.

Parry, R. (1982) 'Public expenditure in Scotland', in D. McCrone (ed.), *The Scottish Government Yearbook 1983*, Edinburgh, Unit for the Study of Government in Scotland.

Parry, R. (1987) 'The Centralization of the Scottish Office', in R. Rose (ed.), *Ministers and Ministries: A Functional Analysis*, Oxford, Clarendon Press.

Paterson, H. M. (1975) 'Godfrey Thomson and the development of psychometrics in Scotland, 1925-1950', paper presented at a conference of the British Educational Research Association, University of Stirling.

Paterson, H. M. (1983) 'Incubus and ideology: The development of secondary schooling in Scotland 1900-1939', in W. M. Humes & H. M. Paterson (eds), *Scottish Culture and Scottish Education 1800-1980*, Edinburgh, John Donald.

Pattison, M. (1980) 'Intergovernmental relations and the limitations of central control: Reconstructing the politics of comprehensive education', *Oxford Review of Education*, vol.6, no.1, 63-89.

Pedley, R. (1963) *The Comprehensive School*, Harmondsworth, Penguin.

Petch, A. (1986) 'Rezoning: An exercise in compromise', University of Edinburgh, Department of Social Policy and Social Work, unpublished mimeograph.

Peters, B. G. (1978) *The Politics of Bureaucracy: A Comparative Perspective*, New York & London, Longman.

Phillipson, N. T. (1969) 'Nationalism and ideology', in J. N. Wolfe (ed.), *Government and Nationalism in Scotland*, Edinburgh, Edinburgh University Press.

Pickard, W. (1983) 'Younger backs traditional role of Inspectorate', *Times Educational Supplement (Scotland)*, 1 April, 3.

Pile, Sir W. (1979) *The Department of Education and Science*, London, George Allen & Unwin.

Pliatzky, L. (1982) *Getting and Spending: Public Expenditure, Employment and Inflation*, Oxford, Basil Blackwell.

Pollard, M. (1974) *The Teachers*, Lavenham, Eastland Press.

Polsby, N. W. (1963) *Community Power and Political Theory*, New Haven, Yale

University Press.

Pottinger, G. (1979) *The Secretaries of State for Scotland 1926-76: Fifty Years of the Scottish Office*, Edinburgh, Scottish Academic Press.

Pringle, S. M. (1985) 'Influences on policy for and practices in the Scottish primary school, from 1946 to the present day', unpublished dissertation presented in part fulfilment of the M Ed degree, University of Edinburgh.

Profitt, T. (1968) 'Great Britain', in F. Ridley (ed.), *Specialists and Generalists*, London, George Allen & Unwin.

Raab, C. D. (1982a) 'The quasi-government of Scottish education', in A. Barker (ed.), *Quangos in Britain: Government and the Networks of Public Policy-Making*, London, Macmillan.

Raab, C. D. (1982b) 'Mapping the boundaries of education policy systems: The case of Scotland', *Public Administration Bulletin*, no.39, 40-57.

Raab, C. (1987a) 'The "leadership class" dismissed: Humes' critique of Scottish education', in D. McCrone (ed.), *The Scottish Government Yearbook 1987*, Edinburgh, Unit for the Study of Government in Scotland.

Raab, C. (1987b) 'Oral history as an instrument of research into Scottish educational policy-making', in G. Moyser & M. Wagstaffe (eds), *Research Methods for Elite Studies*, London, George Allen & Unwin.

Raffe, D. (ed.) (1984a) *Fourteen to Eighteen: The Changing Pattern of Schooling in Scotland*, Aberdeen, Aberdeen University Press.

Raffe, D. (1984b) 'Youth unemployment and the M S C: 1977-1983', in D. McCrone (ed.), *Scottish Government Yearbook 1984*, Edinburgh, Unit for the Study of Government in Scotland.

Ranson, S. (1980) 'Changing relations between centre and locality in education', *Local Government Studies*, vol.6, no.6, 3-23.

Ranson, S. (1985a) 'Contradictions in the government of educational change', *Political Studies*, vol. X X X I I I, no.1, 56-72.

Ranson, S. (1985b) 'Education', in S. Ranson, G. Jones & K. Walsh (eds), *Between Centre and Locality: The Politics of Public Policy*, London, George Allen & Unwin.

Ranson, S. & Tomlinson, J. (1986) 'An alternative view of education and society', in S. Ranson & J. Tomlinson (eds), *The Changing Government of Education*, London, George Allen & Unwin.

Regan, D. E. (1979) *Local Government and Education*, 2nd edn, London, George Allen & Unwin.

Reid, J. (1975) 'The inspectorate's role', *Times Educational Supplement (Scotland)*, 4 April, 1.

Reynolds, D. & Sullivan, M. (1980) 'Towards a new socialist sociology of education', in L. Barton, R. Meighan & S. Walker (eds), *Schooling, Ideology and the Curriculum*, Lewes, Falmer.

Rhodes, G. (1976) 'Local government finance 1918-1966', in Department of the Environment, Scottish Office, and Welsh Office, *Local Government Finance: Appendix 6 to the Report of the Committee of Inquiry under the Chairmanship of Frank Layfield Esq., Q.C.*, London, H M S O.

Rhodes, G. (1981) *Inspectorates in British Government*, London, George Allen & Unwin.

Rhodes, R. A. W. (1981) *Control and Power in Central-Local Government Relations*, London, Gower.

Rhodes, R. A. W. (1985a) 'Power-dependence, policy communities and inter-governmental networks', *Public Administration Bulletin*, no.49, 4-31.

Rhodes, R. A. W. (1985b) 'Corporatism, pay negotiations and local government', *Public Administration*, vol.63, no.3, 287-307.

Rhodes, R. A. W. (1986a) 'Power-dependence theories of central-local relations: A critical assessment', in M. Goldsmith (ed.), *New Research in Central-Local Relations*, Aldershot, Gower.

Rhodes, R. A. W. (1986b) *The National World of Local Government*, London, George Allen & Unwin.

Ribbins, P. M. & Brown, R. J. (1979) 'Policy making in English local government: The case of secondary school reorganization', *Public Administration*, vol.57, no.2, 187-202.

Richardson, J. J. & Jordan, A. G. (1979) *Governing Under Pressure: The Policy Process in a Post-Parliamentary Democracy*, Oxford, Martin Robertson.

Richardson, J. J., Jordan, A. G. & Kimber, R. H. (1978) 'Lobbying, administrative reform and policy styles: The case of land drainage', *Political Studies*, vol.xxvi, no.1, 47-64.

Robertson, J. J. (1957) 'The Advisory Council's report on secondary education – ten years after', *Scottish Educational Journal*, 12 April, 213-15, with correction, 243.

Robertson, J. J. (1964) *Godfrey Thomson*, Edinburgh, Moray House College of Education.

Robertson, J. J. (1966) 'Snakes and ladders', *Times Educational Supplement (Scotland)*, 9 September, 467.

Robertson, J. J. (1969a) 'Climate of dissatisfaction', *Times Educational Supplement (Scotland)*, 28 March, 1033.

Robertson, J. J. (1969b) 'Still room for a challenge', *Times Educational Supplement (Scotland)*, 11 April, 1179.

Robertson, J. J. (1969c) 'Not always appreciated', *Times Educational Supplement (Scotland)*, 4 April.

Robertson, J. J. (1969d) 'Impressions and comments', in J. Nisbet and G. Kirk (eds), *Scottish Education Looks Ahead*, Edinburgh, Chambers.

Robertson, J. J. (1970) 'The place of classical studies in education', mimeograph in the authors' possession.

Robertson, J. J. & Wright, E. (1962) Transcript of BBC TV interview, 4 April.

Robertson, R. (1986) 'The GTC: An idiot's guide to non-election', *Times Educational Supplement (Scotland)*, 12 September, 2.

Ross, J. M. (1981) *The Secretary of State for Scotland and the Scottish Office*, Studies in Public Policy No.87, Glasgow, University of Strathclyde, Centre for the Study of Public Policy.

Ross, W. (1978) 'Approaching the archangelic?', in H. M. Drucker & M. G. Clarke (eds), *The Scottish Government Yearbook 1978*, Edinburgh, Paul Harris.

Roxburgh, J. M. (1971) *The School Board of Glasgow 1873-1919*, London, University of London Press.

Royal Commission on Local Government in Scotland (RCLGS) (1967) *Written Evidence 3*, Edinburgh, HMSO.

Royal Commission on Local Government in Scotland (1968a) *Written Evidence 7*, Edinburgh, HMSO.

Royal Commission on Local Government in Scotland (1968b) *Minutes of Evidence 11*, Edinburgh, HMSO.

Royal Commission on Local Government in Scotland (1968c) *Written Evidence 11*, Edinburgh, HMSO.

Royal Commission on Scottish Affairs 1952-54 (RCSA) (1954) *Report*, Edinburgh, HMSO, Cmnd 9212 (the Balfour report).

Rush, M. (1985) 'The Education, Science and Arts Committee', in G. Drewry (ed.), *The New Select Committees: A Study of the 1979 Reforms*, Oxford, Clarendon Press.

References

Salter, B. & Tapper, T. (1981) *Education, Politics and the State: The Theory and Practice of Educational Change*, London, Grant McIntyre.

Salter, B. & Tapper, T. (1985) *Power and Policy in Education: The Case of Independent Schooling,* London & Philadelphia, The Falmer Press.

Saltire Society (1941) *Scotland Tomorrow*, Proceedings of a conference held by the Saltire Society, 15 February 1941, Edinburgh, Saltire Society.

Saltire Society (1948) *List of Members*, Edinburgh, Saltire Society.

Saunders, L. J. (1950) *Scottish Democracy 1815-1840: The Social and Intellectual Background*, Edinburgh & London, Oliver & Boyd.

Saunders, P. (1985) 'Corporatism and urban service provision', in W. Grant (ed.), *The Political Economy of Corporatism*, London, Macmillan.

Saville, R. (1985) 'The industrial background to the post-war Scottish economy', in R. Saville (ed.), *The Economic Development of Modern Scotland 1950-1980*, Edinburgh, John Donald.

Schattschneider, E. E. (1960) *The Semisovereign People: A Realist's View of Democracy in America*, New York, Holt, Rinehart & Winston.

Schmitter, P. C. (1979a) 'Still the century of corporatism?', in P. C. Schmitter & G. Lehmbruch (eds), *Trends Towards Corporatist Intermediation*, Beverly Hills & London, Sage.

Schmitter, P. C. (1979b) 'Modes of interest intermediation and models of societal change in Western Europe', in P. C. Schmitter & G. Lehmbruch (eds), *Trends Towards Corporatist Intermediation*, Beverly Hills & London, Sage.

Schmitter, P. C. & Lehmbruch, G. (eds) (1979) *Trends Towards Corporatist Intermediation*, Beverly Hills & London, Sage.

Scotland, J. (1969) *The History of Scottish Education: Volume 2. From 1872 to the Present Day*, London, University of London Press.

Scotland, J. (1978) 'A watchdog for 80,000 teachers', *GTC News*, no. 10, October, 1.

Scottish Central Committee for Mathematics, Science and Technical Education (SCCMSTE) (1975) 'Science: A curriculum model for the 1980s', *Occasional Paper 1*, Edinburgh, SCCMSTE, quoted in G. Kirk (1982) *Curriculum and Assessment in the Scottish Secondary School: A Study of the Munn and Dunning Reports*, London, Ward Lock Educational, 14.

Scottish Certificate of Education Examination Board (SCEEB) (annual 1965-) *Report*, Edinburgh (1966-75) and Dalkeith (1976-), SCEEB.

Scottish Certificate of Education Examination Board (1968) *Report of Conference on Examinations, April 1968*, Edinburgh, SCEEB.

Scottish Certificate of Education Examination Board (1970) *Report of Conference on Examinations, March 1970*, Edinburgh, SCEEB.

Scottish Certificate of Education Examination Board (1971) *The Scottish Certificate of Education Examination Board and its Work* and *Supplement 1971* (under separate cover), Edinburgh, SCEEB.

Scottish Certificate of Education Examination Board (1972a) 'Ordinary Grade examinations: Scottish Certificate of Education Examination Board proposals', Press Notice, 20 October.

Scottish Certificate of Education Examination Board (1972b) 'Scottish Certificate of Education: Ordinary Grade examination in and after 1973', *Circular Letter*, 21 November.

Scottish Certificate of Education Examination Board (1982) *Full-Time Education after S4: A Statistical Study*, Dalkeith, SCEEB.

Scottish Council (Development and Industry) (SC(DI)) (1961) *Inquiry into the Scottish Economy 1960-1961*, Edinburgh, SC(DI) (the Toothill report).

Scottish Council for Research in Education (SCRE) (1931) *Curriculum for Pupils of*

Twelve to Fifteen Years (Advanced Division), London, University of London Press.

Scottish Council for Research in Education (1933) *The Intelligence of Scottish Children: A National Survey of an Age Group*, London, University of London Press.

Scottish Council for the Training of Teachers (SCTT) (1961) *Minutes of Meetings, vol.I, March 1959-May 1961*, Edinburgh, Darien Press.

Scottish Council for the Training of Teachers (1964) *Minutes of Meetings, vol.II, June 1961-May 1964*, Edinburgh, Darien Press.

Scottish Council for the Training of Teachers (1967) *Minutes of Meetings, vol.III, May 1964-March 1967*, Edinburgh, Darien Press.

Scottish Education Department (SED) (1921) *Circular 44* (no title), London, HMSO.

Scottish Education Department (1941a) *Summary Report for the Years 1939 and 1940*, Edinburgh, HMSO, Cmd 6317.

Scottish Education Department (1942a) *Summary Report on Education in Scotland for the Year 1941*, Edinburgh, HMSO, Cmd 6370.

Scottish Education Department (1943a) *Summary Report on Education in Scotland for the Year 1942*, Edinburgh, HMSO, Cmd 6452.

Scottish Education Department (1944a) *Summary Report on Education in Scotland for the Year 1943*, Edinburgh, HMSO, Cmd 6540.

Scottish Education Department (1944b) *Teachers: Supply, Recruitment and Training in the Period immediately following the War*, Reports of the Advisory Council on Education in Scotland, Edinburgh, HMSO, Cmd 6501.

Scottish Education Department (1945a) *Summary Report on Education in Scotland for the Year 1944*, Edinburgh, HMSO, Cmd 6667.

Scottish Education Department (1946a) *Summary Report on Education in Scotland for the Year 1945*, Edinburgh, HMSO, Cmd 6887.

Scottish Education Department (1946b) *Training of Teachers: A Report of the Advisory Council on Education in Scotland*, Edinburgh, HMSO, Cmd 6723.

Scottish Education Department (1946c) *Technical Education: A Report of a Special Committee of the Advisory Council on Education in Scotland*, Edinburgh, HMSO, Cmd 6786.

Scottish Education Department (1946d) *Primary Education: A Report of the Advisory Council on Education in Scotland*, Edinburgh, HMSO, Cmd 6974.

Scottish Education Department (1947a) *Summary Report on Education in Scotland for the Year 1946*, Edinburgh, HMSO, Cmd 7089.

Scottish Education Department (1947b) *Secondary Education: A Report of the Advisory Council on Education in Scotland*, Edinburgh, HMSO, Cmd 7005.

Scottish Education Department (1947c) *Promotion Schemes*, Edinburgh, SED (Circular 103).

Scottish Education Department (1948a) *Education in Scotland in 1947*, Edinburgh, HMSO, Cmd 7519.

Scottish Education Department (1949a) *Education in Scotland in 1948*, Edinburgh, HMSO, Cmd 7656.

Scottish Education Department (1950a) *Education in Scotland in 1949*, Edinburgh, HMSO, Cmd 7914.

Scottish Education Department (1951a) *Education in Scotland in 1950*, Edinburgh, HMSO, Cmd 8200.

Scottish Education Department (1951b) *Secondary Education: The Report of the Advisory Council*, Edinburgh, SED (Circular 206).

Scottish Education Department (1951c) *Supply of Teachers: First Report of the Departmental Committee appointed by the Secretary of State for Scotland*,

Edinburgh, HMSO, Cmd 8123.

Scottish Education Department (1952a) *Education in Scotland in 1951*, Edinburgh, HMSO, Cmd 8515.

Scottish Education Department (1953a) *Education in Scotland in 1952*, Edinburgh, HMSO, Cmd 8813.

Scottish Education Department (1953b) *Supply of Teachers in Scotland: Second Report of the Departmental Committee appointed by the Secretary of State for Scotland*, Edinburgh, HMSO, Cmd 8721.

Scottish Education Department (1954a) *Education in Scotland in 1953*, Edinburgh, HMSO, Cmnd 9141.

Scottish Education Department (1955a) *Education in Scotland in 1954*, Edinburgh, HMSO, Cmnd 9428.

Scottish Education Department (1955b) *Junior Secondary Education*, Edinburgh, HMSO.

Scottish Education Department (1955c) *Supply of Teachers of Mathematics and Science in Scotland: Report of the Committee appointed by the Secretary of State for Scotland*, Edinburgh, HMSO, Cmd 9419 (the Appleton report).

Scottish Education Department (1956a) *Education in Scotland in 1955*, Edinburgh, HMSO, Cmnd 9722.

Scottish Education Department (1957a) *Education in Scotland in 1956*, Edinburgh, HMSO, Cmnd 162.

Scottish Education Department (1957b) *Supply of Teachers in Scotland: Third Report of the Departmental Committee appointed by the Secretary of State for Scotland*, Edinburgh, HMSO, Cmnd 196.

Scottish Education Department (1958a) *Education in Scotland in 1957*, Edinburgh, HMSO, Cmnd 407.

Scottish Education Department (1958b) *Education in Scotland: The Next Step*, Edinburgh, HMSO, Cmd 603.

Scottish Education Department (1958c) *The Teachers (Training Authorities) (Scotland) Regulations, 1958*, Edinburgh, SED (Circular 389).

Scottish Education Department (1958d) *Draft of the Teachers (Training Authorities) (Scotland) Regulations, 1958*, Edinburgh, SED (Circular 375).

Scottish Education Department (1959a) *Education in Scotland in 1958*, Edinburgh, HMSO, Cmnd 740.

Scottish Education Department (1959b) *Report of the Working Party on the Curriculum of the Senior Secondary School: Introduction of the Ordinary Grade of the Scottish Leaving Certificate*, Edinburgh, HMSO.

Scottish Education Department (1959c) *Report of the Working Party on the Curriculum of the Senior Secondary School*, Edinburgh, SED (Circular 412).

Scottish Education Department (1959d) *Report on Measures to Improve the Supply of Teachers in Scotland: Report of a Special Committee of the Advisory Council on Education in Scotland*, Edinburgh, HMSO, Cmnd 644 (the Knox report).

Scottish Education Department (1960a) *Education in Scotland in 1959*, Edinburgh, HMSO, Cmnd 1018.

Scottish Education Department (1960b) *The Post-Fourth Year Examination Structure in Scotland: A Report of a Special Committee of the Advisory Council on Education in Scotland*, Edinburgh, HMSO, Cmnd 1068.

Scottish Education Department (1961a) *Education in Scotland in 1960*, Edinburgh, HMSO, Cmnd 1359.

Scottish Education Department (1961b) *Transfer from Primary to Secondary Education: A Report of a Special Committee of the Advisory Council on Education in Scotland*, Edinburgh, HMSO, Cmnd 1538.

References

Scottish Education Department (1962a) *Education in Scotland in 1961*, Edinburgh, HMSO, Cmnd 1673.

Scottish Education Department (1962b) *Consultation on Educational Matters: Report of the Working Party on Consultation between the Teachers' Associations and the Scottish Education Department on Educational Matters*, Edinburgh, HMSO.

Scottish Education Department (1962c) *Relations between Education Authorities and Teachers: Report of the Working Party on Appointments to Teaching Posts, Conditions of Tenure of these Posts, and Arrangements for Consultation between Education Authorities and Teachers*, Edinburgh, HMSO.

Scottish Education Department (1962d) *Appointment of Teachers to Education Committees: Report of the Working Party on the Appointment of Teachers in the Employment of Education Authorities in Scotland to the Education Committees of the Authorities*, Edinburgh, HMSO.

Scottish Education Department (1962e) *Pensions for Teachers' Widows: Report of the Working Party on Pensions for Widows, Widowers, Children and Other Dependents of Teachers in Scotland*, Edinburgh, HMSO.

Scottish Education Department (1962f) *Supply of Teachers in Scotland: Fourth Report of the Departmental Committee appointed by the Secretary of State for Scotland*, Edinburgh, HMSO, Cmnd 1601.

Scottish Education Department (1963a) *Education in Scotland in 1962*, Edinburgh, HMSO, Cmnd 1975.

Scottish Education Department (1963b) *From School to Further Education: Report of a Working Party on the Linkage of Secondary and Further Education*, Edinburgh, HMSO (the Brunton report).

Scottish Education Department (1963c) *The Teaching Profession in Scotland: Arrangements for the Award and Withdrawal of Certificates of Competency to Teach*, Edinburgh, HMSO, Cmnd 2066 (the Wheatley report).

Scottish Education Department (1963d) *Teachers and the Administration of Education*, Edinburgh, SED (Circular 548).

Scottish Education Department (1964a) *Education in Scotland in 1963*, Edinburgh, HMSO, Cmnd 2307.

Scottish Education Department (1965a) *Education in Scotland in 1964*, Edinburgh, HMSO, Cmnd 2600.

Scottish Education Department (1965b) *Primary Education in Scotland*, Edinburgh, HMSO.

Scottish Education Department (1965c) *Reorganisation of Secondary Education on Comprehensive Lines*, Edinburgh, SED (Circular 600).

Scottish Education Department (1966a) *Education in Scotland in 1965*, Edinburgh, HMSO, Cmnd 2914.

Scottish Education Department (1966b) *Transfer of Pupils from Primary to Secondary Education*, Edinburgh, SED (Circular 614).

Scottish Education Department (1966c) *Raising the School Leaving Age: Suggestions for Courses*, Edinburgh, HMSO.

Scottish Education Department (1966d) *School Building Programme 1967/68-1969/70*, Edinburgh, SED (Circular 609).

Scottish Education Department (1967a) *Education in Scotland in 1966*, Edinburgh, HMSO, Cmnd 3216.

Scottish Education Department (1967b) *Organisation of Courses Leading to the Scottish Certificate of Education*, CCC Curriculum Paper 2, Edinburgh, HMSO.

Scottish Education Department (1968a) *Education in Scotland in 1967*, Edinburgh, HMSO, Cmnd 3549.

Scottish Education Department (1968b) 'Memorandum No. 75, submitted by the Scottish Education Department, November 1967', in *The Civil Service, vol.5(2): Proposals and Opinions Parts 3 and 4, Organisations and Individuals, Evidence submitted to the Committee under the Chairmanship of Lord Fulton 1966-1968*, London, HMSO.

Scottish Education Department (1969a) *Education in Scotland in 1968*, Edinburgh, HMSO, Cmnd 3949.

Scottish Education Department (1969b) *Consultative Committee on the Curriculum, First Report 1965/8*, Edinburgh, HMSO.

Scottish Education Department (1969c) *Staffing of Secondary Schools in Scotland*, Edinburgh, HMSO.

Scottish Education Department (1969d) *Staffing of Secondary Schools*, Edinburgh, SED (Circular 714).

Scottish Education Department (1970a) *Education in Scotland in 1969*, Edinburgh, HMSO, Cmnd 4312.

Scottish Education Department (1971a) *Education in Scotland in 1970*, Edinburgh, HMSO, Cmnd 4605.

Scottish Education Department (1971b) *Scottish Educational Statistics 1970*, Edinburgh, HMSO.

Scottish Education Department (1971c) *Promoted Posts in Secondary Schools*, Edinburgh, SED (Circular 780).

Scottish Education Department (1972a) *Education in Scotland in 1971*, Edinburgh, HMSO, Cmnd 4887.

Scottish Education Department (1972b) *Consultative Committee on the Curriculum, Second Report 1968/71*, Edinburgh, HMSO.

Scottish Education Department (1972c) *The First Two Years of Secondary Education: Report of a Survey by H. M. Inspectors*, Edinburgh, HMSO.

Scottish Education Department (1972d) *Structure of Promoted Posts in Secondary Schools*, Edinburgh, SED (Circular 826).

Scottish Education Department (1972e) *Secondary School Staffing Survey 1970*, 3 vols, Edinburgh, HMSO.

Scottish Education Department (1973a) *Education in Scotland in 1972*, Edinburgh, HMSO, Cmnd 5246.

Scottish Education Department (1973b) *Secondary School Staffing: A report on Secondary School Staffing in Scotland, with Proposals for New Staffing Standards*, Edinburgh, HMSO (the Red Book).

Scottish Education Department (1973c) *Secondary School Staffing Report*, Edinburgh, SED (Circular 865).

Scottish Education Department (1974a) *Education in Scotland in 1973*, Edinburgh, HMSO, Cmnd 5596.

Scottish Education Department (1975a) *Education in Scotland in 1974*, Edinburgh, HMSO, Cmnd 5908.

Scottish Education Department (1975b) *Education in Aberdeen: A Report by H. M. Inspectors of Schools*, Edinburgh, SED.

Scottish Education Department (1975c) *Consultative Committee on the Curriculum, Third Report 1971/74*, Edinburgh, HMSO.

Scottish Education Department (1976a) *Education in Scotland in 1975*, Edinburgh, HMSO, Cmnd 6421.

Scottish Education Department (1976b) *The Raising of the School Leaving Age in Scotland: A Report by H. M. Inspectors of Schools*, Edinburgh, SED.

Scottish Education Department (1976c) *Modified Procedure for Approval of Education, etc. Building Projects*, Edinburgh, SED (Circular 971).

Scottish Education Department (1977a) *Education in Scotland in 1976*, Edinburgh,

HMSO, Cmnd 6804.

Scottish Education Department (1977b) *Assessment for All: Report of the Committee to Review Assessment in the Third and Fourth Years of Secondary Education in Scotland*, Edinburgh, HMSO (the Dunning report).

Scottish Education Department (1977c) *The Structure of the Curriculum in the Third and Fourth Years of the Scottish Secondary School*, Edinburgh, HMSO (the Munn report).

Scottish Education Department (1977d) *Truancy and Indiscipline in Schools in Scotland*, Edinburgh, HMSO (the Pack report).

Scottish Education Department (1977e) *Education in Lanarkshire: A Report by H. M. Inspectors of Schools*, Edinburgh, SED.

Scottish Education Department (1978a) *Education in Scotland in 1977*, Edinburgh, HMSO, Cmnd 7246.

Scottish Education Department (1979a) *Education in Scotland in 1978*, Edinburgh, HMSO, Cmnd 7549.

Scottish Education Department (1979b) *Statistical Bulletin*, No. 6/A1/1979, April, Edinburgh, SED.

Scottish Education Department (1980a) *Education in Scotland in 1979*, Edinburgh, HMSO, Cmnd 7892.

Scottish Education Department (1980b) *Consultative Committee on the Curriculum, Fourth Report 1974/80*, Edinburgh, HMSO.

Scottish Education Department (1980c) 'Curriculum development in Scotland: The future of the Consultative Committee on the Curriculum and the Scottish Curriculum Development Service', unpublished mimeograph (the Rayner review).

Scottish Education Department (1980d) *The Munn and Dunning Reports: The Government's Development Programme*, Edinburgh, SED.

Scottish Education Department (1980e) *Statistical Bulletin*, No. 5/NI/1980, May, Edinburgh, SED.

Scottish Education Department (1981) *The Staffing of Primary and Secondary Schools: Discussion Paper*, 26 January, Edinburgh, SED.

Scottish Education Department (1982) *The Munn and Dunning Reports: Framework for Decision*, Edinburgh, SED.

Scottish Education Department (1983a) *16-18s in Scotland: An Action Plan*, Edinburgh, SED.

Scottish Education Department (1983b) *Teaching and Learning in the Senior Stages of the Scottish Secondary School: A Report by H. M. Inspectors of Schools*, Edinburgh, HMSO.

Scottish Education Department (1983c) *Consultative Committee on the Curriculum, Fifth Report 1980/83*, Edinburgh, SCDS.

Scottish Education Department (1984) *Learning and Teaching in Scottish Secondary Schools: School Management*, Edinburgh, HMSO.

Scottish Education Department (1985) *Future Strategy for Higher Education in Scotland: Report of the Scottish Tertiary Education Advisory Council on its Review of Higher Education in Scotland*, Edinburgh, HMSO, Cmnd 9676.

Scottish Education Department (1986) 'Consultative Committee on the Curriculum policy review: A report to the Scottish Education Department', unpublished mimeograph (the Crawley review).

Scottish Education Reform Committee (SERC) (1917) *Reform in Scottish Education*, Edinburgh, SERC.

Scottish Home Department (SHD) (1957) *Local Government Finance in Scotland*, Edinburgh, HMSO, Cmnd 208.

References

Scottish Information Office (sio) (1984) *Scottish Education*, Factsheet 15, Edinburgh, sio.

Scottish Office (so) (1954) 'Early school leaving in Scotland', Press Release, 30 December 1954, de 13788/1, Edinburgh, so.

Scottish Office (1977) Press Notice 1323/77, December 9, Edinburgh, so.

Scottish Office (1981) *Scrutiny of H. M. Inspectors of Schools in Scotland*, Edinburgh, so (the Rendle report).

Scottish Office Management Services (soms) (1973) *Future Role and Organisation of H. M. Inspectorate of Schools in Scotland*, Edinburgh, soms Unit.

Scottish Record Office (sro) (1917) ED14/140 *Education (Scotland) Bill, 1917-1918*, Advisory Council, Memoranda and Notes, Struthers' Minute, 12 June.

Scottish Record Office (1945) EB2/1 *Raising of the School Leaving Age to 15*, Cabinet Papers, Memoranda etc., Accommodation Required; Size of Classes etc.

Scottish Record Office (1950) ED8/51 *Scottish Advisory Council on Education in Scotland: Special Committee on the Advisory Council's Report on Secondary Education*, Record of Meetings, Memoranda, Draft Reports etc., 1947-50.

Scottish Record Office (1957) ED8/68 1951-57, Eighth Advisory Council on Education in Scotland: Proposed Reconstitution of Council, Appointments, Remits etc.

Scottish Record Office (1957a) G11/6/1 Papers Leading to Education (Scotland) Advisory Council Order 1952, Proposed Reconstitution of Advisory Council 1955, and Departmental Minutes on Proposal 1956;

Scottish Record Office (1957b) G11/6/2 Reconstitution of Advisory Council on Education in Scotland 1956-57;

Scottish Record Office (1957c) G11/6/3 Advisory Council Remits;

Scottish Record Office (1957d) L11/6/5 Advisory Council on Teacher Supply, Correspondence with Members of Reconstituted Council.

Scottish Record Office (1961a) ED8/84 Eighth Advisory Council on Education in Scotland: Special Committee on Transfer Procedure from Primary to Secondary Education and Post-Fourth Year Examination. Minutes of Meetings etc., L/11/6/36, 1959-61.

Scottish Record Office (1961b) ED8/85 Eighth Advisory Council on Education in Scotland: Special Committee on Transfer Procedure from Primary to Secondary Education and Post-Fourth Year Examinations. Reports, Minutes of Steering Committee etc., L11/6/46A, 1960-61.

Scottish Secondary Teachers' Association (ssta) (1947) *Criticism of the Advisory Council's report on Secondary Education*, Publication No.1, Edinburgh, ssta.

Scottish Secondary Teachers' Association (1957) *Special Bulletin: Teacher-Shortage and the Menace of Dilution*, Edinburgh, ssta.

Secretary of State for Scotland (sss) (1969) *Review of the Constitution and Functions of the General Teaching Council*, Edinburgh, hmso.

Secretary of State for Scotland (1983) 'Scrutiny of H. M. Inspectorate: Policy statement', 24 March.

Seeley, I. W. (1982) 'Over the top in a troubled school: A socio-historical perspective on the crises in a Scottish rural secondary school 1970-1975', unpublished dissertation presented in part fulfilment of the med degree, University of Edinburgh.

Selby-Bigge, Sir L. A. (1927) *The Board of Education*, London and New York, G. P. Putnam's Sons.

Seldon, A. (1981) *Churchill's Indian Summer: The Conservative Government*

1951-55, London, Hodder & Stoughton.

Seldon, A. & Pappworth, J. (1983) *By Word of Mouth: 'Elite' Oral History*, London, Methuen.

Select Committee on Education and Science (SCES) (1968) *Report, Part II*, Her Majesty's Inspectorate (Scotland), House of Commons Papers, Session 1967-68, 400-II, London, HMSO.

Select Committee on Estimates (SC on Estimates) (1953) *Eighth Report: Schools*, House of Commons Papers, Session 1952-53, 186, London, HMSO.

Select Committee on Estimates (1961) *Eighth Report: School Building*, House of Commons Papers, Session 1960-61, 284, London, HMSO.

Select Committee on Expenditure (SC on Expenditure) (1976) *Tenth Report: Policy-Making in the Department of Education and Science*, House of Commons Papers, Session 1975-76, 621, London, HMSO.

Select Committee on Scottish Affairs (SCSA) (1970a) *Report: Economic Planning in Scotland*, House of Commons Papers, Session 1969-70, 267, London, HMSO.

Select Committee on Scottish Affairs (1970b) *Minutes of Evidence . . .*, House of Commons Papers, Session 1969-70, 267-I, London, HMSO.

Self, P. (1972) *Administrative Theories and Politics*, London, George Allen & Unwin.

Self, P. (1985) *Political Theories of Modern Government, Its Role and Reform*, London, George Allen & Unwin.

Self, P. & Storing, H. J. (1962) *The State and the Farmer*, London, George Allen & Unwin.

Sharp, R. (1980) *Knowledge, Ideology and the Politics of Schooling: Towards a Marxist Analysis of Education*, London, Routledge & Kegan Paul.

Sharp, S. (1980) 'Godfrey Thomson and the concept of intelligence', in J. V. Smith & D. Hamilton (eds), *The Meritocratic Intellect: Studies in the History of Educational Research*, Aberdeen, Aberdeen University Press.

Sharpe, L. J. (1985) 'Central coordination and the policy network', *Political Studies*, vol. XXXIII, no.3, 361-81.

Shipman, M. (1984) *Education as a Public Service*, London, Harper & Row.

Silver, H. (1980) *Education and the Social Condition*, London, Methuen.

Silver, H. (1981) 'Policy as history and as theory', *British Journal of Sociology of Education*, vol.2, no.3, 293-9.

Silver, H. (1983) *Education as History: Interpreting Nineteenth- and Twentieth-Century Education*, London, Methuen.

Simmie, J. (1985) 'Corporatism and planning', in W. Grant (ed.), *The Political Economy of Corporatism*, London, Macmillan.

Simpson, M. (1986) 'School-based and centrally directed curriculum development: The uneasy middle ground', in *Scottish Educational Review*, vol.18, no.2, 76-85.

Smith, H. F. (1970) 'Secondary School Staffing Study Group', in *Bulletin – Curriculum Study Group* [later *Inspectorate Bulletin*], no.1, September, 2.

Smout, T. C. (1972) *A History of the Scottish People 1560-1830* (first paperback issue), London, Fontana.

Smout, T. C. (1986) *A Century of the Scottish People 1830-1950*, London, Collins.

Stacey, F. (1975) *British Government 1966 to 1975: Years of Reform*, London, Oxford University Press.

Standing Commission on Pay Comparability (SCPC) (1980) *Report No. 7: Teachers*, London, HMSO, Cmnd 7880 (the Clegg report).

Statutory Instruments (SI) (1952) *The Education (Scotland) Advisory Council Order, 1952*, no.637.

Statutory Instruments (1958a) *The Teachers (Training Authorities) (Scotland) Regulations, 1958*, no.1634.

References

Statutory Instruments (1958b) *The Teachers (Training Authorities) (Scotland) Regulations, 1958*, draft.

Statutory Instruments (1963) *The Scottish Certificate of Education Examination Board Regulations 1963*, no.2131.

Stewart, G. (1927) *The Story of Scottish Education*, London, Pitman.

Stocks, J. (1970) 'Scotland's *ad hoc* authorities, 1919-1930', in History of Education Society, *Studies in the Government and Control of Education since 1860*, London, Methuen.

Stuart, J. (1967) *Within the Fringe*, London, Bodley Head.

Sutherland, G. (1955) 'Sir Godfrey Thomson 1881-1955', *British Journal of Educational Psychology*, vol.25, no.2, 65-6.

Sutherland, G. (1973) *Policy-Making in Elementary Education*, Oxford, Oxford University Press.

Sutherland, G. (1977) 'The magic of measurement: Mental testing and English education 1900-40', *Transactions of the Royal Historical Society*, 5th series, vol.27, 135-53.

Sutherland, G. (1984) (in collaboration with Stephen Sharp) *Ability, Merit and Measurement: Mental Testing and English Education 1880-1940*, Oxford, Clarendon Press.

Thomson, G. H. (1929) *A Modern Philosophy of Education*, London, George Allen & Unwin.

Thorburn, I. (1975) 'Year of the affable conjuror', *Times Educational Supplement (Scotland)*, 19 December, 1.

Thorburn, I. (1976) 'Colleges face closure', *Times Educational Supplement (Scotland)*, 12 March, 1.

Thorburn, I. (1985) 'Mr Strathclyde: Iain Thorburn on Dick Stewart', *Times Educational Supplement (Scotland)*, 1 March, 4.

Thorburn, I. & Munro, N. (1976) 'Contract is the weapon against cuts', *Times Educational Supplement (Scotland)*, 18 June, 88.

Thrasher, M. (1981) 'The concept of a central-local government partnership: Issues obscured by ideas', *Policy and Politics*, vol.9, no.4, 455-70.

The Times (1945 to 1983) *Guide to the House of Commons* (formerly *House of Commons*), London, Times Books.

Torrance, H. (1981) 'The origins and development of mental testing in England and the United States', *British Journal of Sociology of Education*, vol.2, no.1, 45-59.

Treble, J. H. (1979) 'The development of Roman Catholic education in Scotland 1878-1978', in D. McRoberts (ed.), *Modern Scottish Catholicism 1878-1978*, Glasgow, Burns.

Tropp, A. (1957) *The School Teachers: The Growth of the Teaching Profession in England and Wales from 1800 to the Present Day*, London, Heinemann.

Turner, R. H. (1960) 'Sponsored and contest mobility and the school system', *American Sociological Review*, vol.25, no.5, 855-67.

Vaizey, J. & Sheehan, J. (1968) *Resources for Education: An Economic Study of Education in the United Kingdom, 1920-1965*, London, George Allen & Unwin.

Wade, N. (1939) *Post-Primary Education in the Primary Schools of Scotland 1872-1936*, London, University of London Press.

Wake, E. R. (1984) 'Events antecedent to the founding of the Scottish Council for Research in Education', unpublished dissertation presented in part fulfilment of the M Ed degree, University of Edinburgh.

Walker, J. L. (1966) 'A critique of the elitist theory of democracy', *American Political Science Review*, vol. LX, no.2, 285-95.

Walls, A. (1975) Transcript of interview in 'Bon Accord', transmitted by BBC TV as Programme 2 of the Open University Course E203, *Curriculum Design and Development*, 1 July 1975.

Weaver, Sir T. R. (1976) 'What is the good of higher education?', *Higher Education Review*, vol.8, no.3, 3-14.

Weighand, J. E. (1974) 'Post-primary education in Scotland 1918-1930 with particular reference to the "*ad hoc*" Authorities of Dundee and Forfarshire', unpublished dissertation presented in part fulfilment of the MEd degree, University of Dundee.

West, E. G. (1975) *Education and the Industrial Revolution*, London & Sydney, Batsford.

West Midland Group (1956) *Local Government and Central Control: A West Midland Group Study*, London, Routledge & Kegan Paul.

Whiteside, T. & Bernbaum, G. (1979) 'Growth and decline: Dilemmas of a profession', in G. Bernbaum (ed.), *Schooling in Decline*, London, Macmillan.

Who's Who (various dates), also *Who Was Who*, London, Adam & Charles Black.

Wiener, M. J. (1981) *English Culture and the Decline of the Industrial Spirit 1850-1980*, Cambridge, Cambridge University Press.

Willis, P. (1977) *Learning to Labour: How Working Class Kids Get Working Class Jobs*, Farnborough, Saxon House.

Willms, J. D. (1986) 'Social class segregation and its relationship to pupils' examination results in Scotland', *American Sociological Review*, vol.51, no.2, 224-41.

Winkler, J. (1976) 'Corporatism', *Archives Européenes de Sociologie*, vol.XVII, no.1, 100-36.

Wistow, G. & Rhodes, R. A. W. (1987) 'Policy networks and the policy process: The case of "care in the community"', paper presented at a conference of the Political Studies Association of the United Kingdom, Aberdeen, unpublished mimeograph.

Wright, M. (ed.) (1980) *Public Spending Decisions: Growth and Restraint in the 1970s*, London, George Allen & Unwin.

Young, A. (1971) 'Comprehensive reorganisation in Renfrewshire: A case study', unpublished dissertation presented in part fulfilment of the MEd degree, University of Glasgow.

Young, H. (1976) *The Crossman Affair*, London, Hamish Hamilton & Jonathan Cape in association with the *Sunday Times*.

Young, H. & Sloman, A. (1982) *No, Minister*, London, British Broadcasting Corporation.

Young, H. & Sloman, A. (1984) *But, Chancellor*, London, British Broadcasting Corporation.

Young, J. (1986) 'The Advisory Council on Education in Scotland 1920-61', unpublished PhD thesis, University of Edinburgh.

Young, K. (1977) '"Values" in the policy process', *Policy and Politics*, vol.5, no.3, 1-22.

Young, K. & Mills, L. (1978) 'Understanding the "assumptive worlds" of governmental actors: Issues and approaches', a report to the SSRC Panel on Central/Local Government Relations, Bristol.

Young, M. F. D. (1971) *Knowledge and Control: New Directions for the Sociology of Education*, London, Collier-Macmillan.

certification, Highers, O-grade,
Scottish Certificate of Education
Examination Board *and* Standard
Grade

Factories Inspectorate 361
Fairlie, Hugh 308, 309, 316, 338, 380,
381, 395, 445
Fearn, Martin 125, 137, 164, 201, 343
federalism 130–1
Ferguson, John 142n1
Fife 169, 355–8, 378n3, 380
finance ii, 176–88, 197–8, 200, 201,
206–7, 217, 232–3, 365, 484
for colleges of education 283
see also salaries *under* teachers
Fletcher, Alex 162
Flett, Ian 448n6
Forbes, A.K. 142n1
Forsyth, James 107
Fowler, G. 5n3, 149
France 39
Franks report 57
Fraser, Tom 182
Frizell, James 193, 450, 451
Fullwood, Neville 303, 304, 305
Fulton report 129, 140–1, 142
further education 30, 251, 361, 496–7
Fyfe, Sir William Hamilton 78

General Teaching Council x, 226, 243,
261, 262, 263, 266, 275–90, 443,
463
origins 161, 267, 270
registration 276, 289, 290
SED and 462
geology 335–7, 338
Gillett, Eric 167n7
Gilmour, Sir John 126, 130
Gilmour report 126, 127, 128–9
Glasgow 31, 40–1, 162, 188, 189,
190–1, 286, 415, 426, 444, 451–2
appointments of head teachers 425
comprehensive reorganisation in
381–2
schools 169, 198, 394
teachers 225, 267, 272
Glenkinglas, Lord *see* Noble, Michael
Goschen formula 177, 178–9, 180–1,
214
government 154–5, 162–3
central/local divisions of
responsibility iii, 3–4, 10
central-local relationships iii, ix–x,
176, 177, 179–80, 191–5, 197–204,

217, 251, 484–7, 493
see also centralisation
see also Ministers, Parliament *and*
state
Graham, John 362
Graham, Sir Norman 30n3, 58, 61, 103,
115, 116, 123–4, 125, 134, 139,
185, 199, 200, 230, 279
and CCC 319–21, 327–42 *passim*
and GTC 266
and Inspectorate 319–21
and local authorities 198, 200, 444–5
and Schools Council 327
and teachers' unions 438–9
assessments of 65
Brunton on 136
Clark on 136–9
evidence to Select Committee on
Education and Science 142–3, 145,
146
on civil service 141, 164
on comprehensive reorganisation 373
on curriculum 328
on 'democratic tradition' 414
on differences between Scotland and
England 406
on examinations 305–6
on finance allocation 185
on Inspectorate 139–40, 142, 144,
145, 146–7
on middle schools 382–3
on Ministers 160, 164
on perceptions of staffing needs 229
on 'personalisation' 65
on policy community 428
on resources 176, 185
on SCEEB 299, 302, 337
on SED 124–6, 139–40, 142, 144, 198
on teachers 220
on teachers' salaries 216
style 67
Grainger–Stewart T. 121, 122, 227
Gramsci, A. 149
Grant, N. 4n2, 5n3, 29n2, 32, 35n4, 53
Grant, W. 7n7
Gray, George D. 58, 210, 412, 422
and GTC 275–6, 280–1, 283, 285, 287
on Brunton 95, 97–8, 144
on classics 83
on control of colleges of education
281–2
on SCTT 284, 422
on SED 227
on teachers (distribution) 225, 227

proportion in cities 383
school 178, 186, 203, 204, 218, 219, 250, 351
power ii, iii–iv, vi, xiv, 4–5, 456, 457–79
centralisation 418–2, 484–98
communication and 12
divisions, and dual roles in 65–6
individual vii
statutory authority 4
teachers and 4
see also pluralism, policy and 'policy community'
press 109n2, 441–2
Pringle, George 102, 282n3, 310, 419
Brunton on 80
Rodger on 86, 105
privilege 420–5
see also inequality
professionalism 267–70
see also status under teachers
psychology 436
see also intelligence testing
Public Expenditure Survey Committee 180, 184–5
pupils 45, 89, 112, 248–55, 257, 263, 416, 418, 419
achievements 477, 498
and examinations 306–8, 309
and 'vocational' courses 361
Catholic 498
choice of leaving age 375, 418, 484, 486
differentiation 250
see also selection
education outside schools 361
experience of schooling 55
girls 498
influence 347
motivation 416, 419
numbers see under population (school)
promotion by age/stage 45–6
rights 368
transfers 370
truancy 263

qualifications see certification and examinations and under teachers (qualifications)

Radcliffe, Lord 57, 64n3
Raising of the School-Leaving Age see ROSLA
Ranson, S. 4n1, 19n11

Raphael, David 462
rate-capping 484
rate-support grant 180, 184
rates 180, 200, 365
Rayner review 147, 319, 343
reality vi, 9, 498–501
testing 63–7, 70;
see also interview methods
'reality' 253–4, 359
recession 483–7
'Red Book' 230–1, 286, 463
Regan, D.E. 4nn1,2, 5n3, 194
regional economic policy 126, 131
Reith, George 59, 383, 395, 450
religion 36, 39–40, 84, 191, 325
see also Catholic schools and churches
Rendle, Peter 147–8, 343
Rendle report 30n3, 147–8, 149n2, 151, 320
Renfrewshire 182, 351
comprehensive reorganisation 380–1, 397
Labour Party 378n3
quota posts for teachers 225
representation/representativeness 295–301, 304, 306, 330–1, 420–5, 463–4, 469–71, 500
geographical 298, 299
Research Council see Scottish Council for Research in Education
resources viii–ix, 176–97, 206–7, 445
and power 466
Rhodes, G. 149, 179
Rhodes, R. 4n1, 5n4, 7n7
Rifkind, Malcolm 162
Robbins report 98, 261n5
Roberts, Dame Jean 225
Roberts Committee 225–6, 229
Robertson, Sir James J. 63, 74, 77–9, 109–10, 111, 210, 222, 257, 314n6, 328–9, 353n4, 390, 412, 415–16, 459, 468–9
Brunton and 79–80, 109–10, 111
and classics 83
and Committee of Principals 282
and teachers' unions 82, 83
on CCC 330
on CCEM 262n6
on examinations 85
report on secondary education see under Scottish Advisory Council on Education
TV broadcast 61

549